Security Studies

M000035872

This reader brings together key contributions from many of the leading scholars in the field, offering students an informed overview of the most significant work in security studies.

The editors chart the development of the key theoretical and empirical debates in security studies in the Cold War and post-Cold War periods, introducing the ideas of the most influential 'past masters' and contemporary thinkers on security in the UK, the US and elsewhere.

The book is divided into five parts:

- What is Security?
- Security Paradigms
- Security Dimensions and Issues
- Security Frameworks and Actors
- The Future of Security.

In order to guide students through the issues, the book has a substantial critical introduction exploring the development of security studies, as well as introductory essays that provide an overview of each section, highlighting clearly how the readings fit together. Suggestions for further reading and key questions for discussion are also included.

Security Studies is an invaluable resource for all students of security studies and international relations.

Christopher W. Hughes is Professor of International Politics and Japanese Studies, Department of Politics and International Studies, University of Warwick, UK.

Lai Yew Meng is Senior Lecturer in Politics and International Relations at the Centre for the Promotion of Knowledge and Language Learning (CPKLL), Universiti Malaysia Sabah.

This collection of classic essays and contemporary scholarship illustrates the scope, substance and debates of the field of security studies. Hughes and Meng guide the reader by describing the themes and issues that animate security studies, explaining how they form a coherent way of thinking about world politics. This outstanding volume introduces the reader to important works in the field, while illustrating emerging trends in theory, politics and policy.

James J. Wirtz, Naval Postgraduate School, Monterey, CA

Security Studies

A reader

**Edited by Christopher W. Hughes
and Lai Yew Meng**

Routledge
Taylor & Francis Group

LONDON AND NEW YORK

First published 2011 by Routledge

2 Park Square, Milton Park, Abingdon, Oxon, OX14 4RN

Simultaneously published in the USA and Canada
by Routledge
270 Madison Avenue, New York, NY 10016

Routledge is an imprint of the Taylor & Francis Group, an informa business

Typeset in Perpetua and Bell Gothic by Glyph International
Printed and bound in Great Britain by TJ International Ltd,
Padstow, Cornwall

British Library Cataloguing in Publication Data
A catalogue record for this book is available from the British Library

Library of Congress Cataloging in Publication Data
Security studies : a reader / edited by Christopher W. Hughes and
Lai Yew Meng.
    p. cm.
1. Security, International. 2. National security. I. Hughes,
Christopher W. II. Lai, Yew Meng.
JZ5588.S42977 2011
355'.033–dc22   2010032073

ISBN 13: 978-0-415-32600-1 (hbk)
ISBN 13: 978-0-415-32601-8 (pbk)

Contents

The editors   xi
Preface   xiii
Acknowledgements   xvii

PART 1   **1**
What is Security?

Introduction   1

1.1   National security as an ambiguous symbol   5
       ARNOLD WOLFERS

1.2   Redefining security   11
       RICHARD ULLMAN

1.3   The national security problem in international relations   18
       BARRY BUZAN

1.4   The concept of security   24
       DAVID BALDWIN

1.5   Security and emancipation   36
       KEN BOOTH

1.6   Feminism and security   44
       J. ANN TICKNER

1.7 The Third World and security studies   52
    AMITAV ACHARYA

1.8 Redefining security (2)   64
    JESSICA TUCHMAN MATTHEWS

1.9 Human security   71
    ROLAND PARIS

1.10 The renaissance of security studies   80
    STEPHEN M. WALT

1.11 Securitization   93
    OLE WÆVER

Discussion questions   99

PART 2   **101**
Security Paradigms

Introduction   101

2.1 The nemesis of utopianism   105
    E. H. CARR

2.2 A realist theory of international politics   118
    HANS J. MORGENTHAU

2.3 The concept of order in world politics   124
    HEDLEY BULL

2.4 Anarchic orders and balances of power   130
    KENNETH N. WALTZ

2.5 Cooperation under the security dilemma   137
    ROBERT JERVIS

2.6 The false promise of international institutions   142
    JOHN J. MEARSHEIMER

2.7 Economics and the moral case for war   151
    NORMAN ANGELL

2.8 Neoliberal institutionalism   157
    ROBERT KEOHANE

2.9 Democratic peace   165
    MICHAEL W. DOYLE

2.10 Neo-Kantian perspective   173
      BRUCE RUSSETT

2.11 The social construction of power politics   179
      ALEXANDER WENDT

2.12 Norms, identity, and national security   187
      THOMAS U. BERGER

Discussion questions   191

PART 3   **193**
Security Dimensions and Issues

Introduction   193

3.1   Nuclear deterrence   195
      NED LEBOW AND JANICE GROSS STEIN

3.2   Arms races   203
      BARRY BUZAN AND ERIC HERRING

3.3   Why do states build nuclear weapons?   222
      SCOTT SAGAN

3.4   New military conflict   230
      LAWRENCE FREEDMAN

3.5   Technology and war   240
      MICHAEL O'HANLON

3.6   Resources and conflict   246
      THOMAS HOMER-DIXON

3.7   Migration and security   253
      MYRON WEINER

3.8   Transnational crime and security   265
      PHIL WILLIAMS

3.9   AIDS/HIV and security   271
      P. W. SINGER

3.10 Economics and security   278
      JONATHAN KIRSHNER

Discussion questions   293

PART 4   **295**
Security Frameworks and Actors

Introduction   295

4.1 The Long Peace   297
JOHN LEWIS GADDIS

4.2 The unipolar illusion   305
CHRISTOPHER LAYNE

4.3 Alliance politics   315
GLENN SNYDER

4.4 Alliance futures   320
STEPHEN M. WALT

4.5 Multilateralism   330
JOHN GERARD RUGGIE

4.6 Regimes   334
ROBERT JERVIS

4.7 Security communities   339
EMANUEL ADLER

4.8 Interventionism   345
ADAM ROBERTS

4.9 Economic sanctions   351
ROBERT A. PAPE

4.10 Private military companies   356
DAVID SHEARER

Discussion questions   362

PART 5   **363**
The Future of Security

Introduction   363

5.1 Security in the twenty-first century   365
BARRY BUZAN

5.2 Instability in Europe?   375
JOHN J. MEARSHEIMER

5.3 Security dilemmas in East Asia?   381
THOMAS J. CHRISTENSEN

5.4 Structural Realism redux   391
KENNETH N. WALTZ

5.5 Security and global transformation   398
KEN BOOTH

5.6 Globalization and security   406
VICTOR D. CHA

5.7 Terrorism   417
WALTER LAQUEUR

5.8 The war on terrorism   422
MICHAEL HOWARD

Discussion questions   427

Suggestions for further reading   428
Index   435

The editors

Christopher W. Hughes is Professor of International Politics and Japanese Studies, Department of Politics and International Studies, University of Warwick, UK. Previous positions include the *Asahi Shimbun* Visiting Chair of Mass Media and Politics, Faculty of Law, University of Tokyo; Research Associate at the International Institute for Strategic Studies (IISS); and Visiting Scholar at the East Asia Institute, the Free University of Berlin. In 2009–10, he was the Edwin O Reischauer Visiting Professor of Japanese Studies at the Department of Government, Harvard University, and is currently an Associate in Research at Harvard's Reischauer Institute of Japanese Studies. He is author of *Japan's Economic Power and Security: Japan and North Korea* (Routledge, 1999) and *Japan's Security Agenda: Military, Economic and Environmental Dimensions* (Lynne Rienner, 2004), *Japan's Re-mergence as a 'Normal' Military Power?* (Oxford University Press, 2004), and *Japan's Remilitarisation* (Routledge, 2009), and co-author of *Japan's International Relations: Politics: Economics and Security* (Routledge, 2001 and 2005).

Lai Yew Meng is Senior Lecturer in Politics and International Relations at the Centre for the Promotion of Knowledge and Language Learning (CPKLL), Universiti Malaysia Sabah. His Ph.D thesis, entitled 'Nationalism and Power Politics in Japan's Relations with China: A Neoclassical Realist Interpretation', was completed at the Department of Politics and International Studies, University of Warwick. He was also formerly attached to the Japan Institute of International Affairs (JIIA) as a Visiting Research Fellow. His research interests include Japanese and Chinese foreign policy, and East Asian security. He is currently pursuing a Malaysian Higher Education Ministry-funded research on the politics of power and identity in contemporary Indonesia-Malaysia relations.

Preface

Why study security and why use this Reader?

S **ECURITY AND THE STUDY** of it are everywhere. In the aftermath of
the events of 11 September 2001 and the 'War on Terror', security has returned
to the forefront of the policy and social science agendas. If grappling with the diverse
challenges of the unwinding of the Cold War system was not already enough, policy-
makers post-9/11 are now thinking through the ramifications of transnational terrorism for their security of their publics and the international system. Similarly,
researchers and students of politics increasingly need to focus on security in order to
understand not just traditional problems of political violence and conflict but also
how these spill over into a range of subfields of international politics and related
disciplines. Security now penetrates into and generates insights from the fields of
International Relations, International Political Economy, Development Studies,
Economics, Sociology and International Law, to name but a few. Moreover, academic analysts are charged with the responsibility not simply to study the impact of
security on international politics *per se*, but also where possible to provide the necessary expertise to critically examine how policy-makers may devise and utilise security agendas.

Hence, policy-makers, researchers and students now face fundamental questions
regarding the future of the global and regional security orders, and the study of
security has never been more complex or interconnected with other fields of enquiry.
Given this growing imperative for the study of security, and yet the increasing complexity of doing so, the objective of this volume is to provide a practical pathway into
the analysis of International Security or Security Studies. This Reader seeks to provide a comprehensive and sophisticated but user-friendly overview of the past, current and developing trends in Security Studies. The Reader is designed with both the

advanced researcher or teacher and student in mind, and aims to instruct in a number
of areas:

- It provides in one text a series of carefully selected readings, organised thematically and interlinked with each other. The Reader does not try to prescribe
  one particular understanding of Security Studies, but instead to offer a systematically organised 'menu' of options for understanding the diverse field.
- It provides an overview of the key theoretical and empirical debates in Security
  Studies in the Cold War and post-Cold War periods.
- The Reader provides an introduction to the ideas of some of the most influential
  'past masters' and contemporary thinkers on security in the UK, the US and
  elsewhere; or in other words, the 'state of the art' in security thinking. Many of
  the readings will be well known to readers already because of their prominence
  in the field, others are perhaps less well known but they have been chosen
  because of the intrinsic insights that they present.
- The volume provides a sample of works which enables researchers and students
  to discover the progression in theoretical thinking about security, and thus
  enables them to associate and navigate their way around different theories. In
  turn, it will be possible to build from these theories an overall conceptual framework to get a grasp of such a diverse range of security issues.
- In addition to theory, the Reader provides a sample of more empirical or policy-
  focused works which detail past and contemporary security issues in traditional
  and more non-traditional security dimensions.

The Reader more specifically seeks to provide a broadly five-pronged structure to
assist researchers and students.

- Part 1 'What is Security?' provides a set of readings which deal with how the
  definitions of the object and scope of Security Studies have undergone contesta-
  tion and evolution in the Cold War and post-Cold War periods. Contributions
  from a number of key authors demonstrate how understandings of security have
  shifted from a so-called 'traditional' agenda focused on inter-state conflict and
  drawing on the ideas of Political Realism, to a far more diverse set of 'non-
  traditional' issues, encompassing individual and group security and the dimensions of economics and the environment. This part further offers critical
  viewpoints on security from the perspective of Feminism and the developing
  world.
- Part 2 'Security Paradigms' seeks to orient Security Studies within a broader
  canon of theoretical literature that provides contending explanations for
  the generation of violent conflict. Hence, Security Studies is embedded within
  evolving notions of Classical Realism and Neorealism, Liberalism and Neoliberal
  Institutionalism, and Constructivism.
- Part 3 'Security Dimensions and Issues' introduces readings which examine
  particular types of traditional and non-traditional security issues and forms of
  armed conflict, including the proliferation of nuclear weapons, the arms race,
  the Revolution in Military Affairs, environmental degradation, migrations,
  transnational crime, infectious diseases, and economic dislocation.

- Part 4 'Security Frameworks and Actors' turns attention to examining the various structures, organisations and actors and forms of power that have been important in determining global and regional security. It investigates how structures of polarity, unipolar, bipolar or multipolar, may influence security; the role of alliances and multilateralism in contributing to security; and the functions of interventionism, economic sanctions and private military companies in contemporary conflict.
- Part 5 'The Future of Security' provides readings which speculate on the future shape of security post-Cold War, under conditions of globalisation, and post-9/11. It demonstrates contending perspectives which see perpetuation or containment of conflict; the renewal of old security agendas or a range of new issues; and the geographical displacement of conflict to other regions.

How to use this Reader

Once again, to be clear, the objective of this Reader is not to cajole researchers and students into accepting one interpretation of Security Studies. Instead, the aim is to make clear the diversity and complexity of the field, while at the same time offering a structured and balanced pathway to understanding Security Studies. To this end, the Reader can be utilised in a number of ways. The Reader can be read through as a consistent whole in order, almost as a textbook written by many leading figures in the field. Alternatively, the Reader can be dipped into thematically by using each of the Parts where appropriate in order to support ongoing studies in other areas or course. The Reader can also be used to simply provide background reading or more specialised readings in conjunction with courses and other literature.

Each of the parts is organised to assist researchers and students in these different usages. At the opening of every part is a short introductory essay which essentially overviews the content of the upcoming contributions and seeks to show how they fit together and feed off each other in generating understandings of security. At the end of each part, there is also a set of discussion questions linked to the preceding readings, which can be used to reflect back on the key concepts and issues covered. These can be used as seminar discussion or essay questions. Furthermore, there is a set of additional readings at the end of the volume, organised thematically, which enable deeper research into key theoretical and empirical issues highlighted. Finally, although this Reader strives to be comprehensive while user-friendly, it is also advisable that it be read alongside key original texts in the field so as flesh out the structure it provides for comprehending Security Studies.

Acknowledgements

The task of putting together a Reader of this size is not inconsiderable. We would like to thank Craig Fowlie and Nicola Parkin at Routledge for inspiring and guiding this project through to completion. At the University of Warwick, invaluable research assistance was provided at various times by Tomonori Taki and Victoria Tuke.

PART 1

What is Security?

Introduction

ARNOLD WOLFERS'S CLASSIC ESSAY from 1962 starts off this section, providing an insight into competing definitions of security prevalent during the Cold War. Wolfers's key point is that while security is a crucial concept in international relations, it is also (even at the height of the Cold War) extremely subjective in nature. States and nations will tend to perceive differently their 'acquired values' and the degree of danger they face; the degree to which they seek to protect 'core' and 'marginal' values, given resource trade-offs; and the means by which they provide for security, ranging from alliance and arms races to neutrality and the pacifist non-use of force. Hence, Wolfers reminds us that it is a 'sweeping generalisation' that all states tend to pursue a 'uniform and imitable policy of security'; as well as highlighting the malleability of the term and how it is important to be aware of the term's manipulation by policy-makers. **Richard Ullman**, writing in the latter stages of the Cold War, follows up on these themes, arguing that traditional security conceptions have been too narrow and military-oriented. He reminds us that security is not necessarily an absolute value, and needs to be balanced against other key values, and most particularly potential infringements of liberty in the name of the pursuit of security. Ullman's analysis is prescient in pointing to a number of non-military threats, including resource scarcity and basic human needs, which have subsequently become the focus of the post-Cold War security agenda. However, Ullman argues that the redefinition of security in these terms can only be made possible through a change in the conceptual mindset of policy-makers and the engagement of civil society.

Barry Buzan's contribution moves forward the debate on security in the early post-Cold War period by acknowledging that, while security is an essentially contested concept, it should be possible to offer categorisations and greater analytical coherence to the evolving security agenda. Buzan innovates by presenting a systematic list of sectors: military, political, economic, environmental and societal security. He further points out the importance of thinking of how these sectors apply to a range of different referent objects of security, and how the security of one sector or referent cannot be thought of in isolation from the others, thus laying the ground for thinking of security in holistic terms. **David Baldwin** counters Buzan's assertion that security is a contested concept and instead posits that it has simply been inadequately explicated. He then proceeds to specify security in terms of 'security for whom' and 'security for which values'; plus he offers additional specifications such as 'how much security', 'from what threats', 'by what means', 'at what cost' and 'in what time period'. Baldwin agrees that security is a subjective term and concludes that its relative importance can only be assessed through a marginal value approach – asking how far security can be traded off against other important values in order to mobilise policy resources.

Ken Booth picks up on the themes above by advocating further new definitions of security. Booth, writing in 1991, and although eschewing the term post-Cold War for the alternative the 'interregnum', points out the decline in inter-state conflict but the continuance of intra-state violence. Consequently, he argues that, instead of the traditional notions of power and order, security should be understood in terms of 'emancipation' – the freeing of people from all types of constraints on their freedom, including not just war, but also issues of poverty, education and political oppression. Indeed, Booth asserts that the prime object of security should be the individual, and that states are simply a means, not an end in security, thus pointing the way towards the widening of security current in the present day. **J. Ann Tickner** adds a further corrective to traditional notions of security by introducing the importance of feminist perspectives. Tickner demonstrates how the study of International Relations and security has often been a male-centric domain with the concomitant marginalisation of women's experiences. She argues that these biases need to be redressed by embracing the voices of the oppressed 'Others', including women, with the result that new insights can be offered on issues such as militarism and structural violence; fundamental international relations concepts often dominated in the past by 'patriarchal' perspectives; and traditional binary oppositions of domestic and foreign, and order and anarchy.

Amitav Acharya highlights and seeks to redress another past failing of Security Studies, namely the tendency towards a 'Eurocentric' view of conflict. Acharya argues that the experience of the so-called 'Third World' has been marginalised in the mainstream of the discipline, despite the fact that this is where most world conflicts occur. The result has been that Security Studies pays insufficient attention to the intrastate conflict and to non-military sources of conflict. Acharya adds another corrective in stressing the need to understand that much of the conflict originates from local regional conditions rather than simple international system transformation, and hence that much of structural realism may need to be rethought. All in all, Acharya demonstrates again the need to redefine and broaden conceptions of security in the post-Cold War period.

Jessica Tuchman Matthews adds depth to these calls for redefinition with an early call to take the environment seriously as a security issue. Tuchman Matthews argues that the environment deserves attention due to its potential for generating armed conflict, as well as in its own right as a threat to human quality of life. Similarly,

Roland Paris pushes forward attempts to redefine security and its referent objects by grappling with the current concept of Human Security. Paris offers a somewhat sceptical view of the often overly broad Human Security concept, but in doing so still demonstrates the importance of a new research agenda concerned with non-military threats to the safety of societies, groups and individuals.

The penultimate chapter of this part, however, points out some counter-arguments and also the risks of redefining security. **Stephen Walt** contends that any attempt to expand the concept of security to include topics such as poverty, the environment, infectious diseases, runs the risk of over-expanding the field to the point that it loses intellectual coherence. Walt argues that the outcome could be to hamper attempts to deal with these policy issues as well as more traditional military security concerns. Walt stresses that the possibility of inter-state conflict, if declining, has not been eliminated, and thus the core agenda of security studies should remain military, although there is room to expand this agenda to include variables in conflict genera-tion such as domestic politics and the power of ideas. Finally, **Ole Wæver** introduces the concept of 'securitization' whereby policy-makers through the 'speech act' iden-tify and place issues within the category of security. In turn, securitisation empowers policy-makers to mobilise all necessary resources in pursuit of their objectives. Wæver points out the risk of securitisation in removing issues from the normal realm of policy discussion in the name of national security, and that in fact, the de-securitisation of politics may help us to perceive certain types of public policy issues more clearly.

Arnold Wolfers

NATIONAL SECURITY AS AN AMBIGUOUS SYMBOL

Source: *Discord and Collaboration: Essays on International Politics* (Baltimore, MD: The Johns Hopkins University Press, 1962), pp. 147–65.

T ODAY [...] THE FORMULA of the national interest has come to be practically synonymous with the formula of national security. Unless they explicitly state some other intent, spokesmen for a policy which would take the national interest as its guide can be assumed to mean that priority shall be given to measures of security, a term to be analyzed.[1] [...]

The term national security, like national interest, is well enough established in the political discourse of international relations to designate an objective of policy distinguishable from others. We know roughly what people have in mind if they complain that their government is neglecting national security or demanding excessive sacrifices for the sake of enhancing it. Usually those who raise the cry for a policy oriented exclusively toward this interest are afraid their country underestimates the external dangers facing it or is being diverted into idealistic channels unmindful of these dangers. Moreover, the symbol suggests protection through power and therefore figures more frequently in the speech of those who believe in reliance on national power than of those who place their confidence in model behavior, international cooperation, or the United Nations to carry their country safely through the tempests of international conflict. For these reasons it would be an exaggeration to claim that the symbol of national security is nothing but a stimulus to semantic confusion, although used without specifications it leaves room for more confusion than sound political counsel or scientific usage can afford.

The demand for a policy of national security is primarily normative in character. It is supposed to indicate what the policy of a nation should be in order to be either expedient – a rational means toward an accepted end – or moral, the best or the least evil course of action. [Besides] [t]he value judgments implicit in these normative exhortations [...], attention should [also] be drawn to an assertion that is implicit if not explicit in most appeals for a policy guided by national security. Such appeals usually assume that nations have made security their goal except when idealism or utopianism of their leaders has led them to stray from the traditional path. If such conformity of behavior actually existed, it would be proper to infer that a country deviating from the established pattern of conduct would risk being penalized. This would greatly strengthen the normative arguments. The trouble with the contention of fact, however, is that the term "security" covers a range of goals so wide that highly divergent policies can be interpreted as policies of security.

Security points to some degree of protection of values previously acquired. In Walter Lippmann's words, a nation is secure to the extent to which it is not in danger of having to sacrifice core values, if it wishes to avoid war, and is able, if challenged, to maintain them by victory in such a war.[2] This definition implies that security rises and falls with the ability of a nation to deter an attack, or to defeat it. This is in accord with common usage of the term.

Security is a value, then, of which a nation can have more or less and which it can aspire to have in greater or lesser measure.[3] It has much in common, in this respect, with power or wealth, two other values of great importance in international affairs. But while wealth measures the amount of a nation's material possessions, and power, its ability to control the actions of others, security, in an objective sense, measures the absence of threats to acquired values, in a subjective sense, the absence of fear that such values will be attacked. In both respects a nation's security can run a wide gamut from almost complete insecurity or sense of insecurity at one end, to almost complete security or absence of fear at the other.[4]

The possible discrepancy between the objective and subjective connotations of the term is significant in international relations although the chance of future attack can never be measured "objectively"; it must always remain a matter of subjective evaluation and speculation. [...] It is well known that nations, and groups within nations, differ widely in their reaction to one and the same external situation. Some tend to exaggerate the danger while others underestimate it. With hindsight it is sometimes possible to tell exactly how far they deviated from a rational reaction to the actual or objective state of danger existing at the time. Even if for no other reason, this difference in the reaction to similar threats suffices to make it probable that nations will differ in their efforts to obtain more security. Some may find the danger to which they are exposed entirely normal and in line with their modest security expectations while others consider it unbearable to live with these same dangers. [...]

Another and even stronger reason why nations must be expected not to act uniformly is that they are not all or constantly faced with the same degree of danger. [...]

This point, however, should not be overstressed. There can be no quarrel with the generalization that most nations, most of the time – the great powers particularly – have shown, and had reason to show, an active concern about some lack of security and have been prepared to make sacrifices for its enhancement. Danger and the awareness of it have been and continue to be sufficiently widespread to guarantee some uniformity in this respect. But a generalization that leaves room both for the frantic kind of struggle for more security which characterized French policy at times and for the neglect of security apparent in American foreign policy after the close of both world wars throws little light on the behavior of nations. The demand for conformity would have meaning only if it could be said – as it could under the conditions postulated in the working hypothesis of pure power politics – that nations normally subordinate all other values to the maximization of their security. This, however, is obviously not the case.

There have been many instances of struggles for more security taking the form of an unrestrained race for armaments, alliances, strategic boundaries, and the like; but one need only recall the many heated parliamentary debates on arms appropriations to realize how uncertain has been the extent to which people will consent to sacrifice for additional increments of security. Even when there has been no question that armaments would mean more security, the cost in taxes, the reduction in social benefits, or the sheer discomfort involved have militated effectively against further effort. [...]

Instead of expecting a uniform drive for enhanced or maximum security, a different hypothesis may offer a more promising lead. Efforts for security are bound to be experienced as a burden; security after all is nothing but the absence of the evil of insecurity, a negative value so to speak. As a consequence, nations will be inclined to minimize these efforts, keeping them at the lowest level that will provide them with what they consider adequate protection. This level will often be lower than what statesmen, military leaders, or other particularly security-minded participants in the decision-making process believe it should be. In any case, together with the extent of the external threats, numerous domestic factors such as national character, tradition, preferences, and prejudices will influence the level of security that a nation chooses to make its target.

It might be objected that in the long run nations are not so free to choose the amount of effort they will put into security. [...] This objection again would make sense only if the hypothesis of pure power politics were a realistic image of actual world affairs. A quick glance at history is enough, however, to show that survival has only exceptionally been at stake, particularly for the major powers. If nations were not concerned with the protection of values other than their survival as independent states, most of them most of the time would not have had to be seriously worried about their security, despite what manipulators of public opinion engaged in mustering greater security efforts may have said to the contrary. What "compulsion" there is, then, is a function not merely of the will of others, real or imagined, to destroy the nation's independence but of national desires and ambitions to retain a wealth of other values such as rank, respect, material possessions, and special privileges. It would seem to be a fair guess that the efforts for security by a particular nation will tend to vary, other things being equal, with the range of values for which protection is being sought.

In respect to this range, there may seem to exist a considerable degree of uniformity. All over the world today peoples are making sacrifices to protect and preserve what to them appear as the minimum national core values: national independence and territorial integrity. But there is deviation in two directions. Some nations seek protection for more marginal values as well. There was a time when United States policy could afford to be concerned mainly with the protection of the foreign investments or markets of its nationals, its "core values" being out of danger, or when Britain was extending its national self to include large and only vaguely circumscribed "regions of special interest." It is a well-known and portentous phenomenon that bases, security zones, and the like may be demanded and acquired for the purpose of protecting values acquired earlier; and they then become new national values requiring protection themselves. Pushed to its logical conclusion, such spatial extension of the range of values does not stop short of world domination.

A deviation in the opposite direction of a compression of the range of core values is hardly exceptional in our days either. There is little indication that Britain is bolstering the security of Hong Kong although colonies were once considered part of the national territory. The Czechs lifted no finger to protect their independence against the Soviet Union and many West Europeans are arguing today that rearmament has become too destructive of values they cherish to be justified even when national independence is obviously at stake.

The lack of uniformity does not end here. A policy is not characterized by its goal – in this case, security – alone. To establish its character, the means used to pursue the goal must be taken into account as well. Thus, if two nations were both endeavoring to maximize their security but one were placing all its reliance on armaments and alliances, the other on meticulous neutrality, a policy-maker seeking to emulate their behavior would be at a loss where to turn. Those who call for a policy guided by national security are not likely to be unaware of this fact, but they take for granted that they will be understood to mean a security policy based on power, and on military power at that. Were it not so, they would be hard put to prove that their government was not already doing its best for security, though it was seeking to enhance it by such means as international co-operation or by the negotiation of compromise agreements – means which in one instance may be totally ineffective or utopian but in others may have considerable protective value.

It is understandable why it should be assumed so readily that a quest for security must necessarily translate itself into a quest for coercive power. Since security is being sought against external violence – coupled perhaps with internal subversive violence – it seems plausible at first sight that the response should consist in an accumulation of the same kind of force for the purpose of resisting an attack or of deterring a would-be attacker. The most casual reading of history and of contemporary experience, moreover, suffices to confirm the view that such resort to "power of resistance" has been the rule in nations grappling with serious threats to their security, however much the specific form of this power and its extent may differ. Why otherwise would so many nations which have no acquisitive designs maintain costly armaments? [...]

But again, the generalization that nations seeking security usually place great reliance on coercive power does not carry one far. The issue is not whether there is regularly some such reliance but whether as between nations there are no significant differences concerning their overall choice of the means upon which they place their trust. [...] [C]oncerning [...] future security [...], one cannot help drawing the conclusion that, in the matter of means, the roads that are open may lead in diametrically opposed directions.[5] The choice in every instance will depend on a multitude of variables, including ideological and moral convictions, expectations concerning the psychological and political developments in the camp of the opponent, and inclinations of individual policy-makers.[6]

After all that has been said, little is left of the sweeping generalization that in actual practice nations, guided by their national security interest, tend to pursue a uniform and therefore imitable policy of security. Instead, there are numerous reasons why they should differ widely in this respect, with some standing close to the pole of complete indifference to security or complete reliance on nonmilitary means, others close to the pole of insistence on absolute security or of complete reliance on coercive power. It should be added that there exists still another category of nations which cannot be placed within the continuum connecting these poles because they regard security of any degree as an insufficient goal; instead they seek to acquire new values even at the price of greater insecurity. In this category must be placed not only the "mad Caesars" who are out for conquest and glory at any price, but also idealistic statesmen who would plunge their country into war for the sake of spreading the benefits of their ideology, for example, or of liberating enslaved peoples. [...]

Notes

1   Hans Morgenthau's *In Defense of the National Interest* (Alfred A. Knopf, New York, 1951) is the most explicit and impassioned recent plea for an American foreign policy which shall follow "but one guiding star – the National Interest." While Morgenthau is not equally explicit in regard to the meaning he attaches to the symbol "national interest," it becomes clear in the few pages devoted to an exposition of this "perennial" interest that the author is thinking in terms of the national security interest, and specifically of security based on power. The United States, he says, is interested in three things: a unique position as a predominant power without rival in the Western Hemisphere and the maintenance of the balance of power in Europe as well as in Asia, demands which make sense only in the context of a quest for security through power.

2   Walter Lippmann, *U.S. Foreign Policy: Shield of the Republic* (Little, Brown & Co., Boston, 1943), p. 51.

3   This explains why some nations that seem to fall into the category of status quo powers par excellence may nevertheless be dissatisfied and act very much like "imperialist" powers, as Morgenthau calls nations with acquisitive goals. They are dissatisfied with the degree of security they enjoy under the status quo and are out to enhance it. France's occupation of the Ruhr in 1923 illustrates this type of behavior. Because the demand for more security may induce a status quo power even to resort to the use of violence as a means of attaining more security, there is reason to beware of the easy and often self-righteous assumption that nations which desire to preserve the status quo are necessarily "peace-loving."

4   Security and power would be synonymous terms if security could be attained only through the accumulation of power, which will be shown not to be the case. The fear of attack – security in the subjective sense – is also not proportionate to the relative power position of a nation. Why, otherwise, would some weak and exposed nations consider themselves more secure today than does the United States? Harold D. Lasswell and Abraham Kaplan in *Power and Society* (Yale University Press, New Haven, 1950), defining security as "high value expectancy," stress the subjective and speculative character of security by using the term "expectancy"; the use of the term "high," while indicating no definite level, would seem to imply that the security-seeker aims at a position in which the events he expects – here the continued unmolested enjoyment of his possessions – have considerably more than an even chance of materializing.

5   Myres S. McDougal, "Law and Peace," *American Journal of International Law*, Vol. 46, No. 1 (January, 1952), pp. 102 ff. He rightly criticizes Hans Morgenthau for his failure to appreciate the role that nonpower methods, such as legal procedures and moral appeals, may at times successfully play in the pursuit of security. But it is surprising how little aware McDougal appears to be of the disappointing modesty

of the contributions which these "other means" have actually made to the enhancement of security and the quite insignificant contributions they have made to the promotion of changes of the status quo. This latter failure signifies that they have been unable to remove the main causes of the attacks that security-minded peoples rightly fear.

6   On the problem of security policy (Sicherheitspolitik) with special reference to "collective security," see the comprehensive and illuminating study of Heinrich Rogge, "Kollektivsicherheit Buendnispolitik Voelkerbund," *Theorie der nationalen und internationalen Sicherheit* (Berlin, 1937), which deserves attention despite the fact that it was written and published in Nazi Germany. It bears a distinctly "revisionist" slant.

Richard Ullman

REDEFINING SECURITY

Source: *International Security*, vol. 8, no. 1, 1983, pp. 129–53.

S INCE THE ONSET of the Cold War in the late 1940s, every administration in Washington has defined American national security in excessively narrow and excessively military terms. Politicians have found it easier to focus the attention of an inattentive public on military dangers, real or imagined, than on nonmilitary ones; political leaders have found it easier to build a consensus on military solutions to foreign policy problems than to get agreement on the use (and, therefore, the adequate funding) of the other means of influence that the United States can bring to bear beyond its frontiers.

Just as politicians have not found it electorally rewarding to put forward conceptions of security that take account of nonmilitary dangers, analysts have not found it intellectually easy. They have found it especially difficult to compare one type of threat with others, and to measure the relative contributions toward national security of the various ways in which governments might use the resources at their disposal.

[…] [However,] defining national security merely (or even primarily) in military terms conveys a profoundly false image of reality. That false image is doubly misleading and therefore doubly dangerous. First, it causes states to concentrate on military threats and to ignore other and perhaps even more harmful dangers. Thus it reduces their total security. And second, it contributes to a pervasive militarization of international relations that in the long run can only increase global insecurity.

Security versus what?

One way of moving toward a more comprehensive definition of security may be to ask: what should we be willing to give up in order to obtain more security? how do we assess the tradeoffs between security and other values? The question is apposite because, of all the "goods" a state can provide, none is more fundamental than security.

Security, for [traditional thinkers like] Hobbes, was an absolute value. [...] [However], [f]or most of us, security is not an absolute value. We balance security against other values. Citizens of the United States and other liberal democratic societies routinely balance security against liberty. Without security, of course, liberty — except for the strongest — is a sham, as Hobbes recognized. But we are willing to trade some perceptible increments of security for the advantages of liberty. Were we willing to make a Hobbesian choice, our streets would be somewhat safer, and conscription would swell the ranks of our armed forces. But our society would be — and we would ourselves feel — very much more regimented.

The tradeoff between liberty and security is one of the crucial issues of our era. In virtually every society, individuals and groups seek security against the state, just as they ask the state to protect them against harm from other states. Human rights and state security are thus intimately related. [...]

The most profound of all the choices relating to national security is, therefore, the tradeoff with liberty, for at conflict are two quite distinct values, each essential to human development. At its starkest, this choice presents itself as: how far must states go, in order to protect themselves against adversaries that they regard as totalitarian, toward adopting totalitarian-like constraints on their own citizens? In the United States it is a tension that arises every day in the pulling and hauling between police and intelligence agencies and the Constitution. At a practical level, the choices become: what powers do we concede to local police? to the F.B.I.? to the C.I.A. and the other arms of the "intelligence community"?

Other security choices may seem equally vexing if they are not equally profound. One is the familiar choice between cure and prevention. Should the U.S. spend a (large) sum of money on preparations for military intervention in the Persian Gulf in order to assure the continued flow of oil from fragile states like Saudi Arabia, or should it be spent instead on nonmilitary measures — conservation, alternate energy sources, etc. — that promise substantially (although not rapidly) to reduce American dependence upon Persian Gulf oil? A second choice involves collaboration with regimes whose values are antithetic to America's own. Should the United States government forge a relationship of greater military cooperation with the Republic of South Africa, and risk racial conflict in its cities at home? Or should it continue to treat South Africa as an international outlaw and perhaps enhance domestic racial harmony — an important characteristic of a secure society — at the cost of enabling the Soviet navy to pose a greater potential challenge to the safety of the sea lanes around Africa upon which so much vital cargo flows? A third choice involves military versus economic assistance to poor countries. Should U.S. policy aim at strengthening Third World governments against the military threats that they assert they perceive to come from the Soviet Union and its allies, or at helping their citizens develop greater self-reliance so as, perhaps, ultimately to produce more healthful societies with lower rates of birth and thus relieve the rising pressure on global resources? Finally, many choices juxtapose international and domestic priorities. If a stretched national budget cannot afford both increased outlays for military forces and for a more effective criminal justice system at home, programs that create work opportunities for poor inner-city teenagers, or measures to improve the quality of the air we breathe and the water we drink, which expenditures enhance "security" more?

The tradeoffs implied in these and many other similar questions are not as profound as that between security and liberty. But they are nevertheless capable of generating conflicts of values – between alternate ways of viewing national security and its relationship to what might be called global security.

There is, in fact, no *necessary* conflict between the goal of maintaining a large and powerful military establishment and other goals such as developing independence from Persian Gulf oil, promoting self-sustaining development in poor countries, minimizing military reliance on repressive governments, and promoting greater public tranquility and a more healthful environment at home. All these objectives could be achieved if the American people chose to allocate national resources to do so. But it is scarcely likely that they – or their Congressional representatives – will choose to make all the perceived sacrifices that such large governmental programs entail. [...]

A redefinition of threats

In addition to examining security tradeoffs, it is necessary to recognize that security may be defined not merely as a goal but as a consequence – this means that we may not realize what it is or how important it is until we are threatened with losing it. In some sense, therefore, security is defined and valorized by the threats which challenge it.

We are, of course, accustomed to thinking of national security in terms of military threats arising from beyond the borders of one's own country. But that emphasis is doubly misleading. It draws attention away from the nonmilitary threats that promise to undermine the stability of many nations during the years ahead. And it presupposes that threats arising from outside a state are somehow more dangerous to its security than threats that arise within it.

A more useful (although certainly not conventional) definition might be: a threat to national security is an action or sequence of events that (1) threatens drastically and over a relatively brief span of time to degrade the quality of life for the inhabitants of a state, or (2) threatens significantly to narrow the range of policy choices available to the government of a state or to private, nongovernmental entities (persons, groups, corporations) within the state. Within the first category might come the spectrum of disturbances and disruptions ranging from external wars to internal rebellions, from blockades and boycotts to raw material shortages and devastating "natural" disasters such as decimating epidemics, catastrophic floods, or massive and pervasive droughts. [...]

The second category is perhaps less obviously apposite. [...] It is easy to think of degradation of the quality of life or a diminution of the range of policy choices as "national security" problems when the source of these undesirable conditions is a large, powerful, antagonistic state such as Nazi Germany or Stalin's U.S.S.R. And it is even (relatively) easy to organize responses to such clear and present dangers. But it is much more difficult to portray as threats to national security, or to organize effective action against, the myriads of other phenomena, some originating within a national society, many coming from outside it, which also kill, injure, or impoverish persons, or substantially reduce opportunities for autonomous action, but do so on a smaller scale and come from sources less generally perceived as evil incarnate. Interruptions in the flow of critically needed resources or, indeed, a dwindling of the available global supply; terrorist attacks or restrictions on the liberty of citizens in order to combat terrorism; a drastic deterioration of environmental quality caused by sources from either within or outside a territorial state; continuing violence in a major Third World state chronically unable to meet the basic human needs of large numbers of its citizens; urban conflict at home perhaps (or perhaps not) fomented by the presence of large numbers of poor immigrants from poor nations – all these either degrade the quality of life and/or reduce the range of policy options available to governments and private persons.

For a leader trying to instill the political will necessary for a national society to respond effectively to a threat to its security, a military threat is especially convenient. The "public good" is much more easily defined; sacrifice can not only be asked but expected; particular interests are more easily co-opted or, failing that, overridden; it is easier to demonstrate that "business as usual" must give way to extraordinary measures; dissent is more readily swept aside in the name of forging a national consensus. A convenient characteristic of military threats to national security is that their possible consequences are relatively apparent and, if made actual, they work their harm rapidly. Therefore, they are relatively noncontroversial.[1]

The less apparent a security threat may be – whether military or nonmilitary – the more that preparations to meet it are likely to be the subject of political controversy. [...] [For instance] the generally unenthusiastic reception given to programs aimed at aiding poor countries, ameliorating the disaffection of poor persons at home, halting environmental degradation, stockpiling strategically important materials, or other such measures is striking but scarcely surprising. Proponents of such programs in fact frequently do justify them on the ground that they promote national security. But because their connection to security is often not immediately apparent, opponents find it easy to reject or simply ignore such arguments, if not to refute them.[2] [...]

Assessing vulnerability

In every sphere of policy and action, security increases as vulnerability decreases.[3] At the most basic level of individual survival, this is a law of nature, seemingly as well understood by animals as by humans. At that level it is a reflexive response. Reducing vulnerability becomes a matter of policy, rather than of reflex action, when it seems necessary to calculate the costs and benefits involved. How much security do we buy when we expend a given increment of resources to reduce vulnerability? That is a difficult question even in relatively simple situations, such as a householder stockpiling a commodity against the possibility of a disruption in accustomed channels of supply. At the level of the community, rather than the individual, it becomes very much more difficult: different members assess risks differently, and they may well be differently damaged by a disrupting event. An investment in redundancy that seems worthwhile to one family may seem excessively costly to another. Neither will know which is correct unless the crunch actually comes. And even then they might disagree. They might experience distress differently.

At the level discussed in this paper, where states are the communities involved and where the problems are for the most part considerably more complicated than a simple disruption in an accustomed channel of supply, the relationship between decreased vulnerability and increased security is formidably difficult to measure. Consider even the relatively simple measure of adding crude oil to the U.S. Strategic Petroleum Reserve, the (for the most part) underground stockpile whose purpose is to make it possible for the nation to ride out a cutoff in deliveries from one or more major foreign oil suppliers. We know, of course, the cost of buying and storing a given increment of crude oil. But until mid-1981 the government of Saudi Arabia (the world's major exporter of oil) took the position that U.S. stockpiling of oil was an unfriendly act. It claimed that it maintained high levels of oil production to provide immediate benefits – "moderate" prices – to Western (and other) consumers, not to make it possible for Washington to buy insurance against the day when the Saudi leadership might want to cut production so as, say, to influence U.S. policy toward Israel. Successive administrations in Washington have regarded the retention of Saudi good will as something close to a vital American interest, on both economic and strategic grounds. They therefore dragged their feet on filling the Strategic Petroleum Reserve.[4]

Who can say with assurance that those administrations were wrong? Who could measure – before the event – the effects of putting Saudi noses out of joint? It may well have been that even so seemingly modest a measure as adding to the oil stockpile would ripple through Saudi and Middle Eastern politics in such a manner as ultimately to bring about just that calamity against which the stockpile is intended to offer insulation, that is, a production cutback. Moreover, being finite in size; the stockpile may not offer sufficient insulation against a protracted deep cutback. But, by the same token, who can be sure that even if the reserve remains unfilled (its level is still far below the total originally planned[5]), and even if the United States takes other additional measures to mollify the Saudis, an event will not occur that will trigger a supply disruption in any case? If that occurs, the nation would clearly be better off if it possessed a healthy reserve of stored oil, even one insufficient to cushion the entire emergency. [...]

This discussion has sought to show that we generally think about – and, as a polity, dispose of – resource allocations for military and for nonmilitary dimensions of security in quite different ways. Regarding military forces, although analysts and interest groups may have their own ideas about such issues as the appropriate size of the American fleet or the composition of its air wings, there is general agreement on the principle that there must in the end be a single, authoritative determination, and that such a determination can come only from the central government of the polity. Because we acknowledge that there is no marketplace in which we can purchase military security (as distinguished from some of its components), we would not look to private individuals or firms or legislators or regional governments to make such a determination, even though we might disagree with the determination that the federal government makes.

By contrast, as indicated above, there is no consensus about the need for a single, authoritative determination regarding the nonmilitary dimensions of security. The polity as a whole is therefore much more responsive to allegations that a given investment in, say, a commodity stockpile is "inefficient" than it is responsive to the same allegation regarding a given investment in military forces. Moreover, the alleged inefficiency is far more easily demonstrated. The situation is similar regarding measures for coping with the other problems mentioned in this paper: rapid population growth, explosive urbanization, deforestation, and the like. [...]

Changing the consensus

Because of these preconceptions regarding the appropriate role of governmental authority both in defining problems and in proposing solutions, the tendency of American political leaders to define security problems and their solutions in military terms is deeply ingrained. The image of the President as Commander in Chief is powerful. When in this role he requests additional funds for American military forces the Congress and the public are reluctant to gainsay him. When he requests funds for economic assistance to Third World governments, he is much more likely to be disputed even though he may contend that such expenditures also provide the United States with security.

Altering that pattern will require a sustained effort at public education. It is not an effort that administrations themselves are likely to undertake with any real commitment, particularly in times when the economy is straightened and when they find it difficult enough to find funds for the military goals they have set for themselves. The agents for any change in public attitudes are therefore likely to be nongovernmental.

Over the past decade or so a vast array of public interest organizations have begun to put forward alternate conceptions of national security. Nearly all are devoted to particular issues – limiting population growth, enhancing environmental quality, eradicating world hunger, protecting human rights, and the like. Some are overt lobbies expressly seeking to alter political outcomes. Others devote themselves to research and educational activities, but are equally concerned with changing governmental behavior. Jointly they have succeeded in substantially raising public awareness of the vulnerability of the society to a variety of harms nonmilitary in nature, and of the limitations of military instruments for coping with many types of political problems.

One should not overestimate the achievements of these nongovernmental organizations, however. Awareness on the part of a substantial informed minority is one thing. Embodying it in public policy is a very much larger step. A society's consciousness changes only gradually – usually with the change of generations. The likelihood is that for the foreseeable future the American polity will continue to be much more willing to expend scarce resources on military forces than on measures to prevent or ameliorate the myriad profoundly dislocating effects of global demographic change. Yet those effects are likely to intensify with the passage of time. [...]. And while political will and energy are focused predominately on military solutions to the problems of national security, the nonmilitary tasks are likely to grow ever more difficult to accomplish and dangerous to neglect.

Notes

1   This is not to say that there are not recriminations following wars or military crises. Indeed, the governments that lead nations when war is thrust upon them – or when they initiate war themselves – are often subject to pillory. It may be alleged that their complacence allowed their nations' defenses to atrophy to a point where their military forces no longer deterred attack. Or they may be accused of recklessness that brought on a needless and expensive war. But while the war is still in prospect,

or while it is actually underway, there are too seldom any questions of leaders' abilities to command the requisite resources from their perceptibly threatened countrymen.

2   The same is true, it should be noted, about some "ordinary" foreign threats. In 1975 a majority of Senators and members of Congress did not believe that the presence of Soviet-supported Cuban troops in Angola posed a significant threat to U.S. security, and legislated limits on potential American involvement. Three years earlier they imposed a cutoff on U.S. bombing of targets in Cambodia and North Vietnam on the supposition that continued bombing would no longer (if it ever did) promote U.S. security, For a discussion of these Congressional curbs on the President's ability to commit American military resources, see Thomas M. Franck and Edward Weisband, *Foreign Policy By Congress* (New York: Oxford University Press, 1979), esp. pp. 13–23 and 46–57.

3   Some might argue that this is not the case in the strategic nuclear relationship between the United States and the Soviet Union, and that it is the knowledge within each government that its society is highly vulnerable to nuclear attacks by the other that keeps it from ever launching such an attack itself. Security is thus a product of vulnerability. This argument has considerable force as a logical construct. Yet, not surprisingly, neither superpower is content to act upon it. As technological developments seem to make possible the limitation of damage from at least some forms of nuclear attack, each pursues them for fear that the other will secure a momentary advantage. We are therefore faced with the worst of situations, in which one or the other may be unduly optimistic regarding the degree to which it might limit damage to its own society if it were to strike first. Decreased vulnerability accurately assessed may well enhance security even in strategic nuclear relations; misleadingly assessed it may bring disaster.

4   See, e.g., Walter S. Mossberg, "Kowtowing on the Oil Reserve," *The Wall Street Journal,* May 14, 1980, p. 20, and Sheilah Kast, "Filling Our Strategic Oil Reserve," *Washington Star,* February 9, 1981, the latter quoting Secretary-of-State-designate Alexander M. Haig, Jr., as calling the Saudi position "oil blackmail."

5   The Energy Information Administration's *Monthly Energy Review* (Washington: U.S. Department of Energy) presents a running tally of the size of the Strategic Petroleum Reserve. For a technical account of how the reserve is maintained, see Ruth M. Davis, "National Strategic Petroleum Reserve," *Science,* Vol. 213 (August 7, 1981), pp. 618–22. See also David A. Deese and Joseph S. Nye, eds., *Energy and Security* (Cambridge, Mass.: Ballinger, 1981), pp. 326–28, 399–403.

Barry Buzan

THE NATIONAL SECURITY PROBLEM
IN INTERNATIONAL RELATIONS

Source: *People, States and Fear: An Agenda for International Security Studies in the Post-Cold War Era* (London: Harvester Wheatsheaf, 1991), pp. 1–34.

FEW PEOPLE WOULD deny that security, whether individual, national, or international, ranks prominently among the problems facing humanity. National security is particularly central because states dominate many of the conditions that determine security at the other two levels, and states seem unable to coexist with each other in harmony. [...]

In order to have a proper understanding of the national security problem one must first understand the concept of security. In much of its prevailing usage, especially by those associated with state policy-making, this concept is so weakly developed as to be inadequate for the task. I seek to demonstrate that a simple-minded concept of security constitutes such a substantial barrier to progress that it might almost be counted as part of the problem. By simple-minded I mean an understanding of national security that is inadequately aware of the contradictions latent within the concept itself, and/or inadequately aware of the fact that the logic of security almost always involves high levels of interdependence among the actors trying to make themselves secure. [...]

Security is not the only concept through which the national security problem can be approached. Traditionally, most of the literature that attempted analysis or prescription was, and to some extent still is, based on the concepts of power and peace. Those who favour the approach through power derive their thinking from the Realist school of International Relations represented by writers such as E. H. Carr and Hans Morgenthau.[1] It can be argued that power not only reveals the basic pattern of capabilities in the international system but also highlights a prime motive for the behaviour of actors. Those who favour the approach through peace are more loosely associated into the Idealist school. Idealists argue that their concept leads them not only to see the problem in holistic terms, as opposed to the necessarily fragmented view of the Realists, but also that it focuses attention directly on the essential issue of war. Since war is the major threat arising from the national security problem, a solution to it would largely eliminate the problem from the international agenda.

Until the 1980s, these two approaches dominated thinking about the national security problem [...] [which] usually led [...] to highly polarized and conflicting prescriptions. Within this universe of debate the concept of security played a subsidiary role. Realists tended to see security as a derivative of power: an actor with enough power to reach a dominating position would acquire security as a result. This view was easy to take when power was defined in the very broad terms sketched by Morgenthau.[2] Although security was rightly placed as the goal, the understanding that power was the route to it was inherently self-defeating. Idealists tended to see security as a consequence of peace: a lasting peace would provide security for all.

[...] I argue that the concept of security is, in itself, a more versatile, penetrating and useful way to approach the study of international relations than either power or peace. It points to a prime motive for behaviour which is different from, but no less significant than, that provided by power. It also leads to a comprehensive perspective which is likewise different from, but no less useful than, that provided by peace. In combination, these add up to an analytical framework which stands comparison with anything available from the more established concepts. A more fully developed concept of security can be seen to lie between the extremes of power and peace, incorporating most of their insights, and adding more of its own. It provides many ideas which link the established conventions of the other two schools and help to bridge the political and intellectual gulf which normally, and to their mutual detriment, separates them.

* * *

It is almost no longer controversial to say that traditional conceptions of security were (and in many minds still are) too narrowly founded. That advance does not, however, mean that a consensus exists on what a more broadly constructed conception should look like. It is still a useful exercise to survey the ground on which any broader view must be built. In other words, it is necessary to map the domain of security as an essentially contested concept. This cartographic exercise is inevitably more abstract than empirical because its purpose is to define the conceptual sub-structures on which the mass of empirical studies by strategists and others rests. In trying to transcend criticisms aimed at too narrow a focus on national security, analysts must detach themselves from the pressures of day-to-day policy issues and the conventional modes of thought that have grown up around them. [...]

[In other words, one must] look more at the idea of security itself than at the contemporary empirical conditions in which security policy has to be formulated. What does security mean, in a general sense? How is this general meaning transferred to the specific entities such as people and states that must be the objects of security policy? What exactly is the referent object of security when one refers to national security? If it is the state, what does that mean? Is one to take the state as meaning the sum of the individuals within it, or is it in some sense more than the sum of its parts? In either case, how do individuals relate to an idea like national security in terms of their own interests? At the other extreme, what does international security mean? Does it apply to some entity higher than states, or is there some sense in which security among states is an indivisible phenomenon?

The character of this exercise is as much philosophical as empirical. Because security is an essentially contested concept it naturally generates questions as well as answers.

It encompasses several important contradictions and a host of nuances all of which can cause confusion if not understood. Major contradictions include that between defence and security, that between individual security and national security, that between national security and international security, and that between violent means and peaceful ends. Add to these the difficulties of determining the referent object of security (i.e. what is it that is to be made secure) and the pitfalls of applying the idea across a range of sectors (military, political, economic, environmental and societal), and the scope of the task becomes clear.

The object of the exercise is not to try to resolve these conundrums, but rather to explore them, and thereby clarify the difficulties – and the opportunities – that they pose for any attempt to apply the concept to real problems. The easy part of the exercise is using these insights to demolish the logic of simple-minded applications of security which ignore some of the contradictions they contain. For example, defence policies that raise threats by provoking the fears of other states may decrease security more than they increase it. The German naval challenge to Britain before the First World War is a case in point. The harder part of the exercise is finding derived concepts which enable the concept of security to be applied to practical situations in the full knowledge of the contradictions involved. The great merit of ideas like non-provocative defence is that they start from a solid understanding of both the necessity of, and the contradictions inherent within, the pursuit of military security.

As argued above, the nature of security defies pursuit of an agreed general definition. [...] But both the desire for intellectual neatness and the attempt to clarify the ends of security policy naturally create a demand for definition, and it is instructive to survey the results. Wolfers warned about the ambiguity of security, and Charles Schultze argues explicitly that: "The concept of national security does not lend itself to neat and precise formulation. It deals with a wide variety of risks about whose probabilities we have little knowledge and of contingencies whose nature we can only dimly perceive."[3] Despite these warnings, quite a number of writers have been unable to resist the temptation to try:

József Balázs: International security is determined basically by the internal and external security of the various social systems, by the extent, in general, to which system identity depends on external circumstances. Experts generally define social security as internal security. Its essential function is to ensure the political and economic power of a given ruling class, or the survival of the social system and an adequate degree of public security.[4]

Ian Bellany: Security itself is a relative freedom from war, coupled with a relatively high expectation that defeat will not be a consequence of any war that should occur.[5]

Penelope Hartland-Thunberg: [National security is] the ability of a nation to pursue successfully its national interests, as it sees them, any place in the world.[6]

Walter Lippmann: A nation is secure to the extent to which it is not in danger of having to sacrifice core values if it wishes to avoid war, and is able, if challenged, to maintain them by victory in such a war.[7]

Michael H. H. Louw: [National security includes traditional defence policy and also] the non-military actions of a state to ensure its total capacity to survive as a political entity in order to exert influence and to carry out its internal and international objectives.[8]

Giacomo Luciani: National security may be defined as the ability to withstand aggression from abroad.[9]

Laurence Martin: [Security is the] assurance of future well being.[10]

John E. Mroz: [Security is] the *relative freedom* from harmful threats.[11]

National Defence College (Canada): [National Security is] the preservation of a way of life acceptable to the [...] people and compatible with the needs and legitimate aspirations of others. It includes freedom from military attack or coercion, freedom from internal subversion and freedom from the erosion of the political, economic and social values which are essential to the quality of life.[12]

Frank N. Trager and F. L. Simonie: National security is that part of government policy having as its objective the creation of national and international political conditions favourable to the protection or extension of vital national values against existing and potential adversaries.[13]

Richard Ullman: A threat to national security is an action or sequence of events that (1) threatens drastically and over a relatively brief span of time to degrade the quality of life for the inhabitants of a state, or (2) threatens significantly to narrow the range of policy choices available to the government of a state or to private, nongovernmental entities (persons, groups, corporations) within the state.[14]

Ole Wæver: One can view 'security' as that which is in language theory called a speech act: ... it is the utterance itself that is the act ... By saying 'security' a state-representative moves the particular case into a specific area; claiming a special right to use the means necessary to block this development.[15]

Arnold Wolfers: Security, in any objective sense, measures the absence of threats to acquired values, in a subjective sense, the absence of fear that such values will be attacked.[16]

These definitions do a useful service in pointing out some of the criteria for national security, particularly the centrality of values, the timing and intensity of threats and the political nature of security as an objective of the state. But they can do a disservice by giving the concept an appearance of firmness which it does not merit. For purely semantic reasons, it is difficult to avoid the absolute sense of security. The word itself implies an absolute condition – something is either secure or insecure – and does not lend itself to the idea of a graded spectrum like that which fills the space between hot and cold. Most definitions avoid one or more crucial questions. What are 'core values'? Are they a fixed or a floating reference point? Are they in themselves free from contradictions? What sources of change are acceptable and what are not? Does 'victory' mean anything under contemporary conditions of warfare? Are subjective and objective aspects of security separable in any meaningful way? Is war the only form of threat relevant to national security? How can relative security goals be adequately defined? Is national security really national, or merely an expression of dominant groups? What right does a state have to define its security values in terms which require it to have influence beyond its own territory, with the almost inevitable infringement of others' security interests that this implies? How are terms like 'threat' and 'aggression' defined in relation to normal activity? The inadequacy of these definitions should be neither surprising nor discouraging. Years of effort have also failed to produce a generally accepted definition or measure for power. The concept of justice requires legions of lawyers to service its ambiguities. There is no reason to think that security will be any easier to crack, and as with power and justice, the absence of a universal definition does not prevent constructive discussion. Although precise definitions will always be controversial, the general sense of what one is talking about is nevertheless clear: the political effects of physical capabilities in the case of power; the pursuit of fair outcomes when behaviour is contested in the case of justice.

In the case of security, the discussion is about the pursuit of freedom from threat. When this discussion is in the context of the international system, security is about the ability of states and societies to maintain their independent identity and their functional integrity. In seeking security, state and society are sometimes in harmony with each other, sometimes opposed. Its bottom line is about survival, but it also reasonably includes a substantial range of concerns about the conditions of existence. Quite where this range of concerns ceases to merit the urgency of the 'security' label and becomes part of the everyday uncertainties of life, is one of the difficulties of the concept. Security is primarily about the fate of human collectivities, and only second-arily about the personal security of individual human beings. In the contemporary international system, the standard unit of security is thus the sovereign territorial state. The ideal type is the nation-state, where ethnic and cultural boundaries line up with political ones, as in Japan and Denmark. But since nations and states do not fit neatly together in many places, non-state collectivities, particularly nations, are also an important unit of analysis. Because the structure of the international system is anarchic (without central authority) in all of its major organizational dimensions (political, economic, societal), the natural focus of security concerns is the units. Since states are the dominant units, 'national security' is the central issue, both in its normal, but ambiguous, reference to the state and in its more direct application to ethno-cultural units. Since some military and ecological threats affect the conditions of survival on the entire planet, there is also an important sense in which security applies to the collectivity of humankind as a whole.

The security of human collectivities is affected by factors in five major sectors: military, political, economic, societal and environmental. Generally speaking, mili-tary security concerns the two-level interplay of the armed offensive and defensive capabilities of states, and states' perceptions of each other's intentions. Political secur-ity concerns the organizational stability of states, systems of government and the ideologies that give them legitimacy. Economic security concerns access to the resources, finance and markets necessary to sustain acceptable levels of welfare and state power. Societal security concerns the sustainability, within acceptable condi-tions for evolution, of traditional patterns of language, culture and religious and national identity and custom. Environmental security concerns the maintenance of the local and the planetary biosphere as the essential support system on which all other human enterprises depend. These five sectors do not operate in isolation from each other. Each defines a focal point within the security problematique, and a way of ordering priorities, but all are woven together in a strong web of linkages. [...]

[...] What is the referent object for security? What are the necessary conditions for security? [...]

Security as a concept clearly requires a referent object, for without an answer to the question 'The security of what?' the idea makes no sense. To answer simply 'The state', does not solve the problem. Not only is the state an amorphous, multifaceted, collective object to which security could be applied in many different ways, but also there are many states, and the security of one cannot be discussed without reference to the others. The search for a referent object of security goes hand-in-hand with that for its necessary conditions. One soon discovers that security has many potential referent objects. These objects of security multiply not only as the membership of the society of states increases, but also as one moves down through the state to the level of individuals, and up beyond it to the level of the international system as a whole. Since the security of any one referent object or level cannot be achieved in isolation from the others, the security of each becomes, in part, a condition for the security of all.

Notes

1   E. H. Carr, *The Twenty Years Crisis* (London, Macmillan: 1946, 2nd edn); Hans Morgenthau, *Politics Among Nations* (New York: Knopf, 1973, 5th edn). See also, for a more recent Neorealist view, Kenneth N. Waltz, *Theory of International Politics* (Reading, Mass.: Addison-Wesley, 1979). Realism in this context should not be confused with the philosophical school of the same name.

2   Peter Gellman, 'Hans J. Morgenthau and the legacy of political realism', *Review of International Studies*, 14:4 (1988), pp. 50–58.

3   Charles L. Schultze, 'The economic content of national security policy', *Foreign Affairs*, 51:3 (1973), pp. 529–30.

4   József Balázs, 'A note on the interpretation of security', *Development and Peace*, 6 (1985) (note 39), p. 146.

5   Ian Bellany, 'Towards a theory of international security', *Political Studies*, 29:1 (1981), p. 102.

6   Penelope Hartland-Thunberg, 'National economic security: interdependence and vulnerability', in Frans A.M. Alting von Geusau and Jacques Pelkmans (eds), *National Economic Security* (Tilburg: John F. Kennedy Institute, 1982), p. 50.

7   Cited in Arnold Wolfers, *Discord and Collaboration* (Baltimore: Johns Hopkins University Press, 1962), p. 150.

8   Michael H. H. Louw, *National Security* (Pretoria: ISS-University of Pretoria, 1978); the quote is from the introductory note titled 'The purpose of the symposium'.

9   Giacomo Luciani, 'The economic content of security', *Journal of Public Policy*, 8:2 (1989), p. 151.

10   Lawrence Martin, 'Can there be national security in an insecure age?' *Encounter*, 60:3 (1983), p. 12.

11   John E. Mroz, *Beyond Security: Private perceptions among Arabs and Israelis* (New York: International Peace Academy, 1980), p. 105 (emphasis in original).

12   Course documents, National Defence College of Canada, Kingston, 1989.

13   Frank N. Trager and Frank L. Simonie, 'An introduction to the study of national security', in F. N. Trager and P. S. Kronenberg, *National Security and American Society* (Lawrence: University Press of Kansas, 1973), p. 36.

14   Richard H. Ullman, 'Redefining security', *International Security,* 8:1 (1983) (note 32), p. 133.

15   Ole Wæver, 'Security, the speech act: analysing the politics of a word', unpublished second draft, Centre for Peace and Conflict Research, Copenhagen, 1989 (note 38), pp. 5–6.

16   Arnold Wolfers, 'National security as an ambiguous symbol', *Discord and Collaboration* (Baltimore: Johns Hopkins University Press, 1962), (note 45), p. 150.

David Baldwin

THE CONCEPT OF SECURITY

Source: *Review of International Studies*, vol. 23, no. 5, 1997, pp. 5–26.

Security as a contested concept

[...] SOME SCHOLARS have depicted security as an 'essentially contested concept'.[1] This contention must be addressed before we proceed to analyse the concept of security, for three reasons: First, there is some ambiguity as to what this means. Second, security may not fulfil the requirements for classification as an 'essentially contested concept'. And third, even if security were to be so classified, the implications for security studies may be incorrectly specified.[2]

Essentially contested concepts are said to be so value-laden that no amount of argument or evidence can ever lead to agreement on a single version as the 'correct or standard use'.[3] The stronger variants of this position lead to a radical sceptical nihilism in which there are no grounds for preferring one conception of security to another.[4] Acceptance of this position would make the kind of conceptual analysis undertaken here futile. There are, however, weaker forms of this position that allow one to differentiate between better and worse conceptualizations, even though ultimately none of the better conceptualizations can ever be said to be the best.[5] Since the analysis undertaken here purports only to improve on current usage, and not to identify the single best usage, it is compatible with the weaker variant of the essential contestedness hypothesis.

It is not clear, however, that security should be classified as an essentially contested concept. Of the several requirements for such a classification, two are especially questionable with respect to the concept of security. In the first place, the concept must be '*appraisive* in the sense that it signifies or accredits some kind of valued achievement'.[6] W. B. Gallie uses the concept of a 'champion' in sports to illustrate the point, i.e., to label a team as champion is to say that it plays the game better than other teams. Is the concept of security similar to the concept of a champion?

Neorealists seem to imply that it is. For them security is the most important goal a state can have in the same way that winning a championship is presumably the goal of all teams in Gallie's example. Just as teams compete to be champions, so states compete for security. And just as the champion is better at playing the game than other teams, so states with more security than other states are better at playing the neorealist version of the 'game' of international politics.[7] From the neorealist perspective, then, it is plausible to treat security as an appraisive concept.

Wolfers, however, presents a different view of security. He contends that states vary widely in the value they place on security and that some states may be so dissatisfied with the *status quo* that they are more interested in acquiring new values than in securing the values they have.[8] From this perspective, saying that one state has more security than another does not imply that one state is better than another any more than saying that one state has more people or land area implies that one state is better than another. For Wolfers international politics is not a 'game' in which all states play by the same 'rules' and compete for the same 'championship'.

Is security an appraisive concept? For neorealists, it may be. For others, such as Wolfers, it is not. The purpose of this discussion is not to settle the issue, but only to point out that this question is more difficult to answer than those who classify security as an essentially contested concept imply.

A second requirement for classifying a concept as essentially contested – indeed, the defining characteristic of such concepts – is that it must actually generate vigorous disputes as to the nature of the concept and its applicability to various cases. Gallie deliberately rules out policy disputes in 'practical life' that reflect conflicts of 'interests, tastes, or attitudes'. These, he suggests, are more likely to involve special pleading and rationalization than deep-seated philosophical disagreement.[9] Thus, much of the contemporary public policy debate over whether to treat the environment, budget deficits, crime or drug traffic as national security issues does not qualify as serious conceptual debate by Gallie's standards. For Gallie, essential contestedness implies more than that different parties use different versions of a concept. Each party must recognize the contested nature of the concept it uses, and each must engage in vigorous debate in defence of its particular conceptual viewpoint.[10] Yet the security studies literature, as the previous section pointed out, is virtually bereft of serious conceptual debate. The neorealists may have a different conception of security than Wolfers, but they do not debate his position; they ignore it.[11] Writers often fail to offer any definition of security. And if one is offered, it is rarely accompanied by a discussion of reasons for preferring one definition rather than others. This is hardly the kind of toe-to-toe conceptual combat envisioned by Gallie with respect to such matters as what constitutes justice, democracy, or a good Christian.

Even if security were to be classified as an essentially contested concept, some of the implications suggested by Buzan are questionable. One cannot use the designation of security as an essentially contested concept as an excuse for not formulating one's own conception of security as clearly and precisely as possible. Indeed, the whole idea of an essentially contested concept is that various parties purport to have a clearer and more precise understanding of the concept than others. Yet Buzan explicitly disavows any intention of formulating a precise definition and suggests that to attempt to do so is to misunderstand the function of essentially contested concepts in social science.[12]

'Such a conclusion', as Ken Booth points out, 'is unsatisfying. If we cannot name it, can we ever hope to achieve it?'[13]

Another consequence Buzan attributes to the essential contestability of security is a set of 'contradictions latent within the concept itself'.[14] It is not entirely clear what this means, but such 'contradictions' seem to include those between the individual and the state, between national and international security, between violent means and peaceful ends, between blacks and whites in South Africa, between the Jews and Nazi Germany, and so on. Indeed, Buzan's assertion that the 'principal security contradiction' for most states is between their own security and that of other states suggests that the Cold War itself could be described as a 'contradiction' between the security of the NATO allies and the Warsaw Pact countries.[15] It is true, of course, that the state's pursuit of security for itself may conflict with the individual's pursuit of security; but this is an empirical fact rather than a conceptual problem. Most of the phenomena designated by Buzan as conceptual 'contradictions' could more fruitfully be called instances of empirically verifiable conflict between various actors or policies.

In sum, the alleged essential contestedness of the concept of security represents a challenge to the kind of conceptual analysis undertaken here only in its strong variants. There are some grounds for questioning whether security ought to be classified as an essentially contested concept at all. And even if it is so classified, the implications may be misspecified. Insofar as the concept is actually contested this does not seem to stem from 'essential contestability'. Security is more appropriately described as a confused or inadequately explicated concept than as an essentially contested one. [...]

Specifying the security problematique

National security, as Wolfers suggested, can be a dangerously ambiguous concept if used without specification. The purpose of this section is to identify some specifications that would facilitate analysing the rationality of security policy. The discussion begins with specifications for defining security as a policy objective and proceeds to specifications for defining policies for pursuing that objective.

The point of departure is Wolfers' characterization of security as 'the absence of threats to acquired values',[16] which seems to capture the basic intuitive notion underlying most uses of the term security. Since there is some ambiguity in the phrase 'absence of threats', Wolfers' phraseology will be reformulated as 'a low probability of damage to acquired values'. This does not significantly change Wolfers' meaning, and it allows for inclusion of events such as earthquakes, which Ullman has argued should be considered 'threats' to security.[17] The advantage of this reformulation can be illustrated as follows: In response to threats of military attack, states develop deterrence policies. Such policies are intended to provide security by lowering the probability that the attack will occur. In response to the 'threat' of earthquakes, states adopt building codes. This does not affect the probability of earthquakes, but it does lower the probability of damage to acquired values. Thus the revised wording focuses on the preservation of acquired values and not on the presence or absence of 'threats'. With this reformulation, security in its most general sense can be defined in terms of two specifications: Security for whom? And security for which values?

Security for whom?

As Buzan rightly points out, a concept of security that fails to specify a 'referent object' makes little sense.[18] For Buzan, however, a simple specification, such as 'the state' or 'the individual', does not suffice. Since there are many states and individuals, and since their security is interdependent, he argues that the 'search for a referent object of security' must go 'hand-in-hand with that for its necessary conditions'.[19] As noted above, however, this approach confuses concept specification with empirical observation. For purposes of specifying the concept of security, a wide range of answers to the question, 'Security for whom?' is acceptable: the individual (some, most, or all individuals), the state (some, most, or all states), the international system (some, most, or all international systems), etc. The choice depends on the particular research question to be addressed.

Security for which values?

Individuals, states, and other social actors have many values. These may include physical safety, economic welfare, autonomy, psychological well-being, and so on. The concept of national security has traditionally included political independence and territorial integrity as values to be protected; but other values are sometimes added. The former American Secretary of Defense Harold Brown, for example, includes the maintenance of 'economic relations with the rest of the world on reasonable terms' in his conception of national security.[20] Failure to specify which values are included in a concept of national security often generates confusion. Wolfers distinguished between objective and subjective dimensions of security.[21] His purpose was to allow for the possibility that states might overestimate or underestimate the actual probability of damage to acquired values. In the former case, reducing unjustified fears might be the objective of security policy; while in the latter case, a state might perceive itself as secure when it was not. The definition proposed above clearly includes the objective dimension, and the subjective dimension can be accommodated by designating 'peace of mind' or the 'absence of fear' as values that can be specified. Whether one wants to do this, of course, depends on the research task at hand.

It should be noted that specification of this dimension of security should not be in terms of 'vital interests' or 'core values' [...] [f]or [...] this prejudges the value of security as a policy objective, and thus prejudices comparison of security with other policy objectives.

Although the two specifications above suffice to define the concept of security, they provide little guidance for its pursuit. In order to make alternative security policies comparable with each other and with policies for pursuing other goals, the following specifications are also needed.

How much security?

Security, according to Wolfers, is a value 'of which a nation can have more or less and which it can aspire to have in greater or lesser measure'.[22] Writing during the same period as Wolfers, Bernard Brodie observed that not everyone views security as a matter of degree. He cited as an example a statement by General Jacob L. Devers:

> National security is a condition which cannot be qualified. We shall either
> be secure, or we shall be insecure. We cannot have partial security. If we
> are only half secure, we are not secure at all.[23]

Although Brodie, Wolfers, and others have criticized such views, the idea of security
as a matter of degree cannot be taken for granted. Knorr has noted that treating
national security threats as 'matters of more or less causes a lot of conceptual uneasi-
ness'.[24] And Buzan refers to similar difficulties:

> The word itself implies an absolute condition – something is either secure
> or insecure – and does not lend itself to the idea of a graded spectrum like
> that which fills the space between hot and cold.[25]

If this were true, it would be necessary to depart from common usage in defining
security as an analytical concept. This, however, does not appear to be the case. It is
quite common in ordinary language to speak of varying degrees of security.
    One reason it is important to specify the degree of security a country has or seeks
is that absolute security is unattainable. Buzan recognizes this, but treats it as a 'logical
problem' arising from 'the essentially contested nature of security as a concept'.[26] If
security is conceived of as a matter of degree, Buzan observes, 'then complicated and
objectively unanswerable questions arise about how much security is enough'.[27] This,
of course, is precisely why security should be so conceived. It is not clear why such
questions should be described as 'objectively unanswerable'. They are precisely the
kind of questions that economists have been addressing for a long time, i.e., how to
allocate scarce resources among competing ends.[28] Nor is there anything peculiar
about the unattainability of absolute security. As Herbert Simon notes, the 'attain-
ment of objectives is *always* a matter of degree'.[29]
    In a world in which scarce resources must be allocated among competing objec-
tives, none of which is completely attainable, one cannot escape from the question
'How much is enough?' and one should not try.

From what threats?

Those who use the term security usually have in mind particular kinds of threats. [...]
Since threats to acquired values can arise from many sources, it is helpful if this dimension is clearly specified. Vague references to the 'Communist threat' to national security during the Cold War often failed to specify whether they referred to ideological
threats, economic threats, military threats, or some combination thereof, thus impeding rational debate of the nature and magnitude of the threat. The concept of threat
referred to in this specification differs from that used by many students of international politics and national strategy. Such scholars often use the term threat to refer
to actions that convey a conditional commitment to punish unless one's demands are
met.[30] In ordinary language, however, one often finds references to epidemics, floods,
earthquakes, or droughts as 'threats' to acquired values. Ullman and others have
argued that the concept of security should be expanded to include such phenomena.[31]
There seems to be no reason not to use this more expansive concept of threats, especially since it comports with common usage. Those who wish to refer to conditional

commitments to punish by social actors as security threats may make that clear when specifying this dimension of security.

By what means?

Like wealth, the goal of security can be pursued by a wide variety of means. [...] Specification of this dimension of security is especially important in discussions of international politics. Since the publication of Wolfers' article, 'security studies' has emerged as a recognized subfield in international relations. The tendency of some security studies scholars to define the subfield entirely in terms of 'the threat, use, and control of military force'[32] can lead to confusion as to the means by which security may be pursued. It can also prejudice discussion in favour of military solutions to security problems.

At what cost?

The pursuit of security always involves costs, i.e., the sacrifice of other goals that could have been pursued with the resources devoted to security. Specification of this dimension of security policy is important because writers sometimes imply that costs do not matter. [...] From the standpoint of a rational policy-maker, however, [...] [c]osts always matter. [...]

[...] In thinking about security, as in thinking about other policy goals, it is helpful to remember the TANSTAAFL principle, i.e., 'There ain't no such thing as a free lunch'.[33]

Wolfers suggests an additional reason for specifying this dimension of security. Arguing against those who would place national security policy beyond moral judgment, he contends that the sacrifice of other values for the sake of security inevitably makes such policies 'a subject for moral judgment'.[34] Given the crimes that have been committed in the name of 'national security', this is a helpful reminder.

In what time period?

The most rational policies for security in the long run may differ greatly from those for security in the short run. In the short run, a high fence, a fierce dog, and a big gun may be useful ways to protect oneself from the neighbours. But in the long run, it may be preferable to befriend them.[35] Short-run security policies may also be in conflict with long-run security policies.[36] [...]

The question remains, however: 'How much specification is enough?' Must all of these dimensions be specified in detail every time one uses the concept of security? Obviously not. Both the number of dimensions in need of specification and the degree of specificity required will vary with the research task at hand. Each of the dimensions can be specified in very broad or very narrow terms. Not all of the dimensions need to be specified all the time. For most purposes, however, meaningful scientific communication would seem to require at least some indication of how much security is being sought for which values of which actors with respect to which threats. For purposes of systematic comparison of policy alternatives, the last three specifications, i.e., means, costs, and time period, must be specified.

Although the dimensions of security can be specified very broadly, the utility of the concept does not necessarily increase when this is done. For example, if security is specified in terms of threats to *all* acquired values of a state, it becomes almost synonymous with national welfare or national interest and is virtually useless for distinguishing among policy objectives.[37]

The value of security

Security is valued by individuals, families, states, and other actors. Security, however, is not the only thing they value; and the pursuit of security necessitates the sacrifice of other values. It is therefore necessary to ask how important is security relative to other values. Three ways of answering this question will be discussed [...].

The prime value approach

One way of determining the value of security is to ask what life would be like without it. The most famous answer to this question is that by Thomas Hobbes to the effect that life would be 'solitary, poor, nasty, brutish, and short'.[38] Such reasoning has led many scholars to assert the 'primacy' of the goal of security.[39] The logic underlying this assertion is that security is a prerequisite for the enjoyment of other values such as prosperity, freedom, or whatever.

The fallacy in this line of argument is exposed by asking the Hobbesian question with respect to breathable air, potable water, salt, food, shelter or clothing. The answer is roughly the same for each of these as it is for security; and a plausible case for the 'primacy' of each can be made. This exercise, of course, merely underscores a truth King Midas learned long ago, i.e., that the value of something – gold, security, water, or whatever – is not an inherent quality of the good itself but rather a result of external social conditions – supply and demand. The more gold one has, the less value one is likely to place on an additional ounce; and the more security one has, the less one is likely to value an increment of security.

To the extent that the prime value approach implies that security outranks other values for all actors in all situations, it is both logically and empirically indefensible. Logically, it is flawed because it provides no justification for limiting the allocation of resources to security in a world where absolute security is unattainable. Empirically it is flawed because it fails to comport with the way people actually behave. Prehistoric people may have lived in caves for security, but they did not remain there all the time. Each time they ventured forth in pursuit of food, water or adventure, they indicated a willingness to sacrifice the security of the cave for something they presumably valued more. And in choosing places to live, settlers often forgo the security of high mountain-tops in favour of less secure locations with more food or water. Likewise, modern states do not allocate all of their resources to the pursuit of security, even in wartime. Even the most beleaguered society allocates some of its resources to providing food, clothing, and shelter for its population.

Even if 'absolute' security were a possibility, it is not obvious that people would seek it. As Robert Dahl and Charles Lindblom observed long ago, 'probably most people do not really want "absolute" security, if such a state is imaginable; "optimum" security would probably still leave an area of challenge, risk, doubt, danger, hazard, and anxiety. Men are not lotus-eaters'.[40]

The core value approach

The core value approach allows for other values by asserting that security is one of several important values. Although this approach mitigates the logical and empirical difficulties associated with the prime value approach, it does not eliminate them. One is still confronted with the need to justify the classification of some values as core values and other values as non-core values. And if core values are always more important than other values, this approach cannot justify allocating any resources whatsoever to the pursuit of non-core values.

The marginal value approach

The marginal value approach is the only one that provides a solution to the resource allocation problem. This approach is not based on any assertion about the value of security to all actors in all situations. Instead, it is rooted in the assumption that the law of diminishing marginal utility is as applicable to security as it is to other values. Asserting the primacy of security is like asserting the primacy of water, food, or air. A certain minimum amount of each is needed to sustain life, but this does not mean that the value of a glass of water is the same for a person stranded in a desert and a person drowning in a lake. As King Midas learned, the value of an increment of something depends on how much of it one has.

According to the marginal value approach, security is only one of many policy objectives competing for scarce resources and subject to the law of diminishing returns. Thus, the value of an increment of national security to a country will vary from one country to another and from one historical context to another, depending not only on how much security is needed but also on how much security the country already has. Rational policy-makers will allocate resources to security only as long as the marginal return is greater for security than for other uses of the resources.

There is nothing new about treating national security as one of many public policy objectives competing for scarce resources and subject to diminishing returns. Wolfers and his contemporaries used this approach, and defence economists have long advocated it.[41] Its neglect in recent writings on national security, however, suggests the need to reiterate its importance.[42]

Critical theorists, feminist theorists, Realists, neorealists, liberals, Third World theorists, and globalists all live in a world of scarce resources. In the end, all must confront the question posed by Booth of 'how many frigates to build'.[43] Even pacifists, who answer 'none', must decide how to allocate resources among competing non-military uses. The analytical tools of marginal utility analysis are available for use by any or all of the schools mentioned above.

It is not always clear whether statements about the importance of security as a goal are empirical observations or part of the definition of security. The 'high politics/ low politics' distinction, however, suggests that some scholars may be making the value of security a matter of definition. Buzan, for example, includes in security only those concerns that 'merit the urgency of the "security" label', thus suggesting that urgency is part of his definition of security. And when he refers to 'attempts to *elevate* particular economic issues onto the national security agenda', he seems to imply the inherent superiority of that agenda. Likewise, the intensity of the threat seems to be a defining characteristic of security for Buzan.[44]

Ullman's proposed definition of national security threats also includes elements that prejudge the importance of security. Thus, he does not include all threats that 'degrade the quality of life for the inhabitants of a state', but only those that do so 'drastically' and quickly. And he does not include all threats that 'narrow the range of policy choices available to the state', but only those that do so 'significantly'.[45] Both Buzan and Ullman seem to rule out the possibility of a minor or trivial national security threat by conceptual fiat.

Policy advocates, of course, often try to win acceptance for their proposals by declaring them to be 'security issues'. Navies wanting frigates, educators wanting scholarships, environmentalists wanting pollution controls, and so on are likely to portray their respective causes as matters of 'national security'. In this context the declaration that something is a security issue is a way of asserting its importance. Thus one may argue that building urgency into the concept of security is a common practice.[46] If this practice is followed, however, the concept becomes useless for rational policy analysis because the value of security relative to other goals will have been conceptually prejudged. [...]

Notes

1   Barry Buzan, *People, States and Fear: An Agenda for International Security Studies in the Post-Cold War Era,* 2nd edn (Boulder, CO, 1991), and Barry Buzan, 'Peace, Power and Security: Contending Concepts in the Study of International Relations', *Journal of Peace Research,* 21 (1984), pp. 109–25; and Richard E. Little, 'Ideology and Change', in Barry Buzan and R. J. Barry Jones (eds.), *Change and the Study of International Relations: the Evaded Dimension* (New York, 1981), pp. 30–45. For the original formulation, see W. B. Gallie, 'Essentially Contested Concepts', *Proceedings of the Aristotelian Society, N.S.,* 56 (1956), pp. 167–98.

2   It should also be noted that the concept of an 'essentially contested concept' has itself been contested. For references, see Christine Swanton, 'On the "Essential Contestedness" of Political Concepts', *Ethics,* 95 (1985), pp. 811–27; Alasdair MacIntyre, 'The Essential Contestability of Some Social Concepts', *Ethics,* 84 (1973), pp. 1–9; John N. Gray, 'On the Contestability of Social and Political Concepts', *Political Theory,* 5 (1977), pp. 330–48; and Felix E. Oppenheim, *Political Concepts: A Reconstruction* (Chicago, 1981), pp. 182–85.

3   Gallie, 'Essentially Contested Concepts', p. 168.

4   Gray, 'On the Contestability', p. 343; Swanton, 'On the "Essential Contestedness"', pp. 813–14.

5   Swanton, 'On the "Essential Contestedness"', pp. 813–14.

6   Gallie, 'Essentially Contested Concepts', p. 171. Not all value judgments are appraisive. Appraisal presupposes an accepted set of criteria. Examples suggested by Oppenheim include 'grading apples or student papers, evaluating paintings in terms of their market value, [and] wine tasting'. *Political Concepts,* pp. 170–76.

7   Cf. Kenneth N. Waltz, *Theory of International Politics* (Reading, MA, 1979), and 'The Emerging Structure of International Politics', *International Security*, 18 (1993), pp. 44–79; and John J. Mearsheimer, 'Disorder Restored', in Graham Allison and Gregory F. Treverton (eds.), *Rethinking America's Security* (New York, 1992), pp. 213–37.

8   Arnold Wolfers, '"National Security" as an Ambiguous Symbol', *Political Science Quarterly*, 67 (1952), pp. 491–92.

9   Gallie, 'Essentially Contested Concepts', p. 169.

10 Ibid., p. 172.

11 In Waltz's *Theory*, for example, security is posited as the principal goal of states; but little attention is given to defining it or defending the definition against other conceptions of security. Wolfers is never cited. What Tickner describes as 'a fully fledged debate about the meaning of security' beginning in the 1980s is better characterized as a series of attacks on Realism and neorealism. See J. Ann Tickner, 'Re-visioning Security', in Ken Booth and Steve Smith (eds.), *International Relations Theory Today* (Oxford, 1995), p. 177. A debate implies that there are two sides. With the possible exception of Buzan, no example of a Realist or neorealist engaging critics in serious conceptual debate has come to this author's attention. And Buzan cannot fairly be described as a defender of traditional Realist or neorealist conceptions of security.

12 Buzan, *People, States*, pp. 16, 374; and 'Peace, Power', p. 125.

13 Ken Booth, 'Security and Emancipation', *Review of International Studies*, 17 (1991), p. 317. On Buzan's claim regarding the essential contestability of security, see also Peter Digeser, 'The Concept of Security', paper delivered at the 1994 Annual Meeting of the American Political Science Association, 14 September 1994.

14 Buzan, *People, States*, pp. 1–2, 15, 364.

15 Ibid., p. 364.

16 Wolfers, 'National Security', p. 485.

17 Richard H. Ullman, 'Redefining Security', *International Security*, 8 (1983), pp. 129–53.

18 Buzan, *People, States*, p. 26.

19 Ibid.

20 Harold Brown, *Thinking About National Security: Defense and Foreign Policy in a Dangerous World* (Boulder, CO, 1983), p. 4.

21 Wolfers, 'National Security', p. 485.

22 Ibid., p. 484.

23 Bernard Brodie, *National Security Policy and Economic Stability*, Yale Institute for International Studies Memorandum No. 33 (New Haven, CT, 1950), p. 5.

24 'Economic Interdependence and National Security', in Klaus Knorr and Frank N. Trager (eds), *Economic Issues and National Security* (Lawrence, KS, 1977), p. 18.

25 Buzan, *People, States*, p. 18.

26 Ibid., p. 330.

27 Ibid.

28 Cf. Thomas C. Schelling, *International Economics* (Boston, MA, 1958), pp. 518–19; Alain C. Enthoven and K. Wayne Smith, *How Much Is Enough?* (New York, 1971); Charles J. Hitch and Roland N. McKean, *The Economics of Defense in the Nuclear Age* (Cambridge, MA, 1960); James R. Schlesinger, *The Political Economy of National Security* (New York, 1960); and Thomas C. Schelling and Malcolm Palmatier, 'Economic Reasoning in National Defense', in Alan A. Brown, Egon Neuberger and

Malcolm Palmatier (eds.), *Perspectives in Economics: Economists Look at their Fields of Study* (New York, 1971), pp. 143–59.

29   Herbert A. Simon, *Administrative Behaviour*, 3rd edn (New York, 1976), p. 177. On this point, see also David A. Baldwin, *Economic Statecraft* (Princeton, 1985), p. 131.

30   On the concept of threats, see David A. Baldwin, *Paradoxes of Power* (Oxford, 1989), pp. 45–81.

31   Ullman, 'Redefining Security'. See also Graham Allison and Gregory F. Treverton (eds.), *Rethinking America's Security: Beyond Cold War to New World Order* (New York, 1992).

32   Stephen M. Walt, 'The Renaissance of Security Studies', *International Studies Quarterly*, 35 (1991), p. 212. See also Klaus Knorr, 'National Security Studies: Scope and Structure of the Field', in Frank N. Trager and Philip S. Kronenberg (eds.), *National Security and American Society: Theory, Process and Policy* (Lawrence, KS, 1973), p. 6; and Richard Schultz, Roy Godson and Ted Greenwood (eds.), *Security Studies for the 1990s* (New York, 1993), p. 2.

33   Edwin G. Dolan, *TANSTAAFL* (New York, 1971), p. 14.

34   Wolfers, 'National Security', pp. 498–99.

35   Cf. Kenneth E. Boulding, 'Towards a Pure Theory of Threat Systems', *American Economic Review*, 53 (1963), pp. 424–34.

36   See Robert A. Dahl and Charles E. Lindblom, *Politics, Economics and Welfare* (New York, 1953), pp. 50–51.

37   'Virtually' rather than 'totally' useless because even the term 'national interest' distinguishes between national interests and international or subnational interests. And even a very broad concept of security distinguishes between protecting *acquired* values and attempts to acquire additional values.

38   *The Leviathan* (1651), Part I, Ch. XIII.

39   See Richard Smoke, 'National Security Affairs', in Fred I. Greenstein and Nelson W Polsby (eds.), *Handbook of Political Science, Vol. 8: International Politics* (Reading, MA, 1975), pp. 247–48; Mearsheimer, 'Disorder', pp. 221–22; Waltz, *Theory*, p. 126; Joseph M. Grieco, *Cooperation Among Nations: Europe, America, and Non-Tariff Barriers to Trade* (Ithaca, NY, 1990), p. 39; Robert G. Gilpin, 'The Richness of the Tradition of Political Realism', in Robert O. Keohane (ed.), *Neorealism and Its Critics* (New York, 1), p. 305; and Lawrence Freedman, 'The Concept of Security', in Mary Hawkesworth and Maurice Kogan (eds.), *Encyclopedia of Government and Politics*, vol. 2 (London, 1992), p. 730.

40   Dahl and Lindblom, *Politics, Economics*, p. 50. Recent writers who have expressed similar doubts about the value of security include: Barry Buzan, 'Response to Kolodziej', *Arms Control*, 13 (1992), p. 484; James Der Derian, 'The Value of Security: Hobbes, Marx, Nietzsche, and Baudrillard', in Ronnie Lipschutz (ed.), *On Security* (New York, 1995), pp. 24–45; and Ole Wæver, 'Securitization and Desecuritization', ibid., pp. 46–86.

41   E.g. Wolfers, 'National Security'; Frederick S. Dunn, 'The Present Course of International Relations Research', *World Politics*, 2 (1949), p. 94; Bernard Brodie, 'Strategy as a Science', *World Politics*, 1 (1949), pp. 467–88; Schelling, *International Economics*; Charles J. Hitch, 'National Security Policy as a Field for Economics Research', *World Politics*, 12 (1960), pp. 434–52; and Schlesinger, *Political Economy*. 'It is peculiar to the training of an economist that he is continually aware of the need to optimize rather than just to maximize, of the need to weight explicitly the value

of more progress toward one objective at the expense of progress toward another. By training, he is suspicious of any analysis that singles out one conspicuous variable, some "dominant" feature, on which all attention is to be focused, and which is to be maximized by putting arbitrary limits on the other variables.' Schelling and Palmatier, 'Economic Reasoning', p. 148.

42   Buzan's *People, States* contains only passing references to costs and no reference to diminishing returns.

43   Booth, 'Security and Emancipation', p. 325.

44   Ibid., pp.119, 131, 134. Emphasis added.

45   Ullman, 'Redefining Security', p. 133.

46   For a strong defence of this approach, see Wæver, 'Securitization and Desecuritization'.

Ken Booth

SECURITY AND EMANCIPATION

Source: *Review of International Studies*, vol. 17, no. 4, 1991, pp. 313–26.

Word problems and world problems

OUR WORK IS our words, but our words do not work any more. They have not worked for some time. [...] As a result [...], we cannot expect to deal successfully with world problems if we cannot sort out our word problems.

The interregnum

One of the interesting word problems at the moment involves the difficulty of giving a satisfactory name to the present stage of world affairs. The phrase 'post-Cold War world' is widely used, but it is not apposite. The end of the Cold War obviously partly defines when we are living, but there is, and has been for years, much more to this turbulent era: the growth of complex interdependence, the erosion of sovereignty, amazing advances in communications, the declining utility of force, the degradation of nature, huge population growth, the internationalization of the world economy, the spread of global life styles, constant technological innovation, the dissemination of modern weaponry, the growing scope for non-state actors and so on. [...] Rosenau describes our times as 'post-international politics'. This is meant to suggest the decline of long-standing patterns, as more and more of the interactions that sustain world politics do not directly involve states.

Economic and loyalty patterns are becoming more complex. A recent book asks: 'Are Korean stocks purchased in London by a Turk part of the Korean, British or Turkish economy?' The answer it gives breaks out of the state framework and concludes that they are clearly part of a more complicated global economy.[1] Meanwhile, there is the simultaneous development of both more local and more global identities, as people want meaning and authenticity in their lives, as well as economic well-being. The local/global sense of identification is not mutually exclusive; it is part of the development of the more complex and overlapping identities which will characterize the future. The result will be the breaking down of the statist Tebbit *prinzip*: *ein* passport, *ein* leader, *ein* cricket team.

If we must name things correctly before we can 'live in truth', as Vaclev Havel has put it, we need to name when we are living.[2] *Marxism Today*'s label, 'New Times', is the most helpful so far. But if an entirely satisfactory label is still to be conceived, there is at least one neat form of words, from 60 years ago, which speaks exactly to the present. 'The old is dying', Gramsci wrote, 'and the new cannot be born; in this interregnum there arises a great diversity of morbid symptoms.'[3] An 'interregnum' is a useful way to think about the present. [...]

A turning point for inter-state war

The forces shaping the new context for world politics, as ever, offer both dangers and opportunities. What demands our pressing attention is the unprecedented destruction threatened by modern military technology and environmental damage. Since the direct and indirect costs of failure in what might be termed global management are now so high, conscious cultural evolution is imperative.[4] One area where this has become increasingly apparent is security, which has been the first obligation of governments and is the transcendent value of strategic studies, a dominant sub-field of international politics since the mid-1950s.

Until recently the security problematic was well-focused. A group of people like us, turning up at a conference like this, could predict what a speaker would talk about if 'security' was in the title of a talk. It is not long ago when issues such as Cruise, Pershing, SDI and the SS-20 made strategists out of all of us; and gave President Reagan sleepless afternoons. The dominating security questions were: Is the Soviet threat growing? What is the strategic balance? And would the deployment of a particular weapon help stability? In that period of looking at world politics through a missile-tube and gun-sight, weapons provided most of the questions, and they provided most of the answers – whatever the weapon, whatever the context, and whatever the cost. [...]

Military questions will obviously continue to have an important part in the concerns of all students of international politics. However, it is doubtful whether they will be as central a preoccupation, except for some obvious regional conflicts. This is because the institution of inter-state war is in historic decline. [....] Today states will only fight, with the odd deviant, if they or their allies and associates are actually attacked. Otherwise states are running out of motives for war. Within states it is a different matter; there is no diminution of internal violence.

Given the changing costs and benefits of inter-state war, it is too soon in history to describe the international system and the logic of anarchy as immutably a 'war system'. Indeed, there are accumulating signs that world politics is fitfully coming to the end of a 350-year span of history, which was dominated by the military competition between the technologically advanced states of the north, with realist outlooks, Machiavellian ethics and a Clausewitzian philosophy of war.

The period of history just described – the 'Westphalian system' – produced a game, in Raymond Aron's noted formulation, played by diplomats and soldiers on behalf of statesmen. Through these centuries the security game states learned to play was 'power politics', with threats producing counterthreats, alliances, counteralliances, and so on. This has been the basic raw material of strategic studies for the past thirty years. The question we now face is: what security game should be played in the 'New Times' which do not yet have a suitable name?

Security in our new times

The elements of the new security game I want to propose should not be unfamiliar. The ingredients include ideas from such diverse sources as the World Society School, alternative security thinking, classical international relations, critical theory, peace research, strategic studies, and neo-realism. If these different approaches are conceived as tramlines, some are to be extended, some bent and others turned back on themselves, until they all reach a common point. I call this point of convergence utopian realism. It is a mixture of what William T. R. Fox called 'empirical realism'[5] with some notion of what others would call global ethics, or world order principles.

The most obvious difference between security from a utopian realist perspective and traditional security thinking lies in the former's holistic character and non-statist approach. The last decade or so has seen a growing unease with the traditional concept of security, which privileges the state and emphasizes military power. [...]

The unease with traditional security thinking has expressed itself in a frequent call for a 'broadening' or 'updating' of the concept of security. In practice little actual new thinking has taken place. A notable exception, of course, was Barry Buzan's *People, States and Fear,* first published in 1983. [...] But even that book, excellent as it is, can primarily be read as an explanation of the difficulties surrounding the concept. The book not only argues that security is an 'essentially contested concept' defying pursuit of an agreed definition, but it asserts that there is not much point struggling to make it uncontested. Such a conclusion is unsatisfying. If we cannot name it, can we ever hope to achieve it? [...]

The pressures to broaden and update the concept of security have come from two sources. First, the problems with the traditionally narrow military focus of security have become increasingly apparent. It is only necessary here to mention the greater awareness of the pressures of the security dilemma, the growing appreciation of security interdependence, the widespread recognition that the arms race has produced higher levels of destructive power but not a commensurate growth of security, and the realization of the heavy burden on economies of extravagant defence spending. The second set of pressures has come from the strengthening claim of other issue areas for inclusion on the security agenda. The daily threat to the lives and well-being of most people and most nations is different from that suggested by the traditional military perspective. Old-fashioned territorial threats still exist in some parts of the world. [...] For the most part, however, the threats to the well-being of individuals and the interests of nations across the world derive primarily not from a neighbour's army but from other challenges, such as economic collapse, political oppression, scarcity, overpopulation, ethnic rivalry, the destruction of nature, terrorism, crime and disease.

In most of the respects just mentioned people are more threatened by the policies and inadequacies of their own government than by the Napoleonic ambitions of their neighbour's. To countless millions of people in the world it is their own state, and not 'The Enemy' that is the primary security threat. In addition, the security threat to the regimes running states is often internal rather than external. It is almost certainly true that more governments around the world at this moment are more likely to be toppled by their own armed forces than by those of their neighbours. [...]

The broader security problems [...] are obviously not as cosmically threatening as was the Cold War. But they are problems of profound significance. They already cost many lives and they could have grave consequences if left untreated. The repression of human rights, ethnic and religious rivalry, economic breakdown and so on can create dangerous instability at the domestic level which in turn can exacerbate the tensions that lead to violence, refugees and possibly inter-state conflict. [...]

Communities which are wealthy and have a significant level of social justice do not seem to fight each other. There has not been a war since 1945 between the 44 richest countries.[6] 'Security communities' – islands of what Kenneth Boulding called 'stable peace'[7] – have developed in several parts of the world. For whatever reason there does seem to be a correlation between democracy and freedom on the one hand and warlessness (within security communities) on the other. As a result even relatively conservative thinkers about international politics seem increasingly to accept that order in world affairs depends on at least minimal levels of political and social justice. This is where, finally, emancipation comes in.

Emancipation versus power and order

Emancipation should logically be given precedence in our thinking about security over the mainstream themes of power and order. The trouble with privileging power and order is that they are at somebody else's expense (and are therefore potentially unstable). [...] During the Cold War of the 1960s and 1970s there was military stability in Europe (hot war would not pay for either side) but there was no political stability (because millions were oppressed). In the end the vaunted 'order' created by dividing Europe into the two most heavily armed camps in history proved so unstable that it collapsed like a house of cards (and miraculously almost without violence). True (stable) security can only be achieved by people and groups if they do not deprive others of it.

'Security' means the absence of threats.[8] Emancipation is the freeing of people (as individuals and groups) from those physical and human constraints which stop them carrying out what they would freely choose to do. War and the threat of war is one of those constraints, together with poverty, poor education, political oppression and so on. Security and emancipation are two sides of the same coin. Emancipation, not power or order, produces true security. Emancipation, theoretically, is security. Implicit in the preceding argument is the Kantian idea that we should treat people as ends and not means. States, however, should be treated as means and not ends. It is on the position of the state where the conception of security as a process of emancipation parts company with the neo-realist conception as elaborated in *People, States and Fear*. The litmus test concerns the primary referent object: is it states, or is it people?

Whose security comes first? I want to argue, following the World Society School, buttressed on this point by Hedley Bull that individual humans are the ultimate referent. Given all the attention he paid to order between states, it is often overlooked that Bull considered 'world order' – between people – to be 'more fundamental and primordial' than international order: 'the ultimate units of the great society of all mankind', he wrote, 'are not states [...] but individual human beings, which are permanent and indestructible in a sense in which groupings of them of this or that sort are not'.[9]

Those entities called 'states' are obviously important features of world politics, but they are unreliable, illogical and too diverse in their character to use as the primary referent objects for a comprehensive theory of security:

- States are unreliable as primary referents because whereas some are in the business of security (internal and external) some are not. It cannot serve the theory and practice of security to privilege Al Capone regimes. The traditional (national) security paradigm is invariably based upon a text-book notion of 'the state', but the evidence suggests that many do not even approximate it. Can 'security' be furthered by including the regimes of such as Hitler, Stalin or Saddam Hussein among the primary referents of theory or practice?
- It is illogical to place states at the centre of our thinking about security because even those which are producers of security (internal and external) represent the means and not the ends. It is illogical to privilege the security of the means as opposed to the security of the ends. An analogy can be drawn with a house and its inhabitants. A house requires upkeep, but it is illogical to spend excessive amounts of money and effort to protect the house against flood, dry rot and burglars if this is at the cost of the well-being of the inhabitants. There is obviously a relationship between the well-being of the sheltered and the state of the shelter, but can there be any question as to whose security is primary?
- States are too diverse in their character to serve as the basis for a comprehensive theory of security because, as many have argued over the years, the historical variety of states, and relations between them, force us to ask whether a theory of the state is misplaced.[10] Can a class of political entities from the United States to Tuvalu, and Ancient Rome to the Lebanon, be the foundation for a sturdy concept of security?

When we move from theory to practice, the difference between the neo-realist and the utopian realist perspective on the primary referent should become clearer. It was personified in the early 1980s by the confrontation between the women of Greenham Common and Margaret Thatcher on the issue of nuclear weapons. Thatcher demanded Cruise and Trident as guarantors of British sovereignty. In the opinion of the prime minister and her supporters the main threat was believed to be a Soviet occupation of Britain and the overthrow of the Westminster model of democracy. It was believed that British 'sovereignty', and its traditional institutions safeguarded the interests of the British people. Thatcher spoke for the state perspective. The Greenham women sought denuclearization. The main threat, they and anti-nuclear opinion believed, was not the Soviet Union, but the nuclear arms build-up. They pinned tokens of family life, such as photographs and teddy bears, on the perimeter fence of the Greenham missile base, to indicate what was ultimately being threatened by nuclear war.

People could survive occupation by a foreign power, they argued, but could not survive a nuclear war, let alone nuclear winter. By criticizing nuclearism, and pointing to the dangers of proliferation and ecological disaster, the women of Greenham Common were acting as a home counties chapter of the world community.

The confrontation between the Greenham women and the Grantham woman sparked interesting arguments about principle and policy. I thought the Greenham women right at the time, and still do. But the path to nuclear abolition cannot be quick or easy; nor is it guaranteed. The hope of some anti-nuclear opinion for a grand abolition treaty (a sort of Hobbes today, Kant tomorrow) is not feasible.[11] But it is rational to act as though abolition is possible. Indeed, to do otherwise is to perpetuate the belief that there is ultimately no stronger basis for human coexistence than genocidal fear. Over a long period such minimalist thinking seems to be a recipe for disaster, The search for nuclear abolition has value as part of a process of extending the idea of moral and political community (which even realists like Carr saw as the ultimate foundation of security). Kant would have seen the search for total global abolition as a 'guiding ideal'; he might have called it a 'practical impracticality'.

The case for emancipation

It is appropriate to place emancipation at the centre of new security thinking in part because it is the spirit of our times […] [which] refers to the whole of the twentieth century. […] This century has seen the struggle for freedom of the colonial world, women, youth, the proletariat, appetites of all sorts, homosexuals, consumers, and thought.[12] The struggle for emancipation goes on in many places. Some groups have done and are doing better than others. For the moment there is a spirit of liberty abroad. In the struggle against political oppression, one striking feature of recent years has been the remarkable success of non-violent 'people power' in many countries, ranging from Poland to the Philippines.

In the study of world politics, emphasizing emancipation is one way to help loosen the grip of the neo-realist tradition. Neo-realism undoubtedly highlights important dynamics in relations between states, and these cannot be disregarded. But to make world politics more intelligible it is necessary to go beyond these important but limited insights. The tradition of critical theory is helpful in this regard; its most important potential contribution in the present state of the subject lies in recapturing the idea that politics is open-ended and based in ethics.[13] From this perspective strategy becomes not the study of the technological variable in inter-state politics, but a continuation of moral philosophy with an admixture of firepower. The next stage of thinking about security in world affairs should be marked by moving it out of its almost exclusively realist framework into the critical philosophical camp.

In parallel with such a move it is necessary to reconsider much traditional thinking about liberty, which has tended to place freedom before equality. This tradition was clearly expressed by Theodore Sumberg in an argument about foreign aid as a moral obligation. The central value for Americans, it was asserted, is liberty not the abolition of poverty.[14] Liberty is also the central value of emancipation, but emancipation implies an egalitarian concept of liberty. When the homeless are told, for example, that they now have more liberty, by people with hearts of pure polyester, because they can buy shares in privatized industries, that 'liberty' is meaningless. Whether the focus is Britain or the globe, liberty without economic status is propaganda. [...]

Integral to emancipation is the idea of the reciprocity of rights. The implication of this is the belief that 'I am not truly free until everyone is free'. This is a principle everyone can implement in everyday life, and it has implications for international relations. Since 'my freedom depends on your freedom', the process of emancipation implies the further breaking down of the barriers we perpetuate between foreign and domestic policy. In this world of turbulent change it is less and less tenable to see the 'external world' – the subject-matter of traditional international politics – as a 'domain of its own'. In the interpenetrating world of global politics, economics and cultures, we need better attend to the linkages between 'domestic' and 'foreign' politics. Frontiers these days do not hold back either 'internal' or 'external' affairs.

The continuing sharp distinction between what is 'domestic' and what is 'foreign' is one manifestation of the way the study of international politics has been bedevilled by unhelpful dichotomies. What are convenient labels for teaching can actually be misleading. It is only necessary to mention the polarization of order and justice, domestic and foreign policy, internal order and external anarchy, utopianism and realism, political and international theory, high and low politics, and peace research and strategic studies. Security conceived as a process of emancipation promises to integrate all these. It would encompass, for example, the 'top down' northern 'national security' view of security and the 'bottom up' southern view of 'comprehensive security' concerned with problems arising out of underdevelopment or oppression.[15] Overall, therefore, the concept of emancipation promises to bring together Martin Wight's 'theories of the good life', and 'theories of survival' into a comprehensive approach to security in world politics.

* * *

Today it is difficult to think of issues more important than those on the expanded security agenda mentioned earlier. Understanding such issues in the 1990s will be the equivalent of what the Great War was in the 1920s. It is already evident that in the 1990s insecurity in one form or another will be all around. Fortunately, in this post-international politics/post-foreign policy world nobody has to wait for the Douglas Hurds. Some governments can exercise enormous power, but they are not the only agents, and they are not immune to influence. The implementation of an emancipatory strategy through process utopian steps is, to a greater or lesser extent, in the hands of all those who want it to be – the embryonic global civil society. In a world of global communications few should feel entirely helpless. Even in small and private decisions it is possible to make choices which help rather than hinder the building of a world community. Some developments depend on governments, but some do not. We can begin or continue pursuing emancipation in what we research, in how we teach, in what we put on conference agendas, in how much we support Greenpeace, Amnesty International, Oxfam and other groups identifying with a global community, and in how we deal with each other and with students. And in pursuing emancipation, the bases of real security are being established.

Notes

1   John Naisbitt and Patricia Aburdene, *Megatrends 2000. Ten New Directions for the 1990s* (New York, 1990), p. 19.

2   Vaclav Havel, *Living in Truth* (London, 1986), especially ch. 2, 'The Power of the Powerless'.

3   Nadine Gordimer took this quotation as the starting point for a novel on black-white relations in South Africa: see her *July's People* (London, 1981). I took it as the starting point for thinking about the present era in international politics: see *New Thinking about Strategy and International Security* (London, 1991).

4   This is the theme of Robert Ornstein and Paul Ehrlich, *New World, New Mind* (London, 1989).

5   W. T. R. Fox, 'E. H. Carr and Political Realism: Vision and Revision', *Review of International Studies*, 11 (1985), pp. 1–16.

6   Naisbitt and Aburdene, *Megatrends 2000*, p. 29.

7   Kenneth Boulding, *Stable Peace* (Austin, 1979), passim.

8   The most thorough discussion is Barry Buzan, *People, States and Fear* (Hemel Hempstead, 2nd edn, 1991). For some definitions, see pp. 16–18.

9   Hedley Bull, *The Anarchical Society: A Study of Order in World Politics* (London, 1977), p. 22.

10 See, for example, David Held, 'Central Perspectives on the Modern State', pp. 1–55 in David Held et al. (eds.), *States and Societies* (Oxford, 1983).

11 As, for instance, in Jonathan Schell, *The Abolition* (London, 1984).

12 See Modris Eksteins, *Rites of Spring. The Great War and the Birth of the Modern Age* (Boston, 1989), especially pp. xiii–xvi.

13 See, by way of introduction, Mark Hoffman, 'Critical Theory and the Inter-Paradigm Debate', *Millennium*, 16 (1987), pp. 231–49, and Andrew Linklater, *Beyond Realism and Marxism. Critical Theory and International Relations* (London, 1990).

14 Theodore Sumberg, *Foreign Aid as Moral Obligation?* The Washington Papers, no. 10 (Beverly Hills, 1973) discussed in Stanley Hoffmann, *Duties Beyond Borders* (Syracuse, 1981), p. 153.

15 See, for example, Caroline Thomas, 'New Directions in Thinking about Security in the Third World', pp. 267–89 in Ken Booth (ed.), *New Thinking About Strategy and International Security* (London; 1991), and Caroline Thomas and Paikiasothy Saravanamuttu, eds., *Conflict and Consensus in South/North Security* (Cambridge, 1989).

J. Ann Tickner

FEMINISM AND SECURITY

Source: *Gender in International Relations: Feminist Perspectives on Achieving Global Security* (New York: Columbia University Press, 1992), pp. 1–25.

Engendered insecurities: Feminist perspectives on international relations

> Too often the great decisions are originated and given form in bodies made up wholly of men, or so completely dominated by them that whatever of special value women have to offer is shunted aside without expression.
>
> Eleanor Roosevelt

> Representation of the world, like the world itself, is the work of men; they describe it from their own point of view, which they confuse with absolute truth.
>
> Simone De Beauvoir

As Eleanor Roosevelt and countless others have observed, international politics is a man's world. It is a world inhabited by diplomats, soldiers, and international civil servants, most of whom are men. Apart from the occasional head of state, there is little evidence to suggest that women have played much of a role in shaping foreign policy in any country in the twentieth century. In the United States in 1987, women constituted less than 5 percent of the senior Foreign Service ranks, and in the same year, less than 4 percent of the executive positions in the Department of Defense were held by women.[1] Although it is true that women are underrepresented in all top-level government positions in the United States and elsewhere, they encounter additional difficulties in positions having to do with international politics. [...]

[...] [There is] the belief, widely held in the United States and throughout the world by both men and women, that military and foreign policy are arenas of policy-making least appropriate for women. Strength, power, autonomy, independence, and rationality, all typically associated with men and masculinity, are characteristics we most value in those to whom we entrust the conduct of our foreign policy and the defense of our national interest. Those women in the peace movements, whom feminist critics [...] cited as evidence for women's involvement in international affairs, are frequently branded as naive, weak, and even unpatriotic. When we think about the definition of a patriot, we generally think of a man, often a soldier who defends his homeland, most especially his women and children, from dangerous outsiders. [...] [E]ven women who have experience in foreign policy issues are perceived as being too emotional and too weak for the tough life-and-death decisions required for the nation's defense. Weakness is always considered a danger when issues of national security are at stake: the president's dual role as commander in chief reinforces our belief that qualities we associate with "manliness" are of utmost importance in the selection of our presidents.

The few women who do make it into the foreign policy establishment often suffer from this negative perception [...]. The[ir] experiences [...] are examples of the difficulties that women face when they try to enter the élite world of foreign policy decision-making. [...] I believe that these gender-related difficulties are symptomatic of a much deeper issue that I do wish to address: the extent to which international politics is such a thoroughly masculinized sphere of activity that women's voices are considered inauthentic. [...] By analyzing some of the writings of those who have tried to describe, explain, and prescribe for the behavior of states in the international system, we can begin to understand some of the deeper reasons for women's pervasive exclusion from foreign policy-making – for it is in the way that we are taught to think about international politics that the attitudes I have described are shaped.

With its focus on the "high" politics of war and Realpolitik, the traditional Western academic discipline of international relations privileges issues that grow out of men's experiences; we are socialized into believing that war and power politics are spheres of activity with which men have a special affinity and that their voices in describing and prescribing for this world are therefore likely to be more authentic. The roles traditionally ascribed to women – in reproduction, in households, and even in the economy – are generally considered irrelevant to the traditional construction of the field. Ignoring women's experiences contributes not only to their exclusion but also to a process of self-selection that results in an overwhelmingly male population both in the foreign policy world and in the academic field of international relations. This selection process begins with the way we are taught to think about world politics; if women's experiences were to be included, a radical redefinition of the field would have to take place. [...]

Gender in international relations

[...] [T]he marginalization of women in the arena of foreign policy-making through the kind of gender stereotyping that I have described suggests that international politics has always been a gendered activity in the modern state system. Since foreign and military policy-making has been largely conducted by men, the discipline that analyzes these activities is bound to be primarily about men and masculinity. [...] Any attempt to introduce a more explicitly gendered analysis into the field must therefore begin with a discussion of masculinity.

Masculinity and politics have a long and close association. Characteristics associated with "manliness," such as toughness, courage, power, independence, and even physical strength, have, throughout history, been those most valued in the conduct of politics, particularly international politics. Frequently, manliness has also been associated with violence and the use of force, a type of behavior, that, when conducted in the international arena, has been valorized and applauded in the name of defending one's country. [...]

[...] Socially constructed gender differences are based on socially sanctioned, unequal relationships between men and women that reinforce compliance with men's stated superiority. Nowhere in the public realm are these stereotypical gender images more apparent than in the realm of international politics, where the characteristics associated with hegemonic masculinity are projected onto the behavior of states whose success as international actors is measured in terms of their power capabilities and capacity for self-help and autonomy. [...]

[...] Historically, differences between men and women have usually been ascribed to biology. But when feminists use the term *gender* today, they are not generally referring to biological differences between males and females, but to a set of culturally shaped and defined characteristics associated with masculinity and femininity. These characteristics can and do vary across time and place. In this view, biology may constrain behavior, but it should not be used "deterministically" or "naturally" to justify practices, institutions, or choices that could be other than they are. While what it means to be a man or a woman varies across cultures and history, in most cultures gender differences signify relationships of inequality and the domination of women by men. [...]

[Joan] Scott claims that the way in which our understanding of gender signifies relationships of power is through a set of normative concepts that set forth interpretations of the meanings of symbols. In Western culture, these concepts take the form of fixed binary oppositions that categorically assert the meaning of masculine and feminine and hence legitimize a set of unequal social relationships.[2] Scott and many other contemporary feminists assert that, through our use of language, we come to perceive the world through these binary oppositions. Our Western understanding of gender is based on a set of culturally determined binary distinctions, such as public versus private, objective versus subjective, self versus other, reason versus emotion, autonomy versus relatedness, and culture versus nature; the first of each pair of characteristics is typically associated with masculinity, the second with femininity.[3] Scott claims that the hierarchical construction of these distinctions can take on a fixed and permanent quality that perpetuates women's oppression: therefore they must be challenged. To do so we must analyze the way these binary oppositions operate in different contexts and, rather than accepting them as fixed, seek to displace their hierarchical construction.[4] When many of these differences between women and men are no longer assumed to be natural or fixed, we can examine how relations of gender inequality are constructed and sustained in various arenas of public and private life. In committing itself to gender as a category of analysis, contemporary feminism also commits itself to gender equality as a social goal.

Extending Scott's challenge to the field of international relations, we can immediately detect a similar set of hierarchical binary oppositions. But in spite of the seemingly obvious association of international politics with the masculine character-istics described above, the field of international relations is one of the last of the social sciences to be touched by gender analysis and feminist perspectives.[5] The reason for this, I believe, is not that the field is gender neutral, meaning that the introduction of gender is irrelevant to its subject matter as many scholars believe, but that it is so thoroughly masculinized that the workings of these hierarchical gender relations are hidden.

Framed in its own set of binary distinctions, the discipline of international rela-tions assumes similarly hierarchical relationships when it posits an anarchic world "outside" to be defended against through the accumulation and rational use of power. In political discourse, this becomes translated into stereotypical notions about those who inhabit the outside. Like women, foreigners are frequently portrayed as "the other": nonwhites and tropical countries are often depicted as irrational, emotional, and unstable, characteristics that are also attributed to women. The construction of this discourse and the way in which we are taught to think about international politics closely parallel the way in which we are socialized into understanding gender differ-ences. To ignore these hierarchical constructions and their relevance to power is there-fore to risk perpetuating these relationships of domination and subordination. [...]

* * *

Contemporary feminist theories

Just as there are multiple approaches within the discipline of international relations, there are also multiple approaches in contemporary feminist theory that come out of various disciplinary traditions and paradigms. While it is obvious that not all women are feminists, feminist theories are constructed out of the experiences of women in their many and varied circumstances, experiences that have generally been rendered invisible by most intellectual disciplines.

Most contemporary feminist perspectives define themselves in terms of reacting to traditional liberal feminism that, since its classic formulation in the works of Mary Wollstonecraft and John Stuart Mill, has sought to draw attention to and eliminate the legal restraints barring women's access to full participation in the public world.[6] Most contemporary feminist scholars, other than liberals, claim that the sources of dis-crimination against women run much deeper than legal restraints: they are enmeshed in the economic, cultural, and social structures of society and thus do not end when legal restraints are removed. Almost all feminist perspectives have been motivated by the common goal of attempting to describe and explain the sources of gender inequal-ity, and hence women's oppression, and to seek strategies to end them.

Feminists claim that women are oppressed in a multiplicity of ways that depend on culture, class, and race as well as on gender. Rosemary Tong suggests that we can categorize various contemporary feminist theories according to the ways in which they view the causes of women's oppression. While Marxist feminists believe that capitalism is the source of women's oppression, radical feminists claim that women are oppressed by the system of patriarchy that has existed under almost all modes of production. Patriarchy is institutionalized through legal and economic, as well as social and cultural institutions. Some radical feminists argue that the low value assigned to the feminine characteristics described above also contributes to women's oppression. Feminists in the psychoanalytic tradition look for the source of women's oppression deep in the psyche, in gender relationships into which we are socialized from birth.

Socialist feminists have tried to weave these various approaches together into some kind of a comprehensive explanation of women's oppression. Socialist feminists claim that women's position in society is determined both by structures of production in the economy and by structures of reproduction in the household, structures that are reinforced by the early socialization of children into gender roles. Women's unequal status in all these structures must be eliminated for full equality to be achieved. Socialist feminism thus tries to understand the position of women in their multiple roles in order to find a single standpoint from which to explain their condition. Using standpoint in the sense that it has been used by Marxists, these theorists claim that those who are oppressed have a better understanding of the sources of their oppression than their oppressors. "A standpoint is an engaged vision of the world opposed and superior to dominant ways of thinking."[7]

This notion of standpoint has been seriously criticized by postmodern feminists who argue that a unified representation of women across class, racial, and cultural lines is an impossibility. Just as feminists more generally have criticized existing knowledge that is grounded in the experiences of white Western males, postmodernists claim that feminists themselves are in danger of essentializing the meaning of woman when they draw exclusively on the experiences of white Western women: such an approach runs the additional risk of reproducing the same dualizing distinctions that feminists object to in patriarchal discourse.[8] Postmodernists believe that a multiplicity of women's voices must be heard lest feminism itself become one more hierarchical system of knowledge construction.

Any attempt to construct feminist perspectives on international relations must take this concern of postmodernists seriously; as described above, dominant approaches to international relations have been Western-centered and have focused their theoretical investigations on the activities of the great powers. An important goal for many feminists has been to attempt to speak for the marginalized and oppressed: much of contemporary feminism has also recognized the need to be sensitive to the multiple voices of women and the variety of circumstances out of which they speak. Developing perspectives that can shed light on gender hierarchies as they contribute to women's oppression worldwide must therefore be sensitive to the dangers of constructing a Western-centered approach. Many Western feminists are understandably apprehensive about replicating men's knowledge by generalizing from the experiences of white Western women. Yet to be unable to speak for women only further reinforces the voices of those who have constructed approaches to international relations out of the experiences of men.

"[Feminists] need a home in which everyone has a room of her own, but one in which the walls are thin enough to permit a conversation."[9] Nowhere is this more true than in these early attempts to bring feminist perspectives to bear on international politics, a realm that has been divisive in both its theory and its practice. [...]

Feminist theories and international relations

Since, as I have suggested, the world of international politics is a masculine domain, how could feminist perspectives contribute anything new to its academic discourses? Many male scholars have already noted that, given our current technologies of destruction and the high degree of economic inequality and environmental degradation that now exists, we are desperately in need of changes in the way world politics is conducted; many of them are attempting to prescribe such changes. For the most part, however, these critics have ignored the extent to which the values and assumptions that drive our contemporary international system are intrinsically related to concepts of masculinity; privileging these values constrains the options available to states and their policymakers. All knowledge is partial and is a function of the knower's lived experience in the world. Since knowledge about the behavior of states in the international system depends on assumptions that come out of men's experiences, it ignores a large body of human experience that has the potential for increasing the range of options and opening up new ways of thinking about interstate practices. Theoretical perspectives that depend on a broader range of human experience are important for women and men alike, as we seek new ways of thinking about our contemporary dilemmas.

Conventional international relations theory has concentrated on the activities of the great powers at the center of the system. Feminist theories, which speak out of the various experiences of women – who are usually on the margins of society and interstate politics – can offer us some new insights on the behavior of states and the needs of individuals, particularly those on the peripheries of the international system. Feminist perspectives, constructed out of the experiences of women, can add a new dimension to our understanding of the world economy; since women are frequently the first casualties in times of economic hardship, we might also gain some new insight into the relationship between militarism and structural violence.

However, feminist theories must go beyond injecting women's experiences into different disciplines and attempt to challenge the core concepts of the disciplines themselves.

Concepts central to international relations theory and practice, such as power, sovereignty, and security, have been framed in terms that we associate with masculinity. Drawing on feminist theories to examine and critique the meaning of these and other concepts fundamental to international politics could help us to reformulate these concepts in ways that might allow us to see new possibilities for solving our current insecurities. Suggesting that the personal is political, feminist scholars have brought to our attention distinctions between public and private in the domestic polity: examining these artificial boundary distinctions in the domestic polity could shed new light on international boundaries, such as those between anarchy and order, which are so fundamental to the conceptual framework of realist discourse.

Most contemporary feminist perspectives take the gender inequalities that I have described above as a basic assumption. Feminists in various disciplines claim that feminist theories, by revealing and challenging these gender hierarchies, have the potential to transform disciplinary paradigms. By introducing gender into the discipline of international relations, I hope to challenge the way in which the field has traditionally been constructed and to examine the extent to which the practices of international politics are related to these gender inequalities. The construction of hierarchical binary oppositions has been central to theorizing about international relations.[10] Distinctions between domestic and foreign, inside and outside, order and anarchy, and center and periphery have served as important assumptions in theory construction and as organizing principles for the way we view the world. Just as realists center their explanations on the hierarchical relations between states and Marxists on unequal class relations, feminists can bring to light gender hierarchies embedded in the theories and practices of world politics and allow us to see the extent to which all these systems of domination are interrelated.

As Sarah Brown argues, a feminist theory of international relations is an act of political commitment to understanding the world from the perspective of the socially subjugated. "There is the need to identify the as yet unspecified relation between the construction of power and the construction of gender in international relations."[11] Acknowledging, as most feminist theories do, that these hierarchies are socially constructed, also allows us to envisage conditions necessary for their transcendence. [...]

Notes

Roosevelt epigraph from speech to the United Nations General Assembly (1952), quoted in Crapol, ed., *Women and American Foreign Policy*, p. 176; de Beauvoir epigraph from *The Second Sex*, p. 161.

1. McGlen and Sarkees, "Leadership Styles of Women in Foreign Policy," p. 17.
2. Scott, *Gender and the Politics of History*, p. 43. Scott's chapter 2, entitled "Gender: A Useful Category of Historical Analysis," on which my analysis of gender draws, was originally published in the *American Historical Review* (December 1986), 91(5):1053–75.
3. Broverman et al., "Sex-Role Stereotypes: A Current Appraisal." Although the original study was published in 1972, replication of this research in the 1980s confirmed that these perceptions still held in the United States.
4. Scott, *Gender and the Politics of History*, p. 43.
5. As of 1986, a study showed that no major American international relations journal had published any articles that used gender as a category of analysis. See Steuernagel and Quinn, "Is Anyone Listening?" Apart from a special issue of the British international relations journal *Millennium* (Winter 1988),17(3), on women and international relations, very little attention has been paid to gender in any major international relations journal.
6. Tong, *Feminist Thought*, p. 2. My description of the varieties of contemporary feminist thought draws heavily on her chapter 1.
7. Ruddick, *Maternal Thinking*, p. 129. See also Hartsock, *Money, Sex, and Power*, ch. 10.
8. Runyan and Peterson, "The Radical Future of Realism," p. 7.
9. Tong, *Feminist Thought*, p. 7.
10. Runyan and Peterson, "The Radical Future of Realism," p. 3.
11. Brown, "Feminism, International Theory, and International Relations of Gender Inequality," p. 469.

Bibliography

Broverman, Inge K., Susan R. Vogel, Donald M. Broverman, Frank E. Clarkson, and Paul S. Rosenkranz. "Sex-Role Stereotypes: A Current Appraisal." *Journal of Social Issues* 28(2) (1972): 59–78.

Brown, Sarah. "Feminism, International Theory, and International Relations of Gender Inequality." *Millennium: Journal of International Studies* 17(3) (1988): 461–475.

Crapol, Edward P., ed. *Women and American Foreign Policy: Lobbyists, Critics, and Insiders.* New York: Greenwood Press, 1987.

Hartsock, Nancy C. M. *Money, Sex, and Power: Toward a Feminist Historical Materialism.* Boston: Northeastern University Press, 1983.

McGlen, Nancy E. and Meredith Reid Sarkees. "Leadership Styles of Women in Foreign Policy." Unpublished paper, 1990.

Ruddick, Sara. *Maternal Thinking: Toward a Politics of Peace.* New York: Ballantine Books, 1989.

Runyan, Anne Sisson and V. Spike Peterson. "The Radical Future of Realism: Feminist Subversions of IR Theory." *Alternatives* 16(1) (1991): 67–106.

Scott, Joan W. *Gender and the Politics of History.* New York: Columbia University Press, 1988.

Steuernagel, Gertrude A. and Laurel U. Quinn. "Is Anyone Listening? Political Science and the Response to the Feminist Challenge." Unpublished paper, 1986.

Tong, Rosemarie. *Feminist Thought: A Comprehensive Introduction.* Boulder: Westview, 1989.

Amitav Acharya

THE THIRD WORLD AND SECURITY STUDIES

Source: 'The periphery as the core: the Third World and security studies', in Keith Krause and Michael C. Williams (ed.) *Critical Security Studies: Concepts and Cases* (Minneapolis: University of Minnesota Press, 1997), pp. 299–328.

The periphery as the core: The Third World and security studies

THIS CHAPTER LOOKS at another, less pronounced but ultimately more significant, reason why a redefinition of security is called for. The Cold War period was marked by a preoccupation of security studies scholars with issues and problems of a particular segment of the international system. As with other key concepts of International Relations, national security assumed a Eurocentric universe of nation-states and dwelled primarily on the responses of Western governments and societies, particularly the United States, to the problem of war. The issues and experiences within the other segment, collectively labeled as the Third World, were not fully incorporated into the discourse of security studies. Because the international system as a whole was seen as a "transplantation of the European territorial state," the concept of national security was taken to be a general model, "reflecting the universalization of the competitive European style of anarchic international relations."[1]

This exclusion of the Third World from the Cold War security studies agenda was evident in both policy and academic arenas.[2] [...] In the academic literature, what was considered mainstream focused on "the centrality of the East-West divide to the rest of global politics."[3] Attention to problems of regional instability in the Third World was given only to the extent that they had the potential to affect the superpower relationship. Not surprisingly, therefore, [...] "regional security issues (apart from Western Europe) [...] received inadequate attention," a fact attributable to "ethnocentric biases" resulting from "the development of security studies in the United States more than in other countries."[4]

The tendency of security studies to focus on a particular segment of the international system to the exclusion of another is ironic given the fact that it is in the neglected arena that the vast majority of conflicts have taken place.[5] Moreover, the security predicament of the Third World states challenges several key elements of the national security paradigm, especially its state-centric and war-centric universe. The Third World's problems of insecurity and their relationship with the larger issues of international order have been quite different from what was envisaged under the dominant notion.[6]

[...] [A]s security studies adapts itself to post-Cold War realities, the security predicament of Third World states provides a helpful point of departure for appreciating the limitations of the dominant understanding and moving it toward a broader and more inclusive notion of security. This redefinition is crucial to understanding the problems of conflict and order in the post-Cold War period. [...]

National security, regional conflicts, and the emergence of the Third World

The emergence of the Third World challenged the dominant understanding of security in three important respects:

1. Its focus on the interstate level as the point of origin of security threats.
2. Its exclusion of nonmilitary phenomena from the security studies agenda.
3. Its belief in the global balance of power as the legitimate and effective instrument of international order.

During the Cold War, the vast majority of the world's conflicts occurred in the Third World. Most of these conflicts were intrastate in nature (antiregime insurrections, civil wars, tribal conflicts, and so on). [...] Many of them were cases of aggravated tensions emerging from the process of state formation and regime maintenance. The proliferation of such conflicts reflected the limited internal sociopolitical cohesion of the newly independent states, rather than the workings of the globally competitive relationship between the two superpowers.

The roots of Third World instability during the Cold War period were to be found in weak state structures that emerged from the process of decolonization, that is, structures that lacked a close fit between the state's territorial dimensions and its ethnic and societal composition. The concept of national security is of limited utility in this context. Udo Steinbach points out that "the concept of 'nation,' introduced by colonial powers or by small élites who saw in it the prerequisite for the fulfilment of their own political aspirations, materialized in a way which went against territorial, ethnic, religious, geographical or culto-historical traditions."[7] As a result, to quote Mohammed Ayoob, most Third World states lacked a "capacity to ensure the habitual identification of their inhabitants with the post-colonial structures that have emerged within colonially-dictated boundaries."[8] The most common outcome of this was conflicts about national identity, including separatist insurgencies whose peak was recorded in the 1960s.

The relatively brief time available to Third World governments for creating viable political structures out of anticolonial struggles as well as conditions of poverty, underdevelopment, and resource scarcity limited their capacity for pursuing developmental objectives in order to ensure domestic stability. Moreover, domestic conflicts in the Third World were often responsible for a wider regional instability. Revolutions, insurgencies, and ethnic separatist movements frequently spilled over across national boundaries to fuel discord with neighbors. Ethnic minorities fighting the dominant élite rarely honored state boundaries, often seeking sanctuary in neighboring states where the regime and population might be more sympathetic to their cause. Weak states were more vulnerable to foreign intervention, as outside powers, including the superpowers, could take advantage of their domestic strife to advance their economic and ideological interests.

These general patterns of regional instability were compounded by the particular insecurities of the ruling élite in Third World states.[9] Most Third World societies exhibited a lack of consensus on the basic rules of political accommodation, power sharing, and governance. Regime creation and regime maintenance were often a product of violent societal struggles, governed by no stable constitutional framework. The narrow base of Third World regimes and the various challenges to their survival affected the way in which national security policy was articulated and pursued. In such a milieu, the regime's instinct for self-preservation often took precedence over the security interests of the society or the nation. [...]

As a result, the nature of national security as an ambiguous symbol is more pronounced in Third World societies than in the industrial North. The Third World experience challenged the realist image of the state as a provider of security. [...]

Another way in which the emergent Third World challenged the dominant understanding of security relates to the place of nonmilitary issues in the latter. [...] To date, the dominant understanding of security resists the inclusion of nonmilitary phenomena in the security studies agenda.[10] [...]

But the logic of accepting a broader notion of security becomes less contestable when one looks at the Third World experience. From the very outset, resource scarcity, overpopulation, underdevelopment, and environmental degradation were at the heart of insecurity in the Third World. These essentially nonmilitary threats were much more intimately linked to the security predicament of the Third World than that of the developed countries. Economic development and well-being were closely linked not only because "a semblance of security and stability is a prerequisite for successful economic development," but also because "it is also generally understood within the Third World that economic development can contribute to national security; an economically weak nation can be exploited or defeated more easily by foreign powers and may be exposed periodically to the violent wrath of dissatisfied citizens."[11] While problems such as lack of sufficient food, water, and housing are not part of the national security agenda of developed states, they very much hold the balance between conflict and order in the Third World. [...]

The vulnerability of Third World states to [...] [the above] threats was compounded by their lack of material, human, and institutional capacity to deal with these problems [...] [let alone] enjoy[ing] little influence over the international context within which these problems arise. [...]

Finally, the Third World's emergence challenged the legitimacy of the dominant instrument of the Cold War international order. The principal anchor of that order, the global superpower rivalry, was viewed with profound mistrust throughout the Third World. [...] The role of the Non-Aligned Movement (NAM) in demanding a speedy completion of the decolonization process, opposing superpower interference in the Third World, and advocating global disarmament and the strengthening of global and regional mechanisms for conflict resolution testified to the collective resistance of Third World states to the system of international order resulting from superpower rivalry.[12] While the NAM's record in realizing these objectives has attracted much criticism, it was able to provide a collective psychological framework for Third World states to strengthen their independence and to play an active role in international affairs.[13] Membership in the NAM provided many Third World states with some room to maneuver in their relationship with the superpowers and to resist pressures for alliances and alignment.[14]

The Third World's collective attitude toward superpower rivalry has important implications for realist international theory. A structural realist understanding of International Relations (as developed by Ken Waltz or John Mearsheimer) would credit the Cold War and bipolarity for ensuring a stable international order. But this perspective was misleading insofar as the Third World was concerned. The Cold War order, instead of dampening conflicts in the Third World, actually contributed to their escalation. Although rarely a direct cause of Third World conflicts, the Cold War opportunism and influence seeking of superpowers contributed significantly to the ultimate severity of many cases of incipient and latent strife in the Third World.[15] It led to the internationalization of civil wars and the internalization of superpower competition.[16] It also contributed to the prolongation of regional wars by preventing decisive results in at least some theaters, including the major regional conflicts of the 1970s and 1980s in Central America, Angola, the Horn of Africa, Cambodia, Afghanistan, and the Iran-Iraq War.[17]

Thus, superpower rivalry, while keeping the "long peace" in Europe, served to exacerbate the problems of regional conflict and instability in the Third World. [...] While nuclear deterrence prevented even the most minor form of warfare between the two power blocs in Europe, superpower interventions in regional conflicts elsewhere were "permitted" as a necessary "safety valve."[18] [...]

Similarly, the Third World security experience during the Cold War explains why mechanisms for international order that reflected (and were shaped by) superpower balancing strategies were of limited effectiveness in promoting regional security. Steven David argues that for a balance of power approach to be effective, "the determinants of alignment [must] come overwhelmingly from the structure of the international system, particularly from the actual and potential *external* threats that states face." But in the Third World, it is the "internal characteristics of states" that usually influence alignments.[19] Thus, no superpower-sponsored mechanism for international order could be effective unless it would be able to address client states' internal (including regime security) concerns. This factor explains the failure of outward-looking regional security alliances such as the South East Asia Treaty Organization (SEATO) and the Central Treaty Organization (CENTO), and the relative success of more internal-security-oriented regional security arrangements such as the Association of Southeast Asian Nations (ASEAN) and the Gulf Cooperation Council (GCC). [...]

Security in the post-Cold War era: the relevance of the Third World experience

The above-mentioned features of insecurity in the Third World constitute a highly relevant explanatory framework for analyzing the major sources of instability in the post-Cold War era. To begin with, they aid our understanding of the emergence and escalation of conflicts and instability in the new states of Europe and Central Asia, which now constitute some of the most serious threats to the post-Cold War international order. [...]

In a broader context, the Third World security experience suggests the need to view the majority of the post-Cold War conflicts as a product of local factors, rather than of the changing structure of the international system from bipolarity to multipolarity. Some observers have suggested that the Cold War had suppressed "many potential third-world conflicts"; its end will ensure that "other conflicts will very probably arise from decompression and from a loosening of the controls and self-controls" exercised by the superpowers.[20] But such a view obscures the unchanged role of essentially domestic and intraregional factors related to weak national integration, economic underdevelopment, and competition for political legitimacy and control in shaping Third World instability. [...]

The view of regional conflicts as "essentially local expressions of rivalry" also underscores the need to rethink structuralist ideas that tend to analyze regional security in terms of systemic factors. [...]

There is sufficient empirical evidence to support Fred Halliday's view that "since the causes of third world upheaval [were] to a considerable extent independent of Soviet-U.S. rivalry they will continue irrespective of relations between Washington and Moscow."[21] In Africa, which the U.S. Defense Intelligence Agency rates to be "the most unstable region in the Third World,"[22] recent outbreaks of conflict (as in Rwanda and Somalia) are rooted in old ethnic and tribal animosities.[23] In Asia, the end of the two major Cold War conflicts (Afghanistan and Cambodia) leaves a number of ethnic insurgencies and separatist movements. In South Asia, the problems of political instability and ethnic separatism continue to occupy the governments of India (Assam, Kashmir, and the Punjab), Pakistan (demands for autonomy in the Sind province), and Sri Lanka (Tamil separatism).[24] The Southeast Asian governments face similar problems, especially in Indonesia (Aceh, East Timor, Irian Jaya), Myanmar (Karen and Shan guerrillas), and the Philippines (the New People's Army). In the more economically developed parts of the Third World, the primary security concerns of the ruling regimes derive from what Shahram Chubin calls the "stresses and strains of economic development, political integration, legitimation and institutionalization."[25] A good example is the situation in the Persian Gulf, where despite the recent attention to interstate wars (for example, the Iran-Iraq War and the Iraqi invasion of Kuwait), the threat from within remains a central cause of concern about the stability and survival of the traditional monarchies. [...]

There is another reason why the Third World security experience is highly relevant to post-Cold War security analysis. Conflicts in the post-Cold War era are likely to become even more regional in their origin and scope because of the changing context of great power intervention. The post-Cold War era is witnessing a greater regional differentiation in great power interests and involvement in the Third World. [...] This will render conflict formation and management in these areas more localized, subject to regional patterns of amity and enmity and the interventionist role of regionally dominant powers. The diffusion of military power to the Third World is enabling some regional powers to exercise greater influence in shaping conflict and cooperation in their respective areas.

With the end of the Cold War, some parts of the Third World are likely to experience a shift from internal to external security concerns, while others will remain primarily concerned with internal stability. [...] The more developed states in the Third World (such as the newly industrializing countries) are reshaping their defense capabilities from counterinsurgency to conventional warfare postures. [...] A number of major Third World powers, such as India, Indonesia, Nigeria, and Iran, are developing extended power-projection capabilities, which is bound to alarm their neighbors into giving greater attention to external security.

In general, the end of the Cold War is not having a single or uniform effect on Third World stability. [...] [I]t is [therefore] not helpful to interpret conflict structures in the post-Cold War period as the product of a single structural or systemic realignment; a more differentiated view of the post-Cold War disorder is required.

Finally, the Third World security experience suggests the need to focus on economic and ecological changes that are giving rise to new forms of regional conflicts. The issue of economic development remains at the heart of many of these conflicts. Although economically induced instability in the Third World has been traditionally viewed as a function of underdevelopment, such instability is becoming more associated with the strategies for, and the achievement of, developmental success. [...] Numerous empirical studies have established that the Third World is the main arena of conflicts and instability linked to environmental degradation.[26] The view of the environment as a global commons should not obscure the fact that the scale of environmental degradation, its consequences in fostering intra- and interstate conflict, and the problems of addressing these issues within the framework of the nation-state are more acute in the Third World than in the developed states. [...] Moreover, environmental degradation originating in the Third World is increasingly a potential basis for conflict between the North and the South, as poorer nations demand a greater share of the world's wealth and Third World environmental refugees aggravate existing group-identity conflicts (the problems of social assimilation of the migrant population) in the host countries.

The Third World security experience is helpful not only in understanding the sources of insecurity in the post-Cold War era, but also for judging the effectiveness of global-order-maintenance mechanisms. As during the Cold War period, the management of international order today reflects the dominant role of great powers, albeit now operating in a multipolar setting. The sole remaining superpower, the United States, has taken the lead in espousing a "new world order," whose key elements include a revival of collective security and the relatively newer frameworks of humanitarian intervention and nonproliferation. But as during the Cold War period, attempts by the globally dominant actors to manage international order do not correspond with regional realities in the Third World. Moreover, these attempts have contributed to a climate of mistrust and exacerbated North-South tensions.

For example, former President George Bush's vision of a new world order promised a return to multilateralism and the revival of the UN's collective security framework. But the first major test of this new world order, the U.S.-led response to the Iraqi invasion of Kuwait, prompted widespread misgivings in the Third World. Although the UN resolutions against Iraq were supported by most Third World states, this was accompanied by considerable resentment of the U.S. domination of the UN decision-making process. [...] The Gulf War fed apprehensions in the Third World that in the so-called unipolar moment, the United States, along with like-minded Western powers, would use the pretext of multilateralism to pursue essentially unilateral objectives in post-Cold War conflicts. Conflicts in those areas deemed to be vitally important to the Western powers will be especially susceptible to Northern unilateralism.

As with collective security, armed intervention in support of humanitarian objectives has the potential to exacerbate North-South tensions. The use of the humanitarian label in justifying intervention in failed states (as in the case of Somalia or Rwanda) or against regimes accused of gross human rights abuses has created some serious misgivings in the Third World. Many Third World regimes view this as a kind of recycled imperialism, while those taking a more tolerant view worry nonetheless about the effects of such a sovereignty-defying instrument. [...] A third area of North-South tension concerns the Northern approach to arms control and nonproliferation. In particular, supplyside antiproliferation measures developed by the North, such as the Nuclear Non-Proliferation Treaty (NPT) or the Missile Technology Control Regime (MTCR), which seek to restrict the availability of military or dual-use technology to Southern states, have met with Southern objections. These objections focus on the selective application and discriminatory nature of the North's antiproliferation campaign. Chubin finds that the North's antinuclear policy "frankly discriminates between friendly and unfriendly states, focusing on signatories (and potential cheats) like Iran but ignoring actual proliferators like Israel. It is perforce more intelligible in the North than in the South."[27] [...]

In the absence of greater understanding between the North and the South, there is a definite risk that the organizing principles of order devised and enforced by the dominant actors of the international system will have a limited impact as instruments of international order. In this context, regional security arrangements, developed by the Southern actors themselves, could theoretically provide greater opportunity and scope for regional autonomy and help the maintenance of international order.[28] [...] The end of the Cold War is reinvigorating and reshaping the role of Third World regional groupings toward conflict control, peacekeeping, and preventive diplomacy functions. [...]

But the peace and security role of regional groupings remains limited by their lack of the institutional structures required for conflict resolution or a collective military capacity needed for complex peacekeeping operations. Moreover, wide disparities of power within many existing Third World regional groupings create the risk that collective regional action will be held hostage to the narrow interests of a dominant member state. The Third World's continued adherence to the principle of noninterference undermines the prospect for effective regional action with respect to internal conflicts.[29] In addition, regional security arrangements in areas that are deemed to engage the vital interests of the great powers have limited autonomy in managing local conflicts. In these areas, the dependence of local states on external security guarantees (hence frequent great power intervention in local conflicts) will continue to thwart prospects for regional solutions to regional problems.[30] [...]

Nonetheless, regional approaches to peace and security face fewer systemic constraints in the post-Cold War era. They could provide a way of ensuring a greater decentralization of the global peace and security regime, which has assumed greater urgency in view of the limited resources of the UN in the face of an ever-expanding agenda of peacekeeping operations. They are also a means for achieving greater democratization of the global security regime, an important challenge in view of the Third World's resentment of the dominant role of great powers in the UN Security Council. Thus, the post-Cold War era contains an opportunity for a more meaningful division of labor between universal and regional frameworks of security in promoting conflict resolution in the Third World. [...]

There are three principal reasons why the notion of a Third World retains analytical value. First, the existence of North-South divisions continues to be widely acknowledged among scholars and policy makers from Washington to Kuala Lumpur. It has become commonplace to find observations that the end of East-West conflict has left the North-South divide as the main challenge to collective international order. [...]

Second, despite their diversity, the Third World countries continue to share a number of common features in the security and economic arena. These include the primacy of internal threats (as weak states) and a dependence on external security guarantees (as weak powers). Moreover, while the collective bargaining position of the Third World over international economic regimes and the redistribution of wealth might have collapsed, the economic predicament of Third World states, marked by poverty, underdevelopment, resource scarcity, and dependence, remains as a general feature of many of the states that emerged in the post-World War II period. [...] The diversity of the South or the disunity that has afflicted all its major platforms cannot be denied, but these features are nothing new and by themselves should not negate the Third World's claim for a collective label. Indeed, the Third World states have never pretended to be a homogeneous lot. If economic and political differentiation is accepted as the basis for rejecting the notion, then the analytical relevance of similar notions (such as the "West") should also be questioned.

Third, it should be remembered that the term *Third World* was not originally intended to denote a political bloc between the East and the West. Instead, the term was coined by French authors by analogy with the "Third Estate" of prerevolutionary France to refer to social groups other than the most privileged groups of the day, the clergy and nobility. In James Mittleman's view, the relatively inferior position of Third World states within the international system still holds true, especially as a large part of the Third World is facing greater marginalization after the Cold War. In this sense, the term Third World did and continues to refer to "the marginalized strata of the international system." [...]

The end of the Cold War has dramatically shifted the empirical focus of security studies. Today, regional conflicts – conflicts (intra-as well as interstate) in the world's less developed areas, including the new states that emerged out of the breakup of the Soviet empire – are widely recognized as a more serious threat to international order. [...]

[...] [T]he understanding of regional conflicts and security in the post-Cold War period [...] requires conceptual tools and methodology beyond what is provided by orthodox notions of security developed during the Cold War period. [...]

During the Cold War, the exclusion of the Third World's security problems from the mainstream security studies agenda contributed to its narrow and ethnocentric conceptual framework and empirical terrain. The analysis of regional conflict in the contemporary security discourse can benefit from a framework that captures the significantly broader range of issues – involving state and nonstate actors, military and nonmilitary challenges – that lie at the heart of insecurity and disorder in the Third World. In this respect, a greater integration of Third World security issues into international security studies will facilitate the latter's attempt to move beyond its now-discredited realist orthodoxy. [...]

[T]he end of the Cold War should serve as a catalyst for the coming of age of Third World security studies. The true globalization of security studies should be built on a greater regionalization of our understanding of the sources of conflict and the requirements of international order, with the Third World serving as a central conceptual and empirical focus.

Notes

1   The words used here are those of Barry Buzan. While Buzan himself is a strong advocate of the broadening of the focus of security studies to nonmilitary threats and to the Third World, he assumes the larger inter national system to be based on the universal European model. Barry Buzan, *People, States and Fear: An Agenda for International Security Studies in the Post-Cold War Era* (New York: Harvester Wheatsheaf, 1991), 240.

2   The most important exceptions to the general neglect of Third World security issues are Mohammed Ayoob, "Security in the Third World: The Worm about to Turn," *International Affairs* 60:1 (1984), 41–51; Mohammed Ayoob, "Regional Security and the Third World," in Mohammed Ayoob, ed., *Regional Security in the Third World* (London: Croom Helm, 1986), 3–23; Bahgat Korany, "Strategic Studies and the Third World: A Critical Appraisal," *International Social Science Journal* 38:4 (1986), 547–62; Udo Steinbach, "Sources of Third World Conflict," in *Third World Conflict and International Security*, Adelphi Paper no. 166 (London: International Institute for Strategic Studies, 1981), 21–28; Soedjatmoko, "Patterns of Armed Conflict in the Third World," *Alternatives* 10:4 (1985), 477–93; Edward Azar and Chung-in Moon, "Third World National Security: Towards a New Conceptual Framework," *International Interactions* 11:2 (1984), 103–35; Barry Buzan, "The Concept of National Security for Developing Countries with Special Reference to Southeast Asia," paper presented to the Workshop on "Leadership and Security in Southeast Asia," Institute of Southeast Asian Studies, Singapore, 10–12 December 1987; Barry Buzan, "People, States and Fear: The National Security Problem in the Third World," in Edward Azar and Chung-in Moon, eds., *National Security in the Third World* (Aldershot: Edward Elgar, 1988), 14–43; Caroline Thomas, *In Search of Security: The Third World in International Relations* (Brighton: Wheatsheaf Books, 1987); Yezid Sayigh, *Confronting the 1990s: Security in the Developing Countries,* Adelphi Paper no. 251 (London: International Institute for Strategic Studies, 1990); Mohammed Ayoob, "The Security Predicament of the Third World State," in Brian L. Job, ed., *The (In)Security Dilemma: The National Security of Third World States* (Boulder, Colo.: Lynne Rienner, 1992); Mohammed Ayoob, "The Security Problematic of the Third World," *World Politics* 43:2 (1991), 257–83; Steven R. David, "Explaining Third World Alignment," *World Politics* 43:2 (1991), 232–56. Caroline Thomas provides a succinct overview of the place of Third World issues in international security studies in her "New Directions in Thinking about Security in the Third World," in Ken Booth, ed., *New Thinking about Strategy and International Security* (London: HarperCollins; 1991), 267–89.

3   Hugh Macdonald, "Strategic Studies," *Millennium* 16:2 (1987), 333–36.

4   Joseph S. Nye and Sean M. Lynn Jones, "International Security Studies: Report of a Conference on the State of the Field," *International Security* 12:4 (1988), 27. Major theoretical attempts to develop an understanding of Third World regional conflict and security issues in terms of their local, rather than systemic or structural, determinants during the Cold War period include Ayoob's work on regional security in the Third World and Buzan's work on "regional security complexes." Contending that "issues of regional security in the developed world are defined primarily in Cold War terms (NATO versus Warsaw Pact, etc.) and are, therefore, largely indivisible from issues of systemic security," Ayoob convincingly demonstrated that "the salient regional security issues in the Third World have a life of their own independent of superpower rivalry." Buzan similarly urged greater attention to the "set of security dynamics at the regional level" in order to "develop the concepts and language for systematic comparative studies, still an area of conspicuous weakness in Third World studies." His notion of a "security complex," was designed to understand "how the regional level mediates the interplay between states and the international system as a whole." It should be noted, however, that while both Ayoob and Buzan called for greater attention to the regional and local sources of conflict and cooperation, Ayoob's was specifically focused on the Third World. Buzan's approach is also more structuralist, emphasizing the role of systemic determinants such as colonialism and superpower rivalry (which he called "overlays") in shaping regional security trends. This seems to undercut his earlier call for "the relative autonomy of regional security relations." See Ayoob, "Regional Security and the Third World"; Buzan, *People, States and Fear*, 186; and Buzan, "Third World Regional Security in Structural and Historical Perspective," in Job, ed., *The (In)Security Dilemma*, 167–89.

5   Evan Luard estimates that between 1945 and 1986, there were some 117 "significant wars." Out of these, only two occurred in Europe, while Latin America accounted for twenty-six; Africa, thirty-one; the Middle East, twenty-four; and Asia, forty-four. According to this estimate, the Third World was the scene of more than 98 percent of all international conflicts. Evan Luard, *War in International Society* (London: I. B. Tauris, 1986), appendix 5.

6   To say that the Third World's security predicament or experience has not been captured by realist analysis is not to say that the security behavior of Third World states has not followed the tenets of realism. On the contrary, there has been a mismatch between security analysis and security policy and praxis in the case of Third World states. Many Third World governments have pursued policies that enhance the security of the state and the regime while ignoring more unconventional sources of conflict, such as underdevelopment and ecological degradation. This state-centrism in security policy has, in turn, compounded the instability and violence in the Third World.

7   Udo Steinbach, "Sources of Third World Conflict," 21.

8   Ayoob, "Regional Security and the Third World," 9–10.

9   Brian L. Job, "The Insecurity Dilemma," in Job, ed., *The (In)Security Dilemma*.

10   Those who are skeptical of a broader notion of security or who caution against too much broadening include some of the leading contributors to the analysis of the Third World security predicament. Mohammed Ayoob, in his contribution to this volume, argues that "there are major intellectual and practical hazards in adopting unduly elastic definitions of security" and specifically calls for security analysts to

"show greater discrimination in applying security-related vocabulary to matters pertaining to ecological or other global management issues." In his view, for the latter to be considered as security issues, "they must demonstrate the capacity immediately to affect political outcomes." I agree on the need for such caution. But even if one adopts Ayoob's criteria; there remains a wide range of nonmilitary issues that create tension and violence within and between states and destabilize state-society relations. These (such as the conflict-creating potential of underdevelopment or environmental degradation) should be considered as being legitimately within the purview of security studies.

11   H. John Rosenbaum and William G. Tyler, "South-South Relations: The Economic and Political Content of Interactions among Developing Countries," *International Organization* 29:1 (1975) 243–74.

12   On the origins and role of the NAM, see Peter Lyon, *Neutralism* (Leicester: Leicester University Press, 1963); A. W. Singham and S. Hume, *Non-Alignment in the Age of Alignments* (London: Zed Books, 1986); Peter Willetts, *The Non-Aligned Movement* (London: Frances Pinter, 1978); Satish Kumar, "Non-Alignment: International Goals, and National Interests," *Asian Survey* 23:4 (1983), 445–61; Fred Halliday, "The Maturing of the Non-Aligned: Perspectives from New Delhi," in *Third World Affairs* (London: Third World Foundation, 1985); Bojana Tadic, "The Movement of the Non-Aligned and Its Dilemmas Today," *Review of International Affairs* 31:756 (5 October 1981), 19–24; A. W. Singham, ed., *The Non-Aligned Movement in World Politics* (Westport, Conn.: L. Hill, 1977).

13   Pervaiz Iqbal Cheema, "NAM and Security," *Strategic Studies* (Islamabad) 14:3 (1991), 15.

14   Mohammed Ayoob, "The Third World in the System of States: Acute Schizophrenia or Growing Pains," *International Studies Quarterly* 33:1 (1989), 75.

15   Edward A. Kolodziej and Robert Harkavy, "Developing States and the International Security System," *Journal of International Affairs* 34:1 (1980), 63.

16   Shahram Chubin, "The Super-powers, Regional Conflicts and World Order," in *The Changing Strategic Landscape,* Adelphi Papers, no. 237 (London: International Institute for Strategic Studies, 1989), 78.

17   In a comprehensive survey of 107 wars in the Third World between 1945 and 1990, Guy Arnold found that "many would almost certainly have been far shorter in duration and less devastating in their effects had the big powers not intervened." See Arnold, *Wars in the Third World since 1945* (London: Cassell, 1991), xvi.

18   Ayoob, "Regional Security and the Third World," 14.

19   David, "Explaining Third World Alignment," 233–55.

20   Jose T. Cintra, "Regional Conflicts: Trends in a Period of Transition," in *The Changing Strategic Landscape,* Adelphi Paper no. 237 (London: International Institute for Strategic Studies, 1989), 96–97.

21   Fred Halliday, *Cold War, Third World* (London: Hutchinson Radius, 1989), 162.

22   Testimony by Lieutenant General James Clapper to the Senate Armed Services Committee, 22 January 1992, in *Regional Flashpoints Potential for Military Conflict* (Washington, D.C.: United States Information Service, 1992), 5.

23   "Africa's Tribal Wars," *The Economist*, 13 October 1990, 50–51.

24   "Tribalism Revisited," *The Economist*, 21 December 1991 – 3 January 1992, 24.

25   Shahram Chubin, "Third World Conflicts: Trends and Prospects," *International Social Science Journal* 43:1 (1991), 159.

26 For example, much of the evidence cited by Jessica Tuchman Mathews to support her arguments concerning redefining security is from the Third World. See Jessica Tuchman Mathews, "Redefining Security," *Foreign Affairs* 68:2 (1989), 162–77.

27 Shahram Chubin, "The South and the New World Disorder," *The Washington Quarterly* 16:4 (1993), 98.

28 Regional security organizations may perform a variety of roles and may be based on different models such as collective security systems, alliances, or common security forums. Collective security systems should not be confused with alliance-type regional security arrangements such as the Bush administration's idea of a "regional security structure" in the wake of Iraq's expulsion from Kuwait. Collective security refers to the role of a global or regional system in protecting any member state from aggression by another member state. The inward-looking security role of a collective security system is to be contrasted with the outer-directed nature of an alliance that is geared to protect its members from a common external threat. See Ernst B. Haas, *Tangle of Hopes* (Englewood Cliffs, N.J.: Prentice Hall, 1969), 94. For an appraisal of the strengths and limitations of regional security arrangements in the post-Cold War era, see S. Neil MacFarlane and Thomas G. Weiss, "Regional Organizations and Regional Security," *Security Studies* 2:1 (1992); Tom J. Farer, "The Role of Regional Collective Security Arrangements," in Thomas G. Weiss, ed., *Collective Security in a Changing World* (Boulder, Colo.: Lynne Rienner, 1993), 153–86; Amitav Acharya, "Regional Approaches to Security in the Third World: Lessons and Prospects," in Larry A. Swatuk and Timothy M. Shaw, eds., *The South at the End of the Twentieth Century* (London: Macmillan, 1994), 79–94; Paul F. Diehl, "Institutional Alternatives to Traditional U.N. Peacekeeping: An Assessment of Regional and Multinational Options," *Armed Forces and Society* 19:2 (1993); Benjamin Rivlin, "Regional Arrangements and the UN System for Collective Security and Conflict Resolution: A New Road Ahead?" *International Relations* 11:2 (1992), 95–110.

29 MacFarlane and Weiss, "Regional Organizations and Regional Security," 31.

30 See Amitav Acharya, "Regional Military-Security Cooperation in the Third World: A Conceptual Analysis of the Relevance and Limitations of ASEAN," *Journal of Peace Research* 291:1 (1992), 7–21; Amitav Acharya, "The Gulf Cooperation Council and Security: Dilemmas of Dependence," *Middle East Strategic Studies Quarterly* 1:3 (1990), 88–136.

Jessica Tuchman Matthews

REDEFINING SECURITY (2)

Source: 'Redefining security', *Foreign Affairs*, vol. 68, no. 2, Spring 1989, pp. 162–77.

T HE 1990S will demand a redefinition of what constitutes national security. In the 1970s the concept was expanded to include international economics [...]. Global developments now suggest the need for another analogous, broadening definition of national security to include resource, environmental and demographic issues.

The assumptions and institutions that have governed international relations in the postwar era are a poor fit with these new realities. Environmental strains that transcend national borders are already beginning to break down the sacred boundaries of national sovereignty, previously rendered porous by the information and communication revolutions and the instantaneous global movement of financial capital. The once sharp dividing line between foreign and domestic policy is blurred, forcing governments to grapple in international forums with issues that were contentious enough in the domestic arena. [...]

Individuals and governments alike are beginning to feel the cost of substituting for (or doing without) the goods and services once freely provided by healthy ecosystems. Nature's bill is presented in many different forms [...]. Whatever the immediate cause for concern, the value and absolute necessity for human life of functioning ecosystems is finally becoming apparent.

Moreover, for the first time in its history, mankind is rapidly – if inadvertently – altering the basic physiology of the planet. Global changes currently taking place in the chemical composition of the atmosphere, in the genetic diversity of species inhabiting the planet, and in the cycling of vital chemicals through the oceans, atmosphere, biosphere and geosphere, are unprecedented in both their pace and scale. If left unchecked, the consequences will be profound and, unlike familiar types of local damage, irreversible.

Population growth lies at the core of most environmental trends. It took 130 years for world population to grow from one billion to two billion: it will take just a decade to climb from today's five billion to six billion. [...]

The relationship linking population levels and the resource base is complex. Policies, technologies and institutions determine the impact of population growth. These factors can spell the difference between a highly stressed, degraded environment and one that can provide for many more people. [...]

An important paradox to bear in mind when examining natural resource trends is that so-called nonrenewable resources – such as coal, oil and minerals – are in fact inexhaustible, while so-called renewable resources can be finite. [...] There are, thus, threshold effects for renewable resources that belie the name given them, with unfortunate consequences for policy.

The most serious form of renewable resource decline is the deforestation taking place throughout the tropics. [...] Tropical forests are fragile ecosystems, extremely vulnerable to human disruption. Once disturbed, the entire ecosystem can unravel. The loss of the trees causes the interruption of nutrient cycling above and below the soil, the soil loses fertility, plant and animal species lose their habitats and become extinct, and acute fuelwood shortages appear (especially in the dry tropical forests). The soil erodes without the ground cover provided by trees and plants, and downstream rivers suffer siltation, causing floods and droughts, and damaging expensive irrigation and hydroelectric systems. Traced through its effects on agriculture, energy supply and water resources, tropical deforestation impoverishes about a billion people. [...]

The planet's evolutionary heritage – its genetic diversity is heavily concentrated in these same forests. It is therefore disappearing today on a scale not seen since the age of the dinosaurs, and at an unprecedented pace. Biologists estimate that species are being lost in the tropical forests 1,000–10,000 times faster than the natural rate of extinction. As many as 20 percent of all the species now living may be gone by the year 2000. The loss will be felt aesthetically, scientifically and, above all, economically. [...]

[...] The bitter irony is that genetic diversity is disappearing on a grand scale at the very moment when biotechnology makes it possible to exploit fully this resource for the first time.

Soil degradation is another major concern. Both a cause and a consequence of poverty, desertification, as it is generally called, is causing declining agricultural productivity on nearly two billion hectares, 15 percent of the earth's land area. The causes are overcultivation, overgrazing, erosion, and salinization and waterlogging due to poorly managed irrigation. [...]

Finally, patterns of land tenure, though not strictly an environmental condition, have an immense environmental impact. [...] Land reform is among the most difficult of all political undertakings, but without it many countries will be unable to create a healthy agricultural sector to fuel economic growth.

Environmental decline occasionally leads directly to conflict [...]. Generally, however, its impact on nations' security is felt in the downward pull on economic performance and, therefore, on political stability. The underlying cause of turmoil is often ignored; instead governments address the poverty and instability that are its results. [...]

If such resource and population trends are not addressed, as they are not in so much of the world today, the resulting economic decline leads to frustration, resentment, domestic unrest or even civil war. Human suffering and turmoil make countries ripe for authoritarian government or external subversion. Environmental refugees spread the disruption across national borders. [...] Wherever refugees settle, they flood the labor market, add to the local demand for food and put new burdens on the land, thus spreading the environmental stress that originally forced them from their homes. Resource mismanagement is not the only cause of these mass movements, of course. Religious and ethnic conflicts, political repression and other forces are at work. But the environmental causes are an essential factor.

A different kind of environmental concern has arisen from mankind's new ability to alter the environment on a planetary scale. The earth's physiology is shaped by the characteristics of four elements (carbon, nitrogen, phosphorous and sulfur); by its living inhabitants (the biosphere); and by the interactions of the atmosphere and the oceans, which produce our climate.

Mankind is altering both the carbon and nitrogen cycles, having increased the natural carbon dioxide concentration in the atmosphere by 25 percent. This has occurred largely in the last three decades through fossil-fuel use and deforestation. The production of commercial fertilizer has doubled the amount of nitrogen nature makes available to living things. The use of a single, minor class of chemicals, chlorofluorocarbons, has punched a continent-sized "hole" in the ozone layer at the top of the stratosphere over Antarctica, and caused a smaller, but growing loss of ozone all around the planet. Species loss is destroying the work of three billion years of evolution. Together these changes could drastically alter the conditions in which life on earth has evolved.

The greenhouse effect results from the fact that the planet's atmosphere is largely transparent to incoming radiation from the sun but absorbs much of the lower energy radiation reemitted by the earth. This natural phenomenon makes the earth warm enough to support life. But as emissions of greenhouse gases increase, the planet is warmed unnaturally. Carbon dioxide produced from the combustion of fossil fuels and by deforestation is responsible for about half of the greenhouse effect. A number of other gases, notably methane (natural gas), nitrous oxide, ozone (in the lower atmosphere, as distinguished from the protective ozone layer in the stratosphere) and the man-made chlorofluorocarbons are responsible for the other half.

Despite important uncertainties about aspects of the greenhouse warming, a virtually unanimous scientific consensus exists on its central features. If present emission trends continue, and unless some as yet undocumented phenomenon (possibly increased cloudiness) causes an offsetting cooling, the planet will, on average, get hotter because of the accumulation of these gases. Exactly how large the warming will be, and how fast it will occur, are uncertain. Existing models place the date of commitment to an average global warming of 1.5–4.5°C (3–8°F) in the early 2030s. The earth has not been this hot for two million years, long before human society, and indeed, even Homo sapiens, existed.

Hotter temperatures will be only one result of the continuing greenhouse warming. At some point, perhaps quite soon, precipitation patterns are likely to shift, possibly causing dustbowl-like conditions in the U.S. grain belt. Ocean currents are expected to do the same, dramatically altering the climates of many regions. A diversion of the Gulf Stream, for example, would transform Western Europe's climate, making it far colder than it is today. Sea level will rise due to the expansion of water when it is warmed and to the melting of land-based ice. The oceans are presently rising by one-half inch per decade, enough to cause serious erosion along much of the

U.S. coast. The projected rise is one to four feet by the year 2050. Such a large rise in the sea level would inundate vast coastal regions, erode shorelines, destroy coastal marshes and swamps (areas of very high biological productivity), pollute water supplies through the intrusion of salt water, and put at high risk the vastly disproportionate share of the world's economic wealth that is packed along coastlines. The great river deltas, from the Mississippi to the Ganges, would be flooded. Estimates are that a half-meter rise in Egypt would displace 16 percent of the population, while a two-meter rise in Bangladesh would claim 28 percent of the land where 30 million people live today and where more than 59 million are projected to live by 2030. [...]

[...] [H]uman societies, industrial no less than rural, depend on the normal, predictable functioning of the climate system. Climate undergoing rapid change will not only be less predictable because it is different, but may be inherently more variable. Many climatologists believe that as accumulating greenhouse gases force the climate out of equilibrium, climate extremes such as hurricanes, droughts, cold snaps and typhoons will become more frequent and perhaps more intense. [...]

Greenhouse change is closely linked to stratospheric ozone depletion, which is also caused by chlorofluorocarbons. The increased ultraviolet radiation resulting from losses in that protective layer will cause an increase in skin cancers and eye damage. It will have many still uncertain impacts on plant and animal life, and may suppress the immune systems of many species.

Serious enough in itself, ozone depletion illustrates a worrisome feature of man's newfound ability to cause global change. It is almost impossible to predict accurately the long-term impact of new chemicals or processes on the environment. Chlorofluorocarbons were thoroughly tested when first introduced, and found to be benign. Their effect on the remote stratosphere was never considered. [...]

Not only is it difficult to anticipate all the possible consequences in a highly interdependent, complex system, the system itself is poorly understood. [...]

[...] [C]urrent knowledge of planetary mechanisms is so scanty that the possibility of surprise, perhaps quite nasty surprise, must be rated rather high. The greatest risk may well come from a completely unanticipated direction. We lack both crucial knowledge and early warning systems.

Absent profound change in man's relationship to his environment, the future does not look bright. Consider the planet without such change in the year 2050. Economic growth is projected to have quintupled by then. Energy use could also quintuple; or if post-1973 trends continue, it may grow more slowly, perhaps only doubling or tripling. The human species already consumes or destroys 40 percent of all the energy produced by terrestrial photosynthesis, that is, 40 percent of the food energy potentially available to living things on land. While that fraction may be sustainable, it is doubtful that it could keep pace with the expected doubling of the world's population. Human use of 80 percent of the planet's potential productivity does not seem compatible with the continued functioning of the biosphere as we know it. The expected rate of species loss would have risen from perhaps a few each day to several hundred a day. The pollution and toxic waste burden would likely prove unmanageable. Tropical forests would have largely disappeared, and arable land, a vital resource in a world of ten billion people, would be rapidly decreasing due to soil degradation. In short, sweeping change in economic production systems is not a choice but a necessity.

Happily, this grim sketch of conditions in 2050 is not a prediction, but a projection, based on current trends. Like all projections, it says more about the present and the recent past than it does about the future. The planet is not destined to a slow and painful decline into environmental chaos. There are technical, scientific and economical solutions that are feasible to many current trends, and enough is known about promising new approaches to be confident that the right kinds of research will produce huge payoffs. Embedded in current practices are vast costs in lost opportunities and waste, which, if corrected, would bring massive benefits. Some such steps will require only a reallocation of money, while others will require sizable capital investments. None of the needed steps, however, requires globally unaffordable sums of money. What they do demand is a sizable shift in priorities.

For example, family-planning services cost about $10 per user, a tiny fraction of the cost of the basic human needs that would otherwise have to be met. Already identified opportunities for raising the efficiency of energy use in the United States cost one-half to one-seventh the cost of new energy supply. Comparable savings are available in most other countries. Agroforestry techniques, in which carefully selected combinations of trees and shrubs are planted together with crops, can not only replace the need for purchased fertilizer but also improve soil quality, make more water available to crops, hold down weeds, and provide fuelwood and higher agricultural yields all at the same time.

But if the technological opportunities are boundless, the social, political and institutional barriers are huge. Subsidies, pricing policies and economic discount rates encourage resource depletion in the name of economic growth, while delivering only the illusion of sustainable growth. Population control remains a controversial subject in much of the world. The traditional prerogatives of nation states are poorly matched with the needs for regional cooperation and global decision-making. And ignorance of the biological underpinning of human society blocks a clear view of where the long-term threats to global security lie.

Overcoming these economic and political barriers will require social and institutional inventions comparable in scale and vision to the new arrangements conceived in the decade following World War II. Without the sharp political turning point of a major war, and with threats that are diffuse and long term, the task will be more difficult. But if we are to avoid irreversible damage to the planet and a heavy toll in human suffering, nothing less is likely to suffice. A partial list of the specific changes suggests how demanding a task it will be.

Achieving sustainable economic growth will require the remodeling of agriculture, energy use and industrial production after nature's example – their reinvention, in fact. These economic systems must become circular rather than linear. Industry and manufacturing will need processes that use materials and energy with high efficiency, recycle by-products and produce little waste. Energy demand will have to be met with the highest efficiency consistent with full economic growth. Agriculture will rely heavily upon free ecosystem services instead of nearly exclusive reliance on man-made substitutes. And all systems will have to price goods and services to reflect the environmental costs of their provision.

A vital first step, one that can and should be taken in the very near term, would be to reinvent the national income accounts by which gross national product is measured. GNP is the foundation on which national economic policies are built, yet its calculation does not take into account resource depletion. A country can consume its forests, wildlife and fisheries, its minerals, its clean water and its topsoil, without seeing a reflection of the loss in its GNP. Nor are ecosystem services sustaining soil fertility, moderating and storing rainfall, filtering air and regulating the climate-valued, though their loss may entail great expense. The result is that economic. policymakers are profoundly misled by their chief guide.

A second step would be to invent a set of indicators by which global environmental health could be measured. Economic planning would be adrift without GNP, unemployment rates, and the like, and social planning without demographic indicators – fertility rates, infant mortality, literacy, life expectancy – would be impossible. Yet this is precisely where environmental policymaking stands today.

Development assistance also requires new tools. Bilateral and multilateral donors have found that project success rates climb when nongovernmental organizations distribute funds and direct programs. This is especially true in agriculture, forestry and conservation projects. The reasons are not mysterious. Such projects are more decentralized, more attuned to local needs and desires, and have a much higher degree of local participation in project planning. They are usually quite small in scale, however, and not capable of handling very large amounts of development funding. Often, too, their independent status threatens the national government. Finding ways to make far greater use of the strengths of such groups without weakening national governments is another priority for institutional innovation.

Better ways must also be found to turn the scientific and engineering strengths of the industrialized world to the solution of the developing world's problems. The challenges include learning enough about local constraints and conditions to ask the right questions, making such research professionally rewarding to the individual scientist, and transferring technology more effectively. [...]

On the political front, the need for a new diplomacy and for new institutions and regulatory regimes to cope with the world's growing environmental interdependence is even more compelling. Put bluntly, our accepted definition of the limits of national sovereignty as coinciding with national borders is obsolete. [...]

The majority of environmental problems demand regional solutions which encroach upon what we now think of as the prerogatives of national governments. This is because the phenomena themselves are defined by the limits of watershed, ecosystem, or atmospheric transport, not by national borders. Indeed, the costs and benefits of alternative policies cannot often be accurately judged without considering the region rather than the nation. [...]

Dealing with global change will be more difficult. No one nation or even group of nations can meet these challenges, and no nation can protect itself from the actions – or inaction – of others. No existing institution matches these criteria. It will be necessary to reduce the dominance of the superpower relationship which so often encourages other countries to adopt a wait-and-see attitude [...].

The United States, in particular, will have to assign a far greater prominence than it has heretofore to the practice of multilateral diplomacy. This would mean changes [...] that [allow] leadership without primacy, both in the slogging work of negotiation and in adherence to final outcomes. Above all, ways must soon be found to step around the deeply entrenched North-South cleavage and to replace it with a planetary sense of shared destiny. [...]

Today's negotiating models – the Law of the Sea Treaty, the Nuclear Nonproliferation Treaty, even the promising Convention to Protect the Ozone Layer – are inadequate. Typically such agreements take about 15 years to negotiate and enter into force, and perhaps another ten years before substantial changes in behavior are actually achieved. [...] Far better approaches will be needed.

Among these new approaches, perhaps the most difficult to achieve will be ways to negotiate successfully in the presence of substantial scientific uncertainty. The present model is static: years of negotiation leading to a final product. The new model will have to be fluid, allowing a rolling process of intermediate or self-adjusting agreements that respond quickly to growing scientific understanding. [...] [It] will require new economic methods for assessing risk, especially where the possible outcomes are irreversible. It will depend on a more active political role for biologists and chemists than they have been accustomed to, and far greater technical competence in the natural and planetary sciences among policymakers. Finally, the new model may need to forge a more involved and constructive role for the private sector. Relegating the affected industries to a heel-dragging, adversarial, outsiders role almost guarantees a slow process. [...]

International law, broadly speaking, has declined in influence in recent years. With leadership and commitment from the major powers it might regain its lost status. But that will not be sufficient. To be effective, future arrangements will require provisions for monitoring, enforcement and compensation, [...] areas where international law has traditionally been weak. [...]

Reflecting on the discovery of atomic energy, Albert Einstein noted "everything changed." And indeed, nuclear fission became the dominant force – military, geopolitical, and even psychological and social – of the ensuing decades. In the same sense, the driving force of the coming decades may well be environmental change. Man is still utterly dependent on the natural world but now has for the first time the ability to alter it, rapidly and on a global scale. Because of that difference, Einstein's verdict that "we shall require a substantially new manner of thinking if mankind is to survive" still seems apt.

Roland Paris

HUMAN SECURITY

Source: 'Human security: paradigm shift or hot air?' *International Security*, vol. 26, no. 2, 2001, pp. 87–102.

What is human security?

THE FIRST MAJOR statement concerning human security appeared in the 1994. *Human Development Report*, an annual publication of the United Nations Development Programme (UNDP). "The concept of security," the report argues, "has for too long been interpreted narrowly: as security of territory from external aggression, or as protection of national interests in foreign policy or as global security from the threat of nuclear holocaust. [...] Forgotten were the legitimate concerns of ordinary people who sought security in their daily lives."[1] This critique is clear and forceful, but the report's subsequent proposal for a new concept of security – *human security* – lacks precision: "Human security can be said to have two main aspects. It means, first, safety from such chronic threats as hunger, disease and repression. And second, it means protection from sudden and hurtful disruptions in the patterns of daily life – whether in homes, in jobs or in communities.[2] The scope of this definition is vast: Virtually any kind of unexpected or irregular discomfort could conceivably constitute a threat to one's human security. Perhaps anticipating this criticism, the authors of the report identify seven specific elements that comprise human security: (1) economic security (e.g., freedom from poverty); (2) food security (e.g., access to food); (3) health security (e.g., access to health care and protection from diseases); (4) environmental security (e.g., protection from such dangers as environmental pollution and depletion); (5) personal security (e.g., physical safety from such things as torture, war, criminal attacks, domestic violence, drug use, suicide, and even traffic accidents); (6) community security (e.g., survival of traditional cultures and ethnic groups as well as the physical security of these groups); and (7) political security (e.g., enjoyment of civil and political rights, and freedom from political oppression). This list is so broad that it is difficult to determine what, if anything, might be excluded from the definition of human security. Indeed the drafters of the report seem distinctly uninterested in establishing any definitional boundaries. Instead they make a point of commending the "all-encompassing" and "integrative" qualities of the human security concept, which they apparently view as among the concept's major strengths.[3]

Today the UNDP's 1994 definition of human security remains the most widely cited and "most authoritative" formulation of the term,[4] although different members of the human security coalition have customized the definition to suit their own particular interests. [...] Meanwhile the human security network – which, in addition to Canada, Norway, and Japan, includes several other states and a broad assortment of international NGOs – has committed itself to the goal of "strengthening human security with a view to creating a more humane world where people can live in security and dignity, free from want and fear, and with equal opportunities to develop their human potential to the full."[5] The sentiments embodied in these statements are honorable, but they do little to clarify the meaning or boundaries of the human security concept.

Some academic writings on the subject have been similarly opaque. Many works amount to restatements or revisions of the UNDP's laundry list of human security issues. Jorge Nef, for example, devises a fivefold classification scheme, arguing that human security comprises (1) environmental, personal, and physical security, (2) economic security, (3) social security, including "freedom from discrimination based on age, gender, ethnicity, or social status," (4) political security, and (5) cultural security, or "the set of psychological orientations of society geared to preserving and enhancing the ability to control uncertainty and fear."[6] Laura Reed and Majid Tehranian offer their own list of human security's ten constituent elements – including psychological security, which "hinges on establishing conditions fostering respectful, loving, and humane interpersonal relations," and communication security, or the importance of "freedom and balance in information flows."[7] Other scholars avoid the laundry list approach, but offer equally expansive definitions. According to Caroline Thomas, human security refers to the provision of "basic material needs" and the realization of "human dignity," including "emancipation from oppressive power structures – be they global, national, or local in origin and scope."[8] For Robert Bedeski, human security includes "the totality of knowledge, technology, institutions and activities that protect, defend and preserve the biological existence of human life; and the processes which protect and perfect collective peace and prosperity to enhance human freedom."[9] Again, if human security is all these things, what is it *not?*

A guide for research and policymaking?

Policymakers and scholars face different, but related, problems in attempting to put these definitions of human security into practical use. For policymakers, the challenge is to move beyond all-encompassing exhortations and to focus on specific solutions to specific political issues. This is a difficult task not only because of the broad sweep and definitional elasticity of most formulations of human security but also – and perhaps even more problematically – because the proponents of human security are typically reluctant to prioritize the jumble of goals and principles that make up the concept. As noted above, part of the ethic of the human security movement is to emphasize the "inclusiveness" and "holism" of the term, which in practice seems to mean treating *all* interests and objectives within the movement as equally valid. Reed and Tehranian, for instance, after presenting their list of ten constituent categories of human security, conclude with this caveat: "It is important to reiterate that these overlapping categories do not represent a hierarchy of security needs from personal to national, international, and environmental rights. On the contrary, each realm impinges upon the others and is intrinsically connected to wider political and economic considerations."[10] The observation that all human and natural realms are fundamentally interrelated is a truism, and does not provide very convincing justification for treating all needs, values, and policy objectives as equally important. Nor does it help decisionmakers in their daily task of allocating scarce resources among competing goals: After all, not everything can be a matter of national security, with all of the urgency that this term implies. […]

For those who study, rather than practice, international politics, the task of transforming the idea of human security into a useful analytical tool for scholarly research is also problematic. Given the hodgepodge of principles and objectives associated with the concept, it is far from clear what academics should even be studying. Human security seems capable of supporting virtually any hypothesis – along with its opposite – depending on the prejudices and interests of the particular researcher. Further, because the concept of human security encompasses both physical security and more general notions of social, economic, cultural, and psychological well-being, it is impractical to talk about certain socioeconomic factors "causing" an increase or decline in human security, given that these factors are themselves part of the definition of human security. The study of causal relationships requires a degree of analytical separation that the notion of human security lacks.[11] […]

Attempts to narrow the concept

One possible remedy for the expansiveness and vagueness of human security is to redefine the concept in much narrower and more precise terms, so that it might offer a better guide for research and policymaking. […] King and Murray offer a definition of human security that is intended to include only "essential" elements, meaning elements that are "important enough for human beings to fight over or to put their lives or property at great risk."[12] Using this standard, they identify five key indicators of well-being – poverty, health, education, political freedom, and democracy – that they intend to incorporate into an overall measure of human security for individuals and groups. Similarly, another scholar, Kanti Bajpai, proposes construction of a "human security audit" that would include measures of "direct and indirect threats to individual bodily safety and freedom," as well as measures of different societies' "capacity to deal with these threats, namely, the fostering of norms, institutions, and […] representativeness in decisionmaking structures."[13] […]

Both of these projects, however, face problems that seem endemic to the study of human security. First, they identify certain values as more important than others without providing a clear justification for doing so. Bajpai, for instance, proposes inclusion of "bodily safety" and "personal freedom" in his human security audit, and argues that this audit would draw attention to the fact that "threats to safety and freedom are *the most important*" elements of human security.[14] He does not explain, however, why other values are not equally, or perhaps even more, important than the values he champions. What about education? Is the ability to choose one's marriage partner, which is one of Bajpai's examples of personal freedom, really more important than, say, a good education? Perhaps it is, but Bajpai does not address this issue. Similarly, King and Murray state that their formulation of human security includes only those matters that people would be willing to fight over. But they neglect to offer evidence that their five indicators are, in fact, closely related to the risk of violent conflict. [...] Additionally, their decision to exclude indicators of violence from their composite measure of human security creates a de facto distinction between human security and physical security, thereby purging the most familiar connotation of security – safety from violence – from their definition of human security. [...] Thus the challenge for these scholars is not simply to narrow the definition of human security into a more analytically tractable concept, but to provide a compelling rationale for highlighting certain values. [...]

[...] Defining the core values of human security may be difficult not only because there is so little agreement on the meaning of human security, but because the term's ambiguity serves a particular purpose: It unites a diverse and sometimes fractious coalition of states and organizations that "see an opportunity to capture some of the more substantial political interest and superior financial resources" associated with more traditional, military conceptions of security.[15] These actors have in effect pursued a political strategy of "appropriating" the term "security," which conveys urgency, demands public attention, and commands governmental resources.[16] By maintaining a certain level of ambiguity in the notion of human security, moreover, the members of this coalition are able to minimize their individual differences, thereby accommodating as wide a variety of members and interests in their network as possible.[17] Given these circumstances, they are unlikely to support outside calls for greater specificity in the definition of human security, because definitional narrowing would likely highlight and aggravate differences among them, perhaps even to the point of alienating certain members and weakening the coalition as a whole. [...]

Human security as a category of research

To recapitulate my argument so far: Human security does not appear to offer a particularly useful framework of analysis for scholars or policymakers. But perhaps there are other avenues by which the idea of human security can contribute to the study of international relations and security. I would like to suggest one such possibility: Human security may serve as a *label* for a broad category of research in the field of security studies that is primarily concerned with nonmilitary threats to the safety of societies, groups, and individuals, in contrast to more traditional approaches to security studies that focus on protecting states from external threats. Much of this work is relatively new, and our understanding of how such research "fits" within the larger field of security studies is still limited. In other words, even if the concept of human security itself is too vague to generate specific research questions, it could still play a useful taxonomical role in the field by helping to classify different types of scholarship. Using human security in this manner would be compatible with the *spirit* of the term – particularly its emphasis on nonmilitary sources of conflict – while recognizing that there is little point in struggling to operationalize the quicksilver concept of human security itself. [...]

[...] Since the end of the Cold War, in particular, the subject matter of security studies has undergone both a "broadening" and a "deepening."[18] [...]

[...] [I]t is [now] possible to construct a matrix of the security studies field, [...] [that] contains four cells, each representing a different cluster of literature in the field. [...]

- Cell 1 contains works that concentrate on military threats to the security of states. Conventional realists tend to adopt this perspective, which has traditionally dominated academic security studies, particularly in the United States.[19] Most of the articles published in *International Security,* for example, fall into this category.

- Cell 2 contains works that address nonmilitary threats (instead of, or in addition to, military threats) to the national security of states, including environmental and economic challenges. Jessica Tuchman Mathews's much-cited 1989 article, "Redefining Security," is typical of this category. Mathews argues that foreign security policies should incorporate considerations of environmental destruction, among other things, but she still considers the state, rather than substate actors, to be the salient object of security.[20] Other examples of such work include the Palme Commission's 1982 report, *Common Security*, which argued that nuclear weapons posed a threat to the survival of all states; "investigations into the relationship between environmental degradation and international armed conflict," and studies of foreign economic policy and international security.[21]

- Cell 3 includes works that focus on military threats to actors other than states: namely societies, groups, and individuals. The prevalence of intrastate violence since the end of the Cold War has given rise to a large literature on intrastate conflicts, in which substate groups are the principal belligerents.[22] In addition, studies of "democide," or the intentional killing by a state of its own citizens, also fall into this category.[23]

- Cell 4 is concerned with military or nonmilitary threats – or both – to the security of societies, groups, and individuals. Does poverty, for example, fuel violence within societies?[24] Are certain types of domestic political institutions more conducive to domestic peace?[25] Is the degree of urbanization of a society, or access to medical care, associated with the occurrence of civil violence?[26] What other societal conditions pose a particular danger to the survival of groups and individuals? All of these questions would fall into the category of research that I label "human security."

Using the term "human security" to describe this type of scholarship has several advantages. First, [...] [it] echo[es] many of the concerns of the human security coalition [...]. Second, employing human security as a label for a broad category of research eliminates the problem of deriving clear hypotheses from the human security concept itself – a concept that [...] offers little analytical leverage because it is so sprawling and ambiguous. Consequently, scholars working in the "human security branch" of security studies would not need to adjudicate the merit or validity of human security per se, but rather they would focus on more specific questions that could be clearly defined (and perhaps even answered). Third, and relatedly, although many scholars in this branch of security studies may be interested in normative questions as well as empirical ones, the advantage of using human security as a descriptive label for a class of research is that the label would not presuppose any particular normative agenda.[27]

Fourth, mapping the field [...] with human security as one branch – helps to differentiate the principal nontraditional approaches to security studies from one another. With the broadening and deepening of security studies in recent years, it is no longer helpful or reasonable to define the field in dualistic terms: with the realist, state-centric, military-minded approach to security studies at the core and a disorderly bazaar of alternative approaches in the periphery. These alternative approaches actually fall into broad groupings and have become sufficiently important to merit their own classification scheme. Mapping the field in new ways can help us to understand how these approaches relate to more traditional approaches to security studies, and to one another. Finally, the very fashionability of the label "human security" could benefit scholars by drawing attention to existing works within cell 4 and opening up new areas of research in this branch of the field. [...]

Notes

1   United Nations Development Programme, *Human Development Report, 1994* (New York: Oxford University Press, 1994), p. 22.
2   Ibid., p. 23.
3   Ibid., p. 24.
4   John G. Cockell, "Conceptualising Peacebuilding: Human Security and Sustainable Peace," in Michael Pugh, ed., *Regeneration of War-Torn Societies* (London: Macmillan, 2000), p. 21.
5   "Chairman's Summary," Second Ministerial Meeting of the Human Security Network, Lucerne, Switzerland, May 11–12, 2000, http://www.dfaitmaeci.gc.ca/foreignp/humansecurity/Chairman_summary-e.asp (accessed on February 14, 2001).
6   Jorge Nef, *Human Security and Mutual Vulnerability: The Global Political Economy of Development and Underdevelopment,* 2nd ed. (Ottawa: International Development Research Centre, 1999), p. 25.
7   Laura Reed and Majid Tehranian, "Evolving Security Regimes," in Tehranian, *Worlds Apart,* pp. 39 and 47.
8   Caroline Thomas, "Introduction," in Caroline Thomas and Peter Wilkin, eds., *Globalization, Human Security, and the African Experience* (Boulder, Colo.: Lynne Rienner, 1999), p. 3.
9   Robert Bedeski, "Human Security, Knowledge, and the Evolution of the Northeast Asian State," Centre for Global Studies, University of Victoria, February 8, 2000, http:// www.globalcentres.org/does/bedeski.hbnl (accessed on February 14, 2001).
10   Reed and Tehranian, "Evolving Security Regimes," p. 53.
11   Suhrke makes a similar point in "Human Security and the Interests of States." See Astri Suhrke, "Human Security and the Interests of States," *Security Dialogue,* Vol. 30, No. 3 (September 1999), pp. 270–71.

12   Gary King and Christopher Murray, "Rethinking Human Security," Harvard University, May 4, 2000, http://Sking.harvard.edu/files/hs.pdf (accessed on February 14, 2001), p. 8.

13   Kanti Bajpai, "Human Security: Concept and Measurement," Kroc Institute Occasional Paper No. 19:OP:1 (Notre Dame, Ind.: University of Notre Dame, August 2000), http://www.nd.edu/?krocinst/ocpapers/op 19_I.PDF (accessed on February 14, 2001).

14   See "Independent Panel on 'Human Security' To Be Set Up," Agence France-Press, January 24, 2001, p. 53 (emphasis added).

15   King and Murray, "Rethinking Human Security," p. 4. See also Mahbub ul Haq, *Reflections on Human Development,* exp. ed. (Delhi: Oxford University Press, 1998). On the strategic use of the term "security" as a tool for changing policy or obtaining resources, see Emma Rothschild, "What Is Security?" *Dædalus*, Vol. 124, No. 3 (Summer 1995), pp. 58–59.

16   On the urgency that is automatically associated with the concept of national security, see David E. Sanger, "Sometimes National Security Says It All," *New York Times*, Week in Review, May 7, 2000, p. 3.

17   The communiqués of the human security network, for example, describe the concept of human security more vaguely than do Canadian or Japanese government documents on the subject. Compare "Chairman's Summary," Second Ministerial Meeting of the Human Security Network, to the Government of Canada's "Human Security: Safety for People in a Changing World," Department of Foreign Affairs and International Trade, May 1999, and the "Statement by Director-General Yukio Takasu." Bajpai also discusses some of these differences in "Human Security: Concept and Measurement," as does Fen Osler Hampson, "The Axworthy Years: An Assessment," presentation prepared for delivery to the Group of 78, National Press Club, Ottawa, October 31, 2000, http://www.hri.ca/partners/G78/English/Peace/hampsort-axworthyhtrn (accessed on February 14, 2001).

18   I borrow these terms from Richard Wyn Jones, *Security, Strategy, and Critical Theory* (Boulder, Colo.: Lynne Rienner, 1999).

19   See, for example, Stephen M. Walt, "The Renaissance of Security Studies," *International Studies Quarterly*, Vol. 35, No. 1 (March 1991); Richard K. Betts, "Should Strategic Studies Survive?" *World Politics*, Vol. 50, No. 1 (October 1997), pp. 7–33; Michael E. Brown, Owen R. Coté, Jr., Sean M. Lynn-Jones, and Steven E. Miller, eds., *America's Strategic Choices*, rev. ed. (Cambridge, Mass.: MIT Press, 2000); David A. Baldwin, "Security Studies and the End of the Cold War," *World Politics*, Vol. 48, No. 1 (October 1995), pp. 117–41; and Joseph S. Nye, Jr., and Sean M. Lynn-Jones, "International Security Studies: A Report of a Conference on the State of the Field," *International Security*, Vol. 12, No. 4 (Spring 1988), pp. 5–27.

20   Jessica Tuchman Mathews, "Redefining Security," *Foreign Affairs*, Vol. 68, No. 2 (Spring 1989), pp. 162–77. See also Richard H. Ullman, "Redefining Security," *International Security*, Vol. 8, No. 1 (Summer 1983), pp. 129–53; and Joseph J. Romm, *Defining National Security: The Nonmilitary Aspects* (New York: Council on Foreign Relations, 1993).

21   See, for example, Jean-Mare F. Blanchard, Edward D. Mansfield, and Norrin M. Ripsman, eds., *Power and the Purse: Economic Statecraft, Interdependence, and National Security* (London: Frank Cass, 2000), originally published as a special issue of *Security Studies*, Vol. 9, Nos. 1–2 (Autumn 1999–Winter 2000), pp. 1–316; C. Fred Bergsten, "America's Two-Front Economic Conflict," *Foreign Affairs*, Vol. 80, No. 2

(March–April 2001), pp. 16–27; Richard N. Haass, ed., *Economic Sanctions and American Diplomacy* (New York: Council on Foreign Relations, 1998); and Jonathan Kirschner, "Political Economic in Security Studies after the Cold War," *Review of International Political Economy*, Vol. 5, No. 1 (Spring 1998), pp. 64–91.

22   See, for example, John Mueller, "The Banality of 'Ethnic War,'" *International Security*, Vol. 25, No. 1 (Summer 2000), pp. 42–70; Benjamin Valentino, "Final Solutions: The Causes of Mass Killing and Genocide," *Security Studies*, Vol. 9, No. 3 (Spring 2000), pp. 1–59; Barbara F. Walter and Jack Snyder, eds., *Civil Wars, Insecurity, and Intervention* (New York: Columbia University Press, 1999); Beverly Crawford and Ronnie D. Lipschutz, eds., *The Myth of 'Ethnic Conflict': Politics, Economics, and 'Cultural' Violence* (Berkeley: International and Area Studies, University of California, 1998); Chaim Kaufmann, "Possible and Impossible Solutions to Ethnic Civil Wars," *International Security*, Vol. 20, No. 4 (Spring 1996), pp. 136–75; Donald M. Snow, *Uncivil Wars: International Security and the New Internal Conflicts* (Boulder; Colo.: Lynne Rienner, 1996); Michael E. Brown, ed., *Ethnic Conflict and International Security* (Princeton, N.J.: Princeton University Press, 1993); and Roy Licklider, ed., *Stopping the Killing: How Civil Wars End* (New York: New York University Press, 1993).

23   See, for example, R. J. Rummel, *Power Kills: Democracy as a Method of Non-Violence* (New Brunswick, N.J.: Transaction, 1997); Gerald W. Scully, "Democide and Genocide as Rent-Seeking Activities," *Public Choice*, Vol. 93, Nos. 1–2 (October 1997), pp. 77–97; and Matthew Krain, "State Sponsored Mass Murder: The Onset and Severity of Genocides and Politicizes," *Journal of Conflict Resolution*, Vol. 41, No. 3 (June 1997), pp. 331–60.

24   Steve Maistorovic, "Politicized Ethnicity and Economic Inequality," *Nationalism and Ethnic Politics*, Vol. 1, No. 1 (Spring 1995), pp. 33–53; Walker Connor, "Eco- or Ethno-Nationalism," in Connor, *Ethnonationalism: The Quest for Understanding* (Princeton, N.J.: Princeton University Press, 1994), pp. 145–64; Ted Robert Gurr, "Why Minorities Rebel: A Global Analysis of Communal Mobilization and Conflict since 1945," *International Political Science Review*, Vol. 14, No. 2 (April 1993), pp. 161–201; Saul Newman, "Does Modernization Breed Ethnic Conflict?" *World Politics*, Vol. 43, No. 3 (April 1991), pp. 451–78; James B. Rule, *Theories of Civil Violence* (Berkeley: University of California Press, 1988); Steven Finkel and James B. Rule, "Relative Deprivation and Related Theories of Civil Violence: A Critical Review," in Kurt Lang and Gladys Lang, eds., *Research in Social Movements, Conflicts, and Change* (Greenwich, Conn.: JAI, 1986), Vol. 9, pp. 47–69; Ted Robert Gurr, *Why Men Rebel* (Princeton, N.J.: Princeton University Press, 1970); and William Ford and John Moore, "Additional Evidence on the Social Characteristics of Riot Cities," *Social Science Quarterly*, Vol. 51, No. 2 (September 1970), pp. 339–48.

25   Håvard Hegre, Tanja Ellingsen, Nils Petter Gleditsch, and Scott Gales, "Towards a Democratic Civil Peace? Opportunity, Grievance, and Civil War, 1816–1992," paper presented to the workshop Civil Conflicts, Crime, and Violence in Developing Countries, World Bank, Washington, D.C., February 1999; Matthew Krain and Marissa Edson Myers, "Democracy and Civil War: A Note on the Democratic Peace Proposition," *International Interactions*, Vol. 23, No. 1 (June 1997), pp. 109–18; and Michael Engelhardt, "Democracies, Dictatorships, and Counterinsurgency: Does Regime Type Really Matter?" *Conflict Quarterly*, Vol. 12, No. 3 (Summer 1992), pp. 52–63.

26 These two factors, among others, are studied in Daniel C. Esty, Jack A. Goldstone, Ted Robert Gurr Barbara Harff, Marc Levy, Geoffrey D. Dabelko, Pamela T. Surko, and Alan N. Unger, *State Failure Task Force Report: Phase II Findings* (McLean, Va.: Science Applications International Corporation, 1998). For a critique of this report, see Gary King and Langche Zeng, "Improving Forecasts of State Failure," paper prepared for the Midwest Political Science Association meeting in Chicago, Illinois, November 13, 2000, http://gking.harvard.edu/files/civil.pdf (accessed on May 5, 2001).

27 Scholars may conclude, for example, that certain socioeconomic conditions are not associated with any particular threats to human survival.

Stephen M. Walt

THE RENAISSANCE OF SECURITY STUDIES

Source: 'The renaissance of security studies', *International Studies Quarterly*, vol. 35, no. 2, 1991, pp. 211–39.

What is "security studies"?

T HE BOUNDARIES OF intellectual disciplines are permeable; as a result, any effort to delineate the precise scope of security studies is somewhat arbitrary. The main focus of security studies is easy to identify, however: it is the phenomenon of war. Security studies assumes that conflict between states is always a possibility and that the use of military force has far-reaching effects on states and societies (Bull, 1968; Martin, 1980). Accordingly, security studies may be defined as *the study of the threat, use, and control of military force* (Nye and Lynn Jones, 1988). It explores the conditions that make the use of force more likely, the ways that the use of force affects individuals, states, and societies, and the specific policies that states adopt in order to prepare for, prevent, or engage in war. [...]

Military power is not the only source of national security, and military threats are not the only dangers that states face (though they are usually the most serious). As a result security studies also includes what is sometimes termed "statecraft" – arms control, diplomacy, crisis management, for example. These issues are clearly relevant to the main focus of the field, because they bear directly on the likelihood and character of war.

Because nonmilitary phenomena can also threaten states and individuals, some writers have suggested broadening the concept of "security" to include topics such as poverty, AIDS, environmental hazards, drug abuse, and the like (Buzan, 1983; Brown, 1989). Such proposals remind us that nonmilitary issues deserve sustained attention from scholars and policymakers, and that military power does not guarantee well-being. But this prescription runs the risk of expanding "security studies" excessively; by this logic, issues such as pollution, disease, child abuse, or economic recessions could all be viewed as threats to "security." Defining the field in this way would destroy its intellectual coherence and make it more difficult to devise solutions to any of these important problems.

Moreover, the fact that other hazards exist does not mean that the danger of war has been eliminated. However much we may regret it, organized violence has been a central part of human existence for millennia and is likely to remain so for the foreseeable future. Not surprisingly, therefore, preparations for war have preoccupied organized polities throughout history (McNeill, 1982). Any attempt to understand the evolution of human society, let alone the prospects for peace, must take account of the role of military force. Indeed, given the cost of military forces and the risks of modern war, it would be irresponsible for the scholarly community to ignore the central questions that form the heart of the security studies field.[1] […]

* * *

Problems and prospects for security studies

What lies ahead for security studies? On the one hand, the widespread belief that the end of the Cold War has decreased the risk of war may temporarily divert financial support and research energies in other directions. On the other hand, a permanent decline is unlikely for at least three reasons. First, as the war in the Persian Gulf reminds us, military power remains a central element of international politics, and failure to appreciate its importance invariably leads to costly reminders. Second, security studies has been institutionalized within many university departments; indeed, a graduate program lacking qualified experts in this area must now be considered incomplete. Thus, new Ph.Ds will emerge in due course and will enjoy adequate professional opportunities. Most important of all, the collapse of the Cold War order will create new policy problems and new research puzzles. In short, the scholarly agenda in security studies is expanding, not shrinking, and security studies will remain an active sub-field for some time to come.

Potential problems

Despite these grounds for optimism, several dangers could undermine the future development of the field. As noted earlier, the resources at stake in debates over defense and foreign policy create a strong temptation to focus on short-term policy analysis. Moreover, as Hans Morgenthau once warned, active involvement in policy debates inevitably tempts participants to sacrifice scholarly integrity for the sake of personal gain or political effectiveness (Morgenthau, 1970; Walt, 1987:146–60). At the very least, there are powerful incentives to concentrate on consulting work and policy analysis rather than on cumulative scholarly research. If security studies neglects long-term research questions and focuses solely on immediate policy issues, a decline in rigor and quality will be difficult to avoid.

Yet the opposite tendency may pose an even greater danger. On the whole, security studies have profited from its connection to real-world issues; the main advances of the past four decades have emerged from efforts to solve important practical questions. If security studies succumbs to the tendency for academic disciplines to pursue "the trivial, the formal, the methodological, the purely theoretical, the remotely historical – in short, the politically irrelevant" (Morgenthau, 1966:73), its theoretical progress and its practical value will inevitably decline.

In short, security studies must steer between the Scylla of political opportunism and the Charybdis of academic irrelevance. What does this mean in practice? Among other things, it means that security studies should remain wary of the counterproductive tangents that have seduced other areas of international studies, most notably the "post-modern" approach to international affairs (Ashley, 1984; Der Derian and Shapiro, 1989; Lapid, 1989). Contrary to their proponents' claims, post-modern approaches have yet to demonstrate much value for comprehending world politics; to date, these works are mostly criticism and not much theory.[2] As Robert Keohane has noted, until these writers "have delineated [...] a research program and shown [...] that it can illuminate important issues in world politics, they will remain on the margins of the field" (Keohane, 1988:392). In particular, issues of war and peace are too important for the field to be diverted into a prolix and self-indulgent discourse that is divorced from the real world.

The use of formal models should also be viewed with some caution, though their potential value is greater. Formal methods possess obvious virtues: analytic assumptions tend to be stated more explicitly, gaps in evidence can be handled through systematic sensitivity analyses, and advanced mathematical techniques can identify deductive solutions to previously intractable problems (for recent examples, see O'Neill, 1989; Downs and Rocke, 1990; Powell, 1990). Formal analysis can also depict a theory's logical structure with precision, generating counterintuitive propositions and identifying inconsistencies.

Yet despite these strengths, recent formal applications have had relatively little impact on other work in the field. This situation stands in sharp contrast to earlier formal works (Schelling, 1960; Olson and Zeckhauser, 1966), which had a broad and lasting influence. One reason is the tendency for recent works to rely on increasingly heroic assumptions, which render these models both impossible to test and less applicable to important real-world problems. The danger, as Schelling warned, is "the willingness of social scientists to treat the subject [of strategy] as though it were, or should be, solely a branch of mathematics" (1960:10).

Obviously, scholarship in social science need not have immediate "policy relevance." But tolerance for diverse approaches is not a license to pursue a technique regardless of its ultimate payoff; the value of any social science tool lies in what it can tell us about real human behavior. Formal models are useful when they do this, but they should not be viewed as ends in themselves. Unfortunately, despite the impressive technical firepower displayed in many recent formal works, their ability to illuminate important national security problems has been disappointing.

Because scientific disciplines advance through competition, we should not try to impose a single methodological monolith upon the field. To insist that a single method constitutes the only proper approach is like saying that a hammer is the only proper tool for building a house. The above strictures are no more than a warning, therefore; progress will be best served by increased dialogue between different methodological approaches (Downs, 1989).[3]

A research agenda for security studies

Any attempt to define a research agenda will invariably omit important or unforeseen possibilities. Nevertheless, several subjects clearly merit further attention.

The role of domestic politics. Some of the most interesting advances in security studies have come from scholars focusing on different aspects of domestic politics. What unites these disparate theories is the belief that domestic politics is a powerful determinant of national security policy. For example, several prominent studies have argued that liberal democracies do not fight each other (Small and Singer, 1976; Chan, 1984; Weede, 1984; Doyle, 1986; Maoz and Abdolali, 1989); given the importance of this claim, further research is needed to resolve the remaining theoretical and empirical puzzles.[4] Similarly, the long-standing debate over the military's role as a cause of war remains unresolved (Huntington, 1957; Vagts, 1959; Betts, 1977; Snyder, 1984; Van Evera, 1984), along with the validity of the so-called scapegoat and diversionary theories of war (Levy, 1988, 1990). Other recent works suggest that regime change or revolution is a potent cause of conflict as well (Maoz, 1989; Walt, 1990), but further research to measure and explain this effect is still needed. Students of arms races have long stressed the role of domestic factors (York, 1970; Kurth, 1971; Senghaas, 1972; Evangelista, 1988), and Jack Snyder's recent work (1991) on empires argues that the internal politics of rapidly industrializing societies encourages "log-rolled" domestic coalitions to unite behind highly expansionist foreign policies. Given the recent shifts in the domestic politics of the Soviet Union and its Eastern European allies, further work on these different approaches is clearly in order.

The causes of peace and cooperation. Another potential growth area is in greater attention to the causes of peace and cooperation. To be sure, most theories about the causes of war are also theories about peace (Van Evera, 1984; Blainey, 1988), and exploring ways to reduce the risk of war has been part of the field since its inception.[5] In the past, however, security studies tended to view explicit research on peace as utopian or naive, perhaps based on a belief that realists should not be diverted into such idealistic pursuits. For their part, peace researchers tended to assume that the use of force was always irrational, that arms races were a powerful cause of conflict rather than a symptom, and that war was always the result of misperception. The tendency for some peace researchers to view capitalism as a powerful engine of conflict (despite the abundant evidence against this belief) divided the two fields even further.[6]

Over time, however, the two perspectives have begun to converge. As discussed above, scholars in security studies have devoted considerable attention to misperception and domestic politics as causes of war, while some peace researchers have begun to address issues of military strategy and defense policy in a more sophisticated and well-informed way. This trend is perhaps most evident in the literature on "nonoffensive" defense: many of these writings acknowledge the need for military power while investigating alternative force structures that could ameliorate the security dilemma between states (Ahfeldt, 1983; Alternative Defense Commission, 1983; Agrell, 1987; Gates, 1987; Saperstein, 1987; Flanagan, 1988). Although primarily a product of the peace research community, these works bear a strong resemblance to the offense/defense literature in security studies.

Increased interest in peace and cooperation is evident in other ways as well. For example, scholars of security affairs have been understandably skeptical of "security regimes" in the past (Jervis, 1983), but more recent studies suggest that international regimes can have modest positive effects on the ability of states to cooperate on specific security issues (Lynn Jones, 1985; Nye, 1987; George, Farley, and Dallin, 1988).

Although self-help remains the primary imperative in international politics, institutional arrangements could still contribute to peace, particularly if they directly address the primary controllable causes of war identified by previous scholarly work.[7]

Far from being a utopian ideal, efforts to reduce the danger of war are consistent with the central focus of security studies and with realism's traditional pessimism about the prospects for a durable peace. Moreover, preserving peace contributes directly to national security, at least for most states most of the time. Given their belief that war is always a possibility, realists should be especially interested in devising ways to ensure that it does not occur. In short, well-informed research on peace is a realistic response to anarchy and should be part of security studies.

The power of ideas. Finally, interest in the "autonomous power of ideas" has also grown in recent years. The role of "strategic beliefs" in foreign and military policy has been stressed by historians (Howard, 1984), by scholars drawing upon psychology (Jervis, 1976; Kull, 1988), and by studies of military organizations and domestic politics (Snyder, 1984, 1991; Van Evera, 1984; Thomson, 1990). More generally, John Mueller (1989) and James L. Ray (1990) have argued that war is a fading institution among advanced industrial societies, just as dueling and slavery become obsolete in the 19th century. Significantly, their arguments are not based on the dangers posed by nuclear weapons. Instead, they claim that the horrors of conventional war have discredited the earlier belief that it was a noble or heroic activity. This argument remains incomplete, however, for we lack a theory to account for the observed change in attitudes (Kaysen, 1990). Mueller attributes the shift to the dehumanizing experience of World War I, but this does not explain why earlier wars failed to produce a similar result. Without a theory of attitude change, we cannot estimate the durability of current antiwar attitudes or devise a workable strategy for reinforcing them. And as Mueller admits, the outbreak of World War II shows that if most *but not all* states believe war is too horrible to contemplate, those that do not share this view will be more likely to use force precisely because they expect opponents to acquiesce rather than fight. Unless popular revulsion against war becomes universal and permanent, it provides no guarantee that inter-state violence would end. Despite these limitations, the impact of changing attitudes on warfare remains a fascinating question, as part of the general subject of how states learn.

The end of the Cold War. For the past forty years, the two superpowers defined their security policies primarily in response to each other, and the rivalry between them shaped the conduct of most other states as well. Accordingly, the waning of U.S. Soviet rivalry will have a significant impact on security studies.

First, the study of grand strategy will be increasingly important. As discussed earlier, interest in U.S. grand strategy revived during the renaissance of security studies, but there are still no theoretical or comparative works on grand strategy and relatively few studies of other cases.[8] Because both great and lesser powers will need new security arrangements once the Cold War is over, research on alternative grand strategies will be of obvious interest. Under what conditions should states employ military force and for what purposes? With the waning of the Soviet threat, what interests will the other great powers seek to defend? Can the United States and its allies now reduce their military forces, or should they be configured for other contingencies? These issues are certain to receive considerable attention, and some of it should come from experts without a professional interest in the outcome.

Second, the end of the Cold War raises basic issues about the prospects for peace. Will the waning of U.S.-Soviet rivalry reduce the danger of war or allow familiar sources of conflict to reemerge? Will regional powers take more aggressive actions to improve their positions – as Iraq sought to do by invading Kuwait – or will they behave more cautiously in the absence of superpower support? Attempts to answer these and other questions will necessarily build on the existing knowledge base in the field, but will also stimulate new empirical studies and theoretical innovations.

These concerns are already evident in the scholarly debate over the future of Europe. At least four main views can be identified. "Third-image pessimists"[9] argue that the re-emergence of a multipolar Europe will restore the conditions that fueled war in Europe in the past; for this reason, the end of the Cold War will increase the danger of war. They recommend that U.S. military forces remain in Europe to dampen these effects and favor the managed spread of nuclear weapons (to Germany in particular) to alleviate the security fears they believe will accompany the superpowers' withdrawal from Europe (Mearsheimer, 1990). "Second-image pessimists" downplay systemic causes and emphasize the dangers arising from the weak democratic institutions in Eastern Europe and the Soviet Union. They fear that competing interest groups will use foreign policy to enhance their domestic positions; in the worst case, several factions would unite in a coalition combining their separate expansionist agendas, as occurred in Germany and Japan before the two world wars. The recommended antidote is Western assistance to support the new democracies in Eastern Europe, and the rapid integration of these states into the European Community (EC) (Snyder, 1990).

Rejecting these pessimistic views, "second-image optimists" argue that the leveling of European societies, the dampening of militarism, and the extensive rewriting of nationalist history in Europe have removed the main causes of earlier wars. This view sees the possible dissolution of the Soviet Union as the main threat to peace, and favors Western efforts to encourage a peaceful transition and to prevent the reemergence of the domestic forces that fueled aggression in the past (Van Evera, 1990–91). Finally, "institutional optimists" suggest that economic integration and international institutions (such as NATO, the EC, or the Conference on Security and Cooperation in Europe) will be strong enough to safeguard peace in Europe. A full scholarly presentation of this view is not yet available – though Snyder (1990) presents elements of one – but it implies using existing institutions to facilitate arms control and to manage economic and political tensions in an independent and increasingly united Europe (Hoffmann, 1990; Keohane, 1990).

A brief summary cannot do justice to the subtlety and power of these competing views. It is worth noting, however, that all of them rely on scholarship developed or refined during the renaissance of security studies: the scholarly debate on the future of Europe is very much a contest between rival theoretical visions. It is also an issue with far-reaching implications for defense budgets, alliance commitments, and the likelihood of war. Far from signaling a declining role for security studies, in short, the end of the Cold War will keep security issues on the front burner for some time to come.

Economics and security. The relationship between economics and security is of growing interest as well. One obvious dimension is the connection between military spending and economic performance; the debate sparked by Paul Kennedy's *The Rise and Fall of the Great Powers* illustrates the continued dissensus on this question (Kennedy, 1987; Adams and Gold, 1987; Huntington, 1988–89; Friedberg, 1989; Kupchan,

1989; Nye, 1990). Second, despite the attention that resource issues received after the 1973 oil shocks, disputes persist on the strategic importance of economic resources and their role as potential causes of international conflict (Shafer, 1982; Maull, 1984; Finlayson and Haglund, 1987; Johnson, 1989). The recent war in the Persian Gulf highlights the continued relevance of this issue, as well as the potential effectiveness of economic sanctions as a diplomatic instrument.

A third issue linking economics and security is the political influence of the military-industrial complex (MIC). Although several recent works have analyzed the procurement process in detail (Gansler, 1982, 1989; Stubbing, 1986; McNaugher, 1989), there has been little research on the MIC's *political* role in shaping national policy. Even our historical knowledge is deficient; there is still no adequate successor to Huntington's *The Common Defense* (1961), Schilling, Hammond, and Snyder's *Strategy, Politics, and Defense Budgets* (1962), and Enthoven and Smith's How *Much is Enough?* (1971). Indeed, there is no authoritative scholarly analysis of the U.S. defense buildup in the 1980s.[10] Cross-national comparisons would be valuable as well, to supplement the few studies now available (Evangelista, 1988). Given the resources at stake, investigating how such decisions are made seems well worth the effort of economists and security experts alike.

Refining existing theories. The discussion in this section underscores how new theories and approaches have sparked lively scholarly exchanges throughout the renaissance of security studies, on topics such as the impact of offensive and defensive advantages, the effect of domestic politics on war, the causes and consequences of arms races, the requirements of extended deterrence, the sources of military innovation, and the prospects for security cooperation. In most cases, however, competing hypotheses have not been subjected to systematic empirical tests. In addition to the usual efforts to devise new theories, therefore, refining and testing existing hypotheses through well-designed empirical studies should form a central part of future work.

Protecting the data base. As noted earlier, the renaissance of security studies was facilitated by greater access to relevant information. Unfortunately, several recent developments suggest that the information so necessary for scholarship and for an informed public debate is being seriously curtailed. The *Annual Reports* produced by the Defense Department during the Reagan Administration were less informative than earlier versions, and this trend has continued under President Bush.[11] The Reagan Administration was also more aggressive in prosecuting alleged leaks and in manipulating media coverage, thereby inhibiting journalists from investigative reporting and reducing the raw data available for use by scholars (Hertsgaard, 1988).[12] Even more worrisome, a recent volume of the *Foreign Relations of the United States,* the State Department's official record of U.S. diplomacy, contained such serious distortions that the Chairman of its Advisory Committee resigned in protest, accompanied by widespread condemnation from the Historical profession (Cohen, 1990; Kuniholm, 1990; Society of Historians of American Foreign Relations, 1990).[13]

Efforts to shield government policy from outside evaluation pose a grave threat to scholarship in the field. No doubt some government officials would like to deny ordinary citizens the opportunity to scrutinize their conduct; as a central part of that evaluative process, the scholarly profession should resist this effort wholeheartedly. The danger goes beyond the interests of any particular subfield; restricting information threatens the public debate that is central to democracy and essential to sound policy. Events as diverse as the Bay of Pigs invasion, the Iran/contra affair, and the troubled development of the B-2 bomber remind us that excessive secrecy allows ill-conceived programs to survive uncorrected. Instead of limiting the study of security issues to a select group of official "experts," therefore, open debate on national security matters must be preserved. Such a debate *requires* that scholars retain access to a reliable and complete data base. [...]

References

ADAMS, G., AND D. GOLD (1987) *Defense Spending and the Economy: Does the Defense Budget Make a Difference?* Washington, DC: Center for Budget and Policy Priorities.

AGRELL, W. (1987) Offensive versus Defensive Military Strategy and Alternative Defense. *Journal of Peace Research* 24:75–85.

AHFELDT, H. (1983) *Defensive Verteidigung.* Reinbek bei Hamburg: Rowohlt.

ALTERNATIVE DEFENSE COMMISSION (1983) *Defense without The Bomb.* New York: Taylor and Francis.

ART, R. (1968) *The TFX Decision: McNamara and the Military.* Boston: Little, Brown.

ASHLEY, R. (1984) The Poverty of Neo-Realism. *International Organization* 38:225–86.

BEN-HORIN, Y., AND B. R. POSEN (1981) *Israel's Strategic Doctrine.* Research Memorandum R-2845NA. Santa Monica, CA: The RAND Corporation.

BETTS, R. (1977) *Soldiers, Statesmen and Cold War Cases.* Cambridge, MA: Harvard University Press.

BLAINEY, G. (1988) *The Causes of War.* New York: Free Press.

BOULDING, K. (1978) *Stable Peace.* Austin: University of Texas Press.

BRENNAN, D., ed. (1961) *Arms Control, Disarmament and National Security.* New York: George Braziller.

BROWN, N. (1989) Climate, Ecology and International Security. *Survival* 31:519–32.

BULL, H. (1968) Strategic Studies and Its Critics. *World Politics* 20:593–605.

BUZAN, B. (1983) *Peoples, States and Fear: The National Security Problem in International Relations.* Chapel Hill: University of North Carolina Press.

CHAN, S. (1984) Mirror, Mirror on the Wall [...] Are the Democratic States More Pacific? *Journal of Conflict Resolution* 28:617–48.

COHEN, W. I. (1990) At the State Dept., Historygate. *New York Times, May* 8:A29.

COOK, M., AND J. COHEN (1990) How Television Sold the Panama Invasion. *Extra!* 3:1, 3–8.

DANCE, E. H. (1960) *History the Betrayer: A Study in Bias.* London: Hutchinson.

DER DERIAN, J., AND M. SHAPIRO, EDS. (1989) *International/Intertextual Relations: The Boundaries of Knowledge and Practice in World Politics.* Lexington, MA: Lexington Books.

DOWNS, G. W. (1989) The Rational Deterrence Debate. *World Politics* 41:225–37.

DOWNS, G. W., AND D. ROCKE (1990) *Tacit Bargaining, Arms Races, and Arms Control.* Ann Arbor: University of Michigan Press.

DOYLE, M. (1986) Liberalism and World Politics. *American Political Science Review* 80:1151–70.

ENTHOVEN, A., AND K. W. SMITH (1971) *How Much is Enough?: Shaping the Defense Program, 1961–1969.* New York: Harper and Row.

EVANGELISTA, M. (1988) *Innovation and the Arms Race: How the United States and the Soviet Union Develop New Military Technologies.* Ithaca, NY: Cornell University Press.

FALLOWS, J. (1982) *National Defense.* New York: Vintage Press.

FINLAYSON, J. A., AND D. HAGLUND (1987) Whatever Happened to the Resource War? *Survival* 29:403–15.

FLANAGAN, S. (1988) Non-Provocative and Civilian-Based Defense. In *Fateful Visions: Avoiding Nuclear Catastrophe*, edited by J. S. Nye, G. Allison, and A. Carnesale, pp. 93–109. Cambridge, MA: Ballinger Publishers.

FRIEDBERG, A. (1988) *The Weary Titan: Britain and the Experience of Relative Decline, 1895–1905.* Princeton, NJ: Princeton University Press.

—— (1989) The Political Economy of American Strategy. *World Politics* 41:381–406.

GANSLER, J. (1982) *The Defense Industry.* Cambridge, MA: MIT Press.

—— (1989) *Affording Defense.* Cambridge, MA: MIT Press.

GATES, D. (1987) Area Defence Concepts: The West German Debate. *Survival* 29:301–17.

GEORGE, A. L., P. FARLEY, AND A. DALLIN (1988) *U.S.-Soviet Security Cooperation: Achievements, Failures, Lessons.* New York: Oxford University Press.

HANDEL, M. (1973) *Israel's Political-Military Doctrine.* Cambridge, MA: Center for International Affairs, Harvard University.

HERTSGAARD, M. (1988) *On Bended Knee: The Press and the Reagan Presidency.* New York: Farrar, Straus, Giroux.

HOFFMANN, S. (1990) A Plan for a New Europe. *The New York Review of Books*, Jan. 18:18–21.

HOWARD, M. (1984) Men Against Fire: Expectations of War in 1914. *International Security* 9:41–57.

HUNTINGTON, S. (1957) *The Soldier and the Slate: The Theory and Practice of Civil-Military Relations.* Cambridge, MA: Harvard University Press.

—— (1961) *The Common Defense: Strategic Programs and National Politics.* New York: Columbia University Press.

—— (1988–89) The U.S.-Decline or Renewal? *Foreign Affairs* 67:76–96.

INTERNATIONAL INSTITUTE FOR STRATEGIC STUDIES (ISS) (annual) *The Military Balance.* London: IISS.

JERVIS, R. (1976) *Perception and Misperception in International Politics.* Princeton, NJ: Princeton University Press.

—— (1983) Security Regimes. In *International Regimes*, edited by S. Krasner, pp. 173–94. Ithaca, NY: Cornell University Press.

JOHNSON, R. (1989) The Persian Gulf in U.S. Strategy: A Skeptical View. *International Security* 14:122–60.

KENNEDY, P. (1987) *The Rise and Fall of the Great Powers: Economic Power and Military Conflict, 1500–2000.* New York: Random House.

KEOHANE, R. O. (1988) International Institutions: Two Approaches. *International Studies Quarterly* 32:379–96.

—— (1990) Correspondence. *International Security* 15:192–94.

KOTZ, N. (1988) *Wild Blue Yonder: Money, Politics and the B-1 Bomber.* Princeton, NJ: Princeton University Press.

KULL, S. D. (1988) *Minds at War: Nuclear Reality and the Inner Conflicts of Defense Policymakers.* New York: Basic Books.

KUNIHOLM, B. R. (1990) Foreign Relations, Public Relations, Accountability, and Understanding. *Perspectives* 28:1, 11–12.

KUPCHAN, C. (1989) Defense Spending and Economic Performance. *Survival* 31:447–61.

KURTH, J. (1971) A Widening Gyre: The Logic of American Weapons Procurement. *Public Policy* 19:373–404.

LAKATOS, I. (1970) Falsification and the Methodology of Scientific Research Programmes. In *Criticism and the Growth of Knowledge*, edited by I. Lakatos and A. Musgrave, pp. 91–196. Cambridge, MA: Cambridge University Press.

LAPID, Y. (1989) The Third Debate: On the Prospects of International Theory in A Post-Positivist Era. *International Studies Quarterly* 33:235–54.

LEVY, J. (1988) Domestic Politics and War. In *The Origins and Prevention of Major War*, edited by R. Rotberg and T. Raab, pp. 79–99. Cambridge: Cambridge University Press.

—— (1990) The Causes of War: A Review of Theories and Evidence. In *Behavior, Society and Nuclear War, Vol. I*, edited by P. Tetlock *et al.*, pp. 209–333. New York: Oxford University Press.

LUTTWAK, E. (1976) *The Grand Strategy of the Roman Empire: From the First Century A.D. to the Third.* Baltimore, MD: Johns Hopkins University Press.

LYNN-JONES, S. (1985) A Quiet Success for Arms Control: Preventing Incidents at Sea. *International Security* 9:154–84.

MANDELBAUM, M. (1988) *The Fate of Nations: The Search for National Security in the 19th and 20th Centuries.* Cambridge: Cambridge University Press.

MAOZ, Z. (1989) Joining the Club of Nations: Political Development and International Conflict, 1816–1976. *International Studies Quarterly* 33:199–231.

MAOZ, Z., AND N. ABDOLALI (1989) Regime Types and International Conflict, 1816–1976. *Journal of Conflict Resolution* 33:3–36.

MARTIN, L. (1980) The Future of Strategic Studies. *Journal of Strategy Studies* 3:91–99

MAULL, H. (1984) *Energy, Minerals and Western Security.* Baltimore, MD: Johns Hopkins University Press.

MCNAUGHER, T. (1989) *New Weapons, Old Politics: America's Military Procurement Muddle.* Washington, DC: Brookings Institution.

MCNEILL, W. H. (1982) *The Pursuit of Power: Technology, Armed Force and Society since A.D. 1000.* Chicago: University of Chicago Press.

MEARSHEIMER, J. (1990) Back to the Future: Instability in Europe After the Cold War. *International Security* 15:5–56.

MORGENTHAU, H. J. (1966) The Purpose of Political Science. In *A Design For Political Science*, edited by J. C. Charlesworth, pp. 63–79. Philadelphia: American Academy of Political and Social Science.

—— (1970) *Truth and Power: Essays of a Decade, 1960–1970.* New York: Praeger.

MUELLER, J. (1989) *Retreat From Doomsday: The Obsolescence of Major War.* New York: Basic Books.

NYE, J. S. (1987) Nuclear Learning and U.S.-Soviet Security Regimes. *International Organization* 41;371–402.

—— (1990) *Bound to Lead: The Changing Nature of American Power.* New York: Basic Books.

NYE, J. S., AND S. LYNN JONES (1988) International Security Studies: A Report of A Conference on the State of the Field. *International Security* 12:5–27.

O'NEILL, B. (1989) Game Theory and the Study of the Deterrence of War. In *Perspectives on Deterrence*, edited by P. C. Stern, R. Axelrod, R. Jervis, and R. Radner, pp. 134–56. New York: Oxford University Press.

OLSON, M., AND R. ZECKHAUSER (1966) An Economic Theory of Alliances. *Review of Economics and Statistics* 48:266–79.

POWELL, R. (1990) *Nuclear Deterrence Theory: The Search for Credibility.* Cambridge: Cambridge University Press.

QUESTER, G. (1989) International Security Criticisms of Peace Research. In *Peace Studies: Past and Future,* edited by G. A. Lopez, pp. 98–105. *The Annals of the American Academy of Political and Social Science,* 504.

RAY, J. L. (1990) The Abolition of Slavery and the End of International War. *International Organization* 43:405–39.

SAPERSTEIN, A. (1987) An Enhanced Non-Provocative Defense in Europe: Attrition of Aggressive Armored Forces by Local Militaries. *Journal of Peace Research* 24:47–60.

SCHELLING, T. C. (1960) *The Strategy of Conflict.* Cambridge, MA: Harvard University Press.

SCHILLING, W., P. HAMMOND, AND G. SNYDER (1962) *Strategy, Politics and Defense Budgets.* New York: Columbia University Press.

SENGHAAS, D. (1972) *Rustung and Militarismus.* Frankfurt/Main: Suhrkamp.

SHAFER, M. (1982) Mineral Myths. *Foreign Policy* 47:154–71.

SINGER, J. D. (1976) An Assessment of Peace Research. *International Security* 1:118–37.

SMALL, M., AND J. D. SINGER (1976) The War-Proneness of Democratic Regimes, 1816–1965. *Jerusalem Journal of International Relations* 1:50–69.

SNYDER, G. (1984) The Security Dilemma in Alliance Politics. *World Politics* 36:461–95.

SNYDER, J. (1990) Avoiding Anarchy in the New Europe. *International Security* 14:5–41.

—— (1991) *Myths of Empire: Domestic Politics and International Ambitions.* Ithaca, NY: Cornell University Press.

SOCIETY OF HISTORIANS OF AMERICAN FOREIGN RELATIONS (SHAFR) (1990) Resolution on the Integrity of *Foreign Relations of the United States* Documentary History Volumes. *SHAFR Newsletter* 21: 33–40.

STUBBING, R. (1986) *The Defense Game: An Insider Explores the Astonishing Realities of America's Defense Establishment.* New York: Harper and Row.

THOMSON, J. E. (1990) State Practices, International Norms, and the Decline of Mercenarism. *International Studies Quarterly* 34: 23–48.

VAGTS, A. (1959) *A History of Militarism: Civilian and Military.* New York: Meridian Press.

VAN EVERA, S. (1984) Causes of War. Ph.D. dissertation. Berkeley: University of California.

—— (1990–91) Primed for Peace: Europe after the Cold War. *International Security* 15:757.

WALT, S. M. (1987) The Search for a Science of Strategy: A Review Essay of *Makers of Modern Strategy. International Security* 12:140–65.

—— (1990) Revolution and War. Paper presented at the annual meeting of the American Political Science Association, Aug. 27–Sept. 1.

WALTZ, K. (1959) *Man, the State and War: A Theoretical Analysis.* New York: Columbia University Press.

WEEDE, E. (1984) Democracy and War Involvement. *Journal of Conflict Resolution* 28:649–64.

WIBERG, H. (1981) JPR 1964–80: What Have We Learned About Peace? *Journal of Peace Research* 18: 111–48.

YORK, H. (1970) *Race to Oblivion: A Participant's Guide to the Arms Race*. New York: Simon and Schuster.

Notes

1   I am indebted to Michael Desch for discussion on these points.

2   Although Yosef Lapid cites Imre Lakatos's critique of naive positivism approvingly (Lapid, 1989:239, 245), he neglects Lakatos's key argument: theories are only overturned by the development of a superior alternative (Lakatos, 1970).

3   In the past, for example, security studies tended to dismiss quantitative research on conflict as irrelevant, while the latter tended to view security studies as unscientific "policy analysis." Both charges are undoubtedly true in some cases, but a blanket dismissal is increasingly inappropriate. Instead, encouraging both groups to become more familiar with alternative approaches would improve both enterprises. For example, whenever these literatures reach different conclusions – such as on the impact of domestic conflict or regime type on the likelihood of war – there is an obvious opportunity for further work.

4   In addition to problems of definition (were England and Germany liberal states in 1812 and 1914 respectively?) and the lack of independence between cases (many liberal states were formerly united in the British empire), these studies have yet to offer a persuasive explanation for the "liberal peace."

5   For example, deterrence theory identifies the conditions that make decisions for war irrational, surely a worthy goal for opponents of war.

6   For surveys of peace research from a variety of perspectives, see Singer (1976), Boulding (1978), Wiberg (1981), and Quester (1989).

7   Examples include offensive military imbalances, territorial disputes, xenophobia, and hypernationalism. The U.S.-Soviet arms control negotiations helped stabilize their deterrent relationship by limiting anti-ballistic missile systems, and the United Nations Educational, Scientific and Cultural Organization (UNESCO) led a largely successful campaign to eliminate national biases within European textbooks (Dance, 1960).

8   Studies of grand strategy for non-U.S. cases include Handel (1973), Luttwak (1976), Ben-Horin and Posen (1981), Friedberg (1988), and Mandelbaum (1988).

9   "Third-image" theories view war as a result of the anarchic international system, "second-image" theories focus on the internal character of states, and "first-image" theories address causes found in human nature. See Waltz (1959).

10   Instead, most recent writings on U.S. defense policy are journalistic, polemical, or narrowly focused (Fallows, 1982; Stubbing, 1986; or Kotz, 1988).

11   The Defense Department seems proud of its failure to inform us: its 1990 *Annual Report* boasts that it saved $121,800 by "tailoring the report directly to statutory requirements [...] and eliminating unnecessary no-charge distribution." In other words, Secretary Cheney's staff included only what was absolutely required by law and reduced public access to its report!

12   The Bush Administration's handling of the Panama invasion and the Gulf War suggests that it is following a similar approach, aided by a compliant media (Cook and Cohen, 1990).

13   Specifically, Volume X in the 1952–54 series, covering U.S. policy in Iran, makes no mention of Operation AJAX, the U.S.-backed coup that ousted the Mossadegh government in 1953. According to Bruce Kuniholm, an historian of U.S.-Iranian relations and former State Department employee with access to the complete account: "the misleading impression of U.S. non-involvement conveyed in the pages of this volume constitutes a gross misrepresentation of the historical record sufficient to deserve the label of fraud" (Kuniholm, 1990:12).

Ole Wæver

SECURITIZATION

Source: 'Securitization and desecuritization', in Ronnie D. Lipschutz (ed.) *On Security* (New York: Columbia University Press, 1995), pp. 46–86.

[...] [T]HE LABEL "SECURITY" has become the indicator of a specific problematique, a specific *field of practice*. Security is, in historical terms, the field where states threaten each other, challenge each other's sovereignty, try to impose their will on each other, defend their independence, and so on. Security, moreover, has not been a constant field; it has evolved and, since World War II, has been transformed into a rather coherent and recognizable field. In this process of continuous, gradual transformation, the strong military identification of earlier times has been diminished – it is, in a sense, always there, but more and more often in metaphorical form, as other wars, other challenges – while the images of "challenges to sovereignty" and defense have remained central.

If we want to rethink or reconstruct the concept of security, therefore, it is necessary that we keep an eye on the entire field of practice. This is contrary to the now-standard debates on "redefining security," inasmuch as those who want radically to rethink the concept generally tend to cancel out the specific field. The concept is thus reduced to its everyday sense, which is only a semantic *identity,* not the *concept* of security. Of course, both choices are completely legitimate, but this question of language politics depends ultimately on what we wish to accomplish. If our intent is to determine when we are secure, the investigation can address many levels. If, however, we want to add something new to ongoing debates on "security" (in strategic studies) and national interests, we must begin with *those* debates, taking on that problematique, so that we can get at the specific dynamics of that field, and show how these old elements operate in new ways and new places.

The specificity, in other words, is to be found in the *field* and in certain typical *operations* within the field (speech acts – "security" – and modalities – threat-defense sequences), not in a clearly definable objective ("security") or a specific state of affairs ("security"). Beginning from the modality of specific types of interactions in a specific social arena, we can rethink the concept "security" in a way that is true to the classical discussion. By working from the inside of the classical discussion, we can take the concepts of national security, threat, and sovereignty, and show how, on the collective level, they take on new forms under new conditions. We can then strip the classical discussion of its preoccupation with military matters by applying the *same* logic to other sectors, and we can de-link the discussion from the state by applying similar moves to *society* [...]. With this, we maintain a mode of thinking, a set of rules and codes from the field of "security" as it has evolved and continues to evolve.

To start instead from being secure in the everyday sense means that we end up approaching security policy from the *outside,* that is, via another language game. My premise here is, therefore, that we can identify a specific field of social interaction, with a specific set of actions and codes, known by a set of agents as the security field. In international society, for example, a number of codes, rules, and understandings have been established that make international relations an intersubjectively defined social reality possessing its own specific laws and issues.[1] National security is similarly social in the sense of being constituted intersubjectively in a specific field,[2] and it should not be measured against some real or true yardstick of "security" derived from (contemporary) domestic society.

An alternative route to a wider concept of security is to broaden the security agenda to include threats other than military ones. When widening takes place along this axis, it is possible to retain the specific quality characterizing security problems: Urgency; state power claiming the legitimate use of extraordinary means; a threat seen as potentially undercutting sovereignty, thereby preventing the political "we" from dealing with any other questions. With this approach, it is possible that any sector, at any particular time, might be the most important focus for concerns about threats, vulnerabilities, and defense. Historically, of course, the military sector has been most important.[3] [...]

[...] The question remains, however: What made the military sector conspicuous, and what now qualifies the others to almost equal status? [...] Military threats have been primary in the past because they emerged "very swiftly" and with "a sense of outrage at unfair play"; if defeated, a state would find itself laid bare to imposition of the conqueror's will.[4] Such outcomes used to characterize the military sector. But, if the same overturning of the political order can be accomplished by economic or political methods, these, too, will constitute security problems.[5] [...]

From alternative security to security, the speech act

[...] [S]ecurity problems [hence] are developments that threaten the sovereignty or independence of a state in a particularly rapid or dramatic fashion, and deprive it of the capacity to manage by itself. This, in turn, undercuts the political order. Such a threat must therefore be met with the mobilization of the maximum effort.

Operationally, however, this means: *In naming a certain development a security problem, the "state" can claim a special right,* one that will, in the final instance, always be defined by the state and its élites. Trying to press the kind of unwanted fundamental political change on a ruling élite is similar to playing a game in which one's opponent can change the rules at any time s/he likes. Power holders can always try to use the instrument of *securitization* of an issue to gain control over it. By definition, something is a security problem when the élites declare it to be so [...]:

Thus, that those who administer this order can easily use it for specific, self-serving purposes is something that cannot easily be avoided.

What then *is* security? With the help of language theory, we can regard "security" as a *speech act*. In this usage, security is not of interest as a sign that refers to something more real; the utterance *itself is* the act. By saying it, something is done (as in betting, giving a promise, naming a ship).[6] By uttering "security," a state-representative moves a particular development into a specific area, and thereby claims a special right to use whatever means are necessary to block it.[7]

The clearest illustration of this phenomenon [...] occurred in Central and Eastern Europe during the Cold War, where "order" was clearly, systematically, and institutionally linked to the survival of the system and its élites. Thinking about change in East-West relations and/or in Eastern Europe throughout this period meant, therefore, trying to bring about change without generating a "securitization" response by élites, which would have provided the pretext for acting against those who had overstepped the boundaries of the permitted.

Consequently, to ensure that this mechanism would not be triggered, actors had to keep their challenges below a certain threshold and/or through the political process – whether national or international – have the threshold negotiated upward. As Egbert Jahn put it, the task was to turn threats into challenges; to move developments from the sphere of existential fear to one where they could be handled by ordinary means, as politics, economy, culture, and so on. As part of this exercise, a crucial political and theoretical issue became the definition of "intervention" or "interference in domestic affairs," whereby change-oriented agents tried, through international law, diplomacy, and various kinds of politics, to raise the threshold and make more interaction possible.

Through this process, two things became very clear. First, the word "security" is the *act;* the utterance is the primary reality. Second; the most radical and transformational perspective – which nonetheless remained realist – was one of minimizing "security" by narrowing the field to which the security act was applied (as with the European détente policies of the 1970s and 1980s). After a certain point, the process took a different form and the aim became to create a speech act *failure* (as in Eastern Europe in 1989). Thus, the trick was and is to move from a positive to a negative meaning: Security is the conservative mechanism – but we want less security!

Under the circumstances then existing in Eastern Europe, the power holders had among their instruments the speech act "security." The use of this speech act had the effect of raising a specific challenge to a principled level, thereby implying that all necessary means would be used to block that challenge. And, because such a threat would be defined as existential and a challenge to sovereignty, the state would not be limited in what it could or might do. Under these circumstances, a problem would become a *security* issue whenever so defined by the power holders. Unless or until this operation were to be brought to the point of failure – which nuclear conditions made rather difficult to imagine[8] – available avenues of change would take the form of *negotiated limitations* on the use of the "speech act security." Improved conditions would, consequently, hinge on a process implying "less security, more politics!"

To put this point another way, *security* and *insecurity* do not constitute a binary opposition. "Security" signifies a situation marked by the presence of a security problem *and* some measure taken in response. Insecurity is a situation with a security problem and *no* response. Both conditions share the security problematique. When there is no security problem, we do not conceptualize our situation in terms of security; instead, security is simply an irrelevant concern. The statement, then, that security is always relative, and one never lives in complete security, has the additional meaning that, if one has such complete security, one does not label it "security." It therefore never appears. Consequently, transcending a security problem by politicizing it cannot happen *through* thematization in security terms, only *away* from such terms.

An agenda of *minimizing* security in this sense cannot be based on a classical critical approach to security, whereby the concept is critiqued and then thrown away or redefined according to the wishes of the analyst. The essential operation can only be touched by faithfully working *with* the classical meaning of the concept and what is already inherent in it. The language game of security is, in other words, a *jus necessitatis* for threatened élites, and this it must remain.

Such an affirmative reading, not at all aimed at rejecting the concept, may be a more serious challenge to the established discourse than a critical one, for it recognizes that a conservative approach to security is an intrinsic element in the logic of both our national and international political organizing principles. By taking seriously this "unfounded" concept of security, it is possible to raise a new agenda of security and politics. This further implies moving from a positive to a negative agenda, in the sense that the dynamics of securitization and desecuritization can never be captured so long as we proceed along the normal critical track that assumes security to be a positive value to be maximized.

That élites frequently present their interests in "national security" dress is, of course, often pointed out by observers, usually accompanied by a denial of élites' right to do so. Their actions are then labelled something else, for example, "class interests," which seems to imply that authentic security is, somehow, definable independent of élites, by direct reference to the "people." This is, in a word, wrong. All such attempts to define people's "objective interests" have failed. Security is articulated only from a specific place, in an institutional voice, by élites. All of this can be analyzed; if we simply give up the assumption that security is, necessarily, a *positive* phenomenon.

Critics normally address the *what* or *who* that threatens, or the *whom* to be secured; they never ask whether a phenomenon *should* be treated in terms of security because they do not look into "securityness" as such, asking what is particular to security, in contrast to non-security, modes of dealing with particular issues. By working with the assumption that security is a goal to be maximized, critics eliminate other, potentially more useful ways of conceptualizing the problems being addressed. [...]

Viewing the security debate at present, one often gets the impression of the object playing around with the subjects, the field toying with the researchers. The problematique itself locks people into talking in terms of "security," and this reinforces the hold of security on our thinking, even if our approach is a critical one. We do not find much work aimed at *de-securitizing* politics which, I suspect, would be more effective than securitizing problems. [...]

Notes

1   Alexander Wendt, "Anarchy is what states make of it: the social construction of power politics," *International Organization* 46, no. 2 (Spring 1992): 391–426; C. A. W Manning, *The Nature of International Society* (London: London School of Economics, 1962); Martin Wight, *Systems of States* (Leicester: Leicester University Press, 1977); Ole Wæver, "International Society: The Grammar of Dialogue among States?," paper presented at ECPR workshop in Limerich, April 1992; Nicholas Greenwood Onuf, *World of Our Making: Rules and Rule in Social Theory and International Relations* (Columbia: University of South Carolina Press, 1989).

2   "Most seriously, however, even if we admit that we are all now participating in common global structures, that we are all rendered increasingly vulnerable to processes that are planetary in scale, and that our most parochial activities are shaped by forces that encompass the world and not just particular states, it is far from clear what such an admission implies for the way we organize ourselves politically. The state is a political category in a way that the world, or the globe, or the planet, or humanity is not. The security of states is something we can comprehend in political terms in a way that, at the moment, world security can not be understood." R. B. J. Walker, "Security, Sovereignty, and the Challenge of World Politics," *Alternatives* 15, no. 1 (1990): 5. There is nothing inevitable about this way of defining security – it has emerged historically, and might change gradually again – but one has to admit "the extent to which the meaning of security is tied to historically specific forms of political community" (Walker, "Security, Sovereignty"). Only to the extent that other forms of political community begin to become *thinkable* (again), does it make sense to think about *security* at other levels. The main process at the present is a very open and contradictory articulation of the relationship between state (and other political structures) and nation (and other large scale cultural communities). Therefore, the main dynamic of security will play at the interface of state security and societal security (in the sense of the security of large-scale we-identities). Thus, in the section on "Societal Security," I will argue why the study of "societal security" should – although being aware of specific threats to social groups – construct the concept of societal security as distinct from this, as being at a specific level of collectivity, being a social fact.

3   But even here one can argue about the way of defining these standard cases as military or political; Egbert Jahn, Pierre Lemaitre and Ole Wæver, *European Security: Problems of Research on Non-Military Aspects* (Copenhagen: Copenhagen Papers of the Centre for Peace and Conflict Research, 1987), pp. 17–20.

4   Barry Buzan argues more extensively as follows: "Because the use of force can wreak major undesired changes very swiftly, military threats are traditionally accorded the highest priority in national security concerns. Military action can wreck the work of centuries in all other sectors. Difficult accomplishments in politics, art, industry, culture and all human activities can be undone by the use of force. Human achievements, in other words, can be threatened in terms other than those in which they were created, and the need to prevent such threats from being realized is a major underpinning of the state's military protection function. A defeated society is totally vulnerable to the conqueror's power which can be applied to ends ranging from restructuring the government, through pillage and rape, to massacre of the population. and resettlement of the land. The threat of force thus stimulates not only a powerful concern to protect the socio-political heritage of the

state, but also a sense of outrage at the use of unfair forms of competition." Barry Buzan, *People, States and Fear: An Agenda for Security Studies in the Post-Cold War Era* (Boulder: Lynne Rienner, 1991, 2nd ed.), p. 117.

5   Jahn et al., *European Security*, p. 9.

6   More precisely, in the theory of speech acts, "security' would be seen as an *illocutionary* act; this is elaborated at length in Ole Wæver, "Security the Speech Act: Analysing the Politics of a Word," Copenhagen: Centre for Peace and Conflict Research, Working Paper no. 1989/19. See also: J. L. Austin, *How to do Things with Words* (Oxford: Oxford University Press, 1975, 2nd ed.), p. 98.

7   A point to which we will return: The other side of the move will, in most cases, be at least the price of some loss of prestige as a result of needing to use this special resort ("National security was threatened") or, in the case of failure, the act backfires and raises questions about the viability and reputation of the regime. In this sense the move is similar to raising a bet – staking more on the specific issue, giving it principled importance and thereby investing it with basic order questions.

8   The strongest case for the theoretical status of speech act failure being equal to success is given by Jacques Derrida, "Signature Event Context," *Glyph* 1 (1977): 172–97 (originally presented in 1971). The article was reprinted, in a different translation, in Jacques Derrida, *Margins of Philosophy* (Chicago: University of Chicago Press, 1982).

Discussion questions

- What do we mean when we talk about national security?
- Discuss what Arnold Wolfers meant by national security as an 'ambiguous symbol'.
- Is security an 'essentially contested concept'?
- What is/are the referent object/s of, and the necessary conditions for, security?
- Why is there the need to redefine the concept of security?
- How significant is the contribution of IR Realism to the emancipation and primacy of national security?
- How does the feminist perspective change our understanding of international relations and security?
- How does the Third World experience contribute to our understanding and explanation of the problems of (in)security in the post-Cold War era?
- How do the concepts of environmental and human security alter our understanding of national security?
- What are the problems and prospects for the field of security studies in the age of globalisation?
- Why does Ole Wæver consider 'security' as a 'speech act'?

PART 2

Security Paradigms

Introduction

E . H . C A R R in extracts from Chapters three and four of the *Twenty Years'
Crisis* contributes to the foundations of what is often termed the paradigm of
'Classical Realism', emergent in the inter-war and early Cold War periods. Carr's
critique of inter-war 'Utopianism' is based on a rejection of the notion of the role of
public opinion or a balance of economic interest as ensuring international order and
peace. Instead, Carr posits that conflict in the inter-war years was driven by a clash
of economic rivalries between the dominant Anglo-American states and economically
disadvantaged but rising states demanding their perceived fair share of international
power and status. **Hans J. Morgenthau** lays out the main tenets of Classical Realism,
insisting on the rationality of statesmen and their actions in terms of national interest
defined as the pursuit of power. Morgenthau's search for a theory of Realism means
that, while international politics is seen not to be totally indifferent to political ideals,
it is largely governed by successful and prudent political action in the pursuit of
national security. **Hedley Bull** offers a less pessimistic view on the possibilities for
peace among states through articulating the concept of international society. In some
ways, Bull's conception is a bridge between Classical Realism and Liberalism, arguing that states may limit violence among themselves due to bonds, culture, civilisation, international law and diplomacy.

    Kenneth N. Waltz moves the Realist paradigm forward through the provision of a
framework of Neorealism or Structural Realism. In the extract from the *Theory of
International Politics*, Waltz asserts that it is the structure of international anarchy
and lack of an overarching authority to regulate the behaviour of states which
give rise to a self-help system. This system is characterised by competition among
states for power, security and relative gains, making conflict endemic to the system.

Robert Jervis elaborates on some of the assumptions of Neorealism with his explication of the concept of the security dilemma. Jervis illustrates how international anarchy creates a security dilemma which in turn complicates cooperation. Nevertheless, he also points how, even under conditions of anarchy, states may cooperate through constant iterations of the 'Prisoner's Dilemma', thus pointing to a range of subsequent rational choice theory which has demonstrated the possibilities for cooperation under anarchy. **John J. Mearsheimer**, an advocate of 'Offensive Realism', again stresses the belief of Neorealists in the difficulty of international cooperation. Specifically, he demonstrates how the problem of relative gains undermines the efficacy of international institutions in ensuring cooperation, and that, if anything, contemporary theories of Liberalism are adjuncts of Neorealism.

Norman Angell provides a classic statement of early applications of Liberalism to the realm of international politics. Angell, writing in 1933, was forced to modify his earlier pre-World War I view that economic prosperity, built upon a system of interdependent international credit, made large-scale warfare counter-productive and nearly impossible. Instead, Angell retains the Liberal belief that while war will always remain, and despite the fact that men have become increasingly aware of its futility, nevertheless the prospects for conflict can be mitigated through active promotion of economic cooperation and raising the costs of war. **Robert Keohane**, although writing in the more contemporary era, picks up on this Liberal tradition by stressing the importance of international institutions in mediating the possibilities for international conflict. Keohane, in advancing a theory of 'Neoliberal Institutionalism', emphasises the significance of formal and informal institutions – rules, norms, regimes and conventions – in the conduct of world politics. Keohane accepts Neorealism's emphasis on the central role of the state and the constraining condition of international anarchy. However, states may cooperate under anarchy due to the capacity for institutions to facilitate flows of information and lower transaction costs enabling the forging of credible international commitments. Keohane sees the Neoliberal Institutionalism approach as highly relevant to security in the management of alliances and international security agreements. **Michael W. Doyle** offers another variant of Liberalism in his espousing of what is often termed the 'Democratic Peace thesis'. Doyle points out how democratic states do not fight each other due to their domestic accountability which means leaders are restrained in the international arena; their tendency towards negotiation and accommodation in the international arena; and the tendency of liberal democracies to promote international economic interdependency. However, he further points out how liberal states may readily fight non-liberal states which do not share these values and which are inherently distrustful of each other's intentions; so providing an insight into many contemporary wars between the developed powers and so-called 'rogue states'. **Bruce Russett** rounds off the Liberal perspective with a modern version of Immanuel Kant's three Definitive Articles for Perpetual Peace. Russett in 'Neo-Kantian' style emphasises the dynamic and mutually reinforcing triangular relationship between democracy, peace and economic interdependence.

Alexander Wendt introduces Constructivism as the third major paradigm, or at least perspective, on the causes and amelioration of international conflict. Wendt challenges the Neorealist notion that anarchic self-help international system is an immutable given. Instead, he argues that the international system is a social construction based on the interaction of its constituents that brings about a process of identity and interest formation. These inter-subjective identities shape and reshape interests in terms of survival; or, in other words, 'anarchy is what states make of it'. Hence, culture, ideas and identities are core to shaping behaviours, with the result that states may come into conflict, but just as equally they may assume more cooperative identities, so escaping the Neorealist view of conflict as inherent to the international system. **Thomas U. Berger** outlines a second variant of Constructivism which focuses on domestic culture and norms in shaping identities and interests. Berger stresses that culture is constantly evolving and thus political-military cultures will also keep shifting. The implication is that discovering the degree and changing propensity of certain societies to conflict or cooperation will be a product of examinations of different cultures of security.

E. H. Carr

THE NEMESIS OF UTOPIANISM

Source: *Twenty Years' Crisis: An Introduction to the Study of International Relations* (Basingstoke: Papermac, 1981), pp. 25–41, 42–61.

The foundations of utopianism

THE MODERN SCHOOL of utopian political thought must be traced back to the break-up of the mediaeval system, which presupposed a universal ethic and a universal political system based on divine authority. [...] The realists of the Renaissance made the first determined onslaught on the primacy of ethics and propounded a view of politics which made ethics an instrument of politics, the authority of the state being thus substituted for the authority of the church as the arbiter of morality. The answer of the utopian school to this challenge was not an easy one. An ethical standard was required which would be independent of any external authority, ecclesiastical or civil; and the solution was found in the doctrine of a secular 'law of nature' whose ultimate source was the individual human reason. Natural law, as first propounded by the Greeks, had been an intuition of the human heart about what is morally right. [...] In science, the laws of nature were deduced by a process of reasoning from observed facts about the nature of matter [namely that] [...] [t]he moral law of nature could be scientifically established; and rational deduction from the supposed facts of human nature took the place of revelation or intuition as the source of morality. Reason could determine what were the universally valid moral laws; and the assumption was made that, once these laws were determined, human beings would conform to them just as matter conformed to the physical laws of nature. [...]

By the eighteenth century, the main lines of modern utopian thought were firmly established. It was essentially individualist in that it made the human conscience the final court of appeal in moral questions [...]. It was essentially rationalist in that it identified the human conscience with the voice of reason.[1] But it had still to undergo important developments; and it was Jeremy Bentham who [...] gave to nineteenth-century utopianism its characteristic shape. Starting from the postulate that the fundamental characteristic of human nature is to seek pleasure and avoid pain,

Bentham deduced from this postulate a rational ethic which defined the good in the famous formula 'the greatest happiness of the greatest number'. As has often been pointed out, 'the greatest happiness of the greatest number' performed the function, which natural law had performed for a previous generation, of an absolute ethical standard. Bentham firmly believed in this absolute standard, and rejected as 'anarchical' the view that there are 'as many standards of right and wrong as there are men'.[2] In effect, 'the greatest happiness of the greatest number' was the nineteenth-century definition of the content of natural law.

The importance of Bentham's contribution was twofold. In the first place, by identifying the good with happiness, he provided a plausible confirmation of the 'scientific' assumption of the eighteenth-century rationalists that man would infallibly conform to the moral law of nature once its content had been rationally determined. Secondly, while preserving the rationalist and individualist aspect of the doctrine, he succeeded in giving it a broader basis. [...] [By identifying] happiness [as] the criterion, the one thing needful was that the individual should understand where his happiness lay. Not only was the good ascertainable [...] by a rational process, but this process [...] was not a matter of abstruse philosophical speculation, but of simple common sense. Bentham was the first thinker to elaborate the doctrine of salvation by public opinion. The members of the community 'may, in their aggregate capacity, be considered as constituting a sort of judicatory or tribunal – call it [...] The Public-Opinion Tribunal'.[3] [...]

This is not the only argument by which democracy as a political institution can be defended. But this argument was, in fact, explicitly or implicitly accepted by most nineteenth-century liberals. The belief that public opinion can be relied on to judge rightly on any question rationally presented to it, combined with the assumption that it will act in accordance with this right judgement, is an essential foundation of the liberal creed. [...]

The application of these principles to international affairs followed [...]. The Abbé Saint-Pierre, who propounded one of the earliest schemes for a League of Nations, 'was so confident in the reasonableness of his projects that he always believed that, if they were fairly considered, the ruling powers could not fail to adopt them'.[4] Both Rousseau and Kant argued that, since wars were waged by princes in their own interest and not in that of their peoples, there would be no wars under a republican form of government. In this sense, they anticipated the view that public opinion, if allowed to make itself effective, would suffice to prevent war. In the nineteenth century, this view won widespread approval in Western Europe, and took on the specifically rationalist colour proper to the doctrine that the holding of the right moral beliefs and the performance of the right actions can be assured by process of reasoning. Never was there an age which so unreservedly proclaimed the supremacy of the intellect. 'It is intellectual evolution', averred Comte, 'which essentially determines the main course of social phenomena.'[5] [...] The view that the spread of education would lead to international peace was shared by many of Buckle's contemporaries and successors. Its last serious exponent was Sir Norman Angell, who sought, by *The Great Illusion* and other books, to convince the world that war never brought profit to anyone. If he could establish this point by irrefutable argument, thought Sir Norman, then war could not occur. War was simply a 'failure of understanding'. Once the head was purged of the illusion that war was profitable, the heart could look after itself.

[...] Reason could demonstrate the absurdity of the international anarchy; and with increasing knowledge, enough people would be rationally convinced of its absurdity to put an end to it. [...]

Benthamism transplanted

Before the end of the nineteenth century, serious doubts had been thrown from more than one quarter on the assumptions of Benthamite rationalism. The belief in the sufficiency of reason to promote right conduct was challenged by psychologists. The identification of virtue with enlightened self-interest began to shock philosophers. The belief in the infallibility of public opinion had been attractive on the hypothesis of the earlier utilitarians that public opinion was the opinion of educated and enlightened men. It was less attractive, at any rate to those who thought themselves educated and enlightened, now that public opinion was the opinion of the masses; and as early as 1859, in his essay *On Liberty*, J. S. Mill had been preoccupied with the dangers of 'the tyranny of the majority'. After 1900, it would have been difficult to find, either in Great Britain or in any other European country, any serious political thinker who accepted the Benthamite assumptions without qualification. Yet, by one of the ironies of history, these half-discarded nineteenth-century assumptions reappeared, in the second and third decades of the twentieth century, in the special field of international politics, and there became the foundation-stones of a new utopian edifice. The explanation may be in part that, after 1914, men's minds naturally fumbled their way back, in search of a new utopia, to those apparently firm foundations of nineteenth-century peace and security. But a more decisive factor was the influence of the United States, still in the heyday of Victorian prosperity and of Victorian belief in the comfortable Benthamite creed. Just as Bentham, a century earlier, had taken the eighteenth-century doctrine of reason and refashioned it to the needs of the coming age, so now Woodrow Wilson, the impassioned admirer of Bright and Gladstone, transplanted the nineteenth-century rationalist faith to the almost virgin soil of international politics and, bringing it back with him to Europe, gave it a new lease of life. Nearly all popular theories of international politics between the two world wars were reflexions, seen in an American mirror, of nineteenth-century liberal thought. In a limited number of countries, nineteenth-century liberal democracy had been a brilliant success. It was a success because its presuppositions coincided with the stage of development reached by the countries concerned. Out of the mass of current speculation, the leading spirits of the age took precisely that body of theory which corresponded to their needs, consciously and unconsciously fitting their practice to it, and it to their practice. Utilitarianism and *laissez-faire* served, and in turn directed, the course of industrial and commercial expansion. But the view that nineteenth-century liberal democracy was based, not on a balance of forces peculiar to the economic development of the period and the countries concerned, but on certain *a priori* rational principles which had only to be applied in other contexts to produce similar results, was essentially utopian; and it was this view which, under Wilson's inspiration, dominated the world after the first world war. When the theories of liberal democracy were transplanted, by a purely intellectual process, to a period and to countries whose stage of development and whose practical needs were utterly different from those of Western Europe in the nineteenth century, sterility and disillusionment were the inevitable sequel. Rationalism can create a utopia, but cannot make it real. The liberal democracies scattered throughout the world by the peace settlement of 1919 were the product of abstract theory, stuck no roots in the soil, and quickly shrivelled away.

Rationalism and the League of Nations

The most important of all the institutions affected by this one-sided intellectualism of international politics was the League of Nations, which was an attempt 'to apply the principles of Lockeian liberalism to the building of a machinery of international order'.[6] 'The Covenant', observed General Smuts, '[...] simply carries into world affairs that outlook of a liberal democratic society which is one of the great achievements of our human advance.'[7] But this transplantation of democratic rationalism from the national to the international sphere was full of unforeseen difficulties. The empiricist treats the concrete case on its individual merits. The rationalist refers it to an abstract general principle. Any social order implies a large measure of standardization, and therefore of abstraction; there cannot be a different rule for every member of the community. Such standardization is comparatively easy in a community of several million anonymous individuals conforming more or less closely to recognized types. But it presents infinite complications when applied to sixty known states differing widely in size, in power, and in political, economic and cultural development. The League of Nations, being the first large-scale attempt to standardize international political problems on a rational basis, was particularly liable to these embarrassments.

The founders of the League [...] had indeed recognized the dangers of abstract perfection. 'Acceptance of the political facts of the present', remarked the official British Commentary on the Covenant issued in 1919, 'has been one of the principles on which the Commission has worked',[8] and this attempt to take account of political realities distinguished the Covenant not only from previous paper schemes of world organization, but also from such purely utopian projects as the International Police Force, the Briand-Kellogg Pact and the United States of Europe. The Covenant possessed the virtue of several theoretical imperfections. [...] It seemed for the moment as if the League might reach a working compromise between utopia and reality and become an effective instrument of international politics.

Unhappily, the most influential European politicians neglected the League during its critical formative years. Abstract rationalism gained the upper hand, and from about 1922 onwards the current at Geneva set strongly in the utopian direction.[9] It came to be believed, in the words of an acute critic, 'that there can exist, either at Geneva or in foreign offices, a sort of carefully classified card-index of events or, better still, "situations", and that, when the event happens or the situation presents itself, a member of the Council or Foreign Minister can easily recognize that event or situation and turn up the index to be directed to the files where the appropriate action is prescribed'.[10] There were determined efforts to perfect the machinery, to standardize the procedure, to close the 'gaps' in the Covenant by an absolute veto on all war, and to make the application of sanctions 'automatic'. The Draft Treaty of Mutual Assistance, the Geneva Protocol, the General Act, the plan to incorporate the Briand-Kellogg Pact in the Covenant and 'the definition of the aggressor', were all milestones on the dangerous path of rationalization. The fact that the utopian dishes prepared during these years at Geneva proved unpalatable to most of the principal governments concerned was a symptom of the growing divorce between theory and practice.

Even the language current in League circles betrayed the growing eagerness to avoid the concrete in favour of the abstract generalizations. [...] These linguistic contortions encouraged the frequent failure to distinguish between the world of abstract reason and the world of political reality. [...] Once it came to be believed in League circles that salvation could be found in a perfect card-index, and that the unruly flow of international politics could be canalized into a set of logically impregnable abstract formulae inspired by the doctrines of nineteenth-century liberal democracy, the end of the League as an effective political instrument was in sight.

The apotheosis of public opinion

Nor did any better fortune attend the attempt to transplant to the international sphere the liberal democratic faith in public opinion. And here there was a double fallacy. The nineteenth-century belief in public opinion comprised two articles: first (and in democracies this was, with some reservations, true), that public opinion is bound in the long run to prevail; and second (this was the Benthamite view), that public opinion is always right. Both these beliefs, not always clearly distinguished one from the other, were uncritically reproduced in the sphere of international politics.

The first attempts to invoke public opinion as a force in the international world had been made in the United States. [...]

The belief in the compelling power of reason, expressed through the voice of the people, was particularly congenial to [President] Wilson. [...]

America's entry into the war entailed no modification of Wilson's faith in the rightness of popular judgement. He took up the cue in one of the speeches in which he discussed the future conditions of peace [...]. [...]

'Unless the Conference was prepared to follow the opinions of mankind,' he said on his way to Paris, 'and to express the will of the people rather than that of the leaders of the Conference, we should be involved in another break-up of the world.'[11]

Such conceptions did, in fact, play a conspicuous part in the work of the Conference. [...] The communiqué to the Italian people, and the withdrawal of the Italian Delegation from Paris, were the result of this conviction. The problem of disarmament was approached in the same spirit. Once the enemy Powers had been disarmed by force, the voice of reason, speaking through public opinion, could be trusted to disarm the Allies. [...] Most important of all, the whole conception of the League of Nations was from the first closely bound up with the twin belief that public opinion was bound to prevail and that public opinion was the voice of reason. [...]

The ticklish problem of material sanctions was approached reluctantly from the American, and almost as reluctantly from the British, side. Like Taft, Anglo-Saxon opinion felt itself 'very little concerned' over this aspect of the matter; for the recognition of the necessity of sanctions was in itself a derogation from the utopian doctrine of the efficacy of rational public opinion. It was unthinkable that a unanimous verdict of the League should be defied; and even if by some mischance the verdict were not unanimous, 'a majority report would probably be issued, and [...] this', suggested Lord Cecil during the debates in Paris, 'would be likely to carry great weight with the public opinion of the world'.[12] [...] But the argument that public opinion is the all-important weapon is two-edged; and in 1932, during the Manchurian crisis, the ingenious Sir John Simon used it to demonstrate that any other kind of action was superfluous. 'The truth is', he told the House of Commons, 'that when public opinion, world opinion, is sufficiently unanimous to pronounce a firm moral condemnation, sanctions are not needed.'[13] Given the Benthamite and Wilsonian premises, this answer was irrefutable. If public opinion had failed to curb Japan, then – as Lord Cecil had said in 1919 – 'the whole thing is wrong'. [...]

The nemesis of utopianism

The nemesis of utopianism in international politics came rather suddenly. [...] [A] rapid succession of events forced upon all serious thinkers a reconsideration of premises which were becoming more and more flagrantly divorced from reality. The Manchurian crisis had demonstrated that the 'condemnation of international public opinion' [...], was a broken reed. [...] [I]n countries more directly menaced by international crisis, this consoling view no longer found many adherents [...]. Before long the group of intellectuals who had once stressed the relative unimportance of the 'material' weapons of the League began to insist loudly on economic and military sanctions as the necessary cornerstones of an international order. [...]

Moreover, scepticism attacked not only the premise that public opinion is certain to prevail, but also the premise that public opinion is certain to be right. At the Peace Conference, it had been observed that statesmen were sometimes more reasonable and moderate in their demands than the public opinion which they were supposed to represent. [...] Later history provided many examples of this phenomenon. It became a commonplace for statesmen at Geneva and elsewhere to explain that they themselves had every desire to be reasonable, but that public opinion in their countries was inexorable; and though this plea was sometimes a pretext or a tactical manœuvre, there was often a solid substratum of reality beneath it. The prestige of public opinion correspondingly declined. 'It does not help the conciliator, the arbitrator, the policeman or the judge', wrote a well-known supporter of the League of Nations Union recently, 'to be surrounded by a crowd emitting either angry or exulting cheers.'[14] Woodrow Wilson's 'plain men throughout the world', the spokesmen of 'the common purpose of enlightened mankind', had somehow transformed themselves into a disorderly mob emitting incoherent and unhelpful noises. It seemed undeniable that, in international affairs, public opinion was almost as often wrong-headed as it was impotent. But where so many of the presuppositions of 1919 were crumbling, the intellectual leaders of the utopian school stuck to their guns [...]; the rift between theory and practice assumed alarming dimensions. [...]

The problem of diagnosis

In such disasters the obvious explanation is never far to seek. [...] Statesmen of more than one country have been pilloried by disappointed utopians as wreckers of the international order. The few members of the school who have tried to go behind this simple anthropomorphic explanation hesitate between two alternative diagnoses. If mankind in its international relations has signally failed to achieve the rational good, it must either have been too stupid to understand that good, or too wicked to pursue it. Professor Zimmern leans to the hypothesis of stupidity. [...]

The attempt to build a world order has failed not through 'pride or ambition or greed', but through 'muddled thinking'.[15] Professor Toynbee, on the other hand, sees the cause of the breakdown in human wickedness. [...] Some writers combined the charge of stupidity and the charge of wickedness. Much comment on international affairs was rendered tedious and sterile by incessant girding at a reality which refused to conform to utopian prescriptions. [...]

It is not true, as Professor Toynbee believes, that we have been living in an exceptionally wicked age. It is not true, as Professor Zimmern implies, that we have been living in an exceptionally stupid one. Still less is it true, as Professor Lauterpacht more optimistically suggests, that what we have been experiencing is 'a transient period of retrogression' which should not be allowed unduly to colour our thought.[16] It is a meaningless evasion to pretend that we have witnessed, not the failure of the League of Nations, but only the failure of those who refused to make it work. The breakdown of the 1930s was too overwhelming to be explained merely in terms of individual action or inaction. Its downfall involved the bankruptcy of the postulates on which it was based. The foundations of nineteenth-century belief are themselves under suspicion. It may be not that men stupidly or wickedly failed to apply right principles, but that the principles themselves were false or inapplicable. It may turn out to be untrue that if men reason rightly about international politics they will also act rightly, or that right reasoning about one's own or one's nation's interests is the road to an international paradise. If the assumptions of nineteenth-century liberalism are in fact untenable, it need not surprise us that the utopia of the international theorists made so little impression on reality. [...]

The international harmony

Attention has been drawn to the curious way in which doctrines, already obsolete or obsolescent before the war of 1914, were reintroduced in the post-war period, largely through American inspiration, into the special field of international affairs. This would appear to be conspicuously true of the *laissez-faire* doctrine of the harmony of interests. [...] [T]here was a special reason for the ready acceptance of the doctrine in the international sphere. In domestic affairs it is clearly the business of the state to create harmony if no natural harmony exists. In international politics, there is no organized power charged with the task of creating harmony; and the temptation to assume a natural harmony is therefore particularly strong. But [...] [t]o make the harmonization of interests the goal of political action is not the same thing as to postulate that a natural harmony of interests exists;[17] and it is this latter postulate which has caused so much confusion in international thinking.

The common interest in peace

Politically, the doctrine of the identity of interests has commonly taken the form of an assumption that every nation has an identical interest in peace, and that any nation which desires to disturb the peace is therefore both irrational and immoral. This view bears clear marks of its Anglo-Saxon origin. It was easy after 1918 to convince that part of mankind which lives in English-speaking countries that war profits nobody. The argument did not seem particularly convincing to Germans, who had profited largely from the wars of 1866 and 1870, and attributed their more recent sufferings, not to the war of 1914, but to the fact that they had lost it; or to Italians, who blamed not the war, but the treachery of allies who defrauded them in the peace settlement; or to Poles or Czecho-Slovaks who, far from deploring the war, owed their national existence to it; or to Frenchmen, who could not unreservedly regret a war which had restored Alsace-Lorraine to France; or to people of other nationalities who remembered profitable wars waged by Great Britain and the United States in the past. But these people had fortunately little influence over the formation of current theories of international relations, which emanated almost exclusively from the English-speaking countries. British and American writers continued to assume that the uselessness of war had been irrefutably demonstrated by the experience of 1914–18, and that an intellectual grasp of this fact was all that was necessary to induce the nations to keep the peace in the future; and they were sincerely puzzled as well as disappointed at the failure of other countries to share this view.

The confusion was increased by the ostentatious readiness of other countries to flatter the Anglo-Saxon world by repeating its slogans. In the fifteen years after the first world war, every Great Power (except, perhaps, Italy) repeatedly did lip-service to the doctrine by declaring peace to be one of the main objects of its policy.[18] But as Lenin observed long ago, peace in itself is a meaningless aim. [...] The utopian assumption that there is a world interest in peace which is identifiable with the interest of each individual nation helped politicians and political writers everywhere to evade the unpalatable fact of a fundamental divergence of interest between nations desirous of maintaining the *status quo* and nations desirous of changing it.[19] A peculiar combination of platitude and falseness thus became endemic in the pronouncements of statesmen about international affairs. [...] The fact of divergent interests was disguised and falsified by the platitude of a general desire to avoid conflict.

International economic harmony

In economic relations, the assumption of a general harmony of interests was made with even greater confidence; for here we have a direct reflexion of the cardinal doctrine of *laissez-faire* economics, and it is here that we can see most clearly the dilemma which results from the doctrine. When the nineteenth-century liberal spoke of the greatest good of the greatest number, he tacitly assumed that the good of the minority might have to be sacrificed to it. This principle applied equally to international economic relations. If Russia or Italy, for example, were not strong enough to build up industries without the protection of tariffs, then – the *laissez-faire* liberal would have argued – they should be content to import British and German manufactures and supply wheat and oranges to the British and German markets. If anyone had thereupon objected that this policy would condemn Russia and Italy to remain second-rate Powers economically and militarily dependent on their neighbours, the *laissez-faire* liberal would have had to answer that this was the will of Providence and that this was what the general harmony of interests demanded. The modern utopian internationalist enjoys none of the advantages, and has none of the toughness, of the nineteenth-century liberal. The material success of the weaker Powers in building up protected industries, as well as the new spirit of internationalism, preclude him from arguing that the harmony of interests depends on the sacrifice of economically unfit nations. Yet the abandonment of this premise destroys the whole basis of the doctrine which he has inherited; and he is driven to the belief that the common good can be achieved without any sacrifice of the good of any individual member of the community. Every international conflict is therefore unnecessary and illusory. It is only necessary to discover the common good which is at the same time the highest good of all the disputants; and only the folly of statesmen stands in the way of its discovery. The utopian, secure in his understanding of this common good, arrogates to himself the monopoly of wisdom. The statesmen of the world one and all stand convicted of incredible blindness to the interest of those whom they are supposed to represent. Such was the picture of the international scene presented, in all seriousness, by British and American writers, including not a few economists.

It is for this reason that we find in the modern period an extraordinary divergence between the theories of economic experts and the practice of those responsible for the economic policies of their respective countries. [...] The economic expert, dominated in the main by *laissez-faire* doctrine, considers the hypothetical economic interest of the world as a whole, and is content to assume that this is identical with the interest of each individual country. The politician pursues the concrete interest of his country, and assumes (if he makes any assumption at all) that the interest of the world as a whole is identical with it. Nearly every pronouncement of every international economic conference held between the two world wars was vitiated by this assumption that there was some 'solution' or 'plan' which, by a judicious balancing of interests, would be equally favourable to all and prejudicial to none. [...]

[...] It seems altogether rash to suppose that economic nationalism is necessarily detrimental to states which practise it. In the nineteenth century, Germany and the United States, by pursuing a 'strictly nationalistic policy', had placed themselves in a position to challenge Great Britain's virtual monopoly of world trade. No conference of economic experts, meeting in 1880, could have evolved a 'general plan' for 'parallel or concerted action' which would have allayed the economic rivalries of the time in a manner equally advantageous to Great Britain, Germany and the United States. It was not less presumptuous to suppose that a conference meeting in 1927 could allay the economic rivalries of the later period by a 'plan' beneficial to the interests of everyone. Even the economic crisis of 1930–33 failed to bring home to the economists the true nature of the problem which they had to face. The experts who prepared the

'Draft Annotated Agenda' for the World Economic Conference of 1933 condemned the 'worldwide adoption of ideals of national self-sufficiency which cut unmistakably athwart the lines of economic development'.[20] They did not apparently pause to reflect that those so-called 'lines of economic development', which might be beneficial to some countries and even to the world as a whole, would inevitably be detrimental to other countries, which were using weapons of economic nationalism in self-defence. [...] [E]very Power at some period of its history, and as a rule for prolonged periods, has resorted to 'autarkic tendencies'. It is difficult to believe that there is any absolute sense in which 'autarkic tendencies' are always detrimental to those who pursue them. [...]

Economic theory, as opposed to economic practice, was so powerfully dominated in the years between the two world wars by the supposed harmony of interests that it is difficult to find, in the innumerable international discussions of the period, any clear exposition of the real problem which baffled the statesmen of the world. [...]

[...] *Laissez-faire*, in international relations as in those between capital and labour, is the paradise of the economically strong. State control, whether in the form of protective legislation or of protective tariffs, is the weapon of self-defence invoked by the economically weak. The clash of interests is real and inevitable; and the whole nature of the problem is distorted by an attempt to disguise it.

The harmony broken

We must therefore reject as inadequate and misleading the attempt to base international morality on an alleged harmony of interests which identifies the interest of the whole community of nations with the interest of each individual member of it. In the nineteenth century, this attempt met with widespread success, thanks to the continuously expanding economy in which it was made. The period was one of progressive prosperity, punctuated only by minor set-backs. The international economic structure bore considerable resemblance to the domestic economic structure of the United States. Pressure could at once be relieved by expansion to hitherto unoccupied and unexploited territories; and there was a plentiful supply of cheap labour, and of backward countries, which had not yet reached the level of political consciousness. Enterprising individuals could solve the economic problem by migration, enterprising nations by colonization. Expanding markets produced an expanding population, and population in turn reacted on markets. Those who were left behind in the race could plausibly be regarded as the unfit. A harmony of interests among the fit, based on individual enterprise and free competition, was sufficiently near to reality to form a sound basis for the current theory. With some difficulty the illusion was kept alive till 1914. Even British prosperity, though its foundations were menaced by German and American competition, continued to expand. [...]

The transition from the apparent harmony to the transparent clash of interests may be placed about the turn of the century. Appropriately enough, it found its first expression in colonial policies. In the British mind, it was primarily associated with events in South Africa. [...] In North Africa and the Far East, there was a hasty scramble by the European Powers to secure the few eligible sites which were still vacant. Emigration of individuals from Europe, the point of principal tension, to America assumed unparalleled dimensions. In Europe itself, anti-Semitism – the recurrent symptom of economic stress – reappeared after a long interval in Russia, Germany and France.[21] In Great Britain, agitation against unrestricted alien immigration began in the 1890s; and the first act controlling immigration was passed in 1905.

The first world war, which proceeded from this growing tension, aggravated it tenfold by intensifying its fundamental causes. In belligerent and neutral countries in Europe, Asia and America industrial and agricultural production were everywhere artificially stimulated. After the war every country struggled to maintain its expanded production; and an enhanced and inflamed national consciousness was invoked to justify the struggle. One reason for the unprecedented vindictiveness of the peace treaties, and in particular of their economic clauses, was that practical men no longer believed – as they had done fifty or a hundred years earlier – in an underlying harmony of interests between victors and defeated. The object was now to eliminate a competitor, a revival of whose prosperity might menace your own. In Europe, the struggle was intensified by the creation of new states and new economic frontiers. In Asia, India and China built up large-scale manufactures to make themselves independent of imports from Europe. Japan became an exporter of textiles and other cheap goods which undercut European manufactures on the world market. Most important of all, there were no more open spaces anywhere awaiting cheap and profitable development and exploitation. The ample avenues of migration which had relieved the economic pressures of the pre-war period were closed; and in place of the natural flow of migration came the problem of forcibly evicted refugees.[22] The complex phenomenon known as economic nationalism swept over the world. The fundamental character of this clash of interests became obvious to all except those confirmed utopians who dominated economic thought in the English-speaking countries. The hollowness of the glib nineteenth-century platitude that nobody can benefit from what harms another was revealed. The basic presupposition of utopianism had broken down.

What confronts us in international politics today is, therefore, nothing less than the complete bankruptcy of the conception of morality which has dominated political and economic thought for a century and a half. Internationally, it is no longer possible to deduce virtue from right reasoning, because it is no longer seriously possible to believe that every state, by pursuing the greatest good of the whole world, is pursuing the greatest good of its own citizens, and *vice versa*. The synthesis of morality and reason, at any rate in the crude form in which it was achieved by nineteenth-century liberalism, is untenable. The inner meaning of the modern international crisis is the collapse of the whole structure of utopianism based on the concept of the harmony of interests. The present generation will have to rebuild from the foundations. But before we can do this, before we can ascertain what can be salved from the ruins, we must examine the flaws in the structure which led to its collapse; and we can best do this by analysing the realist critique of the utopian assumptions.

Notes

1   While this is the form of utopianism which has been predominant for the past three centuries, and which still prevails (though perhaps with diminishing force) in English-speaking countries, it would be rash to assert that individualism and

rationalism are necessary attributes to utopian thought. Fascism contained elements of a utopianism which was anti-individualist and irrational. These qualities were already latent in the utopian aspects of Leninism – and perhaps even of Marxism.

2   Bentham, *Works*, ed. Bowring, i. p. 31.

3   Bentham, *Works*, ed. Bowring, viii. p. 561.

4   J. S. Bury, *The Idea of Progress*, p. 131.

5   Comte, *Cours de Philosophie Positive*, Lecture LXI.

6   R. H. S. Crossman in J. P. Mayer, *Political Thought*, p. 202.

7   New Year's Eve broadcast from Radio–Nations, Geneva: *The Times*, 1 January 1938.

8   *The Covenant of the League of Nations and a Commentary Thereon*, Cmd. 151 (1919), p. 12. 'The great strength of the Covenant', said the British Government some years later, 'lies in the measure of discretion which it allows to the Council and Assembly in dealing with future contingencies which may have no parallel in history and which therefore cannot all of them be foreseen in advance' (*League of Nations: Official Journal*, May 1928, p. 703).

9   By a curious irony, this development was strongly encouraged by a group of American intellectuals; and some European enthusiasts imagined that, by following this course, they would propitiate American opinion. The rift between the theory of the intellectuals and the practice of the government, which developed in Great Britain from 1932 onwards, began in the United States in 1919.

10   J. Fischer-Williams, *Some Aspects of the Covenant of the League of Nations*, p. 238.

11   *Intimate Papers of Colonel House*, ed. C. Seymour, iv. p. 291.

12   Miller, *The Drafting of the Covenant*, ii. p. 64.

13   House of Commons, *Official Report*, col. 923, 22 March 1932.

14   Lord Allen of Hurtwood, *The Times*, 30 May 1938.

15   *Neutrality and Collective Security*, (1936), Harris Foundation Lectures: Chicago, pp. 8, 18.

16   *International Affairs*, xvii. (September–October 1938), p. 712.

17   The confusion between the two was admirably illustrated by an interjection of Mr Attlee in the House of Commons: 'It was precisely the object of the establishment of the League of Nations that the preservation of peace was a common interest of the world' (House of Commons, 21 December 1937: *Official Report*, col. 1811). Mr Attlee apparently failed to distinguish between the proposition that a natural community of interests existed and the proposition that the League of Nations had been established to create one.

18   'Peace must prevail, must come before all' (Briand, *League of Nations: Ninth Assembly*, p. 83). 'The maintenance of peace is the first objective of British foreign policy' (Eden, *League of Nations: Sixteenth Assembly*, p. 106). 'Peace is our dearest treasure' (Hitler, in a speech in the German Reichstag on 30 January 1937, reported in *The Times*, 1 February 1937). 'The principal aim of the international policy of the Soviet Union is the preservation of peace' (Chicherin in *The Soviet Union and Peace* (1929), p. 249). 'The object of Japan, despite propaganda to the contrary, is peace' (Matsuoka, *League of Nations: Special Assembly 1932–33*, iii. p. 73). The paucity of Italian pronouncements in favour of peace was probably explained by the poor reputation of Italian troops as fighters: Mussolini feared that any emphatic expression of preference for peace would be construed as an admission that Italy had no stomach for war.

19   It is sometimes maintained not merely that all nations have an equal interest in preferring peace to war (which is, in a sense, true), but that war can never in any circumstances bring to the victor advantages comparable with its cost. The latter view does not appear to be true of the past, though it is possible to argue (as does Bertrand Russell, *Which Way Peace?*) that it is true of modern warfare. If accepted, this view leads, of course, to absolute pacifism; for there is no reason to suppose that it is any truer of 'defensive' than of 'offensive' war (assuming the distinction between them to be valid).

20   *League of Nations*: C.48, M.18, 1933, ii. p. 6.

21   The same conditions encouraged the growth of Zionism; for Zionism, as the Palestine Royal Commission of 1937 remarked, 'on its negative side is a creed of escape' (Cmd. 5479, p. 13).

22   'The existence of refugees is a symptom of the disappearance of economic and political liberalism. Refugees are the by-product of an economic isolationism which has practically stopped free migration' (J. Hope Simpson, *Refugees: Preliminary Report of a Survey*, p. 193).

Hans J. Morgenthau

A REALIST THEORY OF INTERNATIONAL POLITICS

Source: *Politics Among Nations: The Struggle for Power and Peace*, Brief Edition, revised by Kenneth W. Thompson (New York: McGraw Hill, 1993), pp. 3–16.

[....] **THE HISTORY** of modern political thought is the story of a contest between two schools that differ fundamentally in their conceptions of the nature of man, society, and politics. One believes that a rational and moral political order, derived from universally valid abstract principles, can be achieved here and now. It assumes the essential goodness and infinite malleability of human nature, and blames the failure of the social order to measure up to the rational standards on lack of knowledge and understanding, obsolescent social institutions, or the depravity of certain isolated individuals or groups. It trusts in education, reform, and the sporadic use of force to remedy these defects.

The other school believes that the world, imperfect as it is from the rational point of view, is the result of forces inherent in human nature. To improve the world one must work with those forces, not against them. This being inherently a world of opposing interests and of conflict among them, moral principles can never be fully realized, but must at best be approximated through the ever temporary balancing of interests and the ever precarious settlement of conflicts. This school, then, sees in a system of checks and balances a universal principle for all pluralist societies. It appeals to historic precedent rather than to abstract principles, and aims at the realization of the lesser evil rather than of the absolute good.

This theoretical concern with human nature as it actually is, and with the historic processes as they actually take place, has earned for the theory presented here the name of realism. What are the tenets of political realism? No systematic exposition of the philosophy of political realism can be attempted here; it will suffice to single out six fundamental principles, which have frequently, been misunderstood.

Six principles of political realism

1. Political realism believes that politics, like society in general, is governed by objective laws that have their roots in human nature. In order to improve society it is first necessary to understand the laws by which society lives. The operation of these laws being impervious to our preferences, men will challenge them only at the risk of failure.

    Realism, believing as it does in the objectivity of the laws of politics, must also believe in the possibility of developing a rational theory that reflects, however imperfectly and one-sidedly, these objective laws. It believes also, then, in the possibility of distinguishing in politics between truth and opinion – between what is true objectively and rationally, supported by evidence and illuminated by reason, and what is only a subjective judgment, divorced from the facts as they are and informed by prejudice and wishful thinking. [...]

    For realism, theory consists in ascertaining facts and giving them meaning through reason. It assumes that the character of a foreign policy can be ascertained only through the examination of the political acts performed and of the foreseeable consequences of these acts. Thus we can find out what statesmen have actually done, and from the foreseeable consequences of their acts we can surmise what their objectives might have been.

    Yet examination of the facts is not enough. To give meaning to the factual raw material of foreign policy, we must approach political reality with a kind of rational outline, a map that suggests to us the possible meanings of foreign policy. In other words, we put ourselves in the position of a statesman who must meet a certain problem of foreign policy under certain circumstances, and we ask ourselves what the rational alternatives are from which a statesman may choose who must meet this problem under these circumstances (presuming always that he acts in a rational manner), and which of these rational alternatives this particular statesman, acting under these circumstances, is likely to choose. It is the testing of this rational hypothesis against the actual facts and their consequences that gives theoretical meaning to the facts of international politics.

2. The main signpost that helps political realism to find its way through the landscape of international politics is the concept of interest defined in terms of power. This concept [...] sets politics as an autonomous sphere of action and understanding apart from other spheres, such as economics (understood in terms of interest defined as wealth), ethics, aesthetics, or religion. Without such a concept a theory of politics, international or domestic, would be altogether impossible, for without it we could not distinguish between political and nonpolitical facts, nor could we bring at least a measure of systemic order to the political sphere.

    We assume that statesmen think and act in terms of interest defined as power, and the evidence of history bears that assumption out. That assumption allows us to retrace and anticipate, as it were, the steps a statesman – past, present, or future – has taken or will take on the political scene. We look over his shoulder when he writes his dispatches; we listen in on his conversation with other statesmen; we read and anticipate his very thoughts. [...] [Also], we think as he does, and as disinterested observers we understand his thoughts and actions perhaps better than he, the actor on the political scene, does himself.

The concept of interest defined as power imposes intellectual discipline upon the observer, infuses rational order into the subject matter of politics, and thus makes the theoretical understanding of politics possible. On the side of the actor, it provides for rational discipline in action and creates that astounding continuity in foreign policy which makes American, British, or Russian foreign policy appear as an intelligible, rational continuum, by and large consistent within itself, regardless of the different motives, preferences, and intellectual and moral qualities of successive statesmen. A realist theory of international politics, then, will guard against two popular fallacies: the concern[s] with motives and [...] ideological preferences.

To search for the clue to foreign policy exclusively in the motives of statesmen is both futile and deceptive. It is futile because motives are the most illusive of psychological data, distorted as they are, frequently beyond recognition, by the interests and emotions of actor and observer alike. [...]

What is important to know, if one wants to understand foreign policy, is not primarily the motives of a statesman, but his intellectual ability to comprehend the essentials of foreign policy, as well as his political ability to translate what he has comprehended into successful political action. It follows that while ethics in the abstract judges the moral qualities of motives, political theory must judge the political qualities of intellect, will, and action.

A realist theory of international politics will also avoid the other popular fallacy of equating the foreign policies of a statesman with his philosophic or political sympathies, and of deducing the former from the latter. Statesmen, especially under contemporary conditions, [...] will distinguish [...] between their "*official* duty," which is to think and act in terms of the national interest, and their "*personal* wish," which is to see their own moral values and political principles realized throughout the world. Political realism does not require, nor does it condone, indifference to political ideals and moral principles, but it requires indeed a sharp distinction between the desirable and the possible – between what is desirable everywhere and at all times and what is possible under the concrete circumstances of time and place.

It stands to reason that not all foreign policies have always followed so rational, objective, and unemotional a course. The contingent elements of personality, prejudice, and subjective preference, and of all the weaknesses of intellect and will which flesh is heir to, are bound to deflect foreign policies from their rational course. Especially where foreign policy is conducted under the conditions of democratic control, the need to marshal popular emotions to the support of foreign policy cannot fail to impair the rationality of foreign policy itself. Yet a theory of foreign policy which aims at rationality must for the time being, as it were, abstract from these irrational elements and seek to paint a picture of foreign policy which presents the rational essence to be found in experience, without the contingent deviations from rationality which are also found in experience. [...]

Political realism contains not only a theoretical but also a normative element. It knows that political reality is replete with contingencies and systemic irrationalities and points to the typical influences they exert upon foreign policy. Yet it shares with all social theory the need, for the sake of theoretical understanding, to stress the rational elements of political reality; for it is these rational elements that make reality intelligible for theory. Political realism presents the theoretical construct of a national foreign policy which experience can never completely achieve.

At the same time political realism considers a rational foreign policy to be good foreign policy; for only a rational foreign policy minimizes risks and maximizes benefits and, hence, complies both with the moral precept of prudence and the political requirement of success. Political realism wants the photographic picture of the political world to resemble as much as possible its painted portrait. Aware of the inevitable gap between good – that is, rational – foreign policy and foreign policy as it actually is, political realism maintains not only that theory must focus upon the rational elements of political reality, but also that foreign policy ought to be rational in view of its own moral and practical purposes. [...]

3.   Realism assumes that its key concept of interest defined as power is an objective category which is universally valid, but it does not endow that concept with a meaning that is fixed once and for all. The idea of interest is indeed of the essence of politics and is unaffected by the circumstances of time and place. [...]

Yet the kind of interest determining political action in a particular period of history depends upon the political and cultural context within which foreign policy is formulated. The goals that might be pursued by nations in their foreign policy can run the whole gamut of objectives any nation has ever pursued or might possibly pursue.

The same observations apply to the concept of power. Its content and the manner of its use are determined by the political and cultural environment. Power may comprise anything that establishes and maintains the control of man over man. Thus power covers all social relationships which serve that end, from physical violence to the most subtle psychological ties by which one mind controls another. Power covers the domination of man by man, both when it is disciplined by moral ends and controlled by constitutional safeguards, as in Western democracies, and when it is that untamed and barbaric force which finds its laws in nothing but its own strength and its sole justification in its aggrandizement.

Political realism does not assume that the contemporary conditions under which foreign policy operates, with their extreme instability and the ever present threat of large-scale violence, cannot be changed. The balance of power, for instance, is indeed a perennial element of all pluralistic societies [...], yet it is capable of operating [...] under the conditions of relative stability and peaceful conflict. If the factors that have given rise to these conditions can be duplicated on the international scene, similar conditions of stability and peace will then prevail there, as they have over long stretches of history among certain nations.

What is true of the general character of international relations is also true of the nation state as the ultimate point of reference of contemporary foreign policy. While the realist indeed believes that interest is the perennial standard by which political action must be judged and directed, the contemporary connection between interest and the nation state is a product of history, and is therefore bound to disappear in the course of history. Nothing in the realist position militates against the assumption that the present division of the political world into nation states will be replaced by larger units of a quite different character, more in keeping with the technical potentialities and the moral requirements of the contemporary world.

The realist parts company with other schools of thought before the all-important question of how the contemporary world is to be transformed [...] [in] that this transformation can be achieved only through the workmanlike manipulation of the perennial forces that have shaped the past as they will the future [...] [not] by confronting a political reality that has its own laws with an abstract ideal that refuses to take those laws into account.

4. Political realism is aware of the moral significance of political action. It is also aware of the ineluctable tension between the moral command and the requirements of successful political action. [...]

Realism maintains that universal moral principles cannot be applied to the actions of states in their abstract universal formulation, but that they must be filtered through the concrete circumstances of time and place. The individual may say for himself: "*Fiat justitia, pereat mundus* (Let justice be done, even if the world perish)," but the state has no right to say so in the name of those who are in its care. Both individual and state must judge political action by universal moral principles, such as that of liberty. Yet while the individual has a moral right to sacrifice himself in defense of such a moral principle, the state has no right to let its moral disapprobation of the infringement of liberty get in the way of successful political action, itself inspired by the moral principle of national survival. There can be no political morality without prudence; that is, without consideration of the political consequences of seemingly moral action. Realism, then, considers prudence – the weighing of the consequences of alternative political, actions – to be the supreme virtue in politics. Ethics in the abstract judges action by its conformity with the moral law; political ethics judges action by its political consequences. [...]

5. Political realism refuses to identify the moral aspirations of a particular nation with the moral laws that govern the universe. [...] All nations are tempted – and few have been able to resist the temptation for long – to clothe their own particular aspirations and actions in the moral purposes of the universe. To know that nations are subject to the moral law is one thing, while to pretend to know with certainty what is good and evil in the relations among nations is quite another. [...]

The lighthearted equation between a particular nationalism and the counsels of Providence is morally indefensible, for it is that very sin of pride against which the Greek tragedians and the Biblical prophets have warned rulers and ruled. That equation is also politically pernicious, for it is liable to engender the distortion in judgment which, in the blindness of crusading frenzy, destroys nations and civilizations – in the name of moral principle, ideal, or God himself.

On the other hand, it is exactly the concept of interest defined in terms of power that saves us from both that moral excess and that political folly. For if we look at all nations, our own included, as political entities pursuing their respective interests defined in terms of power, we are able to do justice to all of them [...] in a dual sense: We are able to judge other nations as we judge our own and, having judged them in this fashion, we are then capable of pursuing policies that respect the interests of other nations, while protecting and promoting those of our own. Moderation in policy cannot fail to reflect the moderation of moral judgment.

6. The difference [...] between political realism and other schools of thought is real, and [...] profound. [...]

The political realist is not unaware of the existence and relevance of standards of thought other than political ones. [...] [H]e cannot but subordinate these other standards to those of politics [and] part[ing] company with other schools when they impose standards of thought appropriate to other spheres upon the political sphere. It is here that political realism takes issue with the "legalistic-moralistic approach" to international politics. [...]

Th[e] realist defense of the autonomy of the political sphere against its subversion by other modes of thought does not imply disregard for the existence and importance of these other modes of thought. It rather implies that each should be assigned its proper sphere and function. Political realism is based upon a pluralistic conception of human nature. [...]

Recognizing that [...] different facets of human nature exist, political realism also recognizes that in order to understand one of them one has to deal with it on its own terms. That is to say, if I want to understand "religious man," I must for the time being abstract from the other aspects of human nature and deal with its religious aspect as if it were the only one. Furthermore, I must apply to the religious sphere the standards of thought appropriate to it, always remaining aware of the existence of other standards and their actual influence upon the religious qualities of man. What is true of this facet of human nature is true of all the others. [...]

It is in the nature of things that a theory of politics which is based upon such principles will not meet with unanimous approval – nor does, for that matter, such a foreign policy. For theory and policy alike run counter to two trends in our culture which are not able to reconcile themselves to the assumptions and results of a rational, objective theory of politics. One of these trends disparages the role of power in society on grounds that stem from the experience and philosophy of the nineteenth century; [...] The other trend, opposed to the realist theory and practice of politics, stems from the very relationship that exists, and must exist, between the human mind and the political sphere. [...] The human mind in its day-by-day operations cannot bear to look the truth of politics straight in the face. It must disguise, distort, belittle, and embellish the truth – the more so; the more the individual is actively involved in the processes of politics, and particularly in those of international politics. For only by deceiving himself about the nature of politics and the role he plays on the political scene is man able to live contentedly as a political animal with himself and his fellow men.

Thus it is inevitable that a theory which tries to understand international politics as it actually is and as it ought to be in view of its intrinsic nature, rather than as people would like to see it, must overcome a psychological resistance the most other branches of learning need not face. [...]

Hedley Bull

THE CONCEPT OF ORDER IN WORLD POLITICS

Source: *The Anarchical Society: A Study of Order in World Politics* (New York: Columbia University Press, 1977), pp. 3–21.

International order

BY INTERNATIONAL ORDER I mean a pattern of activity that sustains the elementary or primary goals of the society of states, or international society. [...]

A *society of states* (or international society) exists when a group of states, conscious of certain common interests and common values, form a society in the sense that they conceive themselves to be bound by a common set of rules in their relations with one another, and share in the working of common institutions. If states today form an international society [...], this is because, recognising certain common interests and perhaps some common values, they regard themselves as bound by certain rules in their dealings with one another, such as that they should respect one another's claims to independence, that they should honour agreements into which they enter, and that they should be subject to certain limitations in exercising force against one another. At the same time they cooperate in the working of institutions such as the forms of procedures of international law, the machinery of diplomacy and general international organisation, and the customs and conventions of war.

An international society in this sense presupposes an international system, but an international system may exist that is not an international society. Two or more states, in other words, may be in contact with each other and interact in such a way as to be necessary factors in each other's calculations without their being conscious of common interests or values, conceiving themselves to be bound by a common set of rules, or co-operating in the working of common institutions. Turkey, China, Japan, Korea and Siam, for example, were part of the European-dominated international system before they were part of the European-dominated international society. That is to say, they were in contact with European powers, and interacted significantly with them in war and commerce, before they and the European powers came to recognise common interests or values, to regard each other as subject to the same set of rules and as co-operating in the working of common institutions. [...]

When, as in the case of encounters between European and non-European states from the sixteenth century until the late nineteenth century, states are participants in a single international system, but not members of a single international society, there may be communication, exchanges of envoys or messengers and agreements – not only about trade but also about war, peace and alliances. But these forms of interaction do not in themselves demonstrate that there is an international society. Communication may take place, envoys may be exchanged and agreements entered into without there being a sense of common interests or values that gives such exchange substance and a prospect of permanence, without any sense that there are rules which lay down how the interaction should proceed, and without the attempt of the parties concerned to co-operate in institutions in whose survival they have a stake. [...]

Whether or not these distinguishing features of an international society are present in an international system, it is not always easy to determine: as between an international system that is clearly also an international society, and a system that is clearly not a society, there lie cases where a sense of common interests is tentative and inchoate; where the common rules perceived are vague and ill-formed, and there is doubt as to whether they are worthy of the name of rules; or where common institutions – relating to diplomatic machinery or to limitations in war – are implicit or embryonic. [...]

A common feature of these historical international societies is that they were all founded upon a common culture or civilisation, or at least on some of the elements of such a civilisation: a common language, a common epistemology and understanding of the universe, a common religion, a common ethical code, a common aesthetic or artistic tradition. It is reasonable to suppose that where such elements of a common civilisation underlie an international society, they facilitate its working in two ways. On the one hand, they may make for easier communication and closer awareness and understanding between one state and another, and thus facilitate the definition of common rules and the evolution of common institutions. On the other hand, they may reinforce the sense of common interests that impels states to accept common rules and institutions with a sense of common values. [...]

[B]y international order is meant a pattern or disposition of international activity that sustains those goals of the society of states that are elementary, primary or universal. What goals, then, are these?

First, there is the goal of preservation of the system and society of states itself. Whatever the divisions among them, modern states have been united in the belief that they are the principal actors in world politics and the chief bearers of rights and duties within it. The society of states has sought to ensure that it will remain the prevailing form of universal political organisation, in fact and in right. [...]

Second, there is the goal of maintaining the independence or external sovereignty of individual states. From the perspective of any particular state what it chiefly hopes to gain from participation in the society of states is recognition of its independence of outside authority, and in particular of its supreme jurisdiction over its subjects and territory. The chief price it has to pay for this is recognition of like rights to independence and sovereignty on the part of other states.

International society has in fact treated preservation of the independence of particular states as a goal that is subordinate to preservation of the society of states itself; this reflects the predominant role played in shaping international society by the great powers, which view themselves as its custodians [...]. Thus international society has often allowed the independence of individual states to be extinguished, as in the great process of partition and absorption of small powers by greater ones, in the name of principles such as 'compensation' and the 'balance of power' that produced a steady decline in the number of states in Europe from the Peace of Westphalia in 1648 until the Congress of Vienna in 1815. In the same way, international society, at least in the perspective of the great powers which see themselves as its guardians, treats the independence of particular states as subordinate to the preservation of the system as a whole when it tolerates or encourages limitation of the sovereignty or independence of small states through such devices as spheres-of-influence agreements, or agreements to create buffer or neutralised states.

Third, there is the goal of peace. By this is meant not the goal of establishing universal and permanent peace, such as has been the dream of irenists or theorists of peace, and stands in contrast to actual historical experience: this is not a goal which the society of states can be said to have pursued in any serious way. Rather what is meant is the maintenance of peace in the sense of the absence of war among member states of international society as the normal condition of their relationship, to be breached only in special circumstances and according to principles that are generally accepted.

Peace in this sense has been viewed by international society as a goal subordinate to that of the preservation of the states system itself, for which it has been widely held that it can be right to wage war; and as subordinate also to preservation of the sovereignty or independence of individual states, which have insisted on the right to wage war in self-defence, and to protect other rights also. The subordinate status of peace in relation to these other goals is reflected in the phrase 'peace and security', which occurs in the United Nations Charter. Security in international politics means no more than safety: either objective safety, safety which actually exists, or subjective safety, that which is felt or experienced. What states seek to make secure or safe is not merely peace, but their independence and the continued existence of the society of states itself which that independence requires; and for these objectives, as we have noted, they are ready to resort to war and the threat of war. The coupling of the two terms together in the Charter reflects the judgement that the requirements of security may conflict with those of peace, and that in this event the latter will not necessarily take priority.

Fourth, it should be noted that among the elementary or primary goals of the society of states are those which, at the beginning of this chapter, were said to be the common goals of all social life: limitation of violence resulting in death or bodily harm, the keeping of promises and the stabilisation of possession by rules of property.

The goal of limitation of violence is represented in international society in a number of ways. States co-operate in international society so as to maintain their monopoly of violence, and deny the right to employ it to other groups. States also accept limitations on their own right to use violence; at a minimum they accept that they shall not kill one another's envoys or messengers, since this would make communication impossible. Beyond this, they accept that war should be waged only for a 'just' cause, or a cause the justice of which can be argued in terms of common rules. They have also constantly proclaimed adherence to rules requiring that wars be fought within certain limits, the *temperamenta belli*.

The goal of the keeping of promises is represented in the principle *pacta sunt servanda*. Among states as among individuals, cooperation can take place only on the basis of agreements, and agreements can fulfil their function in social life only on the basis of a presumption that once entered into they will be upheld. International society adjusts itself to the pressures for change that make for the breaking of treaties, and at the same time salvages the principle itself, through the doctrine of *rebus sic stantibus*.

The goal of stability of possession is reflected in international society not only by the recognition by states of one another's property, but more fundamentally in the compact of mutual recognition of sovereignty, in which states accept one another's spheres of jurisdiction: indeed, the idea of the sovereignty of the state derived historically from the idea that certain territories and peoples were the property or patrimony of the ruler.

The above are among the elementary or primary goals of modern international society, and of other international societies. It is not suggested here that this list is exhaustive, nor that it could not be formulated in some other way. Nor is it any part of my thesis that these goals should be accepted as a valid basis for action, as legislating right conduct in international relations. It should also be said that at this stage in the argument we are concerned only with what may be called the 'statics' of international order and not with its 'dynamics'; we are concerned only to spell out what is involved in the idea of international order, not to trace how it is embodied in historical institutions subject to change. [...]

World order

By world order I mean those patterns or dispositions of human activity that sustain the elementary or primary goals of social life among mankind as a whole. International order is order among states; but states are simply groupings of men, and men may be grouped in such a way that they do not form states at all. Moreover, where they are grouped into states, they are grouped in other ways also. Underlying the questions we raise about order among states there are deeper questions, of more enduring importance, about order in the great society of all mankind.

Throughout human history before the nineteenth century there was no single political system that spanned the world as a whole. The great society of all mankind, to which allusions were made by exponents of canon law or natural law, was a notional society that existed in the sight of God or in the light of the principles of natural law: no actual political system corresponded to it. Before the latter half of the nineteenth century world order was simply the sum of the various political systems that brought order to particular parts of the world.

However, since the late nineteenth century and early twentieth century there has arisen for the first time a single political system that is genuinely global. Order on a global scale has ceased to be simply the sum of the various political systems that produce order on a local scale; it is also the product of what may be called a world political system. Order in the world – say, in 1900 – was still the sum of the order provided within European and American states and their overseas dependencies, within the Ottoman empire, the Chinese and Japanese empires, within the Khanates and Sultanates that preserved an independent existence from the Sahara to Central Asia, within primitive African and Oceanic political systems not yet destroyed by the European impact – but it was also the consequence of a political system, linking them all, that operated all over the world.

The first global political system has taken the form of a global system of states. What is chiefly responsible for the emergence of a degree of interaction among political systems in all the continents of the world, sufficient to make it possible for us to speak of a world political system, has been the expansion of the European states system all over the globe, and its transformation into a states system of global dimension. In the first phase of this process the European states expanded and incorporated or dominated the rest of the world, beginning with the Portuguese voyages of discovery in the fifteenth century and ending with the partition of Africa in the nineteenth. In the second phase, overlapping with the first in point of time, the areas of the world thus incorporated or dominated broke loose from European control, and took their places as member states of international society, beginning with the American Revolution and ending with the African and Asian anticolonial revolution of our own times. It is true that the intermeshing of the various parts of the world was not simply the work of states; private individuals and groups played their part as explorers, traders, migrants, missionaries and mercenaries, and the expansion of the states system was part of a wider spread of social and economic exchange. However, the political structure to which these developments gave rise was one simply of a global system and society of states.

But while the world political system that exists at present takes the form of a system of states, or takes principally this form [...], world order could in principle be achieved by other forms of universal political organisation, and a standing question is whether world order might not better be served by such other forms. Other forms of universal political organisation have existed in the past on a less than global scale; in the broad sweep of human history, indeed, the form of the states system has been the exception rather than the rule. Moreover, it is reasonable to assume that new forms of universal political organisation may be created in the future that do not resemble those that have existed in the past. [...]

Here we need only stress that [...] world order entails something different from international order. Order among mankind as a whole is something wider than order among states; something more fundamental and primordial than it; and also, I should argue, something morally prior to it.

World order is wider than international order because to give an account of it we have to deal not only with order among states but also with order on a domestic or municipal scale, provided within particular states, and with order within the wider world political system of which the states system is only part.

World order is more fundamental and primordial than international order because the ultimate units of the great society of all mankind are not states (or nations, tribes, empires, classes or parties) but individual human beings, which are permanent and indestructible in a sense in which groupings of them of this or that sort are not. This is the moment for international relations, but the question of world order arises whatever the political or social structure of the globe.

World order, finally, is morally prior to international order. To take this view is to broach the question of the value of world order and its place in the hierarchy of human values [...]. It is necessary to state at this point, however, that if any value attaches to order in world politics, it is order among all mankind which we must treat as being of primary value, not order within the society of states. If international order does have value, this can only be because it is instrumental to the goal of order in human society as a whole.

Kenneth N. Waltz

ANARCHIC ORDERS AND BALANCES OF POWER

Source: *Theory of International Politics* (New York: Random House, 1979), pp. 102–28.

1. Violence at home and abroad

THE STATE AMONG STATES, it is often said, conducts its affairs in the brooding shadow of violence. Because some states may at any time use force, all states must be prepared to do so – or live at the mercy of their militarily more vigorous neighbors. Among states, the state of nature is a state of war. This is meant not in the sense that war constantly occurs but in the sense that, with each state deciding for itself whether or not to use force, war may at any time break out. Whether in the family, the community, or the world at large, contact without at least occasional conflict is inconceivable; and the hope that in the absence of an agent to manage or to manipulate conflicting parties the use of force will always be avoided cannot be realistically entertained. Among men as among states, anarchy, or the absence of government, is associated with the occurrence of violence.

The threat of violence and the recurrent use of force are said to distinguish international from national affairs. But in the history of the world surely most rulers have had to bear in mind that their subjects might use force to resist or overthrow them. If the absence of government is associated with the threat of violence, so also is its presence. [...]

If anarchy is identified with chaos, destruction, and death, then the distinction between anarchy and government does not tell us much. Which is more precarious: the life of a state among states, or of a government in relation to its subject? The answer varies with time and place. Among some states at some times, the actual or expected occurrence of violence is low. Within some states at some times, the actual or expected occurrence of violence is high. The use of force, or the constant fear of its use, are not sufficient grounds for distinguishing international from domestic affairs. If the possible and the actual use of force mark both national and international orders, then no durable distinction between the two realms can be drawn in terms of the use or the nonuse of force. No human order is proof against violence.

To discover qualitative differences between internal and external affairs one must look for a criterion other than the occurrence of violence. The distinction between international and national realms of politics is not found in the use or the nonuse of force but in their different structures. But if the dangers of being violently attacked are greater, say, in taking an evening stroll through downtown Detroit than they are in picnicking along the French and German border, what practical difference does the difference of structure make? Nationally as internationally, contact generates conflict and at times issues in violence. The difference between national and international politics lies not in the use of force but in the different modes of organization for doing something about it. A government, ruling by some standard of legitimacy, arrogates to itself the right to use force – that is, to apply a variety of sanctions to control the use of force by its subjects. If some use private force, others may appeal to the government. A government has no monopoly on the use of force, as is all too evident. An effective government, however, has a monopoly on the *legitimate* use of force, and legitimate here means that public agents are organized to prevent and to counter the private use of force. Citizens need not prepare to defend themselves. Public agencies do that. A national system is not one of self-help. The international system is. [...]

2. Interdependence and integration

[...] Differences between national and international structures are reflected in the ways the units of each system define their ends and develop the means for reaching them. In anarchic realms, like units coact. In hierarchic realms, unlike units interact. In an anarchic realm, the units are functionally similar and tend to remain so. Like units work to maintain a measure of independence and may even strive for autarchy. In a hierarchic realm, the units are differentiated, and they tend to increase the extent of their specialization. Differentiated units become closely interdependent, the more closely so as their specialization proceeds. Because of the difference of structure, interdependence within and interdependence among nations are two distinct concepts. [...]

Although states are like units functionally, they differ vastly in their capabilities. Out of such differences something of a division of labor develops [...]. The division of labor across nations, however, is slight in comparison with the highly articulated division of labor within them. Integration draws the parts of a nation closely together. Interdependence among nations leaves them loosely connected. Although the integration of nations is often talked about, it seldom takes place. Nations could mutually enrich themselves by further dividing not just the labor that goes into the production of goods but also some of the other tasks they perform, such as political management and military defense. Why does their integration not take place? The structure of international politics limits the cooperation of states in two ways.

In a self-help system each of the units spends a portion of its effort, not in forwarding its own good, but in providing the means of protecting itself against others. Specialization in a system of divided labor works to everyone's advantage, though not equally so. Inequality in the expected distribution of the increased product works strongly against extension of the division of labor internationally. When faced with the possibility of cooperating for mutual gain, states that feel insecure must ask how the gain will be divided. They are compelled to ask not "Will both of us gain?" but "Who will gain more?" If an expected gain is to be divided, say, in the ratio of two to one, one state may use its disproportionate gain to implement a policy intended to damage or destroy the other. Even the prospect of large absolute gains for both parties does not elicit their cooperation so long as each fears how the other will use its increased capabilities. Notice that the impediments to collaboration may not lie in the character and the immediate intention of either party. Instead, the condition of insecurity – at the least, the uncertainty of each about the other's future intentions and actions – works against their cooperation.

In any self-help system, units worry about their survival, and the worry conditions their behavior. Oligopolistic markets limit the cooperation of firms in much the way that international-political structures limit the cooperation of states. Within rules laid down by governments, whether firms survive and prosper depends on their own efforts. Firms need not protect themselves physically against assaults from other firms. They are free to concentrate on their economic interests. As economic entities, however, they live in a self-help world. All want to increase profits. If they run undue risks in the effort to do so, they must expect to suffer the consequences. [...] [Hence,] [f]irms are constrained to strike a compromise between maximizing their profits and minimizing the danger of their own demise. Each of two firms may be better off if one of them accepts compensation from the other in return for withdrawing from some part of the market. But a firm that accepts smaller markets in exchange for larger profits will be gravely disadvantaged if, for example, a price war should break out as part of a renewed struggle for markets. If possible, one must resist accepting smaller markets in return for larger profits (pp. 132, 217–18). [...] Like nations, oligopolistic firms must be more concerned with relative strength than with absolute advantage.

A state worries about a division of possible gains that may favor others more than itself. That is the first way in which the structure of international politics limits the cooperation of states. A state also worries lest it become dependent on others through cooperative endeavors and exchanges of goods and services. That is the second way in which the structure of international politics limits the cooperation of states. [...] [Furthermore,] states seek to control what they depend on or to lessen the extent of their dependency. This simple thought explains quite a bit of the behavior of states: their imperial thrusts to widen the scope of their control and their autarchic strivings toward greater self-sufficiency.

Structures encourage certain behaviors and penalize those who do not respond to the encouragement. [...] Internationally, many lament the resources states spend unproductively for their own defense and the opportunities they miss to enhance the welfare of their people through cooperation with other states. And yet the ways of states change little. In an unorganized realm each unit's incentive is to put itself in a position to be able to take care of itself since no one else can be counted on to do so. The international imperative is "take care of yourself"! Some leaders of nations may understand that the well-being of all of them would increase through their participation in a fuller division of labor. But to act on the idea would be to act on a domestic imperative, an imperative that does not run internationally. What one might want to do in the absence of structural constraints is different from what one is encouraged to do in their presence. States do not willingly place themselves in situations of increased dependence. In a self-help system, considerations of security subordinate economic gain to political interest.

What each state does for itself is much like what all of the others are doing. They are denied the advantages that a full division of labor, political as well as economic, would provide. Defense spending, moreover, is unproductive for all and unavoidable for most. Rather than increased well-being, their reward is in the maintenance of their autonomy. States compete, but not by contributing their individual efforts to the joint production of goods for their mutual benefit. Here is a second big difference between international-political and economic systems. [...]

3. Structures and strategies

[...] Structures cause actions to have consequences they were not intended to have. [...] [That said,] [s]o long as one leaves the structure unaffected it is not possible for changes in the intentions and the actions of particular actors to produce desirable outcomes or to avoid undesirable ones. Structures may be changed [...] by changing the distribution of capabilities across units. Structures may also be changed by imposing requirements where previously people had to decide for themselves. [...] The only remedies for strong structural effects are structural changes. [...]

Structural constraints cannot be wished away, although many fail to understand this. In every age and place, the units of self-help systems – nations, corporations, or whatever – are told that the greater good, along with their own, requires them to act for the sake of the system and not for their own narrowly defined advantage. [...] The international interest must be served; and if that means anything at all, it means that national interests are subordinate to it. The problems are found at the global level. Solutions to the problems continue to depend on national policies. What are the conditions that would make nations more or less willing to obey the injunctions that are so often laid on them? How can they resolve the tension between pursuing their own interests and acting for the sake of the system? No one has shown how that can be done, although many wring their hands and plead for rational behavior. The very problem, however, is that rational behavior, given structural constraints, does not lead to the wanted results. With each country constrained to take care of itself, no one can take care of the system. [...]

Great tasks can be accomplished only by agents of great capability. That is why states, and especially the major ones, are called on to do what is necessary for the world's survival. But states have to do whatever they think necessary for their own preservation, since no one can be relied on to do it for them. [...]

[...] Over the centuries states have changed in many ways, but the quality of international life has remained much the same. States may seek reasonable and worthy ends, but they cannot figure out how to reach them. The problem is not in their stupidity or ill will, although one does not want to claim that those qualities are lacking. The depth of the difficulty is not understood until one realizes that intelligence and goodwill cannot discover and act on adequate programs. Early in this century Winston Churchill observed that the British-German naval race promised disaster *and* that Britain had no realistic choice other than to run it. States facing global problems are like individual consumers trapped by the tyranny of small decisions. States, like consumers, can get out of the trap only by changing the structure of their field of activity. The message bears repeating: The only remedy for a strong structural effect is a structural change.

4. The virtues of anarchy

To achieve their objectives and maintain their security, units in a condition of anarchy – be they people, corporations, states, or whatever – must rely on the means they can generate and the arrangements they can make for themselves. Self-help is necessarily the principle of action in an anarchic order. A self-help situation is one of high risk – of bankruptcy in the economic realm and of war in a world of free states. It is also one in which organizational costs are low. Within an economy or within an international order, risks may be avoided or lessened by moving from a situation of coordinate action to one of super- and subordination, that is, by erecting agencies with effective authority and extending a system of rules. Government emerges where the functions of regulation and management themselves become distinct and specialized tasks. [...]

Along with the advantages of hierarchic orders go the costs. In hierarchic orders, moreover, the means of control become an object of struggle. Substantive issues become entwined with efforts to influence or control the controllers. The hierarchic ordering of politics adds one to the already numerous objects of struggle, and the object added is at a new order of magnitude. [...]

[...] As hierarchical systems, governments nationally or globally are disrupted by the defection of major parts. In a society of states with little coherence, attempts at world government would founder on the inability of an emerging central authority to mobilize the resources needed to create and maintain the unity of the system by regulating and managing its parts. The prospect of world government would be an invitation to prepare for world civil war. [...] States cannot entrust managerial powers to a central agency unless that agency is able to protect its client states. The more powerful the clients and the more the power of each of them appears as a threat to the others, the greater the power lodged in the center must be. The greater the power of the center, the stronger the incentive for states to engage in a struggle to control it.

States, like people, are insecure in proportion to the extent of their freedom. If freedom is wanted, insecurity must be accepted. Organizations that establish relations of authority and control may increase security as they decrease freedom. If might does not make right, whether among people or states, then some institution or agency has intervened to lift them out of nature's realm. The more influential the agency, the stronger the desire to control it becomes. In contrast, units in an anarchic order act for their own sakes and not for the sake of preserving an organization and furthering their fortunes within it. Force is used for one's own interest. In the absence of organization, people or states are free to leave one another alone. Even when they do not do so, they are better able, in the absence of the politics of the organization, to concentrate on the politics of the problem and to aim for a minimum agreement that will permit their separate existence rather than a maximum agreement for the sake of maintaining unity. If might decides, then bloody struggles over right can more easily be avoided.

Nationally, the force of a government is exercised in the name of right and justice. Internationally, the force of a state is employed for the sake of its own protection and advantage. Rebels challenge a government's claim to authority; they question the rightfulness of its rule. Wars among states cannot settle questions of authority and right; they can only determine the allocation of gains and losses among contenders and settle for a time the question of who is the stronger. Nationally, relations of authority are established. Internationally, only relations of strength result. Nationally, private force used against a government threatens the political system. Force used by a state – a public body – is, from the international perspective, the private use of force; but there is no government to overthrow and no governmental apparatus to capture. Short of a drive toward world hegemony, the private use of force does not threaten the system of international politics, only some of its members. War pits some states against others in a struggle among similarly constituted entities. The power of the strong may deter the weak from asserting their claims, not because the weak recognize a kind of rightfulness of rule on the part of the strong, but simply because it is not sensible to tangle with them. Conversely, the weak may enjoy considerable freedom of action if they are so far removed in their capabilities from the strong that the latter are not much bothered by their actions or much concerned by marginal increases in their capabilities.

National politics is the realm of authority, of administration, and of law. International politics is the realm of power, of struggle, and of accommodation. The international realm is preeminently a political one. The national realm is variously described as being hierarchic, vertical, centralized, heterogeneous, directed, and contrived; the international realm, as being anarchic, horizontal, decentralized, homogeneous, undirected, and mutually adaptive. The more centralized the order, the nearer to the top the locus of decisions ascends. Internationally, decisions are made at the bottom level, there being scarcely any other. In the vertical horizontal dichotomy, international structures assume the prone position. Adjustments are made internationally, but they are made without a formal or authoritative adjuster. Adjustment and accommodation proceed by mutual adaptation (cf. Barnard 1944, pp. 148–52; Polanyi 1941, pp. 428–56). Action and reaction, and reaction to the reaction, proceed by a piecemeal process. The parties feel each other out, so to speak, and define a situation simultaneously with its development. Among coordinate units, adjustment is achieved and accommodations arrived at by the exchange of "considerations," in a condition, as Chester Barnard put it, "in which the duty of command and the desire to obey are essentially absent" (pp. 150–51). Where the contest is over considerations, the parties seek to maintain or improve their positions by maneuvering, by bargaining, or by fighting. The manner and intensity of the competition is determined by the desires and the abilities of parties that are at once separate and interacting.

Whether or not by force, each state plots the course it thinks will best serve its interests. If force is used by one state or its use is expected, the recourse of other states is to use force or be prepared to use it singly or in combination. No appeal can be made to a higher entity clothed with the authority and equipped with the ability to act on its own initiative. Under such conditions the possibility that force will be used by one or another of the parties looms always as a threat in the background. In politics force is said to be the *ultima ratio*. In international politics force serves, not only as the *ultima ratio*, but indeed as the first and constant one. [...] The constant possibility that force will be used limits manipulations, moderates demands, and serves as an incentive for the settlement of disputes. One who knows that pressing too hard may lead to war has strong reason to consider whether possible gains are worth the risks entailed. [...] The possibility that conflicts among nations may lead to long and costly wars has [...] sobering effects. [...]

References

Barnard, Chester I. (1944). "On planning for world government." In Chester I. Barnard (ed.), *Organization and Management*. Cambridge: Harvard University Press, 1948.

Polanyi, Michael (November 1941). "The growth of thought in society." *Economica*, vol. 8.

Robert Jervis

COOPERATION UNDER THE SECURITY DILEMMA

Source: 'Cooperation under the security dilemma', *World Politics*, vol. 30, no. 2, January 1978, pp. 167–214.

I. Anarchy and the security dilemma

T HE LACK OF AN INTERNATIONAL sovereign not only permits wars to occur, but also makes it difficult for states that are satisfied with the status quo to arrive at goals that they recognize as being in their common interest. Because there are no institutions or authorities that can make and enforce international laws, the policies of cooperation that will bring mutual rewards if others cooperate may bring disaster if they do not. Because states are aware of this, anarchy encourages behavior that leaves all concerned worse off than they could be, even in the extreme case in which all states would like to freeze the status quo. This is true of the men in Rousseau's "Stag Hunt." If they cooperate to trap the stag, they will all eat well. But if one person defects to chase a rabbit – which he likes less than stag – none of the others will get anything. Thus, all actors have the same preference order, and there is a solution that gives each his first choice: (1) cooperate and trap the stag (the international analogue being cooperation and disarmament); (2) chase a rabbit while others remain at their posts (maintain a high level of arms while others are disarmed); (3) all chase rabbits (arms competition and high risk of war); and (4) stay at the original position while another chases a rabbit (being disarmed while others are armed).[1] Unless each person thinks that the others will cooperate, he himself will not. And why might he fear that any other person would do something that would sacrifice his own first choice? The other might not understand the situation, or might not be able to control his impulses if he saw a rabbit, or might fear that some other member of the group is unreliable. If the person voices any of these suspicions, others are more likely to fear that he will defect, thus making them more likely to defect, thus making it more rational for him to defect. Of course in this simple case – and in many that are more realistic – there are a number of arrangements that could permit cooperation. But the main point remains: although actors may know that they seek a common goal, they may not be able to reach it.

Even when there is a solution that is everyone's first choice, the international case is characterized by three difficulties not present in the Stag Hunt. First, to the incentives to defect given above must be added the potent fear that even if the other state now supports the status quo, it may become dissatisfied later. No matter how much decision makers are committed to the status quo, they cannot bind themselves and their successors to the same path. Minds can be changed, new leaders can come to power, values can shift, new opportunities and dangers can arise.

The second problem arises from a possible solution. In order to protect their possessions, states often seek to control resources or land outside their own territory. Countries that are not self-sufficient must try to assure that the necessary supplies will continue to flow in wartime. This was part of the explanation for Japan's drive into China and Southeast Asia before World War II. If there were an international authority that could guarantee access, this motive for control would disappear. But since there is not, even a state that would prefer the status quo to increasing its area of control may pursue the latter policy.

When there are believed to be tight linkages between domestic and foreign policy or between the domestic politics of two states, the quest for security may drive states to interfere pre-emptively in the domestic politics of others in order to provide an ideological buffer zone. [...]

More frequently, the concern is with direct attack. In order to protect themselves, states seek to control, or at least to neutralize, areas on their borders. But attempts to establish buffer zones can alarm others who have stakes there, who fear that undesirable precedents will be set, or who believe that their own vulnerability will be increased. When buffers are sought in areas empty of great powers, expansion tends to feed on itself in order to protect what is acquired, as was often noted by those who opposed colonial expansion. [...]

Though this process is most clearly visible when it involves territorial expansion, it often operates with the increase of less tangible power and influence. The expansion of power usually brings with it an expansion of responsibilities and commitments; to meet them, still greater power is required. The state will take many positions that are subject to challenge. It will be involved with a wide range of controversial issues unrelated to its that would be seen as normal if made by a small power would be taken as an index of weakness inviting predation if made by a large one. [...]

The third problem present in international politics but not in the Stag Hunt is the security dilemma: many of the means by which a state tries to increase its security decrease the security of others. In domestic society, there are several ways to increase the safety of one's person and property without endangering others. One can move to a safer neighborhood, put bars on the windows, avoid dark streets, and keep a distance from suspicious-looking characters. Of course these measures are not convenient, cheap, or certain of success. But no one save criminals need be alarmed if a person takes them. In international politics, however, one state's gain in security often inadvertently threatens others. In explaining British policy on naval disarmament in the inter-war period to the Japanese, Ramsey MacDonald said problem was not with British desires, but with the consequences of her policy. In earlier periods, too, Britain had needed a navy large enough to keep the shipping lanes open. But such a navy could not avoid being a menace to any other state with a coast that could be raided, trade that could be interdicted, or colonies that could be isolated. When Germany started building a powerful navy before World War I, Britain objected that it could only be an offensive weapon aimed at her. As Sir Edward Grey, the Foreign Secretary, put it to King Edward VII: "If the German Fleet ever becomes superior to ours, the German Army can conquer this country. There is no corresponding risk of this kind to Germany; for however superior our Fleet was, no naval victory could bring us any nearer to Berlin." The English position was half correct: Germany's navy was an anti-British instrument. But the British often overlooked what the Germans knew full well: "in every quarrel with England, German colonies and trade were [...] hostages for England to take." Thus, whether she intended it or not, the British Navy consti-tuted an important instrument of coercion.[2]

II. What makes security cooperation more likely?

Given this gloomy picture, the obvious question is, why are we not all dead? Or, to put it less starkly, what kinds of variables ameliorate the impact of anarchy and the security dilemma? The workings of several can be seen in terms of the Stag Hunt or repeated plays of the Prisoner's Dilemma. The Prisoner's Dilemma differs from the Stag Hunt in that there is no solution that is in the best interests of all the participants; there are offensive as well as defensive incentives to defect from the coalition with the others; and, if the game is to be played only once, the only rational response is to defect. But if the game is repeated indefinitely, the latter characteristic no longer holds and we can analyze the game in terms similar to those applied to the Stag Hunt. It would be in the interest of each actor to have others deprived of the power to defect; each would be willing to sacrifice this ability if others were similarly restrained. But if the others are not, then it is in the actor's interest to retain the power to defect.[3] [...]

[...] "Given either of the above situations, what makes it more or less likely that the players will cooperate [...]?" The chances of achieving this outcome will be increased by: (1) anything that increases incentives to cooperate by increasing the gains of mutual cooperation [...] and/or decreasing the costs the actor will pay if he cooperates and the other does not [...]; (2) anything that decreases the incentives for defecting by decreasing the gains of taking advantage of the other [...] and/or increas-ing the costs of mutual noncooperation [...] [and]; (3) anything that increases each side's expectation that the other will cooperate.[4]

* * *

IV. Four worlds

The two variables we have been discussing — whether the offense or the defense has the advantage, and whether offensive postures can be distinguished from defensive ones — can be combined to yield four possible worlds.

The first world is the worst for status-quo states. There is no way to get security without menacing others, and security through defense is terribly difficult to obtain.

Because offensive and defensive postures are the same, status-quo states acquire the same kind of arms that are sought by aggressors. And because the offense has the advantage over the defense, attacking is the best route to protecting what you have; status-quo states will therefore behave like aggressors. The situation will be unstable. Arms races are likely. Incentives to strike first will turn crises into wars. Decisive victories and conquests will be common. States will grow and shrink rapidly, and it will be hard for any state to maintain its size and influence without trying to increase them. Cooperation among status-quo powers will be extremely hard to achieve. [...]

In the second world, the security dilemma operates because offensive and defensive postures cannot be distinguished; but it does not operate as strongly as in the first world because the defense has the advantage, and so an increment in one side's strength increases its security more than it decreases the other's. So, if both sides have reasonable subjective security requirements, are of roughly equal power, and the variables discussed earlier are favorable, it is quite likely that status-quo states can adopt compatible security policies. Although a state will not be able to judge the other's intentions from the kinds of weapons it procures, the level of arms spending will give important evidence. Of course a state that seeks a high level of arms might be not an aggressor but merely an insecure state, which if conciliated will reduce its arms, and if confronted will reply in kind. To assume that the apparently excessive level of arms indicates aggressiveness could therefore lead to a response that would deepen the dilemma and create needless conflict. But empathy and skillful statesmanship can reduce this danger. Furthermore, the advantageous position of the defense means that a status-quo state can often maintain a high degree of security with a level of arms lower than that of its expected adversary. Such a state demonstrates that it lacks the ability or desire to alter the status quo, at least at the present time. The strength of the defense also allows states to react slowly and with restraint when they fear that others are menacing them. So, although status-quo powers will to some extent be threatening to others, that extent will be limited. [...]

In the third world there may be no security dilemma, but there are security problems. Because states can procure defensive systems that do not threaten others, the dilemma need not operate. But because the offense has the advantage, aggression is possible, and perhaps easy. If the offense has enough of an advantage, even a status-quo state may take the initiative rather than risk being attacked and defeated. If the offense has less of an advantage, stability and cooperation are likely because the status-quo states will procure defensive forces. They need not react to others who are similarly armed, but can wait for the warning they would receive if others started to deploy offensive weapons. But each state will have to watch the others carefully, and there is room for false suspicions. The costliness of the defense and the allure of the offense can lead to unnecessary mistrust, hostility, and war, unless some of the variables discussed earlier are operating to restrain defection. [...]

The fourth world is doubly safe. The differentiation between offensive and defensive systems permits a way out of the security dilemma; the advantage of the defense disposes of the problems discussed in the previous paragraphs. There is no reason for a status-quo power to be tempted to procure offensive forces, and aggressors give notice of their intentions by the posture they adopt. Indeed, if the advantage of the defense is great enough, there are no security problems. The loss of the ultimate form of the power to alter the status quo would allow greater scope for the exercise of nonmilitary means and probably would tend to freeze the distribution of values. [...]

Notes

1   This kind of rank-ordering is not entirely an analyst's invention, as is shown by the following section of a British army memo of 1903 dealing with British and Russian railroad construction near the Persia-Afghanistan border:
      The conditions of the problem may [...] be briefly summarized as follows:
      a) If we make a railway to Seistan while Russia remains inactive, we gain a considerable defensive advantage at considerable financial cost;
      b) If Russia makes a railway to Seistan, while we remain inactive, she gains a considerable offensive advantage at considerable financial cost;
      c) If both we and Russia make railways to Seistan, the defensive and offensive advantages may be held to neutralize each other; in other words, we shall have spent a good deal of money and be no better off than we are at present. On the other hand, we shall be no worse off, whereas under alternative (b) we shall be much worse off. Consequently, the theoretical balance of advantage lies with the proposed railway extension from Quetta to Seistan.
      W. G. Nicholson, "Memorandum on Seistan and Other Points Raised in the Discussion on the Defence of India" (Committee of Imperial Defence, March 20, 1903). It should be noted that the possibility of neither side building railways was not mentioned, thus strongly biasing the analysis.
2   Quoted in Leonard Wainstein, "The Dreadnought Gap," in Robert Art and Kenneth Waltz, eds., *The Use of Force* (Boston: Little, Brown 1971), 155; Raymond Sontag, *European Diplomatic History, 1871–1932* (New York: Appleton-Century-Croits 1933), 147. The French had made a similar argument 50 years earlier; see James Phinncy Baxter III, *The Introduction of the Ironclad Warship* (Cambridge: Harvard University Press 1933), 149. For a more detailed discussion of the security dilemma, see Jervis, *Perception and Misperception in International Politics* (Princeton: Princeton University Press 1976), 62–76.
3   Experimental evidence for this proposition is summarized in James Tedeschi, Barry Schlenker, and Thomas Bonoma, *Conflict, Power, and Games* (Chicago: Aldine 1973), 135–41.
4   The results of Prisoner's Dilemma games played in the laboratory support this argument. See Anatol Rapoport and Albert Chammah, *Prisoner's Dilemma* (Ann Arbor: University of Michigan Press 1965), 33–50. Also see Robert Axelrod, *Conflict of Interest* (Chicago: Markham 1970), 60–70.

John J. Mearsheimer

THE FALSE PROMISE OF
INTERNATIONAL INSTITUTIONS

Source: 'The false promise of international institutions', *International Security*, vol. 19, no. 3, Winter 1994/95, pp. 5–49.

Liberal institutionalism

LIBERAL INSTITUTIONALISM does not directly address the question of whether institutions cause peace, but instead focuses on the less ambitious goal of explaining cooperation in cases where state interests are not fundamentally opposed.[1] Specifically, the theory looks at cases where states are having difficulty cooperating because they have "mixed" interests; in other words, each side has incentives both to cooperate and not to cooperate.[2] Each side can benefit from cooperation, however, which liberal institutionalists define as "goal-directed behavior that entails mutual policy adjustments so that all sides end up better off than they would otherwise be."[3] The theory is of little relevance in situations where states' interests are fundamentally conflictual and neither side thinks it has much to gain from cooperation. In these circumstances, states aim to gain advantage over each other. They think in terms of winning and losing, and this invariably leads to intense security competition, and sometimes war. But liberal institutionalism does not deal directly with these situations, and thus says little about how to resolve or even ameliorate them.

Therefore, the theory largely ignores security issues and concentrates instead on economic and, to a lesser extent, environmental issues.[4] In fact, the theory is built on the assumption that international politics can be divided into two realms – security and political economy – and that liberal institutionalism mainly applies to the latter, but not the former. [...] Moreover, the likelihood of cooperation is markedly different within these two realms: when economic relations are at stake, "cooperation can be sustained among several self-interested states," whereas the prospects for cooperation are "more impoverished[...]in security affairs."[5] Thus, the theory's proponents pay little attention to the security realm, where questions about war and peace are of central importance.

Nevertheless, there are good reasons to examine liberal institutionalism closely. Liberal institutionalists sometimes assert that institutions are an important cause of international stability. Moreover, one might argue that if the theory shows a strong causal connection between institutions and economic cooperation, it would be relatively easy to take the next step and link cooperation with peace.[6] Some proponents of the theory maintain that institutions contribute to international stability; this suggests that they believe it is easy to connect cooperation and stability.[7] I doubt this claim, mainly because proponents of the theory define cooperation so narrowly as to avoid military issues. [...]

CAUSAL LOGIC. Liberal institutionalists claim to accept realism's root assumptions while arguing that cooperation is nevertheless easier to achieve than realists recognize. [...]

According to liberal institutionalists, the principal obstacle to cooperation among states with mutual interests is the threat of cheating.[8] The famous "prisoners' dilemma," which is the analytical centerpiece of most of the liberal institutionalist literature, captures the essence of the problem that states must solve to achieve cooperation.[9] Each of two states can either cheat or cooperate with the other. Each side wants to maximize its own gain, but does not care about the size of the other side's gain; each side cares about the other side only so far as the other side's chosen strategy affects its own prospects for maximizing gain. The most attractive strategy for each state is to cheat and hope the other state pursues a cooperative strategy. [...]

The key to solving this dilemma is for each side to convince the other that they have a collective interest in making what appear to be short-term sacrifices (the gain that might result from successful cheating) for the sake of long-term benefits (the substantial payoff from mutual long-term cooperation). This means convincing states to accept the second-best outcome, which is mutual collaboration. The principal obstacle to reaching this cooperative outcome will be fear of getting suckered, should the other side cheat. This, in a nutshell, is the problem that institutions must solve.

To deal with this problem of "political market failure," institutions must deter cheaters and protect victims.[10] Three messages must be sent to potential cheaters: you will be caught, you will be punished immediately, and you will jeopardize future cooperative efforts. Potential victims, on the other hand, need early warning of cheating to avoid serious injury, and need the means to punish cheaters.

Liberal institutionalists do not aim to deal with cheaters and victims by changing fundamental norms of state behavior. Nor do they suggest transforming the anarchical nature of the international system. They accept the assumption that states operate in an anarchic environment and behave in a self-interested manner.[11] [...] Liberal institutionalists instead concentrate on showing how rules can work to counter the cheating problem, even while states seek to maximize their own welfare. They argue that institutions can change a state's calculations about how to maximize gains. Specifically, rules can get states to make the short-term sacrifices needed to resolve the prisoners' dilemma and thus to realize long-term gains. Institutions, in short, can produce cooperation.

Rules can ideally be employed to make four major changes in "the contractual environment."[12] First, rules can increase the number of transactions between particular states over time.[13] [...]

Second, rules can tie together interactions between states in different issue areas. [...]

Third, a structure of rules can increase the amount of *information* available to participants in cooperative agreements so that close monitoring is possible. [...]

Fourth, rules can reduce the *transaction costs* of individual agreements.[14] [...]

Liberal institutionalism is generally thought to be of limited utility in the security realm, because fear of cheating is considered a much greater obstacle to cooperation when military issues are at stake.[15] There is the constant threat that betrayal will result in a devastating military defeat. This threat of "swift, decisive defection" is simply not present when dealing with international economics. Given that "the costs of betrayal" are potentially much graver in the military than the economic sphere, states will be very reluctant to accept the "one step backward, two steps forward" logic which underpins the tit-for-tat strategy of conditional cooperation. One step backward in the security realm might mean destruction, in which case there will be no next step – backward or forward.[16]

FLAWS IN THE CAUSAL LOGIC. There is an important theoretical failing in the liberal institutionalist logic, even as it applies to economic issues. The theory is correct as far as it goes: cheating can be a serious barrier to cooperation. It ignores, however, the other major obstacle to cooperation: relative-gains concerns. As Joseph Grieco has shown, liberal institutionalists assume that states are not concerned about relative gains, but focus exclusively on absolute gains.[17] [...]

This oversight is revealed by the assumed order of preference in the prisoners' dilemma game: each state cares about how its opponent's strategy will affect its own (absolute) gains, but not about how much one side gains relative to the other. [...] Nevertheless, liberal institutionalists cannot ignore relative-gains considerations, because they assume that states are self-interested actors in an anarchic system, and they recognize that military power matters to states. A theory that explicitly accepts realism's core assumptions – and liberal institutionalism does that – must confront the issue of relative gains if it hopes to develop a sound explanation for why states cooperate.

One might expect liberal institutionalists to offer the counterargument that relative-gains logic applies only to the security realm, while absolute-gains logic applies to the economic realm. Given that they are mainly concerned with explaining economic and environmental cooperation, leaving relative-gains concerns out of the theory does not matter.

There are two problems with this argument. First, if cheating were the only significant obstacle to cooperation, liberal institutionalists could argue that their theory applies to the economic, but not the military realm. In fact, they do make that argument. However, once relative-gains considerations are factored into the equation, it becomes impossible to maintain the neat dividing line between economic and military issues, mainly because military might is significantly dependent on economic might. The relative size of a state's economy has profound consequences for its standing in the international balance of military power. Therefore, relative-gains concerns must be taken into account for security reasons when looking at the economic as well as military domain. The neat dividing line that liberal institutionalists employ to specify when their theory applies has little utility when one accepts that states worry about relative gains.[18]

Second, there are non-realist (i.e., non-security) logics that might explain why states worry about relative gains. Strategic trade theory, for example, provides a straightforward economic logic for why states should care about relative gains.[19] It argues that states should help their own firms gain comparative advantage over the firms of rival states, because that is the best way to insure national economic prosperity. There is also a psychological logic, which portrays individuals as caring about how well they do (or their state does) in a cooperative agreement, not for material reasons, but because it is human nature to compare one's progress with that of others.[20]

Another possible liberal institutionalist counterargument is that solving the cheating problem renders the relative-gains problem irrelevant. If states cannot cheat each other, they need not fear each other, and therefore, states would not have to worry about relative power. The problem with this argument, however, is that even if the cheating problem were solved, states would still have to worry about relative gains because gaps in gains can be translated into military advantage that can be used for coercion or aggression. And in the international system, states sometimes have conflicting interests that lead to aggression. [...]

I am not suggesting that relative-gains considerations make cooperation impossible; my point is simply that they can pose a serious impediment to cooperation and must therefore be taken into account when developing a theory of cooperation among states. [...]

CAN LIBERAL INSTITUTIONALISM BE REPAIRED? Liberal institutionalists must address two questions if they are to repair their theory. First, can institutions facilitate cooperation when states seriously care about relative gains, or do institutions only matter when states can ignore relative-gains considerations and focus instead on absolute gains? I find no evidence that liberal institutionalists believe that institutions facilitate cooperation when states care deeply about relative gains. They apparently concede that their theory only applies when relative-gains considerations matter little or hardly at all.[21] Thus the second question: when do states not worry about relative gains? The answer to this question would ultimately define the realm in which liberal institutionalism applies.

Liberal institutionalists have not addressed this important question in a systematic fashion, so any assessment of their efforts to repair the theory must be preliminary. What exists are a lengthy response by Keohane to Grieco's original work on relative gains, and two studies responding to Grieco's writings by Robert Powell and Duncan Snidal, which Keohane and other liberal institutionalists point to as exemplars of how to think about the relative-gains problem.[22]

Powell and Snidal offer different arguments about when relative-gains considerations are slight. Nevertheless, both are essentially realist arguments.[23] Neither study discusses how institutions might facilitate cooperation, and both explanations are built around familiar realist concepts.

At the root of Powell's argument is the well-known offense-defense balance made famous by Robert Jervis, George Quester, Jack Snyder, and Stephen Van Evera.[24] Powell maintains that relative-gains considerations matter little, and that states act in accordance with liberal institutionalism when the threat of aggressive war is low and "the use of force is no longer at issue."[25] That situation obtains when the cost of aggression is high, which is, in turn, a function of the "constraints imposed by the underlying technology of war."[26] In other words, when the prevailing military weaponry favors the offense, then the cost of war is low, and relative-gains considerations will be intense. Institutions can do little to facilitate cooperation in such circumstances. However, when defensive technology dominates, the cost of initiating aggression is high and the relative-gains problem is subdued, which allows institutions to cause cooperation.

Snidal maintains that relative-gains concerns might not matter much to states even if they face a serious threat of war. The root concept in his argument is the distribution of power in the international system.[27] Specifically, he maintains that in a multipolar system where more than a small number of states have roughly equal power, states will not worry much about relative gains. Increasing the number of states in the system decreases concern for relative gains. "The reason is that more actors enhance the possibilities of protecting oneself through forming coalitions; and, generally, the less well united one's potential enemies, the safer one is."[28] However, he concedes that "the relative gains hypothesis[...]has important consequences for two-actor situations and, where there are small numbers or important asymmetries among larger numbers, it may modify conclusions obtained from the absolute gains model."[29]

I draw three conclusions from this discussion of the liberal institutionalists' efforts to deal with the relative-gains problem. First, even if one accepts Powell and Snidal's arguments about when states largely ignore relative-gains concerns, those conditions are rather uncommon in the real world. Powell would look for a world where defensive military technologies dominate. However, it is very difficult to distinguish between offensive and defensive weapons, and Powell provides no help on this point.[30] Nuclear weapons are an exception; they are defensive weapons in situations of mutual assured destruction.[31] Still, the presence of massive numbers of nuclear weapons in the arsenals of the superpowers during the Cold War did not stop them from engaging in an intense security competition where relative-gains considerations mattered greatly. Very importantly, Powell provides no historical examples to illustrate his central argument. Snidal would look for a multipolar world with large numbers of roughly equal-sized great powers. However, historically we find multipolar systems with small numbers of great powers – usually five or six – and very often significant power asymmetries within them. Snidal offers no historical examples of multipolar systems in which the great powers largely ignored relative-gains considerations.[32]

Second, liberal institutionalism itself has little new to say about when states worry about relative gains. Proponents of the theory have instead chosen to rely on two realist explanations to answer that question: the offense-defense balance and the distribution of power in the system. Thus, liberal institutionalism can hardly be called a theoretical alternative to realism, but instead should be seen as subordinate to it.[33]

Third, even in circumstances where realist logic about relative gains does not apply, non-military logics like strategic trade theory might cause states to think in terms of relative gains. Liberal institutionalist theory should directly confront those logics. [...]

In summary, liberal institutionalism does not provide a sound basis for understanding international relations and promoting stability in the post-Cold War world. It makes modest claims about the impact of institutions, and steers clear of war and peace issues, focusing instead on the less ambitious task of explaining economic cooperation. Furthermore, the theory's causal logic is flawed, as proponents of the theory now admit. Having overlooked the relative-gains problem, they are now attempting to repair the theory, but their initial efforts are not promising. [...]

Notes

1 Among the key liberal institutionalist works are: Robert Axelrod and Robert O. Keohane, "Achieving Cooperation under Anarchy: Strategies and Institutions," *World Politics*, Vol. 38, No. 1 (October 1985), pp. 226–54; Robert O. Keohane, *After Hegemony: Cooperation and Discord in the World Political Economy* (Princeton, N.J.: Princeton University Press, 1984); Robert O. Keohane, "International Institutions: Two Approaches," *International Studies Quarterly*, Vol. 32, No. 4 (December 1988), pp. 379–96; Robert O. Keohane, *International Institutions and State Power: Essays in International Relations Theory* (Boulder, Colo.: Westview Press, 1989), chap. 1; Charles Lipson, "International Cooperation in Economic and Security Affairs," *World Politics*, Vol. 37, No. 1 (October 1984), pp. 1–23; Lisa L. Martin, "Institutions and Cooperation: Sanctions During the Falkland Islands Conflict," *International Security*, Vol. 16, No. 4 (Spring 1992), pp. 143–78; Lisa L. Martin, *Coercive Cooperation: Explaining Multilateral Economic Sanctions* (Princeton, N.J.: Princeton University Press, 1992); Kenneth A. Oye, "Explaining Cooperation Under Anarchy: Hypotheses and Strategies," *World Politics*, Vol. 38, No. 1 (October 1985), pp. 1–24; and Arthur A. Stein, *Why Nations Cooperate: Circumstance and Choice in International Relations* (Ithaca, N.Y.: Cornell University Press, 1990).

2 Stein, *Why Nations Cooperate*, Chap. 2. Also see Keohane, *After Hegemony*, pp. 6–7, 12–13, 67–69.

3 Helen Milner, "International Theories of Cooperation among Nations: Strengths and Weaknesses," *World Politics*, Vol. 44, No. 3 (April 1992), p. 468.

4 For examples of the theory at work in the environmental realm, see Peter M. Haas, Robert O. Keohane, and Marc A. Levy, eds., *Institutions for the Earth: Sources of Effective International Environmental Protection* (Cambridge, Mass.: MIT Press, 1993), especially chaps. 1 and 9. Some of the most important work on institutions and the environment has been done by Oran Young. See, for example, Oran R. Young, *International Cooperation: Building Regimes for Natural Resources and the Environment* (Ithaca, N.Y.: Cornell University Press, 1989). The rest of my discussion concentrates on economic, not environmental issues, for conciseness, and also because the key theoretical works in the liberal institutionalist literature focus on economic rather than environmental matters.

5 Lipson, "International Cooperation," p. 18.

6 I have suggested a possible line of argument in John J. Mearsheimer, "Back to the Future: Instability in Europe After the Cold War," *International Security*, Vol. 15, No. 1 (Summer 1990), pp. 42–44. Also, Charles Glaser makes the connection between cooperation and peace in "Realists as Optimists: Cooperation as Self-Help," *International Security*, Vol. 19, No. 3 (Winter 1994/95), pp. 50–90.

7 Liberal institutionalists assume that cooperation is a positive goal, although they recognize it has a downside as well. See Keohane, *After Hegemony*, pp. 10–11, 247–57; and Keohane, "International Institutions: Two Approaches," p. 393. The virtues and vices of cooperation are not explored in any detail in the liberal institutionalist literature.

8   Cheating is basically a "breach of promise." Oye, "Explaining Cooperation Under Anarchy," p. 1. It usually implies unobserved non-compliance, although there can be observed cheating as well. Defection is a synonym for cheating in the institutionalist literature.

9   The centrality of the prisoners' dilemma and cheating to the liberal institutionalist literature is clearly reflected in virtually all the works cited in footnote 36. As Helen Milner notes in her review essay on this literature: "The focus is primarily on the role of regimes [institutions] in solving the defection [cheating] problem." Milner, "International Theories of Cooperation," p. 475.

10   The phrase is from Keohane, *After Hegemony*, p. 85.

11   Kenneth Oye, for example, writes in the introduction to an issue of *World Politics* containing a number of liberal institutionalist essays: "Our focus is on non-altruistic cooperation among states dwelling in international anarchy." Oye, "Explaining Cooperation Under Anarchy," p. 2. Also see Keohane, "International Institutions: Two Approaches," pp. 380–81; and Keohane, *International Institutions and State Power*, p. 3.

12   Haas, Keohane, and Levy, *Institutions for the Earth*, p. 11. For general discussions of how rules work, which inform my subsequent discussion of the matter, see Keohane, *After Hegemony*, chaps. 5–6; Martin, "Institutions and Cooperation," pp. 143–78; and Milner, "International Theories of Cooperation," pp. 474–78.

13   See Axelrod and Keohane, "Achieving Cooperation Under Anarchy," pp. 248–50; Lipson, "International Cooperation," pp. 4–18.

14   See Keohane, *After Hegemony*, pp. 89–92.

15   This point is clearly articulated in Lipson, "International Cooperation," especially pp. 12–18. The subsequent quotations in this paragraph are from ibid. Also see Axelrod and Keohane, "Achieving Cooperation Under Anarchy," pp. 232–33.

16   See Roger B. Parks, "What if 'Fools Die'? A Comment on Axelrod," Letter to *American Political Science Review*, Vol. 79, No. 4 (December 1985), pp. 1173–74.

17   See Joseph M. Grieco, "Anarchy and the Limits of Cooperation: A Realist Critique of the Newest Liberal Institutionalism," *International Organization*, Vol. 42, No. 3 (Summer 1988). Other works by Grieco bearing on the subject include: Joseph M. Grieco, "Realist Theory and the Problem of International Cooperation: Analysis with an Amended Prisoner's Dilemma Model," *The Journal of Politics*, Vol. 50, No. 3 (August 1988), pp. 600–624; Grieco, *Cooperation among Nations: Europe, America, and Non-Tariff Barriers to Trade* (Ithaca, N.Y.: Cornell University Press, 1990); and Grieco, "Understanding the Problem of International Cooperation: The Limits of Neoliberal Institutionalism and the Future of Realist Theory," in Baldwin, *Neorealism and Neoliberalism*, pp. 301–38. The telling effect of Grieco's criticism is reflected in ibid., which is essentially organized around the relative gains vs. absolute gains debate, an issue given little attention before Grieco raised it in his widely cited 1988 article. The matter was briefly discussed by two other scholars before Grieco. See Joanne Gowa, "Anarchy, Egoism, and Third Images: *The Evolution of Cooperation* and International Relations," *International Organization*, Vol. 40, No. 1 (Winter 1986), pp. 172–79; and Oran R. Young, "International Regimes: Toward a New Theory of Institutions," *World Politics*, Vol. 39, No. 1 (October 1986), pp. 118–19.

18   My thinking on this matter has been markedly influenced by Sean Lynn-Jones, in his June 19, 1994, correspondence with me.

19   For a short discussion of strategic trade theory, see Robert Gilpin, *The Political Economy of International Relations* (Princeton, N.J.: Princeton University Press, 1987), pp. 215–21. The most commonly cited reference on the subject is

Paul R. Krugman, ed., *Strategic Trade Policy and the New International Economics* (Cambridge, Mass.: MIT Press, 1986).

20   See Robert Axelrod, *The Evolution of Cooperation* (New York: Basic Books, 1984), pp. 110–13.

21   For example, Keohane wrote after becoming aware of Grieco's argument about relative gains: "Under specified conditions – where mutual interests are low and relative gains are therefore particularly important to states – neoliberal theory expects neorealism to explain elements of state behavior." Keohane, *International Institutions and State Power*, pp. 15–16.

22   Keohane, "Institutional Theory and the Realist Challenge," pp. 269–300; Robert Powell, "Absolute and Relative Gains in International Relations Theory," *American Political Science Review*, Vol. 85, No. 4 (December 1991), pp. 1303–20; and Duncan Snidal, "Relative Gains and the Pattern of International Cooperation," *American Political Science Review*, Vol. 85, No. 3 (September 1991), pp. 701–26. Also see Powell, "Anarchy in International Relations Theory: The Neorealist-Neoliberal Debate," *International Organization*, Vol. 48, No. 2 (Spring 1994), pp. 313–44; Snidal, "International Cooperation among Relative Gains Maximizers," *International Studies Quarterly*, Vol. 35, No. 4 (December 1991), pp. 387–402; and Powell and Snidal's contributions to "The Relative-Gains Problem for International Cooperation," pp. 735–42.

23   On this point, see Sean Lynn-Jones, "Comments on Grieco, 'Realist Theory and the Relative Gains Problem for International Cooperation: Developments in the Debate and the Prospects for Future Research'," unpublished memorandum, December 10, 1992.

24   Robert Jervis, "Cooperation under the Security Dilemma," *World Politics*, Vol. 30, No. 2 (January 1978), pp. 167–214; George H. Quester, *Offense and Defense in the International System* (New York: John Wiley, 1977); Jack Snyder, *The Ideology of the Offensive: Military Decision Making and the Disasters of 1914* (Ithaca, N.Y.: Cornell University Press, 1984); and Stephen Van Evera, "The Cult of the Offensive and the Origins of the First World War," *International Security*, Vol. 9, No. 1 (Summer 1984), pp. 58–107.

25   Powell, "Absolute and Relative Gains," p. 1314; also see p. 1311.

26   Ibid., p. 1312. Powell does not use the term "offense-defense" balance in his article.

27   Although Snidal's basic arguments about distribution of power fit squarely in the realist tradition (in fact, Grieco made them in abbreviated form in "Anarchy and the Limits of Cooperation," p. 506), the formal model he develops rests on the non-realist assumption that "gains from cooperation are proportional to the size of the involved states and are shared equally between them." Snidal, "Relative Gains," p. 715. This assumption essentially eliminates the possibility of gaps in gains and thus erases the relative-gains problem. For discussion of this matter, see Grieco's contribution to "The Relative-Gains Problem for International Cooperation," pp. 729–33.

28   Snidal, "Relative Gains," p. 716.

29   Ibid., p. 702.

30   There is general agreement that defensive weapons make conquest difficult and costly, while offensive weapons make conquest cheap and easy. However, there is no recognized set of criteria for assigning specific weapons either offensive or defensive status. See Marion Boggs, *Attempts to Define and Limit "Aggressive" Armament*

in Diplomacy and Strategy (Columbia: University of Missouri, 1941); Jack Levy, "The Offensive/Defensive Balance of Military Technology: A Theoretical and Historical Analysis," *International Studies Quarterly*, Vol. 28, No. 2 (June 1984), pp. 219–38; John J. Mearsheimer, *Conventional Deterrence* (Ithaca, N.Y.: Cornell University Press, 1983), pp. 25–27; and Jonathan Shimshoni, "Technology, Military Advantage, and World War I: A Case for Military Entrepreneurship," *International Security*, Vol. 15, No. 3 (Winter 1990/1991), pp. 187–215.

31   See Shai Feldman, *Israeli Nuclear Deterrence: A Strategy for the 1980s* (New York: Columbia University Press, 1982), pp. 45–49; Charles L. Glaser, *Analyzing Strategic Nuclear Policy* (Princeton, N.J.: Princeton University Press, 1990); Jervis, "Cooperation under the Security Dilemma"; and Stephen Van Evera, *Causes of War*, Vol. II: *National Misperception and the Origins of War*, forthcoming), chap. 13.

32   Keohane actually discusses the prospects for stability in post-Cold War Europe in his response to Grieco; see Keohane, "Institutional Theory and the Realist Challenge," pp. 284–91. Surprisingly, his optimistic assessment pays no attention to either Powell or Snidal's arguments, although earlier in that response, he relies on their arguments to "delimit the scope of both realist and institutionalist arguments." See ibid., p. 276.

33   Liberal institutionalists have not always been clear about the relationship between their theory and realism. For example, Keohane makes the modest claim in *After Hegemony* (p. 14) that his theory is a "modification of Realism. Realist theories [...] need to be supplemented, though not replaced." He made a somewhat bolder claim a few years later, writing that, "despite [certain] affinities with neorealism, neoliberal institutionalism should be regarded as a distinct school of thought." Keohane, *International Institutions and State Power*, p. 8. In that same piece, however, he makes the very bold argument that "we must understand that neoliberal institutionalism is not simply an alternative to neorealism, but, in fact, claims to subsume it." Ibid., p. 15.

Norman Angell

ECONOMICS AND THE MORAL CASE FOR WAR

Source: *The Great Illusion*, *1933* (London: William Heinemann, 1933), pp. 82–98, 325–51.

[...] THE PEACE ADVOCATE pleads for "altruism" in international relationships, and in so doing admits that successful war may be to the interest, though the immoral interest, of the victorious party. That is why the "inhumanity" of war bulks so largely in his propaganda, and why he dwells so much upon its horrors and cruelties.

It thus results that the workaday world and those engaged in the rough and tumble of practical politics have come to look upon the peace ideal as a counsel of perfection which may one day be attained when human nature, as the common phrase is, has been improved out of existence, but not as long as human nature remains what it is. While it remains possible to seize a tangible advantage by a man's strong right arm, the advantage, it is felt, will be seized, and woe betide the man who cannot defend himself.

Nor is this philosophy of force either as brutal, or immoral as its common statement would make it appear. We know that in the world as it exists today, in spheres other than those of international rivalry, the race is to the strong, and the weak get scant consideration. Industrialism and commercialism are as full of cruelties as war itself – cruelties, indeed, that are longer drawn out, more refined, if less apparent, and, it may be, appealing less to the ordinary imagination than those of war. With whatever reticence we may put the philosophy into words, we all feel that conflict of interests in this world is inevitable, and that what is an incident of our daily lives should not be shirked as a condition of those occasional titanic conflicts which mould history.

The virile man doubts whether he ought to be moved by the plea of the "inhumanity" of war. The masculine mind accepts suffering, death itself, as a risk which we are all prepared to run even in the most unheroic forms of money-making. None of us refuses to use the railway train because of the occasional smash, to travel because of the occasional shipwreck. Indeed, peaceful industry demands in the long run a heavier toll even in life and blood than does war. It suffices to note the physique of the thousands – women as well as men – who pour through the factory gates of the north; the health of the children left at home, the kind of life that industry involves for millions, to say nothing of the casualty statistics in railroading, fishing, mining and seamanship, to be persuaded of that fact. Even in the "conscious" brutality which we usually deem special to war, such peaceful industries as fishing and shipping reveal a dreadful plenty.* Our peaceful administration of the tropics not only takes its heavy toll in the health and lives of good men, but much of it involves a moral deterioration of human character as great – as does so much of our "peaceful" industry and trade.

Beside these peace sacrifices the "price of war" does not seem unduly high, and many may well feel that the trustees of a nation's interests ought not to shrink from paying that price should the efficient protection of those interests demand it. If the ordinary man is prepared, as we know he is, to risk his life in a dozen dangerous trades and professions for no object higher than that of improving his position or increasing his income, why should the statesman shrink from such sacrifices as the average war demands, if thereby the great interests which have been confided to him can be advanced? If it be true, as even the pacifist admits that it may be true, that the vital interests of a nation can be advanced by warfare; if, in other words, warfare can play some large part in the protection of the nation's heritage, the promotion of its welfare, then the rulers of a courageous people are justified in disregarding the suffering and the sacrifice that it may involve. And they will continue to receive the support of "the common man" so long as he feels that military predominance gives his nation the efficient protection of rights, its due share in the world's wealth and economic opportunity, enlarged commercial opportunities, wider markets, protection against the aggression of commercial rivals, all translatable into welfare and prosperity, not at all necessarily for himself personally, but for his people – those who should come first, by whom he feels he should stand as a matter of plain and simple loyalty. He faces the risk of war in the same spirit as that in which a sailor or a fisherman faces the risk of drowning, or a miner that of the choke-damp, or a doctor that of a fatal disease, because he would rather take the supreme risk than accept for himself and his dependants a lower situation, a narrower and meaner existence, with complete safety. He also asks whether the lower path is altogether free from risks. He knows that in so very many circumstances the bolder way is the safer way.

When the pacifist in these circumstances falls back upon the moral plea as opposed to economic considerations, he does not seem to realize that he has not met the militarists' – which is here the common man's – moral case, a case for war which is undoubtedly valid if one accepts the economic assumptions that are usually common alike to the pacifist and the militarist.

If it be true that successful war secures for a people enlarged economic opportunities, opportunities which may be necessary for life and welfare, it may be our only available means of preventing the starvation of our children, of making due provision for them. This is an economic task, but moral motives may well underlie it, and moral rights be involved. We can only meet that moral case by disproving the economic one. Yet so often does the pacifist regard it as sordid to discuss economic issues at all. [...]

Now you cannot answer that case merely by invoking righteousness, the higher claims of morals over economic interest, for the moral question itself arises out of the question of economic rights.

The economic fact is the test of the ethical claim: if it really be true that we must withhold sources of food from others because otherwise our own people would starve, there is ethical justification for such use of our power. But if such is not the fact, the whole moral issue is changed, and with it, to the degree to which it is mutually realised, the social outlook and attitude. Furthermore, as voters we are trustees, trustees of our nation, and as such it is our duty to do the best we can for its prosperity. We have here, therefore, a moral obligation to understand economic issues.

So much of pacifist advocacy has never done the militarist the elementary justice of assuming that, however mistaken, the soldier is sincere when he says that he fights for right as he sees it; that he has no other recourse than to fight or to acquiesce in wrong. To retort in that circumstance that all war is wrong is merely to beg the question: the rightness or wrongness is the very thing in dispute. And when the soldier, who honestly believes that he is giving his life for a righteous cause, is met by the pacifist appeal to "righteousness," the plea is apt to excite a not unnatural exasperation.

Not long since, an English Divine said that the root cause of all war was the selfishness and avarice of man. One thought of the spectacle which almost any war affords us, of tens of thousands of youngsters going to their deaths as to a feast, of the mothers who bid them good-bye with smiling faces and breaking hearts; of the fathers who are so proud of them; of the millions who starve, and skimp, and suffer through the years without murmur. Selfishness? Avarice?

War does not arise because consciously wicked men take a course which they know to be wrong, but because good men on both sides pursue a course which they believe to be right, stand, as Lincoln stood when he made war, for the right as they see it. It is a case not of conscious and admitted wrong challenging unquestioned and admitted right; but of misunderstanding of right.

It is not a question of moral intent, as some pacifist advocacy would so persistently imply, but of intellectual error in the interpretation of Right, and the problem is to find at what point and in what manner the mistake arises. The investigation of that misunderstanding is a task rather of intellectual clarification than of moral exhortation; and it must include examination of economic situations, since questions of right and morals arise out of economic conflict, or assumed economic conflict.

This […] is not, therefore, an attempt to set up the economic motive over against the moral; it is an attempt to analyse a moral situation which arises out of alleged economic needs; to examine the economic reasons commonly advanced as morally justifying war.

To criticize such examination as preferring "an appeal to narrow self-interest" to one based on righteousness and morals, involves one of those confusions of thought which frustrate and stultify so much peace advocacy, and perpetuate the misunderstandings which lie at the root of war.

This of course does not imply that the economic motive should dominate life, but rather that it will unless the economic problem is solved: a hungry people is a people thinking first and last of bread. To turn their minds to other things they must be fed. […]

To refuse to face this problem because "economics" are sordid, is to refuse to face the needs of human life, and the forces that shape it. Such an attitude, while professing moral elevation, involves a denial of the right of others to live. Its worst defect, perhaps, is that its heroics are fatal to intellectual rectitude, to truth. No society built upon such foundations can stand.

It is because this fact of the relationship of economics and morals has not been adequately faced that so much peace propaganda has failed; that the public opinion of the countries of Europe, far from restraining the tendency of governments to increase armaments, is pushing them into still greater expenditure. Behind that impulse, and justifying it, are certain universally accepted assumptions, such as that national power means national wealth, national advantage; that expanding territory means increased opportunity for industry; that the strong nation can guarantee opportunities for its citizens that the weak nation cannot. [...]

[...] We have seen that no material advantage is to be achieved by a successful attack upon us, any more than by ours upon someone else; that an enemy, successful in war, could take neither our wealth, our gold, our trade, nor our colonies (since we don't own them); his war would certainly prove economically futile. Is the conclusion, therefore, that we need no defence; that we can abolish our armaments and invite the foreigner to do his worst?

Always have I insisted that this is not the conclusion; that the futility of war will never of itself stop war; that only when men realize the futility will it deter them. They do not at present so realize that futility, or this [...] would never have been written. Policy is determined, not by the facts, but what men believe to be the facts, and that belief may be woefully mistaken. [...]

In this matter it seems fatally easy to secure either one of two kinds of action: that of the "practical man" who limits his energies to securing a policy which will perfect the machinery of war, and disregard anything else; or that of the pacifist, who, persuaded of the brutality or immorality of war, just leaves it at that, implying that national defence is no concern of his. What is needed is the type of activity which will include both halves of the problem; provision for education, for a political reformation in this matter, *as well as* such means of defence as will meantime counterbalance the existing impulse to aggression. To concentrate on either half to the exclusion of the other half is to render the whole problem insoluble. [...]

The essence of truth is degree. This book does not argue that there is not, and could never be, such a thing as a conflict of national interests. It is not necessary to prove such absolutes in order to establish the case which I am trying to establish. But if it be true, broadly, that a nation cannot capture wealth by military means – that wealth in the modern world is of such a nature that the very fact of military seizure causes the thing we want to disappear; if, far from it being true that we *must* fight or starve, it is very much nearer to the truth to say that we shall starve unless we stop fighting; and that only by co-operation can we solve our economic problems, then to prove this is to clear the road to co-operation, to do the thing which must be done if the *will* to co-operate is to be set in motion.

For while it may not be true that, where there is a will, there is a way, it is certainly true that, where there is no will, there is no way; and there can be no will to co-operation so long as each party believes that partnership means dividing limited spoils of which he could secure the whole if only he can "conquer" that other party.

Now, though it may be true that, where you are dependent upon your partner (where, say, two fishermen are working together a fishing smack which would certainly be wrecked if one tried to work it alone), you cannot profitably destroy him, cannot seize his share of the catch without sacrificing your own – even so, it does not mean that you are ready to forgo all means of protecting your rights under the terms of the partnership; does not mean surrendering all measures to ensure that you do not have more than your share of the work and less than your share of the profits.

Thus, though we may decide that fighting each other in order to seize things which cannot be seized is a silly business, and that as civilized men we must learn to co-operate, co-operation needs organizing, perhaps policing.

Collective power, expressed through police, may be necessary to give men – or nations – equality, equality of right. Circumstances give a person or a nation a position of power. There arises a difference – it may well be an honest difference – of view as to which has the rights of the matter. The stronger – fortified by his sense of right – says to the other: "That's my view. I believe I'm right: I intend to carry my view into effect, and, as you are weaker, you will just have to accept it." There is no equality of right here. The material or economic question, as we have seen, soon becomes a question of right. And, by some curious quirk of thought this situation is supposed to justify competition of arms, the armed anarchy of the nations. But that does not ensure right or justice; it imposes injustice; compels the weaker to accept the view of the stronger, however outrageous that view may be.

But if anarchy, the competition of arms does not ensure justice, neither does non-resistance: the unresisted domination of the stronger. Power must act impartially for all, and it can only do that if it is placed behind a law or code that is applied equally to all. Even when civilized individuals, living within the nation, accept completely the principle of social cooperation and do not base their conduct on the assumption that in order to live someone else has to go under – even so, we know that life can only go on by means of established rules and codes, sometimes of great complexity, covering things from motor traffic to marriage laws, banking practice and inheritance of property. Each individual must know that such rights as he possesses will be assured to him other than by his own strength, otherwise he will be his own defender of his own rights and try to be stronger than his neighbour; and that neighbour will claim the same right to be stronger, and you will then get the process of everybody trying to be stronger than everybody else, anarchy and chaos.

That is why I do not believe that the problem of defence can be simply ignored; nor that we can persuade men to accept sheer non-resistance as its solution. The first stage in getting rid of our instruments of coercion, or reducing them to vanishing point, is, as indicated in preceding pages, to transfer them from rival litigants to the law, to the community, to make of our armies and navies the common police of civilization, standing behind a commonly agreed rule. But, before that can be done, there must be created a sense of community, a sense of our interests being common interests, not inherently, "biologically," in conflict. It is futile to lament the fact that there is no police to restrain our rival if we ourselves refuse to co-operate in the creation of a police. Before the police can exist, there must be a community; and before the community can exist, there must be a sense of common interest, and before that can exist, we must shed the false ideas which are incompatible with that sense. To that end finally – the transformation of men's ideas which determine their acts – do we inevitably come.

However we may start, with whatever plan, however elaborated or varied, the end is always the same – the progress of man in this matter depends upon the degree to which his ideas are socially workable. Again we have arrived at the region of platitude. But also again it is one of those platitudes which most people deny. [...]

* * *

We do not believe it impossible to change or reform men's ideas; such a plea would doom us all to silence, and would kill social and political literature. "Public opinion" is not external to men; it is made by men; by what they hear and read, and have suggested to them by their daily tasks, and talk and contact. [...]

If little apparently has been done in the modification of ideas in this matter, it is because little relatively has been attempted. Millions of us are prepared to throw ourselves with energy into that part of national defence which, after all, is a make-shift, into agitation for the building of dreadnoughts and the raising of armies, the things in fact which can be seen. But barely dozens will throw themselves with equal ardour into that other department of national defence, the only department which will really guarantee security, though by means which are invisible – the clarification of ideas. [...]

Admitting his premises – and these premises are the universally accepted axioms of international politics the world over – who shall say that he is wrong?

Note

*   The Matin recently (1908) made a series of revelations, in which it was shown that the master of a French cod-fishing vessel had, for some trivial insubordinations, nearly disembowelled his cabin-boy, put salt into the intestines, and then thrown the quivering body into the hold with the cod-fish. So inured were the crew to brutality that they did not effectively protest, and the incident was only brought to light months later by wine-shop chatter. The Matin quotes this as the sort of brutality that marks the Newfoundland cod-fishing industry in French ships. Again, the German Socialist papers have recently been dealing with what they term "The Casualties of the Industrial Battlefield," showing that the losses from industrial accidents since 1871 – the loss of life during peace, that is – have been enormously greater than the losses due to the Franco-Prussian War.

Robert Keohane

NEOLIBERAL INSTITUTIONALISM

Source: *International Institution and State Power* (Boulder, Colorado: Westview Press, 1989), pp. 1–20.

Neoliberal institutionalism: a perspective on world politics

[...] TO UNDERSTAND WORLD politics, we must keep in mind both decentralization and institutionalization. It is not just that international politics is "flecked with particles of government," as Waltz (1979:114) acknowledges; more fundamentally, it is *institutionalized*. That is, much behavior is recognized by participants as reflecting established rules, norms, and conventions, and its meaning is interpreted in light of these understandings. Such matters as diplomatic recognition, extraterritoriality, and the construction of agendas for multilateral organizations are all governed by formal or informal understandings [...].

Thinking about international institutions

The principal thesis [...] is that variations in the institutionalization of world politics exert significant impacts on the behavior of governments. In particular, patterns of cooperation and discord can be understood only in the context of the institutions that help define the meaning and importance of state action. This perspective on international relations, which I call "neoliberal institutionalism," does not assert that states are always highly constrained by international institutions. Nor does it claim that states ignore the effects of their actions on the wealth or power of other states.[1] What I do argue is that state actions depend to a considerable degree on prevailing institutional arrangements, which affect

- the flow of information and opportunities to negotiate;
- the ability of governments to monitor others' compliance and to implement their own commitments – hence their ability to make credible commitments in the first place; and
- prevailing expectations about the solidity of international agreements.

Neoliberal institutionalists do not assert that international agreements are easy to make or to keep: indeed, we assume the contrary. What we do claim is that the ability of states to communicate and cooperate depends on human-constructed institutions, which vary historically and across issues, in nature (with respect to the policies they incorporate) and in strength (in terms of the degree to which their rules are clearly specified and routinely obeyed) (Aggarwal, 1985:31). States are at the center of our interpretation of world politics, as they are for realists; but formal and informal rules play a much larger role in the neoliberal than in the realist account.

Neoliberal institutionalism is not a single logically connected deductive theory, any more than is liberalism or neorealism: each is a school of thought that provides a perspective on world politics. Each perspective incorporates a set of distinctive questions and assumptions about the basic units and forces in world politics. Neoliberal institutionalism asks questions about the impact of institutions on state action and about the causes of institutional change; it assumes that states are key actors and examines both the material forces of world politics and the subjective self-understandings of human beings.[2]

The neoliberal institutionalist perspective [...] is relevant to an international system only if two key conditions pertain. First, the actors must have some mutual interests; that is, they must potentially gain from their cooperation. In the absence of mutual interests, the neoliberal perspective on international cooperation would be as irrelevant as a neoclassical theory of international trade in a world without potential gains from trade. The second condition for the relevance of an institutional approach is that variations in the degree of institutionalization exert substantial effects on state behavior. If the institutions of world politics were fixed, once and for all, it would be pointless to emphasize institutional variations to account for variations in actor behavior. There is, however, ample evidence to conclude both that states have mutual interests and that institutionalization is a variable rather than a constant in world politics. Given these conditions, cooperation is possible but depends in part on institutional arrangements. A successful theory of cooperation must therefore take into account the effects of institutions. [...]

Organizations, rules, and conventions

[...] I define institutions as "persistent and connected sets of rules (formal and informal) that prescribe behavioral roles, constrain activity, and shape expectations." We can think of international institutions, thus defined, as assuming one of three forms:

1.   *Formal intergovernmental or cross-national nongovernmental organizations.* [...]
2.   *International regimes.* [...]
3.   *Conventions.* [...]

* * *

The significance of institutions

International institutions are important for states' actions in part because they affect the incentives facing states, even if those states' fundamental interests are defined autonomously. International institutions make it possible for states to take actions that would otherwise be inconceivable [...]. They also affect the costs associated with alternatives that might have existed independently [...]. Evasion is often possible, [...] but institutions do affect behavior, even if they do not always attain the desired objective.

[...] Institutions may also affect the understandings that leaders of states have of the roles they should play and their assumptions about others' motivations and perceived self-interests. That is, international institutions have constitutive as well as regulative aspects: they help define how interests are defined and how actions are interpreted.[3] Meanings are communicated by general conventions such those reflecting the principle of reciprocity and by more specific conventions, such as those that indicate what is meant in a diplomatic communiqué by a "full and frank exchange of views." Meanings are also embedded in the rules of international regimes, such as those of the General Agreement on Tariffs and Trade (GATT), which specify and implement the principle of reciprocity[4] [...].

[...] In modern international relations, the pressures from domestic interests, and those generated by the competitiveness of the state system, exert much stronger effects on state policy than do international institutions, even broadly defined. International "social structures" are manifestly weaker than those of small homogeneous communities or even of modern national societies. Thus, although I accept the "structurationist" advice to be alert to the reciprocal interaction between state and international institutions, I do not wish to be interpreted as accepting the view that the causal impact of international institutions on state policy is as strong as that of states on international institutions.

There is no strict relationship between the degree of institutionalization of an institution and its importance to world politics. In addition to asking questions about institutionalization, we need to inquire about effectiveness, which is not necessarily correlated with institutionalization. Highly institutionalized arrangements can become ossified, encapsulated, or irrelevant. [...] Likewise, practices that are not highly institutionalized may be of supreme importance, insofar as they provide the basis for interpretation of action throughout world politics. Sovereign statehood was one such practice even before its rules had been codified. Whether increasing institutionalization leads to greater effectiveness should therefore not be assumed; the issue needs to be addressed with the usual combination of theory (under what conditions does institutionalization increase effectiveness?) and empirical research. [...]

* * *

Neoliberal institutionalism and neorealism

Contemporary neorealist international political theory, as elegantly outlined in Kenneth Waltz's work, has enhanced our understanding of world politics by clarifying the concept of structure, and by using this concept parsimoniously to account for certain prominent patterns of international political behavior, such as the formation of balances of power. [...]

Neoliberal institutionalism [...] shares some important intellectual commitments with neorealism. Like neorealists, neoliberal institutionalists seek to explain behavioral regularities by examining the nature of the decentralized international system. Neither neorealists nor neoliberal institutionalists are content with interpreting texts: both sets of theorists believe that there is an international political reality that can be partially understood, even if it will always remain to some extent veiled. Both also believe in trying to test theories, while recognizing that epistemology is also problematical: neither perspective is committed to the naive notion that reality can be objectively known.

Another reason for associating neoliberal institutionalism with neorealism is that both tendencies regard the international system as decentralized and take state power seriously. [...]

Finally, neoliberal institutionalists agree with neorealists that by understanding the structure of an international system, as defined by neorealists, we come to know "a small number of big and important things" (Waltz, 1986:329). As Waltz notes: "to the extent that dynamics of a system limit the freedom of its units, their behavior and the outcomes of their behavior become predictable" (1979:72). This is not to say that they become *perfectly* predictable: "Systems theories explain why different units behave similarly and, despite their variations, produce outcomes that fall within expected ranges. Conversely, theories at the unit level tell us why different units behave differently despite their similar placement in a system" (Waltz, 1979:72). Since no systems theory can be expected to account for the behavior of the units, we also have to look at policies and the exercise of state power [...].

Yet despite these affinities with neorealism, neoliberal institutionalism should be regarded as a distinct school of thought (Keohane, 1986:25–26, fn. 7). Although neoliberal institutionalists share the neorealists' objective of explaining state behavior insofar as possible through an understanding of the nature of the international system, we find the neorealist conception of structure too narrow and confining. Neorealism can account only for changes that result from shifts in relative state capabilities. [...] Unless the positions of units change relative to one another, the neorealist cannot explain changes in their behavior. Yet, [...] I believe that conventions in world politics are as fundamental as the distribution of capabilities among states: indeed, state action in the sense used by neorealists depends on the acceptance of practices such as sovereign statehood [...]. Thus I accept and generalize John Ruggie's argument that Waltz's conception of structure is unduly truncated, as well as static (Ruggie, 1983). Deeply embedded expectations are as fundamental to world politics as are the power resources of the units.

An implicit version of this appreciation of the role of expectations and conventions in world politics underlay the notion of "complex interdependence" [which] [...] key characteristic [...] is the well-founded expectation of the inefficacy of the use or threat of force among states – an expectation that helps create support for conventions or regimes delegitimating threats of force. [...]

Complex interdependence exemplifies the role of expectations and conventions in world politics – and therefore of institutionalization as defined above. My argument is that neorealism is underspecified because it fails to theorize about variations in the institutional characteristics of world politics. Because neorealists do not properly specify the nature of the international environment, their conclusions about self-help, about reliance on unit-level capabilities, and about sources of shift in patterns of interstate relationships are often wrong or at best misleading. Different international political systems have different degrees of institutionalization. In relatively non-institutionalized systems, the physical capabilities of states are most important: this is presumably what Waltz has in mind when he says of international relations that "authority quickly reduces to a particular expression of capability" (1979:88). But in relatively institutionalized international systems, states may be able to exert influence by drawing on widespread diplomatic norms, on legally institutionalized transnational financial networks, and on those international institutions known as alliances. [...] An adequate understanding of state action in world politics depends on an appreciation of the strengths and weaknesses of institutionalization. [...]

Neoliberal institutionalism and liberalism

Liberalism [...] stresses the importance of international institutions, constructed by states, in facilitating mutually beneficial policy coordination among governments.[5] Another conception of liberalism associates it with a belief in the value of individual freedom. [...]

[...] Liberalism [...] also [...] stresses the role of human-created institutions in affecting how aggregations of individuals make collective decisions. It emphasizes the importance of changeable political processes rather than simply of immutable structures, and it rests on a belief in at least the possibility of cumulative progress in human affairs. [...] Institutions change as a result of human action, and the changes in expectations and processes that result can exert profound effects on state behavior. [...]

Yet [neoliberal institutionalism] [...] diverge[s] from those of much liberal international political theory. Liberalism in international relations is often thought of exclusively in terms of what I have elsewhere called *republican* and *commercial* liberalism (Keohane, 1989). Republican liberalism argues that republics are more peacefully inclined than despotisms. In its naive version, commercial liberalism argues that commerce leads necessarily to peace. The resulting caricature of liberalism posits the "harmony of interests" so tellingly criticized by E. H. Carr (1946). My own view is that republics are remarkably peaceful toward one another, but republics do not necessarily act peacefully toward nonrepublican states or toward societies not organized as states (Doyle, 1983). I believe that an open international economic environment, characterized by opportunities for mutually rewarding exchange under orderly sets of rules, provides incentives for peaceful behavior, but not that it necessitates or ensures such behavior. That is, cooperation must be distinguished from harmony. Cooperation is not automatic, but requires planning and negotiation. It is a highly political process inasmuch as patterns of behavior must be altered – a process that involves the exercise of influence. And influence is secured not only with the aid of persuasion and prestige but also through the use of resources – principally economic resources under conditions of complex interdependence, and military resources when conflicts of interest are very sharp and uses or threats of force are efficacious.[6] Neoliberal institutionalists accept a version of liberal principles that eschews determinism and that emphasizes the pervasive significance of international institutions without [marginalizing] the role of state power. [...]

* * *

Neoliberal institutionalism also insists on the significance of international regimes and the importance of the continued exploration of the conditions under which they emerge and persist. Judging from the literature in international relations journals, this battle has been won in the area of political economy: studies of particular international economic regimes have proliferated.[7] [...] But we need to carry the investigation of international regimes further into the security area, as a number of authors have begun to do.[8]

The third type of international institution discussed [...] is the convention: an informal institution, with implicit rules and understandings, that shapes the expectations of actors. Conventions change over time, although the pace of change may be slow. To understand the changes in world politics over the course of centuries, we need to understand how conventions change. [...]

It has often been assumed that neorealist [theory] is appropriate for the study of security issues; yet on some security [issues] states have substantial mutual interests that can be realized only through institutionalized cooperation. Consider, for example, the phenomenon of international alliances. Currently, the theoretical literature on alliances views them from a neorealist perspective.

According to this literature, alliances result from relations of major antagonism and are formed to supplement the capabilities of the parties (Liska, 1962:14–20; 26–27). They are viewed as fundamentally shaped by the structure of the system, defined in neorealist terms. [...] But none of these otherwise perceptive works takes advantage of the fact that alliances are *institutions*, and that both their durability and strength (the degree to which states are committed to alliances, even when costs are entailed) may depend in part on their institutional characteristics. None of them employs theories of institutions to examine the formal and informal rules and conventions on which alliances rely. Thus questions such as the following are not asked:

- Are formal alliances more durable or stronger than alignments based on informal agreements?
- How much difference do executive heads of alliance organizations, and their bureaucracies, make in terms of the durability or strength of alliances?
- To what extent do alliances provide information to their members that facilitates cooperation, therefore contributing to alliance durability or strength?
- Do alliances ever develop norms that are not subject to calculations of interest, and that are therefore genuine normative commitments for participants? If so, under what conditions (domestic as well as international) do such commitments emerge?
- Do open democratic governments find it easier to maintain alliance ties than closed authoritarian regimes?[9]

I believe that a comparison of neorealist interpretations of alliances with a sophisticated neoliberal alternative would show that neoliberal theory provides richer and more novel insights, without sacrificing the valuable arguments of neorealism. Similar conclusions may hold in other security issues, such as those concerning economic sanctions and unilateral versus multilateral arrangements for military procurement.[10] Indeed, the study of security and cooperation, using neoliberal theory, should be highly worthwhile [...].

Notes

1   Joseph Nye (1988) refers to work such as mine as "neoliberal." Expanding Nye's phrase, Joseph Grieco employs the appropriate label of "neoliberal institutionalism" and provides a number of interesting critiques from the perspective of realist political thought. Unfortunately, however, he misinterprets my discussion of utility functions to imply lack of concern by states for the wealth and power of others. My assumption in *After Hegemony*, to which I continue to adhere, is that states' utility functions are independent of one another. This assumption, however, clearly does not imply that states ignore the effects of their actions on other states' power and welfare, insofar as these changes may affect the states' future actions toward themselves and, hence, their own utilities. Indeed, the focus on strategic interaction in my work clearly implies that actors must be careful to assess the *indirect* effects of their actions on their future payoffs (effects that operate through the power and incentives of their partners). Compare Grieco, 1988:496–97 with Keohane, 1984:Chs. 5–7 (especially p. 123).

2   Example of neoliberal institutionalist thinking can be found in the following, among other works: Krasner, 1983; Oye, 1986; and Aggarwal, 1985.

3   On constitutive and regulative aspects of rules, see Giddens, 1984. My thinking on these issues has been helped by discussions with David Dessler and by a recent paper of his (Dessler, 1988).

4   Some conventions are deeply constitutive, in the sense that their rules cannot change without causing the fundamental nature of the activity to change. I refer to these conventions as *practices* in Chapter 7. In international politics, sovereign statehood is the best example of a practice: if the concept of sovereignty and the rules governing recognition of sovereign actors were to change, international relations as such would be fundamentally transformed. Insofar as they are intrinsically connected with sovereign statehood, diplomatic immunity and reciprocity can also be considered to have the status of practices. Practices originate as conventions, but they may become codified in the form of regimes. It should be emphasized, however, that not all conventions are practices. Many conventions are not sufficiently intrinsic to international relations to qualify as practices; indeed, they may reflect customary behavior that could change without fundamentally affecting the nature of world politics.

5   It would also be mistaken to believe that I am particularly sympathetic to this neoclassical liberalism on normative grounds. I recognize the efficiency advantages of well-functioning markets and the liabilities of state control, but I regard unregulated markets as biased against people disadvantaged by lack of marketable skills, mobility, or sophistication. Some regulation is needed not merely to keep markets functioning efficiently but also to counteract the inequities that they generate.

6   On cooperation and harmony, see Keohane, 1984:51–55. On the conditions of complex interdependence and realism, see Keohane and Nye, 1989:158–62 and Chs. 1 and 2.

7   For a partial listing, see Keohane and Nye, 1987:741, fn. 33.

8   Nye, 1987 (see especially pp. 374–78), cites the relevant works in his discussion of this issue.

9   A speculation to this effect appears in Keohane, 1984:95; but as far as I know, no one has sought to test this proposition.

10   Promising dissertations on these topics are being written at Harvard by Lisa Martin and Andrew Moravcsik, respectively.

References

Aggarwal, Vinod K., 1985. *Liberal Protectionism: The International Politics of Organized Textile Trade* (Berkeley: University of California Press).

Carr, E. H., 1946. *The Twenty Years' Crisis, 1919–1939*, 2nd ed. (London: Macmillan).

Dessler, David, 1988. What's at stake in the agent–structure debate? (Williamsburg, Va.: Unpublished paper, Department of Government, College of William and Mary).

Doyle, Michael W., 1983. Kant, liberal legacies and foreign affairs. *Philosophy and Public Affairs*, vol. 12, nos. 3 and 4 (two-part article), pp. 205–31, 323–53.

Giddens, Anthony, 1984. *The Constitution of Society* (Berkeley: University of California Press).

Grieco, Joseph, 1988. Anarchy and the limits of cooperation: A realist critique of the newest liberal institutionalism. *International Organization*, vol. 42, no. 3 (Summer), pp. 485–508.

Kant, Immanuel, 1795/1949. Eternal peace. In Carl J. Friedrich, ed., *The Philosophy of Kant* (New York: Modern Library, 1949), pp. 430–76.

Keohane, Robert O., 1984. *After Hegemony: Cooperation and Discord in the World Political Economy* (Princeton, N.J.: Princeton University Press).

——, 1989. International Liberalism reconsidered. In John Dunn, ed., *Economic Limits to Modern Politics* (Cambridge: Cambridge University Press).

Keohane, Robert O., ed., 1986. *Neorealism and Its Critics* (New York: Columbia University Press).

Keohane, Robert O., and Joseph S. Nye, Jr., 1987. *Power and Interdependence* revisited. *International Organization*, vol. 41, no. 4 (Autumn), pp. 725–53. Reprinted in Keohane and Nye, 1989.

——, 1989. *Power and Interdependence: World Politics in Transition*, 2nd ed. (Boston: Little, Brown).

Krasner, Stephen D., ed., 1983. *International Regimes* (Ithaca, N.Y.: Cornell University Press).

Liska, George, 1962. *Nations in Alliance: The Limits of Interdependence* (Baltimore: Johns Hopkins University Press).

Nye, Joseph S., Jr., 1987. Nuclear learning. *International Organization*, vol. 41, no. 3 (Summer), pp. 371–402.

——, 1988. Neorealism and neoliberalism. *World Politics*, vol. 40, no. 2 (January), pp. 235–51.

Oye, Kenneth A., ed., 1986. *Cooperation Under Anarchy* (Princeton, NJ.: Princeton University Press).

Ruggie, John Gerard, 1983. Continuity and transformation in the world polity: Toward a neorealist synthesis. *World Politics*, vol. 35, no. 2 (January), pp. 261–85.

Waltz, Kenneth N., 1979. *Theory of International Politics* (Reading, Mass.: Addison-Wesley).

——, 1986. A response to my critics. In Keohane, 1986, pp. 322–45.

Michael W. Doyle

DEMOCRATIC PEACE

Source: 'Liberalism and world politics', *The American Political Science Review*, vol. 80, no. 4, December 1986, pp. 1151–69.

Liberal internationalism

MODERN LIBERALISM carries with it two legacies. They do not affect liberal states separately, according to whether they are pacifistic or imperialistic, but simultaneously.

The first of these legacies is the pacification of foreign relations among liberal states.[1] [...] Beginning in the eighteenth century and slowly growing since then, a zone of peace, which Kant called the "pacific federation" or "pacific union," has begun to be established among liberal societies. More than 40 liberal states currently make up the union. Most are in Europe and North America, but they can be found on every continent. [...]

Here the predictions of liberal pacifists [...] are borne out: liberal states do exercise peaceful restraint, and a separate peace exists among them. This separate peace provides a solid foundation for the United States' crucial alliances with the liberal powers, e.g., the North Atlantic Treaty Organization and our Japanese alliance. This foundation appears to be impervious to the quarrels with our allies that bedeviled the Carter and Reagan administrations. It also offers the promise of a continuing peace among liberal states, and as the number of liberal states increases, it announces the possibility of global peace this side of the grave or world conquest.

Of course, the probability of the outbreak of war in any given year between any two given states is low. The occurrence of a war between any two adjacent states, considered over a long period of time, would be more probable. The apparent absence of war between liberal states, whether adjacent or not, for almost 200 years thus may have significance. Similar claims cannot be made for feudal, fascist, communist, authoritarian, or totalitarian forms of rule (Doyle, 1983a, pp. 222), nor for pluralistic or merely similar societies. More significant perhaps is that when states are forced to decide on which side of an impending world war they will fight, liberal states all wind up on the same side despite the complexity of the paths that take them there. These characteristics do not prove that the peace among liberals is statistically significant nor that liberalism is the sole valid explanation for the peace.[2] They do suggest that we consider the possibility that liberals have indeed established a separate peace – but only among themselves.

Liberalism also carries with it a second legacy: international "imprudence" (Hume, 1963, pp. 346–47). Peaceful restraint only seems to work in liberals' relations with other liberals. Liberal states have fought numerous wars with non-liberal states. [...]

Many of these wars have been defensive and thus prudent by necessity. Liberal states have been attacked and threatened by nonliberal states that do not exercise any special restraint in their dealings with the liberal states. Authoritarian rulers both stimulate and respond to an international political environment in which conflicts of prestige, interest, and pure fear of what other states might do all lead states toward war. War and conquest have thus characterized the careers of many authoritarian rulers and ruling parties, from Louis XIV and Napoleon to Mussolini's fascists, Hitler's Nazis, and Stalin's communists.

Yet we cannot simply blame warfare on the authoritarians or totalitarians, as many of our more enthusiastic politicians would have us do.[3] Most wars arise out of calculations and miscalculations of interest, misunderstandings, and mutual suspicions, such as those that characterized the origins of World War I. However, aggression by the liberal state has also characterized a large number of wars. Both France and Britain fought expansionist colonial wars throughout the nineteenth century. The United States fought a similar war with Mexico from 1846 to 1848, waged a war of annihilation against the American Indians, and intervened militarily against sovereign states many times before and after World War II. Liberal states invade weak nonliberal states and display striking distrust in dealings with powerful nonliberal states (Doyle, 1983b).

Neither realist (statist) nor Marxist theory accounts well for these two legacies. While they can account for aspects of certain periods of international stability (Aron, 1966, pp. 151–54; Russett, 1985), neither the logic of the balance of power nor the logic of international hegemony explains the separate peace maintained for more than 150 years among states sharing one particular form of governance – liberal principles and institutions. Balance-of-power theory expects – indeed is premised upon – flexible arrangements of geostrategic rivalry that include preventive war. Hegemonies wax and wane, but the liberal peace holds. [...]

Kant's theory of liberal internationalism helps us understand these two legacies. [...] *Perpetual Peace*, written in 1795 (Kant, 1970, pp. 93–130), helps us understand the interactive nature of international relations. Kant tries to teach us methodologically that we can study neither the systemic relations of states nor the varieties of state behavior in isolation from each other. Substantively, he anticipates for us the ever-widening pacification of a liberal pacific union, explains this pacification, and at the same time suggests why liberal states are not pacific in their relations with nonliberal states. Kant argues that perpetual peace will be guaranteed by the ever-widening acceptance of three "definitive articles" of peace. When all nations have accepted the definitive articles in a metaphorical "treaty" of perpetual peace he asks them to sign, perpetual peace will have been established.

The First Definitive Article requires the civil constitution of the state to be republican. By *republican* Kant means a political society that has solved the problem of combining moral autonomy, individualism, and social order, [one] [...] that preserved juridical freedom – the legal equality of citizens as subjects – on the basis of a representative government with a separation of powers. Juridical freedom is preserved because the morally autonomous individual is by means of representation a self-legislator making laws that apply to all citizens equally, including himself or herself. Tyranny is avoided because the individual is subject to laws he or she does not also administer (Kant, *PP*, pp. 99–102; Riley, 1983, chap. 5).[4]

Liberal republics will progressively establish peace among themselves by means of the pacific federation, or union (*foedus pacificum*), described in Kant's Second Definitive Article. The pacific union will establish peace within a federation of free states and securely maintain the rights of each state. The world will not have achieved the "perpetual peace" that provides the ultimate guarantor of republican freedom until "a late stage and after many unsuccessful attempts" (Kant, *UH*, p. 47). At that time, all nations will have learned the lessons of peace through right conceptions of the appropriate constitution, great and sad experience, and good will. Only then will individuals enjoy perfect republican rights or the full guarantee of a global and just peace. In the meantime, the "pacific federation" of liberal republics – "an enduring and gradually expanding federation likely to prevent war" – brings within it more and more republics – despite republican collapses, backsliding, and disastrous wars – creating an ever-expanding separate peace (Kant, *PP*, p. 105).[5] [...]

The pacific union is not a single peace treaty ending one war, a world state, nor a state of nations. Kant finds the first insufficient. The second and third are impossible or potentially tyrannical. National sovereignty precludes reliable subservience to a state of nations; a world state destroys the civic freedom on which the development of human capacities rests (Kant, *UH*, p. 50). Although Kant obliquely refers to various classical interstate confederations and modern diplomatic congresses, he develops no systematic organizational embodiment of this treaty and presumably does not find institutionalization necessary (Riley, 1983, chap. 5; Schwarz, 1962, p. 77). He appears to have in mind a mutual non-aggression pact, perhaps a collective security agreement, and the cosmopolitan law set forth in the Third Definitive Article.[6]

The Third Definitive Article establishes a cosmopolitan law to operate in conjunction with the pacific union. The cosmopolitan law "shall be limited to conditions of universal hospitality." In this Kant calls for the recognition of the "right of a foreigner not to be treated with hostility when he arrives on someone else's territory." This "does not extend beyond those conditions which make it possible for them [foreigners] to attempt to enter into relations [commerce] with the native inhabitants" (Kant, *PP*, p. 106). Hospitality does not require extending to foreigners either the right to citizenship or the right to settlement, unless the foreign visitors would perish if they were expelled. Foreign conquest and plunder also find no justification under this right. Hospitality does appear to include the right of access and the obligation of maintaining the opportunity for citizens to exchange goods and ideas without imposing the obligation to trade (a voluntary act in all cases under liberal constitutions). [...]

In tracing the effects of both political and moral development, he builds an account of why liberal states do maintain peace among themselves and of how it will (by implication, has) come about that the pacific union will expand. He also explains how these republics would engage in wars with nonrepublics and therefore suffer the "sad experience" of wars that an ethical policy might have avoided.

The first source of the three definitive articles derives from a political evolution – from a constitutional law. Nature (providence) has seen to it that human beings can live in all the regions where they have been driven to settle by wars. [...] "Asocial sociability" draws men together to fulfill needs for security and material welfare as it drives them into conflicts over the distribution and control of social products (Kant, *UH*, p. 44–45; *PP*, pp. 110–11). This violent natural evolution tends towards the liberal peace because "asocial sociability" inevitably leads toward republican governments, and republican governments are a source of the liberal peace.

Republican representation and separation of powers are produced because they are the means by which the state is "organized well" to prepare for and meet foreign threats (by unity) and to tame the ambitions of selfish and aggressive individuals [...]. States that are not organized in this fashion fail. [...]

Kant shows how republics, once established, lead to peaceful relations, he argues that once the aggressive interests of absolutist monarchies are tamed and the habit of respect for individual rights engrained by republican government, wars would appear as the disaster to the people's welfare that he and the other liberals thought them to be. [...]

Yet these domestic republican restraints do not end war. If they did, liberal states would not be warlike, which is far from the case. They do introduce republican caution – Kant's "hesitation" – in place of monarchical caprice. Liberal wars are only fought for popular, liberal purposes. The historical liberal legacy is laden with popular wars fought to promote freedom, to protect private property, or to support liberal allies against nonliberal enemies. Kant's position is ambiguous. He regards these wars as unjust and warns liberals of their susceptibility to them (Kant, *PP*, p. 106). At the same time, Kant argues that each nation "can and ought to" demand that its neighboring nations enter into the pacific union of liberal states (*PP*, p. 102). Thus to see how the pacific union removes the occasion of wars among liberal states and not wars between liberal and nonliberal states, we need to shift our attention from constitutional law to international law, Kant's second source.

Complementing the constitutional guarantee of caution, international law adds a second source for the definitive articles: a guarantee of respect. The separation of nations that asocial sociability encourages is reinforced by the development of separate languages and religions. These further guarantee a world of separate states – an essential condition needed to avoid a "global, soul-less despotism." Yet, at the same time, they also morally integrate liberal states: "as culture grows and men gradually move towards greater agreement over their principles, they lead to mutual understanding and peace" (Kant, *PP*, p. 114). As republics emerge (the first source) and as culture progresses, an understanding of the legitimate rights of all citizens and of all republics comes into play; and this, now that caution characterizes policy, sets up the moral foundations for the liberal peace. Correspondingly, international law highlights the importance of Kantian publicity. Domestically, publicity helps ensure that the officials of republics act according to the principles they profess to hold just and according to the interests of the electors they claim to represent. Internationally, free speech and the effective communication of accurate conceptions of the political life of foreign peoples is essential to establishing and preserving the understanding on which the guarantee of respect depends. Domestically just republics, which rest on consent, then presume foreign republics also to be consensual, just, and therefore deserving of accommodation. The experience of cooperation helps engender further cooperative behavior when the consequences of state policy are unclear but (potentially) mutually beneficial. At the same time, liberal states assume that nonliberal states, which do not rest on free consent, are not just. Because nonliberal governments are in a state of aggression with their own people, their foreign relations become for liberal governments deeply suspect. [...]

Lastly, cosmopolitan law adds material incentives to moral commitments. The cosmopolitan right to hospitality permits the "spirit of commerce" sooner or later to take hold of every nation, thus impelling states to promote peace and to try to avert war. Liberal economic theory holds that these cosmopolitan ties derive from a cooperative international division of labor and free trade according to comparative advantage. Each economy is said to be better off than it would have been under autarky; each thus acquires an incentive to avoid policies that would lead the other to break these economic ties. Because keeping open markets rests upon the assumption that the next set of transactions will also be determined by prices rather than coercion, a sense of mutual security is vital to avoid security-motivated searches for economic autarky. Thus, avoiding a challenge to another liberal state's security or even enhancing each other's security by means of alliance naturally follows economic interdependence.

A further cosmopolitan source of liberal peace is the international market's removal of difficult decisions of production and distribution from the direct sphere of state policy. A foreign state thus does not appear directly responsible for these outcomes, and states can stand aside from, and to some degree above, these contentious market rivalries and be ready to step in to resolve crises. The interdependence of commerce and the international contacts of state officials help create crosscutting transnational ties that serve as lobbies for mutual accommodation. According to modern liberal scholars, international financiers and transnational and transgovernmental organizations create interests in favor of accommodation. Moreover, their variety has ensured that no single conflict sours an entire relationship by setting off a spiral of reciprocated retaliation (Brzezinski and Huntington, 1963, chap. 9; Keohane and Nye, 1977, chap. 7; Neustadt, 1970; Polanyi, 1944, chaps. 1–2). Conversely, a sense of suspicion, such as that characterizing relations between liberal and nonliberal governments, can lead to restrictions on the range of contacts between societies, and this can increase the prospect that a single conflict will determine an entire relationship.

No single constitutional, international, or cosmopolitan source is alone sufficient, but together (and only together) they plausibly connect the characteristics of liberal polities and economies with sustained liberal peace. Alliances founded on mutual strategic interest among liberal and nonliberal states have been broken; economic ties between liberal and nonliberal states have proven fragile; but the political bonds of liberal rights and interests have proven a remarkably firm foundation for mutual nonaggression. A separate peace exists among liberal states.

In their relations with nonliberal states, however, liberal states have not escaped from the insecurity caused by anarchy in the world political system considered as a whole. Moreover, the very constitutional restraint, international respect for individual rights, and shared commercial interests that establish grounds for peace among liberal states establish grounds for additional conflict in relations between liberal and nonliberal societies. [...]

Notes

1   Clarence Streit (1938, pp. 88, 90–92) seems to have been the first to point out (in contemporary foreign relations) the empirical tendency of democracies to maintain peace among themselves, and he made this the foundation of his proposal for a (non-Kantian) federal union of the 15 leading democracies of the 1930s. In a very interesting book, Ferdinand Hermens (1944) explored some of the policy implications of Streit's analysis. D. V. Babst (1972, pp. 55–58) performed a quantitative study of this phenomenon of "democratic peace," and R. J. Rummel (1983) did a similar study of "libertarianism" (in the sense of laissez faire) focusing on the postwar period that drew on an unpublished study (Project No. 48) noted in Appendix 1 of his *Understanding Conflict and War* (1979, p. 386). I use the term *liberal* in a wider, Kantian sense in my discussion of this issue (Doyle, 1983a). In that essay, I survey the period from 1790 to the present and find no war among liberal states.

2   Babst (1972) did make a preliminary test of the significance of the distribution of alliance partners in World War I. He found that the possibility that the actual distribution of alliance partners could have occurred by chance was less than 1% (Babst, 1972, p. 56). However, this assumes that there was an equal possibility that any two nations could have gone to war with each other, and this is a strong assumption. Rummel (1983) has a further discussion of the issue of statistical significance as it applies to his libertarian thesis.

3   There are serious studies showing that Marxist regimes have higher military spending per capita than non-Marxist regimes (Payne, n.d.), but this should not be interpreted as a sign of the inherent aggressiveness of authoritarian or totalitarian governments or of the inherent and global peacefulness of liberal regimes. Marxist regimes, in particular, represent a minority in the current international system; they are strategically encircled, and due to their lack of domestic legitimacy, they might be said to "suffer" the twin burden of needing defenses against both external and internal enemies. Andreski (1980), moreover, argues that (purely) military dictatorships, due to their domestic fragility, have little incentive to engage in foreign military adventures. According to Walter Clemens (1982, pp. 117–18), the United States intervened in the Third World more than twice as often during the period 1946–76 as the Soviet Union did in 1946–79. Relatedly, Posen and Van Evera (1980, p. 105; 1983, pp. 86–89) found that the United States devoted one quarter and the Soviet Union one tenth of their defense budgets to forces designed for Third World interventions (where responding to perceived threats would presumably have a less than purely defensive character).

4   All citations from Kant are from *Kant's Political Writings* (Kant, 1970), the H. B. Nisbet translation edited by Hans Reiss. The works discussed and the abbreviations by which they are identified in the text are as follows:

PP   *Perpetual Peace* (1795)
UH *The Idea for a Universal History with a Cosmopolitan Purpose* (1784)
CF   *The Contest of Faculties* (1798)
MM *The Metaphysics of Morals* (1797)

5   I think Kant meant that the peace would be established among liberal regimes and would expand by ordinary political and legal means as new liberal regimes appeared. By a process of gradual extension the peace would become global and then perpetual; the occasion for wars with nonliberals would disappear as nonliberal regimes disappeared.

6   Kant's *foedus pacificum* is thus neither a *pactum pacis* (a single peace treaty) nor a *civitas gentium* (a world state). He appears to have anticipated something like a less formally institutionalized League of Nations or United Nations. One could argue that in practice, these two institutions worked for liberal states and only for liberal states, but no specifically liberal "pacific union" was institutionalized. Instead, liberal states have behaved for the past 180 years as if such a Kantian pacific union and treaty of perpetual peace had been signed.

References

Andreski, Stanislav. 1980. On the Peaceful Disposition of Military Dictatorships. *Journal of Strategic Studies*, 3:3–10.

Babst, Dean V. 1972. A Force for Peace. *Industrial Research*. 14 (April): 55–58.

Brzezinski, Zbigniew, and Samuel Huntington. 1963. *Political Power: USA/USSR*. New York: Viking Press.

Clemens, Walter C. 1982. The Superpowers and the Third World. In Charles Kegley and Pat McGowan, eds., *Foreign Policy; USA/USSR*. Beverly Hills: Sage. pp. 111–35.

Doyle, Michael W. 1983a. Kant, Liberal Legacies, and Foreign Affairs: Part 1. *Philosophy and Public Affairs*, 12:205–35.

—— 1983b. Kant, Liberal Legacies, and Foreign Affairs: Part 2. *Philosophy and Public Affairs*, 12:323–53.

Hermens, Ferdinand A. 1944. *The Tyrants' War and the People's Peace*. Chicago: University of Chicago Press.

Hume, David. 1963. Of the Balance of Power. *Essays: Moral, Political, and Literary*. Oxford: Oxford University Press.

Kant, Immanuel. 1970. *Kant's Political Writings*. Hans Reiss, ed. H. B. Nisbet, trans. Cambridge: Cambridge University Press.

Keohane, Robert, and Joseph Nye. 1977. *Power and Interdependence*. Boston: Little Brown.

Neustadt, Richard. 1970. *Alliance Politics*. New York: Columbia University Press.

Payne, James L. n.d. Marxism and Militarism. *Polity*. Forthcoming.

Polanyi, Karl. 1944. *The Great Transformation*. Boston: Beacon Press.

Posen, Barry, and Stephen Van Evera. 1980. Over-arming and Underwhelming. *Foreign Policy*, 40:99–118.

Posen, Barry, and Stephen Van Evera. 1983. Reagan Administration Defense Policy. In Kenneth Oye, Robert Lieber, and Donald Rothchild, eds., *Eagle Defiant*. Boston: Little Brown. pp. 67–104.

Riley, Patrick. 1983. *Kant's Political Philosophy*. Totowa, NJ: Rowman and Littlefield.

Rummel, Rudolph J. 1979. *Understanding Conflict and War*, 5 vols. Beverly Hills: Sage Publications.

Rummel, Rudolph J. 1983. Libertarianism and International Violence. *Journal of Conflict Resolution*, 27:27–71.

Russett, Bruce. 1985. The Mysterious Case of Vanishing Hegemony. *International Organization*, 39:207–31.

Schwarz, Wolfgang. 1962. Kant's Philosophy of Law and International Peace. *Philosophy and Phenomenonological Research*, 23:71–80.

Streit, Clarence. 1938. *Union Now: A Proposal for a Federal Union of the Leading Democracies*. New York: Harpers.

Bruce Russett

NEO-KANTIAN PERSPECTIVE

Source: 'A neo-Kantian perspective: democracy, interdependence, and international organizations in building security communities', in Emanuel Adler and Michael Barnett (eds.), *Security Communities* (Cambridge: Cambridge University Press, 1998), pp. 368–94.

PEACE AMONG REPRESENTATIVE democracies, economic interdependence, and international law clearly emerge in a free translation and late-twentieth century reading of Kant's 1795 work.[1] It is also a view consistent with a definition of human security recently espoused as the protection of states, and their populations, from mortal danger.[2] It is a view subversive of authoritarian and autarchic concepts of state sovereignty, in the interest of popular sovereignty in control of states (liberal internal systems) operating with substantial autonomy but embedded in, and therefore supporting and actively promoting, the production of liberal states in an interdependent international system. It is a view ultimately of a global authority structure, weak but with enough teeth to defend itself against illiberal challengers. In this it is a dynamic view of sovereignty.[3]

Conceptually, a Kantian view fits nicely with the thesis of the former UN Secretary-General Boutros-Ghali that democracy, economic development and interdependence, and peace are inextricably linked, in something of a triangle of positive feedbacks, with the United Nations and other international organizations able to make direct contributions to each. [...]

It does not matter what item one places at any particular corner of the triangle, but for the sake of this discussion peace belongs at the center. The triangular image serves as a description and prescription for an ordered, just, and peaceful society at the domestic or international levels, with wide and equal political participation yet protection of minority rights, equality of opportunity with sharp limits on rents that are derived from control of a market by powerful political or economic actors, and institutions to facilitate and promote cooperation with some – but minimal – elements of coercion.

The basic perspective holds that each of these is interacting and mutually supportive, internationally and domestically as well, in a dynamic mutually reinforcing system. For example, each of the other elements is, or can be, supported and encouraged by international organizations; in turn, a world where international organizations can flourish must be one where peace, development, and democracy also flourish in most of the constituent states. [...]

Democracy and peace

At the international level, the causal arrow from democracy (and perhaps human rights more generally) to peace is arguably the most solidly established generalization of the lot. It is not uncontested, but in my view the critics have yet to seriously dent the "democratic peace" proposition. To this point in time, no one to my knowledge has seriously argued the opposite (that democracies are *more* likely to fight each other than are other states); at most a few articles have held that, especially for particular times and places, the positive association does not appear, or if so is not statistically significant. [...]

For the security community perspective, it is important to note that the "democracies rarely fight each other" effect is specific to democracies. It depends on particular normative perspectives on the rightness of fighting others who share a commitment to peaceful conflict resolution, and on the absence of need to fight those who have political institutions that support peaceful conflict resolution internationally. It may apply to a degree to states which, though not especially democratic, nevertheless share some of the normative perspectives and institutional restraints typical of democracies. But little evidence suggests it is generalizable to other broad categories of political and cultural similarity (e.g., Islamic states, military governments; communist states). Whereas there surely are specific examples of similar "we feelings" that inhibit war-making, applying that expectation broadly risks frequent refutations unless one makes it virtually tautological. (If we don't fight them, despite some opportunity and perhaps cause to do so, it must be because we share mutual identity and we-feeling.) Deutsch's emphasis on compatibility of values rather than similarity seems sounder. I doubt, therefore, that it is necessary to make expectations of a global security community – however distant that may seem – dependent upon widespread acceptance of ideas of global citizenship or adoption of a common global culture. Globally, as well as within states, the need is to create institutions reflecting democratic principles which can protect cultural diversity while preserving a wider sense of common identity.

Within countries the evidence about peace and democracy may be less well developed, but it is still strong. Whereas civil wars do occur within democracies, they are relatively rare. The extreme cases of governments slaughtering their own citizens and otherwise engaging in massive violations of human rights are overwhelmingly concentrated in authoritarian and totalitarian states. Stable democracies, with guarantees of minority rights against majority tyranny, offer means of peaceful conflict resolution and are less likely to experience severe ethnic conflict.[4]

The return arrow plausibly also operates at both the international and national levels. Since democracies usually – 80 percent of the time – win their wars against authoritarian states, and leaders of states who lose wars are more likely to be overthrown, an evolutionary mechanism may operate from democracy to peace.[5] [...]

Peace and economic interdependence

As for the effect of economic interdependence on peace, a long tradition – partly Deutschian and constructivist, partly straight-out rational and nineteenth-century liberal – argues in favor of the proposition. The nineteenth-century liberal version derives primarily from a viewpoint of rational economic interest: it is hardly in my interest to fight you if in fact my markets, my sources of supplies, raw materials, and other imports are in your country. If my investments are located in your country, bombing your industry means, in effect, bombing my own factories. The Deutschian argument is that economic exchange becomes a medium for communicating perspectives, interests, and desires on a broad range of matters not the subject of the economic exchange, and that these communications form an important channel for conflict management. Both these versions probably operate empirically. In these ways dense linkages of economic interdependence are part of a wider variety of international transactions that help build a sense of shared identity among peoples.[6]

It is true that there is a competing proposition, that in many circumstances economic ties, especially in the form of asymmetrical dependence rather than true interdependence, do not promote peaceful relations. The final judgment is not yet in. The preponderance of systematic evidence for at least the post-World War II era, however, suggests that mutual economic interdependence, measured as the share of dyadic trade to GNP in the country where that trade is proportionately smaller, is strongly associated with peaceful relations in subsequent years. This is so even after the now-customary controls – distance, alliance, relative power, democracy, and wealth or economic growth rates – are included in the equation and prove also to have positive independent effects.[7] To this should be added the possibility of an interaction between democracy and interdependence with a stronger effect than just the additive one. For example, Lisa Martin argues within the context of the principal-agent framework that in order to reach credible agreements with other states, democratic executives have to persuade, and accommodate themselves to the perspectives of, their legislatures. In doing so, they make it more likely that they will be able to keep their commitments, that the commitments won't become unglued in quick or arbitrary fashion. She applies this, appropriately, both to security issues and issues of trade and economic interdependence. From it one can plausibly impute not just the direct arrow from democracy to peace, but one running from democracy to interdependence and then to peace. Another kind of interaction may be seen in some "two-level games," whereby interdependence brings extra-state actors into the domestic political process to a degree facilitated by a pluralistic political system.[8]

The possibility of reciprocal effects – states do not allow themselves to become too economically dependent on states with whom they are in military conflict or anticipate such a possibility – is of course also plausible and likely; a full sorting-out of these relationships is in progress.

Democracy and interdependence

The final set of relationships concerns the base of the triangle, between democracy and economic interdependence. At the international level, it may be that economic interdependence supports democracy; at least the European Union seems to operate on this principle, requiring all applicants for admission to the common market to demonstrate their commitment to stable democratic rule and human rights. In the other direction, democratic states presumably feel their security less threatened by other democratic states, and hence can enter into relationships of economic interdependence for absolute gain without worrying as much about the relative gains that so centrally impact the realist model of relationships. One would therefore expect more trade between democracies than between democracies and non-democracies, or between two non-democracies, holding constant other relevant cultural and economic influences.[9] Economic interdependence typically is greater between states with competitive markets (somewhat more common in democracies) than operating under state or private monopolies.

Purely at the domestic level, the relation between economics and democracy requires a conceptual shift away from simply economic interdependence to a broader focus on income levels and distribution, and to a focus on peaceful means of conflict resolution and the maintenance of stable democracy. These relationships are somewhat problematic and in dispute. Most scholars readily agree that there is an association between democracy and per capita income, and that economic development facilitates democratization. But they do not agree on whether any significant causality operates from democracy to development, nor fully on the causal relationship between economics and domestic political stability and peaceful conflict resolution. The role of free markets is also part of the discussion. Arguably, a key component of economic development is the determination of peaceful processes of economic interdependence more by market considerations than by state fiat or ethnic preference. [...]

Notes

1   Daniele Archibugi rightly points out, in "Immanuel Kant, Cosmopolitan Law and Peace," *European Journal of International Relations* 1, 4 (December 1995), pp. 429–56, that this is not a fully accurate rendition of Kant, chiefly in that Kant thought of peaceful democracies primarily as a monadic phenomenon (peaceful in general) rather than a dyadic one (peaceful with one another). The distinction matters as an item of intellectual history, but it nonetheless seems appropriate to credit Kant for most of the basic insights, recognizing that more than 200 years of experience and scholarship modify them somewhat. Hence I use the term "neo-Kantian." The important consideration is whether the theoretical and empirical evidence for this vision, however one labels it, is sound. The question of whether democracies are relatively more peaceful in general is contested. The most persuasive evidence so far indicates that whereas democracies do not behave more pacifically when they are in crises with nondemocratic states, they are less likely to get into such crises in the first place; see David Rousseau, Christopher Gelpi, Dan Reiter, and Paul Huth, "Assessing the Dyadic Nature of the Democratic Peace, 1918–88," *American Political Science Review* 89, 3 (September 1996), pp. 512–33.

2   For use of this term, see Commission on Global Governance, *Our Global Neighbourhood*; Independent Commission, *The United Nations in Its Next Half-Century*; United Nations Development Programme, *World Development Report 1994* (New York: Oxford University Press, 1994).

3   Michael Barnett, "The New UN Politics of Peace," *Global Governance* 1, 1 (January 1995), 79, 98; Mark Zacher, "The Decaying Pillars of the Westphalian System," in James Rosenau and Erst Otto Czempiel, eds., *Governance without Government: Order and Change in World Politics* (Cambridge: Cambridge University Press, 1992), pp. 58–101. Steven Krasner, however, in an important article, shows that the principles of sovereignty as expressed in the Treaty of Westphalia in 1648 have regularly been violated, by conventions and contracts as well as by coercion and imposition, ever since then. It is also worth noting that Krasner, often considered an arch-realist, makes a critical modification to realist understanding: "At the international level, different rulers can champion different principles not only because their interests vary, but because their normative frames of reference, primarily derived from their domestic experiences, also vary." See his "Compromising Westphalia," *International Security* 20, 3 (Winter 1995/96), 115–51; the quotation is from p. 148.

4   Amartya Sen, *Poverty and Famine* (New York: Oxford University Press, 1981); R. J. Rummel, *Death by Government: Genocide and Mass Murder since 1900* (New Brunswick, NJ: Transaction, 1994) and *Power Kills: Democracy as A Method of Nonviolence* (New Brunswick, NJ: Transaction, 1997); Ted Robert Gurr, *Minorities at Risk: A Global View of Ethnopolitical Conflict* (Washington, DC: US Institute of Peace, 1993).

5   David Lake, "Powerful Pacifists; Democratic States and War," *American Political Science Review* 86, 1 (March 1992), pp. 24–37; Bruce Bueno de Mesquita, Randolph Siverson, and Gary Woller, "War and the Fate of Regimes," *American Political Science Review* 86, 3 (September 1992), 638–46; Alan Stam, *Win, Lose, or Draw: Domestic Politics and the Crucible of War* (Ann Arbor: University of Michigan Press, 1996).

6   For early micro-level evidence, see Bruce Russett, *Community and Contention: Britain and America in the Twentieth Century* (Cambridge, MA: MIT Press, 1963). A good review of liberal hypotheses linking interdependence to peace is Arthur Stein, "Governments, Economies, Interdependence, and International Cooperation," in Philip Tetlock et al., eds., *Behavior, Society, and International Conflict*, vol. 3 (Oxford; Oxford University Press, 1989), pp. 244–54. Because of the possibility, cogently presented by Jonathan Mercer, "Anarchy and Identity," *International Organization* 49, 2 (Spring 1995), pp. 229–52, that a sense of mutual identity may well entail characterizing others as "outgroup," it is essential to recognize links of mutual self-interest that do not depend on shared social identity.

7   John Oneal and Bruce Russett, "The Classical Liberals Were Right: Democracy, Interdependence, and Conflict, 1950–85," *International Studies Quarterly* 41, 2 (June 1997), pp. 267–93; Soo Yeon Kim, "Ties that Bind: The Role of Trade in International Conflict Processes, 1950–92" (PhD dissertation, Yale University, 1988). The importance of interdependence is illustrated in the *dependencia* literature, and dates back to Albert Hirschmann, *National Power and the Structure of Foreign Trade* (Berkeley: University of California Press, 1945). Also note that rich countries are unlikely to fight each other. As a realist would probably recognize, the costs of fighting another rich country with a modern, highly destructive military capability now outweigh any possible economic gain in an era when national wealth depends far more on physical capital (skill, technological capacity, organization) than on land or natural resources. See John Mueller, *Retreat from Doomsday: The Obsolescence of Major War* (New York: Basic Books, 1988), and Carl Kaysen, "Is War Obsolete?" *International Security* 14, 4 (Spring 1990), pp. 42–64.

8   Lisa Martin, "Democratic Commitments: Legislatures and International Cooperation" (manuscript, Harvard University). For evidence that democracies are

able to enter into longer-term commitments with each other, see Kurt Taylor Gaubatz, "Democratic States and Commitment in International Relations, *International Organization* 50, 1 (Winter 1996), pp. 109–39. Other versions of the link from democracy and free trade to peace include Daniel Verdier, *Democracy and International Trade: Britain, France, and the United States, 1860–1990* (Princeton, NJ: Princeton University Press, 1994); Erich Weede, "Economic Policy and International Security: Rent-Seeking, Free Trade, and Democratic Peace," *European Journal of International Relations* 1, 4 (December 1995), pp. 519–37; Robert Putnam, "Diplomacy and Domestic Politics: The Logic of Two-Level Games," *International Organization* 42, 3 (Summer 1988), pp. 427–62.

9   See Harry Bliss and Bruce Russett, "Democratic Trading Partners: The Liberal Connection," *Journal of Politics*, 58, 4 forthcoming November 1998, for strong evidence of this, with a data base and method similar to that of Oneal and Russett, "The Classical Liberals Were Right," and Kim, "Ties that Bind."

Alexander Wendt

THE SOCIAL CONSTRUCTION OF POWER POLITICS

Source: 'Anarchy is what states make of it: the social construction of power politics', *International Organization*, vol. 46, no. 2, Spring 1992, pp. 391–425.

[...] [THERE ARE] SOCIAL theories which seek to explain identities and interests do exist. Keohane has called them "reflectivist";[1] because I want to emphasize their focus on the social construction of subjectivity and minimize their image problem, following Nicholas Onuf I will call them "constructivist."[2] Despite important differences, cognitivists, poststructuralists, standpoint and postmodern feminists, rule theorists, and structurationists share a concern with the basic "socio-logical" issue bracketed by rationalists – namely, the issue of identity- and interest-formation. [...] [B]oth modern and postmodern constructivists are interested in how knowledgeable practices constitute subjects, which is not far from the strong liberal interest in how institutions transform interests. They share a cognitive, intersubjective conception of process in which identities and interests are endogenous to interaction, rather than a rationalist-behavioral one in which they are exogenous. [...]

Constructivists [...] argue that self-help and power politics do not follow either logically or causally from anarchy and that if today we find ourselves in a self-help world, this is due to process, not structure. There is no "logic" of anarchy apart from the practices that create and instantiate one structure of identities and interests rather than another; structure has no existence or causal powers apart from process. Self-help and power politics are institutions, not essential features of anarchy. *Anarchy is what states make of it.* [...]

* * *

[...] A fundamental principle of constructivist social theory is that people act toward objects, including other actors, on the basis of the meanings that the objects have for them.[3] States act differently toward enemies than they do toward friends because enemies are threatening and friends are not. Anarchy and the distribution of power are insufficient to tell us which is which. U.S. military power has a different significance for Canada than for Cuba, despite their similar "structural" positions, just as British missiles have a different significance for the United States than do Soviet missiles. The distribution of power may always affect states' calculations, but how it does so depends on the intersubjective understandings and expectations, on the "distribution of knowledge," that constitute their conceptions of self and other.[4] [...] It is collective meanings that constitute the structures which organize our actions.

Actors acquire identities – relatively stable, role-specific understandings and expectations about self – by participating in such collective meanings.[5] Identities are inherently relational: "Identity, with its appropriate attachments of psychological reality, is always identity within a specific, socially constructed world," Peter Berger argues.[6] Each person has many identities linked to institutional roles, such as brother, son, teacher, and citizen. Similarly, a state may have multiple identities as "sovereign," "leader of the free world," "imperial power," and so on.[7] The commitment to and the salience of particular identities vary, but each identity is an inherently social definition of the actor grounded in the theories which actors collectively hold about themselves and one another and which constitute the structure of the social world.

Identities are the basis of interests. Actors do not have a "portfolio" of interests that they carry around independent of social context; instead, they define their interests in the process of defining situations.[8] [...] Sometimes situations are unprecedented in our experience, and in these cases we have to construct their meaning, and thus our interests, by analogy or invent them de novo. More often they have routine qualities in which we assign meanings on the basis of institutionally defined roles. [...] The absence or failure of roles makes defining situations and interests more difficult, and identity confusion may result. This seems to be happening today in the United States and the former Soviet Union: without the cold war's mutual attributions of threat and hostility to define their identities, these states seem unsure of what their "interests" should be.

An institution is a relatively stable set or "structure" of identities and interests. Such structures are often codified in formal rules and norms, but these have motivational force only in virtue of actors' socialization to and participation in collective knowledge. Institutions are fundamentally cognitive entities that do not exist apart from actors' ideas about how the world works.[9] This does not mean that institutions are not real or objective, that they are "nothing but" beliefs. As collective knowledge, they are experienced as having an existence "over and above the individuals who happen to embody them at the moment."[10] In this way, institutions come to confront individuals as more or less coercive social facts, but they are still a function of what actors collectively "know." Identities and such collective cognitions do not exist apart from each other; they are "mutually constitutive."[11] On this view, institutionalization is a process of internalizing new identities and interests, not something occurring outside them and affecting only behavior; socialization is a cognitive process, not just a behavioral one. Conceived in this way, institutions may be cooperative or conflictual, a point sometimes lost in scholarship on international regimes, which tends to equate institutions with cooperation. There are important differences between conflictual and cooperative institutions to be sure, but all relatively stable self-other relations – even those of "enemies" – are defined intersubjectively.

Self-help is an institution, one of various structures of identity and interest that may exist under anarchy. Processes of identity-formation under anarchy are concerned first and foremost with preservation or "security" of the self. Concepts of security therefore differ in the extent to which and the manner in which the self is identified cognitively with the other,[12] and, I want to suggest, it is upon this cognitive variation that the meaning of anarchy and the distribution of power depends. Let me illustrate with a standard continuum of security systems.[13]

At one end is the "competitive" security system, in which states identify negatively with each other's security so that ego's gain is seen as alter's loss. Negative identification under anarchy constitutes systems of "realist" power politics: risk-averse actors that infer intentions from capabilities and worry about relative gains and losses. [...]

In the middle is the "individualistic" security system, in which states are indifferent to the relationship between their own and others' security. This constitutes "neoliberal" systems: states are still self-regarding about their security but are concerned primarily with absolute gains rather than relative gains. One's position in the distribution of power is less important, and collective action is more possible (though still subject to free riding because states continue to be "egoists").

Competitive and individualistic systems are both "self-help" forms of anarchy in the sense that states do not positively identify the security of self with that of others but instead treat security as the individual responsibility of each. Given the lack of a positive cognitive identification on the basis of which to build security regimes, power politics within such systems will necessarily consist of efforts to manipulate others to satisfy self-regarding interests.

This contrasts with the "cooperative" security system, in which states identify positively with one another so that the security of each is perceived as the responsibility of all. This is not self-help in any interesting sense, since the "self" in terms of which interests are defined is the community; national interests are international interests.[14] In practice, of course, the extent to which states' identification with the community varies, from the limited form found in "concerts" to the full-blown form seen in "collective security" arrangements.[15] Depending on how well developed the collective self is, it will produce security practices that are in varying degrees altruistic or prosocial. This makes collective action less dependent on the presence of active threats and less prone to free riding.[16] Moreover, it restructures efforts to advance one's objectives, or "power politics," in terms of shared norms rather than relative power.[17]

On this view, the tendency in international relations scholarship to view power and institutions as two opposing explanations of foreign policy is therefore misleading, since anarchy and the distribution of power only have meaning for state action in virtue of the understandings and expectations that constitute institutional identities and interests. Self-help is one such institution, constituting one kind of anarchy but not the only kind. Waltz's three-part definition of structure therefore seems underspecified. In order to go from structure to action, we need to add a fourth: the intersubjectively constituted structure of identities and interests in the system.

This has an important implication for the way in which we conceive of states in the state of nature before their first encounter with each other. Because states do not have conceptions of self and other, and thus security interests, apart from or prior to interaction, we assume too much about the state of nature if we concur with Waltz that, in virtue of anarchy, "international political systems, like economic markets, are formed by the coaction of self-regarding units."[18] We also assume too much if we argue that, in virtue of anarchy, states in the state of nature necessarily face a "stag hunt" or "security dilemma."[19] These claims presuppose a history of interaction in which actors have acquired "selfish" identities and interests; before interaction (and still in abstraction from first- and second-image factors) they would have no experience upon which to base such definitions of self and other. To assume otherwise is to attribute to states in the state of nature qualities that they can only possess in society.[20] Self-help is an institution, not a constitutive feature of anarchy. [...]

Anarchy and the social construction of power politics

If self-help is not a constitutive feature of anarchy, it must emerge causally from processes in which anarchy plays only a permissive role.[21] This reflects a second principle of constructivism: that the meanings in terms of which action is organized arise out of interaction.[22] [...]

Conceptions of self and interest tend to "mirror" the practices of significant others over time. This principle of identity-formation is captured by the symbolic interactionist notion of the "looking-glass self," which asserts that the self is a reflection of an actor's socialization.

Consider two actors – ego and alter – encountering each other for the first time.[23] Each wants to survive and has certain material capabilities, but neither actor has biological or domestic imperatives for power, glory, or conquest (still bracketed), and there is no history of security or insecurity between the two. What should they do? Realists would probably argue that each should act on the basis of worst-case assumptions about the other's intentions, justifying such an attitude as prudent in view of the possibility of death from making a mistake. Such a possibility always exists, even in civil society; however, society would be impossible if people made decisions purely on the basis of worst-case possibilities. Instead, most decisions are and should be made on the basis of probabilities, and these are produced by interaction, by what actors *do*. [...]

This process of signaling, interpreting, and responding completes a "social act" and begins the process of creating intersubjective meanings. It advances the same way. The first social act creates expectations on both sides about each other's future behavior: potentially mistaken and certainly tentative, but expectations nonetheless. Based on this tentative knowledge, ego makes a new gesture, again signifying the basis on which it will respond to alter, and again alter responds, adding to the pool of knowledge each has about the other, and so on over time. The mechanism here is reinforcement; interaction rewards actors for holding certain ideas about each other and discourages them from holding others. If repeated long enough, these "reciprocal typifications" will create relatively stable concepts of self and other regarding the issue at stake in the interaction.[24]

It is through reciprocal interaction, in other words, that we create and instantiate the relatively enduring social structures in terms of which we define our identities and interests. [...]

The simple overall model of identity- and interest-formation proposed [...] applies to competitive institutions no less than to cooperative ones. Self-help security systems evolve from cycles of interaction in which each party acts in ways that the other feels are threatening to the self, creating expectations that the other is not to be trusted. Competitive or egoistic identities are caused by such insecurity; if the other is threatening, the self is forced to "mirror" such behavior in its conception of the self's relationship to that other.[25] Being treated as an object for the gratification of others precludes the positive identification with others necessary for collective security; conversely, being treated by others in ways that are empathic with respect to the security of the self permits such identification.[26]

Competitive systems of interaction are prone to security "dilemmas," in which the efforts of actors to enhance their security unilaterally threatens the security of the others, perpetuating distrust and alienation. The forms of identity and interest that constitute such dilemmas, however, are themselves ongoing effects of, not exogenous to, the interaction; identities are produced in and through "situated activity."[27] We do not *begin* our relationship with the aliens in a security dilemma; security dilemmas are not given by anarchy or nature. Of course, once institutionalized such a dilemma may be hard to change (I return to this below), but the point remains: identities and interests are constituted by collective meanings that are always in process. As Sheldon Stryker emphasizes, "The social process is one of constructing and reconstructing self and social relationships."[28] If states find themselves in a self-help system, this is because their practices made it that way. Changing the practices will change the intersubjective knowledge that constitutes the system.

Notes

1   Robert Keohane, "International Institutions: Two Approaches," *International Studies Quarterly* 32 (December 1988), pp. 379–96.

2   See Nicholas Onuf, *World of Our Making* (Columbia: University of South Carolina Press, 1989).

3   See, for example, Herbert Blumer, "The Methodological Position of Symbolic Interactionism," in his *Symbolic Interactionism: Perspective and Method* (Englewood Cliffs, N.J.: Prentice-Hall, 1969), p. 2. Throughout this article, I assume that a theoretically productive analogy can be made between individuals and states. There are at least two justifications for this anthropomorphism. Rhetorically, the analogy is an accepted practice in mainstream international relations discourse, and since this article is an immanent rather than external critique, it should follow the practice. Substantively, states are collectivities of individuals that through their practices constitute each other as "persons" having interests, fears, and so on. A full theory of state identity- and interest-formation would nevertheless need to draw insights from the social psychology of groups and organizational theory, and for that reason my anthropomorphism is merely suggestive.

4   The phrase "distribution of knowledge" is Barry Barnes's, as discussed in his work *The Nature of Power* (Cambridge: Polity Press, 1988); see also Peter Berger and Thomas Luckmann, *The Social Construction of Reality* (New York: Anchor Books, 1966). The concern of recent international relations scholarship on "epistemic communities" with the cause-and-effect understandings of the world held by scientists, experts, and policymakers is an important aspect of the role of knowledge in world politics; see Peter Haas, "Do Regimes Matter? Epistemic Communities and Mediterranean Pollution Control," *International Organization* 43 (Summer 1989), pp. 377–404; and Ernst Haas, *When Knowledge Is Power*. My constructivist approach

would merely add to this an equal emphasis on how such knowledge also *constitutes* the structures and subjects of social life.

5   For an excellent short statement of how collective meanings constitute identities, see Peter Berger, "Identity as a Problem in the Sociology of Knowledge," *European Journal of Sociology*, vol. 7, no. 1, 1966, pp. 32–40. See also David Morgan and Michael Schwalbe, "Mind and Self in Society; Linking Social Structure and Social Cognition," *Social Psychology Quarterly* 53 (June 1990), pp. 148–64. In my discussion, I draw on the following interactionist texts: George Herbert Mead, *Mind, Self, and Society* (Chicago: University of Chicago Press, 1934); Berger and Luckmann, *The Social Construction of Reality*; Sheldon Stryker, *Symbolic Interactionism: A Social Structural Version* (Menlo Park, Calif.: Benjamin/Cummings, 1980); R. S. Perinbanayagam, *Signifying Acts: Structure and Meaning in Everyday Life* (Carbondale: Southern Illinois University Press, 1985); John Hewitt, *Self and Society: A Symbolic Interactionist Social Psychology* (Boston: Allyn & Bacon, 1988); and Turner, *A Theory of Social Interaction*. Despite some differences, much the same points are made by structurationists such as Bhaskar and Giddens. See Roy Bhaskar, *The Possibility of Naturalism* (Atlantic Highlands, N.J.: Humanities Press, 1979); and Anthony Giddens, *Central Problems in Social Theory* (Berkeley: University of California Press, 1979).

6   Berger, "Identity as a Problem in the Sociology of Knowledge," p. 111.

7   While not normally cast in such terms, foreign policy scholarship on national role conceptions could be adapted to such identity language. See Kal Holsti, "National Role Conceptions in the Study of Foreign Policy," *International Studies Quarterly* 14 (September 1970), pp. 233–309; and Stephen Walker, ed., *Role Theory and Foreign Policy Analysis* (Durham, N.C.: Duke University Press, 1987). For an important effort to do so, see Stephen Walker, "Symbolic Interactionism and International Politics: Role Theory's Contribution to International Organization," in C. Shih and Martha Cottam, eds., *Contending Dramas: A Cognitive Approach to Post-War International Organizational Processes* (New York: Praeger, forthcoming).

8   On the "portfolio" conception of interests, see Barry Hindess, *Political Choice and Social Structure* (Aldershot, U.K.: Edward Elgar, 1989), pp. 2–3. The "definition of the situation" is a central concept in interactionist theory.

9   In neo-Durkheimian parlance, institutions are "social representations." See Serge Moscovici, "The Phenomenon of Social Representations," in Rob Farr and Serge Moscovici, eds., *Social Representations* (Cambridge: Cambridge University Press, 1984), pp. 3–69. See also Barnes, *The Nature of Power*. Note that this is a considerably more socialized cognitivism than that found in much of the recent scholarship on the role of "ideas" in world politics, which tends to treat ideas as commodities that are held by individuals and intervene between the distribution of power and outcomes. For a form of cognitivism closer to my own, see Emanuel Adler, "Cognitive Evolution: A Dynamic Approach for the Study of International Relations and Their Progress," in Emanuel Adler and Beverly Crawford, eds., *Progress in Postwar International Relations* (New York: Columbia University Press, 1991), pp. 43–88.

10   Berger and Luckmann, *The Social Construction of Reality*, p. 58.

11   See Giddens, *Central Problems in Social Theory*; and Alexander Wendt and Raymond Duvall, "Institutions and International Order," in Ernst-Otto Czempiel and James Rosenau, eds., *Global Changes and Theoretical Challenges* (Lexington, Mass.: Lexington Books, 1989), pp. 51–74.

12   Proponents of choice theory might put this in terms of "interdependent utilities." For a useful overview of relevant choice-theoretic discourse, most of which has

focused on the specific case of altruism, see Harold Hochman and Shmuel Nitzan, "Concepts of Extended Preference," *Journal of Economic Behavior and Organization* 6 (June 1985), pp. 161–76. The literature on choice theory usually does not link behavior to issues of identity. For an exception, see Amartya Sen, "Goals, Commitment, and Identity," *Journal of Law, Economics, and Organization* 1 (Fall 1985), pp. 341–55; and Robert Higgs, "Identity and Cooperation: A Comment on Sen's Alternative Program," *Journal of Law, Economics, and Organization* 3 (Spring 1987), pp. 140–42.

13   Security systems might also vary in the extent to which there is a functional differentiation or a hierarchical relationship between patron and client, with the patron playing a hegemonic role within its sphere of influence in defining the security interests of its clients. I do not examine this dimension here; for preliminary discussion, see Alexander Wendt, "The States System and Global Militarization," Ph.D. diss., University of Minnesota, Minneapolis, 1989; and Alexander Wendt and Michael Barnett, "The International System and Third World Militarization," unpublished manuscript, 1991.

14   This amounts to an "internationalization of the state." For a discussion of this subject, see Raymond Duvall and Alexander Wendt, "The International Capital Regime and the Internationalization of the State," unpublished manuscript, 1987. See also R. B. J. Walker, "Sovereignty, Identity, Community: Reflections on the Horizons of Contemporary Political Practice," in R. B. J. Walker and Saul Mendlovitz, eds., *Contending Sovereignties* (Boulder, Colo.: Lynne Rienner, 1990), pp. 159–85.

15   On the spectrum of cooperative security arrangements, see Charles Kupchan and Clifford Kupchan, "Concerts, Collective Security, and the Future of Europe," *International Security* 16 (Summer 1991), pp. 114–61; and Richard Smoke, "A Theory of Mutual Security," in Richard Smoke and Andrei Kortunov, eds., *Mutual Security* (New York: St. Martin's Press, 1991), pp. 59–111. These may be usefully set alongside Christopher Jencks' "Varieties of Altruism," in Jane Mansbridge, ed., *Beyond Self-Interest* (Chicago: University of Chicago Press, 1990), pp. 53–67.

16   On the role of collective identity in reducing collective action problems, see Bruce Fireman and William Gamson, "Utilitarian Logic in the Resource Mobilization Perspective," in Mayer Zald and John McCarthy, eds., *The Dynamics of Social Movements* (Cambridge, Mass.: Winthrop, 1979), pp. 8–44; Robyn Dawes et al., "Cooperation for the Benefit of Us – Not Me, or My Conscience," in Mansbridge, *Beyond Self-Interest*, pp. 97–110; and Craig Calhoun, "The Problem of Identity in Collective Action," in Joan Huber, ed., *Macro-Micro Linkages in Sociology* (Beverly Hills, Calif.: Sage, 1991), pp. 51–75.

17   See Thomas Risse-Kappen, "Are Democratic Alliances Special?" unpublished manuscript, Yale University, New Haven, Conn., 1991. This line of argument could be expanded usefully in feminist terms. For a useful overview of the relational nature of feminist conceptions of self, see Paula England and Barbara Stanek Kilbourne, "Feminist Critiques of the Separative Model of Self: Implications for Rational Choice Theory," *Rationality and Society* 2 (April 1990), pp. 156–71. On feminist conceptualizations of power, see Ann Tickner, "Hans Morgenthau's Principles of Political Realism: A Feminist Reformulation," *Millennium* 17 (Winter 1988), pp. 429–40; and Thomas Wartenberg, "The Concept of Power in Feminist Theory," *Praxis International* 8 (October 1988), pp. 301–16.

18   Waltz, *Theory of International Politics*, p. 91.

19   See Waltz, *Man, the State, and War*; and Robert Jervis, "Cooperation Under the Security Dilemma," *World Politics* 30 (January 1978), pp. 167–214.

20   My argument here parallels Rousseau's critique of Hobbes. For an excellent critique of realist appropriations of Rousseau, see Michael Williams, "Rousseau, Realism, and Realpolitik," *Millennium* 18 (Summer 1989), pp. 188–204. Williams argues that far from being a fundamental starting point in the state of nature, for Rousseau the stag hunt represented a stage in man's fall. On p. 190, Williams cites Rousseau's description of man prior to leaving the state of nature: "Man only knows himself; he does not see his own well-being to be identified with or contrary to that of anyone else; he neither hates anything nor loves anything; but limited to no more than physical instinct, he is no one, he is an animal." For another critique of Hobbes on the state of nature that parallels my constructivist reading of anarchy, see Charles Landesman, "Reflections on Hobbes: Anarchy and Human Nature," in Peter Caws, ed., *The Causes of Quarrel* (Boston: Beacon, 1989), pp. 139–48.

21   The importance of the distinction between constitutive and causal explanations is not sufficiently appreciated in constructivist discourse. See Wendt, "The Agent-Structure Problem in International Relations Theory," pp. 362–65; Wendt, "The States System and Global Militarization," pp. 110–13; and Wendt, "Bridging the Theory/Meta-Theory Gap in International Relations," *Review of International Studies* 17 (October 1991), p. 390.

22   See Blumer, "The Methodological Position of Symbolic Interactionism," pp. 2–4.

23   This situation is not entirely metaphorical in world politics, since throughout history states have "discovered" each other, generating an instant anarchy as it were. A systematic empirical study of first contacts would be interesting.

24   On "reciprocal typifications," see Berger and Luckmann, *The Social Construction of Reality*, pp. 54–58.

25   The following articles by Noel Kaplowitz have made an important contribution to such thinking in international relations: "Psychopolitical Dimensions of International Relations: The Reciprocal Effects of Conflict Strategies," *International Studies Quarterly* 28 (December 1984), pp. 373–406; and "National Self-Images, Perception of Enemies, and Conflict Strategies: Psychopolitical Dimensions of International Relations," *Political Psychology* 11 (March 1990), pp. 39–82.

26   These arguments are common in theories of narcissism and altruism. See Heinz Kohut, *Self-Psychology and the Humanities* (New York: Norton, 1985); and Martin Hoffmann, "Empathy, Its Limitations, and Its Role in a Comprehensive Moral Theory," in William Kurtines and Jacob Gewirtz, eds., *Morality, Moral Behavior, and Moral Development* (New York: Wiley, 1984), pp. 283–302.

27   See C. Norman Alexander and Mary Glenn Wiley, "Situated Activity and Identity Formation," in Morris Rosenberg and Ralph Turner, eds., *Social Psychology: Sociological Perspectives* (New York: Basic Books, 1981), pp. 269–89.

28   Sheldon Stryker, "The Vitalization of Symbolic Interactionism," *Social Psychology Quarterly* 50 (March 1987), p. 93.

Thomas U. Berger

NORMS, IDENTITY, AND NATIONAL SECURITY

Source: 'Norms, identity, and national security in Germany and Japan', in Peter J. Katzenstein (ed.) *The Culture of National Security: Norms and Identity in World Politics* (New York: Columbia University Press, 1996), pp. 317–56.

The concept of political-military culture

C OMMON TO ALL theories of culture is the notion that human behavior is guided by socially shared and transmitted ideas and beliefs.[1] Cultures as such comprise beliefs about the way the world is – including at the most basic level beliefs that define the individual's and the group's identities – and ideas about the way the world ought to be.[2] Political culture refers to those cultural beliefs and values that shape a given society's orientations toward politics.[3] Political-military culture in turn refers to the subset of the larger political culture that influences how members of a given society view national security, the military as an institution, and the use of force in international relations.

Although influenced by the real world, cultures (including political-military cultures) are not merely subjective reflections of objective reality. Two individuals or groups with different cultural backgrounds are likely to behave differently even when confronted with identical situations. For example, if French or American policy makers found themselves in geostrategic positions similar to Japan's or Germany's, they might be expected to behave in a very different way than their German and Japanese counterparts do because they come from cultural backgrounds with very different norms and values regarding the military and the use of force.

Cultures – and by extension political-military cultures – are not static entities hovering above society, directing behavior while they themselves remain immune to social, economic, and political forces. They are transmitted through the often imperfect mechanisms of primary and secondary socialization and are under constant pressure from both external developments and internal contradictions.[4] Cognitive beliefs about the world are constantly tested by actual events. While failures and surprises can be reinterpreted so that they do not contradict existing norms and beliefs, they also create pressures that can lead to a reevaluation and modification of the culture.

In extreme cases, if a culture totally fails to meet the expectations of its members, large-scale defections to other cultural systems are likely to result.[5] The collapse of Communism may serve as a case in point.

Such adaptation, however, is neither quick nor easy. Simple, instrumental beliefs can be discarded easily. More abstract or emotionally laden beliefs and values that make up the core of a culture (such as a preference for democracy or belief in monotheism) are more resistant to change.[6] Ordinarily such change takes place slowly and incrementally. Occasionally more rapid change in core beliefs and values occurs, but only after they have been thoroughly discredited and the society is under great strain. Individuals and groups are then forced to reexamine their old beliefs and seek new ways of making sense of the world and new solutions to the problems confronting them. Such rapid and fundamental change tends to be accompanied by psychological distress and is broadly similar to Thomas Kuhn's description of paradigm shifts in the natural sciences.[7]

The reexamination of the core beliefs and values of a particular nation is a complicated affair. At any one time there exists a multiplicity of political actors – motivated by their own distinctive experiences and interests – who seek to establish their understandings as binding for the rest of the society. In pluralistic political systems, however, usually no one group is able to impose its views on the rest. In order to pursue their agenda, political actors are compelled to enter into debates and negotiations with other groups, making compromises and concessions along the way. These compromises, however, have to be legitimated, both internally within the group and externally in the rest of society. Such legitimations often involve a reinterpretation of past events, current conditions, and future goals. In this way, politics is a question not only of who gets what but of who persuades whom in an ongoing negotiation of reality.

At first such compromises are precarious. Political actors are keenly aware of their arbitrary and artificial nature, and many may hope to reverse the agreed-upon compromises at the earliest possible opportunity. Once agreed upon, however, these negotiated realities are typically institutionalized in the political system and cannot be easily changed even if there is a shift in the balance of power among the different political actors. Decision-making rules, such as the requirement of a two-thirds majority to revise a constitution, may create high barriers to the reversal of agreed-upon policies, while the credibility of leaders may be damaged by a constant shifting of positions. Moreover, over time the legitimations offered on behalf of these compromises – particularly if they are perceived as successful – are reified and become what Emile Durkheim called "social facts."[8] Subsequent generations of decision makers come to take for granted these legitimations and the beliefs and values on which they are based. What may have been an ad hoc response to historical necessities at one time becomes hallowed social truth at another. These legitimations thus become part of the political culture of the nation and can have a lasting impact on state behavior long after the circumstances that gave birth to them have passed.

The study of the political-military culture of an entire nation requires a detailed, multilayered research strategy, involving three central empirical tasks. First, it is necessary to investigate the original set of historical experiences that define how a given society views the military, national security, and the use of force, paying careful attention to the interpretation of these events among different groups in the society.

Second, one needs to examine the political process through which actual security policy was made and how particular decisions were subsequently legitimated. In this context it is important to define the essential features of both the political-military culture and the security policy associated with it at a *particular point in time*. Third, it is necessary to examine the evolution of both the political-military culture and defense policies over time, monitoring how they evolved in response to historical events.

Such a longitudinal analysis allows us to escape the trap of deriving culture from behavior, which leads to the kind of tautological, ad hoc reasoning of which cultural analysis is often accused.[9] While in practice it is nearly impossible to separate culture from behavior, for analytical purposes it is possible to disaggregate policy behavior and the meanings that political actors and the general public attach to those policies, as reflected in public opinion polls, parliamentary debates, books and articles written by opinion leaders, newspaper editorials, and so forth. This procedure allows us to judge the degree of consistency between behavior and expressed beliefs and values over time. If culture (in this case, political-military culture) changes without any corresponding shift in behavior, there are grounds to question the posited relationship between the two. Likewise, if behavior changes without any change in the expressed beliefs and values that have been associated with earlier policies, then again we have reason to doubt that the two factors influence one another. In other words, expressed cultural beliefs and values should develop in tandem with behavior – in this case defense and national security policy. When there is a disjuncture between the two, an appropriate degree of tension should be observable in the political system.

According to the model of cultural change explicated above, under normal circumstances culture should change only incrementally in response to ordinary historical events such as shifts in the balance of power or the formation of international institutions. When major new policy initiatives violating existing norms and values are proposed, resistance in the form of demonstrations, political confrontations, and changes in government should be observable. If major changes occur without generating such resistance, then the presumed relationship between political-military culture and defense policy can be considered to have been falsified.

In this sense, political-military culture often acts as a source of inertia in policy making, at least in the short run. At the same time, how nations choose to behave can have significant, system-level effects in the long run as well, especially if they are important actors like Germany and Japan. For example, isolationism in the United States before 1941 significantly delayed the American entry into World War II, creating a window of opportunity in which the Axis powers could have achieved military victory. While from a structural realist point of view the only significant difference would have been that Western Europe would have been organized under the aegis of a Nazi German rather than a democratic American hegemon, the character of the international system would have been profoundly different.[10]

Notes

1   For an excellent yet succinct summary of the main features of a cultural theory of action, see Harry Eckstein, "A Culturalist Theory of Political Change," in Eckstein,

Regarding Politics: Essays on Political Theory, Stability, and Change, pp. 267–71 (Berkeley: University of California Press, 1992).

2   For an interesting discussion of the relationship between national identity and national interest, see William Bloom, *Personal Identity, National Identity, and International Relations* (New York: Cambridge University Press, 1990), esp. ch. 4; and Alexander Wendt, "Anarchy Is What States Make of It: The Social Construction of Power Politics," *International Organization* 46, no. 2 (Spring 1992): 391–425.

3   The classic formulation of the concept of political culture can be found in Gabriel Almond and Sydney Verba, *The Civic Culture* (Boston: Little, Brown, 1965), pp. 11–14.

4   For an example of the kind of internal contradictions that may emerge out of a culture over time, see Daniel Bell, *The Cultural Contradictions of Capitalism* (New York: Basic Books, 1976).

5   Michael Thompson, Richard Ellis, and Aaron Wildavsky, *Cultural Theory* (Boulder: Westview, 1990), ch. 5.

6   For more on the process of social learning, see Milton Rokeach, *The Open and Closed Mind* (New York: Basic Books, 1960); Lloyd Etheridge, *Can Governments Learn?* (New York: Pergamon, 1985); and Ernst Haas, "Why Collaborate? Issue Linkage and International Relations," *World Politics* 32, no. 3 (April 1980): 357–405.

7   Thomas Kuhn, *The Structure of Scientific Revolutions*, 2d ed. (Chicago: University of Chicago Press, 1970).

8   Emile Durkheim, *The Rules of the Sociological Method*, trans. Sarah A. Solovay and John D. Mueller, ed. George E. G. Catlin (Chicago: University of Chicago Press, 1938), pp. 1061–62.

9   See Brian Barry, *Sociologists, Economists, and Democracy* (London: Collier-Macmillan, 1970); and Carole Pateman, "Political Culture, Political Structures, and Political Change," *British Journal of Sociology* 1, no. 3 (July 1971): 291–306.

10   For a similar type of argument, see John Gerard Ruggie, "Multilateralism: The Anatomy of an Institution," in Ruggie, ed., *Multilateralism Matters: The Theory and Praxis of an Institutional Form* (New York: Columbia University Press, 1993), pp. 24–31.

Discussion questions

- Identify and discuss the flaws of utopianism that led to the eventual obsolescence of the League of Nations.
- Do you find the principles of classical realism relevant and convincing in explaining contemporary international relations/security?
- What are the specific features of an 'international society' that distinguish it from an 'international system'?
- What do Neorealist advocates mean by 'structure'?
- What is a security dilemma?
- Why do states become 'like-units' in an anarchical international order?
- Identify the major differences between Morgenthau's classical realism and the Neorealism of Kenneth Waltz.
- How do Realists and Liberals differ in their understanding of war and peace?
- What makes cooperation more likely under the security dilemma?
- In what manner does the flaw in the causal logic of liberal institutionalism undermine its understanding of international relations, and its ability to promote stability in the post-Cold War world?
- To what extent is Neoliberal Institutionalism similar to Neorealism in terms of their intellectual commitments?
- What is meant by a 'democratic peace'?
- Do you agree with Alexander Wendt's conviction that 'anarchy is what states make of it'?
- Do ideas and discourse influence and shape state behaviour and preferences?
- How does constructivism's view of international security differ from that of Neorealism and Neoliberal Institutionalism?
- How do culture and identity affect state behaviour and preferences?

PART 3

Security Dimensions and Issues

Introduction

NED LEBOW AND JANICE GROSS STEIN offer a discussion of nuclear war as the apogee of the use of armed force, and focus on typologies of nuclear deterrence and the contribution to international stability. Lebow and Stein point out that mutually assured destruction (MAD) did ensure relative peace during the Cold War, but also that deterrence can be self-defeating. Deterrence, if mishandled, may induce the very kind of reckless behaviour in adversaries that it was originally designed to prevent, fuelling dangerous arms races and even aggression. **Barry Buzan** and **Eric Herring** expand on the theme of arms races, presenting the two models of Action-Reaction and Domestic Structure. The former model reflects the Realist logic of the security dilemma, whereby any action by a hostile state to increase its military strength will heighten the sense of insecurity in other states and provoke an arms build-up. Conversely, any attempt to build down armaments should induce a reduction in military tensions. Buzan and Herring in presenting the Domestic Structure model, though, highlight an important complementary or alternative dynamic to explain arms races. They draw attention to the role of bureaucratic-military complexes and the proprietors of defence technologies in perpetuating arms build-ups even in the absence of external threats, thus offering an important corrective to the dominant Realist view. **Scott Sagan**'s piece adds further depth to the understanding of arms races through an examination of the motivations for states to join the ranks of nuclear proliferators. The first model of proliferation, the Security Model, follows the Realist logic of the security dilemma and external threat. The second model of Domestic Politics emphasises the role of internal bureaucratic and political actors in encouraging the acquisition of nuclear weapons for their own parochial interests. The final model of Norms suggests that states' normative attachment to or repellence from nuclear weapons will be a key determinant in choices over whether to proliferate or not. These models offer a menu of explanations to understand in more sophisticated terms the current impulse of certain states towards retaining or procuring nuclear weapons.

Lawrence Freedman's contribution points to new potential loci and forms of armed conflict. Freedman argues that, while major war is becoming obsolete, war and violence are still very much apparent, whether within or occasionally between states. In particular, he argues, the international security scene will see the emergence of new forms of unorthodox warfare and new sub-state actors which do not play by the normal rules of military engagement. Freedman opines that states must come to terms with these new forms of warfare, utilising the Revolution in Military Affairs (RMA) and gaining an 'information advantage' for conduct of effective military operations, and for more effective 'public relations' to win hearts and minds in emerging complex struggles. **Michael O'Hanlon** expands on the theme of the RMA, explaining how the rapid development and innovation of military and information technologies lead to the introduction of new tactics and strategy, which will inevitably influence the future shape of warfare. O'Hanlon provides a typology of thinking about the RMA and the ways in which it is seen to expand US global military reach but also to introduce potential new military vulnerabilities.

Thomas Homer-Dixon illustrates the linkages between resource scarcity and the perpetration of violence. Homer-Dixon argues that states tend to wage war over nonrenewable resources such as fossil fuels and minerals, rather than renewable resources such as agricultural land and fishing grounds, because these can be used to augment state power and because weaker states are more reliant on the latter and have less national power for aggression. Homer-Dixon points to water as the most likely renewable resource to generate conflict. In addition, he demonstrates the causal linkage between environmental scarcity and economic and social disruption, which then trigger 'deprivation' conflicts such as civil strife and insurgency. **Myron Weiner** advances the issue of migration as another potential trigger for armed conflict, both within and between states. Weiner presents a number of ways in which migrants can be perceived as political, cultural and economic threats to both sending and receiving states.

Phil Williams introduces yet another source of non-traditional contemporary conflict in the shape of transnational criminal organisations (TCO). TCOs pose a threat of violence to individual and state apparatus, as well as undermining governance structures. Williams also indicates the risk of collaboration between TCOs and 'rogue states' in the trafficking of WMD. **P. W. Singer** further widens out the non-traditional threat agenda to examine the linkages between AIDS and security. Singer highlights the high incidence of HIV/AIDS infections in militaries, and how this may serve to weaken not only the security functions of states but also their very institutional stability. Singer indicates that the AIDS epidemic is likely to create more orphans, thus exacerbating the issue of child soldiers, and that the disease can even be used as a weapon of war and genocide through the crime of rape. Finally in this section, **Jonathan Kirshner** looks at the issue of the role of economics in contemporary warfare. Kirshner outlines how economic growth and dislocation can produce conditions for conflict. He also examines how economic sanctions are used as a form of warfare.

Ned Lebow and Janice Gross Stein

NUCLEAR DETERRENCE

Source: 'Nuclear lessons of the Cold War', in Ken Booth (ed.) *Statecraft and Security: The Cold War and Beyond* (Cambridge: Cambridge University Press, 1998), pp. 71–86.

Nuclear lessons of the Cold War

S TUDENTS OF NUCLEAR deterrence distinguish between general and immediate deterrence (Morgan, 1977). General deterrence relies on the existing power balance to prevent an adversary from seriously considering a military challenge because of its expected adverse consequences. It is often a country's first line of defence against attack. Leaders resort to the strategy of immediate deterrence only after general deterrence has failed, or when they believe that a more explicit expression of their intent to defend their interests is necessary to buttress general deterrence. If immediate deterrence fails, leaders will find themselves in a crisis, as President Kennedy did when US intelligence discovered Soviet missiles in Cuba [...]. General and immediate deterrence represent a progression from a diffuse if real concern about an adversary's intentions to the expectation that a specific interest or commitment is about to be challenged.

Both forms of deterrence assume that adversaries are most likely to resort to force or threatening military deployments when they judge the military balance favourable and question the defender's resolve. General deterrence pays particular importance to the military dimension; it tries to discourage challenges by developing the capability to defend national commitments or inflict unacceptable punishment on an adversary. General deterrence is a long-term strategy. Five-year lead times and normally longer are common between a decision to develop a weapon and its deployment.

Immediate deterrence is a short-term strategy. Its purpose is to discourage an imminent attack or challenge of a specific commitment. The military component of immediate deterrence must rely on forces in being. To buttress their defensive capability and display resolve, leaders may deploy forces when they anticipate an attack or challenge, as Kennedy did in the aftermath of the Vienna summit meeting with Soviet Premier Nikita Khrushchev in June 1961. In response to Khrushchev's ultimatum on

Berlin, he sent additional ground and air forces to Germany and strengthened the US garrison in Berlin. These reinforcements were designed to communicate the administration's will to resist any encroachment against West Berlin or Western access routes to the city.

General deterrence: The origins of the Cuban missile crisis indicate that general deterrence, as practised by both superpowers, was provocative rather than preventive. Soviet officials testified that US strategic buildup, deployment of missiles in Turkey and assertions of nuclear superiority, made them increasingly insecure. The president viewed all of these measures as prudent, defensive precautions. His actions had the unanticipated consequence of convincing Khrushchev of the need to protect the Soviet Union and Cuba from US military and political challenges.

Khrushchev was hardly the innocent victim of US paranoia. His unfounded claims of nuclear superiority and nuclear threats were the catalyst for Kennedy's decision to increase the scope and pace of the US strategic buildup. The new US programmes and the Strategic Air Command's higher state of strategic readiness exacerbated Soviet perceptions of threat and contributed to Khrushchev's decision to send missiles to Cuba. In attempting to intimidate their adversaries, both leaders helped to bring about the kind of confrontation they were trying to avoid.

Kennedy later speculated, and Soviet officials have since confirmed, that his efforts to reinforce deterrence also encouraged Khrushchev to stiffen his position on Berlin (Schlesinger, 1965: 347–48; see also George and Smoke, 1974: 429, 579). The action and reaction that linked Berlin and Cuba were part of a larger cycle of insecurity and escalation that reached well back into the 1950s, if not to the beginning of the Cold War. The Soviet challenge to the Western position in Berlin in 1959–61 was motivated by Soviet concern about the viability of East Germany and secondarily by Soviet vulnerability to US nuclear-tipped missiles stationed in Western Europe. The US missiles had been deployed to assuage NATO fears about the conventional military balance on the central front, made more acute by the creation of the Warsaw Pact in 1955. The Warsaw Pact itself was an attempt by Moscow to consolidate its political and physical control over an increasingly restive Eastern Europe (Remmington, 1967; Jones, 1981; Holloway and Sharp, 1984).

Once the Cuban missile crisis erupted, general deterrence played an important moderating role. Kennedy and Khrushchev moved away from confrontation and towards compromise because they both feared war. Kennedy worried that escalation would set in motion a chain of events that could lead to nuclear war. Khrushchev's decision to withdraw the missiles indicated that he too was prepared to make sacrifices to avoid war. His capitulation in the face of US military pressure was a humiliating defeat for the Soviet Union and its leader. Soviet officials confirm that it was a crucial factor in his removal from power a year later.[1] For many years, Americans portrayed the crisis as an unalloyed US triumph. Kennedy's secret promise to remove the Jupiter missiles from Turkey within six months of the end of the missile crisis, and his willingness on Saturday night, 27 October, to consider making that concession public, indicate that when the superpower leaders were 'eyeball to eyeball' both sides blinked. One reason they did so was their fear of nuclear war and its consequences. [...]

Immediate deterrence is intended to forestall a specific military deployment or use of force. For immediate deterrence to succeed, the defender's threats must convince adversaries that the likely costs of a challenge will more than offset any possible gains.[2]

Immediate deterrence did not prevent the missile crisis. After Khrushchev had decided to send missiles to Cuba, Kennedy warned that he would not tolerate the introduction of Soviet missiles in Cuba. The president issued his threat in the belief that Khrushchev had no intention of establishing missile bases in Cuba. Despite the president's warnings, Khrushchev nevertheless proceeded with the secret deployment; he was convinced that they were necessary to protect Cuba from invasion, redress the strategic balance and establish psychological equality with the United States (Lebow and Stein, 1994: 19–66).

Students of the crisis disagree about why deterrence failed. Some contend that the strategy could not have worked while others insist that Kennedy attempted deterrence too late (Lebow, 1983). Whatever the cause, the failure of deterrence exacerbated the most acute crisis of the Cold War. By making a public commitment to keep Soviet missiles out of Cuba, Kennedy dramatically increased the domestic political and foreign policy costs of allowing the missiles to remain after they were discovered. A threat originally intended to deflect pressures on the administration to invade Cuba would have made that invasion very difficult to avoid if Soviet-leaders had not agreed to withdraw their missiles. [...]

Deterrence had diverse and contradictory consequences for superpower behaviour. General and immediate deterrence were principal causes of the missile crisis, but general deterrence also facilitated its resolution. [...]

The strategy of deterrence attempts to manipulate the risk of war for political ends. For much of the Cold War, Soviet and US policymakers doubted that their opposites were deterred by the prospect of nuclear war. They expended valuable resources trying to perfect the mix of strategic forces, nuclear doctrine and targeting policy that would succeed in restraining their adversary. They also used military build-ups, force deployments and threats of war to try to coerce one another into making political concessions. In Berlin [...], these attempts were unsuccessful but succeeded in greatly aggravating tensions.

The reality of deterrence derived from the inescapable fact that a superpower nuclear conflict would have been an unprecedented catastrophe for both sides. Superpower leaders understood this; by the late 1960s, if not earlier, they had come to believe that their countries could not survive a nuclear war. Fear of war, independent of the disparity in the strategic capabilities of the two sides, helped to keep both US and Soviet leaders from going over the brink and provided an important incentive for the mutual concessions that resolved the Cuban missile crisis. The moderation induced by the reality of deterrence helped to curtail the recklessness associated with the strategy of deterrence in the late 1950s and early 1960s. [...]

When and why does deterrence work?

Proponents of deterrence have advanced two constraining reasons for its putative success. The conventional wisdom holds that deterrence restrained the Soviet Union by convincing its leaders that any military action against the United States or its allies would meet certain and effective opposition. Those who credit deterrence with preserving the peace assume that in its absence the Soviet Union would have been tempted to use force against its Western adversaries or their allies [...].

[...] [Indeed] [t]he conventional wisdom [...] assumed that Soviet aggression would wax and wane as a function of Soviet perceptions of US military capability and resolve. Soviet leaders would be most restrained when they regarded the military balance as unfavourable and US resolve as unquestionable (NSC 68, 1950: 264; Pipes, 1977; Aspaturian, 1980; Podhoretz, 1980; Luttwak, 1980).

The evidence from the crises in 1962 [...] do[es] not support this assessment of deterrence. [...] The alternative interpretation holds that fear of nuclear war made both superpowers more cautious than they otherwise would have been in their competition for global influence, and thereby kept the peace. While far more convincing than the argument which credits the strategy of nuclear deterrence with preserving the peace, this explanation also is not fully persuasive. The reality of nuclear deterrence had a restraining effect on both Kennedy and Khrushchev in 1962 [...]. When superpower leaders believed that they were approaching the brink of war, fear of war pulled them back.[3]

It is difficult to judge how much of the fear of war can be attributed to nuclear weapons, but the pattern of war avoidance was well set before the 1960s when the strategic nuclear arms race greatly accelerated (MccGwire, 1994: 215–17). At the time of the Korean War, the United States had only a limited nuclear arsenal, but Stalin may have exaggerated US ability to launch extensive nuclear strikes against the Soviet Union.[4] Secretary of Defense Robert McNamara subsequently testified that President Kennedy worried primarily that the missile crisis would lead to a conventional war with the Soviet Union (Welch, 1989). Other members of the Ex Comm disagree; they say it was the threat of nuclear war that was in the back of their minds, and probably, the president's (Welch, 1989). [...]

Soviet leaders during the missile crisis also worried about war, but neither the written record nor the testimony of Soviet officials offers any evidence of the kind of war Khrushchev thought most likely. There is no evidence that Khrushchev or Kennedy speculated about war scenarios; they were desperately trying to resolve the crisis. They had no political or psychological incentive to investigate the consequences of failure – quite the reverse. Their fear of war remained strong but diffuse. [...]

The absence of superpower war is puzzling only if at least one of the superpowers was expansionist and aggressive. On the basis of the evidence now available, the image that each superpower held of the other as opportunity-driven aggressors can be discredited as crude stereotypes. Khrushchev and Brezhnev felt threatened by what they considered the predatory policies of their adversary, as did US leaders by Soviet policies. For much of the Cold War, Soviet leaders were primarily concerned with preserving what they had, although, like their US counterparts, they were not averse to making gains that appeared to entail little risk or cost. Serious confrontations between the superpowers arose only when one of them believed that its vital interests were threatened by the other.

With the benefit of hindsight it is apparent that although both superpowers hoped to remake the world in their image, neither Moscow nor Washington was ever so dissatisfied with the status quo that it was tempted to go to war with the other, or even threaten war, to force a change. It was not only the absence of *opportunity* that kept the peace, but also the absence of a strong *motive* for war. Without a compelling motive, leaders were unwilling to assume the burden and responsibility for war, even if they thought its outcome would be favourable. In the late 1950s and early 1960s, when the

United States might have destroyed the Soviet Union in a first strike with relatively little damage to itself, US leaders never considered a preventive war. The Soviet Union never possessed such a strategic advantage, but there is no reason to suspect that Khrushchev or Brezhnev had any greater interest than Eisenhower and Kennedy in going to war. The reality of deterrence helped to restrain leaders on both sides, but their relative satisfaction with the status quo was an important cause of the long peace.

Deterrence in hindsight

The Cold War began as a result of Soviet – US competition in Central Europe in the aftermath of Germany's defeat. Once recognised spheres of influence were established, confrontations between the superpowers in the heart of Europe diminished. Only Berlin continued to be a flashpoint until the superpowers reached a tacit understanding about the two Germanies in the mid-1960s.

The conventional and nuclear arms buildup that followed in the wake of the crises of the early Cold War was a reaction to the mutual insecurities they generated. By the 1970s, the growing arsenal and increasingly accurate weapons of mass destruction that each superpower aimed at the other had become the primary source of mutual insecurity and tension. Moscow and Washington no longer argued about the status quo in Europe but about the new weapons systems each deployed to threaten the other. Each thought that deterrence was far less robust than it was. Their search for deterrence reversed cause and effect and prolonged the Cold War.

The history of the Cold War provides compelling evidence of the pernicious effects of the open-ended quest for nuclear deterrence. Michael MccGwire captured the pernicious effects of deterrence dogma on Western attitudes, ethics and policies, which he summarised under seven major indictments; he argued consistently that the Western theory of nuclear deterrence had a particular dogmatic quality which was not shared by the more practical approach of the Soviets (MccGwire, 1985/6). Be that as it may, nuclear weapons also moderated superpower behaviour, once leaders in Moscow and Washington recognised and acknowledged to the other that a nuclear war between them would almost certainly lead to their mutual destruction.

Since the late 1960s, when the Soviet Union developed an effective retaliatory capability, both superpowers had to live with nuclear vulnerability. There were always advocates of preemption, ballistic missile defence or other illusory visions of security in a nuclear world. But nuclear vulnerability could not be eliminated. Mutual Assured Destruction (MAD) was a reality from which there was no escape short of the most far-reaching arms control. Even after the dissolution of the Soviet Union and the proposed deep cuts in nuclear weapons, Russia and the United States will still possess enough nuclear weapons to destroy each other many times over.[5]

Nuclear vulnerability distinguished the Soviet – US conflict from conventional conflicts of the past or present. In conventional conflicts, leaders could believe that war might benefit their country. Leaders have often gone to war with this expectation although, more often than not, they have been proved wrong. The consequences of war turned out very differently than leaders in Iraq in 1980, Argentina in 1982 and Israel in 1982 expected.

Fear of the consequences of nuclear war not only made it exceedingly improbable that either superpower would deliberately seek a military confrontation with the other; it made their leaders extremely reluctant to take any action that they considered would seriously raise the risk of war. Over the years they developed a much better appreciation of each other's interests. In the last years of the Soviet–US conflict, leaders on both sides acknowledged and refrained from any challenge of the other's vital interests.

The ultimate irony of nuclear deterrence may be the way in which the strategy of deterrence undercut much of the political stability the reality of deterrence should have created. The arms build-ups, threatening military deployments, and the confrontational rhetoric that characterised the strategy of deterrence effectively obscured deep-seated, mutual fears of war. Fear of nuclear war made leaders inwardly cautious, but their public posturing convinced their adversaries that they were aggressive, risk-prone and even irrational.

This reckless kind of behaviour was consistent with the strategy of deterrence. Leaders on both sides recognised that only a madman would use nuclear weapons against a nuclear adversary. To reinforce deterrence, they therefore tried, and to a disturbing degree, succeeded in convincing the other that they might be irrational enough or sufficiently out of control to implement their threats. Each consequently became less secure, more threatened and less confident of the robust reality of deterrence. The strategy of deterrence was self-defeating; it provoked the kind of behaviour it was designed to prevent.

The history of the Cold War suggests that nuclear deterrence should be viewed as a very dangerous medicine. Arsenic, formerly used to treat syphilis and schistosomiasis, or chemotherapy, routinely used to treat cancer, can kill or cure a patient. The outcome depends on the virulence of the disease, how early the disease is detected, the amount of drugs administered, and the resistance of the patient to both the disease and the cure. So it is with nuclear deterrence. Mutual deterrence can prompt mutual caution. Too much deterrence, or deterrence applied inappropriately to a frightened and vulnerable adversary, can fuel an arms race that makes both sides less rather than more secure and provoke the aggression that it is designed to prevent.

The superpowers 'overdosed' on deterrence. It poisoned their relationship, but their leaders remained blind to its consequences. Instead, they interpreted the tension and crises that followed as evidence of the need for even more deterrence. In retrospect, both sides would probably have been more secure without any nuclear weapons. But once nuclear weapons were developed and used against Japan it became impossible to put the nuclear genie back in the bottle with a secure stopper at its mouth. Despite its rhetoric to the contrary, the United States was unprepared to give up its advantage, and the Soviet Union was committed to developing its own nuclear arsenal. Still, the superpowers would have been wise to have resisted the temptation to develop thermonuclear weapons, intercontinental ballistic missiles and multiple independently targeted re-entry vehicles (MIRVs). MIRVs were particularly destabilising because they conferred an advantage to offence, and made both sides feel more insecure and more committed to programmes that seemed to confirm the other's worst case assumptions about their motives.

The superpowers were unique in their resources, level of technical sophistication and numbers of nuclear weapons that they developed and deployed. We have to be careful in drawing wider lessons. Bearing this caveat in mind, there do seem to be some important political parallels. Nowhere do nuclear weapons appear to have conferred real security benefits. In the Middle East, the Indian subcontinent, and in Argentina and Brazil until changes of government in both those countries put an end to their nuclear weapons programme, the attempt or actual development of nuclear weapons was the catalyst for adversaries to develop their own weapons of mass destruction. As with the superpowers, this made both sides more insecure because it made them feel vulnerable and was taken as evidence of the other's hostile intentions. The superpower experience should serve as a cautionary tale for the leaders of these countries and of those countries contemplating the possible development of nuclear arsenals.

Notes

1   Interview with Leonid Zamyatin, Moscow, 16 December 1991 (see also Khrushchev, 1990: 156–57; Troyanovsky, 1992).

2   See Lebow, 1981, pp. 82–97, for a discussion of the four traditional prerequisites of deterrence. For an alternative set of hypotheses about the conditions essential to deterrent success, see Lebow and Stein, 1990: 59–69.

3   There is also evidence that the fear of war influenced Soviet behaviour in Korea. Joseph Stalin had encouraged Kim Il Sung to attack South Korea in June 1950 in the expectation that the UnitedStates would not intervene. When Washington did intervene, Stalin, afraid that the North Korean attack would provoke a Soviet–US war, quickly signalled interest in a cease-fire (Schecter with Luchkov, 1990: 144–47).

4   Oleg Grinevsky contends that Stalin feared that even a few atomic bombs dropped on Moscow would have been enough to destroy the communist experiment (interview with Oleg Grinevsky, Stockholm, 24 Oct. 1992).

5   By 2003, if the cuts proposed in the START II treaty are implemented, Russia will cut its missiles to 504 and its warheads to 3,000 and the United States will reduce its missiles to 500 and its warheads to 3,500.

References

Aspaturian, Vernon (1980) 'Soviet Global Power and the Correlation of Forces', *Problems of Communism*, no. 20 (May–June).

George, Alexander L. and Smoke, Richard (1974) *Deterrence in American Foreign Policy: Theory and Practice* (New York: Columbia University Press).

Holloway, David and Sharp, Jane M. O. (eds.) (1984) *The Warsaw Pact: Alliance in Transition?* (London: Macmillan).

Jones, Christopher D. (1981) *Soviet Influence in Eastern Europe: Political Autonomy and the Warsaw Pact* (New York: Praeger).

Khrushchev, Sergei (1990) *Khrushchev on Khrushchev: An Inside Account of the Man and His Era*, trans. William Taubman (Boston: Little, Brown).

Kissinger, Henry (1982) *Years of Upheaval* (Boston: Little, Brown).

Lebow, Richard Ned (1981) *Between Peace and War: The Nature of International Crisis* (Baltimore: Johns Hopkins University Press).

—— (1983) 'The Cuban Missile Crisis: Reading the Lessons Correctly', *Political Science Quarterly*, no. 98 (Fall).

—— (1987) *Nuclear Crisis Management: A Dangerous Illusion* (Ithaca: Cornell University Press).

Lebow, Richard Ned and Gross Stein, Janice (1990) *When Does Deterrence Succeed and How Do We Know?* (Ottawa: Canadian Institute for International Peace and Security).

—— (1994) *We All Lost The Cold War* (Princeton: Princeton University Press).

Luttwak, Edward N. (1980) 'After Afghanistan', *Commentary*, no. 69 (April).

MccGwire, Michael (1985/6) 'Deterrence: The Problem – Not The Solution', *International Affairs*, vol. 62 (1). Also in *SAIS Review*, no. 5, Summer – Fall 1985, pp. 105–24.

Morgan, Patrick M. (1977) *Deterrence: A Conceptual Analysis* (Beverley Hills: Sage Library of Social Science).

NSC 68 (1950) 'United States Objectives and Programs for National Security', *Foreign Relations of the United States, 1950*, vol. I (Washington, DC: Government Printing Office, 1977), 14 April.

Pipes, Richard (1977) 'Why the Soviet Union Thinks It could Fight and Win a Nuclear War', *Commentary*, no. 64 (July).

Podhoretz, Norman (1980) 'The Present Danger', *Commentary*, no. 69 (April).

Remmington, Robin Allison (1967) *The Changing Soviet Perception of the Warsaw Pact* (Cambridge: MIT Center for International Studies).

Schecter, Jerrold L. with Luchkov, Vyacheslav L. (trans.) (1990) *Khrushchev Remembers: The Glasnost Tapes* (Boston: Little Brown).

Schlesinger, Arthur (1965) *A Thousand Days: John F. Kennedy in the White House* (London: Deutsch).

Troyanovsky, Oleg (1992) 'The Caribbean Crisis: A View from the Kremlin', *International Affairs* (Moscow), no. 4–5 (April/May).

Welch, David A. (ed.) (1989) *Proceedings of the Hawk's Cay Conference on the Cuban Missile Crisis. CSIA Working Papers, No. 89–1* (Cambridge, MA: Center for Sciences and International Affairs) mimeograph.

Barry Buzan and Eric Herring

ARMS RACES

Source: *The Arms Dynamic in World Politics* (Boulder, CO: Lynne Rienner, 1998), pp. 83–118.

The action–reaction model

T HE ACTION–REACTION MODEL is the classical view of arms racing and provides the basis for the metaphor of a race. Most attempts to define arms racing are rooted in it. The basic proposition of the action–reaction model is that states strengthen their armaments because of the threats the states perceive from other states. The theory implicit in the model explains the arms dynamic as driven primarily by factors external to the state. An action by any potentially hostile state to increase its military strength will raise the level of threat seen by other states and cause them to react by increasing their own strength (Rathjens 1973). In theory this process also works in reverse. If states are driven to arm by external threats, then domestic economic pressures to apply resources to other items on the political agenda should lead them to build down in proportion to reductions in military capability by others. Whether action–reaction works with equal facility in both directions has important implications for disarmament.

The action–reaction model posits something like an international market in military strength. States will arm themselves either to seek security against the threats posed by others or increase their power to achieve political objectives against the interests of others. Military power can be used to achieve objectives through use of force, implicit or explicit threats, or symbolism [...]. Balances (including balances in political status as well as balances of military power) will emerge at higher or lower levels of armament, depending on how willing states are to drive up the price of achieving their objectives. Counterpressure to open-ended arms competition is created both by the responses of other states to attempts by one to increase its military power and by domestic resource constraints. [...]

The action–reaction model does not depend on the process by which techno-logical innovation causes continual improvement in military technology. However, if such innovation exists it becomes part of the action–reaction process. Even if the quality of military technology was static, and evenly distributed in the international system, the action–reaction process could still be the mechanism by which states compete militarily in purely quantitative terms. Increases in the number of battle-ships in one state would still create pressure for countering increases in other states. For this reason, the action–reaction model can more easily be applied than the domestic structure model to cases that occurred before the onset of the industrial revolution. Some authors nevertheless take the view that arms racing has only become a distinctive international phenomenon since the industrial revolution unleashed the forces of mass production and institutionalized innovation into the international system (Huntington 1958: 41, 43; Hammond 1993: 11).

When military competition reflects a power struggle between states, as before both world wars; during the Cold War; or between Iran and Iraq, India and Pakistan, or Israel and its Arab neighbors, it can be intense and highly focused – especially when the parties see war as a likely outcome. Even when there is no specific power struggle, or only a weak one, the action–reaction process still works at the lower levels of com-petition and maintenance of the military status quo. States will usually have some sense of who they consider to be possible sources of attack even when they see the probability of war as being low. This perception will ensure an element of action–reaction in military policy, albeit of a much more subdued kind than in an arms race. For build-down, maintenance, and competition as for racing, action–reaction expresses itself not only in the size of armed forces, but also in the type of forces acquired and the level of concern about modernization and readiness for combat. The action–reaction model therefore applies to the arms dynamic as a whole. [...]

There is considerable blending of power and security motives in the behavior of states. Most military instruments can be used for offensive as well as defensive pur-poses. It is therefore difficult for any state to distinguish between measures other states take to defend themselves and measures they may be taking to increase their capability for aggression. Because the consequences of being wrong may be very severe, it is a commonplace dictum that prudence requires each state to adjust its own military measures in response to a worst-case view of the measures taken by others. [...]

There are problems associated with different aspects of this dictum. First, what is described as worst-case analysis is often something more moderate (worse rather than worst-case analysis) in that the real worst case is dismissed or seen as unlikely. Second, worst-case analysis is often adopted not due to prudence but as a conscious symbolic and ideological exaggeration to ensure support for military expenditure and the use of threats and force. [...] Third, worst-case analysis can be as dangerous as, and more wasteful of resources than, a more balanced threat assessment in that it can unnecessarily escalate a rivalry (Garthoff 1978, 1984). Finally, since each adjustment may be seen by some other states as a possible threat, even a system in which all states seek only their own defense can produce competitive accumulations of military strength. The set of circumstances that produces this tendency is known as the "secur-ity dilemma" (Herz 1950; Butterfield 1951; Snyder 1984; Jervis 1978, 1985; Snyder 1985; Buzan 1991: chapter 8; Wheeler and Booth 1992). It is a dilemma because states cannot easily take measures to strengthen their own military security without making others feel less secure. If others feel less secure they may take countermeasures that may negate the measures taken by the first state. That state in turn may feel pressured to restore its preferred ratio of strength by further increases in its own armaments, and so on. The workings of the security dilemma are thus closely related to those of the action–reaction model. [...]

The idea of the action–reaction model is simple, but its operation in practice is complex. The model says little about motives other than that each side feels threatened by the other. Neither does it indicate whether the two actors are aware of, and are seeking to control, the process in which they are engaged. In practice, the only thing that may be clear is that their behavior is influenced in part by their sense of external threat. The specific details of the action–reaction process may be difficult to identify. This point needs to be considered in detail because the validity of the action–reaction model is widely questioned on the grounds that its supposed process is often difficult to see in practice. First the idiom of action and reaction will be examined: that is to say, the types of action that states can take within the process. Then other variables in the pattern of response will be identified, particularly magnitude, timing, and the awareness of the actors of the process in which they are engaged. Finally, it is necessary to look at the motives of the actors, which can have a considerable influence on the other variables in the action–reaction process. However, this does not mean that intentions with regard to weapons acquisition are necessarily oriented toward competition with other states: they may also be a deliberate part of domestic politics. [...]

The idioms of action and reaction

The idioms of action and reaction are numerous. The simplest is like that of [...] two states compet[ing] in terms of a single, similar weapon system, and where the strength of the rivals can be compared directly because the weapons are designed primarily to fight each other. [...] The idiom may be in terms of dissimilar weapons systems, or sets of systems, such as antisubmarine, antiaircraft, or antimissile systems versus submarines, bombers, and missiles. In such cases, the calculation of relative strengths is complicated by the large uncertainties that always surround estimates of how different, but opposed, weapons will work in combat. However, this contrast should not be overdrawn. Predicting combat outcomes between similar weapon systems is still very difficult because there are so many additional important variables such as weather, terrain, and communications or the skill, experience, and morale of the operators of those weapon systems (and the commanders of those operators). [...] The action–reaction process may not be single weapon systems, but instead be in terms of the overall arsenals of states, with each trying to measure its relative overall capability to make war (Rattinger 1976; Baugh 1984: chapter 4). [...]

In competitions over military technology the distinction between quality and quantity is important (Huntington 1958: 65–89; Gray 1971: 46–48). Potential combatants will compare not only the numbers of their weapons but also their quality. [...] However, assessments of the quality and quantity of hardware have to be accompanied by assessments about the quality of the software and "wetware" (human beings) that accompany the weapons. Weapons per se often prove to be less important during war than other factors such as morale, strategy, logistics, or alliance politics.

Although this section is concerned primarily with what explains arms competition rather than what arms competition explains, it is worth flagging Huntington's interesting argument that qualitative arms races are less war prone than quantitative ones. His argument is that increases of quantity provide what is perceived (to a great extent falsely, considering the history of war) as a known ability to fight, whereas constant changes in quality both undermine the value of quantitative accumulation and increase the difficulty of calculating the outcome of a resort to arms (Huntington 1958: 71–79). [...] The effects of this factor are seen most clearly where the arms dynamic is bilateral and focused on a single main weapon system. However, arms dynamics involve mixes of both – quality being used to offset quantity and vice versa, and quality and quantity being sought by both sides (Hammond 1993: 48, 274–75). We suspect that quantitative arms competitions or races will indicate either an intention to begin a war or an expectation of imminent war rather than being causes of wars, which appear to begin for other reasons (Blainey 1973; Lebow 1981; Gray 1993). Competitions or races in armies, whether quantitative or qualitative, are much more a sign than competitions or races in navies or air forces that war is likely (Hammond 1993: 248–49). It is worth emphasizing that wars are rarely begun when the military balance is optimal (Lebow 1984). Instead, they are more likely to occur in response to perceived threats to interests and/or to psychological biases that lead to over-estimation of the chances of military success (Lebow 1981; Herring 1995).

When the action–reaction dynamic is in terms of overall military strength, then military expenditure may become in itself an idiom of interaction. It can also play a symbolic role. This was the case with President Kennedy's announcements in May and July 1961 of increases in spending on conventional forces during the Berlin crisis. Such spending – and the increase in military spending ordered in June 1961 by Soviet leader Nikita Khrushchev – could have no practical military value in the short term for the crisis then under way: the intention was to symbolize resolve (Herring 1995: 139). [...]

When reliable data can be obtained, military expenditure is perhaps more useful to indicate the difference between arms racing and maintenance of the military status quo than it is to measure a specific action–reaction dynamic between states. For this purpose, absolute levels of military expenditure are less important than military expenditure expressed as a percentage of GNP. If military expenditure is a constant or declining percentage of GNP, then one is probably observing maintenance or build-down, especially where GNP itself tends to rise at a steady but not spectacular rate. Although absolute amounts spent will tend to rise, the increase will mostly reflect the rising costs of modern weapons compared with the older generations they replace. But if military expenditure is rising as a percentage of GNP, then the state is increasing the level of its military activity at the expense of its other activities. Such an increase cannot be sustained indefinitely. The increase's appearance indicates either a shift away from maintenance toward racing, or at least competition, or else a state caught in the squeeze of economic growth too weak to support its desired range of military commitments.

Although very useful as an indicator of the intensity of the arms dynamic, the measure of military expenditure as a percentage of GNP has to be used with caution.

Different rates of growth can have a large impact on interpretation of the figures. Slow or no growth of the figure in a rapidly expanding economy may disguise a considerable military expansion, as it did in the case of Japan until recently, and as was also the case in much of East Asia during the 1990s. A rise in the figure for a static or slow-moving economy may indicate more a holding action than an expansion of military capability. Furthermore, a rise in military spending may be a necessary transitional cost in conducting a build-down. This was seen at the end of the Cold War, when the hoped for peace dividend (reduced military spending leading to tax cuts or increased social spending) turned out in some ways to be a peace tax. Dismantling weapons, reconfiguring forces, demobilizing and rehousing military personnel, redeploying military capabilities, and so on has proven to be expensive.

The idiom of action–reaction can take a variety of other forms, economic and political, as well as military. As long as the idiom remains military the process is still within the arms dynamic. Action and reaction options other than increases in military strength or expenditure are available. States can, for example, change the deployment patterns of their armed forces in ways that make them more threatening and/or less vulnerable to an opponent. Motives are usually mixed. Khrushchev claimed that in deploying nuclear missiles in Cuba, he was reacting to the invasion threat posed by the United States to Cuba. But much more than that was in play. He also wanted to react strategically to the nuclear superiority established by the United States, and symbolically to the deployment of NATO missiles on the Soviet periphery, especially in Turkey. By giving the United States a taste of its own medicine and establishing symbolic partial nuclear equality, he hoped to create the diplomatic leverage that would broaden that equality to many areas of U.S.-Soviet relations and that would let him shift resources to nonmilitary activities (Herring 1995: chapter 8, especially 154–56). [...]

States can change their operational or declaratory strategic doctrine in response to actions (including doctrinal innovations) by an opponent. Such doctrines are a key element in actual military strength, as the Germans demonstrated with their imaginative use of the rapid mechanized warfare doctrine, known as blitzkrieg, in the early years of World War II. Because they are perceived as changes in intentions, changes in doctrine (such as the U.S. shift toward a declaratory policy of warfighting strategies of nuclear deterrence starting in the 1970s) can carry just as much weight in the eyes of an opponent as increases or decreases in the size and quality of armed forces (Gray 1976: 7; McGwire 1987, 1991; Garthoff 1990; Zisk 1993). Kimberley Zisk (1993) describes reactive doctrinal innovation between rival states as "doctrine races," although such a label will often exaggerate the pace of the innovation and the effort put into it.

When the idiom moves into the economic and political domains, the action–reaction process of the arms dynamic joins the more general one of foreign policy, and the subject shifts from strategic studies and peace studies to world politics and international political economy. The area of overlap should not be ignored. Restrictions on trade may become part of the action–reaction process, as in the long-standing attempts by NATO to prevent such dual-use technologies (militarily useful civil technologies) as computers from reaching the Soviet Union, and post-Cold War concerns regarding the spread of dual-use technologies (especially in the areas of nuclear and missile technology) to LICs.

General shifts in perception, and therefore in the character of political relations, also play an important role in the action–reaction process. Shifts toward (or away from) more negative and hostile views of an opponent can mark a major shift toward (or away from) competition or racing within the arms dynamic. Negative shifts occurred in Britain toward Germany during the late 1930s and in the United States toward the Soviet Union during the mid-1940s. Positive, or "desecuritizing" ones (Wæver 1995; Buzan, Wæver, and de Wilde 1998) – that is, ones that move issues from the security agenda and into the realm of normal politics – occurred in southern Africa with the end of apartheid. Most notably, they accompanied Gorbachev's new political thinking in international relations, which, coupled with unilateral arms reductions, triggered the end of the Cold War. A political action may also trigger a military reaction, as when states increase their military strength in response to an unleashing of revolutionary energy in a rival, as Iraq did after the revolution in Iran. Iraq saw Iran as politically more threatening but militarily weakened and therefore decided (unwisely, in view of the outcome) to attack. This kind of interplay is where the arms dynamic blends into the broader patterns of world politics.

One cannot assume that states will display consistency in the idiom of their actions and reactions [...]. Consistent responses are more likely when the rate of technological innovation is low and when the weapons concerned are ones that can be expected to fight each other, such as tanks, battleships, and fighter aircraft. Inconsistent responses are more likely when technological innovation offers opportunities to degrade the effectiveness of existing weapons systems. Such responses are also more likely when existing defensive capability looks more attractive than a matching offensive capability or when resource constraints force one side to take unorthodox measures to stay in the competition. [...]

Magnitude, timing, and awareness in the action–reaction process

To the variety of idioms in which the dialogue of the arms dynamic can be pursued must be added the variables that attend the process of action–reaction itself. These variables are magnitude (what proportion the reaction bears to the triggering action), timing (speed and sequence of interaction), and awareness (the extent to which the parties involved in the process are conscious of their impact on each other, and whether they govern their own behavior in the light of that consciousness). [...]

Magnitude

The magnitude of possible reactions within the arms dynamic covers a wide range. If the dynamic progresses by mutual overreaction, then moves to outdo one's opponent can range from acquisition of greater forces to preventive war (attacking an opponent before it becomes too strong) or preemptive war (striking the first blow in the belief that an attack by the opponent was imminent). [...] Where the rivals are equal, the relationship between the existing level of capability and the scale of the new acquisition becomes important. Parity at low levels means that the balance can change quickly.

When they are unequal, the leader may be able to tolerate some disproportion in the magnitude of the measures taken by itself and its rival.

Huntington (1958: 60) suggests that the probability of war in arms racing is at its highest when the dynamics of the race are close to resulting in a shift in the balance of power. Indeed, war may be the desired outcome for one of the parties, with arms racing as a necessary preparation for it. However, in the nuclear context, this is unlikely to be the case, because of the potential political and physical costs of using nuclear weapons. If Huntington is right, equality of military strength at low levels between nonnuclear rivals is an unstable condition because only small changes are needed to shift the balance of power.

This issue is of great importance in that much of the theory and practice of arms control and disarmament is predicated on the notion of equality as a stabilizing factor (on the grounds that neither side will have any confidence that it can start and win a war). Geoffrey Blainey (1973) argues that peace is most likely when there is a clear *im*balance of power favoring one side. Perhaps this ought to be amended to say that peace is most likely when there is a clear imbalance of power against the state that wishes to go to war. The problem with this is that motives may change so that the state that has the imbalance of power in its favor might decide to go to war. This brings us back to the idea that a broad band of equality might be the best option for preventing war. The extent to which a balance is perceived to be stable is not a technical matter. Perceptions of virtually the same balance can change radically in a short time span. [...] To underline the point, stability rests much more on perceptions than on technology. [...]

Responses of lower magnitude may also indicate a lack of resources or political will on the part of the challenged state. Or the responses may indicate a reasoned political judgment that the arms dynamic should be allowed to generate a peaceful change in the international balance of power and status. Such a judgment reflects a decision that new realities in the international system are so basic as to be very difficult to stop, and not so adverse that they are worth opposing by war. [...]

Although the idea of measured responses is clear enough in theory, in reality it is often very difficult to find reliable measures by which actions and reactions can be compared. [...]

Timing

The variable of timing poses even greater difficulties of measurement than that of magnitude. It is perhaps the main weakness in attempts to apply the action–reaction model to the study of the arms dynamic. The basic model assumes a clear sequence of action and reaction like that in a chess game. In theory, such a process should display a distinct pattern of move and countermove that would enable the pace of the action–reaction cycle to provide one measure of the intensity of interaction. Slow versus rapid patterns of response would give a useful insight into the character of the arms dynamic and is part of the process of distinguishing racing from maintenance. [...] Although delayed responses may result in a more intense arms dynamic than would otherwise have been the case (Huntington 1958: 58–63), one must not generalize too readily. States may decide to catch up without believing there is a compelling need to do so as swiftly as possible. [...]

Awareness

How aware are the actors of the process in which they are engaged? In particular, do they understand their impact on each other, and do they try to manipulate the action–reaction dynamic either to their own or to mutual advantage (Schelling 1966: chapter 7)? The action–reaction model high-lights the dangers of actors that are not aware of their impact on each other. It is a virtual truism of states that, like most individuals, they are more aware of the threats that others pose to them than they are of the threats that they pose to others (Jervis 1976). This unbalanced perception is an important element of the security dilemma in fueling an escalatory cycle of provocation and overreaction. If actors are sensitive to their impact on each other, then there is potential for managing the relationship so as to pursue balance and avoid overreaction. Such management can be approached cooperatively, in the form of negotiated agreements to restrain the arms dynamic, or unilaterally, in the form of actions by one side designed to avoid overstimulating the threat sensitivities of the other. This approach is known as reassurance (Stein 1991a, 1991b; Herring 1995: especially 51–53). […] Among other things, the institutionalization of a long-term rivalry that cannot rationally be solved by war provides considerable incentives for joint management. However, as Gray (1971: 56) points out, awareness also has its dangers. If one side is more keen to manage the arms dynamic than the other, it makes itself vulnerable to having its enthusiasm exploited and its relative strength weakened. […] When suspicions arise that an attempt to manage the arms dynamic is being cynically exploited by one side, then the arms control process can itself become the mechanism that heightens the intensity of arms competition. […]

The impact of strategic objectives on the arms dynamic

Strategic objectives within a rivalry have a major impact on other variables within the action–reaction process. It is, for example, reasonable to conjecture that the action–reaction dynamic between two status quo rivals each interested in maintaining its position through deterrence will be much less intense in terms of the pace and magnitude of its interactions, and much more restrained in its idiom, than a dynamic between two rivals both interested in changing their position, and both prepared to fight a war in order to do so. Eight pairs of concepts capture the most important elements of the impact upon the arms dynamic of strategic objectives. […]

The first pair concerns the balance of power (economic and ideological as well as military) between the actors, and the distinction is whether their strategic objectives are to change it or to preserve their existing positions. The former is a status quo orientation and the latter a revisionist orientation. Revisionism aimed at territorial expansion has the most obvious potential for war. Status quo actors are concerned primarily with security and loss avoidance: revisionist actors are more interested in power maximization and pursuit of gain (Buzan 1991: 298–310; Schweller 1994; Herring 1995: especially 47–49). If any major state seeks to change its international status as a high priority, then the probability arises that it will seek to increase its military strength. Its moves in this direction are likely to lead to an arms race or at least a military competition with those whose interests are challenged by its ambitions. […]

The second pair concerns the value of peace: the higher the value of peace, the more stable and less intense the arms dynamic may be, all other things being equal (Herring 1995: 42–43, 242–43). The value of peace is likely to be high when both sides have nuclear weapons. Attachment of a low value to peace can lead to arms competition or racing because warfighting preparations generate open-ended military needs. When war is considered to be a rational instrument of policy, then there is no absolute ceiling on the force requirements of either side. The needs of each are determined according to the capability of the other in a potentially endless cycle of action and reaction. The existence of exaggerated cycles of over-reaction may be a signal that war is increasingly likely to occur. If the value of peace is high, then there are possibilities for avoiding open-ended competitive accumulations. From the mutually assured destruction (MAD) perspective, nuclear deterrence can in theory be achieved by possession of a guaranteed capability to devastate one's opponent. Such a capability is considerably less sensitive to increases in an opponent's strength than is the case in warfighting rivalries. [...]

[...] The third relates to how secure are the states involved: insecure states are more likely than secure states to be involved in an escalatory arms dynamic (Glaser 1992). The fourth concerns the military strategies of the actors: reliance on defensive military strategies is more stabilizing than reliance on the offensive. Fifth, an emphasis on deterrence is more stabilizing than an emphasis on compellence. Sixth, reassurance of the opponent as well as the use of threats is more stabilizing than reliance solely on threats. Seventh, risk aversion is more stabilizing than willingness to take risks, although risk aversion by one side and risk acceptance by the other leads to a deteriorating situation for the risk-averse side. Eighth, a state willing to take on difficult tasks is more likely to fuel action–reaction processes than one averse to such tasks.

Despite the obvious importance of strategic objectives in the action–reaction dynamic, their role in practice is difficult to assess for a number of reasons. First, strategic objectives may be attributes of situations rather than (or as well as) actors; the objectives cannot be detached completely from the constraints, dangers, and opportunities posed by the distribution of power in the international system or by the vagaries of internal politics. [...]

Second, states usually adopt a set of strategic objectives that incorporate [both status quo and revisionist] elements [...]. Only in propagandist fantasies (or theoretical exercises) is one side the risk-averse, status quo oriented, defensive, deterrent, reassuring actor and the other a risk-acceptant, revisionist, offensive, compellent, threatening actor. [...]

Third, it can be difficult to distinguish between the pairs of strategic objectives [...]. Indeed, not only do decisionmakers often find it difficult to decide how secure they feel, how much they value peace, how averse they are to risk, and so on, but they may not even address these questions. [...]

While strategic objectives appear to be important elements in the action–reaction process, they pose great difficulties for both analysis and policy because they often cannot be either isolated or identified accurately. If the response to this uncertainty is to assume the worst, then valuable opportunities for cooperation may be lost and the operation of the security dilemma may be intensified sufficiently to cause arms competition, arms racing, or even war. If assumptions about strategic objectives are too optimistic, there is a danger that one's opponent will interpret conciliation as weakness and, by seeking to exploit the situation, create the conflict that the conciliatory behavior was aimed at avoiding. [...]

The domestic structure model

The domestic structure model rests on the idea that the arms dynamic is generated by forces within the state. It functions as an alternative to the action–reaction model only in the sense that the two models compete for primacy of place in ability to explain observed behavior within the arms dynamic. [...]

The proponents of the domestic structure model did not argue that the rivalry between the superpowers was irrelevant, but that the process of the arms dynamic had become so deeply institutionalized within each state that domestic factors largely supplanted the crude forms of action and reaction as the main engine of the arms dynamic. The external factor of rivalry still provided the necessary motivation for the arms dynamic. But when "reactions" become anticipatory, the state has, in effect, restructured itself internally on a long-term basis to deal with the arms dynamic. R&D laboratories work to push the frontiers of military technology ever forward. Arms production facilities are kept going with orders so as to maintain capacity, and over time (and along with other military facilities) they get absorbed into the budgetary and electoral processes of the state.

An almost exclusively domestically oriented arms dynamic is sometimes referred to as "autism" (Dedring 1976: 79–81). Autism exists when the military behavior of states is generated much more by internal considerations than by any rational response to external threats. If need be, external threats will be manufactured to bolster domestic unity. Military capability may be acquired more for prestige, or to reinforce the government's hold on the country, than in relation to external threats. Where autism takes hold, the consequences for vigorous interstate rivalries are serious. Excessive egocentrism in the behavior of rival states is an almost certain path to friction and paranoia in relations among them. If autism is taken to extremes, it makes the domestic structure model of the arms dynamic an alternative, rather than a complement, to the action–reaction model. If the arms dynamic is driven powerfully from within states, then it becomes much more difficult to damp down. Any state that reduces its own military strength in hope of a response from its rival will be disappointed if its rival's armaments are determined more by internal than by external factors. Autism looks rather different when it refers to the behavior of states concerned almost exclusively with internal security. Such states, if they do not produce their own arms, will suck them in from the world arms trade or as military aid from friendly states. In some cases the weapons are sold or military aid given not to the government but, if it exists, the military opposition to the government.

Extreme autism is rare, and so the interesting question about the domestic structure model is not whether it is better than the action–reaction model in some general sense, but what proportion and aspects of observed behavior each model explains for any given case. Which structures and mechanisms within the state become the main carriers of the arms dynamic? [...]

· The domestic structure model offers a whole range of factors to explain the arms dynamic. The principal ones are the institutionalization of military R&D; the institutionalization of military production; economic management; electoral politics; the military-industrial complex; organizational politics; the unifying and identity-creating roles of military threats; and internal repression and civil war. [...]

Domestic structure explanations of the arms dynamic

Institutionalization of military research and development

The institutionalization of military R&D plays a major role in the domestic structure model (Gray 1976: 39–43; Thee 1986: chapters 3, 5; Adams and Kosiak 1993; Farrell 1995, 1997: chapter 3). [...]

However, given that only a small number of major arms-producing states spend heavily on military R&D, the logic of this factor can only be applied in a few cases. The role of R&D relates closely to the discussions of technological revolutions and the technological imperative [...]. What makes R&D distinctive within the domestic structure model are the measures that arms-producing states take when the rhythm of technological development puts pressure on them to adopt a long view of military procurement. The increasing involvement of the state in military R&D is a historical trend that began to gather force in the nineteenth century and culminated in the symbiosis of state and science in the nuclear age (Pearton 1982). In the modern era, military technology is so capital intensive and takes so long to develop that any state wishing to be at the leading edge has no choice but to create or encourage a permanent R&D establishment. No state can become a major arms producer without its own R&D base, and since technological improvement is a continual process, the establishments that support it necessarily become permanent. A fully independent R&D base now appears to be beyond the reach of all states: the trend since the 1980s has been for the flattening of the top of the hierarchy of arms-producing states.

On the one hand, R&D establishments are created because the complex and expensive nature of technology requires them. On the other hand, the establishments become mechanisms that set ever higher standards of expense and complexity, increase the pace of technological advance, and work relentlessly to make their own products obsolete. In promoting their own organizational security they necessarily become promoters of technological change. Although their offerings are not always accepted for production, [...] they do mount a continual challenge to accepted standards of adequate military technology. Thus what starts as a response to a problem becomes part of the process by which the problem is continuously re-created and even exacerbated. These establishments reflect the technological conditions stemming from industrial society. They may also have become important in shaping the civil economy by giving preferential boosts to a variety of dual-use technologies, most notably in the aerospace, nuclear, and computer fields (Buzan and Sen 1990).

Despite its domestic roots, and its self-contained nature, the institutionalization of military R&D can in one sense be viewed as part of the action–reaction model. States competing at the leading edge of technology must have an R&D establishment to be in the game at all – and up to a point, so must states seeking to sell less sophisticated technology, though the resources involved are far smaller than in the leading-edge states. [...] Since the end of the Cold War, the justification for the enterprise of R&D has shifted significantly (but not entirely) toward trade rather than interstate rivalry. If the leading edge of military technology is continually moving forward, one effect of R&D is to complicate the task of differentiating arms competition from maintenance of the military status quo. The continual background of qualitative improvement means that in both cases states will tend to upgrade their military technologies. [...]

The dramatic cut in global military R&D due to the end of the Cold War ($60 billion in the mid-1990s – down 50 to 55 percent in real terms since the mid-1980s) undermines any claims of a self-sustaining, autistic process (Arnett 1996b). The United States, and perhaps the Europeans and the Japanese, may try to maintain relatively high levels of military R&D while cutting back on production and deployment. This could reflect a desire to be able to get back into the game should a new military challenger arise, or to maintain a substantial qualitative edge over the many countries around the world now equipped with modern weapons supplied by the major producers. [...]

Institutionalization of military production

The forces leading to the institutionalization of R&D are both linked to and similar to those for the institutionalization of military production, and so this factor is also limited to the small group of major arms producers. Production and R&D often share close organizational links in high-technology industries. Furthermore, for a particular weapon system, R&D and production may be concurrent rather than consecutive (Farrell 1995, 1997: chapter 3). Arms-producing states perceive the same need to maintain military production capabilities in being as they do to maintain a permanent R&D establishment (Kaldor 1982: 60–65; Adams and Kosiak 1993). Maintaining military production capabilities in turn normally involves government support for the whole range of basic industries on which military production depends, so bringing a wide range of industrial interests into the picture (Sen 1984). This constellation of capabilities is usually known as the defense industrial base, although we prefer military-industrial base, because its products are not necessarily used for defensive purposes.

The need to maintain a standing capacity for arms production is reinforced where there is a long-term rivalry. A long-term rivalry is usually seen as requiring not only a degree of permanent mobilization in case there is a rapid move toward war, but also the capacity to expand production quickly to support the war effort. A policy of weaponized deterrence, as opposed to weaponless deterrence or deterrence through strategic nonviolence, is usually also seen as requiring a substantial degree of permanent mobilization to keep the necessary forces in being and up to date. During the Cold War, the high level of activity in the R&D sector speeded up the cycle of obsolescence and so required production capability to keep up with the flow of replacement weapon systems. A factor working against this is the way in which much civil technology can be converted to military uses, and a state can adopt a policy of preparing for rapid civil to military conversion should it be seen as necessary. In the post–Cold War world, it will be interesting to see whether the leading producers will maintain high levels of R&D while cutting back production capacity.

One way of squaring this circle is to encourage arms exports. Excluded from the arms trade are some nuclear weapon delivery systems, notably missile submarines,

ICBMs, and heavy bombers, which are seldom transferred to other countries. Aside from these systems, governments seek to generate both sufficient volume and sufficient continuity of orders to keep their military industries going. This is not just a matter of keeping plant in being but also of maintaining skilled teams of designers and workers. As the market for conventional weapons is saturated in the post–Cold War world, so subsidies for arms exports have increased. Governments trumpet loudly about the jobs secured through arms exports deals but keep as quiet as possible about the subsidies used to secure those deals (World Development Movement 1995). [...]

The other way to square the circle is to provide a volume of orders for one's own armed forces that is sufficiently large and regular to keep in being an armaments industry of the desired size and scope. In this way, the desire to maintain capacity results in the creation of an internalized push for arms production up to a level sufficient to meet the needs of the industry. That push will produce a pattern of arms production that bears no direct relation to any action–reaction dynamic with a rival power, even though the need to maintain a capacity of a given size is defined by the existence, and the character, of the external rival.

Economic management

The interests of political leaders are served by having predictable military budgets, and this contributes to the shaping of military procurement by organizational momentum. If military budget decisions can be made routine, then less time has to be spent arguing over them. More planning stability can then be given both to organizations concerned with military affairs and to programs that compete with military requirements in the annual process of budgetary resource allocation. Domestic political interests can also impinge on the budgetary process in several ways that feed into the arms dynamic. The government may decide to use increased military spending as a means of stimulating demand within the economy – though again this only applies to the small group of significant arms producers. This technique is especially useful in a country like the United States, where Keynesian measures of economic stimulation might, in themselves, attract ideological opposition. It is easier to get taxpayers (and legislators) to consent to subsidies for high-technology industries if they are justified as necessary to the military security of the country. [...] Military spending tends to be less controversial than welfare measures and other public works, and governments are more in control of the variables that govern the need for military measures. The international system may oblige by providing threats that are real enough to be exaggerated if the need to do so for economic reasons arises.

Electoral politics

Political factors can influence military spending more directly, particularly when electoral considerations come into play (Gray 1971: 74–75). For arms-producing states, military procurement decisions can make a big impact on patterns of employment and income in specific electoral districts or constituencies. Whether in terms of new investment and new jobs, or the maintenance of existing plants and jobs, such decisions cannot avoid entanglement in the political process by which individual politicians and political parties seek to enhance their electoral appeal. [...] On a larger scale electoral considerations can shape the way that parties campaign on military issues (Baugh 1984: 101–3; Gray 1976: 33–36). The U.S. presidential campaigns leading up to the Kennedy administration in 1960 and the Reagan administration in 1980 are instructive in this regard. In both cases the winning candidates raised alarms about military weakness created by their predecessors and promised to build up the armed forces. It is always difficult to separate genuine concern from calculation of electoral advantage in such cases. James Lindsay (1991) argues that members of the U.S. Congress are concerned with good policy as well as pork barrel politics for electoral purposes. What we can say is that, in many states, pointing to foreign threats is frequently an effective means of getting political support. Only when states and their societies either take up antimilitary attitudes (as in Japan and Costa Rica) or become firmly embedded in security communities (the European Union) does this ploy cease to be easily available.

The military-industrial complex

There is an obvious parallel interest among the organizations concerned with R&D and production, those concerned with consuming military goods, and the politicians with their economic and electoral concerns. This parallel interest underlies the idea of a "military-industrial complex." [...] The concept of a military-industrial complex had the merit of pointing to the importance of domestic structural inputs into the arms dynamic. It led to the more detailed studies of the individual components of domestic structure reviewed here. It also drew attention to the possibility that the process of arms acquisition had a momentum of its own that might not serve whatever was defined as the national interest, and that was both strong enough and independent enough to be an important part of the arms dynamic. In other words, coalitions of particular military-industrial interests sometimes deliberately cooperate to promote their own interests, even at the expense of the national interests they are meant to serve. [...] However, military-industrial interests collectively do not form a single unit or political actor and do not dominate national policy: they are usually deeply divided and in competition with each other (Sarkesian 1972; Gray 1976; Rosen 1973; Koistinen 1980; Kaldor 1982; Graham 1994). Key questions for any weapons procurement process are whether it can be subordinated to broader security goals and whether it can be made accountable to the public (Singh 1997). [...]

Organizational politics

The military-industrial complex style of analysis of the arms dynamic was preceded and arguably has been superseded by the evolution of a variety of organizational politics approaches. The excessively sweeping nature of the military-industrial complex perspective has been a key element in its downfall. [...]

Armed services organizations often develop fairly fixed views of their missions and the mainstream weapons systems that they prefer. These views are shaped as much by national historical experience, by the traditions of the individual services, and by the interests of organizational survival, as by considerations of what the opponent is doing. Service views play a major role in which systems get built or bought. The U.S. Air Force, for example, has a long-standing attachment to bombers. This attachment owes at least as much to air force traditions and self-image as it does to the rather strained argument that bombers add necessary flexibility to a long-range bombardment capability that is more effectively and cheaply achieved with cruise and ballistic missiles (Kotz 1988; Brown 1992; Farrell 1997). At its mildest, the conservatism of the armed forces results in types of weapons being kept in service longer than the evolution of technology would dictate. [...] At worst, it results in the syndrome that Mary Kaldor (1982) labels "baroque technology," in which favored weapons are developed to such a pitch of complexity that their ability to function in combat becomes doubtful. [...] Theo Farrell (1995, 1997) has rightly argued that much more attention should be paid to what he calls "macro-wastage" of billions of dollars on weapon systems that are not needed or do not work than to "micro-wastage" of millions of dollars on cost overruns and overcharging by manufacturers. Even interservice rivalry often gets channeled into a routine "fair shares" principle of budget allocation.

Because military organizations tend to be conservative, the question arises as to the source of innovation in such organizations. In a very useful review essay that tackles this issue, Farrell (1996) applies the distinctions drawn by W. Richard Scott (1992) between organizations as rational, natural, or open systems. The rational systems view is that organizations innovate to pursue clear goals more effectively and resist innovation that seems to be inefficient. According to natural systems theory, organizations seek to survive – they resist innovations that threaten their existence and back those that protect them. This is the classic bureaucratic politics approach developed by Graham Allison (1971) (cf. Rhodes 1994). Finally, open systems theory – also known as "the new institutionalism" – presents organizations as socially constructed by factors internal and external to them: they embody rules and cultures. Innovation here is a product of changes in the forces of social construction. [...]

The unifying and identity-creating roles of military threats, real and unreal

The general line of the more nuanced military-industrial complex and organizational politics arguments can be expanded from mere electoral considerations and applied to the functioning of the whole state as a political organism (Gray 1976: 31–33; Burton 1984; Kaldor 1985, 1990). The basic case here is that states are relatively fragile political structures and that the task of governing them is made possible in some cases, and easier in others, by cultivating the unifying force of military threats. Such threats will thus be positively sought out and amplified by governments even where the objective basis for them is weak. Without the threats, domestic divisions and dissatisfactions would rise to higher priority on the political agenda, either threatening the status of the ruling élite or making the process of government more difficult. Such arguments have an obvious relevance to politically weak states like Pakistan, where the religious basis of the military and political rivalry with India helps to hold together a country otherwise threatened by serious ethnic and ideological splits. The threats also apply, albeit in a milder fashion, to such military postures as France's strategic nuclear forces designed to emphasize national prestige. [...]

Civil war and internal repression

For many weak states (Buzan 1991: 96–107), the primary way in which domestic politics and the arms dynamic interact is that arms are acquired to have the means to fight civil wars or repress domestic populations. In these cases, unity and identity by means of external military threats may not have been attempted or may have failed. In 1995 thirty major armed conflicts were being waged, and every single one was taking place primarily within, not between, states. If the opponents of state repression are fighting back, the demand for arms and military training is likely to be higher and the involvement in the arms dynamic deeper. Where the state is weak, and internal violence is a major feature of domestic political life, then that violence may become the principal determining factor in how that state relates to the arms dynamic.

In nearly all cases of civil war and internal repression there is significant involvement by other states, often the United States and the Soviet Union (and now Russia) – Serbia and Croatia in the war in Bosnia-Herzegovina; Pakistan in Afghanistan; Israel, Syria, and Iran in Lebanon; and both South Africa and Cuba in Angola and Mozambique provide other examples, often in terms of arms supplies and military training for strategic, ideological, or economic reasons (Harkavy 1985; Neuman 1988; Pearson, Brzoska, and Crantz 1992; Herring 1997). Liberal democracies ostensibly have values antithetical to supporting internal repression, but in practice varying combinations of perceived economic and political interests have ensured that these democracies frequently arm brutal dictatorships or states headed by leaders chosen through unfree elections. Although the member states of the Organization for Security and Cooperation in Europe passed a declaration in 1993 that opposes arms sales that might be used for internal repression or exacerbate existing conflict, the arms trade and military aid have been essentially unaffected (World Development Movement 1995). [...]

Although this aspect of the arms dynamic is mostly of low technology and involves relatively small resources compared with those spent on major weapons systems, its political and human impact is large and widespread (Wolpin 1986). [...]

The problem is not only that small arms are being distributed for political reasons, but that they are cheap and readily available through both legal and illegal channels. In this sense, the low-technology, low-pace aspect of the arms dynamic is a source of problems even for states generally identified with the high-technology, high-pace end of the arms business. Small-arms proliferation is a minor part of the arms dynamic but it has major consequences for world politics. [...]

Bibliography

Adams, Gordon and Steven M. Kosiak (1993) "The United States: Trends in Defence Procurement and Research and Development Programmes," in Herbert Wulf (ed.) *Arms Industry Limited* (Oxford: Oxford University Press for the Stockholm International Peace Research Institute), 29–49.

Allison, Graham (1971) *Essence of Decision: Explaining the Cuban Missile Crisis* (Boston: Little Brown & Co.).

Arnett, Eric (1996b) "Military Research and Development," in *SIPRI Yearbook: Armaments, Disarmament and International Security* (Oxford: Oxford University Press for the Stockholm International Peace Research Institute), 381–409.

Baugh, William H. (1984) *The Politics of the Nuclear Balance* (New York: Longman).

Blainey, Geoffrey (1973) *The Causes of War* (New York: The Free Press).

Brown, Michael E. (1992) *Flying Blind: The Politics of the U.S. Strategic Bomber Program* (Ithaca: Cornell University Press).

Burton, John W. (1984) *Global Conflict: The Domestic Sources of International Crisis* (Brighton: Harvester Wheatsheaf).

Butterfield, Herbert (1951) *History and Human Relations* (London: Collins).

Buzan, Barry (1991) *People, States, and Fear: An Agenda for International Security in the Post-Cold War Era* (Hemel Hempstead: Wheatsheaf; and Boulder, CO: Lynne Rienner Publishers), second edition.

Buzan, Barry and Gautam Sen (1990) "The Impact of Military Research and Development Priorities on the Development of the Civil Economy in Capitalist States," *Review of International Studies*, 16:4, 321–339.

Buzan, Barry, Ole Wæver, and Jaap de Wilde (1998) *Security: A New Framework for Analysis* (Boulder, CO: Lynne Rienner Publishers).

Dedring, J. (1976) *Recent Advances in Peace and Conflict Research* (Beverly Hills, CA: Sage).

Farrell, Theo (1995) "Waster in Weapons Acquisition: How the Americans Do it All Wrong," *Contemporary Security Policy*, 16:2, 192–218.

—— (1996) "Figuring Out Fighting Organisations: The New Organisational Analysis in Strategic Studies," *Journal of Strategic Studies*, 19:1, 128–142.

—— (1997) *Weapons Without a Cause: The Politics of Weapons Acquisition in the United States* (London: Macmillan).

Garthoff, Raymond L. (1978) "On Estimating and Imputing Intentions," *International Security*, 3:2, 22–32.

—— (1984) "Worst case Assumptions: Uses, Abuses and Consequences," in Gwyn Prins (ed.) *The Choice: Nuclear Weapons Versus Security* (London: Chatto & Windus), 98–108.

—— (1990) *Deterrence and Revolution in Soviet Military Doctrine* (Washington, DC: The Brookings Institution).

Glaser, Charles L. (1992) "Political Consequences of Military Strategy. Expanding and Refining the Spiral and Deterrence Models," *World Politics*, 44:4, 497–538.

Graham, Norman A. (1994) *Seeking Security and Development: The Impact of Military Spending and Arms Transfers* (Boulder, CO: Lynner Rienner Publishers).

Gray, Colin S. (1971) "The Arms Race Phenomenon," *World Politics*, 24: 1, 39–79.

—— (1976) *The Soviet-American Arms Race* (Westmead: Saxon House).

—— (1993) *Weapons Don't Make War: Policy, Strategy and Military Technology* (Lawrence: University of Kansas Press).

Hammond, Grant T. (1993) *Plowshares in Swords: Arms Races in International Politics* (Columbia: University of South Carolina Press).

Harkavy, R. (1985) "Arms Resupply During Conflict: A Framework for Analysis," *Jerusalem Journal of International Relations*, 7:3, 5–41.

Herring, Eric (1995) *Danger and Opportunity: Explaining International Crisis Outcomes* (Manchester: Manchester University Press).

—— (1997) "The Uneven Killing Field: The Manufacture of Consent for the Arms Embargo on Bosnia-Hercegovina," in Malcolm Evans (ed.) *Aspects of Statehood and Institutionalism in Contemporary Europe* (Darmouth: Dartmouth Press), 159–182.

Herz, John H. (1950) "Idealist Internationalism and the Security Dilemma," *World Politics*, 2, 157–180.

Huntington, Samuel P. (1958) "Arms Races: Prerequisites and Results," *Public Policy*, 8, 1–87.

Jervis, Robert (1976) *Perception and Misperception in International Politics* (Princeton: Princeton University Press).

—— (1978) "Cooperation Under the Security Dilemma," *World Politics*, 30:2, 167–214.

—— (1985) "From Balance to Concert: A Study of International Security Cooperation," *World Politics*, 38:1, 58–79.

Kaldor, Mary (1982) *The Baroque Arsenal* (London: Andre Deutsch).

—— (1985) "The Concept of Common Security," in *Policies for Common Security* (London: Taylor & Francis for the Stockholm International Peace Research Institute).

—— (1990) *Imaginary War: Understanding the East-West Conflict* (Oxford: Blackwell).

Koistinen, Paul A. C. (1980) *The Military-Industrial Complex: An Historical Perspective* (New York: Praeger).

Kotz, Nick (1988) *Wild Blue Yonder: Money, Politics and the B-1 Bomber* (Princeton: Princeton University Press).

Lebow, Richard Ned (1981) *Between War and Peace: The Nature of International Crisis* (Baltimore: The Johns Hopkins University Press).

—— (1984) "Windows of Opportunity: Do States Jump Through Them?" *International Security*, 98:3, 431–458.

Lindsay, James M. (1991) *Congress and Nuclear Weapons* (Baltimore: The Johns Hopkins University Press).

MccGwire, Michael (1987) *Military Objectives in Soviet Foreign Policy* (Washington, DC: The Brookings Institution).

—— (1991) *Perestroika and Soviet National Security* (Washington, DC: The Brookings Institution).

Neuman, Stephanie G. (1988) "International Stratification and the Third World Military Industries," *International Organization*, 38, 167–197.

Pearson, Frederic S., Michael Brzoska, and Christer Crantz (1992) "The Effects of Arms Transfers on Wars and Peace Negotiations," in *SIPRI Yearbook 1992: World Armaments and Disarmament* (Oxford: Oxford University Press for SIPRI), 339–415.

Pearton, Maurice (1982) *The Knowledgeable State: Diplomacy, War and Technology Since 1830* (London: Burnett Books).

Rathjens, George W. (1973) "The Dynamics of the Arms Race," in Herbert York (ed.) *Arms Control* (San Francisco: Freeman).

Rattinger, Hans (1976) "From War to War: Arms Races in the Middle East," *International Studies Quarterly*, 20, 501–531.

Rhodes, Edward (1994) "Do Bureaucratic Politics Matter? Some Discomforting Findings from the Case of the U.S. Navy," *World Politics*, 47:1.

Rosen, Steven (ed.) (1973) *Testing the Theory of the Military-Industrial Complex* (Lexington, MA: Lexington Books).

Sarkesian, Sam C. (ed.) (1972) *The Military-Industrial Complex: A Reassessment* (London: Sage).

Schelling, Thomas (1966) *Arms and Influence* (New Haven: Yale University Press).

Schweller, Randall L. (1994) "Bandwagoning for Profit: Bringing the Revisionist State Back In," *International Security*, 19:1, 72–107.

Scott, W. Richard (1992) *Organizations: Rational, Natural and Open Systems* (London: Prentice Hall).

Sen, Gautam (1984) *The Military Origins of Industrialisation and International Trade Rivalry* (London: Frances Pinter).

Singh, Ravinder Pal (ed.) (1997) *Arms Procurement Decision-Making Processes. China, India, Israel, Japan and South Korea* (Oxford: Oxford University Press for the Stockholm International Peace Research Institute).

Snyder, Glenn H. (1984) "The Security Dilemma in Alliance Politics," *World Politics*, 36:4, 461–495.

Snyder, Jack L. (1985) "Perceptions of the Security Dilemma in 1914," in Robert Jervis, Richard Ned Lebow, and Janice Gross Stein, *Psychology and Deterrence*, with contributions by Patrick L. Morgan and Jack L. Snyder (Baltimore: The Johns Hopkins University Press), 153–179.

Stein, Janice Gross (1991a) "Deterrence and Reassurance," in Philip E. Tetlock, Jo L. Husbands, Robert Jervis, Paul C. Stern, and Charles Tilly (eds.), *Behavior, Society and Nuclear War, 2* (New York: Oxford University Press), 8–72.

—— (1991b) "Reassurance in International Conflict Management," *Political Science Quarterly*, 106, 431–451.

Thee, Marek (1986) *Military Technology, Military Strategy and the Arms Race* (London: Croom Helm).

Wæver, Ole (1995) "Securitization and Desecuritization," in Ronnie Lipschutz (ed.) *On Security* (New York: Columbia University Press), 46–86.

Wheeler, Nicholas J. and Ken Booth (1992) "The Security Dilemma," in John Baylis and Nicholas J. Rengger (eds.) *Dilemmas of World Politics* (Oxford: Clarendon Press), 29–60.

Wolpin, Miles D. (1986) *Militarization, Internal Repression and Social Welfare in the Third World* (London: Croom Helm).

World Development Movement (1995) *Gunrunners' Gold: How the Public's Money Finances Arms Sales* (London: World Development Movement).

Zisk, Kimberly Martin (1993) *Engaging the Enemy: Organization Theory and Soviet Military Intervention, 1955–1991* (Princeton: Princeton University Press).

Scott Sagan

WHY DO STATES BUILD NUCLEAR WEAPONS?

Source: Scott Sagan, 'Why do states build nuclear weapons?: Three models in search of a bomb', *International Security*, vol. 21, no. 3, Winter 1996/97, pp. 54–86.

The security model: nuclear weapons and international threats

ACCORDING TO NEOREALIST THEORY in political science, states exist in an anarchical international system and must therefore rely on self-help to protect their sovereignty and national security.[1] Because of the enormous destructive power of nuclear weapons, any state that seeks to maintain its national security must balance against any rival state that develops nuclear weapons by gaining access to a nuclear deterrent itself. This can produce two policies. First, strong states do what they can: they can pursue a form of internal balancing by adopting the costly, but self-sufficient, policy of developing their own nuclear weapons. Second, weak states do what they must: they can join a balancing alliance with a nuclear power, utilizing a promise of nuclear retaliation by that ally as a means of extended deterrence. For such states, acquiring a nuclear ally may be the only option available, but the policy inevitably raises questions about the credibility of extended deterrence guarantees, since the nuclear power would also fear retaliation if it responded to an attack on its ally.

Although nuclear weapons could also be developed to serve either as deterrents against overwhelming conventional military threats or as coercive tools to compel changes in the status quo, the simple focus on states' responses to emerging nuclear threats is the most common and most parsimonious explanation for nuclear weapons proliferation.[2] George Shultz once nicely summarized the argument: "Proliferation begets proliferation."[3] Every time one state develops nuclear weapons to balance against its main rival, it also creates a nuclear threat to another state in the region, which then has to initiate its own nuclear weapons program to maintain its national security. [...]

Policy implications of the security model

Several basic predictions and prescriptions flow naturally from the logic of the security model. First, since states that face nuclear adversaries will eventually develop their own arsenals unless credible alliance guarantees with a nuclear power exist, the maintenance of U.S. nuclear commitments to key allies, including some form of continued first-use policy, is considered crucial.[4] Other efforts to enhance the security of potential proliferators – such as confidence-building measures or "negative security assurances" that the nuclear states will not use their weapons against non-nuclear states – can also be helpful in the short-run, but will likely not be effective in the long-term given the inherent suspicions of potential rivals produced by the anarchic international system.

Under the security model's logic, the NPT is seen as an institution permitting non-nuclear states to overcome a collective action problem. Each state would prefer to become the only nuclear weapons power in its region, but since that is an unlikely outcome if it develops a nuclear arsenal, it is willing to refrain from proliferation if, and only if, its neighbors remain non-nuclear. The treaty permits such states to exercise restraint with increased confidence that their neighbors will follow suit, or at a minimum, that they will receive sufficient advance warning if a break-out from the treaty is coming. It follows, from this logic, that other elements of the NPT regime should be considered far less important: specifically, the commitments that the United States and other nuclear states made under Article VI of the treaty – that the nuclear powers will pursue "negotiations in good faith on measures relating to cessation of the nuclear arms race at an early date and to nuclear disarmament" – are merely sops to public opinion in non-nuclear countries. The degree to which the nuclear states follow through on these Article VI commitments will not significantly influence the actual behavior of non-nuclear states, since it will not change their security status.

Under realist logic, however, U.S. nonproliferation policy can only slow down, not eliminate, the future spread of nuclear weapons. Efforts to slow down the process may of course be useful, but they will eventually be countered by two very strong structural forces that create an inexorable momentum toward a world of numerous nuclear weapons states. First, the end of the Cold War creates a more uncertain multipolar world in which U.S. nuclear guarantees will be considered increasingly less reliable; second, each time one state develops nuclear weapons, it will increase the strategic incentives for neighboring states to follow suit.[5] [...]

Problems and evidence

[...] The security model is parsimonious; the resulting history is conceptually clear; and the theory fits our intuitive belief that important events in history (like the development of a nuclear weapon) must have equally important causes (like national security). A major problem exists, however, concerning the evidence, for the realist history depends primarily on first, the statements of motivation by the key decision-makers, who have a vested interest in explaining that the choices they made served the national interest; and second, a correlation in time between the emergence of a plausible security threat and a decision to develop nuclear weapons. [...]

These problems suggest that a more serious analysis would open up the black box of decision-making and examine in more detail how governments actually made their nuclear decisions. Any rigorous attempt to evaluate the security model of proliferation, moreover, also requires an effort to develop alternative explanations, and to assess whether they provide more or less compelling explanations for proliferation decisions. [...]

The domestic politics model: nuclear pork and parochial interests

A second model of nuclear weapons proliferation focuses on the domestic actors who encourage or discourage governments from pursuing the bomb. Whether or not the acquisition of nuclear weapons serves the national interests of a state, it is likely to serve the parochial bureaucratic or political interests of at least some individual actors within the state. Three kinds of actors commonly appear in historical case-studies of proliferation: the state's nuclear energy establishment (which includes officials in state-run laboratories as well as civilian reactor facilities); important units within the professional military (often within the air force, though sometimes in navy bureaucracies interested in nuclear propulsion); and politicians in states in which individual parties or the mass public strongly favor nuclear weapons acquisition. When such actors form coalitions that are strong enough to control the government's decision-making process – either through their direct political power or indirectly through their control of information – nuclear weapons programs are likely to thrive.

Unfortunately, there is no well-developed domestic political theory of nuclear weapons proliferation that identifies the conditions under which such coalitions are formed and become powerful enough to produce their preferred outcomes.[6] The basic logic of this approach, however, has been strongly influenced by the literature on bureaucratic politics and the social construction of technology concerning military procurement in the United States and the Soviet Union during the Cold War.[7] In this literature, bureaucratic actors are not seen as passive recipients of top-down political decisions; instead, they create the conditions that favor weapons acquisition by encouraging extreme perceptions of foreign threats, promoting supportive politicians, and actively lobbying for increased defense spending. This bottom-up view focuses on the formation of domestic coalitions within the scientific-military-industrial complex. [...]

Realists recognize that domestic political actors have parochial interests, of course, but argue that such interests have only a marginal influence on crucial national security issues. The outcome of bureaucratic battles, for example, may well determine whether a state builds 500 or 1000 ICBMs or emphasizes submarines or strategic bombers in its nuclear arsenal; but a strong consensus among domestic actors will soon emerge about the need to respond in kind when a potential adversary acquires nuclear weapons. In contrast, from this domestic politics perspective, nuclear weapons programs are not obvious or inevitable solutions to international security problems; instead, nuclear weapons programs are solutions looking for a problem to which to attach themselves so as to justify their existence. Potential threats to a state's security certainly exist in the international system, but in this model, international threats are seen as being more malleable and more subject to interpretation, and can therefore produce a variety of responses from domestic actors. Security threats are therefore not the central cause of weapons decisions according to this model: they are merely windows of opportunity through which parochial interests can jump. [...]

* * *

Policy implications of the domestic politics model

With respect to U.S. nonproliferation policy, a domestic politics approach both cautions modest expectations about U.S. influence and calls for a broader set of diplomatic efforts. Modest expectations are in order, since the key factors that influence decisions are domestic in origin and therefore largely outside the control of U.S. policy. Nevertheless, a more diverse set of tools could be useful to help create and empower domestic coalitions that oppose the development or maintenance of nuclear arsenals.

A variety of activities could be included in such a domestic-focused nonproliferation strategy. International financial institutions are already demanding that cuts in military expenditures be included in conditionality packages for aid recipients. More direct conditionality linkages to nuclear programs – such as deducting the estimated budget of any suspect research and development program from IMF or U.S. loans to a country – could heighten domestic opposition to such programs.[8] Providing technical information and intellectual ammunition for domestic actors – by encouraging more accurate estimates of the economic and environmental costs of nuclear weapons programs and highlighting the risks of nuclear accidents[9] – could bring new members into anti-proliferation coalitions. In addition, efforts to encourage strict civilian control of the military, through educational and organizational reforms, could be productive, especially in states in which the military has the capability to create secret nuclear programs (like Brazil in the 1980s) to serve their parochial interests. Finally, U.S. attempts to provide alternative sources of employment and prestige to domestic actors who might otherwise find weapons programs attractive could decrease nuclear incentives. To the degree that professional military organizations are supporting nuclear proliferation, encouraging their involvement in other military activities (such as Pakistani participation in peacekeeping operations or the Argentine Navy's role in the Persian Gulf) could decrease such support. Where the key actors are laboratory officials and scientists, assistance in non-nuclear research and development programs (as in the current U.S.-Russian "lab-to-lab" program) could decrease personal and organizational incentives for weapons research.

A different perspective on the role of the NPT also emerges from the domestic politics model. The NPT regime is not just a device to increase states' confidence about the limits of their potential adversaries' nuclear programs; it is also a tool that can help to empower domestic actors who are opposed to nuclear weapons development. The NPT negotiations and review conferences create a well-placed élite in the foreign and defense ministries with considerable bureaucratic and personal interests in maintaining the regime. The IAEA creates monitoring capabilities and enforcement incentives against unregulated activities within a state's own nuclear power organizations. The network of non-governmental organizations built around the treaty supports similar anti-proliferation pressure groups in each state.

According to this model, the U.S. commitment under Article VI to work for the eventual elimination of nuclear weapons is important because of the impact that the behavior of the United States and other nuclear powers can have on the domestic debates in non-nuclear states. Whether or not the United States originally signed Article VI merely to placate domestic opinion in non-nuclear states is not important; what is important is that the loss of this pacifying tool could influence outcomes in potential proliferators. In future debates inside such states, the arguments of anti-nuclear actors – that nuclear weapons programs do not serve the interest of their states – can be more easily countered by pro-bomb actors whenever they can point to specific actions of the nuclear powers, such as refusals to ban nuclear tests or the maintenance of nuclear first-use doctrines, that highlight these states' continued reliance on nuclear deterrence.

The norms model: nuclear symbols and state identity

A third model focuses on norms concerning weapons acquisition, seeing nuclear decisions as serving important symbolic functions – both shaping and reflecting a state's identity. According to this perspective, state behavior is determined not by leaders' cold calculations about the national security interests or their parochial bureaucratic interests, but rather by deeper norms and shared beliefs about what actions are legitimate and appropriate in international relations. [...]

The sociologists' arguments highlight the possibility that nuclear weapons programs serve symbolic functions reflecting leaders' perceptions of appropriate and modern behavior. The political science literature reminds us, however, that such symbols are often contested and that the resulting norms are spread by power and coercion, and not by the strength of ideas alone. Both insights usefully illuminate the nuclear proliferation phenomenon. Existing norms concerning the non-acquisition of nuclear weapons (such as those embedded in the NPT) could not have been created without the strong support of the most powerful states in the international system, who believed that the norms served their narrow political interests. Yet, once that effort was successful, these norms shaped states' identities and expectations and even powerful actors became constrained by the norms they had created.[10] The history of nuclear proliferation is particularly interesting in this regard because a major discontinuity – a shift in nuclear norms – has emerged as the result of the NPT regime.

Although many individual case studies of nuclear weapons decisions mention the belief that nuclear acquisition will enhance the international prestige of the state, such prestige has been viewed simply as a reasonable, though diffuse, means used to enhance the state's international influence and security. What is missing from these analyses is an understanding of why and how actions are granted symbolic meaning: why are some nuclear weapons acts considered prestigious, while others produce opprobrium, and how do such beliefs change over time? Why, for example, was nuclear testing deemed prestigious and legitimate in the 1960s, but is today considered illegitimate and irresponsible? An understanding of the NPT regime is critical here, for it appears to have shifted the norm concerning what acts grant prestige and legitimacy from the 1960s notion of joining "the nuclear club" to the 1990s concept of joining "the club of the nations adhering to the NPT." Moreover, the salience of the norms that were made explicit in the NPT treaty has shifted over time. [...]

* * *

Policy implications of the norms model

If the norms model of proliferation is correct, the key U.S. policy challenges are to recognize that such norms can have a strong influence on other states' nuclear weapons policy, and to adjust U.S. policies to increase the likelihood that norms will push others toward policies that also serve U.S. interests. Recognizing the possibility that norms can influence other states' behavior in complex ways should not be difficult. After all, the norms of the NPT have already influenced U.S. nuclear weapons policy in ways that few scholars or policymakers predicted ahead of time: in January 1995, for example, the Clinton administration abandoned the long-standing U.S. position that the Comprehensive Test Ban Treaty (CTBT) must include an automatic escape clause permitting states to withdraw from the treaty after ten years. Despite the arguments made by Pentagon officials that such a clause was necessary to protect U.S. security, the administration accepted the possibility of a permanent CTBT because senior decision-makers became convinced that the U.S. position was considered illegitimate by non-nuclear NPT members, due to the Article VI commitment to eventual disarmament, and might thereby jeopardize the effort to negotiate a permanent extension of the NPT treaty.[11]

Adjusting U.S. nuclear policies in the future to reinforce emerging nonproliferation norms will be difficult, however, because many of the recommended policies derived from the norms perspective directly contradict recommendations derived from the other models. Focusing on NPT norms raises especially severe concerns about how existing U.S. nuclear first-use doctrine influences potential proliferators' perceptions of the legitimacy or illegitimacy of nuclear weapons possession and use.[12] To the degree that such first-use policies create beliefs that nuclear threats are what great powers do, they will become desired symbols for states that aspire to that status. The norms argument against U.S. nuclear first-use doctrine, however, contradicts the policy advice derived from the security model, which stresses the need for continued nuclear guarantees for U.S. allies. Similarly, the norms perspective suggests that current U.S. government efforts to maintain the threat of first use of nuclear weapons to deter the use of biological or chemical weapons would have a negative impact on the nuclear nonproliferation regime.[13] Leaders of non-nuclear states are much less likely to consider their own acquisition of nuclear weapons to deter adversaries with chemical and biological weapons illegitimate and ill-advised if the greatest conventional military power in the world can not refrain from making such threats.

Other possible policy initiatives are less problematic. For example, if norms concerning prestige are important, then it would be valuable for the United States to encourage the development of other sources of international prestige for current or potential proliferators. Thus, a policy that made permanent UN Security Council membership for Japan, Germany, and India conditional upon the maintenance of non-nuclear status under the NPT might further remove nuclear weapons possession from considerations of international prestige.

Finally, the norms model produces a more optimistic vision of the potential future of nonproliferation. Norms are sticky: individual and group beliefs about appropriate behavior change slowly, and over time norms can become rules embedded in domestic institutions.[14] In the short run, therefore, norms can be a brake on nuclear chain reactions: in contrast to more pessimistic realist predictions that "proliferation begets proliferation," the norms model suggests that such nuclear reactions to emerging security threats can be avoided or at least delayed because of normative constraints. The long-term future of the NPT regime is also viewed with more optimism, for the model envisions the possibility of a gradual emergence of a norm against all nuclear weapons possession. [...] This emphasis on emerging norms therefore highlights the need for the nuclear powers to reaffirm their commitments to global nuclear disarmament, and suggests that it is essential that the U.S. and other governments develop a public, long-term strategy for the eventual elimination of nuclear weapons.[15] The norms model cannot, of course, predict whether such efforts will ever resolve the classic risks of nuclear disarmament: that states can break treaty obligations in crises, that small arsenals produce strategic instabilities, and that adequate verification of complete dismantlement is exceedingly difficult. But the model does predict that there will be severe costs involved if the nuclear powers are seen to have failed to make significant progress toward nuclear disarmament. [...]

Notes

1   The seminal text of neorealism remains Kenneth N. Waltz, *Theory of International Politics* (New York: Random House, 1979). Also see Kenneth N. Waltz, "The Origins of War in Neorealist Theory," in Robert I. Rotberg and Theodore K. Rabb, eds., *The Origin and Prevention of Major Wars* (New York: Cambridge University Press, 1989), pp. 39–52; and Robert O. Keohane, ed., *Neorealism and Its Critics* (New York: Columbia University Press, 1986).

2   The Israeli, and possibly the Pakistani, nuclear weapons decisions might be the best examples of defensive responses to conventional security threats; Iraq, and possibly North Korea, might be the best examples of the offensive coercive threat motivation. On the status quo bias in neorealist theory in general, see Randall L. Schweller, "Bandwagoning for Profit: Bringing the Revisionist State Back In," *International Security*, Vol. 19, No. 1 (Summer 1994), pp. 72–107, and Richard Rosecrance and Arthur A. Stein, eds., *The Domestic Bases of Grand Strategy* (Ithaca, N.Y.: Cornell University Press, 1993).

3   George Shultz, "Preventing the Proliferation of Nuclear Weapons," *Department of State Bulletin*, Vol. 84, No. 2093 (December 1984), p. 18.

4   See Lewis Dunn, *Controlling the Bomb* (New Haven, Conn.: Yale University Press, 1982); May, "Nuclear Weapons Supply and Demand," p. 535; and Benjamin Frankel, "The Brooding Shadow: Systemic Incentives and Nuclear Weapons Proliferation," in Zachary S. Davis and Benjamin Frankel, eds. *The Proliferation Puzzle*, special issue of *Security Studies*, Vol. 2, No. 3/4 (Spring/Summer 1993), pp. 47–54.

5   See Kenneth N. Waltz, "The Emerging Structure of International Politics," *International Security*, Vol. 18, No. 2 (Fall 1993), pp. 44–79; and John J. Mearsheimer, "Back to the Future: Instability in Europe after the Cold War," *International Security*, Vol. 15, No. 1 (Summer 1990), pp. 5–56.

6   This is a serious weakness shared by many domestic-level theories in international relations, not just theories of proliferation. On this issue, see Ethan B. Kapstein, "Is Realism Dead? The Domestic Sources of International Politics," *International Organization*, Vol. 49, No. 4 (Autumn 1995), pp. 751–74.

7   The best examples of this literature include Morton H. Halperin, *Bureaucratic Politics and Foreign Policy* (Washington, D.C.: The Brookings Institution, 1974); Matthew Evangelista, *Innovation and the Arms Race: How the United States and Soviet Union Develop New Military Technologies* (Ithaca, N.Y.: Cornell University Press, 1988); and Donald MacKenzie, *Inventing Accuracy: A Historical Sociology of Nuclear Missile Guidance* (Cambridge, Mass.: MIT Press, 1990). For a valuable effort to apply insights from the literature on social construction of technology to proliferation problems, see Steven Flank, "Exploding the Black Box: The Historical Sociology of Nuclear Proliferation," *Security Studies*, Vol. 3, No. 2. (Winter 1993/94), pp. 259–94.

8   Etel Solingen, *The Domestic Sources of Nuclear Postures*, Institute of Global Conflict and Cooperation, Policy Paper No. 8, October 1994, p. 11.

9   On these costs and risks, see Kathleen C. Bailey, ed., *Weapons of Mass Destruction: Costs Versus Benefits* (New Delhi: Manohar Publishers, 1994); Stephen I. Schwartz, "Four Trillion and Counting," *Bulletin of the Atomic Scientists*, Vol. 51, No. 6 (November/December 1995); Bruce G. Blair, *The Logic of Accidental Nuclear War* (Washington, D.C.: The Brookings Institution, 1993); and Scott D. Sagan, *The Limits of Safety: Organizations, Accidents, and Nuclear Weapons* (Princeton, N.J.: Princeton University Press, 1993).

10   For an excellent analysis of how such a process can work in other contexts, see Michael Byers, "Custom, Power, and the Power of Rules," *Michigan Journal of International Law*, Vol. 17, No. 1 (Fall 1995), pp. 109–80.

11   Douglas Jehl, "U.S. in New Pledge on Atom Test Ban," *New York Times*, January 31, 1995, p. 1; Dunbar Lockwood, "U.S. Drops CTB 'Early Out' Plan; Test Moratorium May Be Permanent," *Arms Control Today*, Vol. 25, No. 2 (March 1995), p. 27.

12   On this issue, see Barry M. Blechman and Cathleen S. Fisher, "Phase Out the Bomb," *Foreign Policy*, No. 97 (Winter 1994–95), pp. 79–95; and Wolfgang K.H. Panofsky and George Bunn, "The Doctrine of the Nuclear-Weapons States and the Future of Non-Proliferation," *Arms Control Today*, Vol. 24, No. 6 (July/August 1994), pp. 3–9.

13   For contrasting views on this policy, see George Bunn, "Expanding Nuclear Options: Is the U.S. Negating its Non-Use Pledges?" *Arms Control Today*, Vol. 26, No. 4 (May/June 1996), pp. 7–10; and Gompert, Watman, and Wilkening, "Nuclear First Use Revisited."

14   For useful discussions, see Abram Chayes and Antonia Handler Chayes, *The New Sovereignty: Compliance with International Regulatory Agreements* (Cambridge, Mass.: Harvard University Press, 1995); and Andrew P. Cortell and James W. Davis Jr., "How Do International Institutions Matter?: The Domestic Impact of International Rules and Norms," *International Studies Quarterly*, Vol. 40, No. 4 (December 1996), pp. 451–78.

15   For important efforts to rethink the elimination issue, see "An Evolving U.S. Nuclear Posture," Report of the Steering Committee of the Project on Eliminating Weapons of Mass Destruction, Henry L. Stimson Center, Washington, D.C., December 1995; and Donald MacKenzie and Graham Spinardi, "Tacit Knowledge, Weapons Design, and the Uninvention of Nuclear Weapons," *American Journal of Sociology*, Vol. 101, No. 1 (July 1995), pp. 44–100.

Lawrence Freedman

NEW MILITARY CONFLICT

Source: Lawrence Freedman, 'The changing forms of military conflict', *Survival*, vol. 40, no. 4, Winter 1998–99, pp. 39–56.

THE FUTURE DEVELOPMENT of the military art will be more the result of the changed structure of international politics than of advances in military technology. Strong states are no longer compelled to fight by great-power competition or colonial acquisition, but must constantly address situations in which only they can calm instability, contain disorder, pacify belligerents and right wrongs. As a result, the conduct of future warfare will not so much be shaped by the most substantial military powers, as conditioned by the possibility of their intervention. [...]

The big players have not ruled out fighting each other again, but at the moment it is hard to see why they should. Those among the smaller players, even the smallest, who still have things to fight about must therefore set their own standards. They cannot, however, do this without regard to the major actors. They see them as potential resources, possibly available to themselves or their adversaries, which, if tapped, might turn the course of a war. Their strategies must always be formulated with this in mind.

Some historians of traditional models of warfare, such as John Keegan and Martin van Creveld, argue that these models have been invalidated by contemporary trends.[1] [...] The means by which states prepare for battle, the degree of economic and social mobilisation required and the implications of the tendency Clausewitz identified towards absolute violence have [...] been questioned in the light of modern experience and the changing character of the international system. [...]

The current challenge to this model is based on the changing character of warfare from the perspective of the world's major players. To be sure, extrapolating from past trends, let alone from recent events, is rarely reliable. The incidence of major war, for example, has not been constant; military activity is always spasmodic and variable. Truly large, world-shaking wars have been rare. The fact that they appeared to be the norm during the first half of the twentieth century was an unusual misfortune brought about by a combination of deep enmities caused by imperial competition, the rise of nationalism and fundamental ideological rivalries. These conflicts were given an unusually vicious character by the industrialisation of violence. This was an exceptional period, although it was feared that it would continue until the struggle between communism and capitalism ended. Precisely because those involved appreciated the trends, especially once these took in nuclear weapons, they held back from all-out war. This allowed time for the struggle to be concluded through more peaceful ideological competition. The move out of this exceptional period, confirmed by the end of the Cold War, has led to the thesis that major war is becoming obsolete.[2]

Yet war itself is hardly obsolescent. As a result of decolonisation, there are now more states than ever; as a result of the arms trade, many have been able to acquire significant military capabilities, which have often spread to sub-state groups – secessionist movements, religious organisations, criminal gangs, disaffected political parties and cultish terrorists. Some states are quite strong militarily compared to their neighbours, but not in relation to the great powers. Some have regimes oriented to the global economy and hopeful of future prosperity. Others risk being left behind because they have failed to adapt to new post-socialist economic conditions, and because the equipment of their large military establishments is approaching obsolescence. Many are weak, lacking economic strength and dogged by deep social cleavages with which their political institutions can barely cope. Violence within, and occasionally between, states is still quite common.

So while it may not be necessary for the major powers to worry too much about how they would cope with each other in battle, it is sensible for them to focus on how they should deal with weaker powers fighting in an unorthodox way. These states may well fight among themselves as 'peer competitors'. If so, they will be drawn to the same issues that, in one way or another, have preoccupied generations of military theorists. […]

* * *

A new way of warfare

[…] [D]eveloping the military art in its most advanced form now appears to be the responsibility of the US. The dominant approach to this task reflects a long-standing objective to develop a military instrument capable of such sharp and efficient direction that it can mitigate war's terrors and bring hostilities to swift and relatively clean conclusions, before too much damage has been done. According to the proponents of the 'revolution in military affairs' (RMA), the technologies of the information age should allow military power to be employed to its maximum efficiency with speed, precision and minimum human cost. There is no need to target civilians intentionally, nor even to hit them inadvertently. There is no need, except for presentational purposes, to rely on allies.[3]

A lone superpower can push a successful winning-formula to its logical conclusion. The favoured model envisages professional forces engaging in a form of combat with a high political pay-off, yet a low human cost. It postulates battles for information advantage, with stand-off strikes reducing the need to commit too many forces to close combat, thereby keeping down the number of casualties suffered, while the precision of the attacks will limit the number imposed. Such a 'Way of Warfare' would reflect not only what is now technically possible, but also what is politically and morally tolerable.[4] Western governments would find it difficult to develop a mandate for a more vicious approach, unless their societies were in mortal danger. They may have been ready in the past to threaten genocide to deter aggression, but only because the risk of actually having to implement the threat, although sufficient for the required deterrent effect, was small.

Yet the fact that relying on nuclear weapons – the most complete of all threats to civil society – was until very recently a centrepiece of Western strategy should be warning enough that this developing Western model is unlikely to be followed. It has been adopted by Western countries not because their armed forces are more in tune with technological trends, let alone can boast a more acute moral sense, but because it is hard to see how they could lose a war fought in this way, assuming that the US participates. The US now leads the world, in quality if not always in quantity, in all types of conventional military capability. To fight on American terms is to court defeat. [...]

This unassailable superiority in regular forces means that the US and its allies would be surprised, indeed shocked, but probably not frightened if anyone took up arms against them, as long as the war focused on a conventional battle fought apart from civil society. Enemies like this are, however, hard to find. They would not only have to have acquired substantial, advanced military capabilities, but would also inhabit the same moral universe. Could the West demonise an enemy so committed to sparing civil society and keeping down casualties on all sides? A readiness to allow civilians their sanctuaries, to honour the Geneva Conventions and to target systems rather than people would not suggest a propensity to barbarism. Such approaches do not make the blood run cold: those who win wars fought in this way are bound to treat the vanquished with courtesy and respect.

This judgement does not alter if the West confronts opponents who seek to compensate for conventional weakness by developing a capacity for strategic information warfare, aiming for disorientation rather than destruction. Some analysts have argued that civil society has become excessively dependent upon information systems susceptible to enemy interference. Frequently cited examples of what an opponent might attempt are attacks on air-traffic-control or banking systems.[5] Concern over the 'Millennium Bug' has brought home the growing reliance of Western societies on information systems, some of which are vulnerable to external attack.[6] There are good reasons to be wary of malevolent or politically motivated hackers, malcontent employees or extortionists. Whether an opponent could coerce Western governments through threats of chaos is, however, questionable. This would seem to be the sort of attack upon which the perpetrator would be unwise to rely and from which the victim could expect to recover, especially if the precautions that most information managers now take as a matter of course – redundancy and backup systems, for example – are in place. Military systems tend to be less vulnerable than civilian ones because they are less familiar to hackers and virus developers. [...]

Concern about information warfare of this nature, along with plans to conduct future wars according to the dictates of the RMA, may reflect a tendency to picture an opponent with a similar perspective to our own, one that not only appreciates the importance of information technology, but also prefers to use brains rather than brawn and is reluctant to cause too much hurt. Unfortunately, the logic of this clear

Western preference for a certain way of war encourages opponents to push matters in the opposite direction. In all credible contingencies, an enemy will be significantly less well-endowed with military capabilities, except possibly manpower, and so must find compensating advantages. These might lie in geography (short supply-lines and opportunities for urban warfare); a higher threshold of pain (a readiness to accept casualties); patience (leading to frustration in Western capitals); and a lack of human-itarian scruples (allowing the war to extend into civil society).[7]

New possibilities for maximising the human cost of war are emerging. The technological trend represented by nuclear-weapon and missile technologies has done more to expand the means of destruction and to extend the range over which they can be applied than it has to mitigate their effects, for example through improv-ing anti-missile defences. There are fears that breakthroughs in biotechnology could lead to new types of weapons with unusually insidious properties. If the main busi-ness of warfare is to eliminate or paralyse an opponent's military capacity, these forms of destruction appear unnecessarily cruel and ruinous. But if its main pur-pose is to intimidate, coerce or simply avenge, it makes a sort of sense to target civil society.

What appears to frighten today's public most is no longer a formidably equipped fighting force that can conquer land and force people into subjugation, nor even the sophisticated information warrior [but] the sort of vicious warfare that is still the norm in parts of the world where everyday life is desperate and political passions intense. This alternative model to the Western Way of Warfare tends to be crude, militia-based and timeless in its brutality and methods. [...]

This explains why so much of the foreign-policy debate in Western countries tends to consider the possibility of insulation from this sort of warfare. In practice, Western states have often, although not invariably, been impelled to act – to extract expatriate communities, stem refugee flows, deliver humanitarian relief, punish the guilty, prevent genocide, reverse aggression, contain fighting within its current boundaries, or impose or reinforce a settlement. This intervention has usually taken a multinational form, and has been designed to rescue a conflict's most conspicuous victims and to encourage a general de-escalation. As they weigh such decisions, Western governments fear that they will become vulnerable to the savage sort of warfare with which these conflicts are associated. [...]

When the demands of contemporary conflict are phrased in these terms, the West becomes wary of involvement. The fact that the first requirement of interven-tion in a conflict is now a credible exit strategy [...] is symptomatic of a lack of con-fidence. Another symptom is the search for ways to influence events from a safe distance, especially through air power. This fits with the notion that we are dealing with criminal elements who must be punished if they cannot be coerced.

Opponents thus become the strategic equivalents of street gangs who menace strangers and mug the helpless, louts who engage in mindless brawls or the youth described as a 'loner' and 'obsessed with guns' just after he has shot his way through a schoolyard or shopping mall. These metaphors can be suggestive, for the military attributes often now required involve the ability to confront physical intimidation, the antennae of the street-wise, the capacity to improvise with whatever is at hand and the staying-power of the survivor. But such images can also mislead because they fail to address the rationality of opponents, and the possibility that their security concerns may be real and deeply felt. Their strategic sense may be underestimated, while their propensity for mindless violence is exaggerated.

These misleading images were evident during the debate surrounding the bomb attacks against the US embassies in Kenya and Tanzania in August 1998; the subsequent cruise-missile strikes against a terrorist camp in Afghanistan and an alleged chemical-weapons factory in Sudan; and the US government's call for a 'war on terrorism'. There are echoes of the old Vietnam War debates about the merits of 'hearts and minds' versus 'search and destroy' as counter-insurgency methods.[8] All military operations should be judged by their success in turning firepower into a more tradable political currency. As missile strikes cannot eliminate enemies of this type, especially if these attacks can only be carried out from a distance, and if the targets hit can be replaced, these tactics must be judged by their political consequences. These will be positive if the missile strikes persuade the *Taleban* in Afghanistan that Osama bin Laden should no longer use its territory to cause trouble. They will be less positive if anger at the strikes merely increases the number of recruits to the anti-American struggle [...].

In this instance, there appears to exist a broad-based movement animated by a deep hatred of the US, but not linked to a specific government, a definite location or even a single political philosophy. In some ways, it is very modern – global in scope, beyond state control, amorphous rather than tightly organised, working through private enterprise as much as through central direction. In management parlance, bin Laden might consider himself a 'facilitator', rather than a 'leader'. If this threat is to be defeated militarily, it must lose its state backers, sources of recruits and capacity to act with stealth and secrecy.[9] First and foremost, this requires attention to the political context in which the militants operate. Defining the opponent simply by its obnoxious tactics trivialises this context.[10] The starting-point for coming to terms with contemporary conflict must be an appreciation of its origins and a grasp of its dynamics. This does not remove the sense of tragedy from these conflicts, but it does mean that they need no longer seem so mysterious or peculiar. [...]

Forms of intervention

This starting-point directs attention away from those wars that Western countries plan to fight, and even from those that others may plan to fight against them, and towards those that start without them. Non-Western strategy is increasingly geared to the conditions of external, possibly Western, military involvement.[11] Those who have the upper hand will want to persuade outsiders not to meddle; those losing will be searching for ways to draw them in.

There are many ways of intervening other than sending in military forces. Providing training, equipment and diplomatic support and imposing economic pressure can be as important, and can turn the course of a war. Nor, of course, is there anything novel about belligerents conducting their affairs with one eye on the possibilities of others joining in by seeking alliances on the one hand and declarations of neutrality on the other. The novelty may lie in the extent to which the connections between a particular conflict and the rest of the international community have now become crucial to the development of the military art.

Most wars are still largely about territory. The ability to hold on to land remains a vital test of sovereignty: even the loss of a remote, barren and under-populated province can weaken a central government's authority. Some land is especially important because it contains political and financial centres, the hub of a communications network, sacred sites or national monuments. Some important land may be owned by another state, for example that containing water, minerals and fuel and the means to transport these resources. The key requirement for military force remains the ability to take and hold strategically important territory, or at least to control those that live there. Air and sea strategies must therefore always be assessed in terms of their impact on land strategy. This is as close to a constant as we are likely to have in the study of war.

Coercive strategies that work through threatening to hurt the opponent are the potential exception. Air power is considered to lend itself to coercion.[12] The success of coercion depends on the responsiveness of the target: is it stubborn, patient, able to absorb punishment or engage in counter-coercion? It also depends on the credibility of the threat. Is the coercer really prepared to edge towards genocide, or to make peoples' lives miserable to no evident purpose? Coercive threats can succeed, but their indirect quality means that they are unreliable. In practice, air power has been most effective when closely linked with developments on the ground. This is important to Western countries because it means that if they do become involved and do not want to insert their own ground forces, they will become closely linked with – in effect, become inadvertently allied to – one of the belligerents, whose wider political aims they may not support.

Considerations of the conflict's intensity, the intractability of the underlying dispute, the extent to which the interests of potentially intervening powers are affected and how far they can agree on the appropriate form of intervention will determine the degree of external engagement. For the belligerent, the question is how to influence these considerations. For example, if the objective is to minimise the risk of intervention, it would be advisable to move swiftly and to inflict as little damage as possible on civilian life and property. The greater the humanitarian crisis generated by a conflict, the greater the pressure to meddle. Indeed, the faster the movement, the less likely it is that resistance will be faced in populated areas. The strength of the offence as against the defence therefore still requires consideration. However, to launch an effective offensive a degree of mobilisation is required, and this might provide a clue to the enemy, as well as alerting the international community. There are, of course, a variety of ways – staging manoeuvres is one – to obscure an intended offensive. Even when the evidence is clear, a military build-up might still be dismissed as bluff. For the same reasons, the victim of an attack, especially by a militarily stronger opponent, will aim simply to continue resistance in the hope that relief will come. [...]

The information advantage

This is the context in which technological changes, especially those connected with the 'information age', must be viewed. It is unlikely that disparities in information systems will compensate for great disparities in firepower and mobility. The US has not had to address this issue because it clearly has advantages in all these areas.

In general, high-quality information systems work best when they are linked to a physical capacity to attack enemy assets, or to defend one's own. The focus on information systems as targets misses the point that, today, information is easily stored, reproduced and accessed. The key strategic feature of these systems lies in the accessibility of information. It is becoming easier to acquire a rudimentary information infrastructure by essentially commercial means – laptop computers, a modem to the internet, a global positioning system handset, mobile phones and commercial meteorological and surveillance data can all significantly improve military capability.[13] Dedicated military systems will be more secure, robust and capable than civilian ones, but even relatively unsophisticated armed forces should be able to improve their capacity to gain acceptable intelligence on the enemy, a better sense of their bearings and improved communications between centre and periphery. Much depends on how the system is used: good information can be misinterpreted or lost in background noise, while stupid messages can be sent over the best communication networks. Full exploitation of the potential of information technology can markedly improve a fighting force, but it is not a substitute for good judgement.

It is therefore important not to exaggerate the West's information advantage. Modern sensors come into their own when observing a conventional order of battle, but have more trouble monitoring urban militias, rural guerrillas or crude mortars on trucks. Much can be achieved through a dedicated commitment of photographic and signals intelligence, but this will only become possible once intervention is imminent, and then it will take time to develop the analytical frameworks required to make sense of the raw data. Such frameworks require in turn basic knowledge about local culture and history, and the constellation and character of political and military forces. Despite the wonders of the information age, the fact remains that few outsiders have any notion of what is really going on in many contemporary conflicts. Local actors manipulate outside perceptions, normally by stage-managing events or feeding snippets of information to the Western media.[14] An independent local press, a potentially reliable source, rarely survives a civil war.

As much as anything, information wars tend to be public-relations battles for Western attention, hence the adoption of English as the universal language of protest. It is assumed that the way to Western decision-making is through the media and public opinion. To an extent, the 'CNN effect' – whereby emotive images of suffering are presumed to lead to a near-automatic public demand to 'do something' – is overstated.[15] Media images of distant conflicts can be varied, while a government aware that it can do nothing positive can normally stay passive. Moreover, the media is increasingly subject to budget cuts and editorial caution, resulting in spasmodic and patchy coverage. Browsing the internet for information can seem preferable to journalists on the spot, even though the most important sources are those sensitive to local culture, history and politics. As a conflict gestates, it appears complex, nuanced, speculative and probably boring – a natural loser in the competition for newspaper space, television time and even ministerial in-trays.

An upsurge in violence means that there is a story to be covered. With rumours of atrocities and pictures of refugees, the core issue soon becomes: who is doing what to whom? Once Western forces are engaged, media coverage becomes incessant, even when hard news is absent. Armed forces can no longer assume secrecy. The media now approaches wars as public spectacles to be covered from all sides. The enemy will seek to engender a sense of shame, futility or danger; the government will seek to counter this by gaining international support, demonstrating proportionality and economy in its use of force and claiming reasonable and fair objectives.

Even when the danger is clear and present, the difficulties of mobilising democracies for war or deterrence can be substantial. [...] With limited wars, it is much harder to 'sell the threat', and attempts to do so risk demonising serious political movements and turning individuals and groups engaged in revolutionary posturing into credible opponents. The alternative tendency is to 'sell the victim', stressing the misery of the weaker side. Suffering does not, unfortunately, always make for goodness, and when former victims gain the upper hand they often seek revenge. [...]

It is here that the information age and the new international politics come together to change the forms of conflict. Precisely because military engagements have become more discretionary for Western countries, belligerents must work hard to persuade them either to stay out, or to go in. Governments must pay close attention to the quality of rationales for both intervention and non-intervention. If battle is joined, operations will be judged against political criteria relating to casualties and collateral damage, justice and fairness. If conflicts involve persuasion as much as combat, there should be no surprise that their conduct has become a branch of marketing.

There is one important qualification to this line of argument. The thesis works only if it is assumed that, in some cases, there is a serious possibility that Western countries will intervene in a conflict. On the evidence of the 1990s, this is not an unreasonable assumption, but form-books can change and different assumptions can take root. If, when they face the choice, Western governments consistently decide not to become involved – because it is too hazardous or difficult, or because the conflict is remote – the belligerents may conclude that they should no longer attempt to influence what appears to be a foregone conclusion. They will still, however, have to consider the interests of neighbours whose interests will be more directly engaged. As always, the key questions when considering the future of conflict still revolve around how the major powers define their interests. The conduct of war depends not only on their attitudes to specific conflicts, but also on their readiness to be concerned about, and accept a degree of responsibility for, the overall levels of conflict and violence in the international system. [...]

Notes

1   John Keegan, *A History of Warfare* (New York: Knopf, 1993); and Martin van Creveld, *The Transformation of War* (New York: Free Press; 1991).

2   John Mueller, *Retreat from Doomsday: The Obsolescence of Modern War* (New York: Basic Books, 1989).

3   The ambiguous US attitude towards allies engendered by the RMA can be discerned in Joseph Nye and William Owen, 'America's Information Edge', *Foreign Affairs*, vol. 75, no. 2, March – April 1996, pp. 20–36. For an analysis of the developing RMA concept, see Eliot Cohen, 'A Revolution in Warfare', ibid., pp. 37–54.

4   These issues are discussed in Lawrence Freedman, *The Revolution in Strategic Affairs*, Adelphi Paper 318 (Oxford: Oxford University Press for the IISS, 1998).

5   For some customary fare, see Matthew Campbell, 'Britain fights US in Cyber Wargame', *Sunday Times*, 7 June 1998. Campbell refers to vulnerabilities in systems controlling 'airports, hospitals, traffic lights, banks and even nuclear weapons', and reports a proposed war game in London which would open with an attack by computer hackers on the UK's power grid, causing a huge blackout. Concerns such as these have led the US government to identify 'critical infrastructure' and to monitor the development of potential threats. As yet, the emphasis remains defensive; there has been no Presidential Directive allowing work on offensive systems in the US, although some is undoubtedly underway. Bradley Graham, 'In Cyberwar a Quandary over Rules and Strategy', *International Herald Tribune*, 9 July 1998, p. 1. This article noted the considerable requirements of large-scale computer attacks, including detailed intelligence on hardware and software systems, as well as how these relate to the decision-making processes of the opponent. Without this knowledge, it may be difficult to appreciate in advance the likely consequences of an attack.

6   It is arguable that various systemic malfunctions are features of modern life. The large-scale use of animated greetings packages disabled a number of internet nodes in the run-up to Christmas 1997. In May 1998, a failure in PanAmSat's *Galaxy* IV satellite disabled 80–90% of the 45 million pagers in the US.

7   Anatol Lieven has stressed that failure to understand and train for urban warfare was central to Russian reverses in Chechnya. See Anatol Lieven, *Chechnya: Tombstone of Russian Power* (New Haven, CT: Yale University Press, 1998).

8   Michael Shafer, *Deadly Paradigms: The Failure of US Counterinsurgency Policy* (Princeton, NJ: Princeton University Press, 1988); and Michael McClintock, *Instruments of Statecraft: US Guerrilla Warfare, Counter-Insurgency, Counter-Terrorism, 1940–1990* (New York: Pantheon, 1992).

9   Recent reports suggest that *Taleban* leaders are trying to restrain bin Laden.

10   On the risks of insensitivity to political context, in particular a fear that the US in Saudi Arabia is following the same practices that led to the Iranian *débâcle* in 1979, see William Pfaff, 'The US Talk of "War" Can Only Fuel Hatred', *International Herald Tribune*, 1 September 1998, p. 9.

11   These strategies may also be conditioned by non-Western involvement, as the important role played by Angola, Namibia and Zimbabwe in the Democratic Republic of Congo (DROC) in 1998 demonstrates.

12   Robert Pape, *Bombing to Win: Air Power and Coercion in War* (Ithaca, NY: Cornell University Press, 1996).

13   One of the most important campaigns being waged by commercial interests aims to liberalise the availability of encryption technology. Elizabeth Corcoran, 'A Bid to Unscramble Encryption Policy', *International Herald Tribune*, 13 July 1998, p. 13. For an analysis of some of the implications of the growing availability of commercial satellite imagery, see Gerald Steinberg, *Dual Use Aspects of Commercial High-Resolution Imaging Satellites* (Tel Aviv: Begin-Sadat Center for Strategic Studies, February 1998). About 250,000 Global Positioning System (GPS) satellite-navigation receives are sold each month for civil and commercial use. Glenn W. Goodman Jr, 'Hitching a Ride: DoD Seeks to Tap Commercial Space Boom, But So Will Potential Adversaries', *Armed Forces Journal International*, July 1998, vol. 135, no. 12, July 1998, pp. 39–45.

14   For a first-class study of the problems of information-management in less accessible modern conflicts, see Nik Gowing, 'New Challenges and Problems for Information Management in Complex Emergencies: Ominous Lessons from the Great Lakes and Eastern Zaire in late 1996 and early 1997', paper delivered at the conference 'Dispatches from Disaster Zones; The Reporting of Humanitarian Emergencies', London, May 1998.

15   Jonathan Mermin, 'Television News and American Intervention in Somalia: The Myth of a Media-Driven Foreign Policy', *Political Science Quarterly*, vol. 112, no. 3, Autumn 1997, pp. 385–403.

Michael O'Hanlon

TECHNOLOGY AND WAR

Source: 'The so-called Revolution in Military Affairs', in *Technological Change and the Future of Warfare*, Washington, D.C.: Brookings Institution Press, 2000, pp. 7–31.

The so-called revolution in military affairs

I N LIGHT OF THE SPECTACULAR performance of American high-technology weapons in the 1991 Persian Gulf War, as well as the phenomenal pace of innovation in the modern computer industry, many defense analysts have posited that we are on the threshold of a revolution in military affairs (RMA). The RMA thesis holds that further advances in precision munitions, real-time data dissemination, and other modern technologies can help transform the nature of future war and with it the size and structure of the U.S. military. RMA proponents believe that military technology, and the resultant potential for radically new types of warfighting tactics and strategies, is advancing at a rate unrivaled since the 1930s and 1940s. [...]

What do people mean, specifically, when they say that a revolution in military affairs is either under way or within reach? In fact, while definitions do vary from person to person, there is one understanding of the term that is fairly widespread. [...]

At a conceptual level, there are perhaps four main schools of RMA thought. The first three are progressively more bullish in their RMA enthusiasm, the last school is of a different type.

- The *system of systems* school focuses on the potential of rapidly improving computers, communications, and networking to make existing weapons systems function in a much more integrated fashion. [...]
- The *dominant battlespace knowledge* school accepts the premises of the system of systems school, but also assumes radical improvements in sensors that will make future battlefield data much better and more complete. [...]

- The *global reach, global power* school accepts the hypotheses of the system of systems and dominant battlespace knowledge schools, but also envisions the development of far more lethal, agile, and deployable weapons. [...]
- Finally, the less confident *vulnerability school* posits that adversaries may benefit at least as much as the United States from technologies like advanced sea mines, submarines, cruise missiles, ballistic missiles, satellite imaging, computer viruses, radio-frequency weapons, antisatellite weapons, and weapons of mass destruction. [...]

SYSTEM OF SYSTEMS. Virtually all contemporary RMA visions emphasize the concept of a system of systems: that future warfare will be dominated less by individual weapons platforms and munitions than by real-time data processing and networking that tie U.S. forces together synergistically. Proponents point to the fact that computers have been getting much faster for years. Supercomputer computational power has been increasing by a factor of ten every five years.[1] Personal computers have improved almost as quickly, roughly doubling in speed every two years since IBM's personal computer was introduced in 1981.[2] Although the computer's benefits for the economy were unclear for the 1980s and the early 1990s, recent economic evidence suggests that information technology may be largely responsible for the prolonged U.S. economic expansion of the mid-to late 1990s. If this effect is real and sustainable, perhaps computers will soon be just as beneficial for military operations.[3]

Trends in computing power, speed, cost, and size have made it possible to put computers on ballistic missiles, fighter jets, and phased-array radars in the last few decades. Further advancements now make it possible to put computing capability on all significant platforms and to network the systems together. This will allow such systems to gather information from many sources, process it in real time, and rapidly exchange data on the battlefield.[4] To put it differently, radical progress is under way in C4 – or command, control, communications, and computers – technologies, and the U.S. military should be able to derive great benefits from that progress. [...]

DOMINANT BATTLESPACE KNOWLEDGE. Many of those who accept the system of systems concept expect even more from future military technology. Convinced that radical improvements are under way not only in computers but also in sensors that gather information, they have invoked the phrase dominant battlespace knowledge (DBK) to describe a future combat environment in which the United States would be able to promptly find and continuously track virtually all important enemy assets within a combat zone often specified as being 200 nautical miles square. [...]

As its name suggests, the DBK school is much more bullish and ambitious than the system of systems school. It not only presupposes the rapid processing and exchange of information on the battlefield, but also the availability of much better information to process and exchange.[5] In other words, it expects breakthroughs not only in C4 technologies, organizations, and capabilities, but also huge strides in intelligence, surveillance, and reconnaissance (ISR), making for a complete C4-ISR revolution in military affairs. [...]

GLOBAL REACH, GLOBAL POWER. Certain schools of thought place a heavy premium on new types of weaponry to deliver ordnance extremely fast and in new ways.

Proponents of this type of vision contemplate being able to base forces in the United States but deploy them rapidly and decisively overseas within hours or at most a few days; they also see the United States being able to avoid dependence on large fixed bases in combat theaters.

The U.S. Air Force first coined the phrase global reach, global power, and used it to argue for more resources for certain types of air force programs.[6] Given its dominant role in winning the Persian Gulf War – not to mention Operation Allied Force against Serbia in 1999 – this is not surprising. Some additional attributes of air force-oriented force postures are that they promise wars with few U.S. casualties and a rapid U.S. military response to crises or conflicts virtually anywhere on earth.

Although these air force visions vary, they generally emphasize the fire-power and rapid-response capabilities of systems such as stealthier air-to-air fighters, B-2 bombers, advanced reconnaissance capabilities such as UAVs, and "brilliant" munitions like the sensor-fuzed weapon (SFW) with autonomous terminal homing capabilities that do not require human operators in their final approach to a target.[7]

These air force-related visions sometimes include specific force structure proposals that would require cuts in the other services and entrust the air force with more than the 30 percent of total Pentagon resources it has typically received over the last three decades.[8] As such, they make the air force few friends within army, navy, and Marine Corps ranks. Be that as it may, air force proponents offer specific suggestions that can be scrutinized and evaluated. The RMA debate, as well as the general U.S. defense debate, needs such unencumbered proposals. The alternative is to give each of the military services their standard share of the defense budget – in essence making defense strategy in the comptroller's office.[9]

The concept of global reach and global power goes well beyond the air force, however. For example, some envision that ground combat units will be organized in radically different ways, permitting them to deploy very rapidly with only modest amounts of equipment and supplies. They might function in very small mobile teams that conduct tactical reconnaissance and call in precise strikes from distant ships or aircraft as they locate enemy assets difficult to identify from air or space. According to a 1996 Defense Science Board task force: "There is a good chance that we can achieve dramatic increases in the effectiveness of rapidly deployable forces if redesigning the ground forces around the enhanced combat cell [light, agile units with 10 to 20 personnel each] proves to be robust in many environments. There is some chance all this will amount to a true revolution in military affairs by 'eliminating the reliance of our forces on the logistics head as Blitzkrieg freed the offense after World War I from its then decades old reliance on the railhead.'"[10]

The U.S. Marine Corps espouses a related concept. The corps wishes to make future units smaller and to base much of their logistics support on ships or perhaps on mobile offshore bases with enormous carrying capacity, airstrips, and resilience to attack. Those capabilities, combined with longer-range airpower such as the MV-22 Osprey tilt-rotor aircraft, would supercede the traditional marine notion of storming the beach, purportedly allowing the Marines to keep many weapons and logistics assets at sea while sending maneuver and scout forces deep into enemy territory directly from their ships.[11] Recently, the army has gotten into the act as well, with Chief of Staff General Eric Shinseki promoting acquisition of armored vehicles only one-third as heavy as today's that would erase the distinction between light and heavy forces, eliminate tracked combat vehicles from the U.S. military inventory, and permit deployment of a five-division force in one month rather than three.[12]

Some imagine going even further with more futuristic weapons. They envision capabilities such as intercontinental artillery, space-based weapons that could be rapidly unleashed at targets on earth only a few hundred kilometers below, and directed-energy weapons such as lasers.[13]

VULNERABILITY. The final major school of RMA thinking is motivated by worry as much as optimism or "technophilia." It highlights the growing threats posed by enemy cruise, antiship, and ballistic missiles; advanced satellite technologies for communications and targeting; sea mines and advanced diesel submarines; the physical and electronic vulnerabilities of information and communications systems on which the U.S. armed forces increasingly depend; the proliferation of chemical and biological weapons; and the enduring challenges of urban and infantry battle. These technologies could make it much harder for the United States to reach foreign ports safely, keep those ports as well as airfields and other infrastructure safe from enemy attack, and protect troops on the battlefield.[14]

There appears to be ample reason for worry. At present, the United States is easily the world's best military force. It would be very fortunate if its dominance were to grow in the future; the opposite trend may be more likely due to the processes of technological diffusion and proliferation.[15] The vulnerability school of thought frequently invokes the term asymmetric warfare in arguing that future adversaries will choose to attack the United States differently than the United States would choose to fight them. That conclusion applies both to the battlefield, and to the American homeland, since foes might attempt terrorist acts against U.S. civilian and economic centers in an attempt to deter or defeat U.S. military action against them.[16]

OTHER RMA SCHOOLS OF THOUGHT. Others make even bolder claims about future warfare. Some assert that both the economy and the nature of warfare will change more in coming years than at any time since the industrial revolution and the age of Napoleon. [...] The best-known proponents of this "third wave" vision, which places the modern information revolution on historical par with the agricultural and industrial revolutions, are Alvin and Heidi Toffler.[17]

Other bold thinkers have posited possibilities such as essentially limitless energy sources, the complete transparency of the oceans, and other technological breakthroughs for which there is no current scientific basis. Slightly more restrained, but still extremely optimistic, visions of technological progress posit developments like a quintupling in the speed of battlefield maneuver between Desert Storm and 2010, from 40 to 200 kilometers per hour.[18]

To the extent that such visionaries participate in the actual RMA debate today – and many do not, since their time horizons are too long to be immediately relevant to most Pentagon decisionmaking – they can generally be lumped into the global reach, global power school. They envision futuristic warfare as far less dependent on large combat vehicles and, hence, far less constrained by geography and distance than has been the case in the twentieth century.

On the other extreme, another RMA school of thought might be defined to include those who believe that major changes in military affairs are coming but who do not yet claim to understand their implications. By comparison with the revolutionaries described previously, this school of thought is notable for its caution and patience. Its proponents find the contemporary RMA hypothesis appealing but remain undecided about its implications and unconvinced that it is near culmination. They are therefore wary of proposals for any radical makeover of the American military.[19] In this regard, they generally see more eye-to-eye with the system of systems than the DBK or global reach, global power schools. Their belief that the country should focus more attention and resources on defense activities such as experimentation is a point with which I concur [...].

Notes

1   Kenneth Flamm, "Controlling the Uncontrollable," *Brookings Review*, vol. 14 (Winter 1996), pp. 22–25.

2   Martin Libicki, "Technology and Warfare," in Patrick M. Cronin, *2015: Power and Progress* (National Defense University Press, 1996), p. 120.

3   On the reasons for skepticism, see Stephen Biddle, "The Past as Prologue: Assessing Theories of Future Warfare," *Security Studies*, vol. 8 (Autumn 1998), pp. 34–44; on the recent good economic news, see Steve Lohr, "Computer Age Gains Respect of Economists," *New York Times*, April 14, 1999, p. A1.

4   Martin C. Libicki, "DBK and Its Consequences," in Stuart E. Johnson and Martin C. Libicki, eds., *Dominant Battlespace Knowledge* (National Defense University Press, 1996), pp. 23–49.

5   See Johnson and Libicki, *Dominant Battlespace Knowledge*.

6   Sheila E. Widnall, "Report of the Secretary of the Air Force," in William S. Cohen, *Annual Report to the President and the Congress* (Department of Defense, 1997), p. 270.

7   See, for example, Christopher Bowie and others, *The New Calculus: Analyzing Airpower's Changing Role in Joint Theater Campaigns* (Santa Monica, Calif.: RAND, 1993); David A. Ochmanek and others, *To Find, and Not to Yield: How Advances in Information and Firepower Can Transform Theater Warfare* (Santa Monica, Calif.: RAND, 1998); Charles M. Perry, Robert L. Pfaltzgraff Jr., and Joseph C. Conway, *Long-Range Bombers and the Role of Airpower in the New Century* (Cambridge, Mass.: Institute for Foreign Policy Analysis, 1995); Zalmay Khalilzad and David Ochmanek, "Rethinking U.S. Defense Planning," and Benjamin S. Lambeth, "The Technology Revolution in Air Warfare," *Survival*, vol. 39 (Spring 1997), pp. 43–64 and 65–83, respectively; Daniel Goure and Stephen A. Cambone, "The Coming of Age of Air and Space Power," in Daniel Goure and Christopher M. Szara, eds., *Air and Space Power in the New Millennium* (Washington, D.C.: Center for Strategic and International Studies, 1997), pp. 1–47.

8   Office of the Under Secretary of Defense (Comptroller), *National Defense Budget Estimates for FY 2000* (Department of Defense, March 1999), pp. 138–41.

9   M. Thomas Davis, *Managing Defense after the Cold War* (Washington, D.C.: Center for Strategic and Budgetary Assessments, June 1997), p. iv; John Hillen, "Defense's Death Spiral," *Foreign Affairs*, vol. 78 (July – August 1999), pp. 2–7.

10   See Defense Science Board 1996 Summer Study Task Force, *Tactics and Technology for 21st Century Military Superiority*, vol. 1 (Department of Defense, 1996), p. S-4.

11   Richard Danzig, "Report of the Secretary of the Navy," in William S. Cohen, *Annual Report to the President and the Congress* (Department of Defense, 1999), pp. 205–6.

12   Steven Lee Myers, "Army Is Restructuring with Brigades for Rapid Response," *New York Times*, October 13, 1999, p. A16; Robert Suro, "Chief Projects an Army on Wheels," *Washington Post*, October 13, 1999, p. A23.

13   On stealth bombers, see, for example, Perry, Pfaltzgraff, and Conway, *Long-Range Bombers*, and Barry M. Blechman and Paul N. Nagy, *U.S. Military Strategy in the 21st Century* (Arlington, Va.: IRIS Independent Research, 1997); on arsenal ships, see Andrew F. Krepinevich Jr., *A New Navy for a New Era* (Washington, D.C.: Center for Strategic and Budgetary Assessments, 1996); on long-range and space weapons, see Harlan Ullman and others, *Shock and Awe: Achieving Rapid Dominance* (National Defense University Press, 1996), and George Friedman and Meredith Friedman, *The Future of War: Power, Technology, and American World Dominance in the 21st Century* (Crown, 1996); for an army view, see Major General Edward G. Anderson III and Major Michael Linick, "Ensuring Future Victories through Land Power Dominance: The U.S. Army Modernization Strategy," *National Security Studies Quarterly*, vol. 2 (Autumn 1996), pp. 1–18.

14   Andrew F. Krepinevich Jr., *The Conflict Environment of 2016: A Scenario-Based Approach* (Washington, D.C.: Center for Strategic and Budgetary Assessments, 1996); General Charles C. Krulak, "Operational Maneuver from the Sea: Building a Marine Corps for the 21st Century," *National Security Studies Quarterly*, vol. 2 (Autumn 1996), pp. 19–23; Robert J. Bunker, *Five-Dimensional (Cyber) Warfighting: Can the Army after Next Be Defeated through Complex Concepts and Technologies?* (Carlisle Barracks, Pa.: U.S. Army War College Strategic Studies Institute, 1998); Blechman and Nagy, *U.S. Military Strategy in the 21st Century*, pp. 11–16, 68–70.

15   John Arquilla, "The 'Velvet' Revolution in Military Affairs," *World Policy Journal* (Winter 1997–98), p. 42.

16   See Gary Hart and others, *New World Coming: American Security in the 21st Century* (Alexandria, Va.: U.S. Commission on National Security/21st Century, September 1999).

17   Alvin Toffler and Heidi Toffler, *War and Anti-War: Survival at the Dawn of the 21st Century* (Boston: Little, Brown, 1993); Admiral Arthur K. Cebrowski and John J. Garstka, "Network-Centric Warfare: Its Origin and Future," *Proceedings* (U.S. Naval Institute, January 1998), pp. 29–35.

18   This is the view of one of the U.S. Army's leading proponents of the RMA. See Robert H. Scales Jr., "Cycles of War: Speed of Maneuver Will Be the Essential Ingredient of an Information-Age Army," *Armed Forces Journal International*, vol. 134 (July 1997), p. 38. On the transparency of the oceans and limitless energy sources, see Zalmay Khalilzad and David Shlapak, with Ann Flanagan, "Overview of the Future Security Environment," in Zalmay Khalilzad and Ian O. Lesser, eds., *Sources of Conflict in the 21st Century* (Santa Monica, Calif.: RAND, 1998), pp. 35–36.

19   Cohen, Eisenstadt, and Bacevich, *Knives, Tanks, and Missiles*, pp. 7–10.

Thomas Homer-Dixon

RESOURCES AND CONFLICT

Source: 'Environmental scarcities and violent conflict', *International Security*, vol. 19, no. 1, 1994, pp. 5–40.

Simple-scarcity conflicts between states

THERE IS LITTLE EMPIRICAL support for the […] hypothesis that environmental scarcity causes simple-scarcity conflicts between states. Scarcities of renewable resources such as forests and croplands do not often cause resource wars between states. This finding is intriguing because resource wars have been common since the beginning of the state system. For instance, during World War II, Japan sought to secure oil, minerals, and other resources in China and Southeast Asia, and the 1991 Gulf War was at least partly motivated by the desire for oil.

However, we must distinguish between non-renewable resources such as oil, and renewable resources. […]

States have fought more over non-renewable than renewable resources for two reasons, I believe. First, petroleum and mineral resources can be more directly converted into state power than can agricultural land, fish, and forests. Oil and coal fuel factories and armies, and ores are vital for tanks and naval ships. In contrast, although captured forests and cropland may eventually generate wealth that can be harnessed by the state for its own ends, this outcome is more remote in time and less certain. Second, the very countries that are most dependent on renewable resources, and which are therefore most motivated to seize resources from their neighbors, also tend to be poor, which lessens their capability for aggression.

Our research suggests that the renewable resource most likely to stimulate inter-state resource war is river water.[1] Water is a critical resource for personal and national survival; furthermore, since river water flows from one area to another, one country's access can be affected by another's actions. Conflict is most probable when a downstream riparian is highly dependent on river water and is strong in comparison to upstream riparians. Downstream riparians often fear that their upstream neighbors will use water as a means of coercion. This situation is particularly dangerous if the downstream country also believes it has the military power to rectify the situation. [...]

However, our review of the historical and contemporary evidence shows that conflict and turmoil related to river water are more often internal than international. The huge dams that are often built to deal with general water scarcity are especially disruptive. Relocating large numbers of upstream people generates turmoil among the relocatees and clashes with local groups in areas where the relocatees are resettled. The people affected are often members of ethnic or minority groups outside the power hierarchy of their society, and the result is frequently rebellion by these groups and repression by the state. Water developments can also induce conflict over water and irrigable land among a country's downstream users. [...]

Population movement and group-identity conflicts

There is substantial evidence to support the hypothesis that environmental scarcity causes large population movement, which in turn causes group-identity conflicts. But we must be sensitive to contextual factors unique to each socio-ecological system. These are the system's particular physical, political, economic, and cultural features that affect the strength of the linkages between scarcity, population movement, and conflict.

For example, experts emphasize the importance of both "push" and "pull" factors in decisions of potential migrants.[2] These factors help distinguish migrants from refugees: while migrants are motivated by a combination of push and pull, refugees are motivated mainly by push. Environmental scarcity is more likely to produce migrants than refugees, because it usually develops gradually, which means that the push effect is not sharp and sudden and that pull factors can therefore clearly enter into potential migrants' calculations.

Migrants are often people who have been weak and marginal in their home society and, depending on context, they may remain weak in the receiving society. This limits their ability to organize and to make demands. States play a critical role here: migrants often need the backing of a state (either of the receiving society or an external one) before they have sufficient power to cause conflict, and this backing depends on the region's politics. Without it, migration is less likely to produce violence than silent misery and death, which rarely destabilizes states.[3] We must remember too that migration does not always produce bad results. It can act as a safety valve by reducing conflict in the sending area. Depending on the economic context, it can ease labor shortages in the receiving society [...].

Economic deprivation, institutional disruption, and civil strife

[...] [T]he third hypothesis [suggests] that environmental scarcity simultaneously increases economic deprivation and disrupts key social institutions, which in turn causes "deprivation" conflicts such as civil strife and insurgency. Environmental scarcity does produce economic deprivation, and this deprivation does cause civil strife. But more research is needed on the effects of scarcity on social institutions.

Resource degradation and depletion often affect economic productivity in poor countries and thereby contribute to deprivation. [...]

I originally hypothesized that scarcity would undermine a variety of social institutions. Our research suggests, however, that one institution in particular – the state – is most important. Although more study is needed, the multiple effects of environmental scarcity, including large population movements and economic decline, appear likely to weaken sharply the capacity and legitimacy of the state in some poor countries.

First, environmental scarcity increases financial and political demands on governments. For example, to mitigate the social effects of loss of water, soil, and forest, governments must spend huge sums on industry and infrastructure such as new dams, irrigation systems, fertilizer plants, and reforestation programs. Furthermore, this resource loss can reduce the incomes of élites directly dependent on resource extraction; these élites usually turn to the state for compensation. Scarcity also expands marginal groups that need help from government by producing rural poverty and by displacing people into cities where they demand food, shelter, transport, energy, and employment. In response to swelling urban populations, governments introduce subsidies that drain revenues, distort prices, and cause misallocations of capital, which in turn hinders economic productivity. Such large-scale state intervention in the marketplace can concentrate political and economic power in the hands of a small number of cronies and monopolistic interests, at the expense of other élite segments and rural agricultural populations.

Simultaneously, if resource scarcity affects the economy's general productivity, revenues to local and national governments will decline. This hurts élites that benefit from state largesse and reduces the state's capacity to meet the increased demands arising from environmental scarcity. A widening gap between state capacity and demands on the state, along with the misguided economic interventions such a gap often provokes, aggravates popular and élite grievances, increases rivalry between élite factions, and erodes the state's legitimacy.

Key contextual factors affect whether lower economic productivity and state weakening lead to deprivation conflicts. Civil strife is a function of both the level of grievance motivating challenger groups and the opportunities available to these groups to act on their grievances. The likelihood of civil strife is greatest when multiple pressures at different levels in society interact to increase grievance and opportunity simultaneously. Our third hypothesis says that environmental scarcity will change both variables, by contributing to economic crisis and by weakening institutions such as the state. But numerous other factors also influence grievance and opportunity.

Contrary to common belief, there is no clear correlation between poverty (or economic inequality) and social conflict.[4] Whether or not people become aggrieved and violent when they find themselves increasingly poor depends, in part, upon their notion of economic justice. For example, people belonging to a culture that inculcates fatalism about deprivation – as with lower castes in India – will not be as prone to violence as people believing they have a right to economic wellbeing. Theorists have addressed this problem by introducing the variable "relative deprivation."[5] But there is little correlation between measures of relative deprivation and civil conflict.[6]

Part of the problem is that analysts have commonly used aggregate data (such as GNP/capita and average educational levels) to measure individual deprivation.[7] In addition, more recent research has shown that, to cause civil strife, economic crisis must be severe, persistent, and pervasive enough to erode the legitimacy or moral authority of the dominant social order and system of governance. System legitimacy is therefore a critical intervening variable between rising poverty and civil conflict. It is influenced by the aggrieved actors' subjective "blame system," which consists of their beliefs about who or what is responsible for their plight.[8]

Serious civil strife is not likely to occur unless the structure of political opportunities facing challenger groups keeps them from effectively expressing their grievances peacefully, but offers them openings for violence against authority.[9] The balance of coercive power among social actors affects the probability of success and, therefore, the expected costs and benefits of different actions by the state, its supporters, and challenger groups. A state debilitated by corruption, by falling revenues and rising demand for services, or by factional conflicts within élites will be more vulnerable to violent challenges by political and military opponents; also vital to state strength is the cohesiveness of the armed forces and its loyalty to civil leadership.[10]

Challengers will have greater relative power if their grievances are articulated and actions coordinated through well-organized, well-financed and autonomous opposition groups. Since grievances felt at the individual level are not automatically expressed at the group level, the probability of civil violence is higher if groups are already organized around clear social cleavages, such as ethnicity, religion, or class. These groups can provide a clear sense of identity and act as nuclei around which highly mobilized and angry elements of the population, such as unemployed and urbanized young men, will coalesce. Conversely, if economic crisis weakens challenger groups more than the state, or affects mainly disorganized people, it will not lead to violence.

Factors that can influence both grievance and opportunity include the leadership and ideology of challenger groups, and international shocks and pressures such as changes in trade and debt relations and in costs of imported factors of production such as energy.[11] The rapid growth of urban areas in poor countries may have a similar dual effect: people concentrated in slums can communicate more easily than those in scattered rural villages; this may reinforce grievances and, by reducing problems of coordination, also increase the power of challenger groups. Research shows, however, surprisingly little historical correlation between rapid urbanization and civil strife;[12] and the exploding cities of the developing world have been remarkably quiescent in recent decades. This may be changing: India has lately witnessed ferocious urban violence, often in the poorest slums, and sometimes directed at new migrants from the countryside.[13] [...]

A combined model

There are important links between the processes identified in the second and third hypotheses. For example, although population movement is sometimes caused directly by scarcity, more often it arises from the greater poverty caused by this scarcity.

Similarly, the weakening of the state increases the likelihood not only of deprivation conflicts, but of group-identity conflicts.

It is useful, therefore, to bring the hypotheses together into one model of environment-conflict linkages [...]. Decreases in the quality and quantity of renewable resources, population growth, and unequal resource access act singly or in various combinations to increase the scarcity, for certain population groups, of cropland, water, forests, and fish. This can reduce economic productivity, both for the local groups experiencing the scarcity and for the larger regional and national economies. The affected people may migrate or be expelled to new lands. Migrating groups often trigger ethnic conflicts when they move to new areas, while decreases in wealth can cause deprivation conflicts such as insurgency and rural rebellion. In developing countries, the migrations and productivity losses may eventually weaken the state which in turn decreases central control over ethnic rivalries and increases opportunities for insurgents and élites challenging state authority. [...]

The causal role of environmental scarcity

Environmental scarcity often acts as a powerful long-term social stressor, but does it have any independent role as a cause of conflict? Many analysts assume that it is no more than a fully endogenous intervening variable linking political, economic, and social factors to conflict. By this view, environmental scarcity may be an important indicator that political and economic development has gone awry, but it does not merit, in and of itself, intensive research and policy attention at the expense of more fundamental political and economic factors.

But the cases reviewed here highlight three reasons why this view is wrong. First, as we saw in the Senegal and Jordan basins, environmental scarcity can itself be an important force behind changes in the politics and economics governing resource use. In both cases, scarcity caused powerful actors to increase in their own favor the inequities in the distribution of resources. Second, ecosystem vulnerability is often an important variable contributing to environmental scarcity, and this vulnerability is, at least in part, an independent physical factor: the depth of soils in the Filipino uplands and the vulnerability of Israel's aquifers to salt intrusion are not functions of human social institutions or behavior. Third, in many parts of the world – including regions of the Philippines, Haiti, Peru, and South Africa – environmental degradation has crossed a threshold of irreversibility. Even if enlightened social change removes the original political, economic, and cultural causes of the degradation, it will be a continuing burden on society. Once irreversible, in other words, environmental degradation becomes an exogenous variable.

Implications for international security

Environmental scarcity has insidious and cumulative social impacts, such as population movement, economic decline, and the weakening of states. These can contribute to diffuse and persistent sub-national violence. The rate and extent of such conflicts will increase as scarcities worsen.

This sub-national violence will not be as conspicuous or dramatic as interstate resource wars, but it will have serious repercussions for the security interests of both the developed and the developing worlds. Countries under such stress may fragment as their states become enfeebled and peripheral regions are seized by renegade authorities and warlords. Governments of countries [...] have lost control over outer territories [...] [where] environmental stress has [partly] contributed to their fragmentation. Fragmentation of any sizeable country will produce large outflows of refugees; it will also hinder the country from effectively negotiating and implementing international agreements on collective security, global environmental protection, and other matters.

Alternatively, a state might keep scarcity-induced civil strife from causing its progressive enfeeblement and fragmentation by becoming a "hard" regime that is authoritarian, intolerant of opposition, and militarized. Such regimes are more prone to launch military attacks against neighboring countries to divert attention from internal grievances. If a number of developing countries evolve in this direction, they could eventually threaten the military and economic interests of rich countries.

A state's ability to become a hard regime in response to environmentally induced turmoil depends, I believe, on two factors. First, the state must have sufficient remaining capacity – despite the debilitating effects of scarcity – to mobilize or seize resources for its own ends; this is a function of the internal organizational coherence of the state and its autonomy from outside pressures. Second, there must remain enough surplus wealth in the country's ecological-economic system to allow the state, once it seizes this wealth, to pursue its authoritarian course. Consequently, the countries with the highest probability of becoming "hard" regimes, and potential threats to their neighbors, are large, relatively wealthy developing countries that are dependent on a declining environmental base and that have a history of state strength. [...]

Notes

1   Peter Gleick, "Water and Conflict," Occasional Paper No. 1, Project on Environmental Change and Acute Conflict (September 1992); and Gleick, "Water and Conflict: Fresh Water Resources and International Security," *International Security*, Vol. 18, No. 1 (Summer 1993), pp. 79–112.

2   Astri Suhrke, "Pressure Points: Environmental Degradation, Migration, and Conflict," Occasional Paper No. 3, Project on Environmental Change and Acute Conflict (March 1993).

3   Ibid.

4   Some of the best studies of this question have focused on the relationship between poverty and urban violence in the United States. See William Ford and John Moore, "Additional Evidence on the Social Characteristics of Riot Cities," *Social Science Quarterly*, Vol. 51, No. 2 (September 1970), pp. 339–48; and Robert Jiobu, "City Characteristics and Racial Violence," *Social Science Quarterly*, Vol. 55, No. 1 (June 1974), pp. 52–64.

5   People are said to be relatively deprived when they perceive a widening gap between the level of satisfaction they have achieved (usually defined in economic terms) and the level they believe they deserve. Deprivation is said to be relative to some

subjective standard of equity or fairness; the size of the perceived gap depends upon the beliefs about economic justice held by the individual. See Ted Gurr, *Why Men Rebel* (Princeton: Princeton University Press, 1970).

6   Steven Finkel and James Rule, "Relative Deprivation and Related Theories of Civil Violence: A Critical Review," in Kurt and Gladys Lang, eds. *Research in Social Movements, Conflicts, and Change* (Greenwich, Conn.: JAI, 1986), pp. 47–69.

7   Ibid.

8   These beliefs are grounded in historical and economic experience. See, for example, James Scott, *The Moral Economy of the Peasant: Rebellion and Subsistence in Southeast Asia* (New Haven: Yale University Press, 1976), pp. 1–11.

9   Thomas Homer-Dixon, "On the Threshold: Environmental Changes as Causes of Acute Conflict," *International Security*, Vol. 16, No. 2 (Fall 1991), pp. 105–6 and 109–11.

10   See Farrokh Moshiri, "Revolutionary Conflict Theory in an Evolutionary Perspective," in Jack Goldstone, Ted Gurr, and Farrokh Moshiri, eds., *Revolutions of the Late Twentieth Century* (Boulder, Colo.: Westview, 1991), pp. 4–36; and Goldstone, "An Analytical Framework," ibid., pp. 37–51.

11   For a review of some of these factors, see Jack Goldstone, "Theories of Revolution: The Third Generation," *World Politics*, Vol. 32, No. 3 (April 1980), pp. 425–53.

12   Wayne Cornelius, Jr., "Urbanization as an Agent in Latin American Political Instability: The Case of Mexico," *American Political Science Review*, Vol. 63, No. 3 (September 1969), pp. 833–357; and Abdul Lodhi and Charles Tilly, "Urbanization, Crime, and Collective Violence in 19th-Century France," *American Journal of Sociology*, Vol. 79, No. 2 (September 1973), pp. 296–318.

13   Sanjoy Hazarika, "Week of Rioting Leaves Streets of Bombay Empty," *New York Times*, January 12, 1993, p. A3.

Myron Weiner

MIGRATION AND SECURITY

Source: 'Security, stability, and international migration', *International Security,* vol. 17, no. 3, 1992/93, pp. 91–126.

Security, stability, and international migration

MIGRATION AND REFUGEE ISSUES, no longer the sole concern of ministries of labor or of immigration, are now matters of high international politics, engaging the attention of heads of states, cabinets, and key ministries involved in defense, internal security, and external relations. [...]

Examples abound of migration flows – both of economic migrants affected by the push and pull of differentials in employment opportunities and income, and of refugees from the pushes of domestic turmoil and persecution – that have generated conflicts within and between states and have therefore risen to the top of the political agenda. [...] One could go on, drawing examples from the daily press to make three points:

First, international migration shows no sign of abating. Indeed, with the end of the Cold War there has been a resurgence of violent secessionist movements that create refugee flows,[1] while barriers to exit from the former Soviet Union and Eastern Europe have been lifted. The breakup of empires and countries into smaller units has created minorities who now feel insecure.[2] Vast differentials in income and employment opportunities among countries persist, providing the push and pull that motivate economic migrants.[3] Environmental degradation, droughts, floods, famines, and civil conflicts compel people to flee across international borders.[4] And new global networks of communication and transportation provide individuals with information and opportunities for migration.[5]

Second, more people want to leave their countries than there are countries willing or capable of accepting them. The reluctance of states to open their borders to all who wish to enter is only partly a concern over economic effects. The constraints are as likely to be political, resting upon a concern that an influx of people belonging to another ethnic community may generate xenophobic sentiments, conflicts between natives and migrants, and the growth of anti-migrant right-wing parties.

Third, it is necessary to note that while the news media have focused on South/North migration and East/West migration, this focus is narrow and misleading. The movement of migrant workers from North Africa to Western Europe, migration from Asia and Latin America to the United States and Canada, and the increase in the number of people from the Third World and Eastern Europe claiming refugee status in the West represent simply one dimension of the global flows. Only a fraction of the world's seventeen million refugees are in the advanced industrial countries and only a small portion of global migration has flowed to Western Europe (where migrants total 5 percent of the population) or to the United States. Most of the movement has been from one developing country to another; the world's largest refugee flows have been in Africa, South Asia, Southeast Asia, and most recently in the Persian Gulf.[6] [...] Attention has been given by economists to the ways in which economic differentials between countries influence migration,[7] and by some political scientists to the ways in which conflicts within countries lead to refugee flows.[8] But little systematic comparative attention has been given to the ways in which international population movements create conflicts within and between states, that is, to population flows as an independent rather than as a dependent variable. [...]

These features of population movements – a growth propelled by economic differentials, internal political disorder, and global networks of communication and transportation; the political as well as economic constraints on the admission of migrants and refugees; and the truly global character of migration – suggest the need for a security/stability framework for the study of international migration that focuses on state policies toward emigration and immigration as shaped by concerns over internal stability and international security. Such a framework should consider political changes within states as a major determinant of international population flows, and migration, including refugee flows, both as cause and as consequence of international conflict. [...]

A security/stability framework complements rather than replaces an economic analysis by focusing upon the role of states in both creating and responding to international migration. [...]

* * *

When is migration a threat to security and stability?

Migration can be perceived as threatening by governments of either population-sending or population-receiving communities. The threat can be an attack by armed refugees; migrants can be a threat to either country's political stability; or migrants can be perceived as a threat to the major societal values of the receiving country.

"Security" is a social construct with different meanings in different societies. An ethnically homogeneous society, for example, may place a higher value on preserving its ethnic character than does a heterogeneous society and may, therefore, regard a population influx as a threat to its security. Providing a haven for those who share one's values (political freedom, for example) is important in some countries, but not in others; in some countries, therefore, an influx of "freedom fighters" may not be regarded as a threat to security. Moreover, even in a given country, what is highly valued may not be shared by élites and counter-élites. The influx of migrants regarded as radicals may be feared by a monarch, but welcomed by the opposition. One ethnic group may welcome migrants, while another is vehemently opposed to them. The business community may be more willing than the general public to import migrant workers.

Similarly, countries differ in whether or not they regard the mistreatment of their citizens abroad as a threat that calls for state action. While some countries are prepared to take armed action in defense of their overseas citizens, others prefer not to antagonize a government that has enabled its citizens to find employment and a country that is a source of much-needed remittances.

Any attempt to classify types of threats from immigration quickly runs into distinctions between "real" and "perceived" threats, or into absurdly paranoid notions of threat or mass anxieties that can best be described as xenophobic and racist. But even these extreme notions are elements in the reaction of governments to immigrants and refugees. It is necessary to find an analytical stance that, on the one hand, does not dismiss fears, and, on the other, does not regard all anxieties over immigration and refugees as a justification for exclusion.

Before turning to an analysis of how, why, and when states may regard immigrants and refugees as potential threats, it is first necessary to note that some obvious explanations for the response of population-receiving countries are of limited utility. One example is economic absorptive capacity. It is plausible, for example, that a country with little unemployment, a high demand for labor, and the financial resources to provide the housing and social services required by immigrants should regard migration as beneficial, while a country low on each of these dimensions should regard migration as economically and socially destabilizing. Nevertheless, using these criteria, one might expect Japan to welcome migrants and Israel to reject them, when in fact the opposite is the case.[9]

A second plausible but unsatisfactory explanation is the volume of immigration. A country faced with a large-scale influx should feel more threatened than a country experiencing a small influx of migrants. From this perspective one might have expected the Federal Republic of Germany to regard a trickle of Sri Lankan Tamils in the mid-1980s with equanimity, but to move swiftly to halt the 1989 influx of 2,000 East Germans daily, or for the countries of Africa to feel more threatened by the onrush of refugees and hence less receptive than the countries of Western Europe confronted with a trickle from the Third World. Again, however, the opposite has been the case.

Economics does, of course, matter. Even a country willing to accept immigrants when its economy is booming is more likely to close its doors in a recession. But economics does not explain many of the differences between countries, nor does it explain the criteria countries employ to decide whether a particular group of migrants or refugees is acceptable or is regarded as threatening. Similarly, volume can matter, but again it depends upon who is at the door.

The third and most plausible explanation for the willingness of states to accept or reject migrants is ethnic affinity. A government and its citizens are likely to be receptive to those who share the same language, religion, or race, while it might regard as threatening those with whom such an identity is not shared. But what constitutes "ethnic affinity" is, again, a social construct that can change over time. Australians and

Americans, for example, redefined themselves so that Asians are no longer excluded as unassimilable peoples. Many West Europeans now regard East Europeans as fellow-Europeans, more acceptable as migrants than people from North Africa. Who is or is not "one of us" is historically variable. To many nineteenth-century American Protestants, Jews and Catholics were not "one of us," and today, for many Europeans, Muslims are not "one of us." Moreover, what constitutes cultural affinity for one group in a multi-ethnic society may represent a cultural, social, and economic threat to another: note, for example, the hostile response of some African-Americans in Florida to Cuban migrants,[10] Indian Assamese response to Bangladeshis, and Pakistan Sindhi response to Biharis. Cultural affinity – or its absence – clearly plays a critical role in how various communities within countries respond to a population influx [...].

We can identify five broad categories of situations in which refugees or migrants may be perceived as a threat to the country that produces the emigrants, to the country that receives them, or to relations between sending and receiving countries. The first is when refugees and migrants are regarded as a threat – or at least a thorn – in relations between sending and receiving countries, a situation that arises when refugees and migrants are opposed to the regime of their home country. The second is when migrants or refugees are perceived as a political threat or security risk to the regime of the host country. The third is when immigrants are seen as a cultural threat or, fourth, as a social and economic problem for the host society. And the fifth – a new element growing out of recent developments in the Gulf – is when the host society uses immigrants as an instrument of threat against the country of origin.

Refugees and immigrants as opponents of the home regime

Conflicts create refugees, but refugees can also create conflicts. An international conflict arises when a country classifies individuals as refugees with a well-founded fear of persecution,[11] thereby accusing and condemning their country of origin for engaging in persecution. The mere granting of asylum can create an antagonistic relationship.[...] The view of the United Nations High Commission for Refugees (UNHCR) is that the granting of refugee status does not necessarily imply criticism of the sending by the receiving country, but such a view contradicts the conception of the refugee as one with a fear of *persecution*.[12] Moreover, democratic regimes generally allow their refugees to speak out against the regime of their country of origin, allow them access to the media, and permit them to send information and money back home in support of the opposition. The host country's decision to grant refugee status thus often creates an adversary relationship with the country that produces the refugees. The receiving country may have no such intent, but even where its motives are humanitarian the mere granting of asylum can be sufficient to create an antagonistic relationship. [...]

A refugee-receiving country may actively support the refugees in their quest to change the regime of their country of origin. Refugees are potentially a tool in inter-state conflict. [...] Refugee-producing countries may thus have good reason for fearing an alliance between their adversaries and the refugees.

Non-refugee immigrants can also be a source of conflict between receiving and sending countries. A diaspora made up primarily of refugees is, of course, likely to be hostile to the regime of the country from which they fled. But even economic migrants may become hostile, especially if they live in democratic countries while the government of their homeland is repressive. [...]

The home country may take a dim view of the activities of its citizens abroad, and hold the host country responsible for their activities. But host countries, especially if they are democratic, are loath to restrict migrants engaged in lawful activities, especially since some of the migrants have already become citizens. The home country may even plant intelligence operators abroad to monitor the activities of its migrants,[13] and may take steps to prevent further emigration. The embassy of the home country may also provide encouragement to its supporters within the diaspora. The diaspora itself may become a focal point of controversy between the home and host countries, among contending groups within the diaspora, or between sections of the diaspora and the home government.[14] Thus, struggles that might otherwise take place only within a country become internationalized if the country has a significant overseas population.

Refugees and immigrants as a political risk to the host country

Governments are often concerned that refugees to whom they give protection may turn against them if they are unwilling to assist the refugees in their opposition to the government of their country of origin. Paradoxically, the risk may be particularly high if the host country has gone so far as to arm the refugees against their country of origin. Guns can be pointed in both directions, and the receiving country takes the risk that refugees will seek to dictate the host country's policies toward the sending country. [...]

Refugees have launched terrorist attacks within their host country, illegally smuggled arms, allied with the domestic opposition against host-government policies, participated in drug traffic, and in other ways eroded government' willingness to admit refugees. [...]

Such fears, it should be noted, are sometimes exaggerated, and governments have often gone to extreme lengths to protect themselves against low-level threats[15] but these fears are nonetheless not always without foundation, especially in the context of an increase in international terrorism.

Migrants perceived as a threat to cultural identity

How and why some migrant communities are perceived as cultural threats is a complicated issue, involving initially how the host community defines itself. Cultures differ with respect to how they define who belongs to or can be admitted into their community. These norms govern whom one admits, what rights and privileges are given to those who are permitted to enter, and whether the host culture regards a migrant community as potential citizens. A violation of these norms (by unwanted immigrants, for example) is often regarded as a threat to basic values and in that sense is perceived as a threat to national security.

These norms are often embedded in the law of citizenship that determines who, by virtue of birth, is entitled as a matter of right to be a citizen, and who is permitted to become a naturalized citizen. The main distinction is between citizenship laws based on *jus sanguinis*, whereby a person wherever born is a citizen of the state of his parents, and those based on *jus soli*, the rule that a child receives its nationality from the soil or place of birth. The ties of blood descent are broader than merely parentage, for they suggest a broader "volk" or people to whom one belongs in a fictive relationship. [...]

Where such notions of consanguinity dominate citizenship law, the political system is capable of distinguishing between an acceptable and unacceptable influx, without regard either to the numbers or to the condition of the economy into which the immigrants move. In general, countries with norms of consanguinity find it difficult to incorporate ethnically alien migrants, including refugees, into citizenship. These countries are also likely to have political groups that advocate sending immigrants home even though expulsion may impose severe economic consequences for the host as well as the home countries.

A norm of indigenousness may also be widely shared by a section of a country's population and even incorporated into its legal system. This norm prescribes different rights for those who are classified as indigenous and those who, irrespective of the length of time they or their ancestors resided in the country, are not so classified. An indigenous people asserts a superior claim to land, employment, education, political power, and the central national symbols that is not accorded to others who live within the country. [...]

Legal definitions of citizenship aside, most societies react with alarm when there is an unregulated large-scale illegal migration of people who do not share their culture and national identity. Examples abound. Illegal migration into the Sabah state of Malaysia from the Philippines and Indonesia – an estimated 400,000 or more of Sabah's 1.4 million population – has created anxieties there. The government of Malaysia is particularly uneasy since the Philippines lays claim to Sabah and some Filipino leaders insist that, so long as the dispute continues, Malaysia has no right to consider Filipinos as illegal aliens. Should the Filipinos acquire citizenship, it has been noted, they might win a third or more of Sabah's parliamentary seats and pursue a merger with the Philippines. The Philippines might thereby acquire through colonization what it is unable to win through diplomatic or military means.[16]

Colonization as a means of international conquest and annexation can in fact be the deliberate intent of a state. The government of Morocco, for example, moved 350,000 civilians into Western Sahara in an effort to claim and occupy disputed territory. The Israeli government has provided housing subsidies to its citizens to settle on the West Bank. Since the annexation of the Turkic regions of central Asia in the nineteenth century, the Czarist and Soviet regimes have encouraged Russian settlement, while a similar policy of settling Han people has been pursued by the Chinese government in Sinkiang province and other areas.

Many governments are concerned that migration may lead to xenophobic popular sentiments and to the rise of anti-migrant political parties that could threaten the regime. Under such circumstances governments may pursue anti-migration policies in anticipation of public reactions.

Migrants perceived as a social or economic burden

Societies may react to immigrants because of the economic costs they impose or because of their purported social behavior such as criminality, welfare dependency, delinquency, etc. Societies may be concerned because the people entering are so numerous or so poor that they create a substantial economic burden by straining housing, education, and transportation facilities. In advanced industrial societies, services provided by the welfare state to migrant workers, permanent migrants, or refugees may generate local resentment. In less developed countries, refugees may illegally occupy private or government lands; their goats, sheep, and cattle may decimate forests and grazing land; they may use firewood, consume water, produce waste, and in other ways come to be regarded as an ecological threat. The willingness to bear these costs is likely to be low if the host government believes that the government of the sending country is engaged in a policy of population "dumping," by exporting its criminals, unwanted ethnic minorities, and "surplus" population at the cost of the receiving country. [...]

The fears of western countries notwithstanding, however, population dumping has not been a significant element in the flow of migrants from the Third World to advanced industrial countries. To the extent that population dumping has occurred, it has largely been of ethnic minorities; flights – at least before the Yugoslav crisis – have primarily been to neighboring developing countries rather than to advanced industrial countries. [...]

Government officials, otherwise concerned with the plight of refugees, may fear that a decision to grant refugee status to a small number of individuals might open the floodgate beyond what society is prepared to accept. One reason states hesitate to grant refugee and asylum status to those fleeing because of economic and even violent conditions at home – as distinct from having a personal "well-founded fear of persecution" – is the concern that the number of asylum requests would then increase. States prefer restrictive criteria in order to keep the influx small. Since laws of asylum are often imprecise and the policy that states will admit refugees with a well-founded fear of persecution is subject to varied interpretations, individuals who wish to enter a country but cannot do so under existing guestworker and migration laws may resort to claiming political asylum. Western European governments are thus torn between a humanitarian sentiment toward refugees and the recognition that the more generous the law of asylum, the greater the number of applicants. As the number of asylum-seekers grows, governments become more restrictive, insisting on evidence that the individual does indeed have a well-founded fear of persecution, not "merely" a fear of being killed in a violent civil conflict. [...]

Migrants as hostages: risks for the sending country

Recent actions of the governments of Iran, Iraq, and Libya all demonstrate how migrants can be used as an instrument of statecraft in order to impose restraints upon the actions of the home government. Following the invasion of Kuwait on August 2, 1990, the government of Iraq announced a series of measures using migrants as instruments for the achievement of political objectives. [...]

While the Iraqi strategy of using their control over migrants for international bargaining is thus far unique, the mere presence of migrants in a country from which they could be expelled has been for some time an element affecting the behavior of the migrants' home country. [...] [They] have recognized that any sudden influx of returning migrants would create a major problem for domestic security as remittances came to an end, balance of payments problems were created, families dependent upon migrant income were threatened with destitution, and large numbers of people were thrown into labor markets where there already existed substantial unemployment. Since the Gulf War, all of these fears have materialized. Sending governments aware of these potential consequences have hesitated to criticize host governments for the treatment of migrant workers.[17] When workers have been expelled for strikes and other agitational activities, the home governments have sought to pacify their migrants – and the host government – in an effort to avoid further expulsions. Governments have often remained silent even when workers' contracts have been violated. [...]

A security threat, as Robert Jervis has reminded us, is often a matter of perception.[18] What are the enemy's capabilities? What are its intentions? Perceptions similarly shape decision-makers' assessments of whether refugees and migrants constitute a security threat. Time and again we have seen how different are the assessments that various governments make of the threat posed by a population influx. [...] [Furthermore,] perceptions of risk change. [...] Moreover, a country's concern that a refugee influx is the result of population "dumping" by its neighbor – clearly a matter of perception of intentions – is likely to be greatest when there is a history of enmity between sending and receiving countries, as in the case of Pakistan and India. Countries almost always feel threatened if their neighbor seeks to create a more homogeneous society by expelling its minorities – the phrase now is "ethnic cleansing"[19] – but we have also seen that there can be circumstances when a population "exchange" or an orderly "return" of an ethnic minority can be regarded as non-threatening by the receiving country.

How governments assess one another's intentions with respect both to economic migrants and political refugees is thus critical to how conflictual population movements may become. A government is more likely to accommodate a refugee flow from a neighboring country if it believes that the flight is the unfortunate and unintended consequences of a civil conflict than if it believes that the flight of the refugees is precisely what is intended.[20] Similarly, a government's response to reports that its citizens abroad are maltreated will depend upon whether it believes that the host country is culpable.

But perception is not everything. As we have seen, there are genuine conflicts of interests among countries on matters of migrants and refugees. Countries quarrel over each other's entry and exit rules as some countries want those whom another will not let go, while some countries force out those whom others do not want.[21] How states react to international population flows can itself be a source of international conflict. [...]

Notes

1   On secessionist movements, see Allen Buchanan, *Secession: The Morality of Political Divorce from Fort Sumter to Lithuania and Quebec* (Boulder, Colo.: Westview Press, 1991). This otherwise excellent analysis by a political philosopher does not deal with the problem of minorities that remain in successor states.

2   Democratization and political liberalization of authoritarian regimes have enabled people to leave who previously were denied the right of exit. An entire region of

the world, ranging from Central Europe to the Chinese border, had imprisoned those who sought to emigrate. Similar restrictions continue to operate for several of the remaining communist countries. If and when the regimes of North Korea and China liberalize, another large region of the world will allow its citizens to leave. See Alan Dowty, *Closed Borders: The Contemporary Assault on Freedom of Movement* (New Haven: Yale University Press, 1987), which provides a useful account of how authoritarian states engaged both in restricting exodus and in forced expulsions. For an analysis of the right to leave and return, see H. Hannum, *The Right to Leave and Return in International Law and Practice* (London: Martinus Nijhoff, 1987). As has happened twice before in this century, the breakup of an empire is producing large-scale ethnic conflict and emigration. With the withdrawal of Soviet power from Eastern Europe and the disintegration of the Soviet state itself, conflicts have erupted between Turks and Bulgarians in Turkey; Romanians and Hungarians in Transylvania; Armenians and Azeris in the Caucasus; Albanians, Croatians, Slovenians, Bosnians, and Serbs in former Yugoslavia; Slovaks and Czechs in Czechoslovakia; and among a variety of ethnic groups in Georgia, Moldova, Ukraine, and in the new states of Central Asia. There is a high potential for continued emigration of minorities among each of these states. See F. Stephen Larrabee, "Down and Out in Warsaw and Budapest: Eastern Europe and East-West Migration," *International Security*, Vol. 16, No. 4 (Spring 1992), pp. 5–33.

3   A long-term decline in the birth rate in advanced industrial countries combined with continued economic growth may lead employers to seek low-wage laborers from abroad. Transnational investment in manufacturing industries may reduce some manpower needs, but the demand for more workers in the service sector seems likely to grow, barring technological breakthroughs that would replace waiters, bus conductors, nurses, and household help. Employers in Japan, Singapore, and portions of the United States and Western Europe are prepared to hire illegal migrants, notwithstanding the objections of their governments and much of the citizenry. So long as employer demand remains high, borders are porous, and government enforcement of employer sanctions is limited, illegal migration seems likely to continue and in some countries to increase.

4   There have already been mass migrations within and between countries as a result of desertification, floods, toxic wastes (chemical contamination, nuclear reactor accidents, hazardous waste), and threats of inundation as a result of rising sea levels. According to one estimate, two million Africans were displaced in the mid-1980s as a result of drought. See Jodi L. Jacobson, *Environmental Refugees: A Yardstick of Habitability*, Worldwatch Paper No. 86 (Washington, D.C.: Worldwatch Institute, 1988).

5   Information concerning employment opportunities and changes in immigration and refugee laws is quickly transmitted to friends and relatives. Not only do many people in the Third World view the United States and Europe as potential places for migration, but differences and opportunities *within* the Third World are also becoming better known. Indonesians, for example, are seeking (illegal) employment in peninsular Malaysia, Sabah, and Sarawak. Malaysians and others are aware of opportunities in Singapore. Oil-rich Brunei attracts workers from Malaysia, the Philippines, Thailand, and Indonesia. Taiwan, Hong Kong, and South Korea export manpower, but also attract illegal immigrant workers drawn by their reputation for employment at high wages. Migrants continue to be attracted to the oil-producing countries of the Middle East. For one account of large-scale migration among Third

World countries, see Michael Vatikiotis, "Malaysia: Worrisome Influx; Foreign Workers Raise Social, Security Fears," *Far Eastern Economic Review*, August 6, 1992, p. 21, which describes the concerns in Malaysia over the influx of an estimated one million migrants from Indonesia.

6   An estimated 5.5 million people from forty countries were temporarily or permanently displaced by the Gulf War. The largest single group was an estimated 1–1.5 million Yemenis who were forced to leave Saudi Arabia to return to Yemen. The other main displaced peoples were Kurds, Kuwaitis, Palestinians, and South Asians. See Elizabeth N. Offten, "The Persian Gulf War of 1990–91: Its Impact on Migration and the Security of States" (M.S. dissertation, Department of Political Science, MIT, June 1992).

7   See Sidney Klein, ed., *The Economics of Mass Migration in the Twentieth Century* (New York: Paragon House, 1987); Brinley Thomas, *Migration and Economic Growth: A Study of Great Britain and the Atlantic Economy* (Cambridge: Cambridge University Press, 1954); Charles P. Kindleberger, *Europe's Postwar Growth: The Role of Labor Supply* (Cambridge: Harvard University Press, 1967), chap. 9; Theodore W. Schultz, "Migration: An Economist's View," in William H. McNeill and Ruth S. Adams, eds., *Human Migration: Patterns and Policies* (Bloomington: Indiana University Press, 1987), pp. 377–86. These and other works by economists deal with the benefits and costs as well as the determinants of migration. For a useful bibliography on the economics of migration, see Julian L. Simon, *The Economic Consequences of Immigration* (New York: Basil Blackwell, 1989).

8   Aristide R. Zolberg, Astri Suhrke, and Sergio Aguayo, *Escape from Violence: Conflict and the Refugee Crisis in the Developing World* (New York: Oxford University Press, 1989); and Michael R. Marrus, *The Unwanted: European Refugees in the Twentieth Century* (New York: Oxford University Press, 1985), are among the most comprehensive treatments of the major world regions that have produced refugees in this century.

9   In fact, when Soviet Jewish migration reached 200,000 in one year, there were "euphoric expectations of a million-and-a-half newcomers within two or three years," wrote the editor of the Jerusalem *Post*. David Bar-Illan, "Why Likud Lost — And Who Won," *Commentary*, Vol. 94, No. 2 (August 1992), p. 28.

10   The ambivalent attitude of African-Americans toward immigration is described by Lawrence H. Fuchs, "The Reactions of Black Americans to Immigration," in Virginia Yans-McLaughlin, ed., *Immigration Reconsidered: History, Sociology and Politics* (New York: Oxford University Press, 1990).

11   The language is from the 1951 United Nations Convention Relating to the Status of Refugees, subsequently modified in a 1967 protocol. The Convention states that a refugee is a person who "owing to a well-founded fear of being persecuted for reasons of race, religion, nationality, membership of a particular social group or political opinion, is outside the country of his nationality and is unable, or unwilling to avail himself of the protection of that country." This definition is the centerpiece of most Western law dealing with refugees. Some critics (see Zolberg, Suhrke, and Aguayo, *Escape from Violence*) believe that the definition is too narrow because it excludes those who only flee from violence. For a defense of the United Nations definition, see David A. Martin, "The Refugee Concept: On Definitions, Politics, and the Careful Use of Scarce Resources," in Howard Adelman, ed., *Refugee Policy: Canada and the United States* (Toronto: York Lanes Press, 1991), pp. 30–51. A wider definition of refugee was adopted in 1969 by the Organization

of African Unity in its Refugee Convention, according to which the term refugee applies to every person who "owing to external aggression, occupation, foreign domination or events seriously disturbing public order in either part or the whole of his country of origin or nationality, is compelled to leave his place, of habitual residence in order to seek refuge in another place outside his country of origin or nationality."

12   For an analysis of the UNHCR's concept of protection, see Leon Gordenker, *Refugees in International Politics* (New York: Columbia University Press, 1987), pp. 27–46.

13   On the role played by the Taiwanese security apparatus in attempts to thwart support for Taiwanese independence sentiments within the Taiwanese community in the United States, see Myron Weiner, "Asian Immigrants and U.S. Foreign Policy," in Tucker, Keely, and Wrigley, *Immigration and U.S. Foreign Policy*, p. 197.

14   Examples include conflicts between Turkish Muslim fundamentalists and their opponents within Germany and, earlier, among Indians in Britain who were divided in their attitude toward Prime Minister Indira Gandhi's government after she declared an emergency in 1975 and arrested members of the opposition.

15   One of the more extreme responses was the McCarran-Walter Immigration Act passed by the U.S. Congress in 1952, which excluded any aliens who might "engage in activities which would be prejudicial to the public interest, or endanger the welfare, safety or security of the United States." The Immigration and Naturalization Service interpreted the act to go beyond barring known or suspected terrorists to exclude writers and politicians known to be critical of the United States.

16   Concern over colonization, it should be noted, can also be an internal affair in multi-ethnic societies. Territorially-based ethnic groups may consider an influx of people from other parts of the country as a cultural and political threat. Hence, the Moros in Mindanao revolted at the in-migration of people from other parts of the Philippines, Sri Lanka's Tamils oppose settlement by Sinhalese in "their" region, Nicaragua Miskito Indians object to the migration of non-Miskito peoples into "their" territory on the Atlantic coast, and a variety of India's linguistic communities regard in-migration as a form of colonization. In some cases such settlements can provoke an internal conflict between migrants and indigenes, with international consequences.

17   For a description of working conditions of South Asian migrants in the Persian Gulf, and the reluctance of South Asian governments to protest the mistreatment of migrants, see Myron Weiner, "International Migration and Development: Indians in the Persian Gulf," *Population and Development Review*, Vol. 8, No. 1 (March 1988), pp. 1–36. For accounts of the benefits to Asian countries of migration to the Gulf see Godfrey Gunatilleke, ed., *Migration of Asian Workers to the Arab World* (Tokyo: United Nations University, 1986); and Rashid Amjad, ed., *To the Gulf and Back: Studies in the Economic Impact of Asian Labour Migration* (Geneva: International Labor Organization, 1989).

18   Robert Jervis, *Perception and Misperception in International Politics* (Princeton: Princeton University Press, 1976).

19   The older expression "unmixing of peoples" was reportedly used by Lord Curzon to describe the situation during the Balkan Wars; Michael R. Marrus, *The Unwanted: European Refugees in the Twentieth Century* (New York: Oxford University Press, 1985), p. 41.

20   The European Community stiffened its views toward Serbia when it became clear that Serbs were seeking to force the exodus of Croatians and Bosnians; many German officials then concluded that their willingness to accommodate refugees was enabling the Serbs to achieve their objective of clearing areas of non-Serbs.

21   For an analysis of how the congruence or incongruence of rules of entry and exit influence the patterns of conflict and cooperation among states, see Myron Weiner, "On International Migration and International Relations," *Population and Development Review*, Vol. 11, No. 3 (September 1985), pp. 441–55.

Phil Williams

TRANSNATIONAL CRIME
AND SECURITY

Source: 'Transnational criminal organisations and international security', *Survival*, vol. 36, no. 1, Spring 1994, pp. 96–113.

Transnational criminal organisations and international security

The changing international environment

ORGANISED CRIME has a long history, and has traditionally been seen as a domestic law-and-order problem. Over the past two decades, however, crime has taken on new international dimensions and criminal organisations have developed to resemble transnational corporations. Although these TCOs [transnational criminal organisations] are usually based partly on familial ties and kinship – at least at the top level – their structures make them highly proficient, adaptable and able to 'treat national borders as nothing more than minor inconveniences to their criminal enterprises'.[1]

The emergence of TCOs is partly a result of underlying changes in global politics and economics, which have been conducive to the development of all transnational organisations. The emergence and development of the 'global village' in the second half of the twentieth century have fundamentally changed the context in which both legitimate and illegitimate businesses operate. This has, moreover, created unprecedented opportunities for international criminal activity. Increased interdependence between nations, the ease of international travel and communications, the permeability of national boundaries, and the globalisation of international financial networks have facilitated the emergence of what is, in effect, a single global market for both licit and illicit commodities. There has been a vast increase in transnational activity – the movement of information, money, physical objects, people, and other tangible or intangible items across state boundaries – in which at least one of the actors involved in the transaction is non-governmental.[2] [...]

The scale of these activities largely reflects the opportunities resulting from changes in both international relations and within states. The second half of the twentieth century has not only witnessed a great increase in transactions across national boundaries that are neither initiated nor controlled by states, but has also seen a decline in state control over its territory. TCOs are both contributors to, and beneficiaries of, these changes. [...]

The rise of transnational criminal organisations

Just as the modern industrial economy and the rise of mass consumer markets encouraged the growth of organised crime [...] so [have] growing opportunities for transnational activities [...] facilitated the growth of TCOs. Not only is transnational activity as open to criminal groups as it is to legitimate multinational corporations, but the character of criminal organisations also makes them particularly suited to exploit these new opportunities. Since criminal groups are used to operating outside the rules, norms and laws of domestic jurisdictions, they have few qualms about crossing national boundaries illegally. In many respects, therefore, TCOs are transnational organisations *par excellence*. They operate outside the existing structures of authority and power in world politics and have developed sophisticated strategies for circumventing law enforcement in individual states and in the global community of states.

Samuel Huntington has argued that transnational organisations conduct centrally directed operations in the territory of two or more nation-states, mobilise resources and pursue optimising strategies across national boundaries, are functionally specific, and seek to penetrate and not acquire new territories.[3] This is also true of TCOs. Criminal enterprises, however, differ from transnational organisations that operate legally in one crucial respect: most transnational organisations seek access to territory and markets through negotiations with states[4] while TCOs obtain access not through consent, but through circumvention. They engage in systematic activities to evade government controls, which is possible because the conditions that have given rise to their emergence also make it very difficult for governments to counter them.

Transnational criminal organisations vary in size and scale. Some, such as the Colombian cartels, focus almost exclusively on drug trafficking while others, such as the Chinese triads or Japanese yakuza, engage in a wide range of criminal activities, including extortion, credit card fraud, prostitution and drug trafficking. [...]

TCOs are diverse in structure, outlook and membership. What they have in common is that they are highly mobile and adaptable and are able to operate across national borders with great ease. They are able to do this partly because of the conditions identified above and partly because of their emphasis on networks rather than formal organisations. It is of interest that legitimate transnational corporations have also adopted more flexible, fluid network structures, which enable them to exploit local conditions more effectively. Perhaps not surprisingly, this is one area where TCOs have taken the lead as their illegality has compelled them to operate covertly and to de-emphasise fixed structures.

Another important trend among transnational corporations has been the growth of strategic alliances, especially between regional transnational corporations that want to develop globally. For legitimate corporations, alliances facilitate production where costs are low and allow corporations to take advantage of local knowledge and experience in marketing and distribution. TCOs pursue strategic alliances for similar reasons. Even if these organisations circumvent state structures, they may still have to negotiate with national and local criminal organisations, and strategic alliances permit them to cooperate with, rather than compete against, indigenously entrenched criminal organisations. Moreover, these alliances enhance the ability of TCOs to circumvent law enforcement agencies, facilitate risk sharing and make it possible to use existing distribution channels. Finally, strategic alliances enable drug trafficking organisations to exploit differential profit margins in different markets.

Although it is difficult to make a definitive analysis of the links between and among TCOs, there is considerable evidence that these alliances exist. [...]

These links between various groups, especially those engaged in drug trafficking, have made TCOs an increasingly serious problem for governments. [...]

The threat to security

It is tempting to say that the activities of TCOs have little impact on national and international security. Unlike revolutionary or terrorist groups, TCOs have predominantly economic objectives. Moreover, it is arguable that even illicit enterprises add to national wealth, create jobs and provide a safety net against recession. TCOs also employ entrepreneurial and managerial skills that would otherwise be wasted. The profits from their activities are enormous and at least some of them are ploughed back into local and national economies, usually with some multiplier effects. In these circumstances, one might conclude that TCOs do not pose a threat to national and international security.

Such an assessment is based on a narrow military conception of security. If one defines security as not just external military threats but as a challenge to the effective functioning of society, then drug trafficking is much more serious than many issues that have traditionally been seen as a threat to security. Drug trafficking poses one of the most serious challenges to the fabric of society in the US, Western Europe and even many drug-producing countries, which have also become consumers of their product. The threats to security are more complex and subtle than more traditional military challenges. Nevertheless, drug trafficking was designated a national security threat by the Reagan Administration in 1986 and subsequent US administrations have concurred with this assessment. Taking this further, it is clear that TCOs pose threats to security at three levels: the individual, the state and the international system of states.[5]

At the individual level, security is the provision of a relatively safe environment in which citizens do not fear violence or intimidation. TCOs have had a profound geosocial impact on this security. Indeed, if individual security is inversely related to the level of violence in society – the greater the violence, the less the security enjoyed by citizens – then drug trafficking and its associated activities pose a serious security threat.

This is partly because of the close connection between drugs and violence. There are three kinds of violence usually associated with the drug industry: violence by criminal organisations to protect their 'turf' and profits; crimes against people and property by drug users who need to pay for illicit drugs; and violence perpetrated by individuals under the influence of mind-altering substances.[6] It has been estimated, for example, that the average heroin user commits 200 crimes a year to feed his habit.[7]

The problems of drug-related violence have become apparent in many societies with a significant number of addicts, including those which have been used for the transhipment of drugs. It is in the US, however, that violence has become the most prevalent. The pervasiveness of gang activity and the emergence of 'no-go zones' for ordinary citizens and even law enforcement officers are associated, in particular, with the trafficking of 'crack' cocaine. While not all violence within US society can be attributed to drug abuse or trafficking, it is clear that there are links between drugs and violence, and that the greater the level of drug abuse within society then the lower the level of security that individual citizens enjoy. Moreover, it is unlikely that these problems can be dealt with adequately as long as the flow of drugs continues unimpeded. Reducing the demand for drugs through education, treatment and reha-bilitation is crucial, but unless more effective curbs are placed on drug supplies, demand reduction is unlikely to be successful. The wholesalers and retailers of the drug business, however, are experts at marketing and they have an insidious product, whose supply helps to create its own demand.

Not only does drug abuse add to the health-care burden and undermine produc-tivity and economic competitiveness, but transnational drug trafficking also results in societies in which violence is more pervasive and individual security is, therefore, more elusive.

Transnational criminal organisations can also pose serious threats to the security of their host and home states. In some cases, their power rivals that of the state itself. Their willingness to use force against the state and its law enforcement agencies chal-lenges the state monopoly on organised violence and can be more destabilising than the activities of revolutionary or terrorist groups. This has certainly been the case in Colombia and Italy, where TCOs have resisted state control and engaged in extensive violence and terrorism. [...]

[...] Moreover, these challenges to state authority may be unavoidable. As one eminent criminologist has noted, 'each crime network attempts to build a coercive monopoly and to implement that system of control through at least two other crimi-nal activities – corruption of public and private officials, and violent terrorism in order to enforce its discipline'.[8] TCOs, therefore, by their very nature undermine civil society, destabilise domestic politics and undercut the rule of law.

Transnational criminal organisations sometimes create chaos, but they also exploit the uncertainty created by other domestic and international developments. Not surprisingly, TCOs flourish in states with weak structures and dubious legiti-macy, which derives from economic inequalities, the dominance of traditional oligar-chies, the lack of congruence between nation and state, poor economic performance and ethnic divisions. In such circumstances, the development of parallel political and economic structures is almost inevitable. Sometimes this follows from the fact that parts of the country are outside the control of central government. In other cases, government institutions may be so corrupt that they no longer have either the incen-tive or the capacity to reassert control. [...]

It is important not to exaggerate the importance of TCOs in causing political upheaval because whenever states lose legitimacy and political authority the prob-lems have deep and extensive roots. Nevertheless, there is an important link between the rise of TCOs, on the one hand, and the crisis of governance and decline in civil society that have become familiar features of the post-Cold War world, on the other.

Whatever the underlying reason for the breakdown in authority structures, political chaos provides a congenial environment for criminal activity. One of the key features of TCOs is that they link 'zones of peace' and 'zones of turbulence' in the international system.[9] They take advantage of the chaos that exists, for example, in countries such as Myanmar, which lacks an effective, legitimate government, is the world's main producer of heroin, and is internationally isolated yet is penetrated transnationally. Moreover, criminal organisations have a vested interest in the continuation of weak government and the conditions which allow them to export heroin from Myanmar with impunity.

Threats to the integrity of states generate challenges to the international state system. Although the field of security studies has traditionally focused on military relations between states, in the future it will also have to consider the relationship between states and powerful non-state actors. The dominance of governments has increasingly been challenged by the emergence of such actors, operating either regionally or globally. Lacking the attributes of sovereignty is often an advantage rather than a constraint for transnational actors – they are sovereignty-free rather than sovereignty-bound and use this freedom and flexibility to engage in activities that are difficult for states to regulate.[10] The issue is control versus autonomy: states want control and transnational actors want autonomy.

Transnational criminal organisations challenge aspects of state sovereignty and security that have traditionally been taken for granted. They prove the permeability of national borders and penetrate societies that are nominally under the control of states. States formally retain sovereignty, but if they are unable to control the importation of arms, people and drugs into their territory then it loses much of its significance. Sovereignty remains a useful basis for the international society of states, but no longer reflects real control over territory. The permeability of national boundaries and the concept of sovereignty do not make easy bedfellows.

It can be argued, of course, that the activities of many transnational organisations undermine state sovereignty. Most of these groups, however, obtain access to national markets and operate on a state's territory only with the permission of the government, a process that revalidates state power and authority.[11] TCOs are different because they obtain access through clandestine methods, minimise the opportunities for state control over their activities, and prevent real sovereignty being exercised. Although the main purpose of their activities is to make a profit, an inevitable by-product is an implicit challenge to state authority and sovereignty. The threat is insidious rather than direct: it is not a threat to the military strength of the state, but is a challenge to the prerogatives that are an integral part of statehood.

This does not mean that all states oppose TCOs. Alliances of convenience between 'rogue' or 'pariah' states and TCOs could pose serious security threats, especially from those trafficking in nuclear material. As soon as a trafficking network is functioning effectively product diversification is easy. Organisations that deal in drugs can also traffick in technology and components for weapons of mass destruction. Whether the recipients of such transfers are terrorist organisations or 'pariah' states, the link between criminal activities and security is obvious.

If non-proliferation and other regulatory regimes are to function effectively in the future, therefore, it will be necessary to curb the activities of TCOs. This will not be easy. [...]

Notes

1   Senator Roth quoted in *The New International Criminal and Asian Organised Crime*, Report made by the Permanent Subcommittee on Investigations of the Committee on Governmental Affairs, United States Senate 102nd Congress, 2nd Session S. Print 102–29 (December 1992), p. 2.

2   Robert Keohane and Joseph Nye, *Transnational Relations and World Politics* (Cambridge MA: Harvard University Press, 1971), p. xii.

3   See Samuel Huntington, 'Transnational Organisations in World Politics', *World Politics*, vol. 25, no. 3 April 1973, pp. 333–68.

4   Ibid., p. 355.

5   The three levels follow Barry Buzan, *People, States and Fear* (Brighton: Wheatsheaf, 1983).

6   P. Goldstein, H. H. Brownstein, P. Ryan and P. Bellucci, 'Crack and Homicide in New York City, 1988: A Conceptually Based Event Analysis', *Contemporary Drug Problems*, vol. 16, no. 4, Winter 1989, pp. 651–87.

7   The Majority Staffs of the Senate Judiciary Committee and the International Narcotics Control Caucus, *The President's Drug Strategy: Has it Worked?*, September 1992, p. vi.

8   R. J. Kelly, 'Criminal Underworlds: Looking down on Society from Below' in R. J. Kelly (ed.), *Organised Crime: A Global Perspective* (Totowa, NJ: Rowman and Littlefield, 1986), pp. 10–31.

9   The concept of the two zones is developed in M. Singer and A. Wildavsky, *The Real World Order* (Chatham, NJ: Chatham House Publishers, 1993).

10   James Rosenau, *Turbulence in World Politics* (Princeton, NJ: Princeton University Press, 1991), p. 253.

11   See Huntington, 'Transnational Organisations in World Politics', p. 363.

P. W. Singer

AIDS/HIV AND SECURITY

Source: 'AIDS and international security', *Survival*, vol. 44, no. 1, Spring 2002, pp. 145–58.

AIDS and international security

AT THE START OF THE NEW CENTURY, the AIDS epidemic is finally receiving high-level attention on the international stage. [...]
   A recurring theme [...] was the growing danger presented by the epidemic, not just in terms of direct victims of the disease itself, but to international security. [...]

The direct danger of AIDS

[...] The death toll from AIDS has already been devastating and over the next decades it portends to kill at almost inconceivable rates. These figures, though, do not tell the full story of the disease's impact: these are fatalities without violence. The complete accounting of AIDS' toll will not just include the obvious direct victims of the disease, but also those who suffer from its wider consequences through warfare.

AIDS and the military

The primary connection between AIDS and conflict appears to come from the unique linkage between the disease and the institution of the military. Studies consistently find that the average infection rates of soldiers are significantly higher than equivalent age groups in the regular civilian population. This is true across the globe, whether in the US, UK, France, or in armies of the developing world where the problem is magnified. Recent studies in Africa have found that military infection rates are around four times that of the civilian population. During periods of war, this figure often soars to as much as 50 times higher.[1]

The reasons for this unhappy link are varied. In addition to being recruited from the most sexually active age groups, soldiers are typically posted away from their communities and families for long periods of time. Besides disconnecting them from traditional societal controls on behaviour, this also means that they are removed from contact with spouses or regular sexual partners. Personnel are often lonely or stressed and typically have more money than the local population, but little to spend it on. Their cloistering in bases thus tends to attract other high-risk populations, including prostitutes and drug dealers. Finally, soldiers live and work inside an institution and culture that tends to encourage risk-taking, so precautions against certain behaviour are often eschewed. In blunt terms, even in peacetime, military bases tend to attract prostitutes and soldiers usually don't use condoms. On deployment, this problem is heightened.[2]

The result is that many armies are the focal point of AIDS infection in their nation and are essentially under direct attack from the disease. [...]

The results are devastating for the military as an institution and can lead to a dangerous weakening of its capabilities. [...] Besides the effect on the regular troops and the general recruiting pool, the disease is particularly costly to military forces in terms of its draining effect on the skilled positions. AIDS is not only killing regular conscripts but also officers and NCOs – key personnel that military forces are least able to lose. Thus, leadership capacities and professional standards are directly suffering from the disease's scourge. [...] This following-out of militaries, particularly at the leadership level, has a number of added implications for security. As human capacity is lost, military organisations' efforts to modernise are undermined. Preparedness and combat readiness deteriorate. Even if a new recruiting pool is found to replace sick troops, cohesion is compromised. As they lose their leadership to an unyielding, demoralising foe, the organisations themselves can unravel.

The higher risk within the military compounds the disease's impact by transferring it to the political level. Commanders in countries with high rates of infection already worry that they are now unable to field full contingents for deployment or to assist their nation's allies. AIDS-weakened militaries also pose the risk of domestic instability and may even invite foreign attack. [...]

AIDS and state failure

AIDS threatens not just the military but the whole state. As the disease spreads and becomes ever more pervasive, 'it destroys the very fibre of what constitutes a nation: individuals, families and communities, economic and political institutions, military and police forces'.[3] The manner in which AIDS can hollow out already weak states parallels its effect on militaries. In contrast to other epidemics, which tended to kill off the weak and infirm first, AIDS in the developing world tends to claim the lives of the more productive members of society, who are not easily replaced. Educated and well-off citizens are more mobile, and thus have often contracted the disease first. Many states have clusters of the disease in the middle and upper levels of management in both business and government, and AIDS is already being blamed for shortages of skilled workers in a number of countries.[4] [...]

The impact is felt not just in governance, but also in economic and social development. Besides acting as a new sort of tax on society, by increasing the health-care costs of business across the board, the disease also discourages foreign investment. Workforce productivity decreases, while revenues go down as the local consumer base is improverished.[5] The disease increases budgetary needs at the same time as it shrinks the tax base. The consequences could well be shattering for already impoverished states. [...]

The precise security threat here is that AIDS causes dangerous weaknesses in the pillars of an otherwise stable state: its military; its governing institutions and economy. The disease is accordingly no longer just a symptom but a fundamental catalyst of state crisis.[6] As public institutions crumble and senior officials succumb to the disease, public confidence in governing bodies is further threatened.[7]

The weakening of state bodies at points of crisis has repeatedly been the spark for coups, revolts and other political and ethnic struggles to secure control over resources. [...] That the disease is concentrating in areas already undergoing tenuous political transitions – such as Africa and the former Soviet Union – only heightens the risk of instability and state failure.

The security danger presented by failed states extends beyond the simple human tragedy played out in the ensuing chaos and collapse. While stable states outside the region might imagine themselves secure and able to stand aside from failed states, the realities of the global system no longer permit this. Major powers have clear national interests in many of the regions most vulnerable to state failure generated or exacerbated by disease. The US, for example, has economic investments in at-risk areas in Africa that are, by some measures, comparable to investments in the Middle East or Eastern Europe.[8] Equally, a number of individual states at risk, such as Angola, Nigeria, and South Africa, are core regional allies, as well as critical suppliers of oil (roughly one-fifth of all US imports) and strategic minerals.[9]

The threats of economic and political collapse from the disease can also lead to new refugee flows. Besides facilitating the spread of the disease, the sudden and massive population movements such collapses provoke have led to heightened region-wide tension and destabilisation.[10] With AIDS likely to reach pandemic levels in the Caribbean and former Soviet Union, American and European governments will have to prepare for refugee crises reminiscent of the Haitian collapse and Balkan wars of the 1990s.

The more direct security threat is that failed states can become havens for the new enemies of global order. [...] Decaying states give extremist groups freedom of operation, with dangerous consequences a world away. This hazard applies even to seemingly disconnected state failures. Sierra Leone's collapse in the 1990s, for example, certainly was of little concern to policy-makers in Washington and had little connection to radical Islamic terrorist groups. Evidence has since emerged, however, that the tiny West African country is connected to al-Qaeda fundraising efforts involving the diamond trade.[11] [...]

The new children of war

The AIDS epidemic also undermines security by creating new pools of combatants who are more likely to go to war. AIDS does not strike with equal weight across age groups. In a 'unique phenomenon in biology', the disease actually reverses death rates to strike hardest at mature, but not yet elderly, adults.[12] The consequence is that population curves shift, eliminating the typical middle-aged hump, almost directly opposite to the manner of previous epidemics.

Such demographic shifts have disturbing security implications. Recent research has found a strong correlation between violent outbreaks, ranging from wars to terrorism, and the ratio of a society's young male population in relation to its more mature segments.[13] Above a ratio of roughly 40 post-adolescent men to every 100 older males, violent conflict in a society becomes far more likely. In several states that are already close to this dangerous threshold, AIDS will likely tip the balance. Young men, psychologically more aggressive under normal circumstances, compete for both social and material resources, and are more easily harnessed to conflict when they outnumber other generational groups. Demagogues, warlords and criminals find it easier to recruit when the population is so distributed. Riots and other social crises are also more likely. Whatever the reason for the correlation, this worrying pattern has held true across history, from ancient times to recent outbreaks of violence in Rwanda, Yugoslavia and the Congo.

The new demographics of AIDS will also heighten security risks by creating a new pool of orphans, magnifying the child-soldier problem. By 2010, over 40m children will lose one or both of their parents to AIDS, including one-third of all children in the hardest-hit countries. [...]

The stigma of the disease, as well as the sheer numbers of victims, will overwhelm the communities and extended families that would normally look after them. This cohort represents a new 'lost orphan generation'.[14] Its prospects are heartrending, as well as dangerous. Besides being malnourished, stigmatised and vulnerable to physical and sexual abuse, this mass of disconnected and disaffected children is particularly at risk of being exploited as child soldiers. Children in such straits are often targeted for recruitment, either through abduction or voluntary enlistment driven by desperation. [...]

Child soldiers have appeared on contemporary battlefields without AIDS being present. The prevalence of a new, globalised mass of orphans, as well as a hollowing of local states and militaries, will make them more widespread. As a result, violent conflicts will be easier to start, greater in loss of life, harder to end and will lay the groundwork for their recurrence in succeeding generations.

Weakening global stability

Just as the disease endangers pillars of the nation-state, so too does it strike at pillars of international stability and governance. In particular, AIDS presents the institution of peacekeeping, a calming influence in many of the world's hotspots, with a unique challenge. [...]

[...] One of the heightening factors is frequency of deployment. During peacekeeping operations, forces from all over the world mix in a poor, post-conflict zone, where the sex industry is one of the few still in business. Not only are peacekeeping forces at risk of infection themselves, but they in turn present a new risk to the areas in which they are deployed and to their home states. Peacekeeping forces are in fact among the primary mechanisms of spreading the disease at a mass level to new areas. [...]

A consequence of high AIDS prevalence in the military is that states will be less able and less willing to contribute their forces to peacekeeping operations. Around

40% of current UN peacekeepers come from countries with soaring infection rates.[15] [...]

The understandable reluctance of countries to accept peacekeepers from regions with high infection rates will thus make the already tough task of finding and deploying a robust peacekeeping operation even more difficult. The disease also provides a new stratagem for local parties to craft the makeup of peacekeeping forces to their own advantage. In the deployment of UNMEE (the UN Mission to Ethiopia and Eritrea), one of the parties used AIDS as a pretence to exclude troops from states that it felt would not be amenable to its own political agenda. The general result is that the already weak institution of peacekeeping is weakened further.

The new costs of war

The AIDS virus represents not only a new weapon of war, but one that makes the impact of war all the more catastrophic and enduring. AIDS has created a new tie between rape and genocide. Rape itself is certainly nothing new to warfare. In the last decade, however, it has become organised for political and strategic purposes.[16] In Bosnia there were camps designated for the purpose, while in Rwanda between 200,000 and 500,000 women were raped in a few short weeks. The introduction of AIDS makes such programs a genocidal practice.[17] The chance of disease transmission is especially high during rape, due to the violent nature of the act. It appears that rape is now being intentionally used to transfer AIDS to target populations. In the conflicts that have taken place over the last years in the Congo, for example, soldiers deliberately raped women of the enemy side with the stated intention of infecting them.[18] Their goal was to heighten the impact of their attacks and create long-lasting harm. [...]

Disease has always been part of the true cost of war.[19] Epidemics decimated armies throughout ancient and biblical times and continued to do so well into the nineteenth century. [...]

The links between AIDS, militaries and warfare may make twenty-first century conflict no different. Of the countries with the highest infection rates in Africa, half are involved in conflict.[20] And during war, as noted above, infection rates within militaries often escalate. The rates within the seven armies that intervened into the Congo are estimated to have reached as high as 50–80%.[21] All these soldiers will die from the disease, making AIDS far more costly in lives than the limited combat that took place.

Such infected forces typically leave a swathe of disease in their wake. The original spread of infection in East Africa can be traced back to the movements made by individual units of the Tanzanian Army.[22] Moreover, the conditions of war hinder efforts to counter the disease's spread. In Sierra Leone and the Congo, for example, all efforts at AIDS prevention were put on hold by the breakdown of order during conflict.[23] Valuable windows of opportunity to arrest epidemics before they reach critical stages are lost.

Wars also lead to the uprooting and amalgamation of populations, bringing groups into contact that otherwise would be unlikely to mix. In the Congo war, for example, soldiers from all over Africa converged, while civilians from rural provinces were brought into urban centres. Such mixing promotes mutations in the virus itself.

Researchers have found that the conflict in the Congo has created a veritable witch's brew of AIDS, bringing together various strains from around the continent. The resulting new strains are called 'strange recombinants'. One scientist noted, 'We are seeing variants [of HIV] never seen before'.[24]

The consequences reach far beyond the scope of the fighting. For those countries who can afford them, the recent development of new multi-drug therapies ('cocktails') have cut the risk of death from AIDS, leading many in the US to think that the disease is, in a sense, cured. Yet, there always remains the possibility of far more dangerous HIV strains: resistant to these latest treatments or even airborne. HIV has always displayed a high rate of genetic mutation, so this may happen regardless of wars or state collapse. That said, if such deadly new strains show up one day in the US or Europe, the multiple linkages of AIDS and warfare mean that its origin will likely be traced back to some ignored and faraway conflict.

Notes

1   UNAIDS, *AIDS and the Military*, May 1998, www.unaids.org; 'Incidence of AIDS Higher Among Soldiers', *Voice of America*, 12 January 2001.

2   UNAIDS, *AIDS and the Military*, 1998. For example, research found that 45% of the Dutch sailors and marines serving in the peacekeeping mission in Cambodia had sexual contact with sex workers or the local population during just a five-month tour.

3   International Crisis Group (ICG), *HIV/AIDS as a Security Threat*, 19 June 2001, www.intl-crisis-group.org, p. 1.

4   Raymond Copson, *AIDS in Africa*, Congressional Research Service Issue Brief IB10050, 14 May 2001.

5   *The Economic Impact of HIV/AIDS in Southern Africa*, Brookings Conference Report, No. 9, September 2001; 'HIV/Aids: The Impact on Social and Economic Development', *Report of Select Committee on International Development*, British House of Commons, 29 March 2001; Copson, *AIDS in Africa*.

6   Helen Epstein, 'AIDS: The Lesson of Uganda', *The New York Review of Books*, 5 July 2001, www.nybooks.com/articles/14309.

7   For example in Ethiopia, there were recently large anti-government protests headed by children orphaned by AIDS. Three million Ethiopians are thought to be infected with HIV and about 900,000 Ethiopian children have been orphaned by the virus. 'Ethiopia: AIDS Orphans Demonstrate', UN Integrated Regional Information Networks (IRIN), 6 August 2001.

8   The US has a range of economic interests, from oil and gas, pharmaceuticals and telecoms, to soft drinks, amounting to just over $15 billion. Direct investment also showed a higher average return, roughly 30% for Africa compared to 17% for the Middle East.

9   'Africa: Clinton Legacy Alive Under Bush', IRIN, 8 February 2001.

10   National Intelligence Council, *The Global Infectious Disease Threat and Its Implications for the United States*; Alan Dowty and Gil Loescher, 'Refugee Flows as Grounds for International Action', *International Security*, vol. 21, issue 1, Summer 1996, pp. 43–71.

11   The rebel RUF and agents of al-Qaeda traded in millions of dollars of 'blood diamonds', with a reported rise in purchasing before the 11 September attacks in New York and Washington DC as the group tried to gain hard assets. Douglas Farah, 'Al Qaeda Cash Tied to Diamond Trade', *Washington Post*, 2 November 2001.

12   Additionally, this is heightened for adult women, killing at even higher rates, such that the death rate for women in Africa in their 20s is twice that of women in their 60s. Rachel Swarns, 'Study Says AIDS is Now Chief Cause of Death in South Africa', www.CNN.com, 16 October, 2001.

13   Christian Mesquida and Neil I. Warner, 'Male Age Composition and Severity of Conflicts', *Politics and Life Sciences*, vol. 18, no. 2, September 1999, pp. 181–89; Richard Morin, 'Boy Trouble', *Washington Post*, 24 June 2001; 'Natural Born Killers', *Profiles*, May 1999, www.yorku.ca. India, Pakistan and some African states are presently at risk if this demographic projection of conflict theory holds true.

14   'South Africa AIDS Orphans Struggle to Survive', www.CNN.com, 21 June 2001; 'HIV/Aids: The Impact on Social and Economic Development', National Intelligence Council, *The Global Infectious Disease Threat and Its Implications for the United States*.

15   'Troops Spread Scourge Worse than War'; *HIV/AIDS as a Security Threat*, ICG Report, p. 23.

16   Lisa Sharlach, 'Rape as Genocide: Bangladesh, the Former Yugoslavia, and Rwanda', *New Political Science*, vol. 22, no. 1, Spring, 2000, p. 98.

17   Vivianne Nathanson, 'Preventing and Limiting Suffering Should Conflict Break Out', *International Review of the Red Cross*, no. 839, 30 September 2000, pp. 601–15.

18   UNAIDS, 'Aids Becoming Africa's Top Human Security Issue, UN Warns', UNAIDS press release, 10 January 2000.

19   See William McNeill, Plagues and Peoples (London: Penguin, 1976), p. 251; Arno Karlen, *Man and Microbes: Disease and Plagues in History and Modern Times* (New York: Touchstone Books, 1996); 'War and Disease', *Mindful*, vol. 1 no. 7, March 1997, http://www.spusa.org/publications/mindfull/mindfullwardis.pdf

20   James Wolfensohn, 'Impact of AIDS on Peace and Security in Africa', Speech delivered to the UN Security Council Special Session, 10 January 2000, www.un.org.

21   Copson, *AIDS in Africa*.

22   Edward Hooper, *The River: A Journey Back to the Source of HIV and AIDS* (London: Penguin, 2000), pp. 42–44.

23   Lansana Fofana, 'Sierra Leone: Conflict Spurs the Spread of HIV/AIDS', *Interpress Service*, 5 July 1999.

24   Laurie Garrett, 'Allies of Aids: Among Warring Factions in Congo, Disease is Mutating', *Newsday*, 9 July 2000.

Jonathan Kirshner

ECONOMICS AND SECURITY

Source: 'Political economy in security studies after the cold war', *Review of International Political Economy*, vol. 5, no.1, Spring 1998, pp. 825–54.

Classical issues: the underlying harmony

C LASSICAL ISSUES [...] link[ing] [...] political economy and security studies [...] include the political economy of power, the economic causes of war, and the role of the national budget constraint on the construction and execution of grand strategy. [...]

The political economy of power

[...] [W]hile the mercantilists and the liberals may have disagreed on a number of issues, both schools of thought perceived an underlying long-run harmony between the national pursuit of wealth and power. The liberal revolution in this regard was to change fundamentally the understanding of what wealth was. Traditional mercantilists stressed the accumulation of treasure – spending power that could buy weapons and support armies. Liberals argued that wealth was represented not by bullion but by productive capacity. On this point, the neo-mercantilist descendants of the discredited mercantilists embraced the liberals' logic. [...] Since that time, few have disputed that productive capacity is the base upon which military power rests. [...]

The economic causes of war

Another subject obviously at the intersection of political economy and security studies [...], is the economic causes of war. Manchester School economists in the nineteenth century saw a negative relationship between free trade and war.[1] Others see conflict emerging from interstate competition over access to markets and raw materials.[2] More generally, Gilpin (1981:67) states that 'in a world of scarcity the fundamental issue is the distribution of the available economic surplus', while Stopford and Strange (1991: 204, see also 209–11) see the post-cold war era as one characterized by states 'more directly engaged in the competition for shares of the world's wealth'.

In practice, there are three principal ways in which economic forces act as a source of war: changes in relative economic growth, internal economic dislocation, and incompatible national economic strategies. *Changes in relative economic growth* are argued to contribute to war by scholars who emphasize the importance of equilibrium between power and privilege in the international system. Under such conditions, states are satisfied with the status quo.[4] According to this school of thought, because states tend to grow at differential rates, there is a natural impetus for the international system to drift away from equilibrium. Since power derives from underlying economic capacity, states that are growing faster perceive a divergence between their power and position in the international pecking order. Such states force a confrontation to revise the status quo, and this is often resolved by war (Gilpin, 1981; Liska, 1957, 1963; Organski, 1968: 364–67; Organski and Kugler, 1980; Doran, 1983; Kennedy, 1980: 291–360).

Internal economic dislocation can contribute to conflict for a number of reasons deriving primarily from the pressures that governments can find themselves under as a consequence of hard times. Such governments may resort to 'military Keynesianism', that is, efforts at pump priming by expanded military spending. These measures can contribute to war by heightening the security dilemma, creating a militaristic mind-set, or by the purposeful extension of military Keynesian tactics. Hard times can also increase the perceived stakes in struggles for international economic opportunity (see, for example, LaFeber, 1963). States may also engage in military adventures to divert attention away from failed domestic policies, or such dislocation may radicalize politics in general (see Pion-Berlin, 1985; also Rosecrance, 1963; Levy, 1989). [...]

Conflicts can also be initiated or exacerbated by *incompatible national strategies*. [...] Often such strategies unintentionally drive conflict as a consequence of the unintended effects of economic policies, as Viner (1948: 29) noted with his claim that mercantilist strategies 'served to poison international relations'. Contrapositively, there is Kennedy's (1983) argument that one of the reasons why the British empire lasted so long was because its liberal international management ruffled few feathers. Additionally, economic strategies may not only be incompatible, they may backfire. French financial diplomacy in the interwar period was intended to influence German policy but may instead have contributed to the deterioration of the situation. [...]

Strategy and the budget constraint

The incompatibility of national economic strategies calls attention to the issue of grand strategies in general. Avoiding unintended (and self-defeating) provocation is a necessary component of strategy, but it is not sufficient. Two central questions remain: how to form an optimal grand strategy, an exercise in setting priorities and reconciling ends and means; and what constraints are imposed on crisis and wartime operations by limited resources. These are issues at the heart of security studies — and they are also fundamentally questions of political economy. [...]

To reiterate, the construction of grand strategy is a fundamentally economic question; further, a state's budget constraint defines the limits of its power. Understanding or failing to recognize these limits often makes the differences between successful and unsuccessful foreign policy. In the context of a crisis or war, retaining international solvency (particularly with regard to the balance of payments), mobilizing and extracting resources from society, and maintaining domestic economic stability are all crucial for success. These issues are ubiquitous and have been highly consequential. [...]

Clearly, there exists a rich tradition of integration between issues associated with political economy and security studies, which is essential to understanding state power as well as the causes and courses of conflict and war.[5] The intellectual history of these issues can be traced to the nineteenth century and before, and the intimate association between the two was commonly assumed and understood prior to the cold war.

Modern issues: action and reaction

Modern issues emerge from the consequences of linkages between political economy and security in the context of a well-developed international economy. The tugging and hauling of international economic influences – exposure to the international economy – and states' efforts to balance their desires for increased wealth and maximal security, create a distinct class of concerns for states. The increasing size of the international economy dating from the last quarter of the nineteenth century presented states with new sets of problems in the first half of the twentieth, and these concepts were developed theoretically in the second half of this century. The larger the state, however, the less intensely these issues are felt. As a result, they were least salient to the extraordinary superpowers, and not typically considered '*high security issues*' during the cold war. With the end of the cold war, the continuing expansion of the international economy, and the growing number of states in the system, these issues will be of increasing consequences in the coming years. In this era, there will be more small states, and, more importantly, all states will be more like small states than they were in the past.

Coercion and punishment

Efforts at economic coercion and punishment, or economic sanctions, have a bad reputation in the public perception and among scholars. Conventional wisdom holds that economic sanctions 'don't work'. This wisdom is flawed, however, and furthermore, economic diplomacy will play an increasingly large role in international relations. With the glue of the Soviet threat no longer in place, conflicts among the western allies will increase and be less constrained. These disputes will almost certainly be fought with economic as opposed to military techniques of statecraft. The collapse of communism has also increased the number of small, market-sensitive economies in the international system, which are particularly vulnerable to economic coercion. Additionally, several great powers, in particular the USA, Germany and

Japan, retain global interests but appear disinclined to use force to resolve most conflicts. For all these reasons students of security studies will need a greater understanding of economic statecraft.

Despite some notable advances in the past decade, particularly David Baldwin's *Economic Statecraft* (1985) and also Hufbauer *et al.*, *Economic Sanctions Reconsidered* (1990), our understanding of economic sanctions remains limited.[6] The consensus regarding their limited utility has left them understudied. But the belief that economic sanctions 'don't work' is based on a number of errors, which are considered at length in Baldwin. In particular, first, the failure to consider why economic sanctions were enacted, second, the failure to compare costs and, third, the failure to consider context, lead to analyses that understate the relative utility of sanctions.

First, economic sanctions, designed to punish a state and change its behavior, are also enacted for additional reasons. One important one is signaling: sanctions can signal to friends and foes alike that you are opposed to an action and will take steps to counter it. It can provide moral support to opposition groups within the target, serve as a warning to others contemplating similar actions, and provide a boat-rocking function – warning that more extreme behavior may result in increasingly dramatic actions.[7] So correctly assessing success or failure depends greatly on the entire range of outcomes the policy was designed to bring about.

Second, in arguing that economic sanctions 'don't work', there is often an implicit comparison to other techniques of statecraft such as military force. But this comparison is almost always left undeveloped. Does military force 'work'? This is an odd question, but a fundamental one. Clearly, force often fails. More importantly, success in statecraft is measured in *political* outcomes. As such, the costs – both political and economic – of a given technique of statecraft must be weighed against the political benefits of success. There may be many instances where military force would be unsuccessful and even more cases where the various costs of using force would be greater than the benefits of success. In those cases, force won't 'work'. Ultimately, it is unproductive to argue whether, in the abstract, economic (or military) statecraft 'doesn't work'. Emphasis should be refocused to elucidate when different tactics will provide states with optimal policies, considering the various costs and benefits associated with different choices. No strategy can guarantee success: all one can hope to do is enact the 'optimal' policy.

Third, finally, it should be noted that it is impossible to evaluate the absolute power of a specific sanction (just as it is impossible to do so for a specific military action). Prospects for success depend on how much the adversary is willing to sacrifice, and this will be different from case to case, depending both on the value the target places on non-compliance and on the objective of the sanction. It is simply impossible to say whether a trade embargo that reduces GNP by 10 percent will 'work' or not. Most likely, there will be cases when it will work and cases when it won't.

Calling attention to these issues still leaves, and in fact increases, the need for additional research on economic sanctions. In particular, two processes require further exploration: the relationship between the imposition of economic sanctions and the level of economic distress in the target, and the relationship between that domestic distress and policy change. [...]

Influence and dependence

More subtle than coercion is the political economy of influence and dependence. Dependence results from asymmetries in economic relationships, and from the ways in which those asymmetries change states' preferences. Influence is the flip side of dependence: that which accrues to the dominant partner in an asymmetric relationship. [...]

But dependence is not mainly about leverage, or coercion. It is distinct from coercion, and similar to what Nye has called 'soft power'. Instead of forcing others to do what you want them to do, soft power is about 'getting others to want what you want'.[8] Engaging in economic relations, especially those that involve discrimination – such as trade agreements or currency areas – alters the domestic political economy of each state. In asymmetric settings, this shift takes place almost entirely in the small state: its interests converge toward those of the dominant state. [...]

It should be made clear that fostering dependence in order to enhance influence is undertaken by states using economic means to advance political goals. This is distinct from *dependency*, in which power is used to enforce economic extraction. Small states in dependent relationships [...] gain economically, both absolutely and relatively: indeed, this is the source of the influence. [...]

As with coercion, the mechanics of influence and dependence need to be more fully explored. This is particularly challenging because it is difficult to measure the 'success' of these policies for large states. Unlike efforts at coercion, which aim to alter existing behavior, this form of statecraft, even when successful, works invisibly. Measuring altered preferences and their impact on policy decisions is problematic, especially given the challenge of establishing relevant counterfactuals. But powerful states have constantly attempted to use their economic resources to expand their influence. This has taken the form not only of efforts at trade and monetary arrangements, but also the manipulation of aid (Baldwin, 1971; Liska, 1960; Montgomery, 1962, 1967; Kaplan, 1967) and financial arrangements (Feis, 1930, 1950; Viner, 1929; Moreau, 1991: 430–53).

Such efforts are not always successful. Many states have been disappointed by the amount of influence they have been able to 'purchase' for a given amount of aid (Liska, 1960; McNeil, 1981; Walt, 1987: 225). [...] But economic influence can be consequential. More importantly, states' interests evolve and are shaped by their economic relationships. This is of particular concern in periods of transition where interests are most contestable.

Autonomy

Influence and dependence refer to interstate relations, including efforts by states to constrain the range of other states' behavior. For example, as recipients of aid or as members in preferential trading areas, states may refrain from engaging in certain behaviors that they expect would be incompatible with the preferences of their benefactors. This limits their options.

At the same time, there are more global international forces at work that challenge state power in a distinct way: they challenge the state's ability to function as an autonomous actor. Questions of autonomy differ from those of influence and dependence in that autonomy, as used here, refers to the power of the state vis-à-vis stateless forces: markets, firms and individuals. These global market forces can limit and constrain policy, eroding overall national power.

There are a number of manifestations of increasing challenges to state autonomy: expanding international financial networks, enormous foreign exchange markets, increasingly complex international intra-firm trade, competition for foreign investment, and large migratory flows. These 'market forces' present three problems for states. First, private actors may engage in patterns of activity that can diverge from the goals of government policy, creating domestic political barriers to some preferred policies (see Cohen, 1986). Second, and especially regarding issues of trade and foreign investment, there is the issue of control: whether the government will have the legal right or the practical capability to execute its chosen policies when dealing with transnational private actors (Vernon, 1971; Graham and Krugman, 1995; Cohey and Aronson, 1992–93; Kapstein, 1994). Included here are concerns for defense autonomy: the perceived need to have such control over industries crucial for national security (see Friedberg, 1991; Davis, 1991; Moran and Mowrey, 1991; Ziegler, 1991; Vernon et al. 1991; Kapstein, 1989–90; Moran, 1990; Borrus and Zysman, 1992). Third, particularly in the areas of finance, foreign exchange and foreign investment, there is the possibility that market reactions will undercut and even force a reversal of preferred policies. States need to be sensitive to the possibility that their policies may lead to capital flight, touch off speculation against their currencies, or discourage foreign investment.

It is this third set of issues which appear the most challenging to state autonomy in the contemporary international economy. Increased financial globalization has reduced macroeconomic policy autonomy, and this affects states' ability to increase defense spending, mobilize their military forces, and even engage in behavior that is perceived to risk war.[9] Markets can be swift and decisive in imposing their discipline [...].

State autonomy is increasingly challenged from many quarters, restricting policy options. In this issue area all states are becoming small states. While these forces can result in a number of different patterns of international relations, growing economic influences on security are inescapable. If states react to the expanding global market forces with a reassertion of their autonomy, then the likely regionalization of the international economy will increase the significance of influence and dependence.[10] If the market is left unchecked, then restrictions on policy autonomy will become more routine, consequential and of necessity integrated into strategic planning.

New classical issues: the economic sustainability of security

All states in coming years will find their security positions increasingly influenced by political economy. This will not be limited to the rise of modern issues: classical issues will also resurface in the post-cold war era, though in some cases, they will take distinct forms, and can be considered 'new classical issues'. New classical issues focus on the classical concern for economic growth as essential to power. In contemporary politics, this takes a number of forms which all focus around the issue of the economic sustainability of security. [...]

The economics of defense

One way in which the issue of the economic sustainability of security surfaces is through the possibility that the myopic pursuit of military might erodes the economic base of the state. [...] This argument had been stated theoretically by Gilpin (1981: 162), who argued that pressure for increased defense spending in mature hegemons was one factor that contributed to decreasing investment and thus slower economic growth.[11] The high military burden of the USA, especially when compared to the spending of prosperous American allies such as Japan, was often cited as a source of economic distress and poor economic performance. Posen and Van Evera (1983: 43) argued that 'wasteful military spending is itself a national security threat, because it contributes to America's economic decline'. Military spending is held to divert resources from the civilian sector, crowd out private investment, and preempt more productive forms of government spending (DeGrasse, 1983).[12]

One comprehensive survey of the issue found that while it can provide a short-term stimulus, in the long run military spending tends to have negative economic consequences (Chan, 1985: 413). But this remains a hotly debated question, and the consequence of this conclusion, which is not universally accepted, is unclear. [...]

More generally, the exact trade-offs between defense spending and economic performance are hard to pin down. The effect of military spending, difficult to measure and compare across states, is also influenced by factors such as a state's level of development and its position in the business cycle (Chan, 1985; Kahler, 1988; Hollenhorst and Ault, 1971: 761; Rothschild, 1973; see also Alexander, 1990; Kiser et al., 1995). In the coming years, this issue is likely to be of more pressing significance among developing countries that are expanding defense expenditures, rather than in developed states paring back from cold war levels.[13]

Regardless of the particular setting, the relationship between defense spending and economic performance remains a complex and contested issue.[14] But the ultimate outcome of this debate does not change the fact that the provision of defense will affect the domestic economy, which in turn shapes the sustainability of state security, and that there remains a need for students of security to understand these relationships.

The locus of production

New classical issues emphasize the crucial role of economic growth in sustaining national security. Nowhere is this clearer than in the concern for the locus of production: what is produced where. This concerns the national interest because the composition of production can affect growth, because certain industries either have inherently superior growth trajectories or provide positive externalities to the greater economy.

The central question is whether government intervention is necessary to support such industries. This rests crucially on the concept of market failure: that the free market, left to its own devices, would produce sub-optimal economic outcomes.[15] Market failures certainly exist,[16] but it is necessary to identify them specifically in each case and explain how they can be eliminated by government intervention. [...]

Some grounds for government intervention appear to be even more straightforward. There is a rich Pigovian tradition regarding externalities – those outputs from production not counted in firms' cost calculation. The existence of externalities means that there can be a divergence between private and societal levels of optimal production. This leads to an overproduction of negative externalities, such as pollution, or an underprovision of positive externalities, such as technologies with spin-off applications. As a result, the government should introduce taxes and subsidies to manipulate the production of externalities so that the private and societal optima are equated (Pigou, 1920: 189–96).

But even this minimal and compelling logic for intervention has been challenged. Coase (1960) has argued that size and scope for Pigovian taxes is much smaller than is usually acknowledged. And even this assumes that externalities can be identified and corrected.[17] The problems mount even further in practice. Even if optimal policies could be calculated, would they be introduced? Critics suggest that 'government failure' could lead to greater costs than market failure, and that industrial policies could lead to wasteful rent seeking and crude protectionism, and invite foreign retaliation (see Grossman, 1986; Krueger, 1990). Finally, there remains the danger that despite avoiding all of the pitfalls mentioned above, the government may still err. [...]

An additional danger regarding strategies designed to affect the locus of production is that they may oversell the importance of trade strategy's contribution to the national economy.[18] Tyson herself (1992:2) notes that 'misguided trade policies can be even worse than ineffective', and that 'flawed domestic choices, not unfair foreign trading practices, are the main cause of the nation's long-run economic slowdown' (see also Bergsten and Noland, 1993).

The social economy

[...] While controversy persists regarding the locus of production, there is increasing consensus that government policies which 'get the basics right' are an important element of economic growth. Instead of targeting sectors, such policies emphasize the economic foundations of society, such as education, infrastructure, incentives for savings and investment, and sound macro-economic policies.[19]

These concerns underscore a more fundamental issue for the sustainability of security – the question of national vitality. Starting with 'the basics' rooted in new growth theory, this also includes issues associated with the sociological foundation of long-run economic growth. The *incentive structure* assures that actors will be encouraged to engage in activities that promote economic growth. Just as the absence of government intervention can lead to a divergence of private and social optima, excessive government regulation and taxation can have the same effect. Clear property rights and predictable legal structures also contribute to a convergence between private and social interests (North, 1981). At the same time, government intervention is crucial in a number of areas, particularly with regard to the provision of public goods, such as a *sound infrastructure*. Economic activity depends on efficient transportation networks, and this includes not only roads, bridges, rails, canals and airports, but also the transmission of information. Further, these assets will not be fully utilized without sufficient investment in human capital, which is increasingly recognized as a fundamental source of economic growth.[20]

The economic sustainability of security is also sensitive to *social cohesion*. The erosion of national vitality, either from internal weakness or domestic conflict, affects not only future economic growth, but also the very ability of states to pursue grand strategies that may require short-term sacrifices for long-run benefits. In Gilpin's model of hegemonic decline, such factors as the corrupting influence of affluence and other social variables figure prominently. [...]

One dimension of social cohesion is income distribution, which is an important new classical security issue that affects both current and future state power. Within regard to current capabilities, sustained or increasing inequality may contribute to insurrection or rebellion (fundamentally reducing state power) (see Hirschman, 1973; Lichbach, 1989; Mueller and Seligson, 1987). But as emphasized above, even in the absence of these outcomes, increasing inequality and social conflict will restrict the state's capability to pursue optimal foreign policies due to the hyper-politicization of fiscal policy. [...] In general, new classical issues serve as a reminder that security has both static and dynamic components. Static concerns, such as current force levels and postures, are certainly important. But security is an inherently dynamic concept, and these dynamics rest on issues associated with political economy. [...]

Notes

1   Representative of Manchester views is Richard Cobden (1848). Similar views were held by US policy makers after the Second World War, who held that the closed international economy had contributed to the war. Highly critical of this argument are E. H. Carr (1946) and Blainey (1975).

2   Access to markets has been a staple of the radical literature, including Lenin (1917), Weisskopf (1974) and Kolko (1988). Economic roots conflicts have been stressed by other writers, such as Robbins (1939) and Howard (1976); securing energy supplies has been a particular focus of attention: see for example Kupchan (1987) and Painter (1986). On raw materials in general, see Lipschutz (1989) and Vernon (1983).

3   Wars can also be fought simply to reap the gains of conquest. See Liberman (1995). While the potential of such gains affects the cost-benefit calculus of going to war, it is only in a secondary sense that such incentives can be characterized an 'economic force' that acts as 'a source of war'. Arguments regarding imperialism, market access and raw materials (see n. 7) derive conflict and war from economic imperatives found within the expansionist state, and fall more obviously into the class of issues at interest here.

4   Satisfied does not mean 'happy'; rather, simply that no state is willing to use force to change the status quo.

5   It should be noted that this relationship runs both ways: war affects state power and capacity. See Brewer (1989), Tilly (1985, 1990) and Desch (1996).

6   On sanctions, see Baldwin (1985), Hufbauer *et al.* (1990), Knorr (1975), Leyton-Brown (1987), Renwick (1981), Doxey (1980, 1987), Daoudi and Dajani (1983) and Kaempfer and Lowenberg (1992).

7   On signaling and boat-rocking in general, see Schelling (1960, 1966).

8   Nye (1990: 188) argues that 'trends today are making{...}soft power resources more important'. See also pp. 189–201.

9   These restraints are not obviously surmountable as, once unleashed, financial deregulation is difficult to contain. See Helleiner (1994: 12, 18, 152, 156, 196–98 especially). See also Goodman and Pauly (1993) and Cosh et al. (1992). For an argument that previous periods witnessed even greater financial integration, see Zevin (1992).

10   Even if autonomy-seeking states move to reestablish control over market forces, regionalism or 'minilateralism', not autarky, is the likely result. This is because security-conscious states must be sensitive to the importance of economic growth. Engaging the international economy provides expanded opportunities and greater prospects for growth. Thus such states face trade-offs between complete autarky and unfettered internationalism in the pursuit of their multiple goals. Regionalism is the obvious compromise, combining relative autonomy with international economic opportunity. This result is predicted by scholars such as Gilpin, who states that 'a mixed system of nationalism, regionalism, and sectoral protectionism is replacing the Bretton Woods system of multilateral liberalization'. Because of these pressures, he concludes, 'loose regional blocs are the likely result' (Gilpin, 1987: 395, 397).

11   Gilpin argued that mature hegemonic states faced pressure to increase both defense spending and domestic consumption. Since gross national product can be divided into three shares – defense spending, consumption (private and public non-defense) and investment – if both defense and consumption are increased, invest-ment must decrease as a share of GNP. Just as importantly, these pressures result in 'an increasingly severe political conflict over the allocation of national income', that 'transforms a relatively benign politics of growth into a more virulent politics of distribution' (Gilpin, 1987: 166–67).

12   For similar (though less rigorous) arguments regarding the British experience, see Chambers (1985).

13   For the debate on the defense spending-growth relationship in developing states, see Benoit (1973), Deger and Smith (1983), Biswas and Ram (1986), Deger (1986), Chowdhury (1991), Stewart (1991), Looney (1994) and Adeola (1996).

14   For recent surveys of this literature, see Chan (1995) and Sandler and Hartley (1995: 200–220 especially).

15   This need not be the justification for government intervention for other reasons, such as to preserve defense autonomy. In that case, economic growth is purpose-fully sacrificed to advance non-economic goals. Here, however, the concern is solely with long-run economic growth, and thus intervention cannot be justified without the demonstration of market failure.

16   See, for example, Akerlof (1970). For a brief summary of the theory of market failure as regards international trade, see Krugman and Obstfeld (1994: 232–36).

17   On the difficulty of addressing externalities in practice, see Krugman (1986).

18   For example, strategic trade policy is about the composition of trade, not the balance of trade. The source of trade deficits is to be found in macroeconomic relationships such as savings rates and can only be corrected by policies which address those more fundamental questions rooted in the domestic economy.

19   On new growth theory, see the various papers in 'The problem of development' (1990) and 'Symposium: new growth theory' (1994). On 'getting the basics right' in practice, see Porter (1990) and World Bank (1993).

20   'Human capital accumulation as the key source of growth and development is one of the major themes of the new economic development literature' (Erlich, 1990: 7). See also Schultz (1961).

References

Adeola, Francis O. (1996) 'Military expenditures, health, and education: bed-fellows or antagonists in Third World development?', *Armed Forces and Society* 22(3) (Spring): 441–67.

Akerlof, George (1970) 'The market for "lemons"', *Quarterly Journal of Economics* 84(3) (August): 488–500.

Alexander, W. Robert J. (1990) 'The impact of defense spending on economic growth', *Defence Economics* 2(1) (1990): 39–55.

Baldwin, David (1971) 'The power of positive sanctions', *World Politics* 24(1) (October): 19–38.

—— (1985) *Economic Statecraft*, Princeton, NJ: Princeton University Press.

Bell, Philip W. (1956) *The Sterling Area in the Postwar World*, Oxford: Clarendon Press.

Benoit, Emile (1973) *Defense and Economic Growth in Developing Countries*, Boston: D. C. Heath.

Bergsten, C. Fred and Noland, Marcus (1993) *Reconcilable Differences? United States-Japan Economic Conflict*, Washington, DC: Institute for International Economics.

Biswas, Basudeb and Ram, Rati (1986) 'Military expenditures and economic growth in less developed countries: an augmented model and further evidence', *Economic Development and Cultural Change* 34(2) (January): 361–72.

Blainey, Geoffrey (1975) *The Causes of War*, New York: Free Press.

Borrus, Michael and Zysman, John (1992) 'Industrial competitiveness and American national security', in Wayne Sandholtz *et al. The Highest Stakes: The Economic Foundations of the Next Security System*, New York: Oxford University Press.

Brewer, John (1989) *The Sinews of Power: War, Money and the English State, 1688–1783*, New York: Knopf.

Carr, E. H. (1946) *The Twenty Years' Crisis, 1919–1939*, 2nd edn, New York: Harper.

Chambers, M. (1985) *Paying For Defense*, London: Pluto Press.

Chan, Steve (1985) 'The impact of defense spending on economic performance', *Orbis* 29 (Summer): 403–34.

—— (1995) 'Grasping the peace dividend: some problems on the conversion of swords into plowshares', *Mershon International Studies Review* 39(s.1) (April): 53–95.

Chowdhury, Abdur R. (1991) 'A causal analysis of defense spending and economic growth', *Journal of Conflict Resolution* 35(1) (March): 80–97.

Coase, R. (1960) 'The problem of social cost', *Journal of Law and Economics* 3 (October): 1–44.

Cobden, Richard (1848/1970) 'Finance', speech delivered in Manchester, 27 January 1848,
reprinted in his *Speeches on Questions of Public Policy*, New York: Klaus Reprint Co., pp. 233–41.

Cohen, Benjamin J. (1986) *In Whose Interest? International Banking and American Foreign Policy*, New Haven, Conn.: Yale University Press.

Cohey, Peter and Aronson, Jonathan (1992–93) 'A new trade order', *Foreign Affairs* 72(1): 183–95.

Cosh, Andrew D., Hughes, Alan and Singh, Ajit (1992) 'Openness, financial innovation, changing patters of ownership, and the structure of financial markets', in Tariq Banuri and Juliet B. Schor (eds) *Financial Openness and National Autonomy: Opportunities and Constraints*, Oxford: Clarendon Press.

Daoudi, M. S. and Dajani, M. S. (1983) *Economic Sanctions: Ideals and Experience*, London: Routledge and Kegan Paul.

Davis, Christopher Mark (1991) 'The exceptional Soviet case: defense in an autarkic system', *Daedalus* 120(4) (Fall): 113–34.

Deger, Saadet (1986) 'Economic development and defense expenditure', *Economic Development and Cultural Change* 35(1) (October): 179–96.

Deger, Saadet and Smith, Ron (1983) 'Military expenditure and growth in less developed countries', *Journal of Conflict Resolution* 27(1) (June): 335–53.

DeGrasse, Robert W. Jr (1983) *Military Expansion, Economic Decline: The Impact of Military Spending on U.S. Economic Performance*, New York: M.E. Sharpe.

Desch, Michael C. (1996) 'War and strong states, peace and weak states?', *International Organization* 50(2) (Spring): 237–68.

Doran, Charles F. (1983) 'War and power dynamics: economic underpinnings', *International Studies Quarterly* 27(4) (December): 419–40.

Doxey, Margaret P. (1980) *Economic Sanctions and International Enforcement*, New York: Oxford University Press.

—— (1987) *International Sanctions in Contemporary Perspective*, New York: St Martin's Press.

Erlich, Issac (1990) 'The problem of development: introduction', *Journal of Political Economy* 98(5/2) (October): s1–s11.

Feis, Herbert (1930/1964) *Europe the World's Banker 1870–1914*, New Haven, Conn.: Yale University Press.

—— (1950/1965) *The Diplomacy of the Dollar: First Era 1919–1932*, Hamden, Conn.: Archon Books.

Friedberg, Aaron (1991) 'The end of autonomy: the United States after five decades', *Daedalus* 120(4) (Fall): 69–90.

Gilpin, Robert (1981) *War and Change in World Politics*, Cambridge: Cambridge University Press.

—— (1987) *The Political Economy of International Relations*, Princeton, NJ: Princeton University Press.

Goodman, John and Pauly, Louis (1993) 'The obsolescence of capital controls? Economic management in an age of global markets', *World Politics* 46(1) (October): 50–82.

Graham, Edward and Krugman, Paul (1995) *Foreign Direct Investment in the United States*, 3rd edn, Washington, DC: Institute for International Economics.

Grossman, Gene (1986) 'Strategic export promotion: a critique', in Krugman (ed.).

Helleiner, Eric (1994) *States and the Reemergence of Global Finance: From Bretton Woods to the 1990s*, Ithaca, NY: Cornell University Press.

Hirschman, Albert O. (1973) 'Changing tolerance for income inequality in the course of economic development', *Quarterly Journal of Economics* 87(4) (November): 544–62.

Hollenhorst, J. and Ault, G. (1971) 'An alternative answer to: who pays for defense', *American Economic Review* 65(3) (September).

Howard, Michael (1976) *War in European History*, Oxford: Oxford University Press.

Hufbauer, Gary Clyde, Schott, Jeffrey J. and Elliot, Kimberly Ann (1990) *Economic Sanctions Reconsidered*, Vol. 1: *History and Current Policy*, Vol. 2: *Supplemental Case Histories*, 2nd edn, Washington, DC: Institute for International Economics.

Kaempfer, William H. and Lowenberg, Anton D. (1992) *International Economic Sanctions: A Public Choice Perspective*, Boulder, Colo.: Westview Press.

Kahler, Miles (1988) 'External ambition and economic performance', *World Politics* 40(4) (July): 419–51.

Kaplan, Jacob J. (1967) *The Challenge of Foreign Aid: Policies, Problems, Possibilities*, New York: Praeger.

Kapstein, Ethan (1989–90) 'Losing control: national security and the global economy', *The National Interest* 18 (Winter): 85–90.

—— (1994) *Governing the Global Economy: International Finance and the State*, Cambridge, Mass.: Harvard University Press.

Kennedy, Paul (1980) *The Rise of the Anglo-German Antagonism*, London: Ashfield Press.

—— (1983) 'Why did the British Empire last so long?', in Paul Kennedy, *Strategy and Diplomacy 1870–1945*, London: George Allen & Unwin.

Kiser, Edgar, Drass, Kriss A. and Brustein, William (1995) 'A century of trade-offs: defense and growth in the Japan and the United States', *International Studies Quarterly* 39(1) (March): 85–108.

Knorr, Klaus (1975) *The Power of Nations*, New York: Basic Books.

Kolko, Gabriel (1988) *Confronting the Third World*, New York: Pantheon.

Krueger, Anne O. (1990) 'Free trade is the best policy', in Robert Z. Lawrence and Charles L. Schultz (eds) *An American Trade Strategy: Options for the 1990s*, Washington, DC: Brookings.

Krugman, Paul (1986) 'Introduction: new thinking about trade policy', in Paul Krugman (ed.) *Strategic Trade Policy and the New International Economics*, Cambridge, Mass.: MIT Press.

Krugman, Paul and Obstfeld, Maurice (1994) *International Economics: Theory and Politics*, 3rd edn, New York: HarperCollins.

Kupchan, Charles (1987) *The Persian Gulf and the West: The Dilemmas of Security*, Boston: Allen & Unwin.

LaFeber, Walter (1963) *The New Empire: An Interpretation of American Expansion 1860–98*, Ithaca, NY: Cornell University Press.

Lenin, V. L. (1917/1985) *Imperialism: The Highest State of Capitalism*, New York: International Publishers.

Levy, Jack (1989) 'The diversionary theory of war: a critique', in Manus Midlarsky (ed.) *Handbook of War Studies*, Boston: Unwin & Hyman.

Leyton-Brown, David (ed.) (1987) *The Utility of International Economic Sanctions*, New York: St Martin's Press.

Liberman, Peter (1995) *Does Conquest Pay? The Exploitation of Occupied Industrial Societies*, Princeton, NJ: Princeton University Press.

Lichbach, Mark Irving (1989) 'An evaluation of "does economic inequality breed conflict" studies', *World Politics* 41(4) (July): 431–70.

Lipschutz, Ronnie D. (1989) *When Nations Clash*, Cambridge: Ballinger.

Liska, George (1957) *International Equilibrium*, Cambridge, Mass.: Harvard University Press.

—— (1960) *The New Statecraft*, Chicago: University of Chicago Press.

—— (1963) 'Continuity and change in international systems', *World Politics* 16(1) (October).

Looney, Robert E. (1994) 'Defense expenditures, investment and crowding out: problems of capital formation in Pakistani manufacturing', *Journal of Third World Studies* 11(2) (Fall): 292–316.

McNeil, Desmond (1981) *The Contradictions of Foreign Aid*, London: Croom Helm.

Montgomery, John D. (1962) *The Politics of Foreign Aid*, New York: Praeger.

Moran, Theodore H. (1990) 'The globalization of America's defense industries: managing the threat of foreign dependence', *International Security* 15(1) (1990): 57–99.

Moran, Theodore H. and Mowrey, David C. (1991) 'Aerospace', *Daedalus* 120(4) (Fall): 135–54.

Moreau, Emile (1991) *The Golden Franc: Memoirs of a Governor of the Bank of France*, Boulder, Colo.: Westview Press.

Mueller, Edward and Seligson, Mitchell (1987) 'Inequality and insurgency', *American Political Science Review* 81(2) (June): 425–51.

North, Douglass (1981) *Structure and Change in Economic History*, New York: Norton.

Nye, Joseph S. Jr (1990) *Bound to Lead: The Changing Nature of American Power*, New York: Basic Books.

Organski, A. F. K. (1968) *World Politics*, 2nd edn, New York: Alfred A. Knopf.

Organski, A. F. K. and Kugler, Jack (1980) *The War Ledger*, Chicago: University of Chicago Press.

Painter, David S. (1986) *Oil and the American Century*, Baltimore, Md.: Johns Hopkins University Press.

Pigou, A. C. (1920) *Economics of Welfare*, London: Macmillan.

Pion-Berlin, David (1985) 'The fall of military rule in Argentina: 1976–83', *Journal of Interamerican Studies and World Affairs* 27(2) (Summer): 55–76.

Porter, Michael (1990) *The Competitive Advantage of Nations*, New York: Free Press.

Posen, Barry and Van Evera, Stephen (1983) 'Defense policy and the Reagan administration: departure from containment', *International Security* 8(1) (Summer): 3–45.

'The Problem of Development' (1990) *Journal of Political Economy* 98(5/2).

Renwick, Robin (1981) *Economic Sanctions*, Cambridge, Mass.: Harvard Studies in International Affairs, No. 45.

Robbins, Lionel (1939) *The Economic Causes of War*, London: Jonathan Cape.

Rosecrance, Richard (1963) *Action and Reaction in World Politics: International Systems in Perspective*, Boston: Little, Brown.

Rothschild, Kurt W. (1973) 'Military expenditure, exports, and growth', *Kyklos* 26 (1973): 804–14.

Sandler, Todd and Hartley, Keith (1995) *The Economics of Defense*, Cambridge: Cambridge University Press.

Schelling, Thomas (1960) *The Strategy of Conflict*, Cambridge, Mass.: Harvard University Press.

—— (1966) *Arms and Influence*, New Haven, Conn.: Yale University Press.

Schultz, Theodore W. (1961) 'Investment in human capital', *American Economic Review* 51(1) (March): 1–17.

Stewart, Douglas B. (1991) 'Economic growth and the defense burden in Africa and Latin America: simulations from a dynamic model', *Economic Development and Cultural Change* 40(1) (October): 189–207.

Stopford, John and Strange, Susan with Henley, John S. (1991) *Rival States, Rival Firms*, Cambridge: Cambridge University Press.

Tilly, Charles (1985) 'War making and state making as organized crime', in Peter Evans, Dietrich Rueschemeyer and Theda Skocpol (eds) *Bringing the State Back In*, Cambridge: Cambridge University Press.

—— (1990) *Coercion, Capital, and European States AD 990–1992*, Cambridge: Blackwell.

Tyson, Laura D'Andrea (1992) *Who's Bashing Whom? Trade Conflict in High Technology Industries*, Washington, DC: Institute for International Economics.

Vernon, Raymond (1971) *Sovereignty at Bay*, New York: Basic Books.

—— (1983) *Two Hungry Giants*, Cambridge, Mass.: Harvard University Press.

Vernon, Raymond, Spar, Deborah and Tobin, Glenn (1991) 'Designing codevelopment: the battle over the FSX fighter', in *Iron Triangles and Revolving Doors*, New York: Praeger.

Viner, Jacob (1929) 'International finance and balance of power diplomacy, 1880–1914', *Political and Social Science Quarterly* IX(4) (March): 408–51.

—— (1948) 'Power vs. plenty as objectives of statecraft in the seventeenth and eighteenth centuries', *World Politics* 1(1) (October): 1–29.

Walt, Stephen (1987) *The Origins of Alliances*, Ithaca, NY: Cornell University Press.

Weisskopf, Thomas E. (1974) 'Capitalism, socialism, and the sources of imperialism', in Steven Rosen and James Kurth (eds) *Testing Theories of Economic Imperialism*, Lexington, Mass.: Lexington books.

World Bank (1993) *The East Asian Miracle*, New York: Oxford University Press.

Zevin, Robert (1992) 'Are world financial markets more open? If so, why and with what effects', in Tariq Banuri and Juliet B. Schor (eds) *Financial Openness and National Autonomy: Opportunities and Constraints*, Oxford: Clarendon Press.

Ziegler, J. Nicholas (1991) 'Semiconductors', *Daedalus* 120(4) (Fall): 155–82.

Discussion questions

- When does nuclear deterrence work, and why?
- What is meant by 'mutual assured destruction' (MAD) and 'nuclear peace'?
- According to the action–reaction model, why do states indulge in arms races?
- What are the principal factors espoused by the domestic structure model to explain the arms dynamic?
- What are the costs and benefits associated with nuclear weapons proliferation?
- In what manner does the so-called Revolution in Military Affairs contribute to the advancement of the American military-industrial complex?
- How does the information age change the forms of conflict?
- Why and how does environmental scarcity generate conflict?
- When does migration become a threat to security and stability?
- Why are transnational criminal organisations considered a serious security threat to both 'host' and 'home' states? How do their activities undermine state sovereignty?
- Explain the linkage between AIDS and military institutions. What are the direct and indirect security threats associated with the spread of the disease?
- What are the economic causes of war?

PART 4

Security Frameworks and Actors

Introduction

JOHN LEWIS GADDIS initiates the discussion on the structures and mechanisms which have been viewed as crucial to maintaining international security.

Gaddis argues for the bipolarity during the Cold War as ensuring a remarkable degree of stability due to the matched strengths of the superpowers and respect for each other's spheres of influence. **Christopher Layne** discusses the possibilities for unipolarity to provide for international security. He argues, based on the logic of Neo-Realism, that unipolarity, such as that of current US dominance, can deliver stability. However, Layne also argues that unipolarity is likely to be short-lived as hegemonic powers lack the strength to maintain the international security system and as other rising powers balance against it. Instead, he argues that the contemporary international system is likely to pass from a phase of US unipolarity and revert to multipolarity.

Glenn Snyder's contribution uses the essential concept of the security dilemma to explain how states in a multipolar system may seek security through the formation of alliances. However, Snyder points out that after this primary phase of alliance creation, there is a secondary phase of states needing to decide how firmly they commit to the alliance. This is because, as Snyder points out, while alliances can provide security, they also involve dilemmas of entrapment and abandonment: the former leading to becoming embroiled in military conflicts, and the latter meaning risks that allies may not come to each other's assistance if their interests do not coincide. **Stephen M. Walt** provides a typology of different types of alliances and their functions, but explores in particular the reasons why alliances persist or come to an end. Walt offers a set of explanations at both the international level in regard to threat perceptions and the credibility of alliance commitments, and at the domestic level including issues of regime change, institutionalisation and ideological solidarity.

John Gerald Ruggie outlines concepts, forms and meanings of multilateralism. Ruggie demonstrates how multilateralism can coordinate relations among states, and provides an example of the demand for and functioning of multilateralism in a collective security scheme. Robert Jervis goes deeper into the issue of security frameworks and the issue of multilateral security through his examination of security regime. Jervis suggests that the commitment of the great powers is essential to the establishment of a security regime, but also a sense of shared values among members to achieving through mutual means the rejection of individualistic approaches. Emanuel Adler looks into the concept of the pluralistic security community, whereby its members obviate the possibility of conflict among themselves through the compatibility of core values and mutual identity. Adler argues that security communities are therefore largely socially constructed, and that liberal democracies and their civic cultures have the strongest tendencies to forge such successful security frameworks.

Adam Roberts's contribution shifts the focus to examine particular forms of force influential in determining contemporary security. Roberts in his study of the 1999 Kosovo campaign highlights the trend towards 'humanitarian war' and interventionism. He raises the issue of how this represents a mixture of idealism and the Realist use of force and the challenges to much theory in Security Studies. Robert A. Pape examines the debate on the role of economic sanctions in contemporary security. He concludes that sanctions have a low success rate due to uncertain commitments by states to enforce a sanctions regime, and due to the fact that states targeted by sanction are strong enough to resist economic pressures, not least because they are buttressed domestically by national sentiment. Pape argues that sanctions cannot serve as a viable alternative to traditional military power. David Shearer's chapter focuses discussion on another facet of contemporary warfare: the rise of private military companies (PMCs) to augment or substitute for the role of nation-states. Shearer demonstrates how the increasing weakness of governments has led to a demand for the skills of PMCs. He does not necessarily condemn so-called mercenary activities, but indicates that PMCs may have an important role in future peacekeeping operations.

John Lewis Gaddis

THE LONG PEACE

Source: 'The Long Peace: elements of stability in the postwar international system', *International Security*, vol. 10, no. 4, Spring 1986, pp. 99–142.

Systems theory and international stability

A PARTICULARLY VALUABLE feature of systems theory is that it provides criteria for differentiating between stable and unstable political configurations: these can help to account for the fact that some international systems outlast others. Karl Deutsch and J. David Singer have defined "stability" as "the probability that the system retains all of its essential characteristics: that no single nation becomes dominant; that most of its members continue to survive; and that large-scale war does not occur." It is characteristic of such a system, Deutsch and Singer add, that it has the capacity for self-regulation: the ability to counteract stimuli that would otherwise threaten its survival, [...]. [...] Self-regulating mechanisms are most likely to function [...] when there exists some fundamental agreement among major states within the system on the objectives they are seeking to uphold by participating in it, when the structure of the system reflects the way in which power is distributed among its respective members, and when agreed-upon procedures exist for resolving differences among them.[1]

Does the post-World War II international system fit these criteria for "stability"? Certainly its most basic characteristic – bipolarity – remains intact, in that the gap between the world's two greatest military powers and their nearest rivals is not substantially different from what it was forty years ago.[2] At the same time, neither the Soviet Union nor the United States nor anyone else has been able wholly to dominate that system; the nations most active within it in 1945 are for the most part still active today. And of course the most convincing argument for "stability" is that, so far at least, World War III has not occurred. On the surface, then, the concept of a "stable" international system makes sense as a way of understanding the experience through which we have lived these past forty years.

But what have been the self-regulating mechanisms? How has an environment been created in which they are able to function? In what way do those mechanisms – and the environment in which they function – resemble or differ from the configuration of other international systems, both stable and unstable, in modern history? What circumstances exist that might impair their operation, transforming self-regulation into self-aggravation? [...]

The structural elements of stability

Bipolarity

Any such investigation should begin by distinguishing the structure of the international system in question from the behavior of the nations that make it up.[3] The reason for this is simple: behavior alone will not ensure stability if the structural prerequisites for it are absent, but structure can under certain circumstances impose stability even when its behavioral prerequisites are unpromising.[4] [...]

[...] The world had had limited experience with bipolar systems in ancient times, it is true: certainly Thucydides' account of the rivalry between Athens and Sparta carries an eerie resonance for us today; nor could statesmen of the Cold War era forget what they had once learned, as schoolboys, of the antagonism between Rome and Carthage.[5] But these had been regional, not global conflicts: not until 1945 could one plausibly speak of a world divided into two competing spheres of influence, or of the superpowers that controlled them. The international situation had been reduced, Hans Morgenthau wrote in 1948, "to the primitive spectacle of two giants eyeing each other with watchful suspicion. [...] Thus contain or be contained, conquer or be conquered, destroy or be destroyed, become the watchwords of the new diplomacy."[6]

Now, bipolarity may seem to many today – as it did forty years ago – an awkward and dangerous way to organize world politics.[7] Simple geometric logic would suggest that a system resting upon three or more points of support would be more stable than one resting upon two. But politics is not geometry: the passage of time and the accumulation of experience has made clear certain structural elements of stability in the bipolar system of international relations that were not present in the multipolar systems that preceded it:

(1)   The postwar bipolar system realistically reflected the facts of where military power resided at the end of World War II[8] – and where it still does today, for that matter. In this sense, it differed markedly from the settlement of 1919, which made so little effort to accommodate the interests of Germany and Soviet Russia. It is true that in other categories of power – notably the economic – states have since arisen capable of challenging or even surpassing the Soviet Union and the United States in the production of certain specific commodities. But as the political position of nations like West Germany, Brazil, Japan, South Korea, Taiwan, and Hong Kong suggests, the ability to make video recorders, motorcycles, even automobiles and steel efficiently has yet to translate into anything approaching the capacity of Washington or Moscow to shape events in the world as a whole.

(2)   The post-1945 bipolar structure was a simple one that did not require sophisticated leadership to maintain it. The great multipolar systems of the 19th century collapsed in large part because of their intricacy: they required a Metternich
or a Bismarck to hold them together, and when statesmen of that calibre were
no longer available, they tended to come apart.[9] Neither the Soviet nor the
American political systems have been geared to identifying statesmen of comparable prowess and entrusting them with responsibility; demonstrated skill in
the conduct of foreign policy has hardly been a major prerequisite for leadership in either country. And yet, a bipolar structure of international relations –
because of the inescapably high stakes involved for its two major actors – tends,
regardless of the personalities involved, to induce in them a sense of caution and
restraint, and to discourage irresponsibility. [...]

(3)   Because of its relatively simple structure, alliances in this bipolar system have
tended to be more stable than they had been in the 19th century and in the
1919–39 period. [...] The reason for this is simple: alliances, in the end, are the
product of insecurity;[10] so long as the Soviet Union and the United States each
remain for the other and for their respective clients the major source of insecurity in the world, neither superpower encounters very much difficulty in maintaining its alliances. In a multipolar system, sources of insecurity can vary in
much more complicated ways; hence it is not surprising to find alliances shifting
to accommodate these variations.[11]

(4)   At the same time, though, and probably because of the overall stability of the
basic alliance systems, defections from both the American and Soviet coalitions – China, Cuba, Vietnam, Iran, and Nicaragua, in the case of the Americans;
Yugoslavia, Albania, Egypt, Somalia, and China again in the case of the Russians –
have been tolerated without the major disruptions that might have attended
such changes in a more delicately balanced multipolar system. The fact that a
state the size of China was able to reverse its alignment twice during the Cold
War without any more dramatic effect upon the position of the superpowers
says something about the stability bipolarity brings [...]. It is a curious consequence of bipolarity that although alliances are more durable than in a multipolar system, defections are at the same time more tolerable.[12] [...]

* * *

"Rules" of the superpower "game"

The question still arises, though: how can order emerge from a system that functions
without any superior authority? Even self-regulating mechanisms like automatic
pilots or engine governors cannot operate without someone to set them in motion;
the prevention of anarchy, it has generally been assumed, requires hierarchy, both at
the level of interpersonal and international relations. [...]

[...] [The] experience [of the postwar international system] has forced students
of international politics to recognize that their subject bears less resemblance to local,
state, or national politics, where order does in fact depend upon legally constituted
authority, than it does to the conduct of games, where order evolves from mutual
agreement on a set of "rules" defining the range of behavior each side anticipates from

the other. The assumption is that the particular "game" being played promises suffi-cient advantages to each of its "players" to outweigh whatever might be obtained by trying to upset it; in this way, rivalries can be pursued within an orderly framework, even in the absence of a referee. Game theory therefore helps to account for the paradox of order in the absence of hierarchy that characterizes the postwar super-power relationship: through it one can get a sense of how "rules" establish limits of acceptable behavior on the part of nations who acknowledge only themselves as the arbiters of behavior. [13]

These "rules" are, of course, implicit rather than explicit: they grow out of a mix-ture of custom, precedent, and mutual interest that takes shape quite apart from the realm of public rhetoric, diplomacy, or international law. They require the passage of time to become effective; they depend, for that effectiveness, upon the extent to which successive generations of national leadership on each side find them useful. They certainly do not reflect any agreed-upon standard of international morality: indeed they often violate principles of "justice" adhered to by one side or the other. But these "rules" have played an important role in maintaining the international system that has been in place these past four decades: without them the correlation one would normally anticipate between hostility and instability would have become more exact than it has in fact been since 1945.

No two observers of superpower behavior would express these "rules" in pre-cisely the same way; indeed it may well be that their very vagueness has made them more acceptable than they otherwise might have been to the nations that have fol-lowed them. [These "rules" included] [...]

(1)   respect spheres of influence. Neither Russians nor Americans officially admit to having such "spheres," but in fact much of the history of the Cold War can be written in terms of the efforts both have made to consolidate and extend them. [...] [W]hat is important from the standpoint of superpower "rules" is the fact that, although neither side has ever publicly endorsed the other's right to a sphere of influence, neither has ever directly challenged it either. [14] [...]

(2)   avoid direct military confrontation. It is remarkable, in retrospect, that at no point during the long history of the Cold War have Soviet and American military forces engaged each other directly in sustained hostilities. The super-powers have fought three major limited wars since 1945, but in no case with each other: the possibility of direct Soviet-American military involvement was greatest – although it never happened – during the Korean War; it was much more remote in Vietnam and has remained so in Afghanistan as well. [...]

Where the superpowers have sought to expand or to retain areas of con-trol, they have tended to resort to the use of proxies or other indirect means to accomplish this. [...] In a curious way, clients and proxies have come to serve as buffers, allowing Russians and Americans to pursue their competition behind a facade of "deniability" that minimizes the risks of open – and presumably less manageable – confrontation.

The two superpowers have also been careful not to allow the disputes of third parties to embroil them directly: this pattern has been most evident in the Middle East, which has witnessed no fewer than five wars between Israel and its Arab neighbors since 1948; but it holds as well for the India-Pakistan conflicts of 1965 and 1971, and for the more recent – and much more protracted – struggle between Iran and Iraq. [...]

(3)   use nuclear weapons only as an ultimate resort. One of the most significant – though least often commented upon – of the superpower "rules" has been the tradition that has evolved, since 1945, of maintaining a sharp distinction between conventional and nuclear weapons, and of reserving the military use of the latter only for the extremity of total war. [...] It is remarkable [...] that the world has not seen a single nuclear weapon used in anger since the destruction of Nagasaki forty-one years ago. Rarely has practice of nations so conspicuously departed from proclaimed doctrine; rarely, as well, has so great a disparity attracted so little public notice. [...]

    [...] [The] limited war situations [mentioned earlier] [...] have confirmed the continued effectiveness of this unstated but important "rule" of superpower behavior, as have the quiet but persistent efforts both Washington and Moscow have made to keep nuclear weapons from falling into the hands of others who might not abide by it.[15] [...]

(4)   prefer predictable anomaly over unpredictable rationality. One of the most curious features of the Cold War has been the extent to which the superpowers – and their respective clients, who have had little choice in the matter – have tolerated a whole series of awkward, artificial, and, on the surface at least, unstable regional arrangements: the division of Germany[;] [...] the arbitrary and ritualized partition of the Korean peninsula, the existence of an avowed Soviet satellite some ninety miles off the coast of Florida, and, not least, the continued functioning of an important American naval base within it. There is to all of these arrangements an appearance of wildly illogical improvisation: none of them could conceivably have resulted, it seems, from any rational and premeditated design.

    And yet, at another level, they have had a kind of logic after all: the fact that these jerry-built but rigidly maintained arrangements have lasted for so long suggests an unwillingness on the part of the superpowers to trade familiarity for unpredictability. [...] For however unnatural and unjust these situations may be for the people whose lives they directly affect, it seems nonetheless incontestable that the superpowers' preference for predictability over rationality has, on the whole, enhanced more than it has reduced prospects for a stable relationship. [...]

(5)   do not seek to undermine the other side's leadership. [...] There have been repeated leadership crises in both the United States and the Soviet Union since Stalin's death: one thinks especially of the decline and ultimate deposition of Khrushchev following the Cuban missile crisis, of the Johnson administration's all-consuming fixation with Vietnam, of the collapse of Nixon's authority as a result of Watergate, and of the recent paralysis in the Kremlin brought about by the illness and death of three Soviet leaders within less than three years. And yet, in none of these instances can one discern a concerted effort by the unaffected side to exploit the other's vulnerability; indeed there appears to have existed in several of these situations a sense of frustration, even regret, over the difficulties its rival was undergoing.[16] From the standpoint of game theory, a "rule" that acknowledges legitimacy of leadership on both sides is hardly

surprising: there have to be players in order for the game to proceed. But when compared to other historical – and indeed other current – situations in which that reciprocal tolerance has not existed,[17] its importance as a stabilizing mechanism becomes clear. [...]

Stability, in great power relationships, is not the same thing as politeness. [...] What stability does require is a sense of caution, maturity, and responsibility on both sides. It requires the ability to distinguish posturing – something in which all political leaders indulge – from provocation, which is something else again. It requires recognition of the fact that competition is a normal rather than an abnormal state of affairs in relations between nations, much as it is in relations between major corporations, but that this need not preclude the identification of certain common – or corporate, or universal – interests as well. It requires, above all, a sense of the relative rather than the absolute nature of security: that one's own security depends not only upon the measures one takes in one's own defense, but also upon the extent to which these create a sense of insecurity in the mind of one's adversary.

It would be foolish to suggest that the Soviet-American relationship today meets all of these prerequisites: the last one especially deserves a good deal more attention than it has heretofore received, on both sides. But to the extent that the relationship has taken on a new maturity – and to see that it has one need only compare the current mood of wary optimism with the almost total lack of communication that existed at the time of the Korean War, or the extreme swings between alarm and amiability that characterized relations in the late 1950s and early 1960s, or the inflated expectations and resulting disillusionments of the 1970s – that maturity would appear to reflect an increasing commitment on the part of both great nations involved to a "game" played "by the rules." [...]

Notes

1   I have followed here, in slightly modified form, criteria provided in Gordon A. Craig and Alexander L. George, *Force and Statecraft: Diplomatic Problems of Our Time* (New York: Oxford University Press, 1983), p. x, a book that provides an excellent discussion of how international systems have evolved since the beginning of the 18th century. But see also Robert Gilpin, *War and Change in World Politics* (New York: Cambridge University Press, 1981), pp. 50–105.

2   See, on this point, Kenneth Waltz, *Theory of International Politics* (Reading, Mass.: Addison-Wesley, 1979), pp. 180–81; also A.W. DePorte, *Europe Between the Super-Powers: The Enduring Balance* (New Haven: Yale University Press, 1979), p. 167.

3   Waltz, *Theory of International Politics*, pp. 73–78; Gilpin, *War and Change in World Politics*, pp. 85–88.

4   "[...][S]tructure designates a set of constraining conditions. [...] [It] acts as a selector, but it cannot be seen, examined, and observed at work. [...] Because structures select by rewarding some behaviors and punishing others, outcomes cannot

be inferred from intentions and behaviors." Waltz, *Theory of International Politics*, pp. 73–74.

5   Robert H. Ferrell, ed., *The Autobiography of Harry S. Truman* (Boulder, Colo.: Colorado Associated University Press, 1980), p. 120; David S. McLellan, *Dean Acheson: The State Department Years* (New York: Dodd, Mead, 1976), p. 116.

6   Hans J. Morgenthau, *Politics Among Nations: The Struggle for Power and Peace* (New York: Alfred A. Knopf, 1949), p. 285. For the transition from bipolarity to multipolarity, see the 1973 edition of *Politics Among Nations*, pp. 338–42; also Waltz, *Theory of International Politics*, p. 162. For an eloquent history of the Cold War that views it as the product of the polarization of world politics, see Louis J. Halle, *The Cold War as History* (New York: Harper and Row, 1967).

7   Among those who have emphasized the instability of bipolar systems are Morgenthau, *Politics Among Nations*, pp. 350–54; and Quincy Wright, *A Study of War*, 2nd ed. (Chicago: University of Chicago Press, 1965), pp. 763–64. See also Geoffrey Blainey, *The Causes of War* (London: Macmillan, 1973), pp. 110–11.

8   "[…][W]hat was dominant in their consciousness," Michael Howard has written of the immediate post-World War II generation of statesmen, "was the impotence, almost one might say the irrelevance, of ethical aspirations in international politics in the absence of that factor to which so little attention had been devoted by their more eminent predecessors, to which indeed so many of them had been instinctively hostile – military power." Michael Howard, *The Causes of Wars*, 2nd ed. (Cambridge, Mass.: Harvard University Press, 1984), p. 55.

9   Henry Kissinger has written two classic accounts dealing with the importance of individual leadership in sustaining international systems. See his *A World Restored* (New York: Grosset and Dunlap, 1957), on Metternich; and, on Bismarck, "The White Revolutionary: Reflections on Bismarck," *Daedalus*, Vol. 97 (Summer 1968), pp. 888–924. For a somewhat different perspective on Bismarck's role, see George F. Kennan, *The Decline of Bismarck's European Order: Franco-Russian Relations, 1875–90* (Princeton, N.J.: Princeton University Press, 1979), especially pp. 421–22.

10 See, on this point, Roger V. Dingman, "Theories of, and Approaches to, Alliance Politics," in Paul Gordon Lauren, ed., *Diplomacy: New Approaches in History, Theory, and Policy* (New York: Free Press, 1979), pp. 245–50.

11 My argument here follows that of Glenn H. Snyder and Paul Diesing, *Conflict Among Nations: Bargaining, Decision Making, and System Structure in International Crises* (Princeton, N.J.: Princeton University Press, 1977), pp. 429–45.

12 Waltz, *Theory of International Politics*, pp. 167–69.

13 My definition here is based on Paul Keal, *Unspoken Rules and Superpower Dominance* (New York: St. Martin's, 1983), pp. 2–3. Other more generalized studies dealing with theories of games and bargaining include Kratochwil, *International Order and Foreign Policy*, passim; Snyder and Diesing, *Conflict Among Nations*, especially pp. 33–182; Anatol Rapaport, *Fights, Games, and Debates* (Ann Arbor: University of Michigan Press, 1960); and Charles Lockhart, *Bargaining in International Conflicts* (New York: Columbia University Press, 1979).

14 "In general terms, acquiescence in spheres of influence has taken the form of A disclaiming what B does and in fact disapproving of what B does, but at the same time acquiescing by virtue of effectively doing nothing to oppose B." Keal, *Unspoken Rules and Superpower Dominance*, p. 115.

15   For a recent review of non-proliferation efforts, see the National Academy of Sciences study, *Nuclear Arms Control: Background and Issues* (Washington: National Academy Press, 1985), pp. 224–73.

16   See, for example, Lyndon B. Johnson, *The Vantage Point: Perspectives of the Presidency, 1963–69* (New York: Holt, Rinehart and Winston, 1971), pp. 468–69; also Henry Kissinger, *Years of Upheaval* (Boston: Little, Brown, 1982), pp. 287–88.

17   I have in mind here the long history of dynastic struggles in Europe up through the wars of the French Revolution; also, and much more recently, the way in which a refusal to acknowledge leadership legitimacy has perpetuated the Iran-Iraq war.

Christopher Layne

THE UNIPOLAR ILLUSION

Source: 'The unipolar illusion: why new great powers will rise', *International Security*, vol. 17, no. 4, Spring 1993, pp. 5–51.

The unipolar illusion: why new great powers will rise

[…] IN A UNIPOLAR system, it is argued, the [predominant state] […] could avoid the unpredictable geopolitical consequences that would attend the emergence of new great powers. Unipolarity would, it is said, minimize the risks of both strategic uncertainty and instability. In effect, the strategy of preponderance aims at preserving the […] status quo [of the prevailing international system]. […]

[…] I use neorealist theory to analyze the implications of unipolarity. I argue that the "unipolar moment" is just that, a geopolitical interlude that will give way to multipolarity. […] I start with a very simple premise: states balance against hegemons, even those […] that seek to maintain their preeminence by employing strategies based more on benevolence than coercion. As Kenneth N. Waltz says, "In international politics, overwhelming power repels and leads other states to balance against it."[1] In a unipolar world, systemic constraints – balancing, uneven growth rates, and the sameness effect – impel eligible states (i.e., those with the capability to do so) to become great powers. […]

[…] A unipolar world is not terra incognita. There have been two other comparable unipolar moments in modern international history. The evidence from those two eras confirms the expectations derived from structural realism: (1) unipolar systems contain the seeds of their own demise because the hegemon's unbalanced power creates an environment conducive to the emergence of new great powers; and (2) the entry of new great powers into the international system erodes the hegemon's relative power and, ultimately, its preeminence. […]

Why great powers rise – the role of systemic constraints

Whether [a preponderant state] […] can maintain its standing as the sole great power depends largely on whether new great powers will rise. To answer that question, we need to understand why states become great powers.[2] This is a critical issue because the emergence (or disappearance) of great powers can have a decisive effect on international politics; a consequential shift in the number of great powers changes the international system's structure. Waltz defines a "consequential" shift as "variations in number that lead to different expectations about the effect of structure on units."[3] Examples are shifts from: bipolarity to either unipolarity or multipolarity; unipolarity to bipolarity or multipolarity; multipolarity to bipolarity or unipolarity; from a multipolar system with three great powers to one of four or more (or vice versa).[4]

Throughout modern international history, there has been an observable pattern of great power emergence. Although neorealism does not, and cannot, purport to predict the foreign policies of specific states, it can account for outcomes and patterns of behavior that happen recurrently in international politics. Great power emergence is a structurally driven phenomenon. Specifically, it results from the interaction of two factors: (1) differential growth rates and (2) anarchy.

Although great power emergence is shaped by structural factors, and can cause structural effects, it results from unit-level actions. In other words, a feedback loop of sorts is at work: (1) structural constraints press eligible states to become great powers; (2) such states make unit-level decisions whether to pursue great power status in response to these structural constraints; (3) if a unit-level decision to seek great power status produces a consequential shift in polarity, it has a structural impact. Rising states have choices about whether to become great powers. However, a state's freedom to choose whether to seek great power status is in reality tightly constrained by structural factors. Eligible states that fail to attain great power status are predictably punished. If policymakers of eligible states are socialized to the international system's constraints, they understand that attaining great power status is a prerequisite if their states are to be secure and autonomous.[5] The fate that befell nineteenth-century China illustrates what can happen to an eligible state when its leaders ignore structural imperatives. [...]

Differential growth rates

The process of great power emergence is underpinned by the fact that the economic (and technological and military) power of states grows at differential, not parallel rates. That is, in relative terms, some states are gaining power while others are losing it. As Robert Gilpin notes, over time, "the differential growth in the power of various states in the system causes a fundamental redistribution of power in the system."[6] The result, as Paul Kennedy has shown, is that time and again relative "economic shifts heralded the rise of new Great Powers which one day would have a decisive impact on the military/territorial order."[7] The link between differential growth rates and great power emergence has important implications for unipolarity. Unipolarity is likely to be short-lived because new great powers will emerge as the uneven growth process narrows the gap between the hegemon and the eligible states that are positioned to emerge as its competitors. [...]

The consequences of anarchy: balancing and sameness

[...] [T]he international political system is a self-help system in which states' foremost concern must be with survival.[8] In an anarchic system, states must provide for their own security and they face many real or apparent threats.[9] International politics thus is a competitive realm, a fact that in itself constrains eligible states to attain great power status. Specifically, there are two manifestations of this competitiveness that shape great power emergence: balancing and the "sameness effect."[10]

BALANCING. The competitiveness of international politics is manifested in the tendency of states to balance.[11] Balancing has especially strong explanatory power in accounting for the facts that unipolarity tends to be short-lived and that would-be hegemons invariably fail to achieve lasting dominance. Structural realism leads to the expectation that hegemony should generate the rise of countervailing power in the form of new great powers.

The reason states balance is to correct a skewed distribution of relative power in the international system. States are highly attentive to changes in their relative power position because relative power shifts have crucial security implications.[12] It is the interaction of differential growth rates – the main cause of changes in the relative distribution of power among states – and anarchy that produces important effects. In an anarchic, self-help system, states must always be concerned that others will use increased relative capabilities against them. By enhancing their own relative capabilities or diminishing those of an adversary, states get a double payoff: greater security and a wider range of strategic options.[13] The reverse is true for states that remain indifferent to relative power relationship. [...]

By definition, the distribution of relative power in a unipolar system is extremely unbalanced. Consequently, in a unipolar system, the structural pressures on eligible states to increase their relative capabilities and become great powers should be overwhelming. If they do not acquire great power capabilities, they may be exploited by the hegemon. Of course, an eligible state's quest for security may give rise to the security dilemma because actions intended to bolster its own security may have the unintended consequence of threatening others.[14]

It can be argued on the basis of hegemonic stability theory and balance of threat theory that a "benign" hegemon might be able to prevent new great powers from emerging and balancing against it.[15] These arguments are unpersuasive. Although hegemonic stability theory is usually employed in the context of international political economy, it can be extended to other aspects of international politics. The logic of collective goods underlying the notion of a benign hegemon assumes that all states will cooperate because they derive absolute benefit from the collective goods the hegemon provides. Because they are better off, the argument goes, others should willingly accept a benign hegemon and even help to prop it up if it is declining. However, as Michael C. Webb and Stephen D. Krasner point out, the benign version of hegemonic stability theory assumes that states are indifferent to the distribution of relative gains.[16] This is, as noted, a dubious assumption. As Joseph Grieco points out, because states worry that today's ally could become tomorrow's rival, "they pay close attention to how cooperation might affect relative capabilities in the future."[17]

Moreover, if stability is equated with the dominant state's continuing preeminence, the stability of hegemonic systems is questionable once the hegemon's power begins to erode noticeably. As Gilpin points out, over time a hegemon declines from its dominant position because: (1) the costs of sustaining its preeminence begin to erode the hegemon's economic strength, thereby diminishing its military and economic capabilities; and (2) the hegemonic paradox results in the diffusion of economic, technological, and organizational skills to other states, thereby causing the hegemon to lose its "comparative advantage" over them.[18] Frequently, these others are eligible states that will rise to great power status and challenge the hegemon's predominance.

This last point suggests that in unipolar systems, states do indeed balance against the hegemon's unchecked power. This reflects the fact that in unipolar systems there is no clear-cut distinction between balancing against threat and balancing against power. This is because the threat inheres in the hegemon's power.[19] In a unipolar world, others must worry about the hegemon's capabilities, not its intentions. The preeminent power's intentions may be benign today but may not be tomorrow. Robert Jervis cuts to the heart of the matter when he notes, "Minds can be changed, new leaders can come to power, values can shift, new opportunities and dangers can arise."[20] Unless they are prepared to run the risk of being vulnerable to a change in the hegemon's intentions, other states must be prepared to counter its capabilities. Moreover, even a hegemon animated by benign motives may pursue policies that run counter to others' interests. Thus, as Waltz says, "Balance-of-power theory leads one to expect that states, if they are free to do so, will flock to the weaker side. The stronger, not the weaker side, threatens them if only by pressing its preferred policies on other states."[21] [...]

It is unsurprising that counter-hegemonic balancing has occurred even during periods of perceived unipolarity. [...] [Indeed] [o]ne of the most important questions concerning international politics today is whether this pattern of balancing against the dominant power in a unipolar system (actual or perceived) will recur in the post-Cold War world.

SAMENESS. As Waltz points out, "competition produces a tendency toward sameness of the competitors"; that is, toward imitating their rivals' successful characteristics.[22] Such characteristics include not only military strategies, tactics, weaponry, and technology, but also administrative and organizational techniques. If others do well in developing effective instruments of competition, a state must emulate its rivals or face the consequences of falling behind. Fear drives states to duplicate others' successful policies because policymakers know that, as Arthur Stein observes, "failure in the anarchic international system can mean the disappearance of their states."[23] From this standpoint, it is to be expected that in crucial respects, great powers will look and act very much alike. It is also to be expected that sameness-effect imperatives will impel eligible states to become great powers and to acquire all the capabilities attendant to that status. [...]

Additional light is shed on the sameness effect by the "second image reversed" perspective, which posits a linkage between the international system's structural constraints and a state's domestic structure. Charles Tilly's famous aphorism, "War made the state, and the state made war" neatly captures the concept.[24] Tilly shows how the need to protect against external danger compelled states in early modern Europe to develop administrative and bureaucratic structures to maintain, supply, and finance permanent military establishments. But there is more to it than that. [...] [E]vidence from 1660–1713 and 1860–1910 suggests that great power emergence reflects an eligible state's adjustment to the international system's structural constraints. Otto Hinze observed that the way in which states are organized internally reflects "their position relative to each other and their overall position in the world" and that "throughout the ages pressure from without has been a determining influence on internal structure."[25]

Great powers are similar because they are not, and cannot be, functionally differentiated. This is not to say that great powers are identical. They may adopt different strategies and approaches; however, ultimately they all must be able to perform satisfactorily the same security-related tasks necessary to survive and succeed in the competitive realm of international politics. The sameness effect reflects the enormous pressure that the international system places on great powers to imitate the successful policies of others. [...]

* * *

History, unipolarity and great power emergence

There is a strong correlation between unipolarity and great power emergence. Late seventeenth-century England and Austria and late nineteenth-century Germany balanced against the dominant pole in the system. Moreover, even when great power emergence was not driven primarily by the need to counterbalance the hegemon's power, the shadow of preeminence was an important factor.[26] This is illustrated by the rise of the United States and Japan to great power status in the late nineteenth century. It is, therefore, apparent that a general tendency exists during unipolar moments: several new great powers simultaneously enter the international system. The events of the late nineteenth century also illustrate how competition from established great powers combined with challenges from rising great powers to diminish Britain's relative power and erode its primacy. During the last years of the nineteenth century, Britain, the most powerful state in the system, was the target of others' balancing policies. "The story of European international relations in the 1890s is the story of the assault of Russia and France upon the territorial position of Britain in Asia and Africa, and the story of the great economic duel between England and her all-too-efficient German rival."[27]

In the late nineteenth century, the growth of American, German, and Japanese naval power compelled Britain to forgo its policy of maintaining global naval supremacy.[28] Indeed, Britain was pressed hard by its rivals on all fronts. By 1900, it was apparent that London could not simultaneously meet the German challenge across the North Sea, defend its imperial and colonial interests from French and Russian pressure, and preserve its position in the Western hemisphere. Britain withdrew from the Western hemisphere because London realized it lacked the resources to compete successfully against the United States and that the naval forces deployed in North American waters could better be used elsewhere.[29] The Anglo-Japanese alliance was driven, from London's standpoint, by the need to use Japanese naval power to protect

Britain's East Asian interests and thereby allow the Royal Navy units in the Far East to be redeployed to home waters. Like the rapprochement with Washington and the alliance with Tokyo, the ententes with France and Russia also evidenced Britain's declining relative power. By 1907, Britain's geopolitical position "depended upon the kindness of strangers." Over the longer term, the great power emergence of the United States and Japan paved the way for Britain's eclipse, first as hegemon and then as a great power. In the 1930s, Japanese power cost Britain its Far Eastern position, and America's relative power ultimately rose to a point where it could displace Britain as hegemon. Such was the result of Britain's policy of benign hegemony, a policy that did not merely abstain from opposing, but actually had the effect of facilitating the emergence of new great powers.

After the Cold War: America in a unipolar world?

[...] [H]istorical evidence [...] strongly supports the hypothesis derived from neo-realist theory: unipolar moments cause geopolitical backlashes that lead to multipolarity. Nevertheless, in principle, a declining hegemon does have an alternative to a policy of tolerating the rise of new great powers: it can actively attempt to suppress their emergence. Thus, if Washington were prepared to contemplate preventive measures (including the use of force), it might be able to beat back rising challengers.[30] But, although prevention may seem attractive at first blush, it is a stop-gap measure. It may work once, but over time the effect of differential growth rates ensures that other challengers will subsequently appear. Given its probable costs and risks, prevention is not a strategy that would lend itself to repetition. [...]

* * *

Reaction to unipolarity: towards a multipolar world

There is ample evidence that widespread concern exists today about America's currently unchallenged dominance in international politics.[31] In September 1991, French Foreign Minister Roland Dumas warned that American "might reigns without balancing weight" and he and European Community Commission President Jacques Delors called for the EC to counterbalance the United States.[32] Some European policy analysts have said that the Soviet Union's collapse means that Europe is now threatened mainly by unchallenged American ascendancy in world politics.[33] This viewpoint was echoed in Japan in the Gulf War's aftermath. A number of commentators worried that the United States – a "fearsome" country – would impose a Pax Americana in which other states would be compelled to accept roles "as America's underlings."[34] China, too, has reacted adversely to America's post-Cold War preeminence. "Chinese analysts reacted with great alarm to President George Bush's 'New World Order' proclamations, and maintained that this was a ruse for extending U.S. hegemony throughout the globe. From China's perspective, unipolarity was a far worse state of affairs than bipolarity. "[35] Similar sentiments have been echoed in the Third World. Although the reactions of these smaller states are not as significant as those of potential new great powers, they confirm that unipolarity has engendered general unease throughout the international system. [...]

[...] [T]he post-Cold War world's geopolitical constellation is not unique. Twice before in international history there have been "unipolar moments." Both were fleeting. On both occasions, the effect of the entry of new great powers in the international system was to redress the one-sided distribution of power in the international system. There is every reason to expect that the pattern of the late seventeenth and nineteenth centuries will recur. The impact of differential growth rates has increased the relative power of Japan and Germany in a way that clearly marks them as eligible states. As their stakes in the international system deepen, so will their ambitions and interests. Security considerations will cause Japan and Germany to emulate the United States and acquire the full spectrum of great power capabilities, including nuclear weapons.[36] It can be expected that both will seek recognition by others of their great power status. [...]

Notes

1   Kenneth N. Waltz, "America as a Model for the World? A Foreign Policy Perspective," *PS*, December 1991, p. 669.

2   As Kenneth Waltz writes, great powers are defined by capabilities: "States, because they are in a self-help system, have to use their combined capabilities in order to serve their interests. The economic, military, and other capabilities of nations cannot be sectored and separately weighed. States are not placed in the top rank because they excel in one way or another. Their rank depends on how they score on all of the following items: size of population and territory; resource endowment; military strength; political stability; and competence." Kenneth N. Waltz, *Theory of International Politics* (Reading, Mass.: Addison-Wesley, 1979), p. 131. Because of their capabilities, great powers tend to behave differently than other states. Jack Levy writes that great powers are distinguished from others by: 1) a high level of military capability that makes them relatively self-sufficient strategically and capable of projecting power beyond their borders; 2) a broad concept of security that embraces a concern with regional and/or global power balances; and 3) a greater assertiveness than lesser powers in defining and defending their interests. Jack Levy, *War and the Modern Great Power System, 1495–1975* (Lexington: University Press of Kentucky, 1983), pp. 11–19.

Recently there have been several questionable attempts to redefine great power status. For example, Joseph S. Nye, Jr., and Samuel P. Huntington argue that only the United States has the "soft" power resources (socio-cultural and ideological attractiveness to other states) that Nye and Huntington claim are a prerequisite of great power status. Nye, *Bound to Lead*; Huntington, "The U.S. – Decline or Renewal?" *Foreign Affairs*, Vol. 67, No. 2 (Winter 1988/89), pp. 90–93. This argument has three weaknesses. First, it is far from clear that others view U.S. culture and ideology in the same positive light that Nye and Huntington do. America's racial, economic, educational, and social problems have eroded others' admiration for the United States. Second, it is not unusual for great powers to see themselves as cultural or ideological role models; examples include nineteenth-century Britain and France, pre-1914 Germany and, of course, the Soviet Union. Finally, when it comes to setting great powers apart from others, soft power may be a helpful supplement to the other instruments of statecraft, but states with the requisite hard power capabilities (per Waltz's definition) are great powers regardless of whether they "stand for an idea with appeal beyond [their] borders."

Another popular intellectual fashion holds that Japan and Germany will carve out niches in international politics as the first "global civilian powers." Hanns Maull, "Germany and Japan: The New Civilian Powers," *Foreign Affairs*, Vol. 69, No. 5 (Winter 1990/91), pp. 91–106. As civilian powers, it is argued, they will eschew military strength in favor of economic power, work through international institutions to promote global cooperation, and "furnish international public goods, such as refugee resettlement, national disaster relief, development of economic infrastructure, and human resources improvements." Yoichi Funabashi, "Japan and America: Global Partners," *Foreign Policy*, No. 86 (Spring 1992), p. 37. In the real world, however, one does not find traditional great powers and "civilian" great powers. One finds only states that are great powers and those that are not.

3   Waltz, *Theory of International Politics*, p. 162.

4   Ibid., pp. 163–70.

5   Kenneth N. Waltz, "A Reply to My Critics" in Robert O. Keohane, ed., *Neorealism and Its Critics* (New York: Columbia University Press, 1986), p. 343.

6   Robert Gilpin, *War and Change in World Politics* (Cambridge: Cambridge University Press, 1981), p. 13. The role of uneven growth rates in the rise of great powers is closely connected to long cycle explanations. See Joshua S. Goldstein, *Long Cycles: Prosperity and War in the Modern Age* (New Haven: Yale University Press, 1988); George Modelski, *Long Cycles in World Politics* (Seattle: University of Washington Press, 1987); and William R. Thompson, "Dehio, Long Cycles, and the Geohistorical Context of Structural Transition," *World Politics*, Vol. 45, No. 1 (October 1992), pp. 127–52.

7   Paul Kennedy, *The Rise and Fall of Great Powers: Economic Change and Military Conflict From 1500 to 2000* (New York: Random House, 1987), p. xxii.

8   Waltz, *Theory of International Politics*, pp. 107, 127.

9   Kenneth N. Waltz, "The Origins of War in Neorealist Theory," in Robert I. Rotberg and Theodore K. Rabb, eds., *The Origin and Prevention of Major Wars* (Cambridge: Cambridge University Press, 1989), p. 43.

10   The phrase "sameness effect" is from Waltz, *Theory of International Politics*, p. 128.

11   For discussion of the differences between bandwagoning and balancing behavior, see Waltz, *Theory of International Politics*, pp. 125–26; Stephen M. Walt, *The Origins of Alliances* (Ithaca: Cornell University Press, 1987), pp. 17–33.

12   Waltz, *Theory of International Politics*, p. 126.

13   Gilpin, *War and Change*, pp. 86–87.

14   John Herz, "Idealist Internationalism and the Security Dilemma," *World Politics*, Vol. 2, No. 2 (January 1950), pp. 157–80.

15   On balance of threat theory, see Walt, *The Origins of Alliances*, pp. 17–26. For an overview of the benevolent and coercive strands of hegemonic stability theory, see Duncan Snidal, "The Limits of Hegemonic Stability Theory," *International Organization*, Vol. 39, No. 4 (Autumn 1985), pp. 579–614.

16   Michael C. Webb and Stephen D. Krasner, "Hegemonic Stability Theory: An Empirical Assessment," *Review of International Studies*, Vol. 15, No. 2 (April 1989), pp. 184–85.

17   Joseph M. Grieco, "Anarchy and the Limits of Cooperation: A Realist Critique of the Newest Liberal Institutionalism," *International Organization*, Vol. 42, No. 3 (Summer 1988), p. 500 (emphasis in original).

18   Gilpin, *War and Change*, pp. 156–210.

19.   Traditional balance-of-power theory postulates that states align against others that are excessively powerful. Stephen Walt refined balance of power theory by arguing that states actually balance against threats rather than against power per se. However, Walt's balance-of-threat analysis is more ambiguous than it might seem at first glance. For example, he admits that every post-1648 bid for European hegemony was repulsed by a balancing coalition. *Origins of Alliances*, pp. 28–29. Why? Because would-be hegemons were powerful or because they were threatening? He does not say directly but one suspects that his answer would be "both." Walt does not downplay the importance of power as a factor in inducing balancing behavior; he simply says it is not the only factor (p. 21). Indeed, power and threat blend together almost imperceptibly. Note that two of his threat variables, geographic proximity and offensive capabilities, correlate closely with military power. When Walt says that states do not necessarily balance against the most powerful actor in the system he essentially is equating power with GNP. When he says that states balance against threat he is saying that they balance against military power (coupled with aggressive intentions). Obviously, power is more than just GNP. What states appear to balance against in reality is actual or latent military capabilities. In a unipolar world, the hegemon's possession of actual or latent military capabilities will result in balancing regardless of its intentions. If, in a unipolar world, capabilities matter more than intentions, the U.S. monopoly on long-range power-projection capabilities – that is, its preponderance of military power – probably will be viewed by others as threatening.

20   Robert Jervis, "Cooperation Under the Security Dilemma," *World Politics*, Vol. 30, No. 2 (January 1978), p. 105.

21   Kenneth N. Waltz, "The Emerging Structure of International Politics," paper presented at the annual meeting of the American Political Science Association, San Francisco, California, August 1990, p. 32.

22   Waltz, *Theory of International Politics*, p. 127.

23   Arthur Stein, *Why Nations Cooperate: Circumstance and Choice in International Relations* (Ithaca, New York: Cornell University Press, 1990), pp. 115–16.

24   Charles Tilly, "Reflections on the History of European State Making," in Charles Tilly, ed., *The Formation of National States in Western Europe* (Princeton: Princeton University Press, 1975), p. 42.

25   Otto Hinze, "Military Organization and the Organization of the State," in Felix Gilbert, ed., *The Historical Essays of Otto Hinze* (Princeton: Princeton University Press, 1975), p. 183.

26   The shadow effect is a consequence of anarchy. The unbalanced distribution of power in the hegemon's favor implicitly threatens others' security. This is because states must react to the hegemon's capabilities rather than to its intentions. In a unipolar system, concern with security is a compelling reason for eligible states to acquire great power capabilities, even if they are not immediately menaced by the hegemon.

27   William L. Langer, *The Diplomacy of Imperialism, 1890–1902*, 2d ed. (New York: Alfred A. Knopf, 1965), p. 415.

28   See Aaron L. Friedberg, *The Weary Titan: Britain and the Experience of Relative Decline, 1895–1905* (Princeton: Princeton University Press, 1988), pp. 135–208.

29   See C. J. Lowe and M. L. Dockrill, *The Mirage of Power, Vol. I: British Foreign Policy, 1902–14* (London: Routledge and Kegan Paul, 1972), pp. 96–106.

30   When a hegemon finds its primacy threatened, the best strategy is "to eliminate the source of the problem." Gilpin, *War and Change*, p. 191.

31   It has been suggested that the Persian Gulf War demonstrates that other states welcome, rather than fear, America's post-Cold War preeminence. However, this simply is not the case. First, it was after the Persian Gulf crisis began that others began voicing their concerns about unipolarity, Second, to the extent that the Gulf War is an example of states bandwagoning with the United States, it is easily explainable. As Walt points out, weak powers threatened by a powerful neighbor will often turn to an outside great power for defensive support. Walt, *Origins of Alliances*, p. 266. Third, as Jean Edward Smith points out, the United States had to exert considerable pressure on both Egypt and Saudi Arabia to get these nations to accept the Bush administration's decision to confront Iraq militarily after the invasion of Kuwait. Jean Edward Smith, *George Bush's War* (New York: Henry Holt and Company, 1992), pp. 63–95. Finally, it should be remembered that during the war, the Arab coalition partners restrained the United States from overthrowing Saddam Hussein and that, in July and August 1992, Egypt, Turkey and Syria restrained the United States when it appeared that the Bush administration was going to provoke a military showdown over the issue of UN weapons inspectors' access to Iraq's Agricultural Ministry.

32   Quoted in "France to U.S.: Don't Rule," *New York Times*, September 3, 1991, p. A8.

33   Rone Tempest, "French Revive Pastime Fretting About U.S. 'Imperialism'," *Los Angeles Times*, February 15, 1989, p. A9.

34   See the views of Waseda University Professor Sakuji Yoshimura, quoted in Paul Blustein, "In Japan, Seeing The War On A Five-Inch Screen," *Washington Post National Weekly Edition*, February 25–March 3, 1991, and of Tokyo University Professor Yasusuke Murakami and Opposition Diet Member Masao Kunihiro, in Urban C. Lehner, "Japanese See A More 'Fearsome' U.S. Following American Success in the Gulf," *Wall Street Journal*, March 14, 1991.

35   David Shambaugh, "China's Security Policy in the Post-Cold War Era," *Survival*, Vol. 34, No. 2 (Summer 1992), p. 92.

36   The nuclear issue is being debated, albeit gingerly, in Japan but not in Germany (or at least not openly). Nevertheless it seems to be widely understood, in the United States and in Germany and Japan, that their accession to the nuclear club is only a matter of time. See Doyle McManus, "Thinking the Once Unthinkable: Japan, Germany With A-Bombs," *Los Angeles Times* (Washington D.C. ed.), June 10, 1992, p. A8. For a discussion of a nuclear Germany's strategic implications, see Mearsheimer, "Back to the Future."

Glenn Snyder

ALLIANCE POLITICS

Source: 'The security dilemma in alliance politics', *World Politics*, vol. 36, no. 4, July 1984, pp. 461–95.

Alliance formation in a multipolar system: the primary alliance dilemma

THE SECURITY DILEMMA IN the alliance game has two phases: primary and secondary. The primary phase occurs during the process of alliance formation, the secondary one after alliances have formed.

In a multipolar system (such as the one that existed before 1945), the primary alliance dilemma among the major states follows the logic of an N-person prisoner's dilemma. Each state has two options: seek allies or abstain from alliances. If all states are about equally strong and are interested only in security, all are fairly well off if all abstain, since each has moderate security against individual others, while alliances involve various costs, such as reduced freedom of action, commitments to defend the interests of others, and so forth. Alliances will form, however, for two reasons: (1) some states may not be satisfied with only moderate security, and they can increase it substantially by allying if others abstain; (2) some states, fearing that others will not abstain, will ally in order to avoid isolation or to preclude the partner from allying against them. Once an alliance forms, a counter-alliance necessarily follows, since there is no way of knowing that the first alliance is intended only for defensive purposes. The eventual result is the division of the system into two rival coalitions. This outcome is worse than all-around abstention because each state has incurred the risks and burdens of alliance with little improvement in its security.[1]

[One can develop a model to portray] the primary alliance security dilemma. Although it is cast in two-person form, it is understood that for player A, the other player, B, means "all other players," and vice versa. The numbers in the cells are ordinal, ranked from 4 (best) to 1 (worst). The first number in each cell represents A's payoff, the second B's. The logical outcome, two rival coalitions, is the second-worst for all players. The best, forming an alliance while others do not, and the second-best, all-around abstention, cannot be obtained, primarily because of uncertainty about the intentions of others and the overwhelming need to guard against the worst outcome, that of isolation.

This model predicts only that alliances will form. It does not predict who will align with whom, or how the benefits, risks, and costs of an alliance will be divided among its members. These matters theoretically are decided by a process of bargaining in which the states compete in offering each other attractive shares of the alliance's "payoff." Each state has two principal aims in the bargaining: to be in the most powerful coalition, and to maximize its share of the alliance's net benefits.[2] These are the "interests" of the state in the alliance game. If these were the only interests at stake, the alliance bargaining process would be completely indeterminate – that is, each state would be equally eligible as the ally or the adversary of every other state.

In the real world, however, the indeterminacy is reduced, though not eliminated, by other interests, which exist apart from the alliance game and which predispose states to align with certain others and against others. Here we must distinguish between "general" and "particular" interests. General interests stem from the anarchic structure of the system and the geographic position of the state. They include, for instance, a state's interest in defending a close neighbor, or in expansion to enhance its security, or even more generally, in preserving a balance of power in the system. [...]

The indeterminacy is further reduced by the "particular" interests of states, which bring them into conflict or affinity with specific other states. These conflicts and commonalities may have some power content or they may stem from ideological, ethnic, economic, or prestige values. [...]

Particular conflicts or affinities of interest establish a tacit pattern of alignment, prior to or apart from any overt alliance negotiations. That is, states will expect to be supported in some degree by those with whom they share interests [and ideology,] and to be opposed by those with whom they are in conflict. [...]

Such conflicts and alignments of interest and ideology establish a background of relationships against which the overt alliance bargaining process takes place, and which affect that process considerably, predisposing the system toward certain alliances and against others. These relationships may foreclose some combinations if the conflict is severe enough; in other cases, the absence of conflict between some pairs may make them natural allies. More likely, however, these conflicts and affinities will narrow the range of indeterminacy rather than eliminate it. Natural partners may fail to ally because one of them overestimates the other's conflicts with third parties and tries to drive too hard a bargain [...]. And natural opponents may be able to overcome their conflicts [...]. Technically, conflicts and commonalities of particular interest enter into the bargaining process by reducing or increasing the total value, or "payoff," of certain alliances, thus reducing or increasing the likelihood that they will form. For example, a state with which one has a conflict will appear as a more likely opponent in war than other states; hence, an alliance *against* it will yield greater value than an alliance *with* it; the latter would require a prior settlement of the conflict, incurring costs in the form of compromised interests. [...]

The choice of allies is also influenced by the internal political configurations of states apart from the general ideological preferences just mentioned. [...]

To summarize: in a multipolar system there is a general incentive to ally with *some* other state or states, following the logic of the N-person prisoner's dilemma, or security dilemma, that is generated by the structure of the system. Who aligns with whom results from a bargaining process that is theoretically indeterminate. The indeterminacy is reduced, though not eliminated, by the prior interests, conflicts, and affinities between states and their internal political make-up.[3]

After alignments form: the secondary alliance dilemma

Once alliances have begun to form, the alliance security dilemma takes on a different character. That is, having already "defected" in the primary dilemma by choosing to make alliances, states move into the second phase of the alliance dilemma, in which their choices are no longer whether to ally or not, but how firmly to commit themselves to the proto-partner and how much support to give that partner in specific conflict interactions with the adversary. The horns of this secondary dilemma may be described by the traditional labels "cooperate" (C) and "defect" (D), where cooperation means a strong general commitment and full support in specific adversary conflicts, and defection means a weak commitment and no support in conflicts with the adversary. The secondary alliance dilemma may or may not be a prisoner's dilemma. (Henceforth in this discussion, the terms "alliance game" and "dilemma" will refer to the secondary game rather than the primary one.)

Each horn of the dilemma has both prospective good and prospective bad consequences; and the "goods" and "bads" for each alternative tend to be the obverse of those of the other. In the alliance security dilemma, the principal "bads" are "abandonment" and "entrapment," and the principal "goods" are a reduction in the risks of being abandoned or entrapped by the ally.[4]

In a multipolar system, alliances are never absolutely firm, whatever the text of the written agreement; therefore, the fear of being abandoned by one's ally is ever-present. Abandonment, in general, is "defection," but it may take a variety of specific forms: the ally may realign with the opponent; he may merely de-align, abrogating the alliance contract; he may fail to make good on his explicit commitments; or he may fail to provide support in contingencies where support is expected. (In both of the latter two variants, the alliance remains intact, but the expectations of support which underlie it are weakened.) Suspicion that the ally is considering realignment may generate an incentive to realign preemptively.

Entrapment means being dragged into a conflict over an ally's interests that one does not share, or shares only partially. The interests of allies are generally not identical; to the extent they are shared, they may be valued in different degree. Entrapment occurs when one values the preservation of the alliance more than the cost of fighting for the ally's interests. It is more likely to occur if the ally becomes intransigent in disputes with opponents because of his confidence in one's support. Thus, the greater one's dependence on the alliance and the stronger one's commitment to the ally, the higher the risk of entrapment. The risk also varies with the ally's inherent degree of recklessness or aggressiveness.

The risks of abandonment and entrapment tend to vary inversely: reducing one tends to increase the other. Thus a "C" strategy of strong commitment to an ally reduces the risk of abandonment by reducing *his* fear of abandonment; he is discouraged from defecting by his confidence in one's support. But this very support may encourage him to excessive boldness in disputes or crises with the adversary, thus exposing one to the risk of a war that one would not wish to fight. Conversely, a "D" strategy of weak or vague commitment, or a record of failing to support the ally in specific conflicts, tends to restrain the ally and to reduce the risk of entrapment; but it also increases the risk of abandonment by casting doubt on one's loyalty, hence devaluing the alliance for the ally. Thus, the resolution of the alliance security dilemma – the choice of strategy – requires chiefly a comparison and trade-off between the costs and risks of abandonment and entrapment.

There are certain other "goods" and "bads" that enter into the alliance security dilemma. A strategy of strong commitment and support will have the undesired effect of reducing one's bargaining leverage over the ally. If he knows he can count on being supported, he is less influenceable. Conversely, bargaining power over the ally is enhanced to the extent he doubts one's commitment because one can then make credible threats of nonsupport. Alliance bargaining considerations thus tend to favor a strategy of weak or ambiguous commitment – a "D" strategy in the alliance game. (Note that the opposite is the case in the adversary game where firm commitments to defend one's interests tend to strengthen bargaining power vis-à-vis the opponent.)

Another negative effect of strong commitment is that it tends to foreclose one's own options of realignment. Despite the general compulsion to align in a multipolar system, states usually want to keep their commitments tentative or vague as long as possible – both to preserve opportunities for shifting partners in case the present one turns out to be unsatisfactory and to maximize bargaining leverage over the current partner by showing that they have alternatives. A strategy of weak commitment has the desirable effect of keeping alignment options open.

Finally, a strong commitment to the ally tends to solidify the adversary alliance by increasing the degree of threat to it. A weak or tentative commitment reduces this effect and may even weaken or divide the opposing alliance by preserving, for states in that alliance, the apparent option of realigning with oneself.

Notes

1   This is, of course, an idealized model based on certain assumptions from which the empirical world will deviate more or less, from time to time. The basic assumptions are that: (1) no state is aggressive, but none can know the intentions of others; (2) the states are roughly equal in military strength; and (3) military technology is such that there is no time to form a successful defense alliance after war begins. Uncertainty about the aims of others is inherent in structural anarchy. If a state clearly reveals itself as expansionist, however, the alliance that forms against it is not "self-defeating" as in the prisoners' dilemma (security dilemma) model. Or, if some states are weaker than others, their motives to ally will be different from the incentives of the prisoner's dilemma. The third assumption has been valid since about 1870. Before then (when the pace of warfare was slower), the compulsion to ally in peacetime was much weaker than suggested by the model. Despite these

qualifications and possibly others, the model does capture some essential dynamics of multipolar alliance formation between 1870 and 1939.

2   "Being in" the most powerful coalition does not necessarily mean that states join the most powerful coalition that is already in existence. Indeed, they will more likely join the weaker one which then becomes the most powerful as a consequence of their joining, because this gives them leverage to bargain for a maximum share of the alliance's payoff. Thus the logic of N-person game theory is consistent with Waltz's argument that states "balance" rather than "bandwagon." See Kenneth N. Waltz, *Theory of International Politics* (Reading, Mass.: Addison–Wesley, 1979), 125–26.

3   Despite the importance of internal politics, this reference will be the only one in this essay. For reasons of theoretical parsimony and space limitations, the analysis is based entirely on what in recently popular academic terminology is called the "rational actor model," the actors being states.

4   The concepts of abandonment and entrapment were first posited, I believe, by Michael Mandelbaum, in *The Nuclear Revolution: International Politics Before and After Hiroshima* (New York: Cambridge University Press, 1981), chap. 6.

Stephen M. Walt

ALLIANCE FUTURES

Source: 'Why alliances endure or collapse', *Survival*, vol. 39, no. 1, Spring 1997, pp. 156–79.

What is an alliance?

A N ALLIANCE IS A FORMAL or informal commitment for security cooperation between two or more states. Although the precise arrangements embodied in different alliances vary enormously, the defining feature of any alliance is a commitment for mutual military support against some external actor(s) in some specified set of circumstances. This concept includes both formal alliances – where the commitment is enshrined in a written treaty – and informal, *ad hoc* agreements based either on tacit understandings or some tangible form of commitment, such as verbal assurances or joint military exercises. Including both formal and informal alliances in this study makes sense because states may provide considerable support to one another even without a formal treaty, and because the presence of a formal agreement often says relatively little about the actual degree of commitment.

The primary purpose of most alliances is to combine the members' capabilities in a way that furthers their respective interests. The form of collaboration and the nature of the commitment varies widely, however. An alliance may be either offensive or defensive, for example, intended either to provide the means for an attack on some third party or intended as a mutual guarantee in the event that another state attacks one of the alliance members. Alliances may also be symmetrical or asymmetrical, depending on whether the members possess roughly equal capabilities and take on broadly identical commitments to each other.[1] An alliance may be a purely expedient arrangement between states with very different regimes and political values – such as the Second World War alliance of the United Kingdom, the United States and the Soviet Union – or it may bring together states whose strategic interests and ideological principles are similar and mutually reinforcing – as in NATO today.

Alliances also vary in their level of institutionalisation. Modern alliances are more than a mechanical combination of independent national assets; they are also social institutions that may involve extensive interactions between the member-states. At one extreme, formal alliances such as NATO are highly institutionalised, with elaborate decision-making procedures and an extensive supporting bureaucracy. This sort of alliance inevitably produces a dense web of élite contacts and subsidiary agreements, and it is likely to exert a more lasting influence on the attitudes and behaviour of each member. At the other extreme are largely *ad hoc* coalitions like the Axis alliance of 1939–45 or most inter-Arab alliances, which were limited partnerships in which each member acted relatively independently.

Third, alliances also differ in the functions that they perform. Most great-power alliances have arisen in order to aggregate power: members pool their resources to achieve some common, or at least compatible, ends. Yet such agreements inevitably allow members to influence each other's conduct, which enables strong states to use the alliance to exercise a restraining influence over allies and adversaries alike. Alliance commitments also impart a greater degree of predictability in international affairs, and can facilitate conflict management among member-states.[2]

Finally, alliances differ in important ways from other forms of security cooperation. An agreement to reduce tensions between adversaries – for example, via an arms-control agreement, a formalised process of détente or a set of 'confidence-building' measures – is not an alliance, because it does not involve a commitment to mutual defence. Thus, the Strategic Arms Reduction Talks (START) Treaty or the 1972 Agreement on Prevention of Incidents at Sea were not alliances, even though they involved cooperation on important security issues.

Similarly, an alliance is not a collective-security agreement. A collective-security arrangement is an inclusive institution: it commits the members to oppose any act of aggression, even one committed by one of its members. By contrast, alliances are exclusive institutions: they entail a commitment to support the other members against states outside the community. Although members of an alliance may also be part of a collective security organisation and may engage in other forms of security cooperation, failure to keep these concepts distinct can lead to misleading analyses and muddy policy-making.[3]

Why do alliances end?

There are several reasons why an existing alliance will erode or dissolve. This article assumes that membership in an alliance entails some costs – for instance, joining an alliance usually reduces a state's autonomy. Accordingly, states will be reluctant to bear these costs if the alliance no longer serves a useful purpose. What sorts of changes might lead states to rethink their alliance commitments?

Changing perceptions of threat

Alliances are most commonly regarded as a response to an external threat. The level of threat is a function of relative power, geographic proximity, offensive capabilities and perceived intentions; other things being equal, an increase in any of these factors will raise the level of threat that a state poses to others. States usually join forces in order to balance against the greatest threat(s) they face, although revisionist states and especially weak states will sometimes 'bandwagon' by allying with a strong or aggressive power.[4]

It follows that alliances will dissolve whenever there is a significant shift in the level of threat that its members face. This sort of shift can occur for a number of different reasons. The most obvious mechanism is a change in the balance of power. An existing alliance is likely to dissolve if the states that posed the original threat become much weaker, because the members of the alliance will have less need for external support. This tendency explains why wartime alliances usually dissolve once victory is won and forms the basis for the belief that NATO will gradually dissolve now that the Soviet threat has evaporated.[5] By the same logic, alliances are also likely to dissolve if one of its members becomes significantly stronger, both because the rising power will have less need for allied support and because the other members may begin to view it as a threat to their security.

Second, an alliance will be prone to deteriorate if the members revise their beliefs about other states' intentions. In particular, if an alliance's members become convinced that their adversaries are not as bellicose as they once feared, or if an alliance member becomes increasingly aggressive, then the alliance itself is less likely to endure. In either case, the magnitude or identity of the main threat to be countered has shifted, triggering a corresponding shift in alliance relations.

These two elements of threat are often related: states whose power is increasing often adopt more ambitious international objectives, thereby alarming both their traditional adversaries and their current allies.[6] [...]

These same tendencies also explain why offensive alliances are generally more fragile than defensive ones. Offensive alliances form in order to attack a specific target; once the victim is defeated, the motivation for the partnership is gone and quarrels over the division of the spoils are likely. [...]

Third, even when the original threat is still present, an alliance may erode if its members acquire other means to protect their interests. Here the need for allies declines not because the external danger is gone, but because one or more members have become more capable of meeting it on their own. Such a shift may occur because the allies' capabilities are growing faster than those of their rival(s), or because changes in the nature of military technology make it more difficult for opponents to attack.[7] [...]

Declining credibility

Because alliances are formed primarily to increase their members' security, anything that casts doubt on their ability to contribute to this goal will encourage the members to re-evaluate their position. Even if the level of threat is unchanged, an alliance will become more fragile if its members begin to doubt that the existing arrangements are sufficient to guarantee their security.[8] [...]

Doubts about the efficacy of an existing alliance may emerge for at least two reasons. First, alliance members may become convinced that they lack the material capabilities to deter or defeat their opponents. If additional resources cannot be found, it may be safer to realign with the enemy or to adopt a neutral position. Weak states are more likely to act this way than strong states are, and this type of behaviour is probably most common during wartime, when the costs of being on the losing side are more apparent. [...]

Second, an alliance may dissolve if its members begin to question whether their partners are genuinely committed to providing assistance. Here the question is one of will rather than capability, and such doubts are more likely to arise when it is no longer obvious that the alliance is in every member's interest. This problem will be more severe when the allies are geographically separate, because a threat to one may not threaten the other; and when there is a large asymmetry of power among the member-states. In the latter case, the weaker members may suspect they are not very important to their more powerful partners, and will fear being abandoned if they are attacked. Skilful aggressors will take advantage of these tendencies by exaggerating their power and portraying their aims as limited in order to raise the perceived cost of resistance and to persuade potential opponents to leave individual victims to their fate.[9] [...]

Domestic politics

The hypotheses just discussed all assume that states are essentially rational actors making decisions in response to shifts in the external environment. An alternative perspective explains alliance dissolution by focusing on political processes within an existing alliance, and especially on political processes within the member states. These hypotheses fall into four main categories.

- *Demographic and Social Trends*. This category explains alliance dissolution by focusing on long-term demographic or social trends. Specifically, if an existing alliance is based to some degree on transnational links between the two societies – such as a common ethnic or cultural background, shared historical experiences and so on – then changes in the internal composition of either society will dilute this unifying force. Similarly, if two states are united by common historical origins, [...] these bonds will inevitably weaken with the passage of time.[10] [...] Such a perspective sees alliances rooted in more than just narrow calculations of power and threat, but in perceptions of a common background, values and heritage as well. If that is indeed the case, then anything that dilutes this social 'glue' could be problematic.
- *Domestic Competition*. An existing alliance may be jeopardised if influential élites decide that they can improve their internal positions by attacking the alliance itself. This problem is more likely to arise when the benefits of the alliance appear biased towards some members (thereby making it appear unfair) or if the terms of the alliance involve measures that are seen as an affront to national sovereignty. In these circumstances, curtailing or ending the alliance may yield domestic political benefits that outweigh any strategic costs. [...]

    [...] [This] suggest[s] that efforts to exploit domestic opposition will be more common when ending the alliance involves modest strategic consequences. [...] Nonetheless, [...] [it] also confirm[s] that a long-standing alliance commitment can deteriorate even when the level of threat is largely unchanged, if it comes to be seen as a domestic political liability.

- *Regime Change.* A third set of hypotheses focuses on the effects of regime change. State interests are not fixed by nature, and different groups within a given society may define these interests differently. If the composition of the government alters – through legitimate or illegitimate means – then the probability of realignment will increase. This effect will be least powerful when the change is relatively minor (for example, when one set of leaders is replaced via a legitimate election), but the impact is likely to increase when the leadership alters because of a change in the basic nature of the regime. Not only are the new leaders likely to prefer policies that differ sharply from those of their predecessors, but they will probably feel little obligation to honour prior commitments.

  Not surprisingly, these effects are especially powerful in the aftermath of a major revolution, and states that undergo a revolution are overwhelmingly likely to make new alliance arrangements. [...]

  The explanation for this pattern is easy to discern. A movement dedicated to overthrowing the regime is unlikely to view its present allies favourably, particularly if these allies are helping the regime retain power. By the same token, the regime's allies are unlikely to welcome its demise, if only because they cannot be certain how its successors will behave. For these and other reasons, relations between the new government and the regime's associates are likely to be extremely suspicious, and existing alliance commitments are unlikely to survive the transfer of power.

- *Ideological Divisions.* A final internal source of alliance dissolution is ideological conflict. A trivial version of this hypothesis blames alliance dissolution on the inevitable disagreements that arise between states espousing different ideologies. Although a grave external threat can overcome ideological antipathies temporarily [...], basic differences in values and objectives will soon drive the former allies apart once the threat is gone.

  A more interesting variation is the tendency for certain ideologies to promote conflict among states that subscribe to similar beliefs. In particular, an ideology that directs its adherents to form a single centralised movement is more likely to be divisive than unifying. The reason is simple: when each regime's legitimacy rests on ideological principles that prescribe obedience to a single central authority, they will inevitably quarrel over who should occupy the leading position. And when differences arise, as they inevitably will, the different factions will regard their own views as entirely justified and the views of their opponents as heretical. [...]

Why do alliances persist?

Hegemonic leadership

An obvious source of alliance durability is the exercise of hegemonic power by a strong alliance leader. Alliance leaders can discourage dissolution by bearing a disproportionate share of the costs, by offering material inducements to make alignment more attractive, or by threatening to punish disloyal regimes. [...]

This source of intra-alliance solidarity rests on two obvious prerequisites. The alliance leader must be strongly committed to preserving the relationship and willing to expend the effort needed to keep its allies from straying. In particular, if changes in the external environment alter the leader's desire for allies, then this source of solidarity will not be available. The alliance leader must also be significantly stronger than its potentially disloyal allies, so that it is able to bear the additional costs of enforcing compliance.

Several implications follow. First, hegemonic leadership is more likely in bipolarity, because the asymmetry of power between leaders and clients will be greater and because the bipolar rivalry gives the two leading states additional incentives to keep their allies in line.[11] Second, hegemonic leadership is most likely when the alliance leader has extensive global interests and faces a serious external threat, because this creates both a desire for allied support and an incentive to acquire influence over other states. Third, hegemonic leadership is most easily exercised against relatively weak clients, which means that this tactic will be most effective for preserving alliance ties that are relatively less valuable.[12] Finally, hegemonic leadership is not a permanent solution to strong centrifugal tendencies. Not only will major external changes affect the leader's interests – and thus its willingness to pay a disproportionate share of the alliance costs – but the additional burdens of alliance leadership will eventually erode the asymmetry of power on which such leadership depends.[13]

Preserving credibility

Alliances are more likely to persist if they have become symbols of credibility or resolve. As discussed above, an alliance is more likely to dissolve if its members begin to question their partners' reliability. To prevent this, a state with many allies may be unwilling to abandon any of them, in case this action is interpreted by its opponents (or by other allies) as a sign of deteriorating resolve. Thus, even when a particular alliance is of little intrinsic value, its members may retain it in order to avoid disturbing other commitments that they regard as more important. [...]

Domestic politics and élite manipulation

Alliances may also survive because self-interested groups in one or more countries need the alliance to support their individual self-interest, even though the alliance may not be in the interest of the larger societies of which they are a part. For example, an alliance may be created and sustained due to pressure from an ethnic group with a powerful attachment to a foreign power, or by élites with large economic interests in the allied state. [...] Similarly, military officials may defend a particular alliance either because it is central to their budgetary demands or because it has become deeply ingrained in their conception of vital interests.[14]

Detecting this source of alliance maintenance can be difficult, because special pleading by interest groups usually disguises itself with patriotic rhetoric. Moreover, the élites who lobby to maintain a particular alliance may genuinely believe that this commitment is both in their own interest and in the broader national interest. They are virtually certain to describe the commitment in terms of the latter, and it may be only with the benefit of hindsight that observers can recognise the extent to which an alliance was sustained by domestic political manipulation.

This sort of alliance will also be rare and relatively fragile, because most states cannot afford to squander resources on commitments that are no longer of value. Furthermore, political élites usually try to avoid being seen as overly loyal to a foreign power, thereby discouraging them from supporting commitments that are only of limited value. Thus, although élite manipulation can delay adjustments to new strategic conditions, it will usually be unable to prevent them. Exceptions are most likely when the state in question is extremely wealthy or secure – and can thus afford to devote resources to marginal interests – or when the costs of the commitment are relatively small.

The impact of institutionalisation

The greater the level of institutionalisation within an alliance, the more likely it is to endure despite an extensive change in the array of external threats. Here 'institution-alisation' means both the presence of formal organisations charged with performing specific intra-alliance tasks (such as military planning, weapons procurement and crisis management), and the development of formal or informal rules governing how alliance members reach collective decisions.

The level of institutionalisation can affect alliance cohesion in several distinct ways. First, if the alliance generates a large formal bureaucracy, this will create a cadre of individuals whose professional perspectives and career prospects are closely tied to maintaining the relationship. Such individuals are likely to view the alliance as intrinsi-cally desirable and will be reluctant to abandon it even when circumstances change. The longer the alliance lasts, the more numerous and influential its advocates will be. [...]

Second, a high level of institutionalisation may create capabilities that are worth keeping even after their original purpose is gone, especially if it costs less to maintain them than it did to create them in the first place.[15] [...]

This type of institutionalisation will operate most powerfully when it creates capacities that are highly adaptable. In general, flexibility will occur when the alli-ances possesses diverse capabilities – which may include military, economic and dip-lomatic assets – and when these capabilities rest on a division of labour that would be difficult to replace. Durability is also increased when the alliance's institutions facili-tate the creation of new rules and principles, thereby making it easier to adapt to new conditions.[16] [...]

The benefits of institutionalisation are bought at a price, however. High levels of institutionalisation may not lead to greater efficiency or effectiveness, especially when an elaborate decision-making process encourages stalemate or inaction. Moreover, an elaborate institutional structure may mask the degree to which the fundamental bases for the alliance are eroding. [...] The danger, of course, is that the alliance may be dead long before anyone notices, and the discovery of the corpse may come at a very incon-venient moment. [...]

Ideological solidarity, shared identities and 'security communities'

'Ideological solidarity' exists when two independent states share common political values and objectives, while continuing to regard themselves as separate political entities. Other things being equal, states will usually prefer to ally with governments whose political outlook is similar to their own and similar regimes may be willing to support each other simply because they believe that doing so contributes to promoting certain intrinsic goods, such as democracy, socialism or Islamic fundamentalism. Ideological solidarity can reduce intra-alliance conflicts, and a commitment to similar basic goals can help sustain an alliance long after its original rationale is gone.

One can also imagine an alliance that persists because its members come to see themselves as integral parts of a larger political community. Here the member-states no longer think of themselves as wholly separable units, and thus find it difficult to imagine dissolving the partnership. This sort of alliance contrasts sharply with the traditional conception of an alliance as a compact between sovereign states. When independent states form an alliance to advance separate national interests, a significant change in the balance of threats will lead each state to rethink its options. But when an alliance either reflects or creates a sense of common identity, then the entire notion of an individual 'national interest' becomes less applicable. If élites and/or publics begin to view their own society as inextricably part of a larger political community, then members will find it difficult to conceive of themselves as separate and will see their interests as identical even if the external environment changes dramatically. As a result, this sort of alliance – if alliance is the correct term – is likely to be extremely robust. [...]

Notes

1   The most extreme form of an asymmetrical alliance is a security guarantee, by which a great power agrees to protect a smaller power but neither requires nor expects its client to do much in return.

2   Robert Osgood thus suggests that 'next to accretion, the most prominent function of alliances has been to restrain and control allies', and Paul Schroeder argues that 'all alliances in some measure functioned as pacts of restraint'. But, as Schroeder's own account makes clear, the leverage that allies use to restrain each other is based largely on the importance each attaches to its partners' capabilities. The distinction between 'power aggregation' and 'mutual restraint' is therefore not a very sharp one. See Robert Osgood, *Alliances and American Foreign Policy* (Baltimore, MD: John Hopkins University Press, 1968), p. 22; and Paul W. Schroeder, 'Alliances, 1815–1945: Weapons of Power and Tools of Management', in Klaus Knorr (ed.), *Historical Dimensions of National Security Problems* (Lawrence, KS: University of Kansas Press, 1976), pp. 230–31.

3   On the distinction between inclusive and exclusive institutions, see John J. Mearsheimer, 'The False Promise of International Institutions', *International Security*, vol. 19, no. 3, Winter 1994–95; and also see Arnold Wolfers, 'Collective Defense vs. Collective Security', in Arnold Wolfers (ed.), *Alliance Policy and the Cold War* (Baltimore, MD: Johns Hopkins University Press, 1959).

4   See Stephen M. Walt, *The Origins of Alliances* (Ithaca, NY: Cornell University Press, 1987), pp. 17–33, 147–80; Walt, 'Testing Theories of Alliance Formation: The Case of Southwest Asia', *International Organization*, vol. 38, no. 2, Spring 1988; and Randall K. Schweller, 'Bandwagoning for Profit: Bringing the Revisionist State Back In', *International Security*, vol. 19, no. 1, Summer 1994. Earlier works advancing similar arguments include Robert Rothstein, *Alliances and Small Powers* (New York:

Columbia University Press, 1968), p. 52; and George Liska, *Nations in Alliance: The Limits of Interdependence* (Baltimore, MD: Johns Hopkins University Press), p. 13.

5   Pessimistic appraisals of NATO's future include John J. Mearsheimer, 'Back to the Future: Instability in Europe after the Cold War', *International Security*, vol. 15, no. 1, Summer 1990; Kenneth N. Waltz, 'The Emerging Structure of International Politics', *International Security*, vol. 18, no. 2, Autumn 1993, especially pp. 75–76; and Walt, *Origins of Alliances*, preface to paperback edition, p. vii.

6   See Robert Gilpin, *War and Change in World Politics* (Cambridge: Cambridge University Press, 1981).

7   In general, states will be less inclined to form an alliance when military technology favours the defensive, both because they have less need of allied assistance and because the costs of war will be higher. See Thomas Christenson and Jack Snyder, 'Chain Gangs and Passed Bucks: Predicting Alliance Patterns in Multipolarity', *International Organization*, vol. 44, no. 2, Spring 1990.

8   Thus Glenn Snyder points out that alliances face an unavoidable trade-off between 'abandonment' and 'entrapment'. Allies must demonstrate their value and commitment in case their partners abandon them for other arrangements. Unfortunately, a state's desire to prove its loyalty will make it easier for its allies to 'entrap' it in an undesirable or unnecessary wars. See Glenn Snyder, 'The Security Dilemma in Alliance Politics', *World Politics*, vol. 36, no. 4, July 1984.

9   Hitler and Napoleon were masters of these tactics during their early careers. By contrast, inept aggressors like Saddam Hussein can provoke otherwise unlikely coalitions through heavy-handed diplomacy and ill-timed acts of aggression.

10   Australian troops fought against Germany in both world wars, even though Germany did not threaten Australia directly in either one. According to one account, the colonies' loyalty to England was 'not one of all to one but of all to all, to the British ideal and way of life wherever it was to be found'. See James A. Williamson, *Great Britain and the Commonwealth* (London: Adam and Charles Black, 1965), pp. 180–81.

11   On the differences in alliance dynamics between bipolar and multipolar systems, see especially Glenn Snyder and Paul Diesing, *Conflict Among Nations: Bargaining, Decisionmaking, and System Structure in International Crises* (Princeton, NJ: Princeton University Press, 1977), pp. 419–29.

12   Soviet control over its Warsaw Pact allies was thus greater than US control over its allies in Western Europe, but the Warsaw Pact contributed less to the overall capabilities of the Soviet bloc than US allies contributed to NATO. See Walt, *Origins of Alliances*, chapter 8 and Appendix II.

13   This factor is a central theme of the literature on 'imperial overstretch'. See, in particular, Paul M. Kennedy, *The Rise and Fall of the Great Powers: Economic Change and Military Conflict from 1500 to 2000* (New York: Random House, 1987); and Gilpin, *War and Change in World Politics*.

14   One would therefore expect the US Navy to be especially vocal in defending present US commitments in Europe and Asia, because these commitments are central justification for a large, blue-water fleet. For a general account of how domestic political struggles can affect the definition of vital interests, see Jack L. Snyder, *Myths of Empire: Domestic Politics and International Ambition* (Ithaca, NY: Cornell University Press, 1994). For a demonstration of how enduring commitments can foster ossified strategic beliefs and impede a state's ability to adapt to new conditions,

see Charles A. Kupchan, *The Vulnerability of Empire* (Ithaca, NY: Cornell University Press, 1994).

15   Robert McCalla, 'NATO's Persistence after the Cold War', *International Organization*, vol. 50, no. 3, Summer 1996, pp. 462–63; and Celeste Wallander and Robert Keohane, 'Why Does NATO Persist? An Institutionalist Approach', unpublished manuscript, Harvard University, Cambridge, MA, March 1996.

16   See McCalla, 'Why NATO Persists', pp. 460–64; Wallander and Keohane, 'Why Does NATO Persist?', especially pp. 19–23; and John S. Duffield, 'NATO's Functions after the Cold War', *Political Science Quarterly*, vol. 109, no. 5, Winter 1994–95.

John Gerard Ruggie

MULTILATERALISM

Source: 'Multilateralism: the anatomy of an institution', *International Organization*, vol. 46, no. 3, Summer 1992, pp. 561–98.

[...] **[W]E CAN BETTER** understand the role of multilateral norms and institutions in the current international transformation by recovering the principled meanings of multilateralism from actual historical practice; by showing how and why those principled meanings have come to be institutionalized throughout the history of the modern interstate system; and by exploring how and why they may perpetuate themselves today, even as the conditions that initially gave rise to them have changed. [...]

[...] Multilateralism is a generic institutional form of modern international life, and as such it has been present from the start. The generic institutional form of multilateralism must not be confused with formal multilateral organizations, a relatively recent arrival and still of only relatively modest importance. Historically, the generic form of multilateralism can be found in institutional arrangements to define and stabilize the international property rights of states, to manage coordination problems, and to resolve collaboration problems. [...]

The meanings of multilateralism

At its core, multilateralism refers to coordinating relations among three or more states in accordance with certain principles. But what, precisely, are those principles? And to what, precisely, do those principles pertain? [...]

Let us examine [...] an institutional arrangement that is generally acknowledged to embody multilateralist principles: a collective security system. None has ever existed in pure form, but in principle the scheme is quite simple. It rests on the premise that peace is indivisible, so that a war against one state is, ipso facto, considered a war against all. The community of states therefore is obliged to respond to threatened or actual aggression, first by diplomatic means, then through economic sanctions, and finally by the collective use of force if necessary. Facing the prospect of such a community-wide response, any rational potential aggressor would be deterred and would desist. Thus, the incidence of war gradually would decline.

A collective security scheme certainly coordinates security relations among three or more states. [...] What is distinct about a collective security scheme is that it comprises, as Sir Arthur Salter put it a half-century ago, a permanent potential alliance "against the *unknown* enemy"[1] – and, he should have added, in behalf of the *unknown* victim. The institutional difference between an alliance and a collective security scheme can be simply put: in both instances, state A is pledged to come to the aid of B if B is attacked by C. In a collective security scheme, however, A is also pledged to come to the aid of C if C is attacked by B. Consequently, as G. F. Hudson points out, "A cannot regard itself as the ally of B more than of C, because theoretically it is an open question whether, if an act of war should occur, B or C would be the aggressor. In the same way B has indeterminate obligations towards A and C, and C towards A and B, and so on with a vast number of variants as the system is extended to more and more states."[2] [...]

We are now in a position to be more precise about the core meaning of multilateralism. Keohane has defined institutions, generically, as "persistent and connected sets of rules, formal and informal, that prescribe behavioural roles, constrain activity, and shape expectations."[3] Very simply, the term "multilateral" is an adjective that modifies the noun "institution." Thus, multilateralism depicts a *generic institutional form* in international relations. How does multilateral modify institution? Our illustrations suggest that multilateralism is an institutional form which coordinates relations among three or more states on the basis of "generalized" principles of conduct – that is, principles which specify appropriate conduct for a class of actions, without regard to the particularistic interests of the parties or the strategic exigencies that may exist in any specific occurrence. MFN treatment is a classic example in the economic realm: it forbids discrimination among countries producing the same product. Its counterpart in security relations is the requirement that states respond to aggression whenever and wherever it occurs – whether or not any specific instance suits their individual likes and dislikes. [...]

Two corollaries follow from our definition of multilateralism. First, generalized organizing principles logically entail an indivisibility among the members of a collectivity with respect to the range of behavior in question. Depending on circumstances, that indivisibility can take markedly different forms, ranging from the physical ties of railway lines that the collectivity chooses to standardize across frontiers, all the way to the adoption by states of the premise that peace is indivisible. But note that indivisibility here is a *social construction*, not a technical condition: in a collective security scheme, states behave as if peace were indivisible and thereby make it so. [...] Second, [...] successful cases of multilateralism in practice appear to generate among their members what Keohane has called expectations of "diffuse reciprocity."[4] That is to say, the arrangement is expected by its members to yield a rough equivalence of benefits in the aggregate and over time. [...]

The obvious next issue to address is the fact that, as Keohane points out, the generic concept of international institution applies in practice to many different types of institutionalized relations among states.[5] So too, therefore, does the adjective multilateral: the generic attribute of multilateralism, that it coordinates relations among three or more states in accordance with generalized principles of conduct, will have different specific expressions depending on the type of institutionalized relations to which it pertains. Let us examine some instances. Common usage in the literature distinguishes among three institutional domains of interstate relations: international orders, international regimes, and international organizations. Each type can be, but need not be, multilateral in form. [...]

[...] An "open" or "liberal" international economic order is multilateral in form [...]. The New Economic Order of the Nazis was not [...], and neither was the European security order crafted by Bismarck. The concept of multilateralism here refers to the constitutive rules that order relations in given domains of international life – their architectural dimension, so to speak. Thus, the quality of "openness" in an international economic order refers to such characteristics as the prohibition of exclusive blocs, spheres, or similar barriers to the conduct of international economic relations. The corresponding quality in an international security order – the quality that would cause it to be described as "collective" – is the condition of equal access to a common security umbrella. To the extent that the characteristic condition or conditions are met, the order in question may be said to be multilateral in form. In short, multilateralism here depicts the character of an overall order of relations among states; definitionally it says nothing about *how* that order is achieved.

A regime is more concrete than an order. Typically, the term "regime" refers to a functional or sectoral component of an order. Moreover, the concept of regime encompasses more of the "how" question than does the concept of order in that, broadly speaking, the term "regime" is used to refer to common, deliberative, though often highly asymmetrical means of conducting interstate relations. [...] But while there is a widespread assumption in the literature that all regimes are, ipso facto, multilateral in character, this assumption is egregiously erroneous. For example, [...] it is entirely possible to imagine the emergence of regimes between *two* states – super-power security regimes, for example, were a topic of some discussion in the 1980s[6] – but such regimes by definition would not be multilateral either. In sum, what makes a regime a *regime* is that it satisfies the definitional criteria of encompassing principles, norms, rules, and decision-making procedures around which actor expectations converge. But in and of themselves, those terms are empty of substance. What makes a regime *multilateral* in form, beyond involving three or more states, is that the substantive meanings of those terms roughly reflect the appropriate generalized principles of conduct. [...]

Finally, formal international organizations are palpable entities with headquarters and letterheads, voting procedures, and generous pension plans. [...] But, again, their relationship to the concept of multilateralism is less self-evident than is sometimes assumed. Two issues deserve brief mention. The first issue, though it may be moot at the moment, is that there have been international organizations that were not multilateral in form. [...] The second issue is more problematic even today. There is a common tendency in the world of actual international organizations, and sometimes in the academic community, to equate the very phenomenon of multilateralism with the universe of multilateral organizations or diplomacy. [...] [D]efinitionally, "multilateral organization" is a separate and distinct type of institutionalized behavior, defined by such generalized decision-making rules as voting or consensus procedures.

In sum, the term "multilateral" is an adjective that modifies the noun institution. What distinguishes the multilateral form from other forms is that it coordinates behavior among three or more states on the basis of generalized principles of conduct. Accordingly, any theory of international institutions that does not include this qualitative dimension of multilateralism is bound to be a fairly abstract theory and one that is silent about a crucial distinction within the repertoire of international institutional forms. Moreover, for analytic purposes, it is important not to (con)fuse the very meaning of multilateralism with any one particular institutional expression of it, be it an international order, regime, or organization. Each can be, but need not be, multilateral in form. In addition, the multilateral form should not be equated with universal geographical scope; the attributes of multilateralism characterize relations within specific collectivities that may and often do fall short of the whole universe of nations. Finally, it should be kept in mind that these are formal definitions, not empirical descriptions of actual cases, and we would not expect actual cases to conform fully to the formal definitions. [...]

Notes

1   Arthur Salter, *Security* (London: Macmillan, 1939), p. 155; emphasis in original.

2   See G. F. Hudson, "Collective Security and Military Alliances," in Herbert Butterfield and Martin Wight, eds., *Diplomatic Investigations* (Cambridge, Mass.: Harvard University Press, 1968), pp. 176–77. See also Charles A. Kupchan and Clifford A. Kupchan, "Concerts, Collective Security, and the Future of Europe," *International Security* 16 (Summer 1991), pp. 114–61.

3   Robert O. Keohane, "Multilateralism: An Agenda for Research," *International Journal* 45 (Autumn 1990), p. 732.

4   Robert O. Keohane, "Reciprocity in International Relations," *International Organization* 40 (Winter 1986), pp. 1–27.

5   Robert O. Keohane, "International Institutions: Two Approaches," *International Studies Quarterly* 32 (December 1988), pp. 379–96.

6   Steve Weber predicted the emergence of a superpower security regime in "Realism, Detente, and Nuclear Weapons," *International Organization* 44 (Winter 1990), pp. 55–82. Robert Jervis discussed the possibility in two of his works: "Security Regimes," in Krasner, *International Regimes*, pp. 173–94; and "From Balance to Concert: A Study of International Security Cooperation," *World Politics* 38 (October 1985), pp. 58–79.

Robert Jervis

REGIMES

Source: 'Security regimes', *International Organization*, vol. 36, no. 2, Spring 1982, pp. 357–78.

BY A SECURITY regime I mean, [...] those principles, rules, and norms that permit nations to be restrained in their behavior in the belief that others will reciprocate. This concept implies not only norms and expectations that facilitate cooperation, but a form of cooperation that is more than the following of short-run self-interest. [...]

* * *

Conditions for forming a security regime

What conditions are most propitious for the formation and maintenance of a security regime? First, the great powers must want to establish it – that is, they must prefer a more regulated environment to one in which all states behave individualistically. This means that all must be reasonably satisfied with the status quo and whatever alterations can be gained without resort to the use or threat of unlimited war, as compared with the risks and costs of less restrained competition. One could not have formed a security regime with [...] a state that sought objectives incompatible with those of the other important states and that would not have been willing to sacrifice those objectives for a guarantee that the others would leave it secure in the borders it had attained.

Second, the actors must also believe that others share the value they place on mutual security and cooperation [...]. In principle this is simple enough; in practice, determining whether others are willing to forgo the chance of forcible expansion is rarely easy. Indeed, decision makers probably overestimate more than underestimate others' aggressiveness.[1] This second condition is not trivial: in several cases security regimes may have been ruled out not by the fact that a major power was an aggressor but by the fact that others incorrectly perceived it as an aggressor.

Third, and even more troublesome, even if all major actors would settle for the status quo, security regimes cannot form when one or more actors believe that security is best provided for by expansion. Statesmen may deny that moderate and cooperative policies can protect them. This belief may be rooted in a general analysis of politics that is common in energetic powers: "That which stops growing begins to rot," in the words of a minister of Catherine the Great.[2] [...]

The fourth condition for the formation of a regime is a truism today: war and the individualistic pursuit of security must be seen as costly. If states believe that war is a good in itself (e.g., because it weeds out the less fit individuals and nations), they will not form a regime to prevent it, although it would still be possible for them to seek one that would impose certain limits on fighting. If states think that building arms is a positive good (e.g., because it supports domestic industries), there will be no incentives to cooperate to keep arms spending down. If states think that arms procurement and security policies can be designed carefully enough so that there is little chance of unnecessary wars, then a major reason to avoid individualistic policies disappears. If hostility in the security area is not believed to spill over into hostility in economic issues, or if decreased cooperation in that sphere is not viewed as a cost, then an important incentive for cooperation will be absent. While it is rare for all these conditions to be met, in some eras the major ones are, thus reducing the pressures to form security regimes.

The possibility for regimes is also influenced by variables that directly bear on the security dilemma. As I have discussed elsewhere,[3] it is not always true that individualistic measures which increase one state's security decrease that of others. It depends on whether offensive measures differ from defensive ones and on the relative potency of offensive and defensive policies. If defensive measures are both distinct and potent, individualistic security policies will be relatively cheap, safe, and effective and there will be less need for regimes. When the opposite is the case – when offensive and defensive weapons and policies are indistinguishable and when attacking is more effective than defending – status quo powers have a great need for a regime, but forming one will be especially difficult because of the strong fear of being taken advantage of. The most propitious conditions for regime formation, then, are the cases in which offensive and defensive weapons and policies are distinguishable but the former are cheaper and more effective than the latter, or in which they cannot be told apart but it is easier to defend than attack. In either of these worlds the costs or risks of individualistic security policies are great enough to provide status quo powers with incentives to seek security through cooperative means, but the dangers of being taken by surprise by an aggressor are not so great as to discourage the states from placing reliance on joint measures. [...]

The balance of power

The balance of power is clearly different [...] [but] [i]s it also a regime? The answer turns on whether the restraints on state action it involves are norms internalized by the actors or arise from the blocking actions of others and the anticipation of such counteractions.[4] Some of the debate between Waltz and Kaplan can be seen in these terms. For Waltz each actor in the balance of power may try to maximize his power; each fails because of the similar efforts of others. The system restrains the actors rather than the actors being self-restrained. Moderation is an unintended result of the clash of narrow self-interests.[5] Although patterns recur, actors share expectations, and aberrant behavior is curbed by the international system, states do not hold back in the belief that others will do likewise and they do not seek to maintain the system when doing so would be contrary to their immediate interests. It is hard to see how the concept of regime helps explain the behavior that results.

Kaplan's view is different. The kind of balance of power that Waltz describes, Kaplan sees as unstable. As one of his students has put it, "A system containing merely growth-seeking actors will obviously be unstable; there would be no provision for balance or restraint."[6] Similarly, Kaplan points out that in his computer model, "if actors do not take system stability requirements into account, a 'balance of power' system will be stable only if some extrasystemic factor[...]prevents a roll-up of the system."[7] For Kaplan, if the system is to be moderate, the actors must also be moderate (a remarkably antisystemic view). Thus two of Kaplan's six rules call for self-restraint: "Stop fighting rather than eliminate an essential national actor," and "Permit defeated or constrained essential national actors to re-enter the system as acceptable role partners..."[8] Of most interest here is that for Kaplan these propositions not only describe how states behave, they are rules that consciously guide statesmen's actions: states exercise self-restraint. In one interpretation – and we will discuss another in the next paragraph – they do so because they seek to preserve the system.[9] This would certainly be a regime [...].

If restraint follows from the ability to predict that immoderate behavior will call up counterbalancing actions by others, does the resulting pattern form a regime? A state may forgo taking advantage of another not because it expects reciprocation, but because it fears that unless it exercises self-restraint others will see it as a menace, increase their arms, and coalesce against it. This is a possible interpretation of Kaplan's rules. He says that states obey them because, by accepting the restraints that they embody, each state is better off than it would be if it broke them: "Under the governing assumptions, states would follow these rules in order to optimize their own security. Thus there is motivation to observe the rules. [...]There is in this system a general, although not necessarily implacable, identity between short-term and long-term interests."[10]

This formulation of the rules is a happy and therefore an odd one. It posits no conflict between the narrow self-interest of each state and the maintenance of the regime.[11] The rules are self-enforcing. This is a logical possibility and can be illustrated by the incentives to follow traffic laws when traffic is heavy. Here it is to one's advantage to keep to the right and to stop when the light turns red. To do otherwise is to get hit; cheating simply does not pay irrespective of whether others cheat.[12] The matter is different when traffic is lighter and cars have more room to maneuver. Then, running a red light or cutting in front of another car does not bring automatic sanctions. Aggressive drivers want others to obey the law while they cut corners. The generally orderly and predictable pattern that facilitates driving is maintained, but they are able to get through a bit faster than the others.

In this interpretation of Kaplan's rules, the states are operating in an environment that resembles heavy traffic.[13] They do not have incentives to take advantage of others' restraint nor do they have to be unrestrained out of the fear that if they are not, others will try to take advantage of them. The dynamics of the security dilemma, the prisoners' dilemma, and public goods, which are so troublesome in situations lacking central authority, are absent. This makes for an unusual systems theory, since these dynamics are a major element in most conceptions of a system. Such a formulation blots out the possibility that all states could be best off if all were moderate, but that each would suffer badly if any of the others were not. It also denies the more likely situation in which each actor prefers taking advantage of others' restraint to mutual cooperation, but prefers mutual cooperation to unrestrained competition. A regime of mutual cooperation is then better for all than no regime, but each actor is constantly tempted to cheat, both to make competitive gains and to protect against others doing so. This is the central problem for most regimes, and indeed for the development of many forms of cooperation. Kaplan has disposed of it in a formula of words, but it is hard to see what arrangement of interests and perceptions could so easily dissolve the difficulties in actual world politics. [...]

Notes

1   Robert Jervis, *Perception and Misperception in International Politics* (Princeton: Princeton University Press, 1976), pp. 73–75, 218–20, 340–41, 350–51.
2   Quoted in Adam Ulam, *Expansion and Coexistence* (New York: Praeger, 1968), p. 5.
3   Robert Jervis, "Cooperation under the Security Dilemma," *World Politics* 30 (January 1978): 167–214.
4   For a different approach to this question, see Richard Ashley, "Balance of Power as a Political-Economic Regime," paper presented at the August 1980 meeting of the American Political Science Association.
5   Kenneth Waltz, *Theory of International Politics* (Reading, Mass.: Addison-Wesley, 1979). This corresponds to Claude's "automatic" version of the balance of power (Inis L. Claude Jr., *Power and International Relations* [New York: Random House, 1962], pp. 43–47). Morton Kaplan also expresses this view in one paragraph of his "Balance of Power, Bipolarity, and Other Models of International Systems" (*American Political Science Review* 51 [September 1957], p. 690), but this paragraph is not repeated in *System and Process in International Politics* (New York: Wiley, 1957) and, as we shall discuss below, is inconsistent with his analysis there.
6   Donald Reinken, "Computer Explorations of the 'Balance of Power,'" in *New Approaches to International Relations*, ed. by Morton Kaplan (New York: St. Martin's, 1968), p. 469. This corresponds to Claude's "manually operated" balance of power (Claude, *Power and International Relations*, pp. 48–50).
7   Morton Kaplan, *Towards Professionalism in International Theory* (New York: Free Press, 1979), p. 136.
8   Kaplan, *System and Process*, p. 23.
9   Kaplan, *Towards Professionalism*, pp. 39, 73, 86. Since states rarely fight wars to the finish and eliminate defeated actors, Kaplan's arguments seem plausible. But this is to confuse result with intent. The desire to maximize power can limit wars and save fallen states. As long as each state views all the others as potential rivals, each will have to be concerned about the power of its current allies. And as long as each views current enemies as potentially acceptable alliance partners in a future war, each will have incentives to court and safeguard the power of states on the other

side. To destroy another state may be to deprive oneself of an ally in the future; to carve up a defeated power is to risk adding more strength to potential adversaries than to oneself. Of the Ottoman Empire in the early nineteenth century, a Russian diplomat said: "If the cake could not be saved, it must be fairly divided" (quoted in Edward Gulick, *Europe's Classical Balance of Power* [New York: Norton, 1967], p. 72). This has it backwards: it was because the cake could not be divided evenly that it had to be preserved. Also see Kaplan, *System and Process*, p. 28.

10   Kaplan, *Towards Professionalism*, p. 139; see also pp. 67, 135.

11   This is partly true because Kaplan excludes some of the main problems when he says that his system assumes that none of the major powers seeks to dominate the system (ibid., p. 136).

12   Thomas Schelling, *Micromotives and Macrobehavior* (New York: Norton, 1978), pp. 120–21.

13   This would seem to contradict Kaplan's argument that the international system is subsystem dominant – i.e, that the environment is not so compelling as to foreclose meaningful national choice (Kaplan, *System and Process*, p. 17).

Emanuel Adler

SECURITY COMMUNITIES

Source: 'Imagined (security) communities: cognitive regions in international relations', *Millennium: Journal of International Studies*, vol. 26, no. 2, pp. 249–77.

Security communities

[...] **IN A PIONEERING** 1957 study, [Karl] Deutsch and his associates introduced the concept of *security community*, that is, a group of people who have become integrated to the point where there is a 'real assurance that the members of that community will not fight each other physically, but will settle their disputes in some other way'.[1] According to Deutsch, security communities may be either 'amalgamated' or 'pluralistic'. In an amalgamated community, two or more (sovereign) states formally merge into an expanded state. On the other hand, a pluralistic security community retains the legal independence of separate states but integrates them to the point that the units entertain 'dependable expectations of peaceful change'.[2] A pluralistic security community develops when its members possess a compatibility of core values derived from common institutions and mutual responsiveness – a matter of mutual identity and loyalty, a sense of 'we-ness', or a 'we-feeling' among states.[3]

More recently, Michael Barnett and I have redefined the concept of pluralistic security communities as those 'transnational regions comprised of sovereign states whose people maintain dependable expectations of peaceful change'.[4] Furthermore, we used the following criteria for distinguishing between loosely and tightly coupled pluralistic security communities: the depth of trust between states, the nature and degree of institutionalisation of the governance system of the region, as well as whether states reside in formal anarchy or are on the verge of transforming it. A 'loosely coupled' pluralistic security community maintains the minimal definitional properties just mentioned. 'Tightly coupled' pluralistic security communities, on the other hand, possess a system of rule that lies somewhere between a sovereign state and a centralised regional government. This system is something of a post-sovereign system, comprised of common supranational, transnational, and national institutions, and some form of a collective security system.[5]

Deutsch, Barnett, and I agree that the existence of security communities does not mean that interest-based behaviour by states will end, that material factors will cease to shape interstate practices, and that security dilemmas will end. Nor do we argue that security communities transcend the mutual dependence between regional orderly security arrangements and stable economic transactions.

To date, according to these criteria, there are only a few pluralistic security communities. These include the European Union, which is tightly coupled, and the Atlantic community, which is partly tightly coupled. Scandinavia as well as the United States and Canada also form security communities. In the future, perhaps, the states that comprise the North American Free Trade Agreement (NAFTA), and the incipient regional communities in South America and in Southeast Asia (revolving around the Association of South East Asian Nations (ASEAN)) may become such communities. Given that we are discussing collective cognitive phenomena, there may be controversy about boundaries and membership. These controversies arise because states may be members of more than one community-region as a result either of their 'liminal' status (*e.g.*, Turkey) or of concentric circles of identity.[6] For example, citizens in the states of the European Free Trade Association (EFTA) 'inhabit' a shared cognitive space with citizens of the European Union, who, in turn, share some core constitutive norms with citizens of Canada and the United States. All of these states together constitute the North Atlantic security community.

Since the end of the Cold War, the states of Eastern Europe, including Russia, have been knocking at the doors of the institutions that symbolically and materially represent this North Atlantic community – the European Union, the North Atlantic Treaty Organization (NATO), the Council of Europe, and even the Western European Union (WEU). These countries are seeking an avenue through which they can exert an influence on politics in the 'West', as well as reap the benefits of Western markets by becoming full members of a political community 'where the very fact of such membership empowers those included in it to contribute to the shaping of a shared collective destiny'.[7] From the perspective of the states already organised in this North Atlantic security community, however, new members can be admitted only after the 'applicants' have learned and internalised their norms. For the original members, 'it's not enough to behave like us, you have to be one of us'. The status of 'partnership', invented by the European Union, the Council of Europe, and NATO, intends to provide a probationary status to states that wish to join the North Atlantic security community. Besides testing the intentions and institutions of applicant states, this probationary status is intended to enable members of the security community to distinguish whether applicants are making instrumental choices or are adopting the shared identity.[8] In addition, their partnership in common economic and security enterprises is meant to play a major role in changing the identities of the applicants to make them 'more like us'.

The OSCE has taken a different approach. Rather than waiting for 'the other' to change its identity and interests before it can be admitted to the security community-building institution, the OSCE has incorporated, from the outset, all states that express a political will to live up to the standards and norms of the security community, hoping to transform their identities and interests. Thus, the OSCE is building security by means of inclusion rather than exclusion or conditional future inclusion. According to Paul Schroeder, since the end of World War II, international order increasingly depends on 'associations' based on a normative consensus that 'certain kinds of international conduct[…]had to be ruled out as incompatible with [states] general security and welfare', and on the power of these associations to offer and deny 'membership' […].[9]

Liberal pluralistic security communities

[…] In communities where ideologies consecrate state goals and condone every possible means that can lead to the achievement of these goals, individuals and states know that one day their fellow community members might stab them in the back, just as they themselves, given the chance, would do. Thus, the mere fact that people in different territorial spaces share knowledge does not lead them to feel safe from organised violence. In other words, while people within totalitarian communities may achieve shared understandings, they are most unlikely to develop mutual trust.[10] The quality of the relationship between people is crucial. Accordingly, security communities are *socially constructed* and rest on *shared practical knowledge* of the peaceful resolution of conflicts.[11] Moreover, security communities are socially constructed because shared meanings, constituted by interaction, engender collective identities.[12] They are dependent on communication, discourse, and interpretation, as well as on material environments.

Practical shared knowledge of the peaceful resolution of conflicts goes a long way in explaining why the majority of existing security communities developed out of *liberal* community-regions. This knowledge, however, characterises only parts of the world, is associated to collective historical experiences, and is related to British hegemony in the nineteenth century and American hegemony in the twentieth century, which helped diffuse and institutionalise liberal values.[13]

Practical liberal knowledge of the peaceful resolution of disputes is not just institutionalised in the memories of élites, but it is also being continually reconstituted through the dense networks of relationships among civil societies and their members. This knowledge becomes an identity marker that helps to create the boundaries between 'us' and 'them'. In other words, liberal community-regions become security communities because of intersubjective understandings among people, their shared sense of identity, and their common notion that they inhabit a non-territorial region, or space, where, being *at home*, they can feel safe.[14] Accordingly, in theory, it is possible to identify a liberal community-region without it being a security community, but it is very likely to become a security community.

However, since security communities are socially constructed, non-liberal community regions may develop into security communities. First, liberal international institutions may socialise non-liberal states into adopting and institutionalising 'selected' liberal practices. Second, non-liberal ideologies – for example, a shared ideology of development perhaps similar to that pursued by Southeast Asian states – may promote a joint project characterised by increasing interdependence and the development of common institutions. Such a project might conceivably promote collective purposes around which emerge a shared identity and, thereafter, dependable expectations of peaceful change.[15] However, liberal and non-liberal community-regions cannot become security communities unless their shared knowledge of the peaceful settlement of disputes is institutionalised in some kind of rule of law or regulation structure that generates trust – 'the expectation that another's behaviour will be predictably friendly'.[16]

In liberal democracies, for example, this practical intersubjective knowledge is part of a 'civic culture',[17] whose concepts of role of government, legitimacy, duties of citizenship, and the rule of law constitute the identities of individuals.[18] The behaviour of member-states in a pluralistic security community reproduces this civic culture, which, in turn, constructs a community-region civic culture. This culture further helps to constitute the identities and interests of the individuals, élites, and organisations whose interactions form the community. Unstable democracies and non-democracies are characterised by an absence of these shared understandings.[19] In a *liberal* community-region, people learn the practices and behaviour that differentiate aggressive states from peaceful states. In other words, each side develops a common knowledge of 'the other's dovishness'.[20] In this sense, the democratic nature of a state becomes an indicator of its 'dovishness'.[21] [...]

Furthermore, liberal democracies and their civic cultures encourage the creation of strong civil societies – and of transnational networks and processes – that promote community bonds and a common identity through the relatively free interpenetration of societies, particularly with regard to the movement and exchange of people, goods, and ideas.[22] [...] Moreover, social networks constituted around liberal norms facilitate the transfer of democratic norms and practices to societies that lack them.[23] [...]

Flows of private transactions in conjunction with transnational institutions (such as epistemic communities and non-governmental organisations (NGOs)) and community law (such as European Union law) can play important roles in transmitting and diffusing shared normative and causal beliefs of a civic culture. [...] International institutions – which provide a forum in which state and non-state representatives debate and bargain about their understandings and interests, and in which ideas flow back and forth between the domestic and international arenas – can play similar, if not, indeed, more important roles than civic cultures.[24] [...]

Notes

1   Karl W. Deutsch, Sidney A. Burrell, Robert A. Kann, Maurice Lee, Jr., Martin Lichterman, Raymond E. Lindgren, Francis L. Lowenheim, and Richard W. Van Wagenen, *Political Community and the North Atlantic Area* (Princeton, NJ: Princeton University Press, 1957), in note 20, p. 5.

2   Ibid., p. 6.

3   Ibid., pp. 36 and 66–67. By 'we-feeling', Deutsch refers to cognition rather than affection.

4   Emanuel Adler and Michael Barnett, 'Governing Anarchy: A Research Agenda for the Study of Security Communities', *Ethics and International Affairs* (Vol. 10, 1996), in note 2, p. 73. See also Emanuel Adler and Michael Barnett (eds.), *Security Communities* (Cambridge: Cambridge University Press, forthcoming 1998).

5   Adler and Barnett, ibid., in note 2, p. 73.

6   Barry Buzan, 'From International System to International Society: Structural Realism and Regime Theory Meet the English School', *International Organization* (Vol. 47, No. 3, 1992), p. 339.

7   Ronald Beiner, *What's the Matter With Liberalism* (Berkeley, CA: University of California Press, 1992), p. 105. See also Andrew Linklater, 'Citizenship and Sovereignty in the Post-Westphalian State', *European Journal of International Relations* (Vol. 2, No. 1, 1996), in note 20.

8   With respect to NATO, see Joseph Lepgold, 'The Next Step Toward a More Secure Europe', *The Journal of Strategic Studies* (Vol. 17, No. 4, 1994), pp. 7–26.

9   Paul W. Schroeder, 'The New World Order: A Historical Perspective', *The Washington Quarterly* (Vol. 17, No. 2, 1994), p. 30.

10 See Barbara A. Misztal, *Trust in Modern Societies* (Cambridge: Polity Press, 1996).

11 *Constructivism* denotes the view that social reality is constructed when individuals come into contact with each other and interact. Constructivists assert that to understand the social world, one must begin with shared understanding and knowledge and, in particular, practices, and investigate how they help to define the institutional and material worlds. Cognitive and institutional structures give meaning to the material world. They provide people with reasons for the way things are and indications as to how they should use their material capabilities and power. In turn, changes in the identities and interests of the agents involved continually transform cognitive and institutional structures. Constructivists do not deny the reality of the material world. They merely point out that the manner in which the material world shapes, modifies, and affects human interaction, which in turn affects it, depends on prior dynamic epistemic and normative interpretations of the material world. See Emanuel Adler, 'Seizing the Middle Ground: Constructivism in World Politics', *European Journal of International Relations* (Vol. 3, No. 3, 1997), pp. 319–63; Friedrich Kratochwil, *Rules, Norms, and Decisions* (Cambridge: Cambridge University Press, 1989); John G. Ruggie, 'Territoriality and Beyond: Problematizing Modernity in International Relations', *International Organization* (Vol. 47, No. 1, 1993), in note 2; and Alexander Wendt, 'Collective Identity Formation and the International State', *American Political Science Review* (Vol. 88, No. 2, 1994), in note 18. For an alternative view on the construction of security communities, see Ole Weaver, 'Insecurity, Security, and Asecurity in the West European Non-War Community', in Adler and Barnett (eds.), op. cit., in note 28.

12 Wendt, op. cit., in note 8.

13 For the ideational effect of American hegemony, see John G. Ruggie, 'Multilateralism: The Anatomy of an Institution', in John G. Ruggie (ed.), *Multilateralism Matters: The Theory and Praxis of an Institutional Form* (New York, NY: Columbia University Press, 1993), pp. 3–47.

14 For the 'democratic peace' thesis, see Michael W. Doyle, 'Kant, Liberal Legacies, and Foreign Affairs: Part 1' *Philosophy and Public Affairs* (Vol. 12, No. 3, 1983), pp. 205–35, and Bruce Russett, *Grasping the Democratic Peace* (Princeton, NJ: Princeton University Press, 1993).

15 See Amitav Acharya, 'Collective Identity and Conflict Resolution in Southeast Asia', in Adler and Barnett (eds.), op. cit., in note 28.

16 Ronald Inglehart, *Culture Shift in Advanced Industrial Societies* (Princeton, NJ: Princeton University Press, 1990), pp. 396–97. See also Diego Gambetta (ed.), *Trust: Making and Breaking Cooperative Relations* (New York, NY: Blackwell, 1988).

17   Gabriel A. Almond and Sidney Verba, *The Civic Culture: Political Attitudes and Democracy in Five Nations* (Boston, MA: Little and Brown, 1963).

18   Robert D. Putnam, *Making DemocracyWork: Civic Traditions in Modern Italy* (Princeton, NJ: Princeton University Press, 1993).

19   Ibid.

20   Harvey Starr, 'Democracy and War: Choice, Learning and Security Communities', *Journal of Peace Research* (Vol. 29, No. 2, 1992), in note 24, p. 210.

21   Ibid., and Bruce Bueno de Mesquita and David Lalman, *War and Reason* (New Haven, CT:Yale University Press, 1992), Chapter 4, in note 24.

22   See, for example, Patricia Chilton, 'Mechanisms of Change: Social Movements, Transnational Coalitions, and the Transformation Processes in Eastern Europe', in Thomas Risse-Kappen (ed.), *Bringing Transnational Relations Back In: Non-State Actors, Domestic Structures and International Institutions* (Cambridge: Cambridge University Press, 1995), pp. 189–226.

23   Chilton, ibid., in note 47, and Daniel Thomas, 'Social Movements and International Institutions: A Preliminary Framework' (paper presented at the annual meeting of the American Political Science Association, Washington, DC, 1991).

24   Emanuel Adler and Michael Barnett, 'A Framework for the Study of Security Communities', in Adler and Barnett (eds.), op. cit., in note 28.

Adam Roberts

INTERVENTIONISM

Source: 'NATO's "Humanitarian War" over Kosovo', *Survival*, vol. 41, no. 3, Autumn 1999, pp. 102–23.

THE 11-WEEK BOMBING campaign conducted by NATO in spring 1999 against the Federal Republic of Yugoslavia (FRY) has many claims to uniqueness. It was the first sustained use of armed force by the NATO alliance in its 50-year existence; the first time a major use of destructive armed force had been undertaken with the stated purpose of implementing UN Security Council resolutions but without Security Council authorisation; the first major bombing campaign intended to bring a halt to crimes against humanity being committed by a state within its own borders; and the first bombing campaign of which it could be claimed that it had on its own, and without sustained land operations, brought about a major change of policy by the target government.

NATO leaders were reluctant to call their action 'war'. However, it was war – albeit war of a peculiarly asymmetric kind. It indisputably involved large-scale and opposed use of force against a foreign state and its armed forces. Because it was justified principally in terms of stopping actual and anticipated Serb killings and expulsions in the Serbian province of Kosovo, the campaign was sometimes colloquially called a 'humanitarian war'. Whatever the nomenclature, *Operation Allied Force* marked a high point in the increasing emphasis on human rights and humanitarian issues which has been a striking feature of international relations in the post-1945 era. For theoreticians of international relations it represented a further remarkable twist in the strange and long-running association between the supposedly hard-nosed and 'realist' factor of force, and the supposedly soft and 'idealist' factor of international humanitarian and human-rights norms.

The date of 24 March 1999 was doubly significant for human rights in international relations. It was the day when the Appeal Chamber of the UK House of Lords, following a second hearing of the matter, announced its decision that, in principle, Chilean ex-President Augusto Pinochet could be extradited to Spain. This ruling was a landmark in the evolution of the idea that there are some crimes so extreme that a leader responsible for them, despite the principle of sovereign immunity, can be extradited and tried in foreign courts. NATO's *Operation Allied Force* was also launched on 24 March. The operation was announced at the start as based on the idea (closely related to the one advanced in the Pinochet decision) that there are some crimes so extreme that a state responsible for them, despite the principle of sovereignty, may properly be the subject of military intervention.

The international human-rights movement – a huge array of individuals, non-governmental organisations (NGOs), inter-governmental bodies and more – was deeply divided over *Operation Allied Force*. This reaction was not surprising: the human-rights movement was naturally unhappy to see human rights and international humanitarian law become a basis for initiating war. In particular it was doubtful about the air campaign, because in the short term it failed to stop, and probably even exacerbated, extreme violence against Kosovars. [...]

* * *

[...] [T]here was an international legal basis for the action taken by NATO over Kosovo. The two main planks of the legal basis (one consisting of requirements in Security Council resolutions, the other drawing on general international law), both placed central emphasis on the protection of the inhabitants of Kosovo. However, any justification of 'humanitarian intervention' along these lines is subject to four important caveats.

- Since no existing international legal instrument provides explicitly for forcible military intervention within a state on humanitarian grounds, neither of the main arguments indicated above gives an incontestable basis for the NATO action. It is thus in the nature of things that different individuals and states see the matter differently.

- The question of the military means pursued by NATO to secure the proclaimed political and humanitarian ends was bound to affect judgements about the legality of the operation. NATO's reliance on bombing did give rise to questions (discussed further below) about its appropriateness so far as protecting the inhabitants of Kosovo was concerned, and about its conformity with the laws of war.

- The argument that a regional alliance has a general right and even a duty to act as vigilante for UN Security Council resolutions, while it may have the considerable merit of ensuring that such resolutions are taken seriously, could also create a risk of undermining international inhibitions against the use of force.

- Questions were inevitably raised about the selectivity of the action taken by NATO. The obvious question raised by Serbs was why NATO had acted over Kosovo when nothing had been done to stop the Croatian government's ethnic cleansing of Serbs from the Krajina in 1995: that episode has been conveniently expunged from Western collective memories, but it is not forgotten in Belgrade, where the refugees from Croatia are still a conspicuous presence. There were many other equally pertinent questions, not least why NATO had not acted with equal resolve against the FRY when Yugoslav forces had attacked Dubrovnik and Vukovar in Croatia in 1991–92.

The motives for the NATO military action included many elements which were not purely humanitarian, and not exclusively concerned with Kosovo. Apart from elements [such as] [...] already mentioned (guilt over past inaction regarding Bosnia, and concern over peace and security in the region generally), factors influencing the decisions of NATO states included their reluctance to accept large numbers of refugees on a permanent basis. A further key element was NATO's credibility: having become deeply involved in 1998 in international diplomacy regarding Kosovo, particularly in making military threats to Belgrade and in underwriting agreements, NATO would indeed have lost credibility had it not acted after it became apparent that agreements were not being observed. Needless to say, other more sinister motives were attributed to NATO. [...]

The available evidence suggests that the critical considerations impelling NATO to take action were those of humanity and credibility. [...]

The reliance on air-power

The NATO campaign was overwhelmingly in the air. [...]

How did it happen that the ancient and ever-contested idea of 'humanitarian intervention' came to be associated with bombing? [...] In the long history of legal debates about humanitarian intervention, there has been a consistent failure to address directly the question of the methods used in such interventions. It is almost as if the labelling of an intervention as 'humanitarian' provides sufficient justification in itself, and there is no need to think further about the aims of the operation or the means employed – or indeed to understand the society in which the intervention occurs. [...]

[...] A problem which has stalked all interventions with a basically humanitarian purpose in the 1990s is that the Western powers that are willing to intervene militarily are reluctant to accept the risk of casualties. This leads to particular modes of operation, such as hesitant and temporary military involvements, and reliance on air-power, that may conflict with the supposed humanitarian aims of the operation. [...]

* * *

The laws of war

While most of the NATO bombing campaign was accurate and was directed at legitimate targets, certain actions did raise questions about whether NATO, in pursuing its humanitarian war, was observing all the requirements of the laws of war (international humanitarian law). These requirements overlap with, and are not necessarily antithetical to, those of military efficiency. [...]

The emphasis on air-power in this campaign, coupled with the reluctance to risk the lives of servicemen, exposed certain problems about the extent to which NATO was able to perform its military tasks effectively and to minimise damage to civilians. In particular, the use of smart weapons, and the practice of bombing from 15,000 feet, were associated with certain problems so far as the safety of civilians and of neutral states were concerned. These included:

- Collateral damage, for example in the cases in which passenger trains and buses were crossing bridges at the moment when bombs hit.
- Errors in identifying and attacking targets, including misidentification of the functions of particular buildings (for example, the Chinese embassy), and weapons going astray.
- Pressure to attack fixed targets such as buildings, bridges and electricity installations, because they are easier to identify and destroy by such means than are moving targets. Since most military assets are either mobile or capable of concealment and hardening, the pressure to attack fixed targets meant, in practice, pressure to attack targets whose destruction had a significant effect on the civilian population.

The damage to civilians and to neutral states which resulted from such problems do not begin to compare, in any grim comparison of losses, with the effects of the ethnic cleansing in Kosovo. Such damage may indeed be inevitable in war. Yet it is a salutary reminder that there are moral problems with the whole idea of the low-risk waging of war. A further difficulty arose from the possible environmental effects of certain NATO actions, including the release of chemicals resulting from certain air attacks, and the use of toxic materials (especially depleted uranium) in weapons and quantities of unexploded ordnance which was a serious hazard after the war.[1] [...]

* * *

[...] Many lessons will be drawn from the Kosovo action, including some hard ones about the virtues, and limits, of operating in a large and disparate alliance. At times, NATO showed the classic problem of a large international organisation in its inability to agree on more than a lowest common denominator. NATO also experienced tensions due to the fact that the US supplied about 85% of the effective power in the bombing campaign, a figure which demands reflection about European readiness for independent security policies. Only with the entry of KFOR into Kosovo in June was the imbalance in military burden-sharing visibly redressed.

During the war, the question was often raised as to whether a general doctrine justifying humanitarian intervention could be developed. As Blair said in his Chicago speech on 22 April:

> The most pressing foreign policy problem we face is to identify the circumstances in which we should get involved in other people's conflicts. Non-interference has long been considered an important principle of international order. And it is not one we would want to jettison too readily ... But the principle of non-interference must be qualified in important respects. Acts of genocide can never be a purely internal matter. When oppression produces massive flows of refugees which unsettle neighbouring countries they can properly be described as 'threats to international peace and security'.[2]

Blair went on to list five major considerations which might help in decisions on 'when and whether to intervene':

First, are we sure of our case? War is an imperfect instrument of righting humanitarian distress; but armed force is sometimes the only means of dealing with dictators. Second, have we exhausted all diplomatic options? We should always give peace every chance, as we have in the case of Kosovo. Third, on the basis of a practical assessment of the situation, are there military operations we can sensibly and prudently undertake? Fourth, are we prepared for the long term? In the past we talked too much of exit strategies. But having made a commitment we cannot simply walk away once the fight is over; better to stay with moderate numbers of troops than return for repeat performances with large numbers. And finally, do we have national interests involved? The mass expulsion of ethnic Albanians from Kosovo demanded the notice of the rest of the world. But it does make a difference that this is taking place in such a combustible part of Europe.

Subsequent attempts to develop any general doctrine regarding the circumstances in which humanitarian intervention may be justified have run into predictable difficulties. Two enduring and inescapable problems are: first, that most states in the international community are nervous about justifying in advance a type of operation which might further increase the power of major powers, and might be used against them; and second, NATO members and other states are uneasy about creating a doctrine which might oblige them to intervene in a situation where they were not keen to do so.

Operation Allied Force will contribute to a trend towards seeing certain humanitarian and legal norms inescapably bound up with conceptions of national interest.[3] It may occupy a modest place as one halting step in a developing but still contested practice of using force in defence of international norms.

However, the unique circumstances in which *Operation Allied Force* took place, and the problems which the campaign exposed, militate against drawing simple conclusions about humanitarian intervention or about the capacity of bombing alone to induce compliance. In the international community, the NATO campaign was the subject of deep differences of opinion, based on diverging perceptions and interests which are not going to change suddenly. The fact that the campaign failed in the intended manner to avert a humanitarian disaster in the short term, even though it did eventually stop it, makes it a questionable model of humanitarian intervention. The uncomfortable paradox involved – that a military campaign against ethnic cleansing culminated in a settlement in which the majority of Serbs resident in Kosovo departed – must reinforce the sense that humanitarian operations cannot suddenly transform a political landscape full of moral complexity. The advanced-weapons-systems bombing, although extraordinarily accurate, gave rise to serious questions about its effectiveness against armed forces and its impact on civilians. The reluctance of NATO governments to risk the lives of their forces, the difficulty in developing a credible threat of land operations and, above all, the narrowness of the line between success and failure, suggest that the many lessons to be drawn from these events should be on a more modest scale than any grand general doctrines of humanitarian intervention.[...]

Notes

1   See especially Mark Fineman, 'Serbia's Nightmare: The Toxic Aftermath of War', *International Herald Tribune*, 7 July 1999, pp. 1, 5; and Dan Eggen, 'Bombs that Still Kill: NATO "Duds" in Kosovo', *International Herald Tribune*, 20 July 1999, p. 4. The environmental effects of warfare have been of considerable concern in recent years, due partly to the salience of the matter in the 1990–91 Gulf War. See, for example, the study in the US Naval War College 'Blue Book' series, Richard J. Grunawalt, John E. King and Ronald S. McClain (eds), *Protection of the EnvironmentDuring Armed Conflict*, US Naval War College, International Law Studies, vol. 69 (Newport, RI: Naval War College, 1996).

2   Tony Blair's speech in Chicago on 22 April 1999 ('Doctrine of the International Community'), is available at: http://dR.www.number-10.gov.uk/public/info/index.html.

3   A point made with particular force by Joseph Nye, 'Redefining the National Interest', *Foreign Affairs*, vol. 78, no. 4, July/August 1999, pp. 22–35.

Robert A. Pape

ECONOMIC SANCTIONS

Source: 'Why economic sanctions do not work', *International Security*, vol. 22, no. 2, Fall 1997, pp. 90–136.

Defining economic sanctions

STATES USE ECONOMIC pressure against other states for a variety of political purposes. There are two main categories of international economic weapons – trade restrictions and financial restrictions – each of which can be employed with varying intensity and scope. For example, trade may be suspended completely or tariffs merely raised slightly; financial flows may be wholly or partially blocked or assets seized; the entire opposing economy may be targeted or just one critical sector. Although the same economic weapons can be employed in support of different political goals, different political purposes yield different strategies. There are three main strategies of international economic pressure: economic sanctions, trade wars, and economic warfare.

Economic sanctions seek to lower the aggregate economic welfare of a target state by reducing international trade in order to coerce the target government to change its political behavior. Sanctions can coerce either directly, by persuading the target government that the issues at stake are not worth the price, or indirectly, by inducing popular pressure to force the government to concede, or by inducing a popular revolt that overthrows the government, resulting in the establishment of a government that will make the concessions.[1] Although coercers may suspend trade either comprehensively or partially, economic sanctions characteristically aim to impose costs on the economy as a whole. Partial trade suspensions are generally adopted either as part of a calculated strategy to signal the potential of still worse pain to come if the target fails to comply, or as a second-best measure because more pressing domestic or international political constraints rule out comprehensive pressure. Accordingly, the most important measure of the intensity of economic sanctions is aggregate gross national product (GNP) loss over time.

A trade war is when a state threatens to inflict economic harm or actually inflicts it in order to persuade the target state to agree to terms of trade more favorable to the coercing state.[2] Because trade wars seek to redirect the course of ongoing trade relations, they typically occur between established trade partners. Unlike economic sanctions, trade wars do not seek to influence the target state's political behavior but rather its international economic policies, and those only to the extent that they affect the wealth of the coercing state. When the United States threatens China with economic punishment if it does not respect human rights, that is an economic sanction; when punishment is threatened over copyright infringement, that is a trade war. Accordingly, the most important measure of the pressure of a trade war is the change in the price that the target state receives (or must pay) for an affected good or service.

Economic warfare seeks to weaken an adversary's aggregate economic potential in order to weaken its military capabilities, either in a peacetime arms race or in an ongoing war. This strategy assumes that the greater a state's overall productive capacity, the greater its ability to produce technologically sophisticated weapons and to mobilize people and wealth for military use. Unlike the first two strategies, economic warfare does not seek to coerce the target by inflicting economic pain. To the extent that it coerces at all, it does so by persuading the target state that its reduced military strength makes certain political objectives unattainable.[3] As a result, the most important measure of the pressure of economic warfare is the change in military production.[4]

Although some might use the term "economic sanctions" to apply to all three strategies, this is not the common practice, because it would be conceptually unwieldy and it would confuse policymakers about what they most want to know: when the strategy of economic sanctions can change another state's behavior without resorting to military force.[5] [...]

Accepting this looser standard for sanctions success would be a mistake for two reasons. First, the determinants of success for different categories of goals are not likely to be the same, and thus require separate theoretical investigations. A standard of success that lumps them all together risks losing information essential to building such theories. For example, knowing whether a certain type of economic sanction often helps the coercer government's standing in the polls tells us little about whether the same sanctions, or other instruments, would be likely to succeed in coercing target states to change their political behavior. Theories of the determinants of success in trade disputes or economic warfare or of international economic threats as a domestic political tool can and should be constructed, but they are not the same as a theory of economic sanctions. Second, beyond a certain point, excessively loose operationalization of dependent variables not only hinders theory building but departs from science altogether. Baldwin argues that the mere imposition of economic sanctions should automatically qualify as a success: "to make the target of an influence attempt pay a price for non-compliance is to be at least partially successful."[6] If failure is defined to be impossible, the dependent variable cannot vary and the theory cannot be falsified. [...]

Evaluating the record of economic sanctions requires a standard of success. Given their coercive purpose, economic sanctions should be credited with success if they meet three criteria: (1) the target state conceded to a significant part of the coercer's demands;[7] (2) economic sanctions were threatened or actually applied before the target changed its behavior; and (3) no more-credible explanation exists for the target's change of behavior. The most common alternative explanations involve the use of force (including military conquest), coercion by the threat of overwhelming military force, and covert use of force, such as foreign-sponsored assassinations and coups. Determining rules for how much credit for the outcome should be assigned to economic sanctions in these mixed cases depends on the type of military force that determined the outcome.

Military conquest, when it occurs, is always a more credible explanation than economic sanctions because the target state's failure to concede before military defeat is in itself evidence of the failure of coercion.[8] Showing that economic pressure weakened the target's military capability and thus accelerated military conquest would count as a success for economic warfare; however, it does not count as evidence that the target state would have conceded had force not been used or if just a little more economic pain had been inflicted. Such cases may tell us that economic pressure can make military force more effective, but they do not imply that economic sanctions alone can achieve comparable goals.

Change of government by assassination or military coup is also evidence of the failure of coercion against the deposed government. Deciding if economic sanctions should be assigned any causal weight depends on whether economic sanctions led to a change in the target state's regime without the sanctioning state either making other, more direct assurances to the coup plotters to inspire them to act or providing them the necessary means to succeed.

Distinguishing coercion by military threat from economic coercion is the most difficult task, because it requires assessing how the target weighed both pressures. The critical evidence is the timing of concessions in relation to specific military threats or economic sanctions. If the concessions were made long after economic sanctions were threatened or imposed but shortly after a military threat, then, barring credible contemporary statements by the target state decision makers to the contrary, military force should be assumed to have determined the outcome. When economic and military threats occur nearly simultaneously, say, only days apart, then the only evidence that can disentangle the weight of these two factors is credible contemporary statements by the target state decision makers. If such statements are unavailable for these cases, they should be coded as indeterminate. [...]

* * *

Why economic sanctions will not become more important

Even if sanctions become somewhat more effective after the Cold War, they still have far to go before they can be a reliable alternative to military force. First, sanctions have been successful less than 5 percent of the time [...]. Thus the world would have to change considerably before sanctions could become a credible alternative to force. Second, it is not clear that the early burst of political cooperation among the world's leading economic powers that we saw in the early 1990s will continue. [...] Third, the key reason sanctions fail is not related to the cooperation of sanctioning states but to the nature of the target. Iraq, for example, has been subjected to the most extreme sanctions in history – 48 percent of its GNP has been eliminated by sanctions for over five years – and it has not buckled. Rather, the key reason that sanctions fail is that modern states are not fragile.[9]

Nationalism often makes states and societies willing to endure considerable punishment rather than abandon their national interests. States involved in coercive disputes often accept high costs, including civilian suffering, to achieve their objectives. Democratization further imbues individual citizens with a personal attachment to national goals. Even in the weakest and most fractured states, external pressure is more likely to enhance the nationalist legitimacy of rulers than to undermine it.[10] In some situations, advances in communication further improve the ability of governments to enhance the legitimacy of the state and its policies. Even much more severe punishment than economic sanctions can possibly inflict rarely coerces. [...] In addition, modern states can adjust to minimize their vulnerability to economic sanctions, because administrative capabilities allow states to mitigate the economic damage of sanctions through substitution and other techniques. Coercers never anticipate all the adjustments and reworking that targets can devise, including endless varieties of conservation, substitution, and more efficient methods of allocation. [...] Economic adjustment also buys time to seek alternatives, such as other trading partners or smuggling, and over time economic and political costs suffered by the sanctioner may increase. [...]

Even unpopular ruling élites can often protect themselves and their supporters by shifting the economic burden of sanctions onto opponents or disenfranchised groups. [...]

Fourth, the deductive case that greater multilateral cooperation will make economic sanctions more effective relies on two expectations: that greater cooperation will increase the economic punishment on target states and, more critically, that increased punishment will make targets more likely to concede. The second proposition is dubious. If it were valid, we should expect to find a significant correlation in past cases between economic loss to the target state and the success of sanctions [...].

Notes

1   Johann Galtung, "On the Effects of International Economic Sanctions: With Examples from the Case of Rhodesia," *World Politics*, Vol. 19, No. 3 (April 1967), pp. 380–81; and Donald L. Losman, *International Economic Sanctions: The Cases of Cuba, Israel, and Rhodesia* (Albuquerque: University of New Mexico Press, 1979), p. 1.

2   On the definition of trade wars, see John C. Conybeare, *Trade Wars: The Theory and Practice of International Commercial Rivalry* (New York: Columbia University Press, 1987), pp. 3–6, 21–28.

3   On the difference between coercion through punishment and denial, see Robert A. Pape, *Bombing to Win: Air Power and Coercion in War* (Ithaca, N.Y.: Cornell University Press, 1996), chap. 2.

4   A fourth strategy, strategic embargo, is a special case of economic warfare; rather than attacking the entire target economy, a strategic embargo denies an adversary

specific critical commodities in order to prevent or delay improvements in its military capabilities. For a comparison of economic warfare and strategic embargo, see Michael Mastanduno, *Economic Containment: CoCom and the Politics of East-West Trade* (Ithaca, N.Y.: Cornell University Press, 1992), pp. 39–52.

5   Works from the 1960s and 1970s by Galtung, Doxey, Knorr, and Losman all evaluate the success or failure of economic sanctions based on their coercive impact. Galtung, "On the Effect of International Economic Sanctions," p. 381; Margaret P. Doxey, *Economic Sanctions and International Enforcement* (New York: Oxford University Press, 1971), p. 14; Klaus Knorr, *The Power of Nations: The Political Economy of International Relations* (New York: Basic Books, 1975), p. 151; and Losman, *International Economic Sanctions*, p. 1. For equivalent formulations more recently, see Lisa L. Martin, *Coercive Cooperation: Explaining Multilateral Economic Sanctions* (Princeton, N.J.: Princeton University Press, 1992), pp. 31–32; and Makio Miyagawa, *Do Economic Sanctions Work?* (New York: St. Martin's, 1992), pp. 8–9.

6   David A. Baldwin, *Economic Statecraft* (Princeton, N.J.: Princeton University Press, 1985), p. 372.

7   Trivial gestures that do not actually change the target state's behavior in the direction demanded by the coercer do not qualify. For example, in 1956 Gamal Abdel Nasser rejected Britain and France's demand for international control of the Suez Canal and its toll revenue. His only "concession" was that foreign ships could use their own pilots, subject to the ultimate authority of an Egyptian pilot.

8   On the distinction between coercion and military victory, see Pape, *Bombing to Win*, chaps. 1 and 2.

9   For an analysis of the weaknesses of economic punishment as a coercive strategy, see Pape, *Bombing to Win*, pp. 21–27.

10   Many have credited the continuing economic sanctions against Iraq with helping to prop up an otherwise extremely unattractive regime. Hunting Mohammed Farah Aideed had the same effect on his stature in Somalia. See "Making Monkeys of the UN," *The Economist*, July 10, 1993, p. 34.

David Shearer

PRIVATE MILITARY COMPANIES

Source: 'Outsourcing war', *Foreign Policy*, no.112, Fall 1998, pp. 68–81.

FOR NEARLY THREE centuries, the accepted international norm has been that only nation-states should be permitted to fight wars. Not surprisingly, the rise of private military companies in the 1990s – and the possibility that they may view conflict as a legitimate business activity – has provoked outrage and prompted calls for them to be outlawed. The popular press has labeled these companies "mercenaries" and "dogs of war," conjuring up images of freebooting and rampaging Rambos overthrowing weak – usually African – governments. [...]

But is this depiction fair? Certainly these soldiers might meet the three most widely accepted criteria defining a mercenary: They are foreign to a conflict; they are motivated chiefly by financial gain; and, in some cases, they have participated directly in combat. They differ significantly, however, from infamous characters such as Irishman "Mad" Mike Hoare and Frenchman Bob Denard, who fought in the Congo and elsewhere in the 1960s. What most sets today's military companies apart is their approach. They have a distinct corporate character, have openly defended their usefulness and professionalism, have used internationally accepted legal and financial instruments to secure their deals, and so far have supported only recognized governments and avoided regimes unpalatable to the international community. [...]

Dismissing private-sector military personnel as little more than modern-day soldiers of fortune would not only be simplistic but would obscure the broader issues that these military companies raise. [...]

These guns for hire

Private military forces are as old as warfare itself. [...]

In the past decade, [...] the increasing inability of weak governments to counter internal violence has created a ready market for private military forces. This demand has also been fueled by a shift in Western priorities. The strategic interests of major powers in countries such as Mozambique, Rwanda, and Sierra Leone have declined with the end of the Cold War. As a result, Western countries are more reluctant to intervene militarily in weak states, and their politicians are disinclined to explain casualties to their electorates. Furthermore, Western armies, designed primarily to fight the sophisticated international conflicts envisaged by Cold War strategists, are ill equipped to tackle low-intensity civil wars, with their complicated ethnic agendas, blurred boundaries between combatants and civilians, and loose military hierarchies. The failed U.S.-led involvement in Somalia in 1993 reinforced American resolve never to enter a conflict unless vital domestic interests were at stake.

Meanwhile, UN peacekeeping efforts have fallen victim to Western governments' fears of sustaining casualties, becoming entangled in expanding conflicts, and incurring escalating costs. The number of personnel in UN operations has fallen from a peak of 76,000 in 1994 to around 15,000 today. Multilateral interventions appear increasingly likely to be limited to situations where the UN gains the consent of the warring parties rather than – as allowed under Chapter VII of the UN Charter – to be designed to enforce a peace on reluctant belligerents. Bilateral, as well as multilateral, commitments have also been trimmed. France's long-standing deployment of troops in its former African colonies, for example, has declined: French troops will be cut by 40 percent to about 5,000 by 2000. Paris has stated that it will no longer engage in unilateral military interventions in Africa, effectively creating a strategic vacuum.

The increasing inability of weak governments to counter internal violence has created a ready market for private military forces

Into this gap have stepped today's private military companies. Most such enterprises hail from South Africa, the United Kingdom, the United States, and occasionally France and Israel. They all share essentially the same goals: to improve their client's military capability, thereby allowing that client to function better in war or deter conflict more effectively. This process might involve military assessments, training, or occasionally weapons procurement. Direct involvement in combat is less common, although two companies, Executive Outcomes (EO) of South Africa and Sandline International of Great Britain, advertise their skills in this area. EO has provided training and strategic advice to the armed forces of Angola and Sierra Leone; its apartheid-era soldiers have fought in both countries.

Other companies, such as Military Professional Resources Incorporated (MPRI), a Virginia-based firm headed by retired U.S. army generals, has limited its services to training and has hired former U.S. military personnel to develop the military forces of Bosnia-Herzegovina and Croatia. Some organizations engage in more passive activities, such as protecting premises and people. The British company Defence Systems Limited, for example, guards embassies and protects the interests of corporations working in unstable areas. Other outfits provide businesses with risk analyses, and several have developed specialist expertise in resolving the kidnapping incidents that plague firms operating in Latin America.

Military companies are unfettered by political constraints. They view conflict as a business opportunity and have taken advantage of the pervasive influence of economic liberalism in the late twentieth century. They have also been quick to adapt to the complex agendas of civil wars. Their ability to operate has been enhanced by an expanded pool of military expertise made available by reductions in Western forces. Many recruits come from highly disciplined military units, such as the British Special Air Service and the South African and American special forces. Likewise, cheap and accessible Soviet-made weaponry has helped strengthen the companies' capabilities. [...]

The lure of rich resources and the risks of exploiting them in unstable areas are powerful incentives for [western mining] companies to [hire private military companies to restore order and] maintain stability in weak states. This motivation can also chime with a government's own wishes. A mining company depends on security to protect its investments; a beleaguered government buys increased security to shore up its rule, while the prospect of mining revenues can supplement its coffers. Furthermore, a military company, while strengthening its client government's military performance, protects a mining company's operations because revenues from these sources guarantee its payment. In the developing world, minerals and hardwoods may soon emerge as the currency of stability. The source of payment is a crucial difference between the intervention of a military company and that of the UN, which is funded by donors, not by the state in question. Coupling multinational companies with an external security force potentially gives foreigners powerful leverage over a government and its affairs – a risk that some governments appear willing to take. [...]

Another trend, reminiscent of the privateers of earlier centuries, is the willingness of private military companies to act as proxies for Western governments [which] [...] allow policymakers to achieve their foreign-policy goals free from the need to secure public approval and safe in the knowledge that should the situation deteriorate, official participation can be fudged. [...]

The future of peacekeeping?

Some private military companies, such as EO, possess sufficient coercive capability to break a stalemate in a conflict. Unlike multinational forces, they do not act impartially but are hired to win a conflict (or deter it) on the client's terms. EO and Sandline International have argued that military force has an underutilized potential to bring conflicts to a close. However, bludgeoning the other side into accepting a peace agreement runs in diametric opposition to most academic studies of conflict resolution [...] These studies center on consent: bringing warring sides together with the implicit assumption that each wants to negotiate an end to the war. [...]

The flaw in this [mainstream] approach is that according to recent empirical studies, outright victories, rather than negotiated peace settlements, have ended the greater part of the twentieth century's internal conflicts. [...]

[...] [This] illustrates that it is better to acknowledge the existence [and participation] of military companies and engage them politically than to ignore them and hope that somehow a peace agreement will stay intact.

Regulating the market

Since the demand for military force is unlikely to end anytime soon, military companies, in their various guises, appear here to stay. Should there be some attempt to regulate them, or is it the right of sovereign states – as with the purchase of weap-onry – to employ who they wish as long as they ensure that their employees behave within acceptable bounds? There is widespread discomfort with a laissez-faire approach, most of it caused by military companies' lack of accountability. Although most military companies have only worked for legitimate governments, there is little to stop them from working for rebel movements in the future.

To make matters even more complicated, deciding which is the "legitimate" side in a civil conflict is not always straightforward. Many modern governments were once classified as "insurgents" or "terrorists" while in opposition, among them South Africa's African National Congress and Ugandan president Yoweri Museveni's National Resistance Army. The governments that grew out of these movements are now inter-nationally recognized.

There is little to stop military companies from working for rebel movements in the future

Military companies are motivated first and foremost by profit and are responsible primarily to their shareholders. Consequently, financial losses, in spite of any strategic or political considerations, may prompt a company to pull out. There are also few checks on their adherence to human-rights conventions. The problem is not a lack of human-rights law. During times of war, the employees of military companies fall under the auspices of Common Article 3 of the Geneva Conventions, which is binding on all combatants. They are also bound by a state's obligations to UN human-rights conventions as "agents" of the government that employs them. What is absent is ade-quate independent observation of their activities – a feature common to all parties in a conflict but especially characteristic of military companies that have no permanent attachments to national governments.

Efforts at controlling mercenaries through international law in the 1960s and 1970s were led by African states that faced a skeptical reception from the United States and major European powers. The most accepted definition of a mercenary, found in Article 47 of the 1977 Additional Protocols to the Geneva Conventions, is so riddled with loopholes that few international-law scholars believe it could withstand the rigors of the courtroom. International apathy is palpable. France and the United States have not signed the Additional Protocols, and the UN's 1989 International Convention against the Recruitment, Use, Financing, and Training of Mercenaries has attracted only 12 signatories. Three of these signatories, Angola, the former Yugoslavia, and the former Zaire, have gone on to employ mercenaries. Most states have domes-tic laws that ban mercenaries but few, if any, have acted on them. Britain's Foreign Enlistment Act, for example, was introduced in 1870, and there has yet to be a pros-ecution. [...]

[...] Military companies are mostly registered offshore and can easily relocate to other countries, making it difficult to pin them down under specific jurisdictions. A growing trend is for international companies to form joint ventures with local com-panies, avoiding the effects of the legislation in any one country. [...] Companies can also easily disguise their activities by purporting to be security companies performing protection services while actually engaging in more coercive military operations.

The principal obstacle to regulating private military companies has been the ten-dency to brand them as "mercenaries" of the kind witnessed in Africa 30 years ago, rather than to recognize them as multinational entrepreneurs eager to solidify their legitimacy. Consequently, regulation can be best achieved through constructive engagement. This process would likely expose governments and international institutions to accusations of sanctioning the use of "soldiers of fortune" to shore up the international system. Yet, this tack offers the international community greater leverage to influence the activities of companies that believe legitimacy is the key to their future growth and prosperity. [...]

Engagement could well begin with dialogue between key multilateral institutions and the private military sector. Liaison at senior levels of the UN, for example, is needed, and the Department of Peacekeeping is an obvious starting point. UN field personnel should be permitted to contact military companies and plan strategies for conflict resolution where appropriate. [...] Direct engagement could also provide an opportunity to lay out a code of conduct that might incorporate more specific operational issues rising from the work of military companies. Observation of companies such as EO to ensure that they adhere to basic principles of warfare is needed, something in which the International Committee of the Red Cross could take a lead.

The prospect that private military companies might gain some degree of legitimacy within the international community begs the question as to whether these firms could take on UN peacekeeping functions and improve on UN efforts. Military companies see this as an area of potential growth and are quick to point out the advantages they offer. There is no denying that they are cheaper than UN operations [...] [and that] [...] there is no doubt that they can mobilize more quickly and appear less sensitive to casualties. However, accepting a UN mandate or conditions may also undermine a company's effectiveness. [...]

Give war a chance

Policymakers and multilateral organizations have paid little attention to private-sector involvement in wars. Yet low-intensity conflicts – the type that military companies have specialized in up to now – will be the wars that prevail in the first part of the twenty-first century. Their virulence and random nature could undermine the viability of many nation-states. These wars defy orthodox means of resolution, thus creating the circumstances that have contributed to the expansion of military companies into this area.

Conflict resolution theory needs to look more closely at the impact of coercion, not dismiss it. Military companies may in fact offer new possibilities for building peace that, while not universal in applicability, can hasten the end to a war and limit loss of life. Moreover, there is no evidence that private-sector intervention will erode the state. Despite the commercial motives of military companies, their interventions, if anything, have strengthened the ability of governments to control their territory. Yet, military companies are unlikely to resolve conflicts in the long term. Political intervention and postconflict peacebuilding efforts are still necessary.

Although the UN's special rapporteur on the use of mercenaries has acknowledged the difficulties in equating military companies with mercenaries, the debate has not moved beyond that point. Admittedly, the UN is in a sticky position. Although some member states have condemned the use of military companies, others have employed their services or condoned their operations. Meanwhile, the future of private military interests looks bright. [...] The most rapid expansion is likely to be linked to the protection of commercial interests, although these can act as a springboard for more aggressive, military actions alongside local companies and power brokers. Mainstream companies, from the United States in particular, are also likely to encroach into low-intensity conflict areas. With backing from a cautious administration not wanting to forego strategic influence, the temptation to use military companies might prove irresistible.

Regulation of military companies will be problematic, given the diversity of their services and the breadth of their market niche. Yet, in many respects, the private military industry is no different from any other sector in the global economy that is required to conform to codes of practice – except that in the former's case, the risk of political instability and social mayhem is amplified if more unscrupulous actors become involved. [...]

Want to know more?

Mercenaries have been around for as long as warfare itself. For detailed accounts of their history, see Anthony Mockler's *Mercenaries* (London: MacDonald, 1969) and Janice Thomson's *Mercenaries, Pirates & Sovereigns: State-Building and Extraterritorial Violence in Early Modern Europe* (New Jersey: Princeton University Press, 1996).

Several recent articles and studies scrutinize private military companies and their activities worldwide: David Shearer's *Private Armies and Military Intervention*, Adelphi Paper 316 (New York: International Institute for Strategic Studies, February 1998); William Shawcross' "In Praise of Sandline" (*The Spectator*, August 1, 1998); Al J. Venter's "Market Forces: How Hired Guns Succeeded Where the United Nations Failed" (*Jane's International Defense Review*, March 1, 1998); Ken Silverstein's "Privatizing War" (*The Nation*, July 28, 1997); and David Isenberg's *Soldiers of Fortune Ltd.: A Profile of Today's Private Sector Corporate Mercenary Firms* (Washington: Center for Defense Information, November 1997).

The legal status of mercenaries is addressed in Françoise Hampson's "Mercenaries: Diagnosis Before Prescription" (*Netherlands' Yearbook of International Law*, No. 3, 1991) and Edward Kwakwa's "The Current Status of Mercenaries in the Law of Armed Conflict" (*Hastings International and Comparative Law Review*, vol. 14, 1990).

Martin van Crevald examines the changing dynamics of conflict in *The Transformation of War* (New York: The Free Press, 1991). Two studies provide empirical evidence that outright victory, rather than negotiated peace, has ended the greater part of the twentieth century's internal conflicts: Stephen John Stedman's *Peacemaking in Civil Wars: International Mediation in Zimbabwe 1974–80* (Boulder: Lynne Rienner, 1991) and Roy Licklider's "The Consequences of Negotiated Settlements in Civil Wars 1954–93" (*American Political Science Review*, September 1995).

On human rights, see a series of reports by the UN's special rapporteur on mercenaries that are available online: *Report on the Question of the Use of Mercenaries as a Means of Violating Human Rights and Impeding the Exercise of the Right of Peoples to Self-Determination*.

For links to this and other relevant Web sites, as well as a comprehensive index of related articles, access www.foreignpolicy.com.

Discussion questions

- What are the implicit 'rules' defining state behaviour in the context of super-power relations/game?
- Why does a unipolar international order tend to encourage the rise of great powers? Explain the strong correlation between unipolarity and great power emergence.
- Why do states form alliances? What is the meaning of 'entrapment' and 'abandonment' in alliance politics?
- Why do some alliances endure while others collapse?
- What is the core meaning of multilateralism?
- What are the conditions favourable to the formation and maintenance of security regimes? Why is the balance of power considered by some to be a regime?
- How do non-liberal community regions potentially develop into liberal security communities?
- To what extent is military force an effective instrument for the advancement of humanitarian values? Why is NATO's military action in the Kosovo crisis considered by observers to be contradictory to its humanitarian objectives?
- Do you agree that war can be morally justified on humanitarian grounds?
- Why do states frequently resort to economic sanction despite its dubious efficacy? Under what conditions is economic sanction likely to be salient?
- Should private military companies be outlawed in view of their 'immoral' propensity to view conflict as a legitimate business activity?

PART 5

The Future of Security

Introduction

BARRY BUZAN, writing in the immediate post-Cold War period, offers a vision of transformation in global patterns of security. He suggest four major changes in great power relations, namely the emergence of a multipolar Europe, a much lower degree of ideological division, global dominance of a security community among the capitalist powers, and the strengthening of international society. However, outside this core dominated by developed powers, the challenges for the periphery states are much great. Buzan predicts problems of the proliferation of WMD, economic underdevelopment, migration flows, clashes of civilisational ideologies and environment degradation. **John J. Mearsheimer**, from an Offensive Realism perspective, offers a very different prognosis for security in Europe following the end of the Cold War. Mearsheimer argues that the Europe is likely to become increasingly multipolar and unstable, especially in the absence of a nuclear balance across the region. He predicts conflicts among Eastern European states, and the re-emergence of hyper-nationalism across the region as fuelling tensions. **Thomas J. Christensen** applies a Neoclassical Realism viewpoint to the East Asia region to divine the prospects for conflict. Christensen argues that any shift in the US commitment to the region through a reduction in its military presence or weakening of the US-Japan alliance will have major ramifications for stability. China and Japan may find themselves in a reinvigorated security dilemma, only exacerbated by legacies of the colonial past and rising nationalism. **Kenneth N. Waltz** offers a discussion of the continuing relevance of Structural Realism to understanding the future trajectory of global security. In line with his theory, he predicts that US unipolarity will inevitably attract counterbalancing behaviour and move towards multipolarity. In East Asia, he predicts that Japan but especially China are likely to rise as great powers.

Ken Booth offers a different focus on contemporary security issues by thinking though the implications of the phenomenon of globalisation for international stability. Booth argues that globalisation is a 'double-edged sword' which has triggered both old and new security issues. In particular, he calls for a new 'global moral science' to think through how security can be provided for in this new era. Victor D. Cha discusses in more specific terms the impact of globalisation on security. He points to the rise of a range of new actors in security able to exploit 'post-sovereign space'; the rise of 'non-physical' security threats, such as information technology security; and the increasing interpenetration of domestic and international security challenges, or what he terms 'intermestic' security. Walter Laqueur discusses terrorism, insisting that it is not a novel threat, but that it is certainly becoming more versatile in nature. Laqueur emphasises the increasingly possibility of terrorist access to WMD and the use of cyber-warfare. Laqueur in many ways, even though writing in 1996, antici-pated many of the terrorist challenges post-11 September. Finally, Michael Howard debates the optimum means to defeat contemporary terrorism, and emphasises the importance of psychological warfare to win 'hearts and minds' and to counter differ-ent cultural assumptions which provide the context for terrorist movements.

Barry Buzan

SECURITY IN THE TWENTY-FIRST CENTURY

Source: 'New patterns of global security in the twenty-first century', *International Affairs,* vol. 67, no. 3, 1991, pp. 431–51.

Into the twenty-first century

[...] THE ENDING OF THE COLD WAR has created a remarkable fluidity and openness in the whole pattern and quality of international relations. [...] There are quite strong indications that the new century will be like the nineteenth in having, at least among the great powers, neither a major ideological divide nor a dominating power rivalry. [...]

Changes in the centre

[...] At this early stage in the new era one can with some confidence suggest four defining features for the new pattern of great-power relations.

1. The rise of a multipolar power structure in place of the Cold War's bipolar one

The term 'superpower' has dominated the language of power politics for so many decades that one is left floundering for words to describe the new power structure that is emerging. The precipitate economic and political decline of the Soviet Union has clearly removed it from this category, despite its still formidable military strength. The decline of the United States has been much less severe, arguably leaving it as the last superpower. But the rise of Europe, particularly the consolidation of the European Community as an economic and political entity, largely removes (and in the case of the Soviet Union inverts) the spheres of influence that were one of the key elements in the claim to superpower status.[1] It seems time to revive the term 'great power'. If one thinks how this term was used before 1945, Russia still qualifies. So do China and India, which might be seen as the contemporary equivalents of regional great powers such as Italy, Austria-Hungary or the Ottoman Empire before 1914. Despite their political oddities, Japan and the EC are strong candidates, albeit still more obviously in the economic than in the military and political spheres. The United States is undoubtedly the greatest of the great powers. The term superpower, however, seems no longer appropriate in a multipolar world with so many independent centres of power and so few spheres of influence.

If one moves away from the strict realist (and neo-realist) conception of power as aggregated capabilities (i.e. military, economic and political strength all together),[2] and towards the disaggregated view of power taken by those who think more in terms of interdependence,[3] then global multipolarity stands out even more clearly. The military inhibitions of Japan and the political looseness of Europe count for less in relation to their standing as major poles of strength and stability in the global political economy. Although not all six great powers are within the global core, multipolarity suggests a centre that is both less rigid and less sharply divided within itself than under bipolarity. A multipolar centre will be more complex and more fluid, and may well allow for the development of militarily hesitant great powers. If military threats are low, such powers can afford – as Japan now does and as the United States did before 1941 – to rest their military security on their ability to mobilize massive civil economies.

A multi-centred core offers more competing points of contact for the periphery. At the same time, the shift from two superpowers to several great powers should mean both a reduction in the intensity of global political concerns and a reduction in the resources available for sustained intervention. This in turn points to the rise of regional politics. Because the great powers are spread across several regions and do not include a dominating ideological or power rivalry within their ranks, they will project their own conflicts into the periphery much less forcefully and systematically than under the zero-sum regime of the Cold War. Because regions are less constrained by the impact of their conflicts on the global scorecard of two rival superpowers, local rivalries and antagonisms will probably have more autonomy. Local great powers such as India, China and perhaps Brazil should also find their regional influence increased.

2. A much lower degree of ideological division and rivalry

Complementing the structural looseness of the new centre is a much reduced level of ideological conflict. [...]

[...] Liberal capitalism, with all its well-known faults, now commands a broad consensus as the most effective and desirable form of political economy available. The difficult formula of political pluralism plus market economics has many critics, but no serious rivals. This development means that the centre is less ideologically divided within itself than it has been since the first spread of industrialization. In conjunction with the shift to multipolarity, this further reduces political and military incentives for competitive intervention into the periphery.

3. The global dominance of a security community among the leading capitalist powers

As the alliance structures of the Cold War dissolve into irrelevance [...], a looming void seems to be appearing at the heart of the international security system. The declining salience of military threats among the great powers makes it unlikely that this void will be filled by new alliances, especially if the European Union is viewed as a single international actor (even though it is still well short of being a single sovereign state). Indeed, the main military structure of the new era requires the viewer to put on different lenses for it to come clearly into focus, for it is inverse in form to traditional alliance structures.

The dominant feature of the post-Cold War era is a *security community* among the major centres of capitalist power. This means a group of states that do not expect, or prepare for, the use of military force in their relations with each other.[4] This is a different and in some ways more profound quality than the collective expectation and preparation to use force against someone else that is the essence of alliance relationships. During the Cold War this security community grew up within, and in its latter days it was masked by, or disguised as, the Western alliance system. The capitalist powers had good reason to form an alliance against the communist states. But equally important is that they developed independent and increasingly dominant reasons for eliminating the use of military force in their relations with each other. The fact that they were able to expunge military rivalry from their own relations was a major factor in their ability to see off the communist challenge without a 'hot' war. [...]

The existence of this capitalist security community – in effect, Europe, North America, Japan and Australia, standing back to back – gives the Western powers an immense advantage in the global political economy. Because they do not have to compete with each other militarily, they can meet other challengers more easily, whether singly or collectively. The relative ease with which the United States was able to construct a military (and financial) coalition to take on Iraq shows both the potential of such a security structure and how it might work to meet other periphery challenges to the stability of the global political economy.

The example of the Second Gulf War suggests a model of concentric circles to complement and modify the raw centre-periphery idea. In the centre circle stood the United States, which was willing to lead only if followed and to fight only if given wide support and assistance. In the second circle were others prepared to fight – some members of the centre (principally Britain and France), and others of the periphery (principally Egypt and Saudi Arabia). In the third circle were those prepared to pay but not to fight, primarily Japan and Germany. In the fourth circle were those prepared to support but not to fight or pay. This group was large, and contained those prepared to vote and speak in favour of the action, some of whom (such as Denmark) also sent symbolic military forces. It also included the Soviet Union and China as well as a mixture of centre and periphery states. The fifth circle contained those states satisfied to be neutral, neither supporting nor opposing the venture, but prepared to accept UN Security Council resolutions. Within these five circles stood the great majority of the international community, and all the major powers. In the sixth circle were those prepared to oppose, mainly verbally and by voting. This contained Cuba, Jordan, Yemen, and a number of Arab states. In the seventh circle stood those prepared to resist – Iraq.

This model does not offer a hard image of the future. It is not a permanent coalition, nor is it likely to recur. But it does suggest the general nature of security relations in a centre-dominated world, the mechanisms available, and the ability of the centre to isolate aggressors who threaten the recognized political order and the workings of the global economy.

The capitalist security community that underpinned this coalition acts as a major moderator to the new multipolar power structure. One danger of multipolarity [...] was that a shifting balance of power, driven by a plethora of antagonisms and security dilemmas, would generate unstable patterns of alliance and periodic lapses into great-power wars. But a multipolar system in which the three strongest powers are also a strong security community is something quite new, and should defuse or perhaps even eliminate most of these old hazards. In the inelegant jargon of systems theory, one could describe the new structure of power relations as multipolar in the sense that several independent great powers are in play, but unipolarized in the sense that there is a single dominant coalition governing international relations. It is the single coalition that gives force to the centre-periphery model and makes the new situation unique.

4. The strengthening of international society

This last defining feature of the new centre is the least certain of the four, but it is a plausible product of the other three. [...]

The foundation of modern international society is the mutual recognition by states of each other's claim to sovereignty. This establishes them as legal equals and provides the foundation for diplomatic relations. The top end of contemporary international society is the whole range of institutions and regimes with which groups of states coordinate their behaviour in pursuit of common goals. Some of these institutions and regimes are already nearly universal – the United Nations, the Law of the Sea regime, the nuclear non-proliferation regime. Others, such as the European Community, have been more restricted. But the EC, though only regional in scope, has now become so deeply institutionalized that many are beginning to see it more as a single actor than as a system of states. During the Cold War the Western states established a particularly rich international societal network of institutions and regimes to facilitate the relatively open economic and societal relations that they wished to cultivate. These included the IMF, the World Bank, the OECD, the GATT and the Group of Seven. As a rule, the development of *global* institutions and regimes was obstructed by the Cold War, almost the only exception being superpower cooperation in the promotion of nuclear non-proliferation. With the ending of the Cold War and of the systemic dominance of the West, it does not seem unreasonable to expect the extension of the Western networks towards more universal standing. Old Marxian arguments that the capitalists were kept united only by their common fear of communism seem to have been overridden by the global scale and deep interdependence of early twenty-first-century capitalism. The eagerness of the ex-Soviet-type systems to join the club is a strong pointer towards consolidation of Western regimes, as is the dramatic upgrading of the UN Security Council as a focus for global consensus-building and legitimation seen in the Gulf crisis. If this occurs, a stronger international society, largely reflecting Western norms and values, will be a powerful element in the security environment of the periphery. [...]

Implications for the periphery

These massive changes in security relations within the centre will have both direct and indirect effects on security within the periphery. [...]

1. Political security

Perhaps the most obvious political impact of the end of the Cold War is the demise of both power bipolarity and ideological rivalry as central features of the centre's penetration into the periphery. One immediate consequence of this is to lower the value of periphery countries as either ideological spoils or strategic assets in great-power rivalry. [...] In the unfolding order of the twenty-first century there will be little or no ideological or strategic incentive for great powers to compete for Third World allegiance. This loss of leverage will be accompanied by the loss of Non-alignment as a useful political platform for the periphery. [...]

Further, many periphery states have found the legitimacy of their one-party systems undermined by the collapse of communism. [...] It remains an open question whether pluralism will fare any better than authoritarianism in the unstable and in many ways unpromising political environment of many Third World states. Theory does not tell us much about the relative virtues of democratic versus command approaches to the early stages of state-building. Experience strongly suggests that state-building is a tricky, difficult, long-term and often violent business under any circumstances – especially so for poorly placed and poorly endowed latecomers under pressure to conform to norms that have already been reached naturally by more powerful states in the international system.

A further blow to the political position of many periphery states comes from the fact that the twentieth century was also the main era of decolonization. Decolonization was a high point in the epic and on-going struggle of the rest of the world to come to terms with the intrusion of superior Western power. A more difficult period is now in prospect in which the euphoria of independence has faded and the reality of continued inferiority has reasserted itself. As the twenty-first century unfolds, with the West in a dominant position, it will become for the periphery states the post-decolonization era. [...] As decolonization becomes remote, many governments in the periphery will find themselves increasingly labouring under the weight of their often dismal performance record, without the support of the colonial rationalizations that might once have forgiven it. They will find it increasingly difficult to evade or parry the rising contempt of both foreigners and their own citizens. Only those few that have made it into the semi-periphery, such as Taiwan and South Korea, can escape this fate.

Particularly in Africa and the Middle East, periphery states may also find it difficult to sustain the legitimacy of the colonial boundaries that have so signally failed to define viable states. [...] Although there is no clear link between the Cold War and the attempt to fix boundaries, the ending of the Cold War is opening up boundary questions in a rather major way. [...]

[...] It is not yet clear whether it is the norm of fixed boundaries that is under assault or only the practice in specific locations. But it is clear that this norm is vulnerable to the counter-norm of national self-determination, and that some of the restraints on boundary change have been weakened by the ending of the Cold War.

A further possible impact of changes in the centre on the political security agenda of the periphery is the pushing of Islam to the front rank of the opposition to Western hegemony. The collapse of communism as the leading anti-Western ideology seems to propel Islam into this role by default, and many exponents of Islam will embrace the task with relish. The anti-Western credentials of Islam are well established and speak to a large and mobilized political constituency. In part this can be seen as a straight clash between secular and spiritual values, albeit underpinned by an older religious antagonism between Christendom and Islam.[5] In part, however, it has to be seen as a kind of civilizational resistance to the hegemony of the West. [...]

Given this combined legacy of historical frustration and ideological antagonism, Islam could become the leading carrier of anti-Western sentiment in the periphery – though it could just as easily be kept impotent by the fierceness of its own numerous internal splits and rivalries. But since the West now dominates the centre, while Islam has a large constituency in Africa and Asia, this old divide may nevertheless define a major political rift between North and South in the coming decades. If it does, one result will be a security problem for Europe and the Soviet Union/Russia, for both share a huge territorial boundary with Islam, and in the case of the Soviet Union this boundary is inside the country. The security issues raised may or may not be military ones, but they will certainly be societal – an aspect to be explored further below. [...]

2. Military security

Developments in the centre can easily be read as pointing to a lowering of militarization in the periphery. A less ideologically divided and more multipolar centre will have less reason to compete politically to supply arms to the periphery. The ending of the Cold War reduces the strategic salience of many military bases in the periphery, and lowers incentives to use arms supply as a way of currying ideological favour with local governments. The outcomes of domestic and even regional political rivalries within the periphery should, other things being equal, be of less interest to the great powers than previously. In the absence of ideological disputes among themselves, the great powers will have fewer reasons to see periphery states as assets, and more reasons to see them as liabilities. The ending of the Cold War thus largely turns off the political mechanism that so effectively pumped arms into the Third World all through the 1960s, 1970s and 1980s. [...]

But this prospect raises an important question about whether the West will use its new pre-eminence to neglect the Third World, or whether it will seek to subject it to stronger collective security and regional management regimes. [...]

Greater control of the conventional arms trade between the centre and the periphery is another development that might be expected from the end of the Cold War, but the likelihood is that two powerful mechanisms will continue to support a substantial flow of military capability into the periphery. The first is the arms trade, driven by an ever-increasing number of suppliers, most eager and some desperate to sell their products. In the fierce commercial competition of the post-Cold War world, arms exports will remain one of the very few industrial areas of comparative advantage for the Soviet Union and China, as well as some smaller states such as Czechoslovakia. [...]

The second mechanism arises from the unbreakable link between industrialization and the ability to make weapons. Industrialization is spreading inexorably across the planet, and all but the most extreme Greens welcome it as an essential ingredient in the development of human civilization. But the arms industry is not separate from the civil economy: think of how the United States transformed itself from being a largely civil economy to being the arsenal of democracy in just a few years during the 1940s. In the 1990s, many of the technologies for making weapons are now old. The knowledge and skills for making poison gas and machine guns were developed more than a century ago, and even nuclear technology dates back nearly half a century. As technologies age, they become easier to acquire even for lightly industrialized countries such as Iraq.

The overlap between civil and military technology is especially obvious in the case of the nuclear and chemical industries, but also applies to engineering, vehicles, aircraft and shipbuilding. In all these industries, there is fierce competition to export both products and manufacturing plant. Any country possessing a full civil nuclear power industry has virtually everything it needs to make a nuclear bomb. Any country that can make basic industrial chemicals can also make poison gas. Any that can make fertilizer can make high explosives. Whoever can make trucks, bulldozers or airliners can make armoured cars, tanks and bombers. The concern over Iraq, Libya, Israel, Pakistan, South Africa, Brazil and other states has as much to do with their industrialization as with their direct imports of arms, and there is no way of stopping the spread of industrial-military capability into the periphery. Any attempt to do so would put the goal of arms restraint into direct opposition with that of economic development.

The combined effect of the arms trade and industrialization means that military capability *will* spread by one mechanism or the other. Attempts to block the arms trade will intensify efforts at military industrialization, as they did in South Africa, so adding to the number of arms suppliers. [...] As a consequence, military security will remain an elusive objective posing difficult policy choices. The ending of the Cold War should result in some diminution of the flow of arms for political motives, but there is no reason to think that it will eliminate the problem of militarization in the periphery. [...]

3. Economic security

If economic security is about access to the resources, finance and markets necessary to sustain acceptable levels of welfare and state power, then the massive political changes of the past few years may well make little difference to the economic security problems of the periphery. The idea of economic security is riddled with contradictions and paradoxes.[6] [...] To the extent that it has any clear meaning in relation to periphery countries, economic security points to the persistent structural disadvantages of late development and a position in the lower ranks of wealth and industrialization. The consequences of such weakness range from inability to sustain the basic human needs of the population (as in Sudan, Bangladesh, Ethiopia, Liberia), through the disruption of fluctuating and uncertain earnings from exports of primary products (as in Zambia, Peru, Nigeria), to inability to resist the policy pressures of outside institutions in return for needed supplies of capital (as in Brazil, Argentina, Tanzania). There seems no reason to expect any fundamental change in the overall problem of the periphery in occupying a weak position in a global market whose prices, trade, finance and technical evolution are all controlled from the centre.

The periphery, in other words, will remain the periphery. [...]

It is not impossible to imagine that in some parts of the periphery, notably those where both imported state structures and economic development have failed totally, there may evolve a kind of de facto institutional recolonization, though some more diplomatic term will need to be found to describe it. There are many potential candidates for this in Africa, and some in South and South – East Asia, Central America and the Caribbean. Given the waning of post-decolonization sensitivities about independence, the harsh realities of economic and political failure and the strengthening global institutions of a Western-dominated international society, a subtle return to 'managed' status for the most hopeless periphery states may well occur. [...]

4. Societal security

Societal security is likely to become a much more prominent issue between centre and periphery, and within both, than it has been during the Cold War era. Societal security is about the threats and vulnerabilities that affect patterns of communal identity and culture. The two issues most prominently on its agenda at the beginning of the twenty-first century in centre – periphery relations are migration[7] and the clash of rival civilizational identities.

Migration threatens communal identity and culture by directly altering the ethnic, cultural religious and linguistic composition of the population. Most societies have resulted from earlier human migrations and already represent a mixture. Many welcome, up to a point, the cultural diversity that further migration brings. But beyond some point, migration becomes a question of numbers. Too great a foreign influx will threaten the ability of the existing society to reproduce itself in the old way, which can easily create a political constituency for immigration control. Uncontrolled immigration eventually swamps the existing culture. [...]

[...] [A]t the beginning of the twenty-first century incentives are rising for more permanent mass population movements in the other direction, from periphery to centre. The advanced industrial cultures of Europe and North America have low birth rates and high, often rising standards of living. Immediately to their south lie dozens of periphery countries with high birth rates and low, often falling standards of living. Substantial immigrant communities from the South already exist in the North. Transportation is not a significant barrier. The economic incentives for large numbers of young people to move in search of work are high, and the markets of the centre have a demand for cheap labour. [...] High incentives to migrate are sustained by the fading of hopes that political independence would bring development and prosperity. In a few places these hopes have been fulfilled, but most face a bleak future in which they seem likely to fall ever further behind the still rapidly evolving political economies of the capitalist centre. Some even face falling behind the dismal standards of their own present.

An acute migration problem between societies can hardly avoid raising barriers and tensions between them. In defending itself against unwanted human influx, a country has not only to construct legal and physical barriers to entry, but also to emphasize its differentiation from the society whose members it seeks to exclude. Questions of status and race are impossible to avoid. The treatment of migrants as a kind of criminal class creates easy ground for antagonism between the societies on both sides.

The migration problem does not exist in isolation. It occurs alongside, and mingled in with, the clash of rival civilizational identities between the West and the societies of the periphery. Here the threat travels mostly in the opposite direction, reflecting the older order of Western dominance. It is much more from the centre to the periphery than the other way around, though the existence of immigrant communities within the centre does mean that there is some real threat from periphery to centre, and a perceived threat of 'fifth column' terrorism. The clash between civilizational identities is most conspicuous between the West and Islam. [...]

The last point is true as between the West and all periphery societies.[8] By its conspicuous economic and technological success, the West makes all others look bad (i.e. underdeveloped, or backward or poor, or disorganized or repressive, or uncivilized or primitive) and so erodes their status and legitimacy. The tremendous energy, wealth, inventiveness and organizational dynamism of the West, not to mention its crass materialism and hollow consumer culture, cannot help but penetrate deeply into weaker societies worldwide. As it does so, it both inserts alien styles, concepts, ideas and aspirations – 'Coca-Colanization' – and corrupts or brings into question the validity and legitimacy of local customs and identities. In the case of Islam, this threat is compounded by geographical adjacency and historical antagonism and also the overtly political role that Islam plays in the lives of its followers. Rivalry with the West is made more potent by the fact that Islam is still itself a vigorous and expanding collective identity.

In combination, migration threats and the clash of cultures make it rather easy to draw a scenario for a kind of societal cold war between the centre and at least part of the periphery, and specifically between the West and Islam, in which Europe would be in the front line. There is no certainty that this scenario will unfold, and much will depend on the performance of (and support given to) moderate governments within the Islamic world, but most of the elements necessary for it are already in place. [...]

This civilizational Cold War could feed into the massive restructuring of relations going on within the centre consequent upon the ending of the East – West Cold War. [...]

5. Environmental security

Much of the environmental agenda falls outside the realm of security and is more appropriately seen as an economic question about how the pollution costs of industrial activity are to be counted, controlled and paid for.[9] Where environmental issues threaten to overwhelm the conditions of human existence on a large scale, as in the case of countries vulnerable to extensive inundation from modest rises in sea level, then casting such issues in security terms is appropriate. [...] There may also be some advantage in treating as international security issues activities that may cause substantial changes in the workings of the planetary atmosphere. These might include the mass production of greenhouse gases or chemicals such as CFCs that erode the protective ozone layer, or exploitative or polluting activities that threaten to diminish the supply of oxygen to the atmosphere by killing off forests and plankton. [...]

[...] [E]nvironmental issues look set to become a regular feature of centre – periphery dialogues and tensions. The holistic quality of the planetary environment will provide the centre with reasons for wanting to intervene in the periphery in the name of environmental security. The periphery will gain some political leverage out of this interest, and will continue to blame the industrialized centre for having created the problem in the first place. This exchange may well stay within the political framework of interdependence, below the threshold of security. But it could also become entangled with the broader debate about development in such a way as to trigger serious conflicts of interest. As others have pointed out, environmental issues, particularly control over water supplies, look likely to generate quite a bit of local conflict within the periphery.[10] [...]

Notes

1   See Barry Buzan, Morten Kelstrup, Pierre Lemaitre, Elzbieta Tromer and Ole Wæver, *The European security order recast: scenarios for the post-Cold War era* (London: Pinter, 1990).

2   Kenneth N. Waltz, *Theory of international politics* (Reading, Mass.: Addison–Wesley, 1979), pp. 129–31.

3   Barry Buzan, Charles Jones and Richard Little, *The logic of anarchy: neorealism to structural realism* (New York: Columbia University Press, forthcoming in 1992), section one.

4   Karl Deutsch and S. A. Burrell, *Political community and the North Atlantic area* (Princeton, NJ: Princeton University Press, 1957).

5   See Edward Mortimer, 'Christianity and Islam', *International Affairs* 67:1 (1991), pp. 7–13.

6   Barry Buzan, *People, states and fear: an agenda for international security studies in the post-Cold War era* (Hemel Hempstead: Harvester–Wheatsheaf, 1991), ch. 6.

7   Jonas Widgren, 'International migration and regional stability', *International Affairs* 66:4 (1990), pp. 749–66; François Heisbourg, 'Population movements in post-Cold War Europe', *Survival* 33:1 (1991), pp. 31–43.

8   Theodore von Laue, *The world revolution of Westernization: the twentieth century in global perspective* (New York: Oxford University Press, 1987).

9   On the risks in the idea of environmental security, see Daniel Deudney, 'The case against linking environmental degradation and national security', *Millennium* 19:3 (1990), pp. 461–76.

10   John Ravenhill, 'The North-South balance of power', *International Affairs* 66:4 (1990), p. 748; *The Economist*, 16 Dec. 1989, p. 70.

John J. Mearsheimer

INSTABILTY IN EUROPE?

Source: 'Back to the future: instability in Europe after the Cold War', *International Security*, vol. 15, no. 1, Summer 1990, pp. 5–56.

Predicting the future: the Balkanization of Europe?

WHAT NEW ORDER will emerge in Europe if the Soviets and Americans withdraw to their homelands and the Cold War order dissolves? What characteristics will it have? How dangerous will it be?

It is certain that bipolarity will disappear, and multipolarity will emerge in the new European order. The other two dimensions of the new order – the distribution of power among the major states, and the distribution of nuclear weapons among them – are not pre-determined, and several possible arrangements could develop. The probable stability of these arrangements would vary markedly. [...]

The distribution and deployment patterns of nuclear weapons in the new Europe is the least certain, and probably the most important, element of the new order. [...]

The best new order would incorporate the limited, managed proliferation of nuclear weapons. This would be more dangerous than the current order, but considerably safer than 1900–1945. The worst order would be a non-nuclear Europe in which power inequities emerge between the principal poles of power. This order would be more dangerous than the current world, perhaps almost as dangerous as the world before 1945. Continuation of the current pattern, or mismanaged proliferation, would be worse than the world of today, but safer than the pre-1945 world.

Europe without nuclear weapons

Some Europeans and Americans seek to eliminate nuclear weapons from Europe, and would replace the Cold War order with a wholly non-nuclear order. Constructing this nuclear-free Europe would require Britain, France and the Soviet Union to rid themselves of nuclear weapons. Proponents believe that a Europe without nuclear weapons would be the most peaceful possible arrangement; in fact, however, a nuclear-free Europe would be the most dangerous among possible post-Cold War orders. The pacifying effects of nuclear weapons – the security they provide, the caution they generate, the rough equality they impose, and the clarity of relative power they create – would be lost. Peace would then depend on the other dimensions of the new order – the number of poles, and the distribution of power among them. However, the new order will certainly be multipolar, and may be unequal; hence the system may be very prone to violence. The structure of power in Europe would look much like it did between the world wars, and it could well produce similar results.

The two most powerful states in post-Cold War Europe would probably be Germany and the Soviet Union. They would be physically separated by a band of small, independent states in Eastern Europe. Not much would change in Western Europe, although the states in that area would have to be concerned about a possible German threat on their eastern flank.

The potential for conflict in this system would be considerable. There would be many possible dyads across which war might break out. Power imbalances would be commonplace as a result of the opportunities this system would present for bullying and ganging up. There would be considerable opportunity for miscalculation. The problem of containing German power would emerge once again, but the configuration of power in Europe would make it difficult to form an effective counterbalancing coalition, for much the same reason that an effective counterbalancing coalition failed to form in the 1930s. Eventually the problem of containing the Soviet Union could also re-emerge. Finally, conflicts may erupt in Eastern Europe, providing the vortex that could pull others into a wider confrontation.

A reunified Germany would be surrounded by weaker states that would find it difficult to balance against German aggression. Without forces stationed in states adjacent to Germany, neither the Soviets nor the Americans would be in a good position to help them contain German power. Furthermore, those small states lying between Germany and the Soviet Union might fear the Soviets as much as the Germans, and hence may not be disposed to cooperate with the Soviets to deter German aggression. This problem in fact arose in the 1930s, and 45 years of Soviet occupation in the interim have done nothing to ease East European fears of a Soviet military presence. Thus, scenarios in which Germany uses military force against Poland, Czechoslovakia, or even Austria become possible.

The Soviet Union also might eventually threaten the new status quo. Soviet withdrawal from Eastern Europe does not mean that the Soviets will never feel compelled to return to Eastern Europe. The historical record provides abundant instances of Russian or Soviet involvement in Eastern Europe. Indeed, the Russian presence in Eastern Europe has surged and ebbed repeatedly over the past few centuries.[1] Thus, Soviet withdrawal now hardly guarantees a permanent exit.

Conflict between Eastern European states is also likely to produce instability in a multipolar Europe. There has been no war among the states in that region during the Cold War because the Soviets have tightly controlled them. This point is illustrated by the serious tensions that now exist between Hungary and Romania over Romanian treatment of the Hungarian minority in Transylvania, a region that previously belonged to Hungary and still has roughly 2 million Hungarians living within its borders. Were it not for the Soviet presence in Eastern Europe, this conflict could have brought

Romania and Hungary to war by now, and it may bring them to war in the future.[2] This will not be the only danger spot within Eastern Europe if the Soviet empire crumbles.[3]

Warfare in Eastern Europe would cause great suffering to Eastern Europeans. It also might widen to include the major powers, because they would be drawn to compete for influence in that region, especially if disorder created fluid politics that offered opportunities for wider influence, or threatened defeat for friendly states. During the Cold War, both superpowers were drawn into Third World conflicts across the globe, often in distant areas of little strategic importance. Eastern Europe is directly adjacent to both the Soviet Union and Germany, and has considerable economic and strategic importance; thus trouble in Eastern Europe could offer even greater temptations to these powers than past conflicts in the Third World offered the superpowers. Furthermore, because the results of local conflicts will be largely determined by the relative success of each party in finding external allies, Eastern European states will have strong incentives to drag the major powers into their local conflicts.[4] Thus both push and pull considerations would operate to enmesh outside powers in local Eastern European wars.

Miscalculation is also likely to be a problem in a multipolar Europe. For example, the new order might well witness shifting patterns of conflict, leaving insufficient time for adversaries to develop agreed divisions of rights and agreed rules of interaction, or constantly forcing them to re-establish new agreements and rules as old antagonisms fade and new ones arise. It is not likely that circumstances would allow the development of a robust set of agreements of the sort that have stabilized the Cold War since 1963. Instead, Europe would resemble the pattern of the early Cold War, in which the absence of rules led to repeated crises. In addition, the multipolar character of the system is likely to give rise to miscalculation regarding the strength of the opposing coalitions.

It is difficult to predict the precise balance of conventional military power that would emerge between the two largest powers in post-Cold War Europe, especially since the future of Soviet power is now hard to forecast. The Soviet Union might recover its strength soon after withdrawing from Central Europe; if so, Soviet power would overmatch German power. Or centrifugal national forces may pull the Soviet Union apart, leaving no remnant state that is the equal of a united Germany.[5] What seems most likely is that Germany and the Soviet Union might emerge as powers of roughly equal strength. The first two scenarios, with their marked inequality between the two leading powers, would be especially worrisome, although there is cause for concern even if Soviet and German power are balanced.

Resurgent hyper-nationalism will probably pose less danger than the problems described above, but some nationalism is likely to resurface in the absence of the Cold War and may provide additional incentives for war. A non-nuclear Europe is likely to be especially troubled by nationalism, since security in such an order will largely be provided by mass armies, which often cannot be maintained without infusing societies with hyper-nationalism. The problem is likely to be most acute in Eastern Europe, but there is also potential for trouble in Germany. The Germans have generally done an admirable job combatting nationalism over the past 45 years, and in remembering the dark side of their past. Nevertheless, worrisome portents are now visible; of greatest concern, some prominent Germans have lately advised a return to greater nationalism in historical education.[6] Moreover, nationalism will be exacerbated by the unresolved border disputes that will be uncovered by the retreat of American and Soviet power. Especially prominent is that of the border between Germany and Poland, which some Germans would change in Germany's favor.

However, it seems very unlikely that Europe will actually be denuclearized, despite the present strength of anti-nuclear feeling in Europe. For example, it is unlikely that the French, in the absence of America's protective cover and faced with a newly unified Germany, would get rid of their nuclear weapons. Also, the Soviets surely would remain concerned about balancing the American nuclear deterrent, and will therefore retain a deterrent of their own.

The current ownership pattern continues

A more plausible order for post-Cold War Europe is one in which Britain, France and the Soviet Union keep their nuclear weapons, but no new nuclear powers emerge in Europe. This scenario sees a nuclear-free zone in Central Europe, but leaves nuclear weapons on the European flanks.

This scenario, too, also seems unlikely, since the non-nuclear states will have substantial incentives to acquire their own nuclear weapons. Germany would probably not need nuclear weapons to deter a conventional attack by its neighbors, since neither the French nor any of the Eastern European states would be capable of defeating a reunified Germany in a conventional war. The Soviet Union would be Germany's only legitimate conventional threat, but as long as the states of Eastern Europe remained independent, Soviet ground forces would be blocked from a direct attack. The Germans, however, might not be willing to rely on the Poles or the Czechs to provide a barrier and might instead see nuclear weapons as the best way to deter a Soviet conventional attack into Central Europe. The Germans might choose to go nuclear to protect themselves from blackmail by other nuclear powers. Finally, given that Germany would have greater economic strength than Britain or France, it might therefore seek nuclear weapons to raise its military status to a level commensurate with its economic status.

The minor powers of Eastern Europe would have strong incentives to acquire nuclear weapons. Without nuclear weapons, these Eastern European states would be open to nuclear blackmail from the Soviet Union and, if it acquired nuclear weapons, from Germany. No Eastern European state could match the conventional strength of Germany or the Soviet Union, which gives these minor powers a powerful incentive to acquire a nuclear deterrent, even if the major powers had none. In short, a continuation of the current pattern of ownership without proliferation seems unlikely.

How stable would this order be? The continued presence of nuclear weapons in Europe would have some pacifying effects. Nuclear weapons would induce greater caution in their owners, give the nuclear powers greater security, tend to equalize the relative power of states that possess them, and reduce the risk of miscalculation. However, these benefits would be limited if nuclear weapons did not proliferate beyond their current owners, for four main reasons.

First, the caution and the security that nuclear weapons impose would be missing from the vast center of Europe. The entire region [...] would become a large zone thereby made "safe" for conventional war. Second, asymmetrical power relations would be bound to develop, between nuclear and non-nuclear states and among non-nuclear states, raising the dangers that attend such asymmetries. Third, the risk of miscalculation would rise, reflecting the multipolar character of this system and the absence of nuclear weapons from a large portion of it. A durable agreed political order would be hard to build because political coalitions would tend to shift over time, causing miscalculations of resolve between adversaries. The relative strength of potential war coalitions would be hard to calculate because coalition strength would depend heavily on the vagaries of diplomacy. Such uncertainties about relative capabilities would be mitigated in conflicts that arose among nuclear powers: nuclear weapons tend to equalize power even among states or coalitions of widely disparate resources, and thus to diminish the importance of additions or defections from each coalition. However, uncertainty would still be acute among the many states that would remain non-nuclear. Fourth, the conventionally-armed states of Central Europe would depend for their security on mass armies, giving them an incentive to infuse their societies with dangerous nationalism in order to maintain public support for national defense efforts

Nuclear proliferation, well-managed or otherwise

The most likely scenario in the wake of the Cold War is further nuclear proliferation in Europe. This outcome is laden with dangers, but also might provide the best hope for maintaining stability on the Continent. Its effects depend greatly on how it is managed. Mismanaged proliferation could produce disaster, while well-managed proliferation could produce an order nearly as stable as the current order. Unfortunately, however, any proliferation is likely to be mismanaged.

Four principal dangers could arise if proliferation is not properly managed. First, the proliferation process itself could give the existing nuclear powers strong incentives to use force to prevent their non-nuclear neighbors from gaining nuclear weapons [...].

Second, even after proliferation was completed, a stable nuclear competition might not emerge between the new nuclear states. The lesser European powers might lack the resources needed to make their nuclear forces survivable; if the emerging nuclear forces were vulnerable, this could create first-strike incentives and attendant crisis instability. [...] Furthermore, their lack of territorial expanse deprives them of possible basing modes, such as mobile missile basing, that would secure their deterrents. [...] Finally, the emerging nuclear powers might also lack the resources required to develop secure command and control and adequate safety procedures for weapons management, thus raising the risk of accidental launch, or of terrorist seizure and use of nuclear weapons.

Third, the élites and publics of the emerging nuclear European states might not quickly develop doctrines and attitudes that reflect a grasp of the devastating consequences and basic unwinnability of nuclear war. There will probably be voices in post-Cold War Europe arguing that limited nuclear war is feasible, and that nuclear wars can be fought and won. These claims might be taken seriously in states that have not had much direct experience with the nuclear revolution.

Fourth, widespread proliferation would increase the number of fingers on the nuclear trigger, which in turn would increase the likelihood that nuclear weapons could be fired due to accident, unauthorized use, terrorist seizure, or irrational decision-making.

If these problems are not resolved, proliferation would present grave dangers. However, the existing nuclear powers can take steps to reduce these dangers. They can help deter preventive attack on emerging nuclear states by extending security guarantees. They can provide technical assistance to help newly nuclear-armed powers to secure their deterrents. And they can help socialize emerging nuclear societies to understand the nature of the forces they are acquiring. Proliferation managed in this manner can help bolster peace. [...]

Notes

1   See, inter alia: Ivo J. Lederer, ed., *Russian Foreign Policy: Essays in Historical Perspective* (New Haven: Yale University Press, 1962); Andrei Lobanov-Rostovsky, *Russia and Europe, 1825–1878* (Ann Arbor, Mich.: George Wahr Publishing, 1954); and Marc Raeff, *Imperial Russia, 1682–1825: The Coming of Age of Modern Russia* (New York: Knopf, 1971), chap. 2.

2   To get a sense of the antipathy between Hungary and Romania over this issue, see *Witnesses to Cultural Genocide: First-Hand Reports on Romania's Minority Policies Today* (New York: American Transylvanian Federation and the Committee for Human Rights in Romania, 1979). The March 1990 clashes between ethnic Hungarians and Romanians in Tîrgu Mures (Romanian Transylvania) indicate the potential for savage violence that is inherent in these ethnic conflicts.

3   See Zbigniew Brzezinski, "Post-Communist Nationalism," *Foreign Affairs*, Vol. 68, No. 5 (Winter 1989/1990), pp. 1–13; and Mark Kramer, "Beyond the Brezhnev Doctrine: A New Era in Soviet-East European Relations?" *International Security*, Vol. 14, No. 3 (Winter 1989/90), pp. 51–54.

4   The new prime minister of Hungary, Jozsef Antall, has already spoken of the need for a "European solution" to the problem of Romania's treatment of Hungarians in Transylvania. Celestine Bohlen, "Victor in Hungary Sees' 45 as the Best of Times," *New York Times*, April 10, 1990, p. A8.

5   This article focuses on how changes in the strength of Soviet power and retraction of the Soviet empire would affect the prospects for stability in Europe. However, the dissolution of the Soviet Union, a scenario not explored here in any detail, would raise dangers that would be different from and in addition to those discussed here.

6   Aspects of this story are recounted in Richard J. Evans, *In Hitler's Shadow: West German Historians and the Attempt to Escape from the Nazi Past* (New York: Pantheon, 1989). A study of past German efforts to mischaracterize history is Holger H. Herwig, "Clio Deceived: Patriotic Self-Censorship in Germany After the Great War," *International Security*, Vol. 12, No. 2 (Fall 1987), pp. 5–44.

Thomas J. Christensen

SECURITY DILEMMAS IN EAST ASIA?

Source: 'China, the US-Japan alliance, and the security dilemma in East Asia', *International Security*, vol. 23, no. 4, Spring 1999, pp. 49–80.

MANY SCHOLARS and analysts argue that in the twenty-first century international instability is more likely in East Asia than in Western Europe. Whether one looks at variables favored by realists or liberals, East Asia appears more dangerous. The region is characterized by major shifts in the balance of power, skewed distributions of economic and political power within and between countries, political and cultural heterogeneity, growing but still relatively low levels of intraregional economic interdependence, anemic security institutionalization, and widespread territorial disputes that combine natural resource issues with postcolonial nationalism.[1]

If security dilemma theory is applied to East Asia, the chance for spirals of tension in the area seems great, particularly in the absence of a U.S. military presence in the region. The theory states that, in an uncertain and anarchic international system, mistrust between two or more potential adversaries can lead each side to take precautionary and defensively motivated measures that are perceived as offensive threats. This can lead to countermeasures in kind, thus ratcheting up regional tensions, reducing security, and creating self-fulfilling prophecies about the danger of one's security environment.[2] If we look at the variables that might fuel security dilemma dynamics, East Asia appears quite dangerous. From a standard realist perspective, not only could dramatic and unpredictable changes in the distribution of capabilities in East Asia increase uncertainty and mistrust, but the importance of sea-lanes and secure energy supplies to almost all regional actors could encourage a destabilizing competition to develop power-projection capabilities on the seas and in the skies. Because they are perceived as offensive threats, power-projection forces are more likely to spark spirals of tension than weapons that can defend only a nation's homeland.[3] Perhaps even more important in East Asia than these more commonly considered variables are psychological factors (such as the historically based mistrust and animosity among regional actors) and political geography issues relating to the Taiwan question, which make even defensive weapons in the region appear threatening to Chinese security.[4]

One way to ameliorate security dilemmas and prevent spirals of tension is to have an outside arbiter play a policing role, lessening the perceived need for regional actors to begin destabilizing security competitions. For this reason, most scholars, regardless of theoretical persuasion, seem to agree with U.S. officials and local leaders that a major factor in containing potential tensions in East Asia is the continuing presence of the U.S. military, particularly in Japan.[5] The historically based mistrust among the actors in Northeast Asia is so intense that not only is the maintenance of a U.S. presence in Japan critical, but the form the U.S.-Japan alliance takes also has potentially important implications for regional stability. In particular, the sensitivity in China to almost all changes in the Cold War version of the U.S.-Japan alliance poses major challenges for leaders in Washington who want to shore up the alliance for the long haul by encouraging greater Japanese burden sharing, but still want the U.S. presence in Japan to be a force for reassurance in the region. To meet these somewhat contradictory goals, for the most part the United States wisely has encouraged Japan to adopt nonoffensive roles that should be relatively unthreatening to Japan's neighbors.

Certain aspects of U.S. policies, however, including joint research of theater missile defenses (TMD) with Japan, are still potentially problematic. According to security dilemma theory, defensive systems and missions, such as TMD, should not provoke arms races and spirals of tension. In contemporary East Asia, however, this logic is less applicable. Many in the region, particularly in Beijing, fear that new defensive roles for Japan could break important norms of self-restraint, leading to more comprehensive Japanese military buildups later. Moreover, Beijing's focus on preventing Taiwan's permanent separation from China means that even defensive weapons in the hands of Taiwan or its potential supporters are provocative to China. Given the bitter history of Japanese imperialism in China and Taiwan's status as a Japanese colony from 1895 to 1945, this certainly holds true for Japan. [...]

Why China would fear a stronger Japan

Chinese security analysts, particularly military officers, fear that Japan could again become a great military great power in the first quarter of the twenty-first century. Such a Japan, they believe, would likely be more independent of U.S. control and generally more assertive in international affairs. If one considers threats posed only by military power and not who is wielding that power, one might expect Beijing to welcome the reduction or even elimination of U.S. influence in Japan, even if this meant China would have a more powerful neighbor. After all, the United States is still by far the most powerful military actor in the Western Pacific.[6] However, given China's historically rooted and visceral distrust of Japan, Beijing would fear either a breakdown of the U.S.-Japan alliance or a significant upgrading of Japan's role within that alliance.[7] This sentiment is shared outside China as well, particularly in Korea. Although Chinese analysts presently fear U.S. power much more than Japanese power, in terms of national intentions, Chinese analysts view Japan with much less trust and, in many cases, with a loathing rarely found in their attitudes about the United States.

The historical legacy

The natural aversion to Japan that sprang from its brutal occupation of China has been preserved in part by Tokyo's refusal to respond satisfactorily to Chinese requests that Tokyo recognize and apologize for its imperial past – for example, by revising history textbooks in the public schools.[8] Chinese sensibilities are also rankled by specific incidents – for example, Prime Minister Ryutaro Hashimoto's 1996 visit to the Yasukuni Shrine, which commemorates Japan's war dead, including war criminals like Tojo.[9] Although some fear that Japan's apparent amnesia or lack of contrition about the past means that Japan could return to the "militarism" (*junguozhuyi*) of the 1930s, such simple historical analogies are relatively rare, at least in Chinese élite foreign policy circles.[10] Chinese analysts' concerns regarding Japanese historical legacies, although not entirely devoid of emotion, are usually more subtle. Many argue that, by downplaying atrocities like the Nanjing massacre and underscoring events like the atomic bombing of Hiroshima and Nagasaki, Japanese élites portray Japan falsely as the victim, rather than the victimizer, in World War II. Because of this, some Chinese analysts fear that younger generations of Japanese citizens may not understand Japan's history and will therefore be insensitive to the intense fears of other regional actors regarding Japanese military power. This lack of understanding will make them less resistant to relatively hawkish élites' plans to increase Japanese military power than their older compatriots, who, because they remember World War II, resisted military buildups during the Cold War.[11] [...]

It may seem odd to the outside observer, but the intensity of anti-Japanese sentiment in China has not decreased markedly as World War II becomes a more distant memory. There are several reasons in addition to those cited above. Nationalism has always been a strong element of the legitimacy of the Chinese Communist Party (CCP), and opposing Japanese imperialism is at the core of this nationalist story. As a result, Chinese citizens have been fed a steady diet of patriotic, anti-Japanese media programming designed to glorify the CCP's role in World War II. Although far removed from that era, most Chinese young people hold an intense and unapologetically negative view of both Japan and, in many cases, its people.[12] [...]

Élite analysts are certainly not immune to these intense anti-Japanese feelings in Chinese society. These emotions, however, have not yet affected the practical, day-to-day management of Sino-Japanese relations. On the contrary, since the 1980s the Chinese government has acted to contain anti-Japanese sentiment in the society at large to avoid damaging bilateral relations and to prevent protestors from using anti-Japanese sentiment as a pretext for criticizing the Chinese government, as occurred several times in Chinese history.[13] But Chinese analysts' statements about the dangers that increased Japanese military power would pose in the future suggest that anti-Japanese sentiment does color their long-term threat assessments, even if it does not always alter their immediate policy prescriptions. Because they can influence procurement and strategy, such longer-term assessments may be more important in fueling the security dilemma than particular diplomatic policies in the present. [...]

Chinese assessments of Japanese military power and potential

In assessing Japan's current military strength, Chinese analysts emphasize the advanced equipment that Japan has acquired, particularly since the late 1970s, when it began developing a navy and air force designed to help the United States contain the Soviet Union's growing Pacific Fleet. [...] They also cite the Japanese defense budget, which, although small as a percentage of gross national product (GNP), is second only to U.S. military spending in absolute size.[14] [...]

[...] [Also,] Chinese analysts understand that Japan can easily do much more militarily than it does. While they generally do not believe that Japan has the requisite combination of material capabilities, political will, and ideological mission to become a Soviet-style superpower, they do believe that Japan could easily become a great military power [...] in the next twenty-five years. [...]

[...] Chinese experts recognize that Japan has practiced a great deal of self-restraint in eschewing weapons designed to project power far from the home islands. [...] [D]espite the long list of current Japanese capabilities mentioned above, Japan certainly is not yet a normal great power because it lacks the required trappings of such a power (e.g., aircraft carriers, nuclear submarines, nuclear weapons, and long-range missile systems)[15] [...] [but] the question is simply if and when Japan will decide to adopt [them] [...]. For this reason, Chinese analysts often view Japan's adoption of even new defensive military roles as dangerous because it may begin to erode the constitutional (Article 9) and nonconstitutional norms of self-restraint (e.g., 1,000-nautical-mile limit on power-projection capability, prohibitions on the military use of space, and tight arms export controls) that have prevented Japan from realizing its military potential. [...]

* * *

The China-Japan security dilemma and U.S. policy challenges

[...] [Furthermore,] [...] most Chinese analysts fear almost any change in the U.S.-Japan alliance. A breakdown of U.S.-Japan ties would worry pessimists and optimists alike. On the other hand, Chinese analysts of all stripes also worry to varying degrees when Japan adopts greater defense burden-sharing roles as part of a bilateral effort to revitalize the alliance. These dual and almost contradictory fears pose major problems for U.S. élites who are concerned that the alliance is dangerously vague and out of date and is therefore unsustainable, but who still want the United States to maintain the reassurance role [...]. Especially before the recent guidelines review, the U.S.-Japan alliance had often been viewed in the United States as lopsided and unfair because the United States guarantees Japanese security without clear guarantees of even rudimentary assistance from Japan if U.S. forces were to become embroiled in a regional armed conflict.[16] [...]

Since the publication of the critically important February 1995 East Asia Strategy Report (also known as the Nye report), U.S. leaders have been expressing very different concerns about the U.S.-Japan relationship. The Nye report, and the broader Nye initiative of which it is a part, placed new emphasis on maintaining and strengthening the security alliance and on keeping economic disputes from poisoning it. The report reaffirms the centrality of U.S. security alliances in Asia, places a floor on U.S. troop strength in East Asia at 100,000, and calls for increased security cooperation between Japan and the United States, including greater Japanese logistics support for U.S. forces operating in the region and consideration of joint research on TMD.[17] [...]

[Undoubtedly,] Chinese security analysts followed these [shifting] trends in U.S.-Japan relations with great interest and concern. [...]

Chinese attitudes and the prospects for regional confidence building

An important prerequisite for resolving a security dilemma is for the actors involved to recognize that one exists. A core factor that underpins the security dilemma is the general lack of empathy among the actors participating in a security competition. Beijing élites may be no better or worse than their counterparts in most other nations on this score. Although they may not use the technical term "security dilemma," Chinese analysts recognize the potential for arms racing and spirals of tension in the region. They even recognize that Japan might build its military out of fear, rather than aggression. China actually supported Japanese buildups in the 1970s and early 1980s in response to the development of the Soviet navy.[18] In 1994 several analysts argued that China did not want North Korea to have nuclear weapons because this might cause Japan to develop them.[19]

Beijing also has demonstrated an ability to understand that others might see China as a threat.[20] But, while many Chinese analysts can imagine some states as legitimately worried about China and can picture Japan legitimately worried about other states, it is harder to find those who believe that Japan's military security policy could be driven by fears about specific security policies in China.[21] Chinese analysts, especially in the past two years, seem to agree that China's overall rise (*jueqi*) is a general source of concern for Japan. They tend not to recognize, however, that particular Chinese actions or weapons developments might be reason for Japan to reconsider aspects of its defense policy. [...]

A different and even more troubling Chinese perspective on China's potential influence on Japanese defense policy has also gained frequency in the past two years. Perhaps because of the relatively high economic growth rates in China compared to Japan in the 1990s, some Chinese experts have expressed more confidence that China would be able to defend its security interests against Japan, even in the absence of a U.S. presence in the region. Although they hardly dismiss the potential threat of a Japan made more assertive by a U.S. withdrawal, they seem relatively confident that China's strength and deterrent capabilities could influence Japan's strategy by dissuading Tokyo from significant Japanese buildups or, at least, later military adventurism.[22] From the security dilemma perspective this attitude may be even more dangerous than the view that China can pose little threat to Japan. If increasing Chinese coercive capacity is seen as the best way to prevent or manage anticipated Japanese buildups, then the danger of China taking the critical first step in an action-reaction cycle seems very high.

There are some more hopeful signs, however. Some Chinese analysts, usually younger experts (appearing to be in their forties or younger) with extensive experience abroad, do recognize that Chinese military strengthening and provocative actions could be seen as legitimate reasons for Japan to launch a military buildup of its own. Given the age of these analysts and the increasing number of Chinese élites with considerable experience abroad, the trends seem to be heading in a positive direction on this score. On a sober note, more than one of these empathetic experts has pointed out that Chinese experts who take Japanese concerns about China seriously are often viewed with suspicion in government circles and sometimes have difficulty when presenting their views to their older and more influential colleagues, particularly in the military.[23]

China's views on multilateral security regimes

One possible way to ameliorate the security dilemma is through multilateral regimes and forums designed to increase transparency and build confidence. For various reasons, Beijing has viewed multilateral confidence building with some suspicion. Many Chinese analysts emphasize that the increased transparency called for by such institutions can make China's enemies more confident and thereby reduce China's deterrent capabilities, particularly its ability to deter Taiwan independence or foreign intervention in cross-strait relations.[24] Especially in the early 1990s they worried that multilateral forums and organizations might be fronts for great powers, and that confidence-building measures might be aspects of a containment strategy designed to keep China from achieving great power status in the military sector.[25]

That said, China has not shunned multilateral forums. China has participated in the ASEAN Regional Forum (ARF) since its first meeting in 1994, and in 1997 Beijing hosted an ARF intersessional conference on confidence-building measures. Although Beijing has prevented any dramatic accomplishments at ARF meetings on important questions such as the territorial disputes in the South China Sea, the precedent of such Chinese participation seems potentially important.[26] [...]

The reduced fear of U.S. domination of the Association of Southeast Asian Nations (ASEAN) and of ASEAN collusion against China, combined with the increased fear of developments in U.S. bilateral diplomacy in the Asia Pacific since 1996, have convinced many formerly skeptical analysts that some form of multilateralism may be the best alternative for China given the risks posed by U.S. bilateral business as usual.[27] Given that China both fears and has little influence over various aspects of current U.S. bilateral diplomacy (such as strengthening the U.S.-Japan alliance or the U.S.-Australia alliance), accepting a bigger role for multilateral dialogue, if not the creation of formal multilateral security institutions, may be the least unpleasant method of reducing the threat that U.S. bilateralism poses.[28] So, in this one sense, the revitalization of the U.S.-Japan alliance may have had some unintended positive results by encouraging China to consider more seriously the benefits of multilateral forums that might reduce mutual mistrust in the region.[29] This phenomenon runs counter to psychological and social constructivist theories on the security dilemma that emphasize how accommodation, not pressure, is the best way to make states adopt more cooperative postures.[30] [...]

* * *

Given China's intense historically based mistrust of Japan, Beijing's concern about eroding norms of Japanese self-restraint, and the political geography of the Taiwan issue, even certain new defensive roles for Japan can be provocative to China. The United States should therefore continue to be cautious about what new roles Japan is asked to play in the alliance. This is particularly true in cases where the United States may be able to play the same roles without triggering the same degree of concern in Beijing.

By maintaining and, where necessary, increasing somewhat U.S. capabilities in Japan and East Asia more generally, not only will the United States better be able to manage and cap future regional crises, it ideally may be able to prevent them from ever occurring. By reassuring both Japan and its potential rivals, the United States reduces the likelihood of divisive security dilemma scenarios and spiral model dynamics in the region. In so doing, the United States can contribute mightily to long-term peace and stability in a region that promises to be the most important arena for U.S. foreign policy in the twenty-first century. [...]

Notes

1   Aaron L. Friedberg, "Ripe for Rivalry: Prospects for Peace in a Multipolar Asia," *International Security*, Vol. 18, No. 3 (Winter 1993/94), pp. 5–33; Richard K. Betts, "Wealth, Power, and Instability," *International Security*, Vol. 18, No. 3 (Winter 1993/94), pp. 34–77; Stephen Van Evera, "Primed for Peace: Europe after the Cold War," *International Security*, Vol. 15, No. 3 (Winter 1990/91), pp. 7–57; and James Goldgeier and Michael McFaul, "A Tale of Two Worlds," *International Organization*, Vol. 46, No. 2 (Spring 1992), pp. 467–92.

2   For the original security dilemma and spiral models, see Robert Jervis, "Cooperation under the Security Dilemma," *World Politics*, Vol. 30, No. 2 (January 1978), pp. 167–74; and Jervis, *Perception and Misperception in International Politics* (Princeton, N.J.: Princeton University Press, 1976), chap. 3.

3   For writings on the destabilizing influence of offensive weapons and doctrines, see Stephen Van Evera, "The Cult of the Offensive and the Origins of the First World War," *International Security*, Vol. 9, No. 1 (Summer 1984), pp. 58–107; Van Evera, "Offense, Defense, and the Causes of War," *International Security*, Vol. 22, No. 4 (Spring 1998), pp. 5–43; and Sean M. Lynn-Jones, "Offense-Defense Theory and Its Critics," *Security Studies*, Vol. 4, No. 4 (Summer 1995), pp. 660–91.

4   My understanding of the Chinese perspectives reflects more than seventy interviews, often with multiple interlocutors, that I conducted during four month-long trips to Beijing in 1993, 1994, 1995, and 1996, and two shorter trips to Beijing and Shanghai in 1998. My interlocutors were a mix of military and civilian analysts in government think tanks as well as academics at leading Chinese institutions. The government think-tank analysts are not decisionmakers, but they advise their superiors in the following key governmental organizations: the People's Liberation Army (PLA), the Foreign Ministry, the State Council, and the Chinese intelligence agencies. For obvious reasons, the individual identities of particular interviewees cannot be revealed.

5   In fact, even optimistic projections for the region are predicated on a long-term U.S. military presence. See, for example, Robert S. Ross, "The Geography of the

Peace: East Asia in the Twenty-first Century," *International Security*, Vol. 23, No. 4 (Spring 1999), pp. 81–118.

6   One might argue that the geographical proximity of Japan alone would make a new regional power a greater threat to China than the more distant United States. In any case, the decision over what poses a larger threat – a distant superpower or a local great power – cannot be reached by analyzing the international balance of power alone. As in the Chinese case, the assessment of which country poses the greater threat will be based on historical legacies and national perceptions. I am grateful to Stephen Walt for helpful comments on this point.

7   For the classic study, see Allen S. Whiting, *China Eyes Japan* (Berkeley: University of California Press, 1989).

8   It is possible that the concerns expressed by Chinese analysts discussed below about Japan and the United States are purely cynical tactics designed to prevent the rise of a new regional power by affecting the debate in the United States and Japan. Such a "spin" strategy could also help justify at home and to regional actors more aggressive Chinese weapons development and diplomacy. Although I believe this probably was the intention of some of my interlocutors, given the large number of interlocutors, the diversity of opinions expressed on various issues over the five years of my discussions, and the controversial positions I sometimes heard expressed on issues such as the Tiananmen massacre or the Chinese missile exercises near Taiwan, I find it difficult to believe that Beijing, or any other government, could manufacture such complex theater over such an extended period of time.

9   Also in that year Japanese rightists built structures on the Diaoyu/Senkaku Islands, which are contested by both Japan and China. Many Chinese analysts saw Tokyo's complicity in their activities, especially after the dispatch of Japanese Coast Guard vessels to prevent protestors from Hong Kong and Taiwan from landing on the Japanese-controlled islands.

10   See Yinan He, "The Effect of Historical Memory on China's Strategic Perception of Japan," paper prepared for the Ninety-forth Annual Meeting of the American Political Science Association," Boston, Massachusetts, September 3–6, 1998. For example, my interlocutors generally did not believe that a militarily stronger Japan would try to occupy sections of the Asian mainland as it did in the 1930s and 1940s.

11   The problem of Japan's lack of contrition was raised in nearly every interview I conducted. See Zhang Dalin, "Qianshi Bu Wang, Houshi Zhi Shi" [Past experience, if not forgotten, is a guide for the future], *Guoji Wenti Yanjiu* [International studies], No. 3 (1995), pp. 6–11. For a critical Japanese perspective on the textbook issue, see Saburo Ienaga, "The Glorification of War in Japanese Education," *International Security*, Vol. 18, No. 3 (Winter 1993/94), pp. 113–33. The Chinese view on the generational issue in Japan is similar to the Japanese pacifist view. See Kunihiro Masao, "The Decline and Fall of Pacifism," *Bulletin of the Atomic Scientists*, Vol. 53, No. 1 (January/February 1997), pp. 35–39.

12   In 1993 government scholars pointed out that, in many ways, China's youth is more actively anti-Japanese than the government. They pointed to student protests against Japanese "economic imperialism" in 1986 as an example.

13   Interviews, 1996. See also Hafumi Arai, "Angry at China? Slam Japan," *Far Eastern Economic Review*, October 3, 1996, p. 21. It is clear that compared to students and other members of the public, the Chinese government was a voice of calm during the 1996 Diaoyu/Senkaku affair.

14 Multiple interviews, 1993–98.

15 Interview, 1996.

16 This common view often ignores the clear benefits to the United States of the Cold War version of the alliance. The United States was guaranteed basing in Japan, and 70–80 percent of those basing costs were covered by the Japanese. Without this basing, the United States would have great difficulty maintaining its presence in the region. For a cost analysis, see Michael O'Hanlon, "Restructuring U.S. Forces and Bases in Japan," in Mike M. Mochizuki, ed., *Toward a True Alliance: Restructuring U.S.-Japan Security Relations* (Washington, D.C.: Brookings, 1997), pp. 149–78.

17 The Nye report, named for former Assistant Secretary of Defense Joseph S. Nye, Jr., is *United States Security Strategy for the East Asia-Pacific Region*, Office of International Security Affairs, Department of Defense, February 1995. For an insider's look at concerns about how acrimonious economic disputes were harming the alliance, see David L. Asher, "A U.S.-Japan Alliance for the Next Century," *Orbis*, Vol. 41, No. 3 (Summer 1997), pp. 343–75, at pp. 346–48.

18 For example, an internally circulated analysis of those Japanese buildups does not suggest opportunism or aggressive intent. See Pan Sifeng, ed., *Riben Junshi Sixiang Yanjiu* [Research on Japanese military thought] (Beijing: Academy of Military Sciences Press, October 1992), pp. 388–92 (internally circulated), chap. 14, and pp. 414–15.

19 Interviews, 1994.

20 For example, Beijing at times has tried to reassure Southeast Asian nations about its desire to settle the Spratly Islands disputes peacefully. Even if these are merely cynical tactics designed to buy time for China to concentrate on the Taiwan problem or develop force projection to handle the Spratlys dispute later, they demonstrate Beijing's ability to conceive of Southeast Asian fears about China.

21 For example, one book takes seriously Japan's fear of the Soviets during the Cold War, but places Japan's concern about China under the heading "Japan's Imagined Enemies," see Pan, *Riben Junshi Sixiang Yanjiu*, pp. 413–16. For another example, see Zhan Shiliang, "Yatai Diqu Xingshi he Zhongguo Mulin Youhao Zhengce" [The Asia-Pacific situation and China's good neighbor policy], *Guoji Wenti Yanjiu* [International studies], No. 4 (1993), pp. 1–3, 7.

22 The increased frequency of such statements over time may be one effect of China's relatively high rates of economic growth in the 1990s in comparison to Japan.

23 In separate interviews in 1994 a military officer and a civilian analyst lamented that the vast majority of Chinese are incapable of thinking in ways empathetic to Japanese concerns about China. In 1996 a civilian analyst complained that too many Chinese leaders and security analysts are unable to separate their analyses of 1930s' Japan and 1990s' Japan.

24 Multiple interviews, 1993–98. In fact, one military officer was even quite critical of China's last round of military exercises in March 1996 because he was afraid that China revealed too much about its military to a vigilant and highly capable U.S. defense intelligence network.

25 China has worked in the past to block the creation of formal multilateral reassurance regimes in East Asia, such as the Organization for Security and Cooperation in Europe, that might lead to condemnation of China's development and/or deployment of its force-projection capabilities. As Jianwei Wang argues, China has been more open to multilateralism in the economic realm than it has been in the security realm. Jianwei Wang, "Chinese Views of Multilateralism," in Yong Deng and Feiling

Wang, *In the Eyes of the Dragon: China Views the World and Sino-American Relations* (Boulder, Colo.: Rowman and Littlefield, forthcoming).

26   For example, at the July 1994 ARF conference and in earlier multilateral meetings with Southeast Asian representatives, China blocked any meaningful discussion of territorial disputes involving Chinese claims. See Allen S. Whiting, "ASEAN Eyes China," *Asian Survey*, Vol. 37, No. 4 (April 1997), pp. 299–322.

27   Interviews, 1996 and 1998. See also Wang, "Chinese Views on Multilateralism," in Deng and Wang, *In the Eyes of the Dragon*; and Wu Xinbo, "Integration on the Basis of Strength: China's Impact on East Asian Security," Asia/Pacific Research Center working paper, February 1998.

28   Interviews, 1996 and 1998. For an excellent analysis of ASEAN concerns and hopes about China, see Whiting, "ASEAN Eyes China.". For Chinese reactions to changes in the U.S.-Japan alliance along these lines, see Zhou Jihua, "RiMei Anbao Tizhi de Qianghua yu Dongya de Anquan" [The strengthening of the U.S.-Japan security structure and the security of East Asia], *Riben Xuekan* [Japan studies], No. 4 (1996), pp. 41–42; and Zhou, "Military Accords Create Suspicions," *China Daily*, October 7, 1996.

29   Interviews, 1996 and 1998. I was impressed that multilateral options, previously often discounted by my interlocutors, were now raised as legitimate alternatives to U.S. bilateralism without my prompting.

30   In the psychological literature on the security dilemma, one is not supposed to try to solve security dilemmas by applying pressure but by reassuring distrustful states. See Jervis, *Perception and Misperception*, chap. 3. In Alexander Wendt's constructivist approach, not only do tough policies merely reproduce realist fear and cynicism, but gentle persuasion and appeasement are prescribed for even truly predatory regimes, such as Hitler's Germany or Stalin's Russia. See Wendt, "Anarchy Is What States Make of It," *International Organization*, Vol. 46, No. 2 (Spring 1992), pp. 391–425, at 409. In fact, recent work on Chinese foreign policy since Tiananmen suggests that the fear of material sanctions and social stigmatization helps explain a broad range of cooperative Chinese foreign policies from a general, more constructive regional strategy to accession to important international arms control institutions, such as the Nuclear Nonproliferation Treaty and the Comprehensive Test Ban Treaty. See Yu Bin, "China's Regional Views and Policies – Implications for the United States," and Hu Weixing, "China and Nuclear Nonproliferation," both in Deng and Wang, *In the Eyes of the Dragon*. See also Alastair Iain Johnston and Paul Evans, "China's Engagement of Multilateral Institutions," in Johnston and Robert S. Ross, eds., *Engaging China: The Management of an Emerging Power* (London: Routledge, forthcoming).

Kenneth N. Waltz

STRUCTURAL REALISM REDUX

Source: 'Structural realism after the Cold War', *International Security*, vol. 25, no. 1, Summer 2000, pp. 5–41.

Balancing power: not today but tomorrow

WITH SO MANY OF THE expectations that realist theory gives rise to confirmed by what happened at and after the end of the Cold War, one may wonder why realism is in bad repute.[1] A key proposition derived from realist theory is that international politics reflects the distribution of national capabilities, a proposition daily borne out. Another key proposition is that the balancing of power by some states against other recurs. Realist theory predicts that balances disrupted will one day be restored. A limitation of the theory, a limitation common to social science theories, is that it cannot say when. [...] Theory cannot say when "tomorrow" will come because international political theory deals with the pressures of structure on states and not with how states will respond to the pressures. The latter is a task for theories about how national governments respond to pressures on them and take advantage of opportunities that may be present. One does, however, observe balancing tendencies already taking place.

Upon the demise of the Soviet Union, the international political system became unipolar. In the light of structural theory, unipolarity appears as the least durable of international configurations. This is so for two main reasons. One is that dominant powers take on too many tasks beyond their own borders, thus weakening themselves in the long run. [...] The other reason for the short duration of unipolarity is that even if a dominant power behaves with moderation, restraint, and forbearance, weaker states will worry about its future behavior. [...] Throughout the Cold War, what the United States and the Soviet Union did, and how they interacted, were dominant factors in international politics. The two countries, however, constrained each other. Now the United States is alone in the world. As nature abhors a vacuum, so international politics abhors unbalanced power. Faced with unbalanced power, some states try to increase their own strength or they ally with others to bring the international distribution of power into balance. [...]

The behavior of dominant powers

Will the preponderant power of the United States elicit similar reactions? Unbalanced power, whoever wields it, is a potential danger to others. The powerful state may, and the United States does, think of itself as acting for the sake of peace, justice, and well-being in the world. These terms, however, are defined to the liking of the powerful, which may conflict with the preferences and interests of others. In international politics, overwhelming power repels and leads others to try to balance against it. With benign intent, the United States has behaved and, until its power is brought into balance, will continue to behave in ways that sometimes frighten others.

For almost half a century, the constancy of the Soviet threat produced a constancy of American policy. Other countries could rely on the United States for protection because protecting them seemed to serve American security interests. [...]

With the disappearance of the Soviet Union, the United States no longer faces a major threat to its security. [...] Constancy of threat produces constancy of policy; absence of threat permits policy to become capricious. When few if any vital interests are endangered, a country's policy becomes sporadic and self-willed.

The absence of serious threats to American security gives the United States wide latitude in making foreign policy choices. A dominant power acts internationally only when the spirit moves it. [...]

Aside from specific threats it may pose, unbalanced power leaves weaker states feeling uneasy and gives them reason to strengthen their positions. The United States has a long history of intervening in weak states, often with the intention of bringing democracy to them. American behavior over the past century in Central America provides little evidence of self-restraint in the absence of countervailing power. [...] Concentrated power invites distrust because it is so easily misused. To understand why some states want to bring power into a semblance of balance is easy, but with power so sharply skewed, what country or group of countries has the material capability and the political will to bring the "unipolar moment" to an end?

Balancing power in a unipolar world

The expectation that following victory in a great war a new balance of power will form is firmly grounded in both history and theory. [...] Victories in major wars leave the balance of power badly skewed. The winning side emerges as a dominant coalition. The international equilibrium is broken; theory leads one to expect its restoration. [...]

The candidates for becoming the next great powers, and thus restoring a balance, are the European Union or Germany leading a coalition, China, Japan, and in a more distant future, Russia. The countries of the European Union have been remarkably successful in integrating their national economies. The achievement of a large measure of economic integration without a corresponding political unity is an accomplishment without historical precedent. On questions of foreign and military policy, however, the European Union can act only with the consent of its members, making bold or risky action impossible. The European Union has all the tools – population, resources, technology, and military capabilities – but lacks the organizational ability and the collective will to use them. [...]

Europe may not remain in its supine position forever, yet signs of fundamental change in matters of foreign and military policy are faint. [...] Now as earlier, European leaders express discontent with Europe's secondary position, chafe at America's making most of the important decisions, and show a desire to direct their own destiny. [...] Europe, however, will not be able to claim a louder voice in alliance affairs unless it builds a platform for giving it expression. If Europeans ever mean to write a tune to go with their libretto, they will have to develop the unity in foreign and military affairs that they are achieving in economic matters. [...]

International structure and national responses

Throughout modern history, international politics centered on Europe. Two world wars ended Europe's dominance. Whether Europe will somehow, someday emerge as a great power is a matter for speculation. In the meantime, the all-but-inevitable movement from unipolarity to multipolarity is taking place not in Europe but in Asia. The internal development and the external reaction of China and Japan are steadily raising both countries to the great power level.[2] China will emerge as a great power even without trying very hard so long as it remains politically united and competent. Strategically, China can easily raise its nuclear forces to a level of parity with the United States if it has not already done so.[3] [...] Economically, China's growth rate, given its present stage of economic development, can be sustained at 7 to 9 percent for another decade or more. Even during Asia's near economic collapse of the 1990s, China's growth rate remained approximately in that range. A growth rate of 7 to 9 percent doubles a country's economy every ten to eight years.

Unlike China, Japan is obviously reluctant to assume the mantle of a great power. Its reluctance, however, is steadily though slowly waning. Economically, Japan's power has grown and spread remarkably. The growth of a country's economic capability to the great power level places it at the center of regional and global affairs. It widens the range of a state's interests and increases their importance. The high volume of a country's external business thrusts it ever more deeply into world affairs. In a self-help system, the possession of most but not all of the capabilities of a great power leaves a state vulnerable to others that have the instruments that the lesser state lacks. Even though one may believe that fears of nuclear blackmail are misplaced, one must wonder whether Japan will remain immune to them.

Countries have always competed for wealth and security, and the competition has often led to conflict. Historically, states have been sensitive to changing relations of power among them. Japan is made uneasy now by the steady growth of China's military budget. Its nearly 3 million strong army, undergoing modernization, and the gradual growth of its sea- and air-power projection capabilities, produce apprehension in all of China's neighbors and add to the sense of instability in a region where issues of sovereignty and disputes over territory abound. The Korean peninsula has more military forces per square kilometer than any other portion of the globe. Taiwan is an unending source of tension. Disputes exist between Japan and Russia over the Kurile Islands, and between Japan and China over the Senkaku or Diaoyu Islands. Cambodia is a troublesome problem for both Vietnam and China. Half a dozen countries lay claim to all or some of the Spratly Islands, strategically located and supposedly rich in oil. The presence of

China's ample nuclear forces, combined with the drawdown of American military forces, can hardly be ignored by Japan, the less so because economic conflicts with the United States cast doubt on the reliability of American military guarantees. Reminders of Japan's dependence and vulnerability multiply in large and small ways. For example, as rumors about North Korea's developing nuclear capabilities gained credence, Japan became acutely aware of its lack of observation satellites. Uncomfortable dependencies and perceived vulnerabilities have led Japan to acquire greater military capabilities, even though many Japanese may prefer not to.

Given the expectation of conflict, and the necessity of taking care of one's interests, one may wonder how any state with the economic capability of a great power can refrain from arming itself with the weapons that have served so well as the great deterrent. For a country to choose not to become a great power is a structural anomaly. For that reason, the choice is a difficult one to sustain. Sooner or later, usually sooner, the international status of countries has risen in step with their material resources. Countries with great power economies have become great powers, whether or not reluctantly. Some countries may strive to become great powers; others may wish to avoid doing so. The choice, however, is a constrained one. Because of the extent of their interests, larger units existing in a contentious arena tend to take on systemwide tasks. Profound change in a country's international situation produces radical change in its external behavior. After World War II, the United States broke with its centuries-long tradition of acting unilaterally and refusing to make long-term commitments. Japan's behavior in the past half century reflects the abrupt change in its international standing suffered because of its defeat in war. In the previous half century, after victory over China in 1894–95, Japan pressed for preeminence in Asia, if not beyond. Does Japan once again aspire to a larger role internationally? Its concerted regional activity, its seeking and gaining prominence in such bodies as the IMF and the World Bank, and its obvious pride in economic and technological achievements indicate that it does. The behavior of states responds more to external conditions than to internal habit if external change is profound.

When external conditions press firmly enough, they shape the behavior of states. Increasingly, Japan is being pressed to enlarge its conventional forces and to add nuclear ones to protect its interests. India, Pakistan, China, and perhaps North Korea have nuclear weapons capable of deterring others from threatening their vital interests. How long can Japan live alongside other nuclear states while denying itself similar capabilities? Conflicts and crises are certain to make Japan aware of the disadvantages of being without the military instruments that other powers command. Japanese nuclear inhibitions arising from World War II will not last indefinitely; one may expect them to expire as generational memories fade.

Japanese officials have indicated that when the protection of America's extended deterrent is no longer thought to be sufficiently reliable, Japan will equip itself with a nuclear force, whether or not openly. Japan has put itself politically and technologically in a position to do so. Consistently since the mid-1950s, the government has defined all of its Self-Defense Forces as conforming to constitutional requirements. Nuclear weapons purely for defense would be deemed constitutional should Japan decide to build some.[4] [...]

Where some see Japan as a "global civilian power" and believe it likely to remain one, others see a country that has skillfully used the protection the United States has afforded and adroitly adopted the means of maintaining its security to its regional environment.[5] Prime Minister Shigeru Yoshida in the early 1950s suggested that Japan should rely on American protection until it had rebuilt its economy as it gradually prepared to stand on its own feet.[6] Japan has laid a firm foundation for doing so by developing much of its own weaponry instead of relying on cheaper imports. [...] Whether reluctantly or not, Japan and China will follow each other on the route to becoming great powers. China has the greater long-term potential. Japan with the world's second or third largest defense budget and the ability to produce the most technologically advanced weaponry, is closer to great power status at the moment.

When Americans speak of preserving the balance of power in East Asia through their military presence,[7] the Chinese understandably take this to mean that they intend to maintain the strategic hegemony they now enjoy in the *absence* of such a balance. When China makes steady but modest efforts to improve the quality of its inferior forces, Americans see a future threat to their and others' interests. Whatever worries the United States has and whatever threats it feels, Japan has them earlier and feels them more intensely. Japan has gradually reacted to them. China then worries as Japan improves its airlift and sealift capabilities and as the United States raises its support level for forces in South Korea.[8] The actions and reactions of China, Japan, and South Korea, with or without American participation, are creating a new balance of power in East Asia, which is becoming part of the new balance of power in the world.

Historically, encounters of East and West have often ended in tragedy. Yet, as we know from happy experience, nuclear weapons moderate the behavior of their possessors and render them cautious whenever crises threaten to spin out of control. Fortunately, the changing relations of East to West, and the changing relations of countries within the East and the West, are taking place in a nuclear context. The tensions and conflicts that intensify when profound changes in world politics take place will continue to mar the relations of nations, while nuclear weapons keep the peace among those who enjoy their protection.

America's policy of containing China by keeping 100,000 troops in East Asia and by providing security guarantees to Japan and South Korea is intended to keep a new balance of power from forming in Asia. By continuing to keep 100,000 troops in Western Europe, where no military threat is in sight, and by extending NATO eastward, the United States pursues the same goal in Europe. The American aspiration to freeze historical development by working to keep the world unipolar is doomed. In the not very long run, the task will exceed America's economic, military, demographic, and political resources; and the very effort to maintain a hegemonic position is the surest way to undermine it. The effort to maintain dominance stimulates some countries to work to overcome it. As theory shows and history confirms, that is how balances of power are made. Multipolarity is developing before our eyes. Moreover, it is emerging in accordance with the balancing imperative.

American leaders seem to believe that America's preeminent position will last indefinitely. The United States would then remain the dominant power without rivals rising to challenge it – a position without precedent in modern history. Balancing, of course, is not universal and omnipresent. A dominant power may suppress balancing as the United States has done in Europe. Whether or not balancing takes place also depends on the decisions of governments. [...] States are free to disregard the imperatives of power, but they must expect to pay a price for doing so. Moreover, relatively weak and divided states may find it impossible to concert their efforts to counter a hegemonic state despite ample provocation. This has long been the condition of the Western Hemisphere.

In the Cold War, the United States won a telling victory. Victory in war, however, often brings lasting enmities. Magnanimity in victory is rare. Winners of wars, facing few impediments to the exercise of their wills, often act in ways that create future enemies. Thus Germany, by taking Alsace and most of Lorraine from France in 1871, earned its lasting enmity; and the Allies' harsh treatment of Germany after World War I produced a similar effect. In contrast, Bismarck persuaded the kaiser not to march his armies along the road to Vienna after the great victory at Königgrätz in 1866. In the Treaty of Prague, Prussia took no Austrian territory. Thus Austria, having become Austria-Hungary, was available as an alliance partner for Germany in 1879. Rather than learning from history, the United States is repeating past errors by extending its influence over what used to be the province of the vanquished.[9] This alienates Russia and nudges it toward China instead of drawing it toward Europe and the United States. Despite much talk about the "globalization" of international politics, American political leaders to a dismaying extent think of East *or* West rather than of their interaction. With a history of conflict along a 2,600 mile border, with ethnic minorities sprawling across it, with a mineral-rich and sparsely populated Siberia facing China's teeming millions, Russia and China will find it difficult to cooperate effectively, but the United States is doing its best to help them do so. Indeed, the United States has provided the key to Russian-Chinese relations over the past half century. Feeling American antagonism and fearing American power, China drew close to Russia after World War II and remained so until the United States seemed less, and the Soviet Union more, of a threat to China. The relatively harmonious relations the United States and China enjoyed during the 1970s began to sour in the late 1980s when Russian power visibly declined and American hegemony became imminent. To alienate Russia by expanding NATO, and to alienate China by lecturing its leaders on how to rule their country, are policies that only an overwhelmingly powerful country could afford, and only a foolish one be tempted, to follow. The United States cannot prevent a new balance of power from forming. It can hasten its coming as it has been earnestly doing. [...]

Notes

1   Robert Gilpin explains the oddity. See Gilpin, "No One Leaves a Political Realist," *Security Studies*, Vol. 5, No. 3 (Spring 1996), pp. 3–28.

2   The following four pages are adapted from Kenneth N. Waltz, "The Emerging Structure of International Politics," *International Security*, Vol. 18, No. 2 (Fall 1993).

3   Nuclear parity is reached when countries have second-strike forces. It does not require quantitative or qualitative equality of forces. See Waltz, "Nuclear Myths and Political Realities," *American Political Science Review*, Vol. 84, No. 3 (September 1990).

4   Norman D. Levin, "Japan's Defense Policy: The Internal Debate," in Harry H. Kendall and Clara Joewono, eds., *Japan, ASEAN, and the United States* (Berkeley: Institute of East Asian Studies, University of California, 1990).

5   Michael J. Green, "State of the Field Report: Research on Japanese Security Policy," *Access Asia Review*, Vol. 2, No. 2 (September 1998), judiciously summarized different interpretations of Japan's security policy.

6   Kenneth B. Pyle, *The Japanese Question: Power and Purpose in a New Era* (Washington, D.C.: AEI Press, 1992), p. 26.

7   Richard Bernstein and Ross H. Munro, *The Coming Conflict with China* (New York: Alfred A. Knopf, 1997); and Andrew J. Nathan and Robert S. Ross, *The Great Wall and the Empty Fortress: China's Search for Security* (New York: W. W. Norton, 1997).

8   Michael J. Green and Benjamin L. Self, "Japan's Changing China Policy: From Commercial Liberalism to Reluctant Realism," *Survival*, Vol. 38, No. 2 (Summer 1996), p. 43.

9   Tellingly, John Lewis Gaddis comments that he has never known a time when there was less support among historians for an announced policy. Gaddis, "History, Grand Strategy, and NATO Enlargement," *Survival*, Vol. 40, No. 1 (Spring 1998), p. 147.

Ken Booth

SECURITY AND GLOBAL TRANSFORMATION

Source: 'Conclusion: security within global transformation?', in Ken Booth (ed.) *Statecraft and Security: The Cold War and Beyond* (Cambridge: Cambridge University Press, 1998), pp. 338–55.

S O FAR IN THE 1990s many of us feel [...] [the] end-of-century gloom; after all, this is not the first time people have complained about incompetent and visionless governments, the collapse of traditional institutions, widespread social and economic distress, appalling disparities in life chances, racism and hypernationalism, private comfort replacing public ideals, and introspection triumphing over internationalism, corruption over service and helplessness over hope. In terms of mood we have been here before, but something is new. The present of world politics is unique in terms of its material conditions: a wired world, a threatened environment, a global population surge, a truly world economy, depleting non-renewable resources, and intercontinental weapons of mass destruction. [...]

In these confusing times, with contested foundations and visions, a major responsibility for students of International Relations is to try to make sense of events without surrendering complexity, to paint pictures of the future without claiming prediction, and to attempt to devise political forms that offer more hope than presently of delivering peace, security and welfare for more of the earth's population. With these points in mind, this Conclusion discusses the changing context of statecraft and security in this, the first truly global age. [...]. [I]t seeks to provide further context for rethinking – resisting and reinventing – in relation to three crucial aspects of global transformation – globalisation, global governance and global moral science.

Globalisation

The context of international relations in the final decades of the twentieth century has changed in a dramatic fashion. This new stage in world history – potentially a step-change in the evolution of human society – cannot easily be reduced to a single word: but to the extent it can, it is encapsulated in the concept of 'globalisation'.

This remains a much debated and contested concept, but for me it embraces those changes that have been taking place in politics, society and economy that result in the daily intermeshing and densification of local lives and global processes, and the impact of this on traditional conceptions of time, space, boundaries, culture, identity and politics. [...]

Wherever one looks, there is movement and challenge in material circumstances and social relations. We are living in an era of spectacular change. At the same time there is a pervasive sense that nobody controls the transformations: instead, the transformations control us. It is only necessary to mention the transnational organisation of production, the liberalisation of markets globally, the growth of world cities, advanced information technology, the 24-hour global finance system, changing consumption patterns and expectations, and the pressures on traditional family relationships, local communities, cultural norms and political authority. The changes are eye-catching at the material level but are profound below the surface, at the level of ontology and political philosophy. For students of International Relations, one outcome of the processes of globalisation is that the familiar textbook notion of the sovereign state is called into question. State borders are increasingly open to external penetration on a minute-by-minute basis, to everything except neighbouring armies, as the autonomy of governments declines over economic planning, social ideas and cultural choice. The sovereign state's power to control its own destiny is eroded by globalisation. James Rosenau's term 'post-international politics' becomes everyday more pertinent (1990). This is certainly not to say that governments and states are henceforth unimportant. They are, and will remain influential conduits in the distribution of social, political and economic goods. They regulate the lives of their citizens in manifold ways, but they themselves are more than ever regulated by outside pressures. If the twentieth-century image of the sovereign state has been that of a juggernaut being driven down an autobahn, towards prosperity and power, the twenty-first-century metaphor is more likely to see governments as traffic cops, at a busy (probably Asian) intersection, gesticulating wildly while trying to direct the teeming flow of people, traffic and goods – all of which have their own imperatives – as best they can. Governments are busier than ever before, with more functions and pressures, but they have less autonomy.

Globalisation, like other human developments, does not everywhere have uniform effects and is a two-edged sword. It offers the promises of inclusiveness and interdependence, and different and more hopeful visions of the human condition, but as a result of certain ruling ideas, it also magnifies disparities between rich and poor, powerful and powerless, and leaves established political authority structures feeling unable to control the companies and cultural ideas that can exploit the time/space opportunities of a globalising planet. These are the circumstances in which apprehension is the dominant mood. The global market promises wealth and choice, but it threatens protectionism, financial crises, the destruction of nature, unemployment, the marginalisation of welfarism, personal anxiety and other negative social consequences and economic reactions. Levels of insecurity rise, and there is fatalism about human agency. The challenge is therefore to inform globalisation with ideas that can maximise its promise in terms of human community and global welfare and minimise its threats in terms of disparity and dislocation. This is the task for what I later call global moral science.

The political economy of globalisation is one of the most powerful forces shaping our times. At its base is the world capitalist economy. (Expressed differently, this aspect of globalisation can be regarded as an extension of US foreign policy by other means.) Capitalism has been an enormously successful economic system in the way it has provided large numbers of people with goods, but as Robert Heilbroner has argued, persuasively and succinctly, its expansionist nature (marked by unbounded science and technology) intrudes into all aspects of human relationships – with nature and with each other. In Heilbroner's words, 'the commodification of life is not only an intrusion of science and technology into the tissues of sociality, but also the means by which a capitalist economy draws energy from its own environment' (1995: 99). [...]

The global market produces particular forms of global competition which in turn means that national economies have to compete by the rules, or wither away. Politics within nations is increasingly shaped by economics above nations, and between national economies and the global economy. Consequently, instead of states aiming to become 'local agents of the world common good', to use Hedley Bull's term (1983: 11–12, 14) they have increasingly been coopted to be local agents of the world capitalist good. It was failure in this competition, for example, which sealed the fate of the militarily super-powerful Soviet Union. To be a stagnant post-Stalinist command economy in a burgeoning post-Fordist capitalist world was historically terminal. The Soviet Union did not collapse, it was coopted. [...]

[...] We live in the age of the Divine Right of the Consumer. As a result the market threatens the welfare of the powerless and tramples over the natural environment. The claim is heard throughout the advanced industrial world – Galbraith's 'culture of contentment' (1992) – that higher levels of public spending cannot be afforded. But what determines the limit is political choice not absolute necessity. Governments face choices between acting as agents of welfare or agents of the marketplace. Today, 'sovereignty-free' international finance disciplines ostensibly sovereign governments. In the West this could result – because of some competitive disadvantages in global terms – in a loss of material living standards; but this in turn need not result in less fulfilling lives. Those who live on or beyond the periphery of today's islands of prosperity, for example, may have plenty to teach in the twenty-first century about how we might live, since they have already accommodated to modest means. Peripheries of the world unite: you have nothing to lose but your centres. That said, the peripheries of the global capitalist system do not presently have much to lose, given their position in the global economy, the unhelpful rules of trade under the World Trade Organisation, the structural adjustment programmes of the IMF and World Bank, limited development help (often still tied to politics rather than helping the poor) and punitive debt repayment burdens.

The implications of globalisation, therefore, are not simple or uniformly beneficial. The two-edged effect is also evident in the field of military security. Long-range weapons of increasing destructive potential, range and accuracy have helped to create a global insecurity community. But note that it was out of common insecurity in the Cold War that the idea of common security emerged. The 'new thinking' of the 1980s showed that in the area of international security the negative aspects of global insecurity could be reversed, though the problem of controlling and ultimately eliminating nuclear weapons remains one of the most urgent challenges for statecraft in the post-Cold War era (MccGwire, 1994).

Globalisation's negative effects are not in principle beyond human control. That control – if it is to be in the human interest – will require new expressions of politics. Globalisation is often seen in extreme terms: by some – the ideologists of the market-place – in a very positive light, while by others – anxious about the impact of these forces on people's lives and traditional national control – in very negative ways. The political project of global moral science discussed later must seek to work with the potentially helpful dynamics of globalisation – the consciousness of 'one worldism' – while encouraging resistance to the destructive effects. It should not be assumed that globalisation in all its forms is irresistible, nor should it be assumed that it must mean homogenisation. It is for these reasons that those who have not given in to globo-pessimism have begun to concern themselves with fundamental questions of political theory and practical wisdom in relation to questions of global governance.

Global governance

[…] [G]lobal governance refers to those theories and practices which seek to provide legitimised procedures for political activities (and not just those of governments) which are of global relevance. The precise shape(s) of global governance for the medium and long-term future are indistinct, but they will obviously have a profound effect on what we now conceive as international security and key questions of international relations. Clearly what emerges institutionally will be of considerable variety, given the multiple interfaces between the local and the global, but they will be critical to the future of world politics, since it will be the task of these mechanisms to distribute (and redistribute) wealth, accommodate the new and cushion change.

There are presently more questions than answers. How will the interplay of global and local forces be mediated through legitimate political control mechanisms? What will replace the Westphalian international system? What political and economic structures will evolve to cope with the decline of national models of economic development in the face of a globalised economic system? Is the most likely shift in political and economic decision-making power away from the soverign state to regional economic collectivities grouped around these traditional units? It is difficult to predict how the patterns of global governance will evolve over the next half-century and beyond. It is as difficult as it would have been to predict the Westphalian system before it took shape. What feels clear is that something profound […] is taking place, but the post-Westphalian pattern of global governance has yet to be worked out. Whether what evolves produces the cosy image of a global village, or a global Johannesburg (a tense city held together, and apart, by razor wire), or any other urban metaphor for our future remains to be seen. But what seems beyond doubt is the verdict that the rationality of statism – the belief that all decision-making power and loyalty should be focused on the sovereign (for the most part multi-nation) state – has reached its culminating point, and that future patterns of global governance will involve complex decentralisation below the state-level, functional organisations above the state level, and a growing network of economic, social and cultural interdependencies at the level of transnational civil society, outside the effective control of governments.

Complexity in forms of governance is likely to be a characteristic of future world politics. [...] [T]he vaunted 'end of history' was not even a pause, still less a finale, and what beckons is not another round of ideological dialectics, but of multilectics about how to run the world, albeit in part rather than in whole. In this cultural babel, the pre-eminence of Western values will be challenged by different voices — some of which will be backed by serious power. The challenge is already present in certain forms of Islam and some so-called Asian values (though the challenge would be better understood and accommodated if the challenge were seen in terms of traditionalist versus modernist values rather than in a cultural essentialist — 'clash of civilisations' — fashion). Cultural essentialism — emphasising cultural continuity, the uniqueness of civilisations, and rejecting the universality of ideas — goes much too far. [...] Values change. Today's Western values, notably individualism, will not flourish on 'lifeboat earth' if the balance of economic and political power shifts to the authoritarian and anti-Western regions of Asia, and if millions of people continue to be born into wretched lives on the margins of existence. Values are a historical rather than a geo-graphical phenomenon. Today's 'Western' values, in different material conditions, will once again reinvent themselves; this, after all, is in the spirit of Enlightenment.

The spread of the term global governance attests to the inadequacy of the ortho-dox language of academic International Relations. Terms such as 'international system', 'great powers', 'balance of power' and even 'foreign policy', today sound increasingly marginal if not actually anachronistic. [...] The traditional discipline of International Relations excludes too much for its own good, and certainly for the good of the vast majority of the world's population. Academic International Relations will not be the site for human emancipation in the twenty-first century if it is impris-oned by the concepts and categories of nineteenth-century language.

Those thinking about the structures and processes of global governance for the decades and half-centuries ahead do not think in traditional global idealist terms — looking towards a world government for example — but instead contemplate multilay-ered, overlapping and multifunctional patterns of legitimate authority. The importance of creating a democratic and law-governed world is central in this project. [...]

The sovereign so-called nation-state with which we are now familiar, and which realists describe (tautologically) as the 'primary actors' in International Relations (defined in terms of 'relations between states') is not a fixed entity — the inevitable product of the political nature of humankind. Sovereign states are historical creations, the product of the political nature of humankind. And times change. Nevertheless, whatever networks of global governance emerge under conditions of globalisation, some form of 'states' will remain an important part of the jigsaw of world politics, though they will not be sovereign in the pure Westphalian sense — any more than they have ever been 'nation states' in the pure Wilsonian sense. Global governance will have to be truer to both language and human needs if a serious and persistent level of violence is to be avoided, and good governance in the human interest is to be fur-thered. If the major task in the theory and practice of international relations during the Cold War was to avoid a superpower nuclear war, the major task for the post-Cold War era is pre-eminently that of developing ideas about global governance that will recapture a sense of the future and of a concept of progress in the interests of human needs, world community and environmental sustainability. A future world which is predictably (soon) to be characterised by system overload has the choice — locally and

globally – of being informed by the values of community or of being driven by mul-
tilevel tribal confrontations. Even a law-governed world will not maximise human
security unless those laws are informed by the values of a just world order. Imagining
a politics and ethics on which to build more helpful structures of global governance is
the task of what I call global moral science.

Global moral science

Global moral science is not the 'objective' moral science that was attempted by the
philosophes but is a call to think systematically about how humans can live together,
globally, in greater security and hope (Booth, 1995). [...]

It is possible to present some truly terrifying scenarios for the decades ahead if
only 'fairly bad-case' assumptions are extrapolated. The nuclear danger could be back
to haunt us, and social stress could lead to Hobbesian nightmares. A world divided,
under conditions of globalisation, would be uniquely insecure and deeply inhumane.
The signs of such possibilities, fuelled by new cold wars of the mind, are not difficult
to find. As the Berlin Wall was being demolished in 1989 – the symbol of the East-
West confrontation and a failed monument to an attempt to stop the movement of
ideas – many more walls were being built to divide the West from the Rest, in an
attempt to stop the movement of peoples. The signs are not encouraging that the
governments of the rich world will be able to persuade their voters to reduce their
material prospects in the interests of a globally richer life.

Despite the endorsement earlier of Heilbroner's view that apprehension is the
dominant mood of today, and the identification of converging global pressures pointing to system-overload, the global future is not inevitably one of permanent and mul-
tilevel confrontation. Such a future is likely, however, if the privileged and powerful
retreat into lives preoccupied by their private and local needs and wants, and if these
fault lines are deepened by ideology. This can only be resisted by the creation of persuasive big pictures of global politics, big pictures that are both inclusive and sensitive
to local outlooks. These big pictures are unlikely to be completely new, but rather the
result of the refinement and modernisation of earlier exercises in global thinking.
Global moral science must seek to reinvent our human future(s) in a manner that is
appropriate for tomorrow's crowded and technological world and anchored in a
knowledge of all the failed projects and false universalisms of the past, including
racism, statism, religious fundamentalism, rampant Westernisation and simple faith in
science and technology. At the centre of reconceiving world politics, the success or
failure of developing a global human rights culture will be crucial. [...]

Statecraft and security

The challenge to students and practitioners of International Relations is no less than
rethinking global politics – from the top down and the bottom up. What has been
explicit in this Conclusion so far has been that global politics are at a crossroads
because of the revolutionary material circumstances in which we find ourselves. The
choice we (the Haves) face is whether to allow regressive thinking to trap us into a
world of private dreams but threatening public nightmares, or whether by resistance

and reinvention to seek to build through dialogue, dollars and determination, a human community and global polity on the foundation of the revolutionary material circumstances. Implicit in crossroads is the question of agency. Who will decide? Who will do the resistance and reinvention? Who will take the necessary practical steps?

At this stage of global politics, the empirical answer to these questions of agency is reasonably clear. The engine room for change – if it is to be progressive – will be global social movements committed to world order values such as non-violence, economic justice, environmental sustainability, good governance and human rights (Ekins, 1992; Falk, 1992). But only so much can be achieved without the agency of the state. As was discussed earlier, the role of the state these days is widely challenged, as the limitations of state-centric politics, environmental policy and economics are all too evident. The sovereign state represents neither an edifying transcendent morality nor the rational unit for determining the politics of a global age. Statism – the ideology which focuses all loyalty and decisionmaking power on the sovereign state – was historically the solution to the disorder of the Thirty Years War. In these terms it can be seen as progressive. But it is not unusual in human life to seek to deal with tomorrow's problems with yesterday's solutions. The continuing strength of statism attests to the fact that state élites in particular learned the lessons of their historical moment too well. We have to begin where we are, and pragmatically the governments of sovereign states will remain important actors in world politics and will continue to serve key functions, inter alia, in the regulation of violence, the development of law, the direction of social policies and the management of external relations. Statecraft will therefore continue to be of significance. Consequently, even if, in practice, states often behave like 'gangsters' rather than 'guardian angels' (Wheeler, 1996), the 'rational hope' must be that more of them will become what Bull called 'local agents of the world common good'. If the evidence for such an outcome is mixed, there are nevertheless grounds for hope, even in the field of international security. [...]

Despite all the warnings, the human sciences have scarcely begun to contemplate the stresses and strains of an overcrowded, overheated planet. In the decades ahead, how much of world politics will resemble what Heilbroner calls 'the rage of the ghetto' (1995: 90)? There is a confident view among some International Relations scholars that international society at the end of the twentieth century is reasonably robust. This is a top down view. Certainly there has not been a major war between the 'great powers' for half a century, and for this we should be thankful. However, when one looks at world politics from the bottom up – from the perspective of the poor, many children, Africa – the picture looks different. Change requires a rejection of the common sense values of the powerful, which have shaped our lives and often depressed our spirits, such as the self-serving homily that 'the poor will always be with us'. The poor are an invention of society. Members of 'primitive societies' have few possessions, but they are not 'poor'. As Marshall Sahlins puts it: 'Poverty is not a certain amount of goods, nor is it just a relationship between means and ends; above all it is a relation between people. Poverty is a social status. As such it is the invention of civilisation' (quoted in Heilbroner, 1995: 28). What we invent, we can reinvent. If such a view is considered utopian and naive, how much more so is the assumption that the human species can survive in good shape in a world dominated by the politics of exclusiveness and the economics of exploitation? But change is obstructed by the historic power of today's ruling ideas about politics and economics, as they have become normalised, naturalised and enshrined as common sense. Ruling ideas always assume their survival, but uncommon sense should warn of the opposite.

To talk of 'beyond' in this Conclusion is not to suppose that there will necessarily be one. 'Humans' as they have evolved may, for a variety of reasons, become extinct as a species, like the Neanderthals. It is in the gap between hope and human achievement (including possible extinction) that this thing called 'international relations' fits, so frustratingly – as a threat and as a promise. Unless, through progress in global moral science, we can develop more rational forms of global governance, then the prospects are, at worst, species elimination, at best a regression into an insecure world of razor wire surrounding one's home and nuclear weapons defending one's country, waiting for catastrophes of greater or lesser magnitude.

For the moment, the progress of human progress has been badly dented. Faith in the future has shrivelled in many societies, although hope for progress remains widespread. [...]

We live, I believe, in the early stages of one of the most decisive periods in human history – the first truly global age, with all that implies for reimagining the human implications of a decisive reinvention of time and space, comparable with a small number of such turning-points over the past 100–150,000 years (learning to ride horses, discovering the world is not flat and the Industrial Revolution). The potential evolutionary implications of globalist reimaginings are enormous, not least for politics and economics, including 'international relations'. [...] In that regard it is important to remember that the Berlin Wall did not fall: it was pushed. It was thought up, built up, unthought and pulled down. This most symbolic material structure of the Cold War was demolished by people changing their minds. Like the Berlin Wall, the political, social, cultural and economic world in which we live today – nuclear missiles, rat-infested shanty-towns, fundamentalist churches and sweat-shops – are also inventions, susceptible of being thought up, built up, unthought and pulled down.

References

Booth, Ken (1995) 'Human Wrongs and International Relations', *International Affairs*, vol. 71(1), 103–26.

Bull, Hedley (1983) 'Order and Justice in International Relations', *Hagey Lectures* (University of Waterloo).

Ekins, Paul (1992) *A New World Order. Grassroots Movements for Global Change* (London: Routledge).

Falk, Richard (1992) *Explorations at the Edge of Time: The Prospects for World Order* (Philadelphia: Temple University Press).

Galbraith, J. K. (1992) *The Culture of Contentment* (London: Sinclair-Stevenson).

Heilbroner, Robert (1995) *Visions of the Future* (New York: Oxford University Press).

MccGwire, Michael (1994) 'Is There a Future for Nuclear Weapons?', *International Affairs*, vol. 70(2), 211–28.

Rosenau, James (1990) *Turbulence in World Politics: A Theory of Change and Continuity* (New York: Harvester Wheatsheaf).

Wheeler, Nicholas J. (1996) 'Guardian Angel or Global Gangster', *Political Studies*, vol. 44(1).

Victor D. Cha

GLOBALIZATION AND SECURITY

Source: 'Globalization and the study of international security', *Journal of Peace Research*, vol. 37, no. 3, May 2000, pp. 391–403.

G **LOBALIZATION IS BEST** understood as a spatial phenomenon.[1] It is not an 'event', but a gradual and ongoing expansion of interaction processes, forms of organization, and forms of cooperation outside the traditional spaces defined by sovereignty. Activity takes place in a less localized, less insulated way as transcontinental and interregional patterns criss-cross and overlap one another.[2]

The process of globalization is analytically distinct from interdependence. The latter, as Reinicke states, denotes growth in connections and linkages between sovereign entities. Interdependence complicates external sovereignty in that sovereign choices have to be made to accommodate these interdependent ties. Globalization processes are not just about linkages but about interpenetration. As Guehenno noted, globalization is defined not just by the ever-expanding connections between states measured in terms of movement of goods and capital but the circulation and interpenetration of people and ideas (Guehenno, 1999: 7). It affects not only external sovereignty choices but also internal sovereignty in terms of relations between the public and private sectors (Reinicke, 1997). Contrary to popular notions of globalization this does not mean that sovereignty ceases to exist in the traditional Weberian sense (i.e. monopoly of legitimate authority over citizen and subjects within a given territory. Instead, globalization is a spatial reorganization of production, industry, finance, and other areas which causes local decisions to have global repercussions and daily life to be affected by global events. [...]

Much of the literature on globalization has focused on its economic rather than security implications.[3] In part, this is because the security effects of globalization often get conflated with changes to the international security agenda with the end of Cold War Superpower competition.[4] It is also because, unlike economics where globalization's effects are manifested and measured everyday in terms of things like international capital flows and Internet use, in security, the effects are inherently harder to conceptualize and measure. To the extent possible, the ensuing analysis tries to differentiate globalization from post-Cold War effects on security. As a first-cut, one can envision a 'globalization – security' spectrum along which certain dialogues in security studies would fall. For example, the notion of selective engagement, pre-emptive withdrawal, democratic enlargement, or preventive defense as viable US grand strategies for the coming century would sit at the far end of this spectrum because they are predominantly security effects deriving from the end of bipolar competition rather than from globalization.[5] Progressively closer to the middle would be arguments about the 'debelicization' of security or the obsolescence of war which do not have globalization as their primary cause, but are clearly related to some of these processes.[6] Also in this middle range would be discussions on 'rogue' or 'pariah' states as this term is a function of the end of the Cold War; at the same time, however, the spread of information and technology exponentially raises the danger of these threats. Similarly, the end of the Cold War provides the permissive condition for the salience of weapons of mass destruction as the Soviet collapse directly affected the subsequent accessibility of formerly controlled substances such as plutonium or enriched uranium. But an equally important driver is globalization because the tech-nologies for creating these weapons have become easily accessible (Falkenrath, 1998). Finally, at the far end of the 'globalization-security' spectrum might be the salience of substate extremist groups or fundamentalist groups because their ability to organize transnationally, meet virtually, and utilize terrorist tactics has been substantially enhanced by the globalization of technology and information. While the US security studies field has made reference to many of these issues, a more systematic under-standing of globalization's security effects is lacking.[7] [...]

Agency and scope of threats

The most far-reaching security effect of globalization is its complication of the basic concept of 'threat' in international relations. This is in terms of both agency and scope. Agents of threat can be states but can also be non-state groups or individuals. While the vocabulary of conflict in international security traditionally centered on interstate war (e.g. between large set-piece battalions and national armed forces), with global-ization, terms such as global violence and human security become common parlance, where the fight is between irregular substate units such as ethnic militias, paramilitary guerrillas, cults and religious organizations, organized crime, and terrorists. Increasingly, targets are not exclusively opposing force structures or even cities, but local groups and individuals (Buzan, 1997a: 6–21; Klare, 1998: 66; Nye, 1989; Väyrynen, 1998; Wæver et al., 1993).

Similarly, security constituencies, while nominally defined by traditional sover-eign borders increasingly are defined at every level from the global to the regional to the individual. [...] Thus the providers of security are still nationally defined in terms of capabilities and resources; however, increasingly they apply these in a post-sovereign space whose spectrum ranges from nonstate to substate to transstate arrangements. For this reason, security threats become inherently more difficult to measure, locate, monitor, and contain (Freedman, 1998a: 56; Reinicke, 1997: 134).

Globalization widens the scope of security as well. As the Copenhagen school has noted, how states conceive of security and how they determine what it means to be secure in the post-Cold War era expand beyond military security at the national level.[8]

Globalization's effects on security scope are distinct from those of the post-Cold War in that the basic transaction processes engendered by globalization – instantaneous communication and transportation, exchanges of information and technology, flow of capital – catalyze certain dangerous phenomena or empower certain groups in ways unimagined previously. In the former category are things such as viruses and pollution. Because of human mobility, disease has become much more of a transnational security concern.[9] Global warming, ozone depletion, acid rain, biodiversity loss, and radioactive contamination are health and environmental problems that have intensified as transnational security concerns precisely because of increased human mobility and interaction (Matthew & Shambaugh, 1998; Väyrynen, 1998; Zurn, 1998).

Globalization also has given rise to a 'skill revolution' that enhances the capabilities of groups such as drug smugglers, political terrorists, criminal organizations, and ethnic insurgents to carry out their agenda more effectively than ever before (Arquilla & Ronfeldt, 1996; Brown, 1998: 4–5; Godson, 1997; Klare, 1998; Rosenau, 1998: 21–23; Shinn, 1996: 38). It is important to note that the widening scope of security to these transnational issues is not simply a short-term fixation with the end of bipolar Cold War competition as the defining axis for security. The threat posed by drugs, terrorism, transnational crime, and environmental degradation has been intensified precisely because of globalization. Moreover, the security solutions to these problems in terms of enforcement or containment increasingly are ineffective through national or unilateral means.[10]

Globalization has ignited identity as a source of conflict. The elevation of regional and ethnic conflict as a top-tier security issue has generally been treated as a function of the end of the Cold War. However, it is also a function of globalization. The process of globalization carries implicit homogenization tendencies and messages,[11] which in combination with the 'borderlessness' of the globalization phenomenon elicits a cultural pluralist response.[12]

At the same time, globalization has made us both more aware and less decisive about our motivations to intervene in such ethnic conflicts. Real-time visual images of horror and bloodshed in far-off places transmitted through CNN make the conflicts impossible to ignore, creating pressures for intervention. On the other hand, the hesitancy to act is palpable, as standard measures by which to determine intervention (i.e. bipolar competition in the periphery) are no longer appropriate, forcing us to grope with fuzzy motivations such as humanitarian intervention.

Non-physical security

Globalization has anointed the concept of non-physical security. Traditional definitions of security in terms of protection of territory and sovereignty, while certainly not irrelevant in a globalized era, expand to protection of information and technology assets. For example, Nye and Owens (1998) cite 'information power' as increasingly defining the distribution of power in international relations in the 21st century. In a similar vein, the revolution in military affairs highlights not greater firepower but greater information technology and 'smartness' of weapons as the defining advantage for future warfare.[13]

These non-physical security aspects have always been a part of the traditional national defense agenda. [...] However, the challenge posed by globalization is that the nation-state can no longer control the movement of technology and information (Simon, 1997). Strategic alliances form in the private sector among leading corporations that are not fettered by notions of techno-nationalism and driven instead by competitive, cost-cutting, or cutting-edge innovative needs. The result is a transnationalization of defense production that further reduces the state's control over these activities.[14]

More and more private companies, individuals, and other non-state groups are the producers, consumers, and merchants of a US$50 billion per year global arms market (Klare & Lumpe, 1998). The end of the Cold War has certainly been a permissive condition for the indiscriminate, profit-based incentives to sell weapons or dual-use technologies to anybody. But globalization of information and technology has made barriers to non-state entry low and detection costs high. Moreover, while enforcement authorities still have the benefit of these technologies, two critical developments have altered the equation: (1) Absence of discrimination: over the past two decades, the private sector, rather than the government, has become the primary creator of new technologies, which in essence has removed any relative advantages state agencies formerly possessed in terms of exclusive access to eavesdropping technology, surveillance, and encryption.[15] Governments once in the position of holding monopolies on cutting edge technologies that could later be 'spun off' in the national commercial sector are now consumers of 'spin-on' technologies. (2) Volume and variety: the sheer growth in volume and variety of communications has overwhelmed any attempts at monitoring or control (Mathews, 1997; Freedman, 1999: 53).[16] [...]

* * *

Intermestic security

[...] Globalization creates an interpenetration of foreign and domestic issues that national governments must recognize in developing policy. One example of this 'intermestic' approach to security policy might be an acceptance that the transnationalization of threats has blurred traditional divisions between internal and external security (Katzenstein, 1996). The obverse would be the frequency with which a state adheres to 'delimiting' security, formulating and justifying policy on the basis of 'national security' interests rather than universal/global interests (Moon Chung-in, 1995: 64). [...]

Multilateralism

[...] As noted above, globalization means that both the agency and scope of threats have become more diverse and non-state in form. This also suggests that the payoffs lessen for obtaining security through traditional means. Controlling pollution, disease, technology, and information transfer cannot be easily dealt with through national, unilateral means but can only be effectively dealt with through the application of national resources in multilateral fora or through encouragement of transnational cooperation. [...]

Thus one would expect globalized security processes reflected in a state's striving for regional coordination and cooperative security. It should emphasize not exclusivity and bilateralism in relations but inclusivity and multilateralism as the best way to solve security problems. At the extreme end of the spectrum, globalization might downplay the importance of eternal iron-clad alliances and encourage the growth of select transnational 'policy coalitions' among national governments, nongovernmental organizations (NGOs), and individuals specific to each problem (Reinicke, 1997: 134).

In conjunction with multilateralism, globalized conceptions of security should be reflected in norms of diffuse reciprocity and international responsibility. This is admittedly more amorphous and harder to operationalize. While some self-serving instrumental motives lie behind most diplomacy, there must be a strong sense of global responsibility and obligation that compels the state to act. Actions taken in the national interest must be balanced with a basic principle that contributes to a universal, globalized value system underpinning one's own values. [...]

Bureaucratic innovation

[...] [There] is the trend toward greater specialization in the pursuit of security. As globalization makes security problems more complex and diverse, national security structures need to be re-oriented, sometimes through elimination of anachronistic bureaucracies or through rationalization of wasteful and overlapping ones. [...]

Another trend engendered by the security challenges of globalization is greater cross-fertilization between domestic law enforcement and foreign policy agencies. This relationship, at least in the USA (less the case in Europe), is at worst non-existent because domestic law enforcement has operated traditionally in isolation from national security and diplomatic concerns, or at best is a mutually frustrating relationship because the two have neither inclination nor interest in cooperating. States that understand the challenges of globalization, particularly on issues of drug-trafficking, environmental crimes, and technology transfer, will seek to bridge this gap, creating and capitalizing on synergies that develop between the two groups. Foreign policy agencies will seek out greater interaction with domestic agencies, not only on a pragmatic short-term basis employing law enforcement's skills to deal with a particular problem, but also on a longer-term and regular basis cultivating familiarity, transparency, and common knowledge. On the domestic side, agencies such as the FBI, Customs, and police departments (of major cities) would find themselves engaged in foreign policy dialogues, again not only at the practitioner's level, but also in academia and think-tank forums.[17]

One of the longer-term effects of specialization and cross-fertilization is that security also becomes more 'porous.' Specialization will often require changes not just at the sovereign national level, but across borders and with substate actors. 'Boilerplate' security (e.g. dealt with by 'hardshell' nation-states with national resources) becomes increasingly replaced by cooperation and coordination that may still be initiated by the national government but with indispensable partners (depending on the issue) such as NGOs, transnational groups, and the media. The obverse of this dynamic also obtains. With globalization, specialized 'communities of choice' (e.g. landmine ban) are empowered to organize transnationally and penetrate the national security agendas with issues that might not otherwise have been paid attention to (Guehenno, 1999: 9; Mathews, 1997).

Aggregating capabilities

The globalization literature remains relatively silent on how globalization processes substantially alter the way in which states calculate relative capabilities. The single most important variable in this process is the diffusion of technology (both old and new). In the past, measuring relative capabilities was largely a linear process. Higher technology generally meant qualitatively better weapons and hence stronger capabilities. States could be assessed along a ship-for-ship, tank-for-tank, jet-for-jet comparison in terms of the threat posed and their relative strength based on such linear measurements. However, the diffusion of technology has had distorting effects. While states at the higher end technologically still retain advantages, globalization has enabled wider access to technology such that the measurement process is more dynamic. First, shifts in relative capabilities are more frequent and have occurred in certain cases much earlier than anticipated. Second, and more significant, the measurement process is no longer one-dimensional in the sense that one cannot readily draw linear associations between technology, capabilities, and power. For example, what gives local, economically backward states regional and even global influence in the 21st century is their ability to threaten across longer distances. Globalization facilitates access to select technologies related to force projection and weapons of mass destruction, which in turn enable states to pose threats that are asymmetric and disproportionate to their size. Moreover, these threats emanate not from acquisition of state-of-the-art but *old and outdated* technology. Thus countries like North Korea, which along most traditional measurements of power could not compare, can with old technology (SCUD and rudimentary nuclear technology) pose threats and affect behavior in ways unforeseen in the past (Bracken, 1998).

Strategies and operational considerations

Finally, the literature on globalization is notably silent on the long-term impact of globalization processes on time-tested modes of strategic thinking and fighting. In the former vein, the widening scope of security engendered by globalization means that the definition of security and the fight for it will occur not on battlefields but in unconventional places against non-traditional security adversaries. [...] [T]he nature of these conflicts may also require new ways of fighting, i.e. the ability to engage militarily with a high degree of lethality against combatants, but low levels of collateral damage. As a result, globalization's widening security scope dictates not only new strategies (discussed below) but also new forms of combat. [...]

Regarding strategy, as the agency and scope of threats diversifies in a globalized world, traditional modes of deterrence become less relevant. Nuclear deterrence throughout the Cold War and post-Cold War eras, for example, was based on certain assumptions. First, the target of the strategy was another nation-state. Second, this deterred state was assumed to have a degree of centralization in the decisionmaking process over nuclear weapons use. Third, and most important, the opponent possessed both counterforce and countervalue targets that would be the object of a second strike. While this sort of rationally based, existential deterrence will still apply to interstate security, the proliferation of weaponized non-state and substate actors increasingly renders this sort of strategic thinking obsolete. They do not occupy sovereign territorial space and therefore cannot be targeted with the threat of retaliation. They also may operate as self-contained cells rather than an organic whole which makes decapitating strikes at a central decisionmaking structure ineffective. [...]

Governments may respond to this in a variety of ways. One method would be, as noted above, greater emphasis on the specialized utilization of whatever state, substate, and multilateral methods are necessary to defend against such threats. A second likely response would be greater attention and resources directed at civil defense preparation and 'consequence' management to minimize widespread panic and pain in the event of an attack. A third possible response is unilateral in nature. Governments may increasingly employ pre-emptive or preventive strategies if rational deterrence does not apply against non-state entities. Hence one might envision two tiers of security in which stable rational deterrence applies at the state – state level but unstable pre-emptive/preventive strategies apply at the state-non-state level. [...]

Notes

1   See Held (1997: 253). As Rosenau (1996: 251) writes, 'It refers neither to values nor structures but to sequences that unfold either in the mind or behavior, to interaction processes that evolve as people and organizations go about their daily tasks and seek to realize their particular goals.'

2   See Mittelman (1994: 427). Or as Goldblatt et al. (1997: 271) note: 'Globalization denotes a shift in the spatial form and extent of human organization and interaction to a transcontinental or interregional level. It involves a stretching of social relations across time and space such that day-to-day activities are increasingly influenced by events happening on the other side of the globe and the practices and decisions of highly localized groups and institutions can have significant global reverberations.'

3   Examples of the non-security bias in the US literature on globalization include Mittelman (1994); Goldblatt et al. (1997); Reinicke (1997); Rosenau (1996); Nye & Owens (1998); Talbott (1997); Falk (1997); Ohmae (1993); Held (1997).

4   Representative of works looking at changing definitions of security at the end of the Cold War are Walt (1991); Gray (1992); Deudney (1990); Chipman (1992); Nye (1989); Lipschutz (1995).

5   For debates on selective engagement and pre-emptive drawback strategies, see Layne (1997); Ruggie (1997). See also Huntington (1999); Betts (1998). On preventive defense see Carter & Perry (1999). European international relations literature that has looked at the post-Cold War effects of security (as distinct from globalization's effects on security) include Kirchner & Sperling (1998); Leatherman & Väyrynen (1995); Buzan (1997a).

6   For the seminal work, see Mueller (1989). See also Mandelbaum (1999); Van Creveld (1991).

7   For a more comprehensive and useful characterization of security studies, see Buzan (1997a), although this categorization takes the post-Cold War rather than globalization as its point of departure.

8   See Buzan (1997a). For applications, see Haas (1995); Cha (1997).

9   For example, the re-emergence of tuberculosis and malaria as health hazards has been related to the development of resistant strains in the South (because of black-market abuses of inoculation treatments), which then reentered the developed North through human mobility.

10   As Matthew & Shambaugh argue, it is not the luxury of the Soviet collapse that enables us to elevate the importance of transnational security but the advances in human mobility, communication, and technology that force us to. See Matthew & Shambaugh (1998: 167). A related example of how security agency and scope have changed is the privatized army. These groups are not a new phenomenon in international politics, dating back to the US revolutionary war (i.e. Britain's hiring of Hessian soldiers) and the Italian city-states of the 14th century (i.e. the *condottiers*). However, their salience today is a function of the changes wrought by the globalization of technology. Increasingly, national armies are retooled to fight high-intensity, high-technology conflicts and less equipped to fight low-intensity conflicts in peripheral areas among ethnic groups where the objectives in entering battle are unclear. This development, coupled with the decreasing Cold War era emphasis on the periphery and the absence of domestic support for casualties in such places, has made the 'jobbing-out' of war increasingly salient. See Shearer (1998); Silverstein (1997); Thomson (1996).

11   Examples of homogenization impulses include the diffusion of standardized consumer goods generally from the developed North; Western forms of capitalism (and not Asian crony capitalism); and Western liberal democracy (not illiberal democracy).

12   As Falk (1997: 131–32) states, 'The rejection of these globalizing tendencies in its purest forms is associated with and expressed by the resurgence of religious and ethnic politics in various extremist configurations. Revealingly, only by retreating to premodern, traditionalist orientations does it now seem possible to seal off sovereign territory, partially at least, from encroachments associated with globalized lifestyles and business operations'. See also Mittelman (1994: 432); Guehenno (1999: 7); and Wæver et al. (1993).

13   These are defined in terms of things such as ISR (intelligence collection, surveillance, and reconnaissance), C4I, and precision force that can provide superior situational awareness capabilities (e.g. dominant battlespace knowledge; 'pre-crisis transparency'). See Nye & Owens (1998); Cohen (1996); Freedman (1998b); Laird & Mey (1999). Freedman correctly points out that the emphasis on information and technology is not in lieu of, but in conjunction with, superior physical military assets. The former cannot compensate for the latter. See Freedman (1999: 51–52).

14   As Goldblatt et al. point out, MNCS now account for a disproportionately large share of global technology transfer as a result of FDI; joint ventures; international patenting; licensing; and knowhow agreements. This means they are more in control of transferring dual-use technologies than traditional states. See Goldblatt et al. (1997: 277–79).

15   On the growing commercial pressure for liberalization of encryption technology, see Freeh (1997). See also Falkenrath (1998: 56–57); Corcoran (1998: 13). On the growing reliance of the US Defense Department on commercial technological advances compared with the 1950–70s, see Carter & Perry (1999: 197–98).

16   The results of this are well known: instantaneous communication by facsimile, cellular phone, satellite phone, teleconferencing, alpha-numeric pagers, e-mail, computer moderns, computer bulletin boards, and federal express are the norm. Approximately 250,000 Global Positioning System satellite navigation receivers are sold *each month* for commercial use.

17   In this vein, it might not be unusual in the future to see the commissioner of New York City Police or the head of the FBI participating in discussions of the Council on Foreign Relations or the Brookings Institution.

References

Arquilla, John & David Ronfeldt, 1996. *The Advent of Netwar*. Santa Monica, CA: RAND.

Betts, Richard, 1998. 'The New Threat of Mass Destruction', *Foreign Affairs* 77(1): 26–41.

Bracken, Paul, 1998. 'America's Maginot Line', *Atlantic Monthly* 282(6): 85–93.

Brown, Seyom Brown, 1998. 'World Interests and the Changing Dimensions of Security', in Klare & Chandrani (4–5).

Buzan, Barry, 1997a. 'Rethinking Security After the Cold War', *Cooperation and Conflict* 32(1): 5–28.

Carter, Ashton & William Perry, 1999. *Preventive Defense: A New Security Strategy for America*. Washington, DC.: Brookings Institution.

Cha, Victor, 1997. 'Realism, Liberalism and the Durability of the U.S.-South Korean Alliance', *Asian Survey* 37(7): 609–22.

Chipman, John, 1992. 'The Future of Strategic Studies' Beyond Grand Strategy', *Survival* 34(1): 109–31.

Cohen, Eliot, 1996. 'A Revolution in Warfare', *Foreign Affairs* 75(2): 37–54.

Corcoran, Elizabeth, 1998. 'A Bid to Unscramble Encryption Policy', *International Herald Tribune*, 13 July.

Deudney, Daniel, 1990. 'The Case Against Linking Environmental Degradation and National Security', *Millennium* 19(3): 461–76.

Falk, Richard, 1997. 'State of Siege: Will Globalization Win Out?', *International Affairs* 73(1): 123–36.

Falkenrath, Richard, 1998. 'Confronting Nuclear, Biological and Chemical Terrorism', *Survival* 40(4): 43–65.

Freedman, Lawrence, 1998a. 'International Security: Changing Targets', *Foreign Policy* 110: 56.

Freedman, Lawrence, 1998b. *The Revolution in Strategic Affairs*, Adelphi Paper 318, Institute for International Security Studies. Oxford: Oxford University Press.

Freedman, Lawrence, 1999. 'The Changing Forms of Military Conflict', *Survival* 40(4): 51–52.

Freeh, Louis J., 1997. 'The Impact of Encryption on Public Safety', statement before the Permanent Select Committee on Intelligence, US House, 9 September, Washington, DC.

Godson, Roy, 1997. 'Criminal Threats to US Interests in Hong Kong and China', testimony before the Senate Foreign Relations Committee, East Asian and Pacific Affairs Subcommittee, 10 April, Washington, DC.

Goldblatt, David; David Held, Anthony McGrew & Jonathan Perraton, 1997. 'EconomicGlobalization and the Nation-State: Shifting Balances of Power', *Alternatives* 22(3): 269–85.

Gray, Colin, 1992. 'New Directions for Strategic Studies: How Can Theory Help Practice', *Security Studies* 1(4): 610–35.

Guehenno, Jean-Marie, 1999. 'The Impact of Globalization on Strategy', *Survival* 40(4): 7.

Haas, Richard, 1995. 'Paradigm Lost', *Foreign Affairs* 74(1): 43–58.

Held, David, 1997. 'Democracy and Globalization', *Global Governance* 3: 253.

Huntington, Samuel, 1999. 'The Lonely Superpower', *Foreign Affairs* 78(2): 35–49.

Katzenstein, Peter, 1996. *Cultural Norms and National Security*. Ithaca, NY: Cornell University Press.

Kirchner, Emil & James Sperling, 1998. 'Economic Security and the Problem of Cooperation in Post-Cold War Europe', *Review International Studies* 24(2): 221–37.

Klare, Michael, 1998. 'The Era of Multiplying Schisms: World Security in the Twenty-First Century', in Klare & Chandrani (59–77).

Klare, Michael & Lora Lumpe, 1998. 'Fanning the Flames of War: Conventional Arms Transfers in the 1990s', in Klare & Chandrani (160–79).

Laird, Robbin & Holger Mey, 1999. 'The Revolution in Military Affairs: Allied Perspectives'. *McNair Paper 60*. Washington, DC: National Defense University.

Layne, Christopher, 1997. 'From Preponderance to Offshore Balancing: America's Future Grand Strategy', *International Security* 22(1): 86–124.

Leatherman, Jamie & Raimo Väyrynen, 1995 'Conflict Theory and Conflict Resolution: Directions for Collaborative Research Policy'. *Cooperation and Conflict* 30(1): 53–82.

Lipschutz, Ronnie, ed., 1995. *On Security*. New York: Columbia University Press.

Mandelbaum, Michael, 1999. 'Is War Obsolete?' *Survival* 40(4): 20–38.

Mathews, Jessica, 1997. 'Power Shift', *Foreign Affairs* 76(1): 50–66.

Matthew, Richard & George Shambaugh, 1998 'Sex, Drugs, and Heavy Metal: Transnational Threats and National Vulnerabilities', *Security Dialogue* 29(2): 163–75.

Mittelman, James, 1994. 'The Globalisation Challenge: Surviving at the Margins', *Third World Quarterly* 15(3): 427–43.

Moon Chung-in, 1995. 'Globalization: Challenges and Strategies', *Korea Focus* 3(3): 64.

Mueller, John, 1989. *Retreat from Doomsday: The Obsolescence of Modern War*: New York: Basic Books.

Nye, Joseph, 1989. *The Contribution of Strategic Studies: Future Challenges*, Adelphi Paper 235. London: IISS.

Nye, Joseph & William Owens, 1998. 'America's Information Edge', *Foreign Affairs* 75(2): 20–36.

Ohmae, Kenichi, 1993. 'The Rise of the Region State', *Foreign Affairs* 72 (Spring): 78–87.

Reinicke, Wolfgang, 1997. 'Global Public Policy', *Foreign Affairs* 76(6): 127–38.

Rosenau, James, 1996. 'The Dynamics of Globalization: Toward an Operational Formulation', *Security Dialogue* 27(3): 18–35.

Rosenau, James, 1998. 'The Dynamism of a Turbulent World', in Klare & Chandrani (21–23).

Ruggie, John, 1997. 'The Past as Prologue? Interests, Identity, and American Foreign Policy', *International Security* 22(1): 89–125.

Shearer, David, February 1998. *Private Armies and Military Intervention*, Adelphi Paper 316. New York: International Institute for Strategic Studies.

Shinn, James, ed., 1996. *Weaving the Net: Conditional Engagement with China*. New York: Council on Foreign Relations.

Silverstein, Ken, 1997. 'Privatizing War', *The Nation*, 28 July.

Simon, Denis Fred, ed., 1997. *Techno-Security in an Age of Globalization*. New York: M. E. Sharpe.

Talbott, Strobe, 1997. 'Globalization and Diplomacy: A Practitioner's Perspective', *Foreign Policy* 108: 69–83.

Thomson, Janice, 1996. *Mercenaries, Pirates, and Sovereigns: State-Building and Extraterritorial Violence in Early Modern Europe*. Princeton, NJ: Princeton University Press.

Van Creveld, Martin, 1991. *The Transformation of War*. New York: Free Press.

Väyrynen, Raimo, 1998. 'Environmental Security and Conflicts: Concepts and Policies', *International Studies* 35(1): 3–21.

Wæver, Ole; Barry Buzan, Marten Kelstrup & Pierre Lemaitre, 1993. *Identity, Migration and the New Security Agenda in Europe*. London: Pinter.

Walt, Stephen M., 1991. 'The Renaissance of Security Studies', *International Studies Quarterly* 35(2): 211–39.

Zurn, Michael, 1998. 'The Rise of International Environmental Politics: A Review of the Current Research', *World Politics* 50(4): 617–49.

Walter Laqueur

TERRORISM

Source: 'Postmodern terrorism', *Foreign Affairs*, vol. 75, no. 5, September/October 1996, pp. 24–37.

New rules for an old game

[...] **TERRORISM HAS BEEN** defined as the substate application of violence or threatened violence intended to sow panic in a society, to weaken or even overthrow the incumbents, and to bring about political change. It shades on occasion into guerrilla warfare (although unlike guerrillas, terrorists are unable or unwilling to take or hold territory) and even a substitute for war between states. In its long history terrorism has appeared in many guises; today society faces not one terrorism but many terrorisms.

Since 1900, terrorists' motivation, strategy, and weapons have changed to some extent. The anarchists and the left-wing terrorist groups that succeeded them, down through the Red Armies that operated in Germany, Italy, and Japan in the 1970s, have vanished; if anything, the initiative has passed to the extreme right. Most international and domestic terrorism these days, however, is neither left nor right, but ethnic-separatist in inspiration. Ethnic terrorists have more staying power than ideologically motivated ones, since they draw on a larger reservoir of public support.

The greatest change in recent decades is that terrorism is by no means militants' only strategy. The many-branched Muslim Brotherhood, the Palestinian Hamas, the Irish Republican Army (IRA), the Kurdish extremists in Turkey and Iraq, the Tamil Tigers of Sri Lanka, the Basque Homeland and Liberty (ETA) movement in Spain, and many other groups that have sprung up in this century have had political as well as terrorist wings from the beginning. The political arm provides social services and education, runs businesses, and contests elections, while the "military wing" engages in ambushes and assassinations. Such division of labor has advantages: the political leadership can publicly disassociate itself when the terrorists commit a particularly outrageous act or something goes wrong. The claimed lack of control can be quite real because the armed wing tends to become independent; the men and women with the guns and bombs often lose sight of the movement's wider aims and may end up doing more harm than good.

Terrorist operations have also changed somewhat. Airline hijackings have become rare, since hijacked planes cannot stay in the air forever and few countries today are willing to let them land, thereby incurring the stigma of openly supporting terrorism. Terrorists, too, saw diminishing returns on hijackings. The trend now seems to be away from attacking specific targets like the other side's officials and toward more indiscriminate killing. Furthermore, the dividing line between urban terrorism and other tactics has become less distinct, while the line between politically motivated terrorism and the operation of national and international crime syndicates is often impossible for outsiders to discern [...]. But there is one fundamental difference between international crime and terrorism: mafias have no interest in overthrowing the government and decisively weakening society; in fact, they have a vested interest in a prosperous economy.

Misapprehensions, not only semantic, surround the various forms of political violence. A terrorist is not a guerrilla, strictly speaking. There are no longer any guerrillas, engaging in Maoist-style liberation of territories that become the base of a counter-society and a regular army fighting the central government – except perhaps in remote places like Afghanistan, the Philippines, and Sri Lanka. The term "guerrilla" has had a long life partly because terrorists prefer the label, for its more positive connotations. It also persists because governments and media in other countries do not wish to offend terrorists by calling them terrorists. [...]

The belief has gained ground that terrorist missions by volunteers bent on committing suicide constitute a radical new departure, dangerous because they are impossible to prevent. But that is a myth, like the many others in which terrorism has always been shrouded. The bomber willing and indeed eager to blow himself up has appeared in all eras and cultural traditions, espousing politics ranging from the leftism of the Baader-Meinhof Gang in 1970s Germany to rightist extremism. When the Japanese military wanted kamikaze pilots at the end of World War II, thousands of volunteers rushed to offer themselves. The young Arab bombers on Jerusalem buses looking to be rewarded by the virgins in Paradise are a link in an old chain.

State-sponsored terrorism has not disappeared. Terrorists can no longer count on the Soviet Union and its Eastern European allies, but some Middle Eastern and North African countries still provide support. Tehran and Tripoli, however, are less eager to argue that they have a divine right to engage in terrorist operations outside their borders [...]. No government today boasts about surrogate warfare it instigates and backs.

On the other hand, Sudan, without fanfare, has become for terrorists what the Barbary Coast was for pirates of another age: a safe haven. Politically isolated and presiding over a disastrous economy, the military government in Khartoum, backed by Muslim leaders, believes that no one wants to become involved in Sudan and thus it can get away with lending support to terrorists from many nations. Such confidence is justified so long as terrorism is only a nuisance. But if it becomes more than that, the rules of the game change, and both terrorists and their protectors come under great pressure. [...]

* * *

The greatest change is that terrorism is not militants' only strategy

Some argue that terrorism must be effective because certain terrorist leaders have become president or prime minister of their country. In those cases, however, the terrorists had first forsworn violence and adjusted to the political process. Finally, the common wisdom holds that terrorism can spark a war or, at least, prevent peace. That is true, but only where there is much inflammable material: as in Sarajevo in 1914, so in the Middle East and elsewhere today. Nor can one ever say with certainty that the conflagration would not have occurred sooner or later in any case.

Nevertheless, terrorism's prospects, often overrated by the media, the public, and some politicians, are improving as its destructive potential increases. This has to do both with the rise of groups and individuals that practice or might take up terrorism and with the weapons available to them. The past few decades have witnessed the birth of dozens of aggressive movements espousing varieties of nationalism, religious fundamentalism, fascism, and apocalyptic millenarianism. [...] [Also] [n]ow, mail-order catalogs tempt militants with readily available, far cheaper, unconventional as well as conventional weapons [...].

In addition to nuclear arms, the weapons of mass destruction include biological agents and man-made chemical compounds that attack the nervous system, skin, or blood. Governments have engaged in the production of chemical weapons for almost a century and in the production of nuclear and biological weapons for many decades, during which time proliferation has been continuous and access ever easier.[1] The means of delivery – ballistic missiles, cruise missiles, and aerosols – have also become far more effective. While in the past missiles were deployed only in wars between states, recently they have played a role in civil wars in Afghanistan and Yemen. Use by terrorist groups would be but one step further.

Until the 1970s most observers believed that stolen nuclear material constituted the greatest threat in the escalation of terrorist weapons, but many now think the danger could lie elsewhere. An April 1996 Defense Department report says that "most terrorist groups do not have the financial and technical resources to acquire nuclear weapons but could gather materials to make radiological dispersion devices and some biological and chemical agents." Some groups have state sponsors that possess or can obtain weapons of the latter three types. [...]

To use or not to use?

If terrorists have used chemical weapons only once and nuclear material never, to some extent the reasons are technical. The scientific literature is replete with the technical problems inherent in the production, manufacture, storage, and delivery of each of the three classes of unconventional weapons.

The manufacture of nuclear weapons is not that simple, nor is delivery to their target. [...]

Chemical agents are much easier to produce or obtain but not so easy to keep safely in stable condition, and their dispersal depends largely on climatic factors. [...] The biological agents are far and away the most dangerous: they could kill hundreds of thousands where chemicals might kill only thousands. They are relatively easy to procure, but storage and dispersal are even trickier than for nerve gases. The risk of contamination for the people handling them is high, and many of the most lethal bacteria and spores do not survive well outside the laboratory. [...]

Given the technical difficulties, terrorists are probably less likely to use nuclear devices than chemical weapons, and least likely to attempt to use biological weapons. But difficulties could be overcome, and the choice of unconventional weapons will in the end come down to the specialties of the terrorists and their access to deadly substances.

Terrorists can order the poor man's nuclear bomb from a catalog

The political arguments for shunning unconventional weapons are equally weighty. The risk of detection and subsequent severe retaliation or punishment is great, and while this may not deter terrorists it may put off their sponsors and suppliers. Terrorists eager to use weapons of mass destruction may alienate at least some supporters, not so much because the dissenters hate the enemy less or have greater moral qualms but because they think the use of such violence counter-productive. Unconventional weapon strikes could render whole regions uninhabitable for long periods. Use of biological arms poses the additional risk of an uncontrollable epidemic. And while terrorism seems to be tending toward more indiscriminate killing and mayhem, terrorists may draw the line at weapons of super-violence likely to harm both foes and large numbers of relatives and friends – say, Kurds in Turkey, Tamils in Sri Lanka, or Arabs in Israel.

Furthermore, traditional terrorism rests on the heroic gesture, on the willingness to sacrifice one's own life as proof of one's idealism. Obviously there is not much heroism in spreading botulism or anthrax. Since most terrorist groups are as interested in publicity as in violence, and as publicity for a mass poisoning or nuclear bombing would be far more unfavorable than for a focused conventional attack, only terrorists who do not care about publicity will even consider the applications of unconventional weapons.

Broadly speaking, terrorists will not engage in overkill if their traditional weapons – the submachine gun and the conventional bomb – are sufficient to continue the struggle and achieve their aims. But the decision to use terrorist violence is not always a rational one; if it were, there would be much less terrorism, since terrorist activity seldom achieves its aims. [...]

* * *

Future shock

Scanning the contemporary scene, one encounters a bewildering multiplicity of terrorist and potentially terrorist groups and sects. [...]

In the past, terrorism was almost always the province of groups of militants that had the backing of political forces like the Irish and Russian social revolutionary movements of 1900. In the future, terrorists will be individuals or like-minded people working in very small groups [...]. An individual may possess the technical competence to steal, buy, or manufacture the weapons he or she needs for a terrorist purpose; he or she may or may not require help from one or two others in delivering these weapons to the designated target. The ideologies such individuals and mini-groups espouse are likely to be even more aberrant than those of larger groups. And terrorists working alone or in very small groups will be more difficult to detect unless they make a major mistake or are discovered by accident.

Thus at one end of the scale, the lone terrorist has appeared, and at the other, state-sponsored terrorism is quietly flourishing in these days when wars of aggression have become too expensive and too risky. As the century draws to a close, terrorism is becoming the substitute for the great wars of the 1800s and early 1900s.

Proliferation of the weapons of mass destruction does not mean that most terrorist groups are likely to use them in the foreseeable future, but some almost certainly will, in spite of all the reasons militating against it. Governments, however ruthless, ambitious, and ideologically extreme, will be reluctant to pass on unconventional weapons to terrorist groups over which they cannot have full control; the governments may be tempted to use such arms themselves in a first strike, but it is more probable that they would employ them in blackmail than in actual warfare. Individuals and small groups, however, will not be bound by the constraints that hold back even the most reckless government.

Society has also become vulnerable to a new kind of terrorism, in which the destructive power of both the individual terrorist and terrorism as a tactic are infinitely greater. Earlier terrorists could kill kings or high officials, but others only too eager to inherit their mantle quickly stepped in. The advanced societies of today are more dependent every day on the electronic storage, retrieval, analysis, and transmission of information. Defense, the police, banking, trade, transportation, scientific work, and a large percentage of the government's and the private sector's transactions are on-line. That exposes enormous vital areas of national life to mischief or sabotage by any computer hacker, and concerted sabotage could render a country unable to function. Hence the growing speculation about infoterrorism and cyberwarfare. [...]

[...] There is little secrecy in the wired society, and protective measures have proved of limited value [...]. The possibilities for creating chaos are almost unlimited even now, and vulnerability will almost certainly increase. Terrorists' targets will change: Why assassinate a politician or indiscriminately kill people when an attack on electronic switching will produce far more dramatic and lasting results? [...] If the new terrorism directs its energies toward information warfare, its destructive power will be exponentially greater than any it wielded in the past – greater even than it would be with biological and chemical weapons. [...]

Note

1   Science fiction writers produced chemical weapons even earlier. In Jules Verne's *The Begum's Fortune*, a (German) scientist aims to wipe out the 250,000 inhabitants of (French) Franceville with one grenade of what he calls carbon acid gas, shot from a supergun.

Michael Howard

THE WAR ON TERRORISM

Source: 'What's in a name? How to fight terrorism', *Foreign Affairs*, vol. 81, no. 1, January/February 2002, pp. 8–14.

W HEN, IN THE IMMEDIATE aftermath of the September 11 attacks on the World Trade Center and the Pentagon, Secretary of State Colin Powell declared that the United States was "at war" with terrorism, he made a very natural but terrible and irrevocable error. Administration leaders have been trying to put it right ever since.

What Powell said made sense if one uses the term "war against terrorism" in the sense of a war against crime or against drug trafficking: that is, the mobilization of all available resources against a dangerous, antisocial activity, one that can never be entirely eliminated but can be reduced to, and kept at, a level that does not threaten social stability.

The British in their time have fought many such "wars" – in Palestine, in Ireland, in Cyprus, and in Malaya (modern-day Malaysia), to mention only a few. But they never called them wars; they called them "emergencies." This terminology meant that the police and intelligence services were provided with exceptional powers and were reinforced where necessary by the armed forces, but they continued to operate within a peacetime framework of civilian authority. If force had to be used, it was at a minimal level and so far as possible did not interrupt the normal tenor of civil life. The objectives were to isolate the terrorists from the rest of the community and to cut them off from external sources of supply. The terrorists were not dignified with the status of belligerents: they were criminals, to be regarded as such by the general public and treated as such by the authorities.

To declare war on terrorists or, even more illiterately, on terrorism is at once to accord terrorists a status and dignity that they seek and that they do not deserve. It confers on them a kind of legitimacy. Do they qualify as belligerents? If so, should they not receive the protection of the laws of war? [...]

But to use, or rather to misuse, the term "war" is not simply a matter of legality or pedantic semantics. It has deeper and more dangerous consequences. To declare that one is at war is immediately to create a war psychosis that may be totally counter-productive for the objective being sought. It arouses an immediate expectation, and demand, for spectacular military action against some easily identifiable adversary, preferably a hostile state – action leading to decisive results.

The use of force is seen no longer as a last resort, to be avoided if humanly possible, but as the first, and the sooner it is used the better. [...] Any suggestion that the best strategy is not to use military force at all but to employ subtler if less heroic means of destroying the adversary is dismissed as "appeasement" by politicians whose knowledge of history is about on a par with their skill at political management. [...]

[...] The qualities needed in a serious campaign against terrorists – secrecy, intelligence, political sagacity, quiet ruthlessness, covert actions that remain covert, above all infinite patience – all these are forgotten or overridden in a media-stoked frenzy for immediate results, and nagging complaints if they do not get them. [...]

* * *

Battle of wits

A struggle against terrorism, as the British have discovered over the past century and particularly in Northern Ireland, is unlike a war against drugs or a war against crime in one vital respect. It is fundamentally a "battle for hearts and minds"; it is worth remembering that that phrase was first coined in the context of the most successful campaign of this kind that the British armed forces have ever fought – the Malayan emergency in the 1950s (a campaign that, incidentally, took some 15 years to bring to an end). Without hearts and minds one cannot obtain intelligence, and without intelligence terrorists can never be defeated. There is not much of a constituency for criminals or drug traffickers, and in a campaign against them the government can be reasonably certain that the mass of the public will be on its side. But it is well known that one man's terrorist is another man's freedom fighter. Terrorists can be successfully destroyed only if public opinion, both at home and abroad, supports the authorities in regarding them as criminals rather than heroes.

In the intricate game of skill played between terrorists and the authorities, as the British discovered in both Palestine and Ireland, the terrorists have already won an important battle if they can provoke the authorities into using over armed force against them. They will then be in a win-win situation: either they will escape to fight another day, or they will be defeated and celebrated as martyrs.

In the process of fighting them a lot of innocent civilians will certainly be hurt, further eroding the moral authority of the government. Who in the United Kingdom will ever forget Bloody Sunday in Northern Ireland, when in 1972 a few salvos of small-arms fire by the British army gave the Irish Republican Army a propaganda victory from which the British government would never recover? And if so much harm can be done by rifle fire, what is one to say about bombing? It is like trying to eradicate cancer cells with a blowtorch. Whatever its military justification, the bombing of Afghanistan, with the inevitable collateral damage, has whittled away the immense moral ascendancy gained as a result of the terrorist attacks in America.

Soon for much of the world that atrocity will be, if not forgotten, then remembered only as history; meanwhile, every fresh picture on television of a hospital hit, or children crippled by land mines, or refugees driven from their homes by Western military action will strengthen the hatred and recruit for the ranks of the terrorists, as well as sow fresh doubts in the minds of America's supporters.

There is no reason to doubt that the campaign in Afghanistan was undertaken only on the best available political and military advice, in full realization of the military difficulties and political dangers and in the sincere belief that there was no alternative. [...] But in compelling the allies to undertake it at all, the terrorists took the first and all-important trick.

The understandable military reasoning that drove the campaign was based on the political assumption that the terrorist network had to be destroyed as quickly as possible before it could do more damage. It further assumed that the network was masterminded by a single evil genius, Osama bin Laden, whose elimination would demoralize if not destroy his organization. Bin Laden operated out of a country the rulers of which refused to yield him up to the forces of international justice. Those rulers had to be compelled to change their minds. The quickest way to break their will was by aerial bombardment, especially since a physical invasion of their territory presented such huge if not insoluble logistical problems. Given these assumptions, what alternative was there?

Weak foundations

But the best reasoning, and the most flawless logic, is of little value if it starts from false assumptions. I have no doubt that voices were raised both in Washington and in Whitehall questioning the need and pointing out the dangers of immediate military action, but if they were, they were at once drowned out by the thunderous political imperative: "Something must be done." The same voices no doubt also questioned the wisdom, if not the accuracy, of identifying bin Laden as the central and indispensable figure in the terrorist network – demonizing him for some people, but for others giving him the heroic status enjoyed by "freedom fighters" throughout the ages.

The allies are now in a horrible dilemma. If they "bring him to justice" and put him on trial they will provide bin Laden with a platform for global propaganda. If, instead, he is assassinated – perhaps "shot while trying to escape" – he will become a martyr. If he escapes he will become a Robin Hood. Bin Laden cannot lose. And even if he is eliminated, it is hard to believe that his global network, apparently consisting of people as intelligent and well educated as they are dedicated and ruthless, will not continue to function effectively until they are traced and dug out by patient and long-term operations of police and intelligence forces, whose activities will not, and certainly should not, make headlines. Such a process, as the British defense chief Admiral Sir Michael Boyce has rightly pointed out, may well take decades, perhaps as long as the Cold War.

Now that the operation has begun it must be pressed to a successful conclusion – successful enough for the allies to be able to disengage with honor and for the tabloid headlines to claim victory (though the very demand for victory and the sub-Churchillian rhetoric that accompanies this battle cry show how profoundly press and politicians still misunderstand the nature of the terrorist problem). Only after achieving an honorable disengagement will it be possible to continue with the real struggle described above, one in which there will be no spectacular battles and no clear victory.

Boyce's analogy with the Cold War is valuable in another respect. Not only did it go on for a very long time, but it had to be kept cold. There was a constant danger that it would be inadvertently toppled into a "hot" nuclear war, which everyone would catastrophically lose. The danger of nuclear war, at least on a global scale, has now ebbed, if only for the moment, but it has been replaced by another threat, and one no less alarming: the likelihood of an ongoing and continuous confrontation of cultures that will not only divide the world but shatter the internal cohesion of our increasingly multicultural societies. And the longer the overt war continues against terrorism, in Afghanistan or anywhere else, the greater is the danger of that confrontation happening.

There is no reason to suppose that Osama bin Laden enjoys any more sympathy in the Islamic world than, say, Northern Ireland's Ian Paisley does in Christendom. The type is a phenomenon that has cropped up several times in British history: a charismatic religious leader fanatically hostile to the West leading a cult that has sometimes gripped an entire nation. There was the Mahdi in the Sudan in the late nineteenth century, and the so-called Mad Mullah in Somaliland in the early twentieth. Admittedly they presented purely local problems, although a substantial proportion of the British army had to be mobilized to deal with the Mahdi and his followers.

Cultural underpinnings

The difference today is that such leaders can recruit followers from all over the world and can strike back anywhere on the globe. They are neither representative of Islam nor approved by Islam, but the roots of their appeal life in a peculiarly Islamic predicament that only intensified over the last half of the twentieth century: the challenge to Islamic culture and values posed by the secular and materialistic culture of the West, and the inability to come to terms with it.

This is a vast subject that must be understood if there is to be any hope, not so much of winning the new cold war as of preventing it from becoming hot. In retrospect, it is quite astonishing how little the West has understood, or empathized with, the huge crisis that has faced that vast and populous section of the world stretching from the Maghreb through the Middle East and Central Asia into South and Southeast Asia and beyond to the Philippines: overpopulated, underdeveloped, being dragged headlong by the West into the postmodern age before their populations have come to terms with modernity.

This is not a problem of poverty as against wealth, and it is symptomatic of Western materialism to suppose that it is. It is the far more profound and intractable confrontation between a theistic, landbased, and traditional culture, in places little different from the Europe of the Middle Ages, and the secular material values of the Enlightenment. The British and the French, given their imperial experiences, ought to understand these problems. But for most Americans it must be said that Islam remains one vast terra incognita — and one, like those blank areas on medieval maps, inhabited very largely by dragons.

This is the region where the struggle for hearts and minds must be waged and won if the struggle against terrorism is to succeed. The front line in the struggle is not in Afghanistan. It is in the Islamic states where modernizing governments are threatened by a traditionalist backlash: Turkey, Egypt, and Pakistan, to name only the most obvious. The front line also runs through the streets of the multicultural cities in the West. For Muslims in Ankara or Cairo, Paris or Berlin, the events of September 11 were terrible, but they happened a long way away and in another world. By contrast, those whose sufferings as a result of Western air raids or of Israeli incursions are nightly depicted on television are people, however geographically distant, with whom Muslims around the world can easily identify.

That is why prolonging the war is likely to be so disastrous. Even more disastrous would be its extension, as U.S. opinion seems increasingly to demand, in a long march through other "rogue states" beginning with Iraq, in order to eradicate terrorism for good so that the world can live at peace. No policy is more likely not just to indefinitely prolong the war but to ensure that it can never be won.

Discussion questions

- What are the defining features for the new pattern of great power relations in the 21st century, and what are the security implications for states in the periphery?
- Why did 'Offensive' Realists like John Mearsheimer consider post-Cold War Europe to be plausibly less stable?
- Do you concur with the theoretical observation commonly shared by Realists, Liberals and Constructivists, alike, regarding the likelihood of international instability in post-Cold War East Asia?
- To what extent do clashing nationalisms and mutual historical mistrust/animosity exacerbate the security dilemma in contemporary Japanese-Chinese relations, in particular, and the East Asian region, in general?
- Can Structural Realism still adequately explain international security in the post-Cold War era? How far have international security developments in the past decade reflected the structural realist perspective? Do you find Waltz's arguments convincing?
- Why is globalisation a 'double-edged sword'? How has the concept of statecraft and security changed following the advent of globalisation?
- What does Ken Booth mean by 'global moral science'?
- What is the most far-reaching security effect of globalisation?
- What are the notable changes that have taken hold on terrorism in recent times?
- How have the forces of globalisation contributed to the rise of terrorism?
- What does one mean by the 'battle for hearts and minds'?
- Why was the declaration of 'war against terrorism' by the US in the immediate aftermath of the '9/11' incident deemed as a natural, yet serious and irrevocable error?

Suggestions for further reading

Part 1 What is Security?

Redefining security studies

Fukuyama, Francis 'The end of history?' *National Interest*, vol. 16, 1989, pp. 3–18.

Romm, Joseph J. *Defining National Security: The Nonmilitary Aspects* (New York: Council on Foreign Relations Press, 1993).

Smith, Steve, 'The increasing insecurity of Security Studies: conceptualizing security in the last twenty years', *Contemporary Security Policy*, vol. 20, no. 3, 1999, pp. 72–101.

Feminist perspectives

Enloe, Cynthia, *Maneuvers: The International Politics of Militarizing Women's Lives* (Berkeley: University of California Press, 2000).

Tickner, J. Ann, 'Man, the state and war: gendered perspectives on national security', in *Gender in International Relations: Feminist Perspectives on Achieving Global Security* (New York: Columbia University Press, 1992), pp. 27–66.

———, 'Re-visioning security', in Ken Booth and Steve Smith (eds) *International Relations Theory Today* (Cambridge: Polity Press, 1995), pp. 175–97.

Post-colonialism and Third World / North-South perspectives

Chowdry, G. and S. Nair (eds), *Power, Postcolonialism and International Relations: Reading Race, Gender and Class* (London and New York: Routledge, 2002).

Lynn Doty, Roxanne, *Imperial Encounters: The Politics of Representation in North-South Relations* (Minneapolis: Minnesota University Press, 1996).

Tickner, Arlene, 'Seeing IR differently: notes from the Third World', *Millennium: Journal of International Studies*, vol. 32, no. 2, 2003, pp. 295–324.

Human security

Human Development Report, *New Dimensions of Human Security* (New York: Oxford University Press, 1994).

King, Gary and Christopher L. Murray, 'Rethinking human security', *Political Science Quarterly*, vol.116. no. 4, 2001/02, pp. 585–610.

Thomas, Caroline, *Global Governance, Development and Human Security: The Challenge of Poverty and Security* (London: Pluto, 2000).

Environmental security/green politics

Barnett, J., *The Meaning of Environmental Security: Ecological Politics and Policy in the New Security Era* (London: Zed Books, 2001).

Diehl, P. F. and N. P. Gleditsch (eds), *Environmental Conflict: An Anthology* (Boulder, CO: Westview Press, 2000).

Kakonen, J. (ed.), *Green Security or Militarised Environment* (Aldershot: Dartmouth, 1994).

Levy, Marc A. 'Is the environment a national security issue?' *International Security*, vol. 20, no. 2, 2000, pp. 35–62.

Copenhagen School/securitisation

Buzan, Barry, Ole, Wæver, and J. De Wilde, *Security: A New Framework for Analysis* (Boulder, CO: Lynne Rienner Publishers, 1998).

Hansen, Lene, 'The Little Mermaid's silent security dilemma and the absence of gender in the Copenhagen School', *Millennium: Journal of International Studies*, vol. 29, 2000, pp. 285–306.

Roe, Paul, 'Actor, audience(s) and emergency measures: securitization and the UK's decision to invade Iraq', *Security Dialogue*, vol. 39, 2008, pp. 615–35.

Williams, Michael C., 'Words, images, enemies: securitization and international politics', *International Studies Quarterly*, vol. 47, no. 4, 2003, pp. 511–31.

Part 2 Security Paradigms

Realism

Aron, Raymond, *Peace and War: A Theory of Peace and War*, translated by Richard Howard and Annette Baker Fox (Garden City, New York: Doubleday, 1996).

Copeland, Dale C., *The Origins of Major War* (Ithaca, N.Y.: Cornell University Press, 2000).

Grieco, Joseph M., 'Anarchy and the limits of cooperation: a Realist critique of the newest Liberal Institutionalism', *International Organization*, vol. 42, no. 3, 1998, pp. 485–507.

Guzzini, Stefano, 'The enduring dilemmas of Realism in international relations', *European Journal of International Relations*, vol. 10, no. 4, 2004, pp. 533–68.

Mearsheimer, John, 'Anarchy and the struggle for power', in *The Tragedy of Great Power Politics* (New York: Norton, 2001), pp. 29–54.

Powell, Robert, 'Absolute and relative gains in International Relations theory', *American Political Science Review*, vol. 85, no. 4, 1991, pp. 1303–20.

Rose, Gideon, 'Neoclassical Realism and theories of foreign policy', *World Politics*, vol. 51, no. 1, 1998, pp. 144–72.

Thucydides, *The Peloponnesian War,* edited and translated by Rex Warner (Baltimore: Penguin, 1954).

Van Evera, Stephen, *Causes of War: Power and Roots of Conflict* (Ithaca, NY: Cornell University Press, 1999).

Liberalism and Neoliberalism

Axelrod, Robert and Robert O Keohane, 'Achieving cooperation under anarchy: strategies and institutions', *World Politics*, vol. 38, 1985, pp. 226–54.

Brown, Michael E., S. M. Lynn-Jones and S. E. Milner (eds) *Debating the Democratic Peace*, (Cambridge, MA: MIT Press, 1996).

Kant, Immanuel, 'To Perpetual Peace: a philosophical sketch', from *Perpetual Peace, and Other Essays on Politics, History, and Morals*, translated by Ted Humphrey (Indianapolis: Hackett Publishing, 1983), pp.110–18.

Lake, David, 'Powerful pacifists: democratic states and war', *American Political Science Review*, vol. 86, 1992, pp. 24–37.

Mastanduno, Michael, 'Do relative gains matter? America's response to Japanese industrial policy', *International Security*, vol. 16, no. 1, 1991, pp. 73–113.

Milner, Helen, 'The assumptions of anarchy in International Relations theory: a critique', *Review of International Studies*, vol. 17, no. 1, 1991, pp. 67–85.

Russett, Bruce and John Oneal, *Triangulating Peace: Democracy, Interdependence, and International Organizations* (New York: Norton, 2001).

International society / English School

Bull, Hedley and A. Watson, *The Expansion of International Society* (Oxford: Clarendon Press, 1984).

Buzan, Barry, 'The English School: an underexploited resource in IR', *Review of International Studies*, vol. 27, no. 3, 2001, pp. 471–88.

——, *From International to World Society?* (Cambridge: Cambridge University Press, 2004).

Martin, Lisa and B. Simmons, 'Theories and empirical studies of international institutions', *International Organization*, vol. 52, no. 4, 1998, pp. 729–57.

Constructivism

Adler, Emanuel, 'Seizing the middle ground: Constructivism in world politics', *European Journal of International Relations*, vol. 3, no. 3, 1997, pp. 319–63.

Desch, Michael C., 'Culture clash: assessing the importance of ideas in Security Studies', *International Security*, vol. 23, no. 1, 1998, pp. 141–70.

Hopf, Ted, 'The promise of Constructivism in International Relations theory', *International Security*, vol. 23, no. 1, 1998, pp. 171–200.

Katzenstein, Peter J. (ed.), *The Culture of National Security: Norms and Identity in World Politics* (New York: Columbia University Press, 1996).

Lapid, Yosef and Friedrich V. Kratochwil (eds), *The Return of Culture and Identity in IR Theory* (Boulder, CO: Lynne Rienner Publishers, 1996).

Part 3 Security Dimensions and Issues

Nuclear proliferation

Allison, Graham, *Nuclear Terrorism: The Ultimate Preventable Catastrophe* (New York: Times Books/Henry Holt, 2004).

Allison, Graham and Phillip Zelikow, *Essence of Decision: Explaining the Cuban Missile Crisis*, 2nd edition (New York: Longman, 1999).

Meyer, Stephen M., *The Dynamics of Nuclear Proliferation* (Chicago: University of Chicago Press, 1984).

Sagan, Scott, 'The perils of proliferation: organization theory, deterrence theory, and the spread of nuclear weapons', *International Security*, vol. 18, no. 4, 1994, pp. 66–107.

——, 'How to keep the bomb from Iran', *Foreign Affairs*, vol. 85, no. 5, 2006, pp. 45–59.

Walt, Kenneth, *The Spread of Nuclear Weapons: More May Be Better*, Adelphi Papers, no. 171, (London: International Institute for Strategic Studies, 1981), available at: http:// www.mtholyoke.edu/acad/intrel/waltz1.htm.

New warfare

Denning, Dorothy, 'Information warfare and security', *EDPACS*, vol. 27, no. 9, 2000, pp. 1–2.

Der Derian, James, *Virtuous War: Mapping the Military-Industrial-Media-Entertainment Network* (Boulder, CO: Westview, 2001).

Dibb, Paul, 'The Revolution in Military Affairs and Asian security', *Survival*, vol. 39, no. 4, 1997, pp. 93–116.

Kalyvas, Stathis N., '"New" and "old" civil wars: a valid distinction?' *World Politics*, vol. 54, no. 1, 2001, pp. 99–118.

Schleher, D. Curtis, *Electronic Warfare in the Information Age*, 1st Edition (Norwood, MA: Artech House, 1996).

Environmental scarcity, degradation, migration and population displacement

Deudney, Daniel, 'The case against linking environmental degradation to national security', *Millennium: Journal of International Studies*, vol.19, no. 3, 1990, pp. 461–76.

Klare, Michael, *Resource War: The New Landscape of Global Conflict* (New York: Metropolitan Books, 2001).

Nevzat, Soguk, *States and Strangers: Refugees and Displacements of Statecraft* (Minneapolis: Minnesota University Press, 1999).

Princen, T., M. Maniates, and K. Conca (eds), *Confronting Consumption* (Cambridge, MA: MIT Press, 2002).

Ross, Michael L., 'Oil, drugs, and diamonds: the varying roles of natural resources in civil war', in Karen Ballentine and Jake Sherman (eds) *The Political Economy of Armed Conflict: Beyond Greed and Grievances* (Boulder, CO: Lynne Rienner, 2003), pp. 47–70.

Transnational crime

Castle, Allan, 'Transnational organised crime and international security', Working Paper No.19 (Institute of International Relations, The University of British Columbia, 1997).

Dupont, Alan, 'Transnational crime, drugs, and security in East Asia', *Asian Survey*, vol. 39 no.3, 1999, pp. 433–55.

Edwards, Adam and Peter Gill, *Transnational Organised Crime: Perspective on Global Security* (London: Routledge, 2003).

Risse-Kappen, Thomas, *Bringing Transnational Relations Back In: Non-state Actors, Domestic Structure, and International Institutions* (Cambridge: Cambridge University Press, 1995).

AIDS, global pandemics, and security

Easterly, William, 'The healers: triumph and tragedy', from *The White Man's Burden: Why the West's Efforts to Aid the Rest Have Done So Much Ill and So Little Good* (New York: Penguin Press, 2006), pp. 238–63.

Garrett, Laurie, 'The next pandemic?', *Foreign Affairs*, vol. 84, no. 4, 2005, pp. 3–23.

Prins, Gwyn, 'AIDS and global security', *International Affairs*, vol. 80, no. 5, 2004, pp. 931–52.

Singer, P. W., 'AIDS and international security', *Survival*, vol. 44, no. 1, 2002, pp. 145–58.

Part 4 Security Frameworks and Actors

Security communities and international regimes

Acharya, Amitav, *Constructing a Security Community in Southeast Asia: ASEAN and the Problem of Regional Order* (New York: Routledge, 2001).

Adler, Emanuel and Michael Barnett (eds), *Security Communities* (New York: Cambridge University Press, 1998).

Rasmussen, M. V., 'Reflexive security: NATO and international risk society', *Millennium: Journal of International Studies*, vol. 30, no. 2, 2001, pp. 285–309.

Risse, Thomas, 'US Power in a liberal security community', in G. John Ikenberry (ed.), *America Unrivaled: The Future of the Balance of Power* (Ithaca, NY: Cornell University Press, 2002).

Security dilemmas, alliance politics, and the balance of power

Cha, Victor D., 'Abandonment, entrapment, and neoclassical realism in Asia: the United States, Japan, and Korea', *International Studies Quarterly*, vol. 44, 2000, pp. 261–91.

Martin, Pierre and Mark R. Brawley (eds), *Alliance Politics, Kosovo, and NATO's War: Allied Force or Forced Allies?* (New York: Palgrave, 2000).

Mastanduno, Michael, 'Preserving the unipolar moment: Realist theories and US grand strategy after the Cold War', *International Security*, vol. 21, no. 4, 1997, pp. 49–88.

Thompson, William R., 'Systemic leadership, evolutionary processes, and International Relations theory: the unipolarity question', *International Studies Review*, vol. 8, no. 1, 2006, pp. 1–22.

Walt, Stephen, *The Origins of Alliances* (Ithaca, NY: Cornell University Press, 1987).

Humanitarian intervention

Chesterman, Simon, *Just War or Just Peace? Humanitarian Intervention and International Law* (Oxford: Oxford University Press, 2001).

Elshtain, Jean B. (ed.), *Just War Theory* (New York: Blackwell, 1992).

Roberts, Adam, 'Humanitarian war: military intervention and human rights', *International Affairs*, vol. 69, no. 3, 1993, pp. 429–49.

Wheeler, N. J., *Saving Strangers: Humanitarian Intervention in International Society* (Oxford: Oxford University Press, 2000).

Economic statecraft

Baldwin, David, *Economic Statecraft* (Princeton, NJ: Princeton University Press, 1985).

Blanchard, Jean-Marc F., Edward D. Mansfield and Norrin M. Ripsman (eds), *Power and the Purse: Economic Statecraft, Interdependence and National Security* (London: Frank Cass and Company, 2000).

Crawford, N.C. and Klotz, A., *How Sanctions Work: Lessons from South Africa* (New York: Palgrave Macmillan, 1999).

Drezner, Daniel W., *The Sanction Paradox: Economic Statecraft and International Relations* (Cambridge: Cambridge University Press, 1999).

Privatisation of military industry

Brooks, Doug, 'Messiah or mercenaries? The future of international private military services', *International Peacekeeping*, vol. 7, no. 4, 2000, pp. 129–44.

Musah, Abdel-Fatau and J. 'Kayode Fayemi (eds), *Mercenaries: An African Security Dilemma* (London: Pluto Press, 2000).

Singer, P. W., 'Corporate warriors: the rise of the privatized military industry and its ramifications for international security', *International Security*, vol. 26, no. 3, 2001/2, pp. 186–220.

Part 5 The Future of Security

International security in the post-Cold War era: trends and developments

Berger, Thomas, 'Set for stability: prospects for conflict and cooperation in East Asia', *Review of International Studies*, vol. 26, no. 3, 2000, pp. 405–28.

Friedberg, Aaron, 'Ripe for rivalry: prospects for peace in a multipolar Asia', *International Security*, vol. 18, no. 3, 1993/4, pp. 5–33.

Glaser, Charles L. and Steve Fetter, 'National missile defense and the future of US nuclear weapons policy', *International Security*, vol. 26, no. 1, 2001, pp. 40–92.

O'Hanlon, Michael, 'Star Wars strikes back', *Foreign Affairs*, vol. 78, no. 6, 1998, pp. 68–82.

Wohlforth, William C., 'Realism and the end of the Cold War', *International Security*, vol. 19 no. 1, 1994/1995, pp. 91–129.

Globalisation and security

Clark, Ian., *Globalisation and International Relations Theory* (Oxford: Oxford University Press, 1999).

Devetak, Richard and Hughes, Christopher W., *The Globalization of Political Violence: Globalization's Shadow* (London: Routledge, 2008).

Hughes, Christopher W., 'Conceptualising the globalisation security nexus in the Asia Pacific', *Security Dialogue*, vol. 32, no. 4, December 2001, pp. 407–21.

Huntington, Samuel P., 'The clash of civilizations?', *Foreign Affairs*, vol. 72, no. 3, 1993, pp. 22–49.

Kaldor, Mary, 'Introduction', *New and Old Wars: Organised Violence in a Global Era* (Cambridge: Polity Press, 2001), pp. 1–13.

Naim, Moises, 'The five wars of globalization', *Foreign Policy*, vol. 134, 2003, pp. 28–37.

Williams, J. and R. Little, *Anarchical Society in a Globalized World* (New York: Palgrave Macmillan, 2006).

Global terrorism

Abrahms, Max, 'Why terrorism does not work', *International Security*, vol. 31, no. 2, 2006, pp. 42–78.

Laquer, Walter, *The New Terrorism: Fanaticism and the Arms of Mass Destruction* (New York: Oxford University Press, 1999).

Pape, Robert, 'The strategic logic of suicide terrorism', *American Political Science Review*, vol. 97, no. 3, 2003, pp. 343–61.

Pearlstein, R. M., *Fatal Future? Transnational Terrorism and the New Global Disorder* (Austin, TX: University of Texas Press, 2004).

Sadowski, Yahya, 'Political Islam: asking the wrong questions?' *Annual Review of Political Science*, vol. 9, 2006, pp. 215–40.

The future of security studies

Krause, Keith and Michael C. Williams, 'Broadening the agenda of Security Studies: politics and methods', *Mershon International Studies Review*, vol. 40, 1996, pp. 229–54.

Wæver, Ole, 'Still a discipline after all these debates?' in Tim Dunne, Milja Kurki and Steve Smith (eds) *International Relations Theories: Discipline and Diversity* (Oxford: Oxford University Press, 2007).

Wæver, Ole and Barry Buzan, 'After the return to theory: the past, present, and future of Security Studies', in A. Collins (ed.) *Contemporary Security Studies* (Oxford: Oxford University Press, 2006), pp. 383–402.

Index

accountability, domestic 102

Acharya, Amitav 2, 52–60

acquired values 1

Adler, Emanuel 296, 339–42

Afghanistan 56, 234, 300, 314, 418, 424, 425, 426

Africa 55, 56, 114, 128, 208, 254, 269, 404; AIDS in 271, 273; significant wars 61n5; US economic interests 273, 276n8

After Hegemony (Keohane) 147n1, 150n33, 163n1

Agreement on Prevention of Incidents at Sea 321

agroforestry techniques 68

aid 41, 69, 282, 331

Aideed, Mohammed Farah 355n10

AIDS 271–6; danger of 271; demographics 273–4, 276n7; effect on peacekeeping operations 274–5; military infection rates 271–2, 275, 276n2; and security 194; threat of 272–3; variants 275–6; victim numbers 274; and violence 274; and war 275–6

air power 233, 235, 347

alliances 162, 169, 170n2, 295–6, 315–8, 320–7, 325; abandonment 317–8, 328n8; bargaining aims 316; bargaining power 318; in bipolar system 299; bureaucracy 326;

commitment to 317–8, 323; credibility 322–3, 325; definition 320; domestic politics and 323, 325–6; ending 321–4; entrapment 317–8, 328n8; formation 315–7; functions 321, 327n2; ideological divisions and 324; ideological solidarity 326–7; impact of globalisation 410; institutionalisation 321, 326; leadership 324–5; liberal 165; motivation 315; persistence of 324–7; purposes 320; and regime change 324; security communities 327; security dilemma 315–7; and threat perceptions 321–2

Allison, Graham 217

al-Qaeda 273, 277n11

altruism 151

anarchic orders 130–6

anarchy 130, 137, 155, 170, 179; balancing 307–8; and great power emergence 307–9; and power politics 182–3; and the security dilemma 138–9

Angell, Norman 102, 106–7, 151–6

Angola 17n2, 55, 218, 238 n11, 273, 357, 359

Annual Reports (US Defense Department) 86

anti-Semitism 115

apocalyptic millenarianism 419

appeasement 390 n30, 423

Archibugi, Daniele 176n1

Argentina 199, 201, 225, 372

armaments, and security 7

Armed services organizations, organizational politics 216–7

arms control 58, 80, 85, 91n7, 201n5, 199, 209, 210, 321, 375–8, 390 n30

arms dynamic, *see* arms races

arms procurement 335

arms producers 213–4, 214–5

arms races 38, 83, 193–4, 203–18, 352; action–reaction model 203–13; autism 212; awareness of participation on 210; and civil war and internal repression 218; domestic structure model 212–8; economic management and 215; electoral politics and 215–6; idioms of action and reaction 205–8; military production and 214–5; military research and development and 213–4; and military threats 217; and the military-industrial complex 216; organizational politics approaches 216–7; qualitative 206; quantitative 206; reaction magnitude 208–9; reaction timing 209; reassurance 210, 211; and strategic doctrine 207; strategic objectives 210–2; worst-case analysis 204–5

arms trade 214–5, 218, 370–1

Arnold, Guy 62n17

Aron, Raymond 38

ASEAN Regional Forum (ARF) 386

Asia 56; significant wars 61n5

asocial sociability 168

Association of South East Asian Nations (ASEAN) 55, 340, 386

assumptions 49

asylum 256, 259

atomic energy 70

Attlee, Clement 116n17

Australia 328n10

autonomy 282–3, 287n10

Ayoob, Mohammed 53, 61n4, 61n10

Babst, Dean V. 170n2

Bajpai, Kanti 73–4

balance of power 55, 121, 166, 188, 189, 209, 210, 308, 313n19, 316, 322, 335–7, 368, 381, 391, 392–3, 395-6, 402

balance of threat theory 307

balancing 307–8

Balázs, József 20

Baldwin, David 2, 24–32, 281, 352–3

Barnard, Chester 135

Barnett, Michael 339, 340

basic human needs 1

Basque Homeland and Liberty (ETA) movement 417

Beauvoir, Simone De 44

Bedeski, Robert 72

behaviour, and culture 189

beliefs 187, 188; strategic 84

Bellany, Ian 20

Bentham, Jeremy 105–6

Benthamism 106, 107–9

Berger, Thomas U. 103, 187–9

Berlin 196, 197, 206

Berlin Wall 403, 405

bin Laden, Osama 234, 424–5

biodiversity 64, 65, 408

biological weapons 419

biotechnology 233

bipolarity 55, 56, 295, 298–9, 325, 369, 375

Blainey, Geoffrey 209

Blair, Tony 348–9

blame systems 249

Bloody Sunday, Northern Ireland (1972) 423

Booth, Ken 2, 26, 36–43, 364, 398–405

Bosnia 275

Bosnia-Herzegovina 218, 357

Boulding, Kenneth 39

boundaries 369–70

Boyce, Sir Michael 424, 425

Brazil 225, 366, 371

Briand-Kellogg Pact 108, 109

British-German naval race 133, 139, 309–10

Brodie, Bernard 27–8

Brown, Harold 27

Brown, Sarah 50

Bull, Hedley 40, 101, 124–9, 400, 404

Bush, George 57

Bush, George W. 310

Bush Administration 91n12

Buzan, Barry 1–2, 18–23, 25–6, 27, 28, 31–2, 38, 39, 60n1, 61n4, 97–8n4, 193, 203–18, 363, 365–74

Cambodia 17n2, 55, 56, 276n2, 393

Campbell, Matthew 238n5

capitalism 47, 83, 231, 366, 368, 400, 413n11

carbon emissions 66
Carr, E. H. 18, 101, 105–15, 161
Carter administration 165
casualties 231–2
Central Treaty Organization (CENTO) 55
Cha, Victor D. 364, 406–12
champion concept 24–5
cheating 144–6, 148n8
chemical weapons 419, 419–20, 421n1
child soldiers 274
China 299, 310, 363, 366, 381, 392; assess-
    ments of Japanese military strength 384;
    economic growth 393; Japanese historical
    legacies 383; military strength 395; and
    multilateral security regimes 386–7;
    regional confidence building 385–6;
    relations with Russia 396; rise of 393;
    Taiwan policy 382, 386, 389n20; threat to
    Japan 385; US policy on 395, 396; and the
    U.S.-Japan alliance 384–5; view of Japan
    382, 388n8
Chinese Communist Party (CCP) 383
choice theory 184n12
Christensen, Thomas J. 363, 381–7
Chubin, Shahram 56, 58
Churchill, Winston 133
citizenship laws 257–8
civic culture 342
civil society 42,182,232, 233, 268, 342, 401
civil strife 248–9, 251
civil wars 53, 174, 218, 357, 419
civilian powers 312n2, 393–5
civilians 231–7, 232; safety of 347–8
civilizational identities, clash of 372, 373
clear and present dangers 13
climate change 64, 374
Clinton administration 227
Coase, R. 285
Coca-Colanization 373
coercive strategies 235
cognitivism 180, 184n9
Cold War 11, 26, 28, 39, 56, 193, 196, 197,
    198, 199, 204, 207, 208, 214, 223, 367,
    369–70, 377, 396, 406, 409; alliances 299;
    bipolarity 55, 298–9; defections 299;
    definitions of security 1; end of 36, 59,
    84–5, 208; global superpower rivalry 54;
    nuclear lessons 195–7; offense-defense
    balance 146; origins 199; rules 299–302;

securitization 95; security studies research
    agenda 84–5; stability 295, 297–302; and
    the Third World 52, 53, 55, 57
collective decision making 161
collective knowledge 180
collective power 155
collective security 10n6, 57–8, 63n28,
    167, 181, 183, 251, 296, 321, 330–1,
    332, 339, 370
Colombia 268
colonial wars 166
colonization 114, 258, 263n16
commercial liberalism 161
Common Defense (Huntington) 86
common interests 124–5, 155
Common Security (Palme Commission) 75
communication 158; information
    advantage 235–6
Communist threat, the 28
communities of choice 411
community, sense of 155
community security 71
compellence 211
complex interdependence 36, 160–1, 161
Comprehensive Test Ban Treaty (CTBT) 227,
    390n30
compromises 188
computers 207, 236, 240-1
conceptual debate 25, 33n11
Conflict resolution theory 360
Congo 274, 275–6, 356
consequential shift 306
constructivism 102–3, 179–83, 343n11
contractual environment 143–4
conventions 102, 157, 158, 159, 160, 162,
    163n4, 359
cooperation 102, 124, 142, 181, 307, 321;
    and anarchy 137–8; causes of 83–4;
    contractual environment 143–4; and
    dependency 132; economic 142–7; gains
    131–2; incentives to defect 138; limits on
    131–3; and Neoliberal institutionalism 161;
    offense-defense balance 145; the Prisoner's
    Dilemma 139, 143; relative-gains
    considerations 144–6; and the security
    dilemma 137–41; social 155; structural
    constraints 133
cooperative security 181, 185n15, 410
Copenhagen school 407

core, multi-centred 366
core values 7–8, 27, 31
cosmopolitan law 167, 169
costs 29
counter-insurgency 234
crime and criminality 258, 265–9, 345–6, 418
critical infrastructure 238n5
critical theory 38, 41
Croatia 357
Cuban missile crisis 195, 196–7, 198, 207, 301
cultural change 187–8, 189
cultural diversity 174, 372
cultural essentialism 402
cultural identity, migrant threat to 257–8
culture 103, 125; and behaviour 189; definition 187; political-military 187–9
cyberwarfare 361, 421
Czechoslovakia 8

Dahl, Robert 30–1
danger, *see also* threats: awareness of 6; evaluation of levels of 6; military 11; nonmilitary 11
data base, protecting the 86–7
David, Steven 55
debelicization 407
decision-making 7, 45, 57, 68, 188, 224, 238, 321, 326, 332, 380, 401
decolonisation 53, 54–5, 231, 369
defence 20; economics of 284; problem of 155
defence policy 20
defence production 409
defence spending 38, 284
Defence Systems Limited 357
defensive systems 140
defensive weapons 149n30
deforestation 15, 65, 66, 67, 68
Delors, Jacques 310
democracy 39, 73, 107 ; and interdependence 175–6; and peace 174
Democratic Peace 102, 165–70, 174; international imprudence 166; Kant's theory of perpetual peace 166–9; liberal states and war 165–6
democratization 58, 176, 260n2, 354
Denard, Bob 356
Denmark 22, 367

Dependence 12, 58, 59, 282, 394
dependency 132, 282
deprivation conflicts 194, 247, 248, 250
desecuritization 3, 96
deterrence 6, 26, 91n5, 193, 195–201, 211, 214, 378–9; assessment of 199–201; consequences 197; general 195, 196–7; immediate 195–6, 196–7; reinforcing 200; success 197–9
Deutsch, Karl 174, 175, 297, 339, 340
development assistance 69
Devers, General Jacob L. 27–8
Diaoyu/Senkaku Islands 388n9
diffuse reciprocity 331, 410
diplomacy 69, 80, 95, 101, 124, 332, 379, 386, 410
disarmament 68, 203, 209, 227
disease 71, 80, 152, 194, 200, 271, 272, 273, 274, 275, 276, 408, 409, 413n9
doctrine races 207
domestic policy 42, 64,
domestic politics, role 83
Doyle, Michael W. 102, 165–70
drug trafficking 266, 267, 267–8, 269, 408
Dumas, Roland 310
Durkheim, Emil 188

East Asia 363; balance of power 393–6; Chinese view of Japan 382, 388n8; Diaoyu/Senkaku Islands 388n9; Japanese historical legacies 383; Japanese military strength 384; multilateral security regimes 386–7; the Nye Report 384–5; postcolonial nationalism 381; psychological factors 381; regional confidence building 385–6; security dilemmas 381–7; spirals of tension 381–2; US involvement 382, 384–5, 386–7, 395; and the U.S.-Japan alliance 384–5
Eastern Europe 85, 95, 196, 253, 254, 261n2, 273, 340, 376, 376–7, 378
economic cooperation 142–7; and war 102, 151–6
economic crisis (1930–33) 113
economic deprivation 247–9, 251n5
economic development 371; Third World 54, 57
economic dislocation 279

economic growth 67, 194, 261n3, 284–5, 285, 287n15, 393; and great power emergence 306; sustainable 68; and war 279

economic harmony 112–4

economic influence 282

economic integration 85, 392

economic interdependence: and democracy 175–6; and peace 175

economic interest 101, 113, 152, 175

economic order, open 332

economic policies 68, 113, 279, 352,

economic sanctions 194, 280–1, 296, 351–4; definition 351–3; effectiveness 353–4; evaluating 352–3; minimising vulnerability to 354; resistance to 354; success rate 353

Economic Sanctions Reconsidered (Hufbauer *et al.*) 281

economic security 22, 71, 72, 371; periphery, twenty-first century security 371–2

Economic Statecraft (Baldwin) 281

economic warfare 351, 352, 353, 354n4,

economics 42, 85, 86, 112, 119, 144, 151, 153, 154, 169, 176, 194, 250, 400, 404, 405, 406; autonomy 282–3, 287n10; budget constraint 279–80; causes of war 278–9; classical issues 278–80; coercion and punishment 280–1; incentive structure 285; income distribution 286; influence and dependence 282; the locus of production 284–5; market forces 283, 287n10; military spending 284; modern issues 280–3; and morals 153–4; national strategies 279, 279–80; and security 85–6; social economy 285–6; soft power 282; sustainability of security 283–6

ecosystem vulnerability 250

Einstein, Albert 70

emancipation 2, 36–43, 402

empirical realism 38

energy use 67, 68

Enthoven, A. 86

environment, the 2, 14

environmental change 64–70; climate change 64, 66–7; and population growth 64–6; refugees from 65–6; regulatory strategies 68–70; resource depletion 69

environmental degradation 14, 49, 54, 57, 250, 253, 408

environmental scarcity, *see* resource scarcity

environmental security 22, 71, 373–4

equality 41–2

essentially contested concepts 24–6

ethics 37, 38, 41, 105, 119, 122, 199, 403

Ethiopia 275, 276n7, 372,

ethnic cleansing 260, 346, 348, 349,

Eurocentrism 2, 52, 393–6

Europe, post-Cold War 363; Balkanization 375; instability in 375–80; multipolar 85, 376–80; nuclear powers 378–9; nuclear proliferation 375, 379–80; nuclear-free 375–8; rise of 365

European Community (EC) 85, 366

European Community Commission 310

European Free Trade Association (EFTA) 340

European Union 176, 340, 367, 392–3

Executive Outcomes (EO) 357, 358, 360

expansionism 138, 335

failed states 58, 273

Falk, Richard 413n12

family-planning services 68

Farrell, Theo 217

fascism 116n1, 419

femininity 46

feminism 2, 44–50; classic 47; definition of gender 46; Marxist 47; perspectives on international relations 44–5, 47–50; postmodern 48; psychoanalytic tradition 48; radical 47–8; socialist 48

firms 132

food security 71

force, use of 97–8n4, 130, 134; private 135; right to legitimate 131; as the *ultima ratio* 135–6

foreign investment 273, 283

foreign policy 6, 9n1, 12, 15, 42, 392, 402, 410; context 121; explanations of 181; and political action 122; rational 121; realism and 119, 120–1

Foreign Relations of the United States (US State Department) 86

foreign threats 17n2, 168, 216, 224,

foreigners 47, 167, 358, 369,

Fox, William T. R. 38

France: African troop deployments 357; colonial wars 166; financial diplomacy 279;

foreign policy 6; nuclear forces 217, 378; occupation of the Ruhr 9n3

Freedman, Lawrence 194, 230–7

freedom 21, 22, 30, 39, 41–2, 73–4, 134, 160, 161, 167-8

freedom fighters 254–5

Gaddis, John Lewis 295, 297–302, 397n9

Galbraith, J. K. 400

Gallie, W. B. 24–5

game theory 300, 301–2, 319n2

gender: differences 46-7; feminist definition 46; hierarchies 49–50; in international relations 45–7; relations 47; in U.S. Foreign Service 44

General Agreement on Tariffs and Trade (GATT) 159

genocide 194, 232, 233, 235, 275–6, 348

Geneva Conventions 232, 359

Germany 20, 139, 189, 279, 280–1, 301, 311, 312n2, 376, 377–8, 378, 392, 396

Gilpin, Robert 278–9, 284, 286, 287n10, 287n11, 306, 307–8

global citizenship 174

global civilian powers 312n2, 393–5

global environmental health indicators 69

global ethics 38

global governance 398, 401–3, 405

global moral science 364, 398, 399–401, 400, 403, 405

global superpower rivalry 54–5

global village, the 265

global warming 66–7, 408,

globalisation 265, 283, 364, 396, 398–405, 406–12, 412n2; definition 399; emergence of 398–401; and global governance 401–3; and global moral science 403, 405; impact on security 403–5, 406–12; impact on states 399, 402, 404, 409; implications of 399–401; intermestic security 409; literature 406, 411; and multilateralism 409–10; non-physical security 408–9; and nuclear deterrence 411–2; and security specialization 410–1; security spectrum 407, 407–8, 410; shifts in relative capabilities 411; and strategy 411–2; transaction processes 408

Goldblatt, David, et al. 412n2, 413n14

governance, global 401–3

government policy, evaluation 86–7

Graham, Bradley 238n5

Gramsci, A. 37

Gray, Colin S. 210

Great Britain: British-German naval race 133, 139; colonial wars 166; decline in status 309–10; and Hong Kong 8; naval disarmament 138–9; naval supremacy 309–10; regions of special interest 7; wars on terrorism 422, 423

Great Illusion, The (Angell) 106–7

great powers 366, 392–3, 402; balancing 307–8; definition 311n2; and differential growth rates 306; emergence of 305–10; hegemonic systems 307–8; historical examples 309–10; local 366; role models 311n2; sameness 308–9

Greeks, Ancient 105

Greenham Common peace protests 40–1

greenhouse effects 66–7

Grey, Sir Edward 139

Grieco, Joseph 144, 145, 163n1, 307

Grinevsky, Oleg 201n4

gross national product 175, 287n11, 313n19, 351; calculation of 68–9; and military expenditure 206–7

Gross Stein, Janice 193, 195–201

Guehenno, Jean-Marie 406

guerrillas 236, 407, 417, 418

Gulf Cooperation Council (GCC) 55

Gulf War, first 57–8, 240, 242, 246, 262n5, 314n31

Gulf War, second 367–8

Halliday, Fred 56

Hamas 417

Hammond, P. 86

hard power 312n2

Hartland-Thunberg, Penelope 20

Hashimoto, Ryutaro 383

Havel, Vaclev 37

health security 71

health-care costs 272–3

hearts and minds 194, 234, 364, 423–4, 425–6

hegemonic stability theory 307

hegemonic systems, stability 307–8

Heilbroner, Robert 400, 403, 404

Herring, Eric 193, 203–18

hierarchic orders 134

high value expectancy 9n4

hijackings 418

Hinze, Otto 309

history 119–20; end of 402

Hitler, Adolf 328n9

Hoare, Mike 356

Hobbes, Thomas 12, 30

Homer-Dixon, Thomas 194, 246–51

Hong Kong 8

hospitality 167, 169

How Much is Enough? (Enthoven and Smith) 86

Howard, Michael 303n8, 364, 422–6

Hudson, G. F. 331

Hufbauer, Gary Clyde, *et al.* 281

Human Development Report (UNDP) 71–2

human nature 105–6, 118, 119, 123, 145, 151

human rights 12, 39, 58, 174, 346, 403

human security 3, 71–6, 173, 403, 407;
    definition 71–2; essential elements 73;
    practical use 72–3; as research category
    74–6; scope 71, 72, 73–4

humanitarian war 58, 296, 345–9; doctrine
    348–9; laws of 347–8; legal basis 346–7

Hungary 376–7, 380n4

Huntington, S. 86, 206, 209, 266, 311n2

idealism 5, 296, 420

Idealists 18–9

ideas 103; autonomous power of 84

identity 103, 187–9; civilizational 373;
    collective 341, 373; common 174; cultural
    257–8; formation 180, 180–1, 183; local/
    global 36–7; mutual 177n6; relational 180;
    shared 326–7; as source of conflict 408;
    state 22; Third World national 53

ideological conflict 366

IMF 225, 368, 394, 400

immigration 14, 256–7; threat 254–6

imperialism 58, 286n3, 382, 383, 388n12

imperialist powers 9n3

In Defense of the National Interest
    (Morgenthau) 9n1

India 56, 57, 217, 260, 366, 393

individual security 20, 267, 268

individuals, and liberalism 161

Indonesia 56, 57, 258, 261n5

industrialization 371

influence 282

information age, the 231–7; the information
    advantage 235–7; military capability 231–2

information power 408

information systems 232, 235–7

information technology 241, 243

information warfare 232–3, 238n5, 421

infoterrorism 421

infrastructure 236, 243, 248, 285, 312

institutional optimists 85

institutionalization 157–8, 159, 160–1, 180;
    alliances 321, 326

institutions: definition 158, 331;
    impact 158; significance of 159;
    structures 180

integration 131–3

intelligence 236

intelligence, surveillance, and
    reconnaissance (ISR) 241

intelligence community, powers 12

interdependence 38, 131, 406; complex
    160–1, 161; and democracy 175–6;
    economic 175

interests: clash of 115; defined as power
    119–22; harmony of 111–2, 114–5;
    identity of 112

intermestic security 409

internal repression 218

internal security 20, 212, 253

international anarchy 101, 102, 106-7

International Atomic Energy Agency
    (IAEA) 225

international authority, lack of 137–41

international economy, growth of 280

international finance 400

international harmony 111–2

international imperative, the 132

international imprudence 166

international institutions 85, 102, 142–7,
    157–64, 333, 342, 368–9; alliances 162;
    conventions 162, 163n4; definition 158;
    and liberalism 161; mutual interests 158;
    significance of 159; and states 159

international law 70, 124, 168–9

international order 124–7, 128; and global
    superpower rivalry 54–5;
    management of 57

international organizations 332

International Police Force 108

international realm, the 135

international regimes 83, 158, 159, 162, 180, 332,
International Relations 1, 2, 54–5; feminist perspectives 44–5, 47–50; gender in 45–7; and globalisation 402; hierarchical binary oppositions 50; Idealist school of 18–9; militarization 11; national security problem in 18–23; Realist School of 18–9; right conduct 127
international responsibility 410
international security 19, 20, 26, 194, 224, 250-1, 254, 265-6, 267, 271, 295, 364, 367, 374, 400, 401, 404, 406
International Security (journal) 75
international social structures 159
international society 124–7, 368–9
international structure 393–6
international system 402; anarchic nature of 22; decentralized 160; institutionalization 160–1; and international society 125
interregnum 36–7
intervention strategies 234–5; objectives 235
interventionism 95, 296, 345–9; doctrine 348–9; laws of war 347–8; legal basis 346–7
intrastate violence literature 75
Iran 57, 58; Operation AJAX 92n13
Iran-Iraq war 208
Iraq 228n2, 259–60, 371, 426; economic sanctions against 354, 355n10; war with Iran 208
Irish Republican Army (IRA) 417, 423
Islam 370, 373, 402, 425–6
Israel 15, 58, 199, 204, 218, 228n2, 255, 258, 300, 357, 371, 420
Italy 113, 268, 366, 417,

Jahn, Egbert 95
Japan 22, 115, 138, 189, 246, 281, 284, 309–10, 310, 311, 312n2, 363, 366, 382, 392, 393–5; Chinese threat 385; Chinese view of 382, 388n8; defence budget 384; historical legacies 383; imperialism 383; militarism 383; military strength 384; regional confidence building 385–6; US alliance 382, 384–5, 386–7
Jervis, Robert 102, 137–41, 145, 260, 296, 308, 334–7

Jones, Nye and Lynn 80
Jordan 250
justice 21, 22, 25, 39, 42, 85, 127, 134, 153, 155, 237, 248, 300, 392, 424

Kaldor, Mary 217
Kant, Immanuel 102, 106, 165, 166–9, 173–6, 176n1
Kaplan, Abraham 9n4, 335, 336–7, 337n9
Keegan, John 230
Kennedy, John F. 195–7, 198, 206
Kennedy, Paul 85, 279, 306
Keohane, Robert 82, 102, 145, 149n21, 150n32, 150n33, 157–64, 179, 331
Khrushchev, Nikita 195–7, 198, 206, 207, 301
King, Gary 73, 74
Kirshner, Jonathan 194, 278–86
Knorr, Klaus 28
knowledge 49; collective 180; shared 341–2
Korean War 201n3, 300, 302
Kosovo and the Kosovo campaign 345–9; air-power 347; legal basis 346–7; lessons of 348–9
Krasner, Stephen D. 307
Krasner, Steven 177n3
Kuhn, Thomas 188
Kuniholm, Bruce 92n13
Kurdish extremists 417

labour, division of across nations 131–3
laissez-faire 107, 111–2, 112–4
Lakatos, Imre 91n2
land reform 65
land tenure 65
language games 93–4
language theory 21, 95
Lapid, Yosef 91n2
Laqueur, Walter 364, 417–21
Lasswell, Harold D. 9n4
Latin America 61n5, 254, 357
"Law and Peace" (McDougal) 9n5
laws: cosmopolitan 167, 169; domestic 410; international 70, 124, 168–9; objective 119; of war 347–8
Layne, Christopher 295, 305–11
League of Nations 106, 108–9, 110, 111, 116n17, 171n6

Lebow, Ned 193, 195–201

legal procedures 9n5

legitimacy 22, 54, 56, 131, 17, 226, 227, 248, 249, 268, 301, 324, 342, 354, 360, 369, 373, 383, 422

liberal capitalism 366

liberal democracy: nineteenth-century 107–8; and public opinion 109–10

liberal institutionalism 142–7

liberal internationalism 165–70, 166–9

liberal pacifists 165

liberal peace 91n4, 166, 168, 169,

Liberal republics 167–8

liberalism 101, 102; commercial 161; and individuals 161; international imprudence 166; and international institutions 161; and Neoliberal institutionalism 161; pacific federation 165; Republican 161

liberty 1, 12, 13, 14, 41–2

Libya 259, 371

life, quality of 13–4, 21, 32

Lindblom, Charles 30–1

Lindsay, James 216

Lippmann, Walter 6, 20

literature 75; globalisation 406, 411; intrastate violence 75; military threats 75; nonmilitary threats 75; security studies 75

local rivalries 56

Louw, Michael H. H. 20

Luard, Evan 61n5

Luciani, Giacomo 21

McCarran-Walter Immigration Act (US) 263n15

MccGwire, Michael 199

MacDonald, Ramsey 138–9

McDougal, Myres S. 9n5

McNamara, Robert 198

Malayan emergency 423

Malaysia 258, 261n5, 422

Manchester School economists 278

Manchurian crisis 110

manliness 45, 46

marginal values 1, 7, 31–2

market, the 169

Martin, Laurence 21

Martin, Lisa 175

Marxism Today 37

masculinity 45, 46, 49,

Mearsheimer, John J. 55, 102, 142–7, 363, 375–80

media, information advantage 236–7

mercenaries 128, 356, 359, 359–60, 361

Middle East, significant wars 61n5

migrants and migration 194, 253–60; acceptance criteria 255–6; burden of 258–9; consanguinity 258; directions 254; economic 255, 260; employment opportunities 261n3, 261n5; environmental 261n4; expulsions 260; home country hostility 256–7; host country risk 257; as hostages 259–60; illegal 258, 261n3; international 253–4; motivation 253; numbers 256; refugee status 256, 259; and resource scarcity 247, 249–50; sending country control of 259–60; state backing 247; threat 254–6, 260; threat to cultural identity 257–8; twenty-first century security 372–3

militarization 11, 370, 371,

military, the, role as cause of war 83

military capability 177, 198, 203, 207, 212, 231–2, 236, 311n2, 353, 357, 370, 371, 411

military competition 37, 204, 205–6, 210

military establishment 13

military force 29

military forces, resource allocation 15

military Keynesianism 279

military power 38, 56, 80, 83, 144, 203

military production 214–5

Military Professional Resources Incorporated (MPRI) 357

military research and development 213–4

military security 3, 22, 26, 37–8, 94; periphery, twenty-first century security 370–1

military spending 85–6, 170n3, 206–7, 215, 217, 225, 279, 284

military stability 39

military strategies 211, 308,

military strength 193, 203, 204, 206, 209, 212, 269, 311n2, 312, 318n1, 352, 365, 384

military technology 204, 205–6, 233, 240–4, 371; organizational politics 216–7; research and development 213–4 military threats 13, 14, 80, 94; and arms races 217; literature 75

military-industrial complex (MIC) 86, 216

militias 233–4, 236, 407

Mill, John Stuart 47, 107

Milner, Helen 148n9

Mindanao 263n16

Missile Technology Control Regime (MTCR) 58

Mittleman, James 59

mixed interests 142

moral appeals 9n5

moral principles, and political action 122

morality, bankruptcy of 115

morals: case for war 151–6; and economics 153–4

Morgenthau, Hans 9n1, 9n3, 9n5, 18, 19, 81, 101, 118–23, 298

Morocco 258

Mozambique 218, 357

Mroz, John E. 21

Mueller, John 84

multilateral organizations 157, 330, 332, 360,

multilateralism 57, 296, 330–3, 386, 389n25, 409–10

multipolarity 299, 365–6, 368, 395; alliance formation and 315–7; European 376–80

Murray, Christopher 73, 74

Muslim Brotherhood 417

mutually assured destruction (MAD) 193, 199, 211

Myanmar 56, 269

Napoleon 166, 243, 328n9

Nasser, Gamal Abdel 355n7

National Defence College (Canada) 21

national interest 5, 20, 30, 45, 101, 120, 216, 223, 284, 325, 327, 349, 410

national politics 135, 299

national security 8–9, 18–23, 27, 94, 96, 187–9; definition 5–9, 11, 20–2; degree of 27–8; demand for a policy of 5–6; Eurocentrism 52; importance of 18; importance of debate 87; and international relations 18–23; marginal values approach 31; problem of 18–23; redefining 16; in the Third World 53–4

nationalism 122, 230-1, 287n10, 354, 363, 377-8, 379, 383, 419

nations, values 1

NATO 196, 320, 321, 322, 340, 345–9, 395

natural law 105, 106, 127

natural systems theory 217

nature, law of 14

nature, state of 130, 186n20

Nazi Germany 13

Nef, Jorge 72

negative security assurances 223

negotiated limitations 95

negotiating models, inadequacy of 70

neoclassical realism 363

neo-Kantianism 102, 173–6

neoliberal institutionalism 102, 157–64; and alliances 162; and conventions 162, 163n4; and cooperation 161; definition of institutions 158; and international regimes 162; and liberalism 161; mutual interests 158; and neorealism 159–61; significance of institutions 159

neorealism 25, 41, 101–2, 222, 295, 305, 306, 310; interpretations of alliances 162; and neoliberal institutionalism 159–61

new world order 57–8, 310

Nigeria 57, 273, 372,

Nixon, Richard 301

Non-Aligned Movement (NAM) 54–5, 369

nongovernmental organizations, lobbying 16

nonmilitary threats 1, 11, 13–4, 80; literature 75; Third World 54

non-physical security 408–9

non-physical threats 364

nonrenewable resources 65, 194

norms 73, 102, 103, 143, 157, 180, 181, 187–9, 226, 227, 257, 258, 266, 332, 334, 335, 340, 349, 369, 387,410

North American Free Trade Agreement (NAFTA) 340

North Korea 228n2, 261, 385, 393, 394, 411

Northern Ireland 423

North-South tensions 57–8, 59, 69

nuclear deterrence 193, 195–201, 222, 378–9; assessment of 199–201; general 195, 196; immediate 195–6, 196–7; impact of globalisation 411–2; reinforcing 200; success 197–9

nuclear energy establishment 224

Nuclear Non-Proliferation Treaty (NPT) 58, 222, 225–6, 226, 227–8 nuclear parity 393, 396n3

nuclear proliferation 193–4, 201, 222–8; bureaucratic actors 224; dangers 379–80; domestic politics model 224–6; Europe 375, 379–80; mismanaged 379; nonproliferation 58, 222, 225–6; the norms model 226–8; parochial interests 224–5, 225; the security model 222–4

nuclear vulnerability 199

nuclear weapons 40, 75, 200–1, 301, 378–9, 393, 405; abolition 41; costs of 225; first-use doctrine 227; negative security assurances 223; nonproliferation 58, 222, 225–6; nuclear-free Europe 375–8; power 222; symbolic functions 226–8; terrorist threat 419, 420; threat of 232, 403; and vulnerability 17n3

Nye, Joseph 163n1, 282, 311n2

objective choices 11–3

offense-defense balance 145–6

Offensive Realism 102, 142–7, 363

O'Hanlon, Michael 194, 240–4

oil 12, 13, 15, 65, 86, 246, 248, 273, 276n8, 393; US Strategic Petroleum Reserve 15

On Liberty (Mill) 107

one-party systems, legitimacy 369

open systems theory 217

Operation AJAX 92n13

Operation Allied Force 242, 345–9

order 2, 39, 95, 124–9; centralized 135; goals 125–7; international 124–7, 128; and peace 126; and treaties 127; value 128; and violence 126–7; world 127–9

organised crime 265–9

Organization for Security and Cooperation in Europe 218, 340, 389n25

Osgood, Robert 327n2

other means, role of 9n5

Others 2, 47, 255–6

Oye, Kenneth 148n10

ozone depletion 66, 67, 408

pacific unions 167

pacifism 117n17

Pakistan 56, 204, 217, 228n2, 260, 371, 393, 426,

Palme Commission 75

Pape, Robert A. 296, 351–4

Paris, Roland 2–3, 71–6

patriarchal perspectives 2, 46, 48

peace: causes of 83–4; and democracy 174; democratic 102, 165–70, 174; and economic interdependence 175; identity of interests 112; and international order 126; Kant's theory of perpetual 166–9; liberal 91n4; neo-Kantian perspective 173–6; and security 19; value of 211

peace sacrifices 152

peace studies 83–4, 207

peacebuilding 360

peacekeeping 58, 225, 274–5, 296, 357, 358, 360

People, States and Fear (Buzan) 38, 39, 97–8n4

periphery, twenty-first century security: boundaries 369–70; clash of civilizational identities 373; economic security 371–2; environmental security 373–4; military security 370–1; political security 369–70; societal security 372–3

Perpetual Peace (Kant) 166–9

Persian Gulf 12, 13, 56, 81, 86

personal, the, political nature of 49

personal security 22, 71

Philippines, the 56, 258, 263n16

Pinochet, Augusto 345–6

police powers 12

policy alternatives, specifications 29–30

policy choices 13, 21, 32, 371,

policy coalitions 410

policy disputes 25

policy relevance 82

politeness 302

political action, moral significance of 122

political economy 142–7, 278, 280, 400; causes of war 278–9

political liberalization 260n2

political market failure 143

political morality 122

political participation 173

political security 22, 71; periphery, twenty-first century security 369–70

political will, mobilisation of 14

political-military culture 187–9

population dumping 259

population growth 64–6, 68

population movement 247, 249–50; see also migrants and migration

Posen, Barry 170, 284
post-international politics 36, 42, 399
post-modern approaches 82
post-sovereign space 364, 407
poverty 2, 3, 39, 41, 53, 59, 65, 73, 80, 248, 404, 425
Powell, Colin 422
Powell, Robert 145–6
power 2, 6, 9n4, 18, 366; balances of 130–6; balancing power 392–3; coercive 8; collective 155; concentrated 392; distribution of 179–80; and economic capacity 279; feminist critique 49; hard 312n2; interest defined as 119–22; military 38, 56, 80, 83, 144, 203; political economy of 278; privileging 39; relations of 121; relative 307; and security 19; soft 282, 286n8, 311n2; state 160; unbalanced 391
Power and Society (Lasswell and Kaplan) 9n4
power of resistance 8
power politics 6, 7–8, 38, 45, 179–83, 365
predictability 160, 301, 321
prime values 30–1
Prisoner's Dilemma, the 139–41, 143, 315–7
private military companies (PMC) 296, 356–61, 413n10; deployment 357; expansion 361; involvement in wars 360; lack of accountability 359; lack of political constraints 357–8; market 356–8; motivation 359; payment 358; peacekeeping role 358; as proxies 358; recruits 358; regulation of 358–60, 361
privileging power 39
psychological warfare 364, 423–4, 425–6
public opinion 109–10, 110, 156; salvation by 106; and terrorism 423
public security 20

Quester, George 145

rape 97n4, 194, 275–6
rationalism 107–9
Ray, James L. 84
Reagan administration 86, 165, 216, 267
realism, classical 55, 101, 118–23, 143, 391; and foreign policy 119, 120–1; fundamental principles 119–23; and human nature 123; interest defined as

power 119–22; the laws of politics 119; and moral judgement 122
realists 18–9, 41, 50, 75, 83,84, 105, 143, 158, 182, 224, 381, 402
reassurance 210, 211, 382, 384
reciprocal interaction 182
reciprocity 42, 159, 331, 410
Reed, Laura 72, 73
referent objects 22–3, 27, 39–40
reflexive response 14
refugees 65–6, 117n22, 253–60, 254, 256, 257, 259, 260, 262n11, 273
regime change 83, 296, 324
regional conflicts 37, 56, 59
regional coordination 410
regional security 58–9; alliances 55; organizations 63n28
regions of special interest 7
relative gains 144–6, 149n27
religious fundamentalism 403, 419
religious fundamentalist leaders 425
religious rivalry 39
renewable resources 65, 194, 246, 250
Republican liberalism 161
republics, liberal 167–8
resource allocation 15, 31, 215
resource degradation 248
resource scarcity 1, 13–4, 65, 69, 86, 246–51; causal role 250; and civil strife 248–9, 251; and economic deprivation 247–9; hard regimes 251; implications for security 250–1; and population movement 247, 249–50; simple-scarcity conflicts 246–7; and violence 194; water 246–7
resource wars 246, 251
resources: control of 138; stockpiling 15
respect 168
Revolution in Military Affairs (RMA) 194, 231–7, 240–4, 408; dominant battlespace knowledge school 240, 241; global reach, global power school 241, 241–3; information warfare 232–3; intervention strategies 234–5; military capability 231–2; militia-based 233–4; system of systems school 240, 241; vulnerability school 241, 243
righteousness 152
rights, reciprocity of 42

Rise and Fall of the Great Powers, The (Kennedy) 85
risk aversion 211
Roberts, Adam 296, 345–9
Rogge, Heinrich 10n6
rogue states 102, 194, 407, 426
Romania 376–7, 380n2, 380n4
Roosevelt, Eleanor 44
Rosenau, James 36, 399, 412n1
Rousseau, Jean-Jacques 106, 137, 186n20
Ruggie, John Gerald 160, 296, 330–3
Ruhr, occupation of the 9n3
rules 143–4, 158, 180, 188, 299–302, 336
Russett, Bruce 102, 173–6
Russia 113, 115, 141n1, 199, 201n5, 298, 309, 310, 340, 366, 370, 390, 392, 393, 396
Rwanda 56, 58, 274, 275, 357

Sabah 258, 261
Saddam Hussein 328n9
Sagan, Scott 193–4, 222–8
Sahlins, Marshall 404
Saint-Pierre, Abbé 106
Salter, Sir Arthur 331
sameness 308–9
Sandline International 357, 358
Saudi Arabia 12, 15, 238n10, 262n6, 314n31, 367
Scandinavia 340
Schelling, T. C. 82
Schilling, W. 86
Schroeder, Paul 327n2, 340–1
Schultze, Charles 20
science fiction 421n1
Scott, Joan 46–7
Scott, W. Richard 217
sea level rises 66–7
second-image pessimists 85
secrecy 87, 234, 236, 421, 423
securitization 3, 93–6
security: absolute sense of 21, 28; affecting sectors 22; and AIDS 194; and armaments 7; articulation 96; categorisations 1–2; champion concept of 24–5; concept of 24–32; conception of 18–23; as contested concept 24–6; contested nature of 19–20; contradictions 20, 26; definition 1, 2, 6, 7, 13, 20–2, 38, 64–70, 95–6, 97n2, 254–5,

267; degree of 27–8; and deterrence 6; economic sustainability of 283–6; and economics 85–6; field 93–4; goals 8; high value expectancy 9n4; impact of globalisation 403–5, 406–12; individual 267; intermestic 409; levels of 6, 7; and liberal institutionalism 144; means 29; minimizing 96; non-physical 408–9; and peace 19; pervasiveness of xii; population influx threat 254–5; power as derivative of 19; redefining 11–6; referent objects 22–3, 27, 39–40; and resource scarcity 250–1; specialization 410–1; subjective nature of 2; temporal dimensions 29–30; twenty-first century 363, 365–74; value approach 30–2; value of 6; and vulnerability 14–5, 17n3
"Security, Sovereignty, and the Challenge of World Politics" (Walker) 97n2
security choices 11–3
security communities 39, 216, 296, 326, 327, 339–42; capitalist 367–8; definition 339; liberal pluralistic 341–2; socially construction 341; twenty-first century 367–8
security constituencies 407
security cooperation, the Prisoner's Dilemma 139
security dilemma, the 38, 83, 102, 137-41, 182, 183, 193, 205, 210, 211, 279, 295, 307, 335, 337, 383, 385, 386, 390n30; alliances 315–7; and anarchy 138–9; and cooperation 137–41; and the Prisoner's Dilemma 139–41; and security regimes 335, 337; status-quo states 139–41
security dilemma theory 381
security guarantees 327n1
security issues 32
security problems, naming 94–5
security regimes 296, 332, 334–7; and the balance of power 335–7; definition 334; East Asia 386–7; formation 334–5; moderation of self-interests 336; and restraint 336; rules 336
security studies: broadening and deepening 75; definition 80–1; formal models 82; literature 75; policy relevance 82; post-modern approaches 82; problems facing 81–2; quantitative research 91n3;

research agenda 82–7; and the Third World
52–60, 61n4
security systems 181, 182, 185n13
security zones 7
self, the 181, 182, 183
self-help systems 131–6, 179, 180–2,
182–3, 307
Senegal 250
September 11 terrorist attacks 422, 426
Serbia and Serbs 264n20, 345, 346, 349
shared knowledge 341–2
Shearer, David 296, 356–61
Shinseki, General Eric 242–3
Shultz, George 222
Sierra Leone 273, 275, 357
Simon, Herbert 28
Simon, Sir John 110
Simonie, F. N. 21
simple-scarcity conflicts 246–7
Singer, David 297
Singer, P. W. 194, 271–6
small-arms proliferation 218
Smith, Jean Edward 314n31
Smith, K. W. 86
Smuts, General Jan 108
Snidal, Duncan 145–6, 149n27
Snyder, Glenn 86, 295, 315–8, 328n8
Snyder, Jack 83, 145
social cohesion 286
social conflict 248–9
social cooperation 155
social economy 285–6
social facts 180, 188
societal security 2, 22, 97n2, 372-3;
periphery, twenty-first century
security 372–3
society of states 124–7
soft power 282, 286n8, 311n2
soil degradation 65, 67
Somalia 56, 58, 355n10, 357
South Africa 12, 273, 371
South Asia 56, 254
South East Asia Treaty Organization
(SEATO) 55
South Korea 201n3, 261n5, 298,
369, 395
sovereignty 125, 137, 163n4, 167, 173,
177n3, 406; and environmental change 64,
69; feminist critique 49; impact of

globalisation 402; popular 173; TCOs
threat to 269
Soviet Union 12, 13, 17n3, 376, 377, 378;
clients 299; and the Cuban missile crisis
196–7, 198; fall of 85, 261n2, 310, 391,
400; involvement in civil war and internal
repression 218; leadership crises 301–2;
nuclear deterrence 195–201; spheres-of-
influence 300; Third World interventions
170n3; threat 392
speech acts 21, 93, 94–6, 98n6
spheres-of-influence 126, 199, 295, 298, 300,
303n14, 365–6
Sri Lanka 56, 263n16, 417, 418, 420
stability 295, 297–302; and bipolarity 298–9;
definition 297; hegemonic systems 307–8;
nuclear Europe 378–9; nuclear-free Europe
378–9; predictable anomalies and 301;
requirements 302; rules 299–302;
spheres-of-influence 300, 303n14
stable peace 39
Stag Hunt 137–9, 182, 186n20
Stalin, Joseph 201n3, 201n4
START II treaty 201n5
state-building 369
statecraft 80, 259, 280, 281, 282, 312, 398,
400, 403–5
states 22; autonomy 282–3, 287n10; backing
for migrants 247; changing capabilities 160;
fragility 217; freedom 134; and
globalisation 399; identity 22; impact of
globalisation 399, 402, 404, 409;
independence 125–6; interdependence
131; interests 135–6, 316; and
international institutions 159; and liberal
institutionalism 144; numbers 231; order
among 127; power 160; as referent objects
40; relative-gains considerations 144–6;
republican 167–8; sameness 308–9;
status-quo 139–41; strategies 133; TCOs
threat to 268–9; Third World
structures 53; values 1
states system, global 127–8
state-sponsored terrorism 418, 421
statism 401, 403, 404
status quo powers 9n3, 140, 335
Stein, Arthur 308
Steinbach, Udo 53
Stopford, John 279

Strange, Susan 279
strategic alliances 266–7
Strategic Arms Reduction Talks (START)
    Treaty 321
strategic beliefs 84, 328n14
strategic doctrine 207
strategic embargos 354n4
strategic objectives 210–2
strategic studies 37–8, 42, 207
strategic trade theory 145,146, 148n19
strategies, economic restraints in 279–80
Strategy, Politics, and Defense Budgets
    (Schilling, Hammond, and Snyder) 86
Streit, Clarence 170n1
structural change 133
structural constraints 133
structural effects 133
structural realism 55, 101, 305, 363, 391–6;
    balancing power 392–3; and dominant
    powers 392; international structure 393–6;
    restoring balance 391
Stryker, Sheldon 183
sub-state groups 231
Sudan 234, 418, 425
Suez crisis 355n7
suicide bombers 418
Sumberg, Theodore 41
superpower behaviour: alliances 299;
    bipolarity 298–9; deniability 300; during
    leadership crises 301–2; predictable
    anomalies and 301; rules 299–302;
    spheres-of-influence 300, 303n14
systems theory 297–8, 368

Taiwan 261n5, 263n13, 369, 381, 382, 386,
    387, 388n8, 389n20, 393
Tamil Tigers 417
technology transfer 410, 413n14
techno-nationalism 409
Tehranian, Majid 72, 73
temporal dimensions 29–30
territorial expansion 138, 210
terrorism 14, 38, 257, 268, 274, 364, 373,
    408, 417–21; war on 234, 422–6
terrorists, legitimacy 422
Thatcher, Margaret 40–1
Theory of International Politics (Waltz) 101
Third World, the 14; civil wars 55; and the
    Cold War 52, 53, 55, 57; common features

59; economic development 54, 57;
    environmental degradation 57; and global
    superpower rivalry 54–5; industrialization
    371; instability 53–4; intrastate conflicts
    53; marginalisation of 2, 52–3, 59; military
    power 56; military security 370–1; national
    identity 53; and national security 53–4;
    nonmilitary threats 54; origin of term 59;
    regional instability 52; regional security
    approaches 58–9; security experience
    55–60; security predicament 52–3, 61n6;
    and security studies 52–60, 61n4;
    significant wars 61n5; stability 57;
    state structures 53
third-image pessimists 85
Thirty Years War, the 404
Thomas, Caroline 72
threat definition 13–4
threat perceptions 295–6, 321–2
threats: absence of 21, 22, 26; AIDS 272–3;
    changing nature of 38–9; and globalisation
    407–8; intensity 32; migrants and
    migration 254–6, 260; non-physical 364;
    sources of 28–9; TCOs 267–9;
    Third World 54
Thucydides 298
Tickner, J. Ann 2, 44–50
Tilly, Charles 308–9
time scales 29–30
Toffler, Alvin and Heidi 243
Tong, Rosemary 47
Towards Professionalism (Kaplan) 337n9
toxic waste 67
trade 175, 283, 287n18, 351
trade wars 351, 352
Trager, Frank N. 21
transnational corporations, strategic
    alliances 266
transnational criminal organisations (TCO)
    194, 265–9; challenges to state authority
    268; emergence of 265–6; objectives 267;
    range of activities 266; rise of 266–7;
    strategic alliances 266–7;
    threat of 267–9
transnational organisations 266, 399
treaties 127
triads 266
Tuchman Matthews, Jessica 2, 64–70, 75
Twenty Years' Crisis (Carr) 101

twenty-first century security 363, 365–74; balance of power 368; clash of civilizational identities 373; economic security 371–2; environmental security 373–4; ideological conflict 366; international society 368–9; migrants and migration 372–3; military security 370–1; multipolarity 365–6, 368; the periphery 369–74; political security 369–70; security communities 367–8; societal security 372–3

Tyson, Laura D'Andrea 285

Ullman, Richard 1, 11–6, 21, 26, 28, 32
unbalanced power 391; danger of 392
uniformity, lack of 7
unipolarity 295, 305–11; and anarchy 307–9; balancing 307–8; balancing power 392–3; counter-hegemonic balancing 308; and differential growth rates 306; distribution of relative power 307; geopolitical backlashes 310; and great power emergence 305–10; historical examples 309–10; life-span 306, 311; moment 392; reaction to 310–1; and sameness 308–9; unbalanced power 391

United Nations 5, 57, 173, 360–1; Charter 126, 357; Department of Peacekeeping 360; peacekeeping operations 357

United Nations Convention Relating to the Status of Refugees 262n11

United Nations Development Programme (UNDP) 71–2

United Nations Educational, Scientific and Cultural Organization (UNESCO) 91n7

United Nations High Commission for Refugees (UNHCR) 256

United Nations Security Council 59, 227, 345, 346, 368–9

United States of America: African economic interests 273, 276n8; alliance with Japan 382, 384–5, 386–7, 394–5; challenges to hegemony 310–1; China policy 395, 396; civil economy 371; clients 299; Cold War victory 396; colonial wars 166; core values 7; and the Cuban missile crisis 196–7, 198; decline in status 365; Defense Department Annual Reports 86; Defense Intelligence Agency 56; drug related violence 268; East Asia involvement 382, 384–5, 386–7, 395;

East Asia Strategy Report (the Nye Report) 384–5; electoral politics 216; emergence as great power 309; energy use 68; and environmental change 69; and the first Gulf War 314n31; foreign policy 6, 9n1, 12, 15, 392; foreign threats 17n2; gender in Foreign Service 44; global interests 280–1; global reach, global power capability 242–3; goals 395–6; grand strategy 84; information advantage 235–6; involvement in civil war and internal repression 218; isolationism 189; leadership crises 301–2; liberal alliances 165; lobbying 16; McCarran-Walter Immigration Act 263n15; military capability 232, 243; military research and development and 214; military spending 215, 284; national security definition 11; nonproliferation policy 222, 225–6, 227; nuclear commitments 223; nuclear deterrence 195–201; nuclear first-use doctrine 227; Operation AJAX 92n13; President 16; as sole superpower 57; spheres-of-influence 300; State Department 86; strategic nuclear relationship 17n3; Strategic Petroleum Reserve 15; Third World interventions 170n3; unipolar moment 392

United States of Europe 108

UNMEE (the UN Mission to Ethiopia and Eritrea) 274–5

unorthodox warfare 194, 230–7, 243–4; human cost 233; the information advantage 235–7; information warfare 232–3; intervention strategies 234–5; militia-based 233–4

U.S. Air Force 217, 242

U.S. Marine Corps 242

Utilitarianism 107

utopianism 6; breakdown of 110–1; critique of 101, 105–15; and economic harmony 112–4; foundations of 105–7; harmony broken 114–5; harmony of interests 111–2, 114; the League of Nations 108–9; and public opinion 106, 109–10, 110; and rationalism 107–9; and war 106–7

values 27, 49, 188; compatibility of 174; core 7–8, 31; marginal 31–2; prime 30–1;

sacrifice of 29; securing 25; shared 296; spatial extension of 7; Western 402

Van Creveld, Martin 230

Van Evera, Stephen 145, 284

Verne, Jules 421n1

Vienna, Congress of 126

Vienna summit, 1961 195–6

Vietnam 17n2, 299, 301, 393

Vietnam War 234, 300

Viner, Jacob 279

violence: and AIDS 274; drugs and 267–8; and human security 74; intrastate literature 75; limitation of 126–7; occurrence of 130; and resource scarcity 194; threat of 130–1

virtue 107, 108, 115, 122, 180, 181

vital interests 27, 58, 152, 198, 200, 325, 392, 394

vulnerability, assessment of 14–5, 17n3

Wæver, Ole 3, 21, 93–6

Walker, R. B. J. 97n2

Walt, Stephen M. 3, 80–7, 295–6, 313n19, 314n31, 320–7

Waltz, Kenneth N. 55, 101, 130–6, 157, 159, 160, 161, 181, 305, 306, 308, 311n2, 335–6, 363, 391–6

war 37–8, 134–5, 337n9; and AIDS 275–6; causes of 153; civil 174, 218, 357; conduct of 237; cost-benefit calculus 286n3; costs of 102, 117n17, 151–6, 335; diversionary theory of 83; economic causes of 278–9; fear of 197, 198, 201n3; horrors of 84; humanitarian 296, 345–9; incidence 230–1; inhumanity of 151–2; just 127; laws of 347–8; liberal 168; liberal states and 165–6; limitation of 126–7; media coverage of 236–7; military's role as cause of 83; moral case for 151–6; motive for 198–9; obsolescence of 407; PMC involvement 360; preparations for 81; probability 165; prudent 166; recriminations 16n1; scapegoat theory of 83; significant 61n5; state of 130; system 37–8; terrorism as substitute for 421; and utopianism 106–7

war on terrorism 234, 422–6

warfare: human cost 233; information 232–3, 238n5; the information advantage 235–7; intervention strategies 234–5; militia-based 233–4; traditional models 230; unorthodox 194, 230–7, 243–4

Warsaw Pact 196, 328n12

water supplies 194, 246–7, 374

wealth 6, 154, 278–9, 280

weapons of mass destruction 364, 407, 419, 419–20, 421

Webb, Michael C. 307

Weiner, Myron 194, 253–60

Wendt, Alexander 102–3, 179–83

Westphalian system 37–8, 126, 177n3

Wight, Martin 42

Williams, Michael 186n20

Williams, Phil 194, 265–9

Wilson, Woodrow 107, 110

Wolfers, Arnold 1, 5–9, 20, 21, 25, 26, 27, 29, 31

Wollstonecraft, Mary 47

women 2; executive positions 44; in the foreign policy establishment 45; in international relations 45–7; oppression 47–8; role 45; value of experiences 49

World Bank 368, 394, 400

World Economic Conference (1933) 114

world government 134, 402

world order principles 38, 127–9

world political system 127–8

World Society School 38–9, 40

World Trade Organisation 400

World War I 84, 115, 166, 170n2

World War II 84, 138, 189, 246, 320, 383

worst-case analysis 204–5

yakuza 266

Yugoslavia 261, 274, 299, 359

Zionism 117n21

Zisk, Kimberley 207

zones of peace 269

zones of turbulence 269